DEVELOPING CHINA'S WEST

A Critical Path to Balanced National Development

Related Titles from The Chinese University Press

Fujian: A Coastal Province in Transition and Transformation
Edited by Y. M. Yeung and David K. Y. Chu (2000)

Guangdong: Survey of a Province Undergoing Rapid Change
(Second Edition)
Edited by Y. M. Yeung and David K. Y. Chu (1998)

Shanghai: Transformation and Modernization under China's Open Policy
Edited by Y. M. Yeung and Sung Yun-wing (1996)

The China Miracle: Development Strategy and Economic Reform
(Revised Edition)
Justin Yifu Lin, Fang Cai and Zhou Li (2003)

Guangdong: Preparing for the WTO Challenge
Edited by Joseph Y. S. Cheng (2003)

New Challenges for Development and Modernization: Hong Kong and the Asia-Pacific Region in the New Millennium
Edited by Yue-man Yeung (2002)

Resource Management, Urbanization and Governance in Hong Kong and the Zhujiang Delta
Edited by Kwan-yiu Wong and Jianfa Shen (2002)

State-owned Enterprise Reform in China
Justin Yifu Lin, Fang Cai and Zhou Li (2001)

China Business: Challenges in the 21st Century
Edited by Oliver H. M. Yau and Henry C. Steele (2000)

China's Regions, Polity, and Economy: A Study of Spatial Transformation in the Post-Reform Era
Edited by Si-ming Li and Wing-shing Tang (2000)

DEVELOPING CHINA'S WEST

A Critical Path to Balanced National Development

Edited by
Y. M. Yeung and Shen Jianfa

The Chinese University Press

Developing China's West: A Critical Path to Balanced National Development
Edited by Y. M. Yeung and Shen Jianfa

ISBN 962–996–157–1

THE CHINESE UNIVERSITY PRESS
The Chinese University of Hong Kong
SHATIN, N.T., HONG KONG
Fax: +852 2603 6692
+852 2603 7355
E-mail: cup@cuhk.edu.hk
Web-site: www.chineseupress.com

Printed in Hong Kong

Contents

Part II: Individual Profiles

Northwest

Southwest

Illustrations

Figures

Tables

Preface

This is the fourth book in a series of regional studies on China's policies of reform and opening up to the outside world since 1978 that have been published by the Urban and Regional Development in Pacific Asia Programme of the Hong Kong Institute of Asia-Pacific Studies at The Chinese University of Hong Kong. In contrast to the previous three volumes — Guangdong (1994, 1998), Shanghai (1996) and Fujian (2000) — that were focused on the fast-paced and rapidly developing coastal region, this book takes a fresh direction by concentrating its attention on China's sprawling but relatively thinly populated western region. This venture differs from the previous volumes in that the contributors have been drawn exclusively from Hong Kong and Mainland China. This "within the family" collaboration was not deliberate, as it was futile to find researchers elsewhere with a track record of having conducted recent important work on any part of the vast region. The impetus to pursue this project was strong, because the market conspicuously lacks a book that brings together theoretical, empirical and policy analyses on China's west, which has been the focus of national and global attention after the Chinese government announced its policy of developing the western region as a long-term strategy for national development.

The year 1999 was a critical one for China. Policy positions were reached that obviously would have a profound impact on the economic development and further openness of the country in the twenty-first century. In that year, China not only promulgated the strategy of western development, but also succeeded in clearing the hurdles with the United States paving the way to its eventual accession to the World Trade Organization in late 2001. Since 1999, the market has been flooded with books in Chinese that have addressed the western region as a whole or in part from a variety of perspectives. However, to our knowledge, a book in the English language that is capable of relating the latest developments in China's west to the social science mainstream in the West had yet to be conceptualized and written. This book has been designed to fulfil this role, but only the reader can judge whether it has succeeded in its objective. The organization of this book is comparable to that of the previous volumes. It aims at the breadth as well as depth of the subject, with a conscious attempt to provide the most up-to-date information and data from published, Internet and other sources. Names are rendered in Chinese, for the convenience of readers.

After spending more than a decade focusing its research on the coastal region of China, the Urban and Regional Development in Pacific Asia Programme decided to take up a new initiative by focusing its energy and resources on China's west. In December 2000, it jointly organized on campus an academic forum addressing the theme of the western region and the new economy. It was attended by a large audience of Hong Kong and Mainland Chinese scholars and policy-makers led by the then Deputy Minister of Science, Dr Xu Guanhua 徐冠華. A book arising from the selected papers was published by the Institute. In December 2002, the research programme took another organizing role with the Shanghai-Hong Kong Development Institute and Yunnan University to host another conference in Kunming on the western region and its neighbouring countries. A book based on the major papers presented at the conference has been published.

This book project was launched in 2001. It has received generous support from the Lippo Group, which has provided an annual grant to the research programme since 1993 to support its research activities. We are especially grateful to Dr Stephen Riady 李宗 and Mr J. P. Lee 李澤培, MBE, OBE, JP, for their unflagging support and cheerful encouragement. Without this, this book project entailing extensive field visits would not have been possible.

The completion of this project makes it incumbent on us to thank other organizations and individuals who have helped us in many ways. In field reconnaissance, the senior editor has been assisted by many friends and scholars, who have shared their knowledge and experience of the western region with him. In July 2000, he took part in a 13-day excursion to northern Xinjiang, under the able guidance of Professor Wang Mingmin 王明敏, of the Xinjiang Ecological and Geographical Research Institute, the Chinese Academy of Sciences in Urumqi. In May 2001, he led a group of geography students on an 11-day visit to southwestern Guangxi, with local assistance provided by Professors Zeng Lingfeng 曾令鋒 and Chen Bingchao 陳炳超, of the Environment and Urban Science Department, Guangxi Normal University in Nanning. Both of these were visits organized by the

Department of Geography and Resource Management at the University. In addition, other field trips were organized to gain a firsthand understanding of Tibet (2001), Sichuan (2001), Yunnan (2001, 2002), Guizhou (2002), Qinghai (2002), Gansu (2002) and Ningxia (2002). For these, the senior editor wishes to thank Professors Zhou Yixing 周一星 and Hu Zhaoliang 胡兆量, of Peking University and Dr Ng Wing-fai 吳永輝 for their wise counsel, careful preparation and enlightened company in the field. In Tibet, we were warmly received by many individuals who provided helpful information and perspectives, including those from Chen Jin 陳錦, of the General Office of Town and Country Construction and Environmental Protection in Lhasa. In Chengdu, we were given an excellent on-site introduction of recent changes in the form and functions of the central city, arranged by Director Zhang Chyau 張樵, of the Sichuan Chengdu Planning Institute. In Ningxia, we benefited from discussions with and the assistance of Professor Wang Yiming 汪一鳴, of Ningxia University. In Gansu and Qinghai, our visits were facilitated by Professor Zhang Zhibin 張志斌, of Northwest Normal University in Lanzhou. The senior editor, in fact, visited the western region in 1983 and 1984, to Chengdu and Xi'an, respectively, and their surroundings, followed by numerous visits to other provincial units since then. The junior editor has also made numerous visits to the western region such as to Yunnan, Guangxi, Shaanxi and Chongqing since 1988. They have been able, therefore, to witness the rapid changes in physical provisions and people's way of life over the years. With the exception of Inner Mongolia, the senior editor has had the opportunity to visit the other 11 provincial units of the western region. Consequently, all of the pictures that appear in this book have been selected from his personal collection taken at different times in the region. The photo credit of Inner Mongolia goes to Dennis Woo 胡兆基, a geography graduate of the University.

As with the previous books, this volume is the product of the devotion and hard work of a strong team. Janet Wong 汪唐鳳萍, the senior editor's personal secretary, doubled up as the project executive, helping him to correspond with the contributors, liaising with The Chinese University Press and generally managing the project. Dora Tsang 曾月蘭 and Jessica Tam 譚穎茜 have provided valuable and conscientious research assistance. S. L. Too 杜仕流 drew all of the maps and illustrations, even returning from retirement for this task. His masterful presentation of maps and figures will be sorely missed. The senior editor wishes to register a personal vote of thanks to him for helping in this vital aspect of his books over the years.

Professor Hu Xuwei 胡序威 of the Institute of Geographical Sciences and Natural Resources Research, Chinese Academy of Sciences, was extremely helpful in identifying and arranging some chapters to be undertaken by Chinese researchers. We also thank the constructive comments from two anonymous referees and have responded to the extent possible. Finally, we are indebted to all of the contributors to this project, who have generously shared their expertise and experience of the part or dimension of the western region with which they are familiar. They have also displayed understanding, goodwill and forbearance in the course of this project. We wish to dedicate this volume, nonetheless, to the people of China's west, for it is their well-being and that of their children that this book is mostly concerned about. We are responsible for any remaining errors and shortcomings.

The editors
January 2004

Abbreviations

ADB	Asian Development Bank
ASEAN	Association of Southeast Asian Nations
BOT	Build-operate-transfer
BTZ	Border Trading Zone
CAD	Comparative-advantage-defying
CAF	Comparative-advantage-following
CCP	Chinese Communist Party
CIS	Commonwealth of Independent States
CV	Coefficient of Variation
DNA	Deoxyribonucleic Acid
FDI	Foreign Direct Investment
FGD	Flue Gas Desulphurization
FIEs	Foreign-invested enterprises
FTA	Free Trade Area
GDP	Gross Domestic Product
GMD	Guomingdang
HTADZ	High-tech Agricultural Demonstration Zone
IBM	International Business Machine Corporation
IC	Integrated Circuits
IT	Information Technology
LPG	Liquefied Petroleum Gas
MEMS	Micro-electric Machine System
MEs	Major state and non-state-owned enterprises
MOFTEC	Ministry of Foreign Trade and Economic Cooperation
PLA	People's Liberation Army
PRC	People's Republic of China

R&D	Research and Development
RMB	Ren Min Bi (Chinese Currency)
RSP	Respirable Particulates
SARS	Severe Acute Respiratory Syndrome
SOE	State-owned Enterprises
TDF	Tibetan Development Fund
TFR	Total Fertility Rate
TV	Television
TVE	Township and Village Enterprises
U.S.	United States
U.K.	United Kingdom
UNDP	United Nations Development Programme
UNEP	United Nations Environment Programme
UNESCO	United Nations Educational, Scientific and Cultural Organization
USSR	Union of Soviet Socialist Republics
VAT	Value-added Tax
WDR	World Development Report
WTO	World Trade Organization
XDZ	Xi'an High-tech Industrial Development Zone

1

Introduction

Y. M. Yeung

The term "China's west" resonates with associations with the country's history, trade and exchange, diplomacy, folk culture and frontier settlement, to mention just a few dimensions. In earlier centuries, the diplomatic exploits of Zhang Qian 張騫 (circa 114 B.C.) and Ban Chao 班超 (A.D. 32–102) are still widely applauded by the Chinese as being the earliest attempts to bring Chinese political and cultural influences to distant lands. Similarly, stoked by the ever-popular *Xi You Ji* 西遊記 (The Journey to the West) by Wu Cheng'en 吳承恩, Xuan Zang's 玄奘 (A.D. 602–664) arduous and adventurous expeditions to procure Buddhist scriptures from India has exerted a lasting impact on the Chinese mind and mythology of a region full of intrigue and mystery.[1]

The range of historical relics and features of great geographical importance that are found in China's west today is unparalleled in the country. As testimonies to human ingenuity and creativity, Lhasa's Potala Palace 拉薩布達拉宮, the Dunhuang Grottoes 敦煌寶窟, Xi'an's terracotta warriors 西安兵馬俑, the recent archaeological finds in Sichuan's 四川 Sanxingdui 三星堆 and the age-old water conservancy works at Dujiangyan 都江堰 are objects of national significance. Tibet 西藏, known as "The Roof of the World," has an average elevation of 4,500 m above sea level. Qinghai 青海 boasts of having China's largest salt-water lake — Qinghai Lake 青海湖 — from which the province derives its name, and is the source of China's major rivers (the Yellow River 黃河, the Yangzi River 長江 and the Lancang River 瀾滄江). Extremely rich in natural resources, Xinjiang 新疆 accounts for one-sixth of the territory of China. Inner Mongolia 內蒙古 possesses the most expansive grasslands in the country, over which the legendary Mongol mounted warriors once freely roamed. Finally, there is the exquisite beauty of the karst topography of Guilin 桂林. The western region is home to 10 of the 28 World Heritage Sites in China designated by United Nations Educational, Scientific and Cultural Organization (UNESCO), an indication of its natural beauty and an acknowledgment of the creativity of the people who inhabited the region.[2]

To be able to adequately describe the extraordinary variety of natural and human landscapes in China's sprawling western region is a challenge. Thus, it is no easy task to convey the meaning and significance of the pronouncement in 1999 of a national policy to focus attention on and greatly increase resources to developing this part of China to pursue balanced and sustainable development. This is a story that is as hard as it is fascinating to tell. To be able to accomplish these objectives between the covers of a book calls for comprehensiveness and objectivity, yet clarity of purpose is vital if the book is to present a lucid and consistent theme.

As the title of the book connotes, the central and organizing thesis of this book is that the underlying principle of initiating a new development strategy for China's west is to minimize the growing social, economic and developmental gaps between the eastern, especially coastal, region and the western region. The strategy of developing the western region is to rectify the existing pattern of uneven development that, if left uncorrected, will lead to national instability.

Towards this end, the book has been divided into two main parts. Part I addresses a number of selected overarching issues across the 12 provincial units of China's west, while Part II systematically presents a profile of the provincial units, with a choice of local themes that are deemed to be pertinent and important in the present and future policy climate. In all of these chapters, attempts have been made to obtain the most up-to-date data and information. Following the style that has been established in this series of regional treatises, Chinese names are rendered for the convenience of the reader.

This introductory piece is intended as a road map for the subsequent chapters, hence frequent references are made to them. To assist the reader in gaining a speedy entry into the subject, this chapter addresses three broad questions. First, how are the diverse physical and human landscapes in China's west to be understood? Second, what are the legacies of past economic development in the region and what do they mean from the standpoint of the regional imbalance that has resulted since 1978, when the country began to pursue policies of openness and reform? Third, how does the new focus on the western region fit into China's national modernization programme and how is it likely to succeed? Finally, a concluding section raising some key questions rounds off this preview of the chapters that follow.

Physical and Human Diversity

China's west exists in most people's minds as a vast territory in the far west of the country. For development purposes, however, national planners have divided the country into several broad regions. With the Seventh Five-year Plan (1986–1990), a three-fold division of China was adopted, under which provinces are classified based on their distance from the coast and level of development. The eastern region consists of 12 provincial units, namely,

Liaoning 遼寧, Hebei 河北, Beijing 北京, Tianjin 天津, Shandong 山東, Jiangsu 江蘇, Shanghai 上海, Zhejiang 浙江, Fujian 福建, Guangdong 廣東, Guangxi 廣西 and Hainan 海南. The central region consists of the 9 provincial units of Heilongjiang 黑龍江, Jilin 吉林, Inner Mongolia, Shanxi 山西, Henan 河南, Anhui 安徽, Hubei 湖北, Hunan 湖南 and Jiangxi 江西. Finally, the western region consists of the 9 provincial units of Shaanxi 陝西, Gansu 甘肅, Ningxia 寧夏, Qinghai, Xinjiang (northwest), Sichuan (including Chongqing 重慶), Yunnan 雲南, Guizhou 貴州 and Tibet (southwest). These broad regional divisions have since been followed in all official documents.

Since the Western Development Strategy was promulgated in 1999, however, China's west has become 12 provincial units, as Chongqing became China's fourth provincial-level municipality in 1997, and Inner Mongolia and Guangxi succeeded becoming included as part of the western region in order to take advantage of the opportunities offered by such a classification. Thus, this book adopts the definition of the western region as one that consists of 12 provincial units; namely, the northwest comprising Inner Mongolia, Shaanxi, Gansu, Qinghai, Ningxia and Xinjiang, and the southwest comprising Guangxi, Chongqing, Sichuan, Guizhou, Yunnan and Tibet. Together, they account for 71.8% of China's land area and 28.5% of its population (Table 1.1, Figure 1.1), figures that convey a sense of imbalance. Where quoting from source materials, references to the west in the following chapters occasionally indicate the original 10 provincial units; however, the 12-unit definition is generally used. The west is so vast that it has sometimes been internally differentiated, for example, as the "Near West" and the "Far West."[3] By contrast, during the Qing 清 dynasty (1644–1911), the west was a broad term referring to the land lying to the west of the Guanzhong Plain 關中平原 (Chapter 2, Li Xiaojian et al.).

A closer look at Figure 1.1 will provide an answer to the apparent imbalance in the amount of land and distribution of population between the east and the west. The famous late geographer, Hu Huanyong 胡煥庸, drew a line in 1933 from Heihe 黑河 (previously Aihui 瑷琿) in Heilongjiang in the northeast of China to Tengchong 騰衝 in Yunnan in the southwest. At that time, that area of China lying northwest of what has since been known as the Hu Huanyong line accounted for only 4% of the country's population but 64% of its land area. By contrast, in the area to the southeast, 96% of the population lived on only 36% of the land. By 1982, a census year, the corresponding figures for the northwest were 5.6% and 57.1%, and for the southeast 94.4% and 42.9%, respectively. Thus, there has been surprisingly

Table 1.1 Key Background Indicators of Western Provincial Units, 2001

Region	Area (sq km)	Population (million)	GDP (billion RMB)	GDP per capita (RMB)	GDP growth rate (%)	Foreign direct investment (actually utilized) (million USD)	Value of import and export by location of commodity management (million USD)	Total investment in fixed assets (billion RMB)
China	9,572,900	1,276.27	9,434.64	7,543	7.3	46.88[1]	509,768.13	3,721.349
Northwest	4,742,600	115.73	644.50	5,769 (average)	9.72 (average)	606.80	7,384.73	283.086
Southwest	2,594,600	248.74	1,170.11	4,774 (average)	9.05 (average)	1,315.39	9,458.20	432.790
Inner Mongolia	1,183,000	23.77	154.58 (24)	6,458	9.6	107.03 (24)	2,034.70 (19)	50.363 (26)
Guangxi	236,700	47.88	223.12 (16)	4,697	8.2	384.16 (17)	1,796.99 (23)	65.563 (23)
Chongqing	82,400	30.97	174.98 (23)	5,655	9	256.49 (22)	1,833.91 (22)	69.703 (21)
Sichuan	485,000	86.40	442.18 (10)	5,250	9.2	581.88 (13)	3,099.16 (15)	161.752 (7)
Guizhou	176,100	37.99	108.49 (26)	2,865	8.8	28.29 (28)	646.45 (28)	53.601 (25)
Yunnan	394,000	42.87	207.47 (18)	4,872	6.5	64.57 (26)	1,988.78 (20)	73.845 (17)
Tibet	1,220,400	2.63	13.87 (31)	5,302	12.6	–	92.91 (31)	8.326 (31)
Shaanxi	205,600	36.59	184.42 (20)	5,015	9.1	351.74 (18)	2,062.00 (18)	77.343 (16)
Gansu	454,400	25.75	107.25 (27)	4,173	9.4	74.39 (25)	778.88 (27)	46.037 (27)
Qinghai	721,200	5.23	30.09 (29)	5,732	12	36.49 (27)	204.90 (30)	19.635 (29)
Ningxia	51,800	5.63	29.81 (30)	5,338	10.1	16.80 (30)	532.77 (29)	19.108 (30)
Xinjiang	1,660,400	18.76	148.35 (25)	7,898	8.1	20.35 (29)	1,771.48 (24)	70.600 (18)

Notes: [1] billion USD
National rank in parentheses

Sources: *China Statistical Yearbook 2002*
Yearbook of China's Foreign Economic Relations and Trade 2002
Website of the National Bureau of Statistics of China — Regional Statistics
http://www.stats.gov.cn/
China Central Western Area Development Yearbook 2002

Figure 1.1 The Geopolitical Setting and Provincial Units of China's Western Region

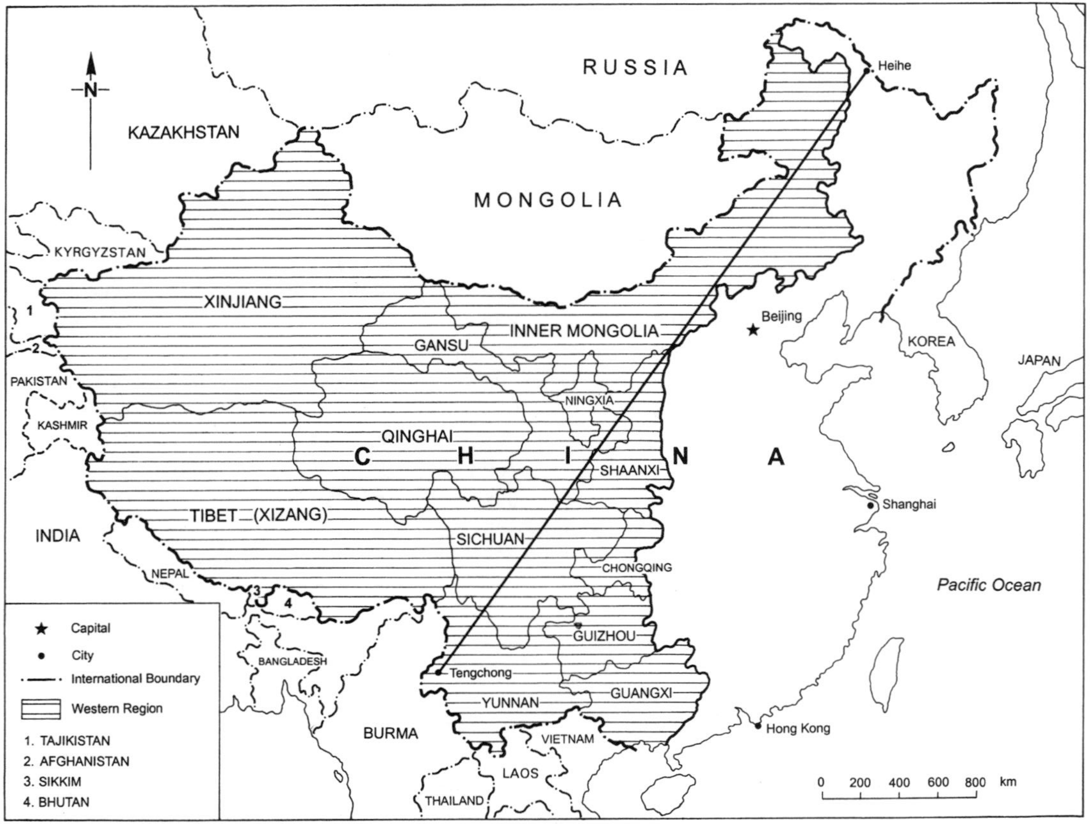

little change over the intervening five decades to the pattern observed in the 1930s, notwithstanding boundary and territorial changes in the interim.[4]

Another look at Figure 1.1 shows that, in fact, the land lying northwest of the Hu Huanyong line includes almost all of the land that is now defined as China's west, although another three complete provincial units and four partial ones have also been included. The vast western region, in physiographical terms, contains the main elements of the country's geography. The landform of China can be said to be made up of three terraces. The first is the Qing-Zang (Qinghai-Tibet) Plateau 青藏高原, which has an average elevation of 3,000 to 4,000 m above sea level and which is where the major rivers originate. The second terrace includes Inner Mongolia, Shanxi, Shaanxi, Gansu and Ningxia, and includes Sichuan, Guizhou and Yunnan in the southwest. In the southwest, the descent of large rivers to the lower plains has endowed the latter provinces with the tremendous potential to generate hydropower (see Chapter 5, Y. M. Yeung et al., for recent efforts to harness this potential). The third terrace refers to the lowland regions in the eastern region. In general, the southwest has a complex geomorphology of typically hilly and little level land, rich water resources and a mild climate. The northwest, on the other hand, has little rainfall, the Gobi Desert 戈壁沙漠, the Loess Plateau 黄土高原 and the bulk of China's grasslands. Both sub-regions have serious ecological problems as well as plentiful natural resources that have yet to be actively exploited (Chapter 3, Niu Wenyuen and David Chen).

China shares 13,000 km of border with 14 countries and has several dozen border towns, most of which are located in the vast western region. To be more specific, 80% of China's land border is located in its western region, and so is about 80% of the population of its many minority nationality groups.[5] Shen Jianfa and Wang Guixin (Chapter 9) analyzed the population dynamics of the 55 minority nationalities and the Han Chinese. They noted that minority nationalities tend to have a higher growth rate than the Han, yet their life expectancy is lower than the national average. Also in the period 1952–1982, the growth of the population in the western region was higher than that of the national average because of high fertility and net migration. The trend has reversed since 1982, owing to the pull factor of the coastal region, which has experienced phenomenal growth. As a result, it is not surprising that of the 40 million people in China who have yet to break free from the cycle of poverty, the majority are located in the minority nationality areas in the western region.[6] The inferior development status of the western region is revealed in its low GDP rankings relative to other provincial units. Similarly, the western provincial units have lagged behind in achievements in investment and trade, with hardly any provincial unit ranking above 15th in the nation (Table 1.1).

Still another look at Figure 1.1 shows that, with the exception of Guangxi, all of the other 11 provincial units in China's west are landlocked. As the only province with access to the sea, Guangxi is especially well positioned to offer its port facilities to provinces in the southwest that seek to export their products and manufactured goods overseas. After having been neglected in development and investment for many years, Guangxi is in a unique position to capitalize on China's "go west" policy. In particular, its border trade with Vietnam has flourished in recent years (Chapter 18, Huang Yefang and Shen Jianfa).[7] Apart from the strategic southwest passage to the sea, the Silk Road was the main link in the early economic and cultural exchanges between China and countries in Central Asia. The overland link is once again becoming important with the recent emergence of the area as a vital transport link in the Euro-Asian continental land bridge, of which 4,143 km is located in China. This land bridge will have a pre-eminent role to play in the twenty-first century, as coastal and continental economies can be married through the flow of goods, people, information and capital.[8] In reviewing the historical links between China's west and its neighbours, one must register the less well-known "Southern Silk Road" or "Dian-Mian Road" 滇緬道, linking present-day Chengdu 成都 to India, Pakistan and Burma via Kunming 昆明 and Dali 大理 from as early as the third century B.C.[9] Present-day Kunming, however, is the focus of Yunnan's efforts to launch a more vigorous and broad-based development focusing on pillar industries, border trade and tourism, notwithstanding the many challenges that lie ahead (Chapter 20, Gan Chunkai and Chen Zhilong).

If the "go west" policy has brought new vitality and stimulated development in Guangxi, then the other western provinces have at least as much to gain from the new policy. China's west has an exceptionally rich natural resources and a mosaic of minority nationalities. An idea of how rich and diversified the physical and human landscape is can be gained from an assembly of images that have been associated with the provinces for centuries, as selectively summarized in Table 1.2. It has to be stressed that the list is selective. Many of these images reflect the traditional strengths and characteristics of the western provinces. Indeed, some provinces do have an idea of how to develop their land under the "go west" policy. For instance, the relatively small Ningxia has highlighted the goal of being

Table 1.2 Some Traditional Images of the Western Region

Provincial unit	Images and characteristics	
Inner Mongolia 內蒙古	Forested East and Industrialized West	東林西鐵
	Southern Granary and Northern Pasture	南糧北牧
	Treasury of Mineral Resources	遍地礦藏
	Windswept Grass Reveals Cattle and Sheep	風吹草低見牛羊
Guangxi 廣西	Mountains and Rivers of Guilin	桂林山水
	The Pearl City	合浦明珠
Chongqing 重慶	The Foggy Capital of Bashan	巴山霧都
	Calm Waters Encircled by Deep Gorges	高峽出平湖
	Economic Hub of The Upper Yangzi River	長江上游的經濟中心
	The Youngest Municipality	最年輕的直轄市
Sichuan 四川	The Heavenly Kingdom	天府之國
	Dujiangyan Engineering Project	都江堰工程
	Travelling to the Shu Province is Harder than Ascending to Heaven	蜀道難，難於上青天
Guizhou 貴州	Captivating Mountains and Rivers	秀色山水
	A Mountainous Land Dotted with Rivers and Fields	八山一水一分田
	Water as Valuable as Oil	水貴如油
	A Province Rich in Resources	資源大省
Yunnan 雲南	Home of Peacocks	孔雀之鄉
	Kingdom of Animals and Plants	動物王國 植物王國
	"Third of the Third Month" Singing Festival	"三月三"歌節
Tibet 西藏	Roof of the World	世界屋脊
	Snow-capped Holy Land	雪域聖地
Shaanxi 陝西	Cradle of Chinese Civilization	中華搖籃
	Imperial Capitals of Qin and Han	秦漢故園
	Qin Terracotta Warriors and Horses	兵馬俑
	Treasure Belt in Guanzhong	關中寶地
Gansu 甘肅	The Silk Road	絲綢之路
	Dunhuang Grottoes	敦煌寶窟
	Home of Non-ferrous Metals	有色金屬之鄉
	The Hexi Corridor	河西走廊
Qinghai 青海	Source of Major Rivers	江河源頭
	High Plateaus and Calm Lakes	高原平湖
Ningxia 寧夏	Jiangnan (Areas South of The Yangzi River) of The North	塞上江南
Xinjiang 新疆	The Majestic Tianshan	巍巍天山
	Home of Music and Dance	歌舞之鄉
	Land of Longevity	長壽之鄉
	Meeting Point of Eastern and Western Cultures	東西文化交匯點
	The Largest Autonomous Region	面積最大的自治區

Source: Adapted and translated from Yang (see note 3), p. 41.

"small but rich, small but strong" 小而富、小而強 (Chapter 13, Hu Xia). In the same vein, Shaanxi envisages its future to lie in "one corridor, two cities, three bases and four pillar industries" 一帶、兩城、三基地、四產業[10] (Chapter 14, Zhao Rong and Zheng Guo). With the rich physical endowments and human contributions that have been briefly sketched, the western region is about to embark on a phase of accelerated development and change that will almost certainly have profound implications for China's future.

Historical Legacy and Regional Imbalance

As Li Xiaojian and others (Chapter 2) and Fan Jie (Chapter 4) have independently detailed, China's west has a history of over 2,000 years. The northwest reached the peak of its prosperity in the Tang 唐 dynasty (A.D. 618–907), with Chang'an 長安 (present-day Xi'an) as the national capital and eastern starting point of the fabulous Silk Road. In the southwest, Sichuan prospered steadily for a long period after the treacherous waters of the Min River 岷江 at Dujiangyan were tamed in the third century B.C. by the father-and-son engineers, Li Bing 李冰 and Li Erlang 李二郎. Not surprisingly, Sichuan has traditionally been called "the Heavenly Kingdom." However, after the Tang dynasty, the northwest began to lose its comparative advantage as the political and economic centre of the nation progressively shifted towards the south and east. This was the beginning of a long period of decline in the northwest, which gradually became a backwater. What is more, despite agricultural and irrigation works that were built under the auspices of the state, frequent warfare, land use and human occupancy of ecologically marginal lands, and sheer neglect have left the western region in a highly precarious ecological condition.

What should be stressed at the outset is that, in contrast to frontier development in the United States and other countries in the past, China's west in the twenty-first century is far from being virgin land. A large proportion of the land has been misused and abused for centuries, such that vast stretches of land have become seriously degraded and will require a tremendous amount of investment before it can be put to economic use. For example, the land along the Silk Road was once bustling with cities and forests, which have been succeeded by abandoned settlements, deserts or semi-deserts. At present, 80% of the 3.6 billion sq m of land in China that is suffering from soil erosion is in the western region. Likewise, most of the 2.4 million sq m of land that becomes desertified annually is in the west. Also serious is the soil erosion in the upper reaches of the Yellow

River and the Yangzi River, desertification in the northwest, and the loss of surface vegetation in the karst regions in Yunnan, Guizhou and Guangxi. Furthermore, air, water and solid waste pollution in the cities of the western region is a matter of international concern. According to an assessment by the World Health Organization, in 1998 eight of the world's ten most polluted cities were in China, with Guiyang 貴陽, Chongqing and Lanzhou 蘭州 ranking first, second and fourth, respectively.[11] Another example of the abuse of land is overgrazing in Inner Mongolia. Over the past two decades, Inner Mongolia has increased its herds by 130,000 heads, to a total of 739,700 heads; overgrazing by mountain goats since has increased 2.3 times since 1983.[12] As Inner Mongolia is the third-largest provincial unit in China with some 60% of its land made up of grasslands, the task of land restoration and ecological construction ranks high in its current development agenda. After all, Inner Monglia is an ecological barrier between Northeast and North China (Chapter 15, Wang Jing'ai and Yang Mingchuan).

The gradual shift of the political and economic centre of the nation away from the west was in part man-made, but was also in part the result of the climate becoming progressively drier, rendering it unsuitable for human settlement and agriculture. Concomitantly, the rise of the coastal region with the emergence of competitive ocean transport from the sixteenth century hastened the regional shift. Nevertheless, the state never gave up the west, taking the view that it formed a crucial component of national territorial integrity. Sustained efforts and campaigns to win the west never ceased, such as the still highly celebrated marriage of the Princess Wencheng 文成公主 to the then ruler of Tubo 吐蕃 (present-day Tibet) during the Tang dynasty (A.D. 641) as a tangible symbol of political and cultural alliance, and the large-scale military expeditions to the northwest, notably in present-day Xinjiang, along with the almost excessive development in the Loess Plateau area in Shaanxi during the Qing dynasty. These are historical antecedents to the "go west" campaigns prior to the twentieth century.

During the twentieth century, the first attempt to "go west" was the relocation of the national capital from Nanjing 南京 to Chongqing in 1940, when the capital and much of coastal China fell to the invading Japanese army. As a temporary capital, Chongqing began a period of transformation into an industrial, cultural and metropolitan centre. In the later years after the founding of the People's Republic of China (PRC) in 1949, the city also benefited considerably from the "Third Front" 三線 campaign and the current "go west" development strategy after it became a Municipality in

1997 (Chapter 17, Chen Yue, Chen Caiti and Lin Hui). Even after 1949, several phases in "go west" development can be distinguished.

Since 1949, the first wave of "go west" development was associated with the First Five-year Plan (1953–1957) when, driven by the goal of "balanced" national development, the state pursued large-scale heavy industrial development, with 156 Soviet-aided projects as the core. These projects were located primarily in the northwest, with Shaanxi assigned 24 projects, the largest number of projects; and Gansu 16 projects. As a result, Lanzhou, Xi'an and Chengdu emerged as newly industrializing cities in the west. The second wave of "go west" development occurred in the period 1965–1975, when a deteriorating international political climate led Chinese leaders to strategically locate the country's new industrial capacity in the "Third Front" in the west, with the southwest gaining the lion's share of the investment. In fact, 33.14% of national investment went to the west, the highest percentage historically, with the southwest acquiring 20.93% and the northwest 12.21%. The third wave of western development began in 1992, when the late Deng Xiaoping 鄧小平 made his historic visit to the southern part of the country and announced an "all front" open policy. East-west co-operation was vigorously promoted until the policy of developing the western region was announced in 1999. "Go west" development has since become a focus of national investment and international attention.[13]

Several bitter lessons have been learned of China's "go west" development. First, short-term economic gains without sufficient regard for long-term impact have led to development approaches that are detrimental to the environment. Second, the first two waves of "go west" development after 1949 were predicated on political, rather than economic principles, thus failing to nourish self-propelling mechanisms for economic growth. Third, policies for developing the west were always top-down, hardly conducive to engendering harmonious relationships between Han Chinese and minority nationalities. Finally, development tended to bypass cities and the choice of industrial locations was somewhat problematic.[14] Particularly worrisome from the standpoints of national stability and regional harmony has been the increasing economic and social disparity between the eastern and western regions in the 1990s.

Many recent studies have underlined the growing inequalities between the eastern and western regions. In the three decades prior to the launching of the open-door policy in 1978, the annual GDP growth rate in the eastern, central and western regions was 7.08%, 6.78% and 7.52%, respectively, with the western region 0.44% ahead of the eastern region. To the relief of central planners and people in the west, the east-west gap had narrowed, as planned. However, in the next two decades, the national GDP grew rapidly at an average annual rate of 9.6%, with the eastern, central and western regions growing at 12.8%, 9.3% and 8.7%, respectively. Thus, on average, the eastern region was growing at a rate of 4.1% faster than the western region, thereby sweeping away the gains of the past three decades in narrowing the gap between the east and the west. In fact, the gap has widened greatly.[15] To be precise, in these two decades, the eastern region has grown 7.8 times, tripling its GDP; whereas the western region has grown 5.7 times, in itself quite impressive. The fastest growing provinces were Guangdong and Fujian, which together had an annual GDP growth of 13.7% in the period. This was far ahead of the rate of 7.2% for the slowest-growing province, Qinghai.[16] More comprehensive and up-to-date data comparing the western with the eastern and central regions over time can be found in Chapter 8 by Gu Chaolin, Shen Jianfa and Yu Taofang.

Table 1.3 shows the trend of economic growth shifting towards the eastern region during the reform period. Since 1979, the proportion of the population among the three major regions has remained largely unchanged, but the shift in economic wealth towards the eastern region, as measured by GDP growth, has been striking. In 1980, the division of GDP among the eastern, central and western regions was 52.17%, 30.3% and 17.53%, respectively, but by 2000, this had changed to 58.86%, 27.55% and 13.58%, respectively. The size of the GDP of the eastern region in relation to the western region has grown from 2.98 times in 1980 to 4.33 times in 2000.[17] Still another indirect gap between east and west is the gap in urban-rural disposal income, which soared from 2.3 times in 1985 to 3.5 times in 1999.[18] It has been noted that this is considerably higher than comparable disparities in Japan in 1955 at 2.94 times, and in Taiwan in 1965 at 2.30 times, at their early stages of industrialization.[19]

Chapter 8 contains a succinct summary of the major theoretical and empirical arguments surrounding the uneven regional development in China during the period of reform, especially as presented in studies conducted in the West, requiring, therefore, no repetition here. The disparity between the eastern and western regions was so glaring that, by the end of the 1990s, some scholars noted that within China, there are four worlds. The first world is represented by high-income developed areas, such as Shanghai, Beijing and Shenzhen 深圳. The second world encompasses large and medium-sized cities and the middle-income areas of the eastern coast, such

Table 1.3 Regional Gaps in GDP in China, 1980–2000

(Unit: %)

Region	1980	1991	1992	1993	1994	1995	1997	1998	1999	2000
National total	100	100	100	100	100	100	100	100	100	100
Eastern region	52.17	54.90	56.55	58.29	59.12	58.30	57.80	58.12	58.70	58.86
Central region	30.30	29.80	28.60	27.25	26.83	27.50	28.19	27.92	27.51	27.55
Western region	17.53	15.30	14.85	14.46	14.05	14.20	14.01	13.96	13.79	13.58
Ratio of eastern region to western region	2.98	3.59	3.81	4.03	4.21	4.11	4.13	4.16	4.26	4.33

Sources: Adapted from Liu et al., *Zhongguo diqu chaju* (see note 15), p. 44, with data drawn from the *China Statistical Yearbook* (various years).

as Tianjin, Guangdong and Zhejiang. The third world includes the middle-income areas of the coastal areas of Hebei, Dongbei (Northeast China) 東北 and Huabei (North China) 華北. The fourth world refers to the central and western regions characterized by poverty-stricken areas, large populations of minority nationalities, and rural and peripheral areas. With the exception of Xinjiang, the per capita GDP of western provincial units ranged from 50% to 75% of the national average. Guizhou, the poorest province in China, can be cited for comparison. In 1990, Shanghai's per capita GDP was 7.3 times that of Guizhou; by 2000, the figure had grown to 12.9 times.[20] Similarly, another study showed that between 1983 and 1999, income disparities between the eastern and western region continued to rise. The "Guizhou phenomenon" of persistent poverty constitutes the background against which creditable progress in economic development and industrial restructuring has been achieved in the reform period (Chapter 19, Chen Zhilong and Zhang Min). The absolute average income gap of RMB325 in 1983 between the eastern and western regions swelled to RMB5,930 in 1999; the coefficient of the relative regional gap soared from 44.4% to 58.7% in the corresponding period.[21]

The widening regional disparities even caught the attention of the UNDP which, in its *Human Development Report* in 1994, cited China as one of the countries where regional inequalities had become excessively large. In their study of uneven development in China, Wang Shaoguang and Hu An'gang concluded that:[22]

> When the government has no intention to reduce regional disparities in the country, regional gaps are unlikely to narrow. Even if the state desires to reduce regional disparities, regional gaps may still expand if the state lacks the capacity to carry out its objectives. Only when the state is both willing and able to intervene on behalf of poor regions may regional disparities decline. The state's ability to intervene is mainly constrained by its extractive capacity (p. 13).

Indeed, since the implementation of economic reforms, the extractive capacity of the central government has been greatly weakened as a consequence of the decentralization of power. Yet the urgency to rectify regional inequalities is real. Wang and Hu further warned:

> The government may be able to persuade people that some must get rich first so that everyone will eventually get rich. But if it persists in failing to distribute the gains from reforms more or less evenly, and if the gap between those who flourish and those who stagnate becomes unacceptably large, the moral foundations of the regime will be shaken (p. 201).

Balanced Development and National Modernization

The pursuit of balanced regional development has been the shared objective of three generations of national leaders in China. Mao Zedong's 毛澤東 programme to rusticate the intelligentsia and the "Third Front" development had the avowed political purpose of tilting the regional balance towards the west, paying no heed to principles of regional comparative advantage. Deng Xiaoping's espousal of the open policy in 1978, leading to a reversal of the pattern of balanced regional development was, in the grand scheme of long-term development, intended to be a temporary phase to accelerate the development of the coast to raise the level of the development of the country as a whole. This was conceived of as the "first situation," in which coastal development was purposely favoured. However, when coastal development reached a certain stage of maturity, it would be incumbent on national leaders to embark on the "second situation," by developing the west to rectify the unbalanced development of the regions.[23] With this historical vision and mission, Jiang Zemin 江澤民 and his colleagues decided in 1999 that it was time to shift the direction of national development towards the west, with the clearly enunciated goal of balanced regional development.

Implicit from the foregoing discussion, developing China's west is a huge, complex and systemic project that demands vast inputs of resources, political will at every level, and the support of people within and outside China. It must be recognized as a long-term campaign likely to run for many decades before balanced development is attained. After all, the development of the frontiers of the United States, Russia and Australia in the past took a similar amount of time. For China, the development of the western region has rightly been viewed as part of the process of national modernization, for the simple reason that, without the modernization of the west, the nation is at best only partially modernized.[24]

The present state of development in China's west has been likened to a person going hungry while holding a golden bowl. This paradoxical circumstance is the result of a mismatch between physical and human factors of production. The exceptionally rich natural resources in the western region have not been effectively exploited for the benefit of the people. Liu and others have attributed 10 factors that have constrained the development of the western region to date, including (1) the faulty strategy of overly orienting national development towards the eastern region; (2) the irreplaceable geographical advantage of the coastal regions prejudicing against the west for development in the 1980s; (3) the lack of capital, preventing the creation of new economic centres; (4) the reduction in educational opportunities; (5) the national economic structure, which is causing wealth to be transferred from the west through inter-regional trade; (6) the lack of collective enterprises in the west as typical of the Sunan model delaying the process of development; (7) sluggish institutional reforms, constraining the advantage of late developers; (8) fossilized thought patterns; (9) uniform national policies that have not been adjusted for the conditions of the west; and (10) weak infrastructure.[25]

Hu has argued that the western region has lagged in development because of the gap in economic, human and knowledge development between the east and the west. The gulf in development indices between the eastern and western regions grew in the 1990s.[26] Another way of explaining the east-west gap is in terms of the traditional regional differences in industrial-agricultural, urban-rural and labour-intensive versus intellect-intensive modes in Chinese society.[27] The alleviation of regional inequities boils down to three basic questions. First, how is the west to rid itself of poverty quickly and urgently? Second, how is it to broaden investment for development outside the government sector? Third, how can a long-term development strategy be combined with a staged uplift in the standard of living of the people? To achieve success in tackling these three questions, the geographical and psychological obstacles with which the western region has been struggling must be overcome.[28]

Developing China's west at the beginning of a new century and in the information era means that, rather than simply imitating the successful experience of the eastern region during the past two decades, new concepts must be found to stimulate fresh development. Many new ideas have been advanced, including shifting from "natural resource base objectives" to "enriching people and place objectives"; from "nation driven externally oriented development" to "self-propelled internally oriented development"; "resource-based exploitation" to "market-oriented exploitation"; "regional comparative advantage" to "regional competitive advantage"; and "extractive development" to "sustainable development."[29] Similarly, Zhou stresses the need to nurture a self-propelling capacity, to build an economic model that is conducive to maximizing the advantages of indigenous resources, and to strenuously improve the investment environment in order to attract foreign capital.[30]

To be able to really build from the bottom, Shi Peijun and others (Chapter 6) have called attention to the problem of backward education and the lack of skilled manpower as critical weaknesses in western development. Nevertheless, the two important centres of Xi'an and Chengdu are well prepared to take on a more central role in strengthening the west, as they have the best universities and research institutes in the region. In the same vein, Mao Hanying and Zhang Li (Chapter 7) have shown that in the present stage of development, the central government's top-down strategy in mobilizing resources and redistributing production factors are critical to achieving success. The education and training of the local people in the long term must accompany preferential policies in the short term.

For decades after 1949, the western region suffered from policies detrimental to its development. The traditional "scissor price" policy (that is, goods from the west sold at artificially low price) has drained the west of its rich natural resources to the benefit of the coastal region. Until very recently, the western region never enjoyed the liberal financial and development policy incentives that had been granted to the coastal region since the early 1980s. Not surprisingly, it has been argued that China's west should be allowed to enjoy a regime of policy incentives even more favourable than those previously enjoyed by the coastal region, in order to compensate for its geographical disadvantages and to attract foreign investment.[31] Indeed, preferential policies can be contemplated in nine domains for the western region, namely, production structure, investment structure, financial arrangement, price levels, measures to attract foreign investment, special policies pertaining to minority groups, poverty-stricken areas and border lands, manpower training, cadre mobility and macro planning.[32]

In the period 2000–2002, preferential policies for the western region have been notable in the area of capital transfers, leading to considerable progress in infrastructure projects. In those years, the central government vastly increased its capital investment in the western region, to more than RMB270 billion, of which RMB200 billion was invested in infrastructure, over RMB50 billion in ecological improvement and environmental protection, and more than RMB10 billion in social undertakings. More than one-third of the funds generated by issuing treasury bonds, to the tune of RMB160 billion, was invested in development. Transfer payments by the central government to the western region reached RMB300 billion. The government launched 36 key construction projects in the western region, with a total investment of over RMB600 billion. By the end of 2000, more than RMB200 had been invested in construction. Key projects underway include the Qinghai-Tibet Railway, West-East Gas Pipeline Project, West-East Power Transmission Project, hydro junctions and trunk highways.[33]

One important and perhaps uniquely Chinese way of pursuing balanced development has been the policy of "paired development" that has been actively implemented since the 1990s. Under this policy, a more developed province or city, usually in the coastal region, is paired with a developing province, autonomous region or city in the west to pursue long-term, co-operative development for their mutual benefit. During the past decade, Tibet has been supported in this policy by the whole nation.[34] This aspect of development for Tibet is the focus of Chapter 21 (Ng Wing-fai), especially from the perspective of regional development and the autonomous region's very special cultural and geographical environment. In 1994, through a directive of the State Council, 13 relatively developed coastal provinces, municipalities and cities were paired in this fashion with 10 developing provinces in the western region populated with minority nationalities to accelerate development.[35] At another level, individual enterprises, such as the Hong Kong-listed electronic company, the Legend Group 聯想集團; the automobile giant, Yiqi 一汽 and the Pearl River Transport Bureau 珠江航務管理局 have begun to actively seek investment and development opportunities in the west.[36]

Other provincial units have equally seized upon the opportunities of the "go west" campaign to pursue development and modernization. Like Tibet, Xinjiang is an autonomous region where the sensitive relationships between Han Chinese and the large minority nationality population has been accorded special attention. K. C. Chau (Chapter 10) has made plain the plans and opportunities Xinjiang has designed for itself, given its unusually rich energy resources and sound agricultural base. Qinghai (Chapter 12, Li Tongshen and Liu Xiaoming), on the other hand, has chosen a pattern of development that emphasizes the construction of the ecological environment and the development of infrastructure, highlighting its unique strategic geographical position for transport links between the east and the west. Still another approach is Gansu's (Chapter 11, Fan Chuanglin and Gary M. C. Shiu) strategy of pursuing development through tourism, following its comparative advantage in this respect, with its plentiful historical sites and relics. Finally, despite Sichuan's (Chapter 16, Qingquan Liu and Gary M. C. Shiu) approach of capitalizing on the strength of its natural resources and strategic location in the southwest, China's recent entry to the World Trade Organization (WTO) and the conclusion of a free trade framework with the Association of Southeast Asian Nations (ASEAN) countries in 2001 have offered the province new challenges and opportunities. As these and other plans of the 12 provincial units come to fruition, China will gradually come to achieve the goal of balance regional development.

Challenges and Opportunities

Developing China's west will be challenging. The sprawling western region is ecologically vulnerable because of improper land-use practices in the past and lack of conservation. Poverty in remote, hilly areas is widespread and intractable. Infrastructure is rudimentary, and the region's rich natural resources have not been exploited and translated into economic wealth. Yet, the enormity of these challenges are matched by the vast opportunities that await the governments and the people of these lands to seize, as the central government has made it a policy commitment to "redevelop" this huge and highly diversified part of China to achieve the goals of national modernization and balanced development.

With China's accession to the WTO in 2001, there is the additional impetus for the western region to accelerate systemic and fundamental changes across a broad front in order to bring about rapid development. Despite the impact of fast-paced globalization over the past two decades on coastal China, the western region has been largely untouched by the growth thus generated. In 2002, the western region accounted for a meagre 3.92% of China's foreign trade, 4.14% of the country's exports, 3.69% of imports and 4.59% of foreign direct investment (FDI).[37] The lack of openness and of external trade and investment have been identified as basic causes of underdevelopment in the western region. Between 1985 and 2000, while the eastern region consistently accounted for upwards of 85% of the FDI of the country, the western region managed a pitifully low one-digit percentage share; for example, 3.9% in 2000.[38] China's entry to the WTO has liberated thought patterns and made it necessary to introduce tangible changes if the western region is to succeed in attracting foreign investment. These include improving the investment environment, changing existing laws and regulations that are incompatible with foreign investment, introducing flexible investment and free trade policies, strengthening the protection of intellectual property rights, broadening the scope and channels of foreign investment, increasing domestic capital to complement foreign investment, and emphasizing the quality and management of foreign investment projects.[39]

The push from the WTO goes hand in hand with the opportunities that beckon from the information age. They enhance the chances for China's west to "leapfrog" in development. New technologies and new methods of business transactions permit the western region to overcome the barrier of distance and skip development stages more readily than ever before. This will enable the western region to fully maximize its comparative advantage as a late developer. The programmes and plans pursued have to be based on local natural resources oriented towards the market and on the people, taking into account location and culture. More than any previous development attempts, a people-based approach is of paramount importance if new development is to be sustainable and have the capacity of translating into better futures for the inhabitants of the region and their children.

National leaders and planners have not underestimated the daunting challenges of developing and modernizing the western region. They have set realistic and realizable goals for transforming the region. The development of China's west is planned to take place over half a century. The first stage, 2000–2010, is intended to arrest ecological deterioration, improve the investment climate, initiate economic development on a virtuous circle and elevate urban-rural living conditions to approximately national levels. This is to be accomplished essentially through massive infrastructure investment, ecological construction and environmental protection. In the second stage, 2011–2030, with the resolution of the problems caused by structural adjustments in the economy, historical legacies and institutional inefficiencies, the western region will enter a period of rapid growth. Rural corporatization, marketization, regional specialization and a rural-urban transfer of labour will achieve a degree of success. The level of urbanization will exceed 50% and the standard of living will approach national levels. In the third and last phase, 2031–2049, the entire western region will have achieved modernization, with different parts arriving at this status at different times. By mid-century, China's west will be economically prosperous, ecologically balanced, ethnically united, socially progressive and culturally advanced. There will be justifiable cause for the centennial celebration of the founding of the PRC.[40]

For two millennia, China has not achieved national economic affluence as measured by the well-being of its people and a balanced space economy. At the threshold of a new century and the conjunction of several favourable internal and external factors in the era of globalization, the time has never been more opportune for the country to confront its long-standing problems in its western region of unrest among minority nationalities, religious strife, ecological/environmental instability, and the various issues troubling the countryside. There are risks and perils in doing so. Yet, the potential payoffs are immense. If development plans go on track and with sustained momentum, the western region will, in 50 years' time, fully propel itself and complement the other regions to make China a truly modernized and developed country.

Notes

1. Wu Cheng'en 吳承恩 (Ming 明), *Xi You Ji* 西遊記 (The Journey to the West) (Taipei: Wenhua tushu gongsi 文化圖書公司, 1992). Also in translation by Anthony Yu, *The Journey to the West*, 4 volumes (Chicago: University of Chicago Press, 1977, 1978, 1980, 1983).
2. See http://whc.unesco.org/nwhc/pages/doc/mainf3.htm. The 10 World Heritage sites in western China are: (1) the Great Wall 萬里長城 (parts of it), (2) Mogao Caves 莫高窟, (3) the Mausoleum of the First Qin Emperor 西安秦始皇兵馬俑, (4) the Jiuzhaigou Valley 九寨溝, (5) the Huanglong scenic and historical interest area 黃龍, (6) the Potala Palace, Lhasa 西藏布達拉宮, (7) Mount Emei, including the Leshan Giant Buddha 峨嵋山及樂山大佛, (8) the old town of Lijiang 雲南麗江古城, (9) the Dazu rock carvings 大足石刻, (10) Mount Qingcheng and the Dujiangyan irrigation system 青城山及都江堰.
3. Yang Kaizhong 楊開忠 et al., *Zhongguo xibu dakaifa zhanlüe* 中國西部大開發戰略 (Strategy of Developing China's West) (Guangzhou: Guangdong jiaoyu chubanshe 廣東教育出版社, 2001), p. 4.
4. Hu Huanyong, *The Past and Future of Population Growth and the Economic Development of China's Eight Regions* (Shanghai: East China Normal University Press, 1986), pp. 17–18.
5. Zeng Peiyan 曾培炎 et al., *Xibu zhinan* 西部指南 (Directory for the West) (Beijing: Zhongguo da baike quanshu chubanshe 中國大百科全書出版社, 2000), p. 3.
6. Zhou Yi 周毅, *Xibu dakaifa qianyan wenti yanjiu* 西部大開發前沿問題研究 (Research on Leading Questions on the Great Western Development) (Xi'an: Shaanxi renmin chubanshe 陝西人民出版社, 2002), p. 430.
7. During a field trip to Guangxi in May 2001, the author noted the especially rapid development of several ports in the province. The ambitious role that Fangchenggang 防城港 had assigned itself as the "gateway to the Southwest" was made explicit, with impressive investment in port facilities to match. The flourishing border trade also invigorated the economies of several border towns. The emergence of the southwest and its potential are reviewed in Wushengqu qifang 五省區七方 (ed.), *Zhongguo da xinan zai jueqi* 中國大西南在崛起 (The Rise of Southwest China) (Nanning: Guangxi jiaoyu chubanshe 廣西教育出版社, 1994).
8. Li Xiangqian 李向前 and Wang Shizhong 王仕忠, *Zhongguo xibu dakaifa*

chulun 中國西部大開發初論 (Introduction to the Development of China's West) (Chengdu: Sichuan cishu chubanshe 四川辭書出版社, 2000), pp. 352–54; Gao Zhen'gang 高振剛 et al., *Xibu dakaifa zhilu — Xin Ya-Ou daluqiao fazhan zhanlüe* 西部大開發之路 — 新亞歐大陸橋發展戰略 (The Road to Western Development — the New Euro-Asian Land Bridge Development Strategy) (Beijing: Jingji kexue chubanshe 經濟科學出版社, 2000), pp. 163–81.

9. Wu Jialun 伍加倫 and Jiang Yuxiang 江玉祥 (eds.), *Gudai xinan sichou zhilu yanjiu* 古代西南絲綢之路研究 (Research on the Ancient Southwest Silk Road) (Chengdu: Sichuan daxue chubanshe 四川大學出版社, 1990), pp. 1–9.
10. Zeng, *Xibu zhinan* (see note 5), p. 142. One corridor refers to a new high-tech development zone with Xi'an as the dragon head in a Guanzhong new high-tech development zone; the two cities include the Yangling agro-industrial city 楊凌農科城 and the Yanliang astronautical city 閻良飛機城; the three bases comprise those for education for R&D, energy and the chemical industry, and water-conserving agriculture; and the four pillar industries are those of fruits, tourism, high-tech production and the military.
11. Zeng, *Xibu zhinan* (see note 5), pp. 10–11.
12. Lu Dadao 陸大道 et al., *2000 Zhongguo quyu fazhan baogao — xibu kaifa de jichu, zhengce yu taishi fenxi* 2000 中國區域發展報告 — 西部開發的基礎、政策與態勢分析 (China Regional Development Report 2000 — Foundation, Policy and Situation Analysis of the Development of Western China) (Beijing: Shangwu yinshuguan 商務印書館, 2001), p. 17.
13. Yang et al., *Zhongguo xibu* (see note 3), pp. 6–9; Liu Yu'an 劉玉安, Jiang Jie 姜杰 and Chen Aiguo 陳愛國, *Zhongguo fazhan de disanci langchao* 中國發展的第三次浪潮 (The Third Wave in China's Development) (Ji'nan: Shandong daxue chubanshe 山東大學出版社, 2000); also Chapter 4 (Fan Jie).
14. *Xibu dakaifa yousilu* 西部大開發憂思錄 (Concerns about the Great Western Development). *Ming Pao Monthly*, March 2000, pp. 19–40.
15. Liu Zhiliang 劉芝良 et al., *Zhongguo diqu chaju yu xibu dakaifa zhanlüe* 中國地區差距與西部大開發戰略 (China's Regional Gaps and the Great Western Development Strategy) (Zhengzhou: Henan renmin chubanshe 河南人民出版社, 2000), pp. 43–44.
16. Zeng, *Xibu Zhinan* (note 5), pp. 9–10. A comprehensive and useful study exploring the regional disparities in China is found in Wang Mengkui 王夢奎 and Li Shantong 李善同, *Zhongguo diqu shehui jingji fazhan bupingheng wenti yanjiu* 中國地區社會經濟發展不平衡問題研究 (Research on the Problem of Regional Inequality and Social Economic Development in China) (Beijing: Shangwu yinshuguan, 2000), especially Part I.
17. Liu et al., *Zhongguo diqu chaju* (see note 15), p. 44.
18. Tian Qiusheng 田秋生 et al., *Rushihou de xibu dakaifa* 入世後的西部大開發 (The Great Western Development after Entry to WTO) (Beijing: Zhongguo shehui chubanshe 中國社會出版社, 2002), p. 202.

19. Zhou, *Xibu dakaifa* (see note 6), p. 431.
20. Hu An'gang 胡鞍鋼 (ed.), *Diqu yu fazhan: Xibu kaifa xinzhanlüe* 地區與發展 — 西部開發新戰略 (Region and Development: New Strategy in Western Development) (Beijing: Zhongguo jihua chubanshe 中國計劃出版社, 2001), pp. 6–10.
21. Wang Luolin 王洛林 and Wei Houkai 魏後凱 (eds.), *Weilai wushinian Zhongguo xibu dakaifa zhanlüe* 未來50年中國西部大開發戰略 (The Coming 50 Years of China's Great Western Development Strategy) (Beijing: Beijing chubanshe 北京出版社, 2002), pp. 10–11.
22. Wang Shaoguang and Hu An'gang, *The Political Economy of Uneven Development: The Case of China* (Armonk, New York: M. E. Sharpe, 1999).
23. Tang Gongzhao 唐公昭 and Xiao Shaoqiu 蕭少秋 (eds.), *Xibu dakaifa zhanlüe zhinan* 西部大開發戰略指南 (Pointers for the Strategy of Developing the Western Region) (Chengdu: Xi'nan caijing daxue chubanshe 西南財經大學出版社, 2000), p. 3; Chen Shupeng 陳述彭, Y. M. Yeung 楊汝萬 and Lin Hui 林琿 (eds.), *Xin jingji yu Zhongguo xibu kaifa* 新經濟與中國西部開發 (The New Economy and China's Western Development) (Hong Kong: Hong Kong Institute of Asia-Pacific Studies, The Chinese University of Hong Kong, 2001), pp. 2–3.
24. Li and Wang, *Zhongguo xibu* (see note 8), p. 3. See also Zhonggong Shanghai shiwei xuanchuanbu lilunchu 中共上海市委宣傳部理論處 (ed.), *Xibu kaifa yu Zhongguo de xiandaihua* 西部開發與中國的現代化 (Western Development and China's Modernization) (Shanghai: Shanghai renmin chubanshe 上海人民出版社, 2002). See also Hongyi Harry Lai, "China's Western Development Program: Its Rationale, Implementation and Prospects," *Modern China*, Vol. 28, No. 4 (2002), pp. 432–66.
25. Liu, *Zhongguo fazhan* (see note 15), pp. 207–26.
26. Hu, *Diqu yu fazhan* (see note 20), pp. 8–16.
27. Li and Wang, *Zhongguo xibu* (see note 8), p. 3.
28. *Xibu dakaifa yousilu* (see note 14).
29. Li and Wang, *Zhongguo xibu* (see note 8), pp. 88–90. Many other authors have emphasized the need to approach western development based on new methods, mechanisms, technology and resources. See, for example, Zhou, *Xibu dakaifa* (see note 6), pp. 51–55, 447–49; Chen et al., *Xin jingji* (see note 23), 47–51.
30. Zhou, ibid.
31. *Xibu dakaifa yousilu* (see note 14).
32. Liu et al., *Zhongguo diqu* (see note 15), pp. 285–92.
33. Western Region Development Office of the State Council, "Progress and Tasks of the Western Region Development Program" (8 March 2003). At http://www.chinawest.gov.cn/english/asp/showinfo.asp?name=200303100001 1.
34. During a reconnaissance trip to Tibet in July 2001, the author had the privilege

of meeting officials and planners from Yangzhou 揚州, Jiangsu, newly posted to Qushui 曲水, about 150 km to the southwest of Lhasa. They had just reported to duty, after two batches of officials had served their respective terms of three years. A modern and almost too extravagant city hall was being completed in a small town with wide and well-paved roads. In Shigatse 日喀則, we stayed in the Shandong Building 山東大廈, donated and built by the Shandong government. Another part of town with wide streets bearing the influence of Shanghai in advertising modes and shops was the responsibility of Shanghai. A sports stadium in Shigatse had also been constructed through this paired development project with the support of Shanghai.

35. Wang and Wei, *Weilai wushinian* (see note 21), pp. 494–511.
36. Zhang Zhiyin 張志銀 et al., *Xibu dakaifa touzi shouce* 西部大開發投資手冊 (Investment Guide to the Great Western Development) (Beijing: Jingji kexue chubanshe 經濟科學出版社, 2000), pp. 25–28.
37. Tian et al., *Ruxihou* (see note 18), pp. 44–47.
38. Ibid., p. 92.
39. Ibid., pp. 76–87.
40. Wang and Wei, *Weilai wushinian* (see note 21), pp. 52–54.

2

Historical Legacy and Future Challenges

Li Xiaojian, Y. M. Yeung and Qiao Jiajun

The development of China's western region can be traced back several thousand years. This sprawling region saw the emergence of some of China's earliest civilizations. The capital of the Chinese state was also located here during some periods, and the region was one of considerable economic importance for a long period. The area's political geography and the spatial configuration of the economic activities that took place there constitute a vital backdrop in studying the processes of change and development in western China. This chapter attempts to outline the early social and economic developments that took place in the region. Particular attention is placed on the historical legacy of the long period of state-aided development. In addition, for the purpose of comparison, the experiences of large-scale frontier developments in the United States, the former Union of Soviet Socialist Republics (USSR), and Brazil are briefly examined.

Historical Changes in Political and Economic Centres

In its long history, China has experienced many changes in the size of its territory. Accordingly, the concept of China's west should vary in different periods. For example, the western boundary of the Qin 秦 dynasty (221–207 B.C.) was drawn along a line that ran from the present-day cities of Yinchuan 銀川 to Lanzhou 蘭州 to Chengdu 成都.[1] The Qin state's economic and political centre was located in the Guanzhong Plain 關中平原 (in the middle of present-day Shaanxi 陝西 province). Despite having no clear definition, the western region during this period may be referred to as the area lying to the west of the Guanzhong Plain. The Chinese state initially controlled only a very limited area to the west of the Guanzhong Plain, but gradually expanded its reach in succeeding dynasties.

The first dynasties with wide-ranging political influence in China, the Xia 夏 (2100–1600 B.C.), Shang 商 (1600–1100 B.C.) and Zhou 周 (1100–221 B.C.) dynasties, tended to locate their capitals in the Yellow River 黃河 basin. The founder of the Qin dynasty (221–207 B.C.), the first unified empire in China, selected Xianyang 咸陽 in present-day Shaanxi as his capital. Thereafter, over a period of about 1,300 years, China's political centre gradually shifted from west to east along the Xi'an 西安-Luoyang 洛陽-Kaifeng 開封 axis. Exceptions occurred in the Eastern Jin 東晉 (A.D. 317–420), when the capital was established in Nanjing 南京, and in the Sui 隋 and Tang 唐 dynasties (A.D. 581–907) when the capital was relocated to Xi'an[2] (Figure 2.1). After this, (barring a short period during which the capital was moved to Hangzhou 杭州), Beijing 北京 became the

Figure 2.1 Locations of Capitals in Pre-Twentieth Century China, 221 B.C.–A.D. 1911

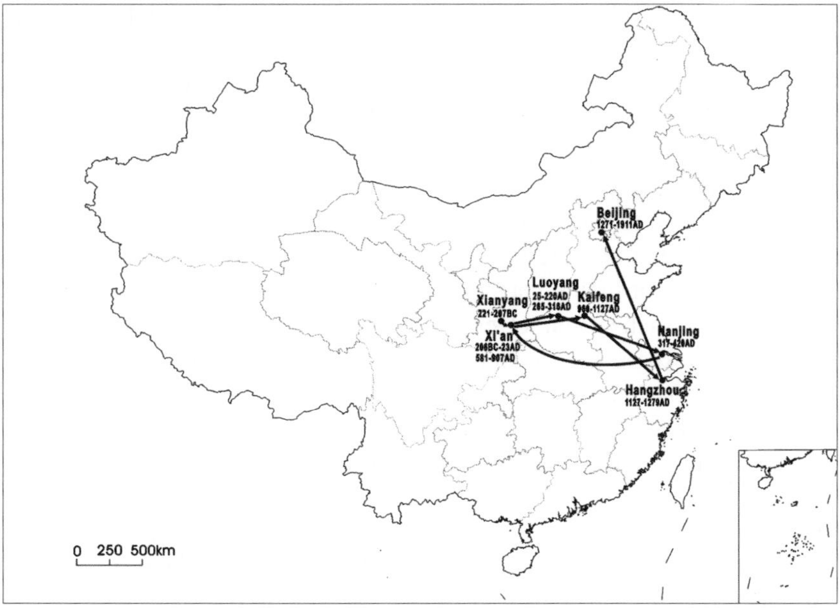

national political centre for several dynasties. If one is to generalize a historical trend, it is that China's political centres were clearly moving from the western area towards the eastern coastal region over time.

It is difficult to trace the historical changes of economic centres in China because of the incompleteness of the regional economic data. However, population records and relevant estimations provide useful bases for inference. As agriculture was the dominant economic activity and such restrictions as may have existed on population mobility during some periods were not always easy to enforce, population density may be used to measure the economic importance of regions in China's history. Thus, according to Hu and Zhang,[3] the largest concentrations of population from the Xia to Han 漢 dynasties (2100 B.C.–A.D. 220) were found in the middle and lower reaches of the Yellow River. In A.D. 2, the population of these regions was estimated to comprise more than 80% of the national total (Figure 2.2, a, region 1-3). At the end of the Western Han 西漢 dynasty (207 B.C.–A.D. 23), the turmoil caused by civil wars adversely affected economic activities in northern China (region 1-3 in Figure 2.2). This, in turn, triggered large-scale migrations to the relatively undeveloped southern China (region 4-7 in Figure 2.2). The population in the north declined to less than 60% in A.D. 140 (Figure 2.2, b). Another downturn occurred in the mid-Tang period. The so-called An-Shi Rebellion 安史之亂 (A.D. 755–762) almost destroyed the economy of previously well-developed regions in the north. The population in these regions again declined, to make up less than 40% of the national total in 1102 (Figure 2.2, c, d). By contrast, the population of southern China grew rapidly, with 22.7% and 20.4% of the total population having migrated to the southeast region (region 4 in Figure 2.2) and the central-south region (region 6), respectively, in the mid-Tang period. This short review demonstrates that the economic centre of China gradually shifted from the north to the south. Over a period of approximately 2,000 years, the middle and lower reaches of the Yangzi River 長江 gradually replaced the Yellow River basin as the most important economic region in China.

It should be mentioned that, for purposes of comparison, the large areas of the present-day western region as defined in Chapter 1 are beyond the boundaries of the main regions in Figure 2.2. In terms of the areas included in the current western region, the northwest (region 3 and 2) and southwest (region 7) regions suffered declines in population. Their proportion of the national total fell from 27.6% in 742 to 19.6% in 1820.

Four Waves of Western Development in China's History

In the long history of China, four waves of development relevant to its western region can be distinguished. The first wave occurred in the Western Han dynasty (207 B.C.–A.D. 23). Three means were employed in the development of China's west to achieve the objectives of the dynasty. First, through war and other auxiliary means, the state conquered many tribal groups in the northwest (mainly those in the present-day Xinjiang Uygur Autonomous Region 新疆維吾爾自治區 and Gansu province) and southwest (mainly the current Yunnan 雲南) and expanded its territory. Second, by establishing a county system, the central government consolidated its administrative control over a vast territory. Third, by allocating free land to farmers, the central government encouraged immigration to this region, followed by agricultural development. According to historical records, land reclamation by servicemen and immigrants in the northwest (the current Xinjiang Uygur Autonomous Region) totalled over 500,000 *mu* 畝 (1 acre = 6.6 *mu*) in the one hundred years of the development of the northwest in the Western Han dynasty.[4]

Figure 2.2 Population Distribution in Ancient China, A.D. 2–1820

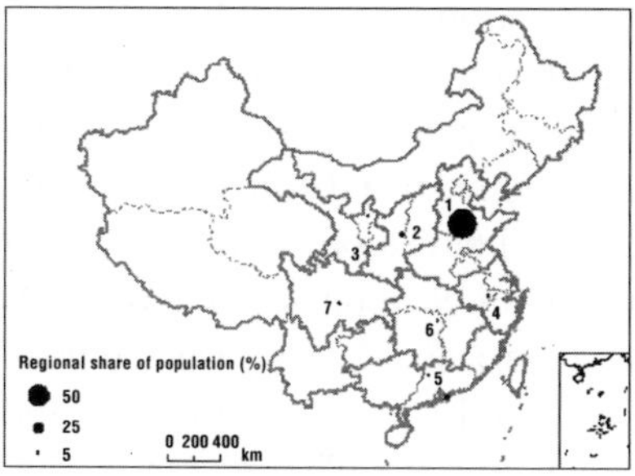

(a) A.D. 2

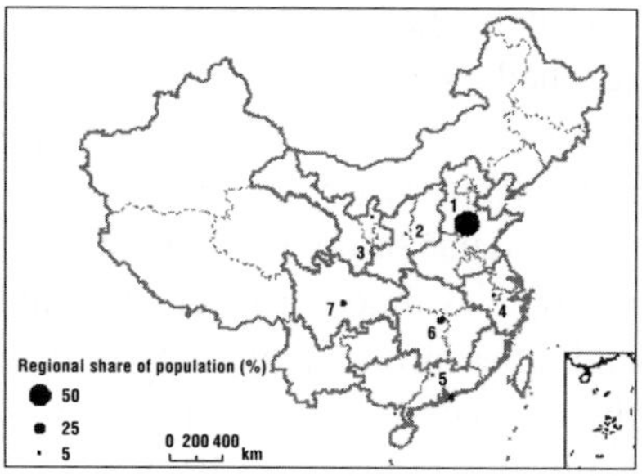

(b) A.D. 140

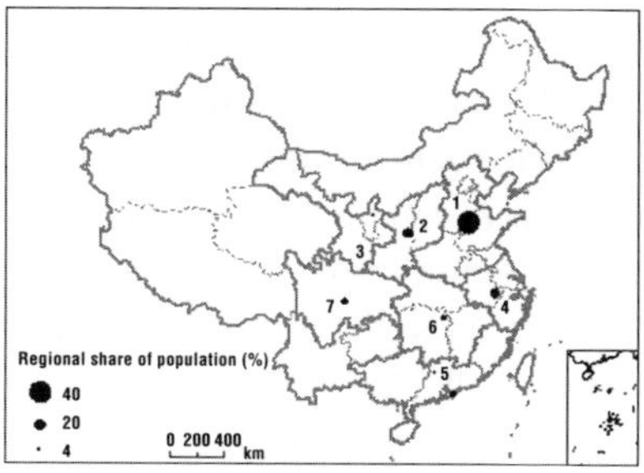

(c) A.D. 742

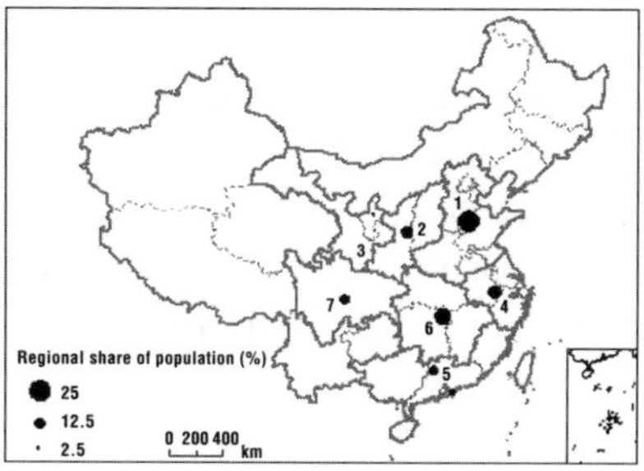

(d) A.D. 1102

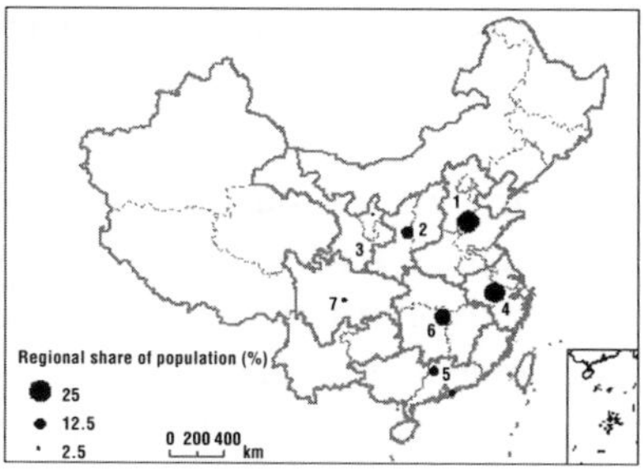

(e) A.D. 1491

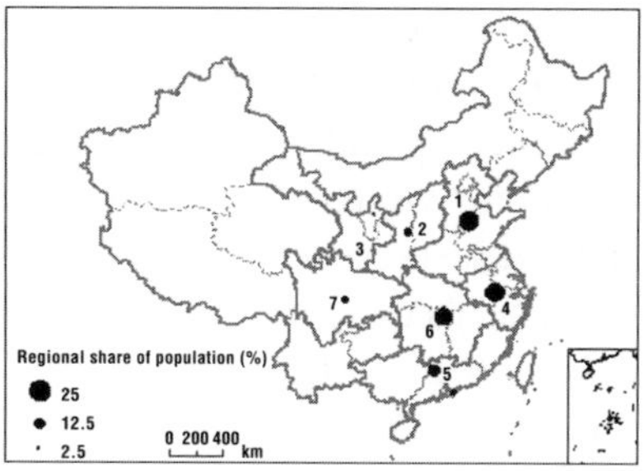

(f) A.D. 1820

Notes: 1. Lower reaches of the Yellow River; 2. Shaanxi 陝西 and Shanxi 山西; 3. Gansu 甘肅 and Ningxia 寧夏; 4. the South of the Huai River 淮河; 5. Guangdong 廣東, Guangxi 廣西 and Fujian 福建; 6. Hunan 河南, Hubei 湖北 and Jiangxi 江西; 7. Sichuan 四川

The second wave of western development in China's history emerged in the Sui (581–618) and Tang dynasties (618–907). This period was a "Golden Age" in China's history. During this period, western development reached a new level. Akin to the first wave, the development of the western region in this period was geographically only part of the development that fanned outwards in all directions from the economical and political ecumene — the Guanzhong Plain. However, the scope of development in the second period was much broader. It included, first of all, the construction of roads and other infrastructure. Domestically, several roads were constructed from the Guanzhong Plain to the northwest, west, southwest, east, northeast and southeast. Internationally, through the fabled "Silk Road" 絲綢之路, Xi'an, the capital of China at the time, was linked to many central, southern and western Asian countries. Second, the period witnessed the widespread construction of land irrigation systems. Although few relevant records are left from the Tang dynasty, over one hundred main channels were discovered to have been constructed in the Dunhuang 敦煌 area alone in this period.[5] Third, the Chinese state actively promoted trade. One emperor of the Sui dynasty chaired an international exposition in Zhangye 張掖 (in present-day Gansu province) in 605. Guests from 27 nations (or tribes) attended this exposition. This promoted commercial growth, attracting many merchants to come to the western region via the "Silk Road." In the following Tang dynasty, the Silk Road was more frequently traversed. Handicraft and commercial industries prospered.[6] The authorities began to turn their attention to setting up institutional structures. Regulations on the selection of government officials, the monitoring of granaries, and on equalized land allocation and irrigation management systems were put in place. The government also favoured immigration from outside the region and promoted agricultural development. In addition, a precedent was set in this period for western development in that the army was encouraged to help support its presence in the region by cultivating land locally.

The Yuan 元 dynasty (1271–1368) started the third wave of western development in Chinese history. Two development strategies adopted in this period need to be mentioned. First, western development was extended to many aspects of the economy. In agriculture, large-scale land reclamations were carried out by the army and farmers, with 1.5 million *mu* of land recorded as having been put to cultivation. In the handicraft industry, a trade management organization was established to promote the growth of the smelting industry, as well as of the weaving and dyeing industries. In transportation, over 60 post stations were established, thereby ensuring that orders from the central government and news of the military situation in the western region would be transmitted quickly.[7] In finance, the currency was unified in the western region to facilitate the development of commerce. In addition, the central government also introduced a policy of light taxation to reduce the burden of farmers in the western region. The second strategy adopted by the central government was to put minority groups in important positions, a policy particularly emphasized in the western region. For instance, a large number of Uyghur statesmen, strategists, scientists and artists emerged. The economy in the western region that had long been in a downturn, recovered, and prospered during the Yuan dynasty.

The fourth wave of China's western development occurred in the Manchu Qing 清 dynasty (1644–1911). The Kangxi 康熙, Yongzheng 雍正 and Qianlong 乾隆 emperors of the early and mid-Qing periods represented another flourishing age in Chinese history. There were two main elements to their policies on the western development. First, various agricultural policies were introduced to accompany a policy of large-scale immigration from China proper and cultivation of the land by soldiers. Regulations were introduced that limited the amount of land that the Manchu nobles and army generals were permitted to occupy, and provided land to demobilized soldiers who had lost their non-agricultural jobs. The government assessment system emphasized performance in land reclamation. The tax-free period for newly cultivated land was extended. The policies on land irrigation listed the relevant responsibilities of government officials at various levels.[8] The second element of western development in the Qing dynasty was its promotion of trade between farmers and herdsmen. Very large "tea and horse markets" 茶馬互市 were held in Shaanxi and Gansu every year. Sales of tea in Gansu are thought to have accounted for around 95% of the national total in the early Qing period.[9] Through this trade, agriculture and animal husbandry in the western region flourished.

The Legacy of Western Development in Pre-Twentieth-Century China

Several points can be made about the very long period of development in China's west under the aegis of the central government. Three will be mentioned here. First, during and following the Tang period, China's economic and political centres were shifting away from the western region. The sparsely populated southern and eastern China attracted large numbers of settlers from other areas of China, and eventually came to overshadow the western region in importance. In addition, marine transport and trade were developing rapidly, bringing new and important international links and strengthening the significance of the coastal area. Furthermore, much of the development that occurred in the western region was a result of government sponsorship. Although government efforts in the eastern and southern regions were not as extensive, these areas steadily grew in demographic and economic importance. Given these trends, one may ask why sustained government support through such a long period did not stop the economic downturn of the western region? Is there an internal logic which human interference cannot reverse? Otherwise, we have to admit that the strategies of the various governments were poorly conceived and ineffectively executed.

Second, throughout this period, agriculture and irrigation works were the main foci of western development. Large tracts of land came under cultivation. The northwest (the present-day provinces of Shaanxi, Gansu and Ningxia) became the main grain-producing area in the Tang dynasty, providing over 90% of the surplus grain purchased by the government (the so-called *hedi canliang* 和糴殘糧).[10] In terms of irrigation works, particularly significant networks were constructed in the Chengdu Plain 成都平原. Moreover, the introduction of grain farming skills in the western region eventually led some nomadic groups to settle down and build permanent homes in suitable locations. Throughout the long history, the local economy was heavily dependent on agriculture.

Third, from the very beginning, western development was very much a product of state intervention. As a common strategy, Chinese emperors encouraged, and even compelled, soldiers and civilians to reclaim land in the west, employing relevant preferential policies. By comparison, development in the southern and eastern regions was driven by local forces. Push (turmoil in their home areas) and pull (favourable natural environment) factors drove people to migrate into these regions from the Yellow River basin. Thus, two different styles of culture were gradually intermingled. While the eastern and southern regions have tended to welcome less state intervention, economic development in the western region has relied on state policy and support.

Fourth, along with immigration and agricultural development, human occupancy was gradually spilling over from river basins to hilly lands such as the Loess Plateau and lower mountainous areas. Some of these areas were, at best, only ecologically marginal for human settlement. The practice of slash-and-burn cultivation put tremendous pressure on the environment and caused serious land degradation. It was estimated that forest coverage in the upper and middle reaches of the Yellow River was 43% in the Qin and Han dynasties but fell to 14% by the end of the Ming 明 dynasty (1368–1644).[11] The area of desertification was gradually expanding in the northwest. Even the once prosperous Silk Road had become partly buried by deserts. This tragic ecological legacy, together with the need to ensure sustainable development, poses critical challenges for the current campaign on western development.

Finally, harmonious relations among ethnic groups appear very important in China's western development. The central government of most of the dynasties in China's history pursued careful ethnic policies, particularly with minority groups. One strategy that government used was to award the leaders of such groups with important political positions in the central administrative system. For example, Hu Bilie 忽必烈, one emperor of the Yuan dynasty, appointed a Tibetan leader master of Buddhism for the whole country, as well as making him the governor of Tibet 西藏. In the early Qing dynasty (1723), imperial ministers for Tibet 欽差駐藏辦事大臣 were sent to Lhasa 拉薩 by the emperor. But the emperor soon granted Dalai and Banchan, Tibetan leaders, equal authority as ministers. In the Ming dynasty, minority group leaders in southwestern China were appointed local officers of the state. Another strategy was to grant local autonomy to many minorities. For example, the central government in the Tang dynasty established two *Duhu Fu* 都護府 (government offices) in the area of present-day Xinjiang, and granted the *Duhu Fu* more power than the equivalent level of government in the provinces of China proper.[12] This tradition lasted for many decades. Although a few conflicts occurred, relations between ethnic groups were generally friendly.

Western Development in the Twentieth Century

The development practices of China in the last century that have had the most impact have been those since 1949. But one should not ignore the first industrial development in the western region during the period of Japanese invasion. The anti-Japanese war damaged the economy in developed regions such as northeastern, eastern and central China. The remote geographical location of the western region meant that this area escaped serious damage. Thus, Chongqing 重慶 was selected as the nation's wartime capital (*peidu* 陪都). Consequently, manufacturing industries were developed. Records show that in 1938–1942, 639 factories, together with

12,000 technicians and workers, were moved from the coastal to the western region. In addition, 4,966 new factories were established in 1937–1944.[13] This led to the rapid growth of manufacturing industries in the western region. But, as expected, development dramatically declined immediately after the end of the anti-Japanese war. Nonetheless, the interlude created a positive impact on industrial development in the region.

The zenith of western development during the twentieth century was reached in 1949–1978. Two main factors forced the central government to focus on inland development. First, dominated by national defense and socialist ideological concerns, the Maoist regime regarded the eastern coast as an unfavourable area for investment. Chinese leaders worried that this border would be vulnerable to possible military attacks from overseas.[14] Another consideration was the concentration of industry (around 70% of industrial assets and output) in the eastern coastal cities, which challenged Chairman Mao Zedong's sense of egalitarianism. Thus, the central government pursued strategies favourable to the development of the interior. The focus of capital investment in state-owned enterprises (SOEs) shifted to the inland provinces (Table 2.1). Two large investment programmes highlighted this trend. The first was the 156 Soviet-aided projects, the country's dominant investment package in the First Five-year Plan of 1953–1957. Urban locations were chosen for most of the projects. Over half were allocated to the interior provinces, including Henan, Shanxi, Gansu and Shaanxi.[15] Second, under the Third Front construction programme in the

Table 2.1 Regional Distribution of Investment in Capital Construction, 1954–1975

(Unit: %)

Period	Coastal	Interior[1]	Third Front area within the interior
1953–1957	41.8	47.8	30.6
1958–1962	42.3	53.9	36.9
1963–1965	39.4	58.0	38.2
1966–1970	30.9	66.8	52.7
1971–1975	39.4	53.5	41.1
1952–1975	40.0	55.0	40.0

Note: [1] The coastal and interior regions do not add up to 100. The discrepancy is due to the purchase of relevant transport equipment which cannot be broken down into individual locations.

Source: Lu Dadao and Victor F. S. Sit 薛鳳旋, *1997 Zhongguo quyu fazhan baogao* 1997 中國區域發展報告 (Regional Development Report 1997) (Beijing: Commercial Press, 1998), p. 6.

period 1966–1975, a large proportion of investment funds flowed to mountainous areas in central China[16] (Table 2.1, last column). The locations of the projects were characterized as in "mountains," "caves" and "diffused."

The two programmes generated very different results in terms of regional economic effects. During the period of its implementation, the per capita income in the project-concentrated provinces as a whole increased from RMB146 to 173, or from 1.19 to 1.22 times the national average (Table 2.2). Possibly as a result of these investments, income levels in the western region also exceeded the national average in 1957. By contrast, the Third Front projects did not witness any positive effects. The provinces in which they were concentrated experienced a decline in per capita national income in terms of their ratio to the national average (from 0.72 to 0.65) in 1965–1975 (Table 2.2, last column).

Three main points can be summarized from the experience of state-aided western development in the period 1949–1978. First, state intervention was clearly aimed at reducing regional disparities in manufacturing industries and securing industrial bases in case of military conflict. Second, the relevant policies might favour — but actually not succeed in — establishing industrial systems in interior China. Certainly, they did not lead to sustained economic development in the region and failed to narrow regional economic gaps. Finally, state strategies more in tune with economic principles would produce more favourable outcomes. Not surprisingly, the 156 projects located mostly in urban areas produced more positive results than the Third Front projects.

Table 2.2 Regional Comparison of Per Capita National Income, 1953–1975

Year	National average (RMB)	Western region (RMB/ratio)	Provinces involved in the 156 projects[1] (RMB/ratio)	Provinces involved in the Third Front projects[2] (RMB/ratio)
1953	122	111(0.91)	146(1.19)	81(0.66)
1957	142	146(1.03)	173(1.22)	111(0.78)
1962	139	149(1.07)	154(1.11)	105(0.75)
1965	194	193(0.99)	208(1.07)	140(0.72)
1970	235	198(0.84)	252(1.07)	156(0.66)
1975	273	238(0.87)	307(1.13)	178(0.65)

Notes: Figures in parentheses denote the ratio of the regional per capita national income to national average.
[1] including Liaoning, Heilongjiang, Jilin, Henan, Shanxi, Gansu and Shaanxi.
[2] including Sichuan, Hubei, Shaanxi, Henan and Guizhou.

Source: National Bureau of Statistics of China, *Statistical Data for the Fifty Years of New China* (Beijing: China Statistical Press, 1999).

A New Era in Western Development

The announcement of the Great Western Development Strategy in 1999 marks the start of a new era in western development. The aims of the Great Western Development Strategy are clearly stated in a State Council policy paper released in 2000.[17] To begin with, the infrastructure and ecological environment of the western region should significantly improve in the next 5 to 10 years. By the mid-twenty-first century, an entirely new west is expected to emerge with a prosperous economy, a more civil society, a modest standard of living, harmonious minority relations and a favourable environment. To reach these goals, the central government has increased capital investment, as well as offered preferential policies. For example, in 2000 the state allocated over RMB70 billion from domestic loans and the national budget to the western region for infrastructure construction, a dramatic increase from past levels of funding. The amount was further increased to RMB300 billion in 2001.[18] Also planned is an allocation of about RMB200 billion to fund reforestation and ecological reconstruction programmes by 2010. According to official documents, the favoured policies are those with a broad reach, including interregional fiscal transfers, land development and afforestation programmes, tax reforms, resource exploitation and conservation programmes, foreign investment and trade projects, and projects on the development of technology and education.[19]

Four areas in the western region have been granted priority in development: (1) the economic corridor along Xi'an-Lanzhou-Xinjiang 隴海–蘭新 railway; (2) the economic belt along the upper reaches of the Yangzi River; (3) the economic region extending along Nanning 南寧-Guiyang 貴陽-Kunming 昆明 axis; and (4) Tibet, Xinjiang and other areas with large minority populations.[20] Apart from the last mentioned one, the three target areas all have denser populations and better infrastructure, which enable them to enjoy advantages in transportation — a pre-condition for development — and access to labour supplies and markets.

There are differences to this new era of western development. First, the government's ability to intervene in the economy is declining. On the one hand, adopting the principles of a market economy, weakening budgetary controls and decentralizing decision-making have seriously weakened the power of the central government to intervene in the economy. On the other hand, WTO principles constrain the ways in which the government can directly intervene in the economy. Thus, not only is the amount of state investment limited, but possibly also the rate of return, especially for domestic loans. Second, the state is confronting a multi-dimensional task. The government has the difficult task of balancing economic growth and improved living standards with environment protection and the sustainable utilization of resources. Third, the central government has learned from past experiences and deliberately selected certain areas to act as poles of growth. It can be seen that market rules have been considered in this selection. Finally, this intervention is a long-term exercise. Given the western region's vastness and remoteness, much time will be needed to realize the government's ambitious goals.

Lessons from Other Countries

Improving the economies of their less-developed regions has been an important goal in many countries, including large ones like the United States, Russia and Brazil. Briefly reviewing the development experience in those countries may yield useful insights for China.

The development of the American West had the following characteristics. First, favourable land policies were devised to attract people and capital. From the latter 1700s to the end of the 1800s, a series of land laws were introduced that favoured settlement. To create demand, the government gradually reduced the unit of sale from 640 acres in 1785 to 160 acres in 1804. The price was lowered from US$2.00 an acre in 1800 to US$1.25 in 1820. The price of land that had no buyers after years on the market could be further lowered to 12.5 cents an acre.[21] Moreover, the Homestead Act of 1862 allowed an American citizen above the age of 21 to have less than 160 acres of land free.[22]

Second, priority was placed on developing transport infrastructure. Supported by favourable Federal Government policies, over 225,300 km of railway were constructed in 1862–1893.[23] Third, development was largely funded by private capital. According to historical data, most of the capital for railway construction in the second half of the nineteenth century (85–90%) came from this source, with some contributions from state governments.[24] Similarly, of the total cost of constructing canals during the period 1790–1909, only 13% came from the Federal Government.[25] Last, agriculture was the main sector in the early stage of development, but was replaced by manufacturing and mining industries in the mid-1900s.

The development of Siberia under the former Union of Soviet Socialist Republics (USSR) provides an example of a centrally planned economy.

This development can be divided into five stages. The first stage (1930s–1940s) focused on the establishment of coal and metal bases in the Ural-Kuznetsk region. To spur development, 322 large enterprises were relocated from the western part of the USSR to this region. The second stage (1950s) concentrated on the utilization of hydro-energy in the Angara-Yenisey region. A series of power stations were constructed, around which over 10 complexes producing specialized products were established. The main projects in the third stage (1960s) involved the exploitation of oil fields in Tyumen and Tomsk. Ten years later, Tyumen became the main oil supplier, producing half of all the oil in the country. The fourth stage (1970s) was characterized by the building of the second trans-Siberian Railroad, extending 3,145 km of line to the undeveloped Far East. The final stage (1980s) focused on the exploitation of natural gas. Two world-famous natural gas fields, Yamburg and Urengoy in the northern part of West Siberia, were developed.[26]

From this brief review of the experience of the former USSR, three points should be mentioned. First, subsequent development has gradually transformed the Siberian resource advantage to an economic advantage. The commodities produced in Siberia have become Russia's main exports and source of foreign currency earnings. This region produces 78% of Russia's oil and 84% of its natural gas, and its petro-chemical industry is expected to increase significantly in the next decade.[27] Second, the development of Siberia has narrowed disparities between eastern and western Russia to some extent. It was estimated that, in 1995, Siberia provided 24% of Russia's industrial output. The indicators of economic efficiency for a majority of Siberian regions and territories were considerably above the Russian average. Average wages in Siberia also exceeded Russia's national average by 32% in the first quarter of 1995.[28] Finally, the two Trans-Siberian Railways have played a very important part in promoting eastward development.[29]

The development of Brazil's interior is considered a successful example of economic improvement in a developing country. The development took place in four stages from the end of World War II. During this half-century, several important strategies have been employed. First, the national government has been fully involved in the development. For a long period, the state annually allocated at least 7% specifically for inland development. Fiscal transfers from developed regions to the interior each year amounted to 15–25% of total industrial output, and about 50% of total investment in supporting provinces. The relocation of the national capital in 1960 from

Rio de Janeiro on the coast to Brasilia in the interior cost the government US$4 billion.[30]

Second, the government constructed highways. The 1960s was the "period of the highway" in Brazil. Many long-distance highways into the interior were built during this period, adding greatly to the current network of national and state highways of 1.5 million km.[31] Third, growth poles were employed as a strategy to promote development. The strategy included the building of a new capital, free trade zones and regional centres. For example, in the 1980s, the Brazilian government initiated an industrial development programme for the Amazon Basin, focused on Manaus. Over 400 companies, many of them leading foreign high-tech firms, have established plants under the sponsorship of the Manaus Free Trade Zone Authority.[32] Fourth, hydropower and water conservancy projects have been stepped up. The country's reservoirs and power stations totalled over 800 in the early 1990s, which have ensured ample supplies of irrigation and energy in the relevant regions.[33]

There are lessons for China's western development in the practices of the above three countries. The following points appear to be particularly relevant. First, the government and other actors should all play a role. Second, infrastructure, such as railways and highways, is an important initiator of development. The economic growth of Siberia, the American West and inland Brazil was all fed by mushrooming transportation networks. Third, cities or regions with great growth potential should be given priority in regional policies. Fourth, the exploitation of resources is a main target for regional development. Finally, ecological and environmental issues should be handled carefully. The exploitation of frontier resources and land in the above countries caused environmental problems. For example, in Brazil, some ecologists maintain that the current development programme in the Amazon Basin, which includes logging, mining and the expansion of settlements, may bring disastrous results in the long term.[34]

The Challenging Future

The historical survey of this chapter has revealed that the state's efforts to develop China's western region has lasted for over two thousand years, despite periods of interruption. However, continuous government support has not raised the region's economic position. Apart from population growth, its economic development still lags far behind that of the coastal region. In fact, a large proportion of the population in this region is economically deprived. Even the areas that have received strong support from the central government, such as those where the Third Front projects were located, show no substantial improvement. Three findings may be summarized from the historical study. First, the economic improvement of a less-developed region presents a real challenge for the government. This is particularly true if the development potential of the target region is weak. The evidence is strong of China's failure to jump-start growth in less-developed areas during the period of central planning, when the state had almost absolute power to allocate national resources. Second, continuous government support over a long period did not generate healthy, local, self-growth mechanisms. Rather, by causing a strong reliance on state assistance, such support may in fact have been negative for regional development. Third, more important than the government's capacity to support a region is the method it adopts to do so. This observation carries a special significance for China, where the political and personal preferences of key decision-makers have strongly influenced the process of policy formulation.

In developing its western region, China can learn from the past experiences of other countries. However, the western region of China differs from the regions of the United States, Russia and Brazil mentioned earlier, both in its development history and in geographical conditions. To be precise, China's west is inhabited by 355.3 million people, although large stretches are comprised of mountains and deserts and are inhospitable to settlement. In terms of carrying capacity, one-fifth of the land area in the western region has been assessed as overloaded.[35] Moreover, as an economy in transition, the Chinese state has many tasks with which to contend when attempting to foster growth in less-developed regions. These include the decentralization of public administration, marketization of economic systems and privatization of economic activities. There is also the factor of global competition, making it harder for the region to move forward. The experience of other countries that have developed their frontier regions may, therefore, not be directly transferable to China. The development of China's western region consequently calls for a new way of thinking and well-designed methods.

First, priority should shift from national industrialization to local interests, especially those of the local people. Western development in history, particularly in the period of the 1950s–1970s, was manifestly driven by national interests. The 156 projects and Third Front programme were conceived mainly for the purpose of building a national industrial system. Although local areas may have benefited from the policy, their socioeconomic development was not a major policy goal. Consequently, government policies in general failed to promote local development. Given the long history of human occupancy in an often harsh environment, the imperative in the current programme to develop the west should focus squarely on "people becoming well-off" rather than on fostering a "booming region." Put differently, not every local area should be developed. In those areas where the ecology is fragile, the residents should migrate to other suitable sites. Urbanization can be facilitated if the migration is channelled to planned towns and cities.

The second suggestion relates to the mechanism of western development. Learning lessons from past experience, state support should be implemented through market rules. At least four points need to be highlighted here. First, state investment should be used as an engine to jump-start the flow of other sources of capital, and not be viewed as the only source of investment. A heavy reliance on state capital is more likely to cause the region to stagnate, rather than result in sustainable economic growth, which requires that investment be multidimensional. Second, economic growth in the region should not be entirely driven by capital investment. Domestic demand and exports should also play a role. The central and provincial governments should pay due attention to the latter two dimensions. Third, when implementing relevant projects, the government should be mindful of the rate of return of state investments. This issue is particularly important because the Chinese government has a tendency to focus on the political or social outcomes of state investment at the expense of economic returns. Finally, the clustering of economic activities is the most distinctive feature of the space economy.[36] The advantages of infrastructure, information, personnel and relevant supporting services enable clusters to have a high potential for development. Following this rule of the market economy, various levels of growth centres, such as cities and towns, can be selected and given priority for development. In this way, rapid economic growth in the western region is more likely to be achieved.

Finally, institutional innovation is fundamental to western development. Why have some provinces such as Zhejiang 浙江 that have received little favourable treatment from the central government yet managed to achieve rapid economic growth since 1978? Why have those provinces in the southeast continued to grow at a rapid rate after government policy has veered to favour the inland areas? There must be some endogenous reasons behind the growth of such areas. Cultural values and "institutional thickness" have played key roles. Compared to the culture in the southeastern coast, where people habitually take risks running industrial and commercial business, the traditional agricultural society of the vast west has not changed a great deal. As long as they have enough to eat, people in the region are content to remain engaged in small-scale, low-return household farming. In terms of the notion of institutional thickness as defined by Amin and Thrift,[37] its main elements — a strong institutional presence, high levels of interaction among the institutions and a common industrial purpose — can be found in the fast-growing provinces. These factors promote the rapid growth of private businesses, which have become the mainstay of the economies of those provinces. For instance, the private and collective sectors accounted for over 80% of the industrial output of Zhejiang, Fujian 福建, Guangdong and Jiangsu 江蘇 in 1995.[38] By contrast, in the western region, the state-owned sector still occupied 65.5% in the same year. The relative lack of private involvement in the economy of the western region is what contributes to the gap that exists between it and the coastal areas. Thus, it is crucial for the western region to learn from the coastal region about institutional innovations. Although these endogenous factors are more or less a local heritage, the government's participation is still important. The government can establish quasi-government organizations for financial and technological promotion and thereby directly foster local institutional networks. Through training and educational programmes, the government can also introduce and spread modern industrial culture and values to the western region. The aim is not to act in defiance of local cultural values but to fertilize the local soil to encourage the growth of economic trees.

Since entering the World Trade Organization (WTO) in December 2001, the development of China's regions is becoming more closely linked to outside forces. Following WTO protocols and adhering to scheduled commitments will bring both opportunities and challenges for China's western development. In this regard, four points may be mentioned. First, strong pressure will be put to reform China's institutions. This will speed up the process of transition from a planned to market system. The growth of multiple forms of ownership will reduce the state-owned sector's share in the economy. This is particularly important for China's west, because this region at present remains one that is most heavily affected by state planning in economic development. Second, more capital and technology will be brought to the west. One channel is through foreign investment. Another opportunity is offered by private capital from coastal China. This capital is more likely to flow into the west, because China's WTO entry will attract large-scale foreign direct investment into the coastal region, which will strongly compete with local private capital. Third, industries are facing various opportunities and pressures. For example, labour-intensive industries, such as textiles and tourism, can be expected to see growth in the west. Animal husbandry, and fruit and vegetable cultivation are also competitive in the international market. By contrast, grain farming in China is facing serious challenges, as costs are much higher than in developed countries. Finally, the situation for employment is serious. Although employment in the sectors with a comparative advantage is likely to expand, the largest economic sector in the west — agriculture — is shrinking. The large numbers of unemployed farmers, with little education and few skills that are in demand in non-agricultural industries, will lead to serious social problems that will challenge governments at different levels.

The many challenges notwithstanding, the success of the Great Western Development Strategy can be predicted in some aspects. First, infrastructure in the western region can be substantially improved. According to the Tenth Comprehensive Five-year Plan for the Development of the west, the government's main priority is on developing a national and inter-provincial network of highways and railways to link the west to the coast and to major cities within the west, as well as to the main airports.[39] As a symbolic project, the 1,100-km Qinghai-Tibet Railway has been under construction in the world's highest plateau. Second, the ecological system and the natural environment of the west are expected to be much improved. The policy of returning cultivated lands to forest and grassland has been implemented. Environmental protection and pollution controls in the upper reaches of the Yangzi and Yellow Rivers have become major concerns for the government. Third, the future offers grounds for optimism in that the region's resource-based industries and tourism industry offer great potential. Finally, the living standards of local people in the west are likely to improve. The Tenth Comprehensive Five-year Plan for the Development of the west emphasizes the principle of encouraging people to become rich.[40] More importantly, the Sixteenth Congress of the Communist Party of China, held in November 2002, announced a new national target for the first two decades of this century — to build a society in which prosperity is broadly based. According to the report delivered by Jiang Zemin on 9 November 2002, this means an all-inclusive search for higher standards, including different groups of people.[41] Certainly, people in the west will benefit from this blueprint.

Acknowledgements

The research for this chapter was supported by a grant from the National Science Foundation of China (No. 40271038) and by the Lippo Urban Research Fund at CUHK. The authors wish to thank Fan Xinsheng 樊新生 for his help in conducting the research for this chapter.

Notes

1. Zhongguo lishi dituji bianjizu 中國歷史地圖集編輯組, *Zhongguo lishi dituji* (di er ce) 中國歷史地圖集（第二冊）(The Historical Atlas of China, Volume 2) (Beijing: Zhonghua ditu xueshe chuban 中華地圖學社出版, 1975), pp. 3–4.
2. Wu Songdi 吳松弟, *Zhongguo gudai ducheng* 中國古代都城 (The Capitals of Ancient China) (Taipei: Taiwan shangwu yinshuguan 台灣商務印書館, 1994), pp. 5–77.
3. Hu Huanyong 胡煥庸 and Zhang Shanyu 張善余, *Zhongguo renkou dili* 中國人口地理 (Population Geography of China) (Shanghai: Huadong shifan daxue chubanshe 華東師範大學出版社, 1984), pp. 16–17.
4. Wu Tingzhen 吳廷楨 and Guo Houan 郭厚安, *Hexi kaifashi yanjiu* 河西開發史研究 (A History of the Development of the Western Region) (Lanzhou: Gansu jiaoyu chubanshe 甘肅教育出版社, 1996), pp. 42–66.
5. Ibid., pp. 225–27.
6. See Volumes 3, 24, 67 of *Sui shu* 隋書.
7. Li Zhian 李治安 and Wang Xiaoxin 王曉欣, *Yuanshixue gailun* 元史學概論 (Introduction to the History of Yuan Dynasty) (Tianjin: Tianjin jiaoyu chubanshe 天津教育出版社, 1989), p. 147.
8. Yang Jianguo 楊建國 and Yao Aiqin 姚愛琴, "Zhongguo dangdai xibu kaifa jingyan zhengce ji qishi" 中國當代西部開發經驗政策及啟示 (A Brief Survey of Western Development Policies in the Contemporary Period and Its Lessons), *Kaifa yanjiu* 開發研究 (Development Studies), No. 6 (2000), pp. 62–63.
9. Yang Chongqi 楊重琦 and Wei Mingkong 魏明孔 (eds.), *Lanzhou jingjishi* 蘭州經濟史 (The Economic History of Lanzhou) (Gansu: Lanzhou daxue chubanshe 蘭州大學出版社, 1991), p. 90.
10. Lu Dadao 陸大道 et al., *1999 Zhongguo quyu fazhan baogao* 1999 中國區域發展報告 (Regional Development Report 1999) (Beijing: Shangwu yinshuguan 商務印書館, 2000), p. 20.
11. Zhu Guangyao 祝光耀, "Guanyu xibu kaifazhong shengtai huanjing baohu de diaocha yu sikao" 關於西部開發中生態環境保護的調查與思考 (Conservation of Ecological Environment in China's West: A Survey and Analysis), *Zhongguo huanjing guanli* 中國環境管理 (China Environment Management), No. 2 (2000), pp. 4–6.
12. Lu, *1999 Zhongguo quyu* (see note 10), pp. 22–23.

13. Zhongguo dabaike quanshu bianji weiyuanhui 中國大百科全書編輯委員會, *Zhongguo dabaike quanshu: Jingji juan* 中國大百科全書：經濟卷 (China Encyclopedia: Economics) (Beijing: Zhongguo dabaike quanshu chubanshe 中國大百科全書出版社, 1988), p. 496.
14. Yue-man Yeung and Xuwei Hu (eds.), *China's Coastal Cities: Catalysts for Modernization* (Honolulu: University of Hawaii Press, 1992), p. 4.
15. The First Five-year Plan released in 1955 identified 156 major Soviet-aided projects. But as 2 of them were counted twice and 4 were not implemented, the actual total is 150. For a detailed discussion of this programme, see Dong Zhikai 董志凱, "Guanyu '156 xiang' de queli" 關於「156項」的確立 (On the Establishment of the 156 Projects), *Zhongguo jingjishi yanjiu* 中國經濟史研究 (China Economic History Studies), Vol. 4 (1999), pp. 93–107.
16. The Third Front refers to a geographical area covering Sichuan, Guizhou, Gansu, Shaanxi and the western parts of Hunan, Hubei and Henan. The Third Front construction programme, starting from 1965 and lasting until 1975, was designed to allocate massive resources to developing defense-oriented industries constructed in the remote Third Front region. See Wei Yehua, Dennis, *Regional Development in China: States, Globalization, and Inequality* (London: Routledge, 2000), pp. 77–79. Also, Barry Naughton, "The Third Front: Defence Industrialization in the Chinese Interior," *The China Quarterly*, No. 115 (1988), pp. 351–86.
17. See *Guowuyuan guanyu shishi xibu dakaifa ruogan zhengce cuoshi de tongzhi* 國務院關於實施西部大開發若干政策措施的通知 (State Council Announcement on the Implementation of the Relevant Policies and Measures on the Great Western Development) (No. 2000-33). This is the basic government document on the Great Western Development, which has guided several succeeding official documents and a five-year overall plan by the Office of Western Development under the State Council.
18. See http://www.developwest.gov.cn/content.asp?filename=txt/20010918001.htm.
19. See note 10 and other two important government documents: *Guanyu xibu dakaifa ruogan zhengce cuoshi de shishi yijian* 關於西部大開發若干政策措施的實施意見 (The Guidelines for Implementing the Policies and Measures on the Great Western Development) released by the Office of Western Development under the State Council on 28 August 2001, and *Shiwu xibu kaifa zongti guihua* 十五西部開發總體規劃 (The Tenth Comprehensive Five-year Plan for the Development of the West) prepared by the same authority in July 2002.
20. Ibid.
21. J. H. Paterson, *North America: A Geography of the United States and Canada,* 9th edition (New York: Oxford University Press, 1994), p. 98.
22. Ibid.

23. Zhang Tian 張天, "Lun Meiguo xibu de kaifa jiqi lishi yiyi" 論美國西部的開發及其歷史意義 (Historical Significance of America's Development of the West), *Ningxia shehui kexue* 寧夏社會科學 (Ningxia Social Science), No. 1 (2001), pp. 78–81.
24. Tian Zuhai 田祖海, "Meiguo xibu kaifa jingyan dui woguo de qishi" 美國西部開發經驗對我國的啟示 (Inspirations from the American Experience on Western Development), *Wuhan Jiaotong Daxue xuebao (shekeban)* 武漢交通大學學報（社科版） (Journal of Wuhan Jiaotong University (Social Science edition)), Vol. 13, No. 3 (2000), pp. 57–61.
25. Sun Ying 孫穎, "Meiguo xibu kaifa jidui woguo de qishi" 美國西部開發及對我國的啟示 (The Development of the American West and Its Inspiration for China), *Jingji zongheng* 經濟縱橫 (Economic Horizon), Vol. 10 (2000), pp. 45–47.
26. Feng Zhijun 馮之浚 (ed.), *Lun xibu kaifa* 論西部開發 (On Western Development) (Hangzhou: Zhejiang jiaoyu chubanshe 浙江教育出版社, 2000), pp. 174–78.
27. Norman Chance and Elena Andreeva. 2002. "Gas Development in Northwest Siberia." At http://arcticcircle.uconn.edu/NatResources/gasdev.html.
28. http://www.friends-partners.org/oldfriends/siberia/eco_bus/f1_2.html.
29. Harm J. de Blij and Peter O. Muller, *Geography: Realms, Regions, and Concepts*, 7th edition (New York: John Wiley & Sons, 1994), p. 158.
30. Xiong Kunxin 熊坤新 and Tao Xiaohui 陶曉輝, "Baxi kaifa bufada diqu de zhongyao jucuo" 巴西開發不發達地區的重要舉措 (Important Methods on Developing Undeveloped Regions of Brazil), *Kaifa yanjiu* 開發研究 (Development Studies), No. 2 (2001), pp. 63–65.
31. Guo Yuanzeng 郭元增, "Baxi kaifa beixibu de jingyan he jiaoxun" 巴西開發北西部的經驗和教訓 (Experience and Lessons from Developing the Northwestern Region in Brazil), *Dangdai shijie* 當代世界 (Contemporary World), No. 5 (2000), pp. 20–22.
32. James S. Fishers, *Geography and Development*, 5th edition (Englewood Cliffs, New Jersey: Prentice Hall, 1995), p. 466.
33. Feng, *Lun xibu* (see note 26), pp. 179–84.
34. Fishers, *Geography and Development* (see note 32), p. 467.
35. Li Baolin 李寶林, Zhou Chenghu 周成虎, Chen Lijun 陳利軍, Feng Xianfeng 馮險峰, Yao Yonghui 姚永慧 and Cheng Weiming 程維明, "Xibu kaifa renkou/tudi chengzaili pinggu" 西部開發人口/土地承載力評估 (Assessment of Population/Land Carrying Capacity in the Western Region), in *Xin jingji yu Zhongguo xibu kaifa* 新經濟與中國西部開發 (The New Economy and China's Western Development), edited by Chen Shupeng 陳述彭, Yeung Yue-man 楊汝萬 and Lin Hui 林琿 (Hong Kong: Hong Kong Institute of Asia-Pacific Studies, 2001), pp. 153–69.
36. Peter Sunley, "Urban and Regional Growth," in *A Companion to Economic*

Geography, edited by Eric Sheppard and Trevor J. Barnes (Oxford: Blackwell Publishers Ltd., 2000), pp. 187–201.

37. See Ash Amin and Nigel Thrift, "Living in the Global," in *Globalization, Institutions, and Regional Development in Europe,* edited by Ash Amin and Nigel Thrift (Oxford: Oxford University Press, 1994), pp. 1–22, and "Globalization, Institutional 'Thickness' and the Local Economy," in *Managing Cities: The New Urban Context,* edited by Patsy Healey, Stuart Cameron, Simin Davoudi, Stephen Graham and Ali Madani-pour (Chichester: John Wiley & Sons, 1995), pp. 91–108.
38. See Wei, *Regional Development in China* (see note 16), p. 106.
39. See *Shiwu xibu kaifa zongti guihua* (see note 19).
40. Ibid.
41. See Jiang Zemin 江澤民, "Quanmian jianshe xiaokang shehui, jianshe you Zhongguo tese shehui zhuyi 全面建設小康社會，建設有中國特色社會主義 (Build a Society in which Prosperity is Broadly Based and Build a Socialism with Chinese Characteristics), *Jingji ribao* 經濟日報 (Economic Daily), 9 November 2002, pp. 2–3.

3

Geographical Background and Sustainable Development

Niu Wenyuan and David Y. Q. Chen

In terms of both territory and population, China is immense. The country covers about 9.6 million km^2 or 6.5% of the world's land area, ranking it third in territorial area after Russia and Canada. With nearly 1.3 billion people, equivalent to about 22% of the earth's human population, China is the most populous country in the world. China is also extremely diverse, both in physical environment and socioeconomic status. As with other large countries with significant regional disparities, the regional divisions can be viewed from different perspectives. In terms of economic development, the regionalization largely demonstrates a gradient from the country's coastal area to its inland territory. This axis stretches from east to west and, therefore, China's west generally implies its interior provinces. This chapter first defines the geographical extent, location and vast territory of the west 西部. The geographical background of the region is illustrated in an introductory discussion of its population, economy, physical environment and natural resources. Based on an analysis of the ecological and environmental challenges facing the region, strategies for sustainable development are mapped out as a critical pathway to the future.

Geographical Extent, Location and Vast Territory

China is currently divided into 23 provinces (including Taiwan 台灣), 4 municipalities and 5 autonomous regions. In addition to these 32 administrative units at the provincial level, there are 2 special administrative regions — Hong Kong 香港 and Macau 澳門. As shown in Table 3.1, China has traditionally been divided into six regions, in addition to the Qinghai-Tibet Plateau. This table presents a broad geographical context for understanding the general concept of the west.[1] Since the founding of the PRC in 1949, the Chinese government has adopted at least three major regionalization schemes, mainly for purposes of economic planning. As shown in Table 3.2, in the early 1950s the country was first divided into two macro regions — the coastal and inland areas.[2] About 10 years later, as a result of changes in both the domestic situation and in the international political climate, China's leaders launched the so-called "Third Front Construction" in the early 1960s. The construction was largely for national defence purposes, to create an entire industrial system within a naturally remote and strategically secure region (Table 3.2).[3] The late 1970s saw an increasing focus on economic development. The state government began to mandate different economic policies for various regions throughout the country, giving some areas priority in financial investment and resource

Table 3.1 Traditional Regional Divisions of Mainland China

Region	Administrative unit
Northeast China 東北	Liaoning 遼寧, Jilin 吉林, Heilongjiang 黑龍江
North China 華北	Beijing 北京, Tianjin 天津, Hebei 河北, Henan 河南, Shandong 山東, Shanxi 山西, Shaanxi 陝西
Central China 華中	Shanghai 上海, Zhejiang 浙江, Jiangsu 江蘇, Hubei 湖北, Hunan 湖南, Jiangxi 江西, Anhui 安徽
South China 華南	Fujian 福建, Guangdong 廣東, Guangxi 廣西, Hainan 海南
Southwest China 西南	Chongqing 重慶, Sichuan 四川, Guizhou 貴州, Yunnan 雲南
Northwest China 西北	Gansu 甘肅, Inner Mongolia 內蒙古, Ningxia 寧夏, Xinjiang 新疆
Qinghai-Tibet Plateau 青藏高原	Qinghai 青海, Tibet 西藏

Note: Taiwan is not included. As provincial-level administrative units, Hainan and Chongqing were established in 1988 and 1997, respectively.
Source: Adopted from Zhao (1986) (see note 1), with modifications.

Table 3.2 Three Schemes of Economic Regionalization in China

Time	Region	Administrative unit
First Five-year Plan (1953–1957)	Coastal 沿海	Liaoning, Beijing, Tianjin, Hebei, Shandong, Shanghai, Zhejiang, Jiangsu, Fujian, Guangdong, Guangxi (11 units)
	Inland 內地	All the other 18 provincial units
Early 1960s–Early 1970s	Third Front 三線	Sichuan, Yunnan, Guizhou, Gansu, Qinghai, Ningxia, a portion of Shaanxi (south of the Qinling mountains) and the western, mountainous portions of Henan, Hubei and Hunan
	First Front 一線 and Second Front 二線	All of the rest
Seventh Five-year Plan (1986–1990)	East 東部	Liaoning, Beijing, Tianjin, Hebei, Shandong, Zhejiang, Jiangsu, Fujian, Guangdong, Guangxi, Hainan (12)
	Central 中部	Heilongjiang, Jilin, Inner Mongolia, Shanxi, Henan, Anhui, Jiangxi, Hubei, Hunan (9)
	West 西部	Sichuan (including Chongqing), Guizhou, Yunnan, Tibet, Shaanxi, Gansu, Qinghai, Ningxia, Xinjiang (9)

allocation. The result was general economic growth, but of a highly unbalanced nature among the regions. It was in the mid-1980s, when the Seventh Five-year Plan (1986–1990) was formulated, that the west first appeared as an economic region in China's development policy. The "East-Central-West" 東部–中部–西部 approach followed in the Seventh Five-year Plan is both a characterization of the geographical divisions in the country as well as a true reflection of the remarkable regional disparities in China's economic development since the "reform and open-door" policy was first introduced in the late 1970s. At the turn of the century, Chinese top leadership clearly recognized the extent to which economic development in the coastal and interior regions had become unbalanced, and insightfully announced the development of the west as a national priority. The central authorities initially derived the definition of the west from the economic regionalization scheme of the Seventh Five-year Plan, and later expanded it to include Inner Mongolia 內蒙古 and Guangxi 廣西. They did this for two reasons. First, both units are autonomous regions of minority nationalities and their economic development lags far behind that of the coastal provinces. Second, there are major barriers to development in the two regions, that is, extensive desertification in Inner Mongolia and large areas of poverty in Guangxi, making it necessary that the two regions be granted some preferential policies. This official 10+2-unit definition demarcates the geographical boundaries and extent of the west (Figure 3.1).

The west is a regional concept with a strong implication of unbalanced socioeconomic development in relation to the rest of the country. An overlay of its administrative boundaries with other geographical features of the nation clearly brings out some of the region's basic characteristics. As shown in Figure 3.1, the west (73°25' – 126°04' E, 20°54' – 53°23' N) is largely located west of the 110°E meridian (except for northeastern Inner Mongolia). Along the 100°E meridian, it can approximately be divided into two parts. The eastern part is the Near West 近西部 (e.g., Shaanxi 陝西 and Sichuan 四川), where population densities and levels of economic development are close to those of the central provinces. The western part is the Far West 遠西部 (e.g., Tibet 西藏 and Xinjiang 新疆), which possesses much stronger "western" characteristics such as a sparse population, backward economy, harsh environment, but plenty of natural resources.

China has a three-stepped topography, with generally declining elevations from the west to the east. As shown in Figure 3.1, the west (except for a large part of Guangxi) mostly occupies the first and second steps

Figure 3.1 Geographical Extent of China's West, along with the Three-stepped Topography and Three Natural Regions of China

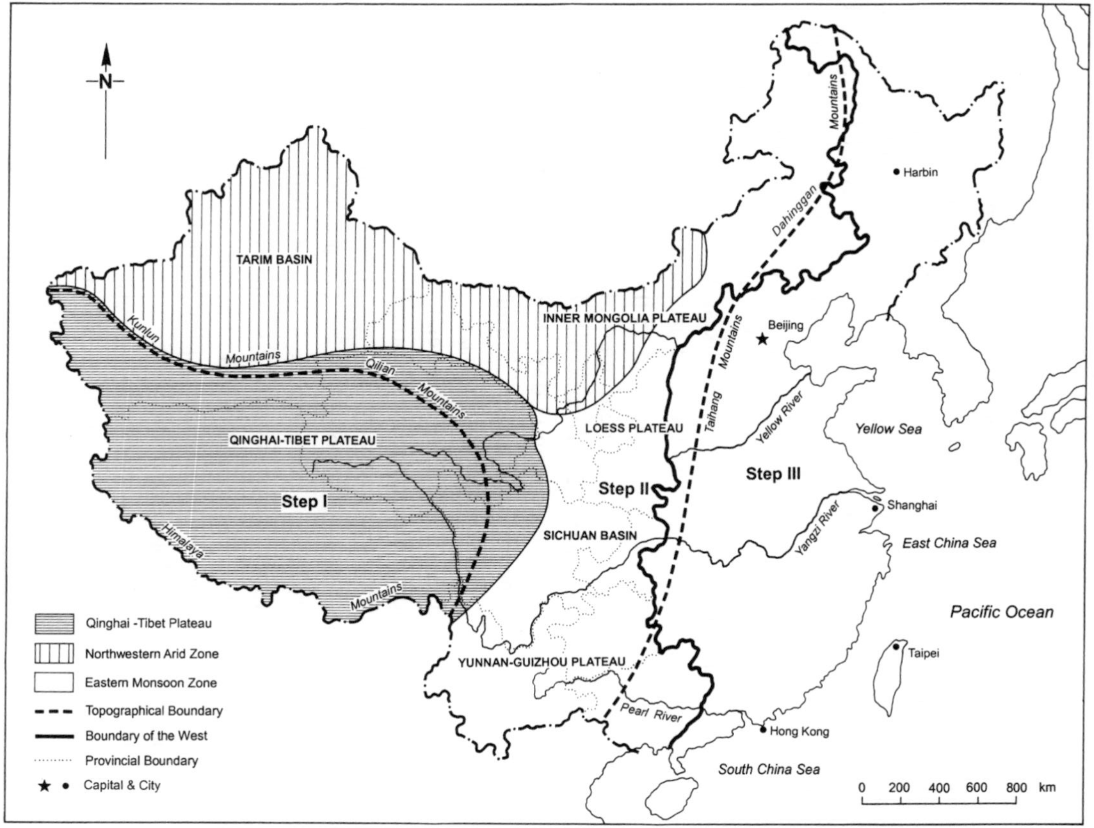

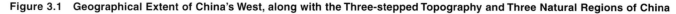

where extensive highlands, mountains and basins largely constitute the regional landform. Based on the natural landscape, particularly climatic conditions, China is broadly divided into three regions, that is, the Eastern Monsoon Zone 東部季風區, the Northwestern Arid Zone 西北乾旱區 and the Qinghai-Tibet (Tibetan) Plateau 青藏高寒區. The greater part of the west is situated within the latter two non-monsoon regions, where environmental conditions are generally harsh. There are severe shortages of water in the northwest and the highland climate of the Qinghai-Tibet Plateau is frigid. The geographical location of the west not only determines the region's physical environment, but also carries enormous geo-political implications that are vital to the stability and peace of China and its neighbouring countries. Situated in the heartland of the Asian continent, China's west shares a 14,970 km borderline (about 2/3 of the country's total) with 14 countries and regions in Central and Southeast Asia, including Mongolia and Russia to the north, Pakistan, Afghanistan, Tajikistan, Kyrgyzstan and Kazakhstan to the west and northwest, and India, Nepal, Bhutan, Myanmar, Laos and Vietnam to the southwest. This strategic location presents both development opportunities and challenges for the west. Trade and other activities of economic co-operation with neighbouring countries have boosted economic development and thus alleviated the disadvantages of the region's largely inland location. In fact, the ancient Silk Road running through the west was historically a key link of enormous cultural and economic importance between China and the rest of the world. On the other hand, however, the west's long borderline is of considerable political and military sensitivity. The countries bordering China are tremendously diverse in terms of ethnicity, culture, religion and political systems; what they have in common are less developed economies, racial divisions and, at times, social instability arising from political or religious conflicts within or between individual countries. Needless to say, these geo-political factors will continue to play a vital role in the long-term socioeconomic development of the west.

That the west has a vast territory is clearly shown by various figures. As presented in Table 3.3, its total area of 6.8 million km^2 comprises about 71% of the country's territory, and the average area of a western province (567,000 km^2) is 1.83 times the national average (310,000 km^2). In China, seven of the eight largest provinces are located in the west. In order of size, they are Xinjiang, Tibet, Inner Mongolia, Qinghai 青海, Sichuan, Heilongjiang 黑龍江, Gansu 甘肅 and Yunnan 雲南. At the same time, while the three largest provinces are most representative of the

Table 3.3 Twelve Administrative Units of the West: Abbreviation, Capital City and Area

Sub-region	Unit	Abbreviation	Type of administration	Capital city	Area	
					Total (1,000 km²)	% of country
Southwest 西南	Chongqing	Yu 渝	Municipality	Chongqing 重慶	82	0.9
	Sichuan	Chuan 川 or Shu 蜀	Province	Chengdu 成都	485	5.1
	Guizhou	Gui 貴 or Qian 黔	Province	Guiyang 貴陽	177	1.8
	Yunnan	Yun 雲 or Dian 滇	Province	Kunming 昆明	394	4.1
	Tibet	Zang 藏	Autonomous region	Lhasa 拉薩	1,200	12.5
	Guangxi	Gui 桂	Autonomous region[1]	Nanning 南寧	236	2.5
Northwest 西北	Shaanxi	Shaan 陝 or Qin 秦	Province	Xi'an 西安	206	2.1
	Gansu	Gan 甘 or Long 隴	Province	Lanzhou 蘭州	454	4.7
	Qinghai	Qing 青	Province	Xining 西寧	722	7.5
	Ningxia	Ning 寧	Autonomous region[2]	Yinchuan 銀川	66	0.7
	Xinjiang	Xin 新	Autonomous region[3]	Urumqi 烏魯木齊	1,600	16.7
	Inner Mongolia	Meng 蒙	Autonomous region	Hohhot 呼和浩特	1,183	12.3
	Regional average				567	5.9
	Regional total				6,805	70.9
	National average				310	3.2
	National total				9,600	100

Notes: [1] Zhuang 壯族; [2] Hui 回族; [3] Uygur 維吾爾族.

Source: Figures of area were obtained from Liang Xiyong 梁希勇 et al. (see note 4), p. 4.

vastness of the western territory (Xinjiang, with one-sixth of the national area; and Tibet and Inner Mongolia, with about one-eighth each), Ningxia 寧夏 (comprising only about 4% of Xinjiang's area) and Chongqing 重慶 are among the smallest provincial-level administrative units in the country. Generally, however, a basic geographical feature of the west as a whole or in terms of its individual units is its territorial immensity.

Diversified Population and Less Developed Economy

In contrast to its vast territory, the west has a relatively small population compared to the central and especially the coastal provinces. As shown in Table 3.4, only 28.1% of the country's population resides in the west, which comprises 70.9% of the nation's territory. For a variety of economic, environmental and historical reasons, population densities are generally lower in the western provinces, particularly in the Far West. On average

Table 3.4 Population and the Ethnic Composition of the West, 2000

Unit	Population			Composition		
	Total (million persons)	% of national total	Density (persons/ km^2)	Ethnic population (%)	Urban (%)	Rural (%)
Inner Mongolia	23.76	1.9	20.1	20.8	42.7	57.3
Guangxi	44.89	3.5	190.2	38.3	28.2	71.8
Chongqing	30.90	2.4	376.8	6.4	33.1	66.9
Sichuan	83.29	6.6	171.7	5.0	26.7	73.3
Guizhou	35.25	2.8	199.2	37.9	23.9	76.1
Yunnan	42.88	3.4	108.8	33.4	23.4	76.6
Tibet	2.62	0.2	2.2	94.1	18.9	81.1
Shaanxi	36.05	2.8	175.0	0.5	32.3	67.7
Gansu	25.62	2.0	56.4	8.7	24.0	76.0
Qinghai	5.18	0.4	7.2	45.5	34.8	65.2
Ningxia	5.62	0.4	85.2	34.5	32.4	67.6
Xinjiang	19.25	1.5	12.0	59.4	33.8	66.2
Regional average	29.61	2.3	52.2	32.0	29.5	70.5
Regional total	355.31	28.1	–	–	–	–
National average	40.83	–	131.9	8.4	36.2	63.8
National total	1,265.83	–	–	–	–	–

Source: The figures were compiled from *Zhongguo tongji nianjian 2001* (see note 5), pp. 92, 100–101, with data originally from the fifth national population census, with zero hour on 1 November 2000 as the reference time.

nationwide, 132 people live in 1 km^2 of land area, but this figure is only 52 in the west. In China, the three provinces with the lowest population densities are all located in the Far West, where mountainous highlands and widespread deserts dominate. They are Tibet (2.2 persons per km^2), Qinghai (7.2 persons per km^2) and Xinjiang (12 persons per km^2). As with territory, population sizes and densities also vary greatly across the region. Tibet, Qinghai and Ningxia are the three least populated provinces in China, and their population is merely a fraction of Sichuan's, the nation's third most populous province. Although the west as a whole is less densely inhabited than the rest of China, five provinces or provincial-level units, in decreasing order — Chongqing, Guizhou 貴州, Guangxi, Shaanxi and Sichuan — have population densities higher than the national average.

The multiplicity of nationalities best illustrates the diversity of the west's population. There are 56 nationalities in China, of which the Han 漢族 is the largest with 91.6% of China's population. The others are called minorities 少數民族, and are tremendously diverse, culturally and racially. According to the latest census data, 71.9% of the ethnic population lives in the west, and 50 of the 55 minority nationalities can be found in the region. As shown in Table 3.4, with the exception of Shaanxi, all of the western provinces have a significant ethnic population; on average, 32.0% of the inhabitants in each province are minorities, almost four times the national figure of 8.4%. Given these figures, it is not surprising that all of the five autonomous regions at the provincial level are located in the west (Table 3.3), and that of the provinces with the highest percentage of ethnic population, the top seven are in the west. In descending order, they are Tibet, Xinjiang, Qinghai, Guangxi, Guizhou, Yunnan and Inner Mongolia (Table 3.4). Another aspect of population composition is the urban-to-rural ratio, shown in Table 3.4. Generally, the western population is less urbanized than the national average (29.5% compared to 36.2%). Inner Mongolia is the only province in the region with an urban population higher than the national average (42.7%).

The move to develop the west has been largely motivated by the unbalanced nature of China's economic growth in the past two decades. In fact, the west is not simply a spatial domain. Rather, it is an administratively defined region with a less developed economy. According to the figures in Table 3.5, the west, which represents 70.9% and 28.1% of the country's land and population, respectively, only contributed 18.6% of the national gross domestic product (GDP) in the year 2000. The combined GDPs of two coastal provinces, Jiangsu 江蘇 and Shandong 山東, slightly exceed half of the west's total. The GDP figure for Beijing 北京, Shanghai 上海

Table 3.5 Gross Domestic Product of the West at Current Prices, 2000

Unit	Total (RMB billion)	Per capita (RMB)	Primary industry (%)	Secondary industry (%)	Tertiary industry (%)
Inner Mongolia	140.1	5,897	25.0	39.7	35.2
Guangxi	205.0	4,567	26.3	36.5	37.2
Chongqing	158.9	5,143	17.8	41.4	40.8
Sichuan	401.0	4,815	23.6	42.4	34.0
Guizhou	99.4	2,819	27.3	39.0	33.7
Yunnan	195.5	4,559	22.3	43.1	34.6
Tibet	11.7	4,483	30.9	23.2	45.9
Shaanxi	166.1	4,607	16.8	44.1	39.1
Gansu	98.3	3,838	19.7	44.7	35.6
Qinghai	26.4	5,089	14.6	43.2	42.1
Ningxia	26.6	4,725	17.3	45.2	37.5
Xinjiang	136.4	7,088	21.1	43.0	35.9
Regional average	138.8	4,803	21.9	40.5	37.6
Regional total	1,665.5	–	–	–	–
National average	288.4	7,078	15.9	50.9	33.2
National total	8,940.4	–	–	–	–

Source: The figures were compiled from *Zhongguo tongji nianjian 2001* (see note 5), pp. 56–57.

and Guangdong 廣東 together is very close to that for the whole of the west. Furthermore, the economic backwardness of the west is clearly exhibited by its per capita GDP and the composition of the regional economy. The average per capita GDP for the region is RMB4,803, 32.1% lower than the national figure of RMB7,078 (Table 3.5). In terms of per capita GDP, almost all of the western provinces (except Xinjiang) are below the national average, and the eight poorest provinces are all located in the west. In descending order, they are Guizhou, Gansu, Tibet, Yunnan, Guangxi, Shaanxi, Ningxia and Sichuan. As a highlight of the sharp contrast in economic development between the east and the west, Shanghai, the richest provincial-level unit in China, enjoys a per capita GDP that is nearly 10 times that of the poorest province, Guizhou. Table 3.5 also shows that in the west, primary industry generally plays a more important role and that a smaller portion of GDP is derived from secondary industry. By and large, this pattern is consistent with the level of economic development in the west as compared to the national average.

Physical Environment

Because of its inland location and high altitudes, the west is generally very different from eastern and central China. Regional characteristics such as a frigid and arid climate, rugged terrain and isolation from the outside world make the west less desirable for human inhabitation. In some areas, very harsh natural conditions prevail. Since the west is an immensely large territory with huge differences in elevation, there are enormous variations and complexities in physical environment and regional landscapes. In general, the west can be divided into six sub-regions. Table 3.6 includes a summary of each sub-region's basic characteristics.[4] Understanding the physical environment and resource availability in the west is crucial to the formulation and implementation of development strategies for the region.

Table 3.6 The Six Sub-regions of the West and Their Basic Characteristics

Sub-region	Extent	Basic characteristics
Northwest Arid Zone	Xinjiang, western Gansu and Inner Mongolia	• The most arid area of China, due to scarce precipitation and huge potential for evaporation, resulting in severe water shortages • Extensive deserts and fragmentary oases in basins surrounded by mountains • Sparse vegetation cover, severe desertification and frequent natural hazards • Plenty of land resources and fine natural grasslands, potentially good for agriculture and animal husbandry • Abundance of mineral resources and enormous reserves of coal, petroleum and natural gas
Loess Plateau	Shaanxi, Ningxia and southeastern Gansu	• Located in a transitional area between the southeast monsoon region and the northwest arid zone and dominated by a generally dry climate • Severe soil erosion on the well-developed loess with sparse vegetation cover • Balanced land use, largely on hillside fields, of agriculture, forestry and animal husbandry • A large variety of mineral resources and the largest reserves of some deposits in China, of which coal is the most advantageous resource
Sichuan Basin	Chongqing and eastern Sichuan	• Dominated by a typical central sub-tropical humid climate with ample precipitation and scarce sunshine

Table 3.6 (Cont'd)

Sub-region	Extent	Basic characteristics
Guangxi Basin	Most of Guangxi, except for the northwest corner	• The main landforms are hills, low mountains and plains. Agriculture flourishes in the western part of the basin where water conservancy is developed • Abundant biological resources and relatively high forest coverage with numerous rare species of flora and fauna • Enormous potential for hydropower, nationally important deposits of metal minerals and natural gas • In the west, the only coastal province and the only area sitting on Step 3 of China's terrain • Dominated by a typical sub-tropical monsoon climate with distinctive seasons — wet and hot summers and dry and warm winters • Abundance of natural resources such as deposits of non-ferrous metal minerals, hydropower and forests
Yunnan-Guizhou Plateau	Yunnan and Guizhou	• Plenty of water and heat resources with large vertical variations in climate, suitable for the development of "stereoscopic" agriculture • Highly developed karst, causing scarcity of surface water and severe soil erosion • The dominant landforms are highlands and mountains, forestry exceeds agriculture in land use due to a shortage of flat land • Abundance of forest resources and great biodiversity, the area with the richest biological resources in China • Great potential for hydropower, resource advantages in metal and chemical minerals, and coal deposits of regional importance in South China
Qinghai-Tibet Plateau	Tibet and most of Qinghai, parts of Xinjiang, Gansu, Sichuan and Yunnan	• Unique highland climate as a result of great heights and plateau landforms • Extensive coverage of glaciers and frozen soils, land use dominated by animal husbandry on grasslands, and over 40% of the land is not in use • Structurally simple ecosystems and frequent natural hazards, highly adverse environmental conditions • Great abundance of renewable energy resources such as solar, wind and hydropower, top rankings in China of some metal and non-metal mineral deposits

Source: Zheng Du 鄭度 et al. (eds.), *Zhongguo xibu diqu ershiyi shiji quyu kechixu fazhan* (see note 6), pp. 30–52.

Landforms

The topography of China can generally be categorized into five types, that is, mountain (33%), plateau (26%), basin (19%), plain (12%) and hills (10%). The dominance of mountains and highlands is apparent.[5] The majority of the mountains and highlands in the country, including the highest and largest in the world, are located in the west, where the most geologically active areas in China can be found. As noted earlier, almost the whole region of the west sits on the first and second steps in the Chinese terrain. On Step 1, the Qinghai-Tibet Plateau has an average elevation of 4,000 m (above mean sea level, and the same below) and is known as the "Roof of the World." It is so high and immense that it controls the regional climate and certainly has an influence on the global climate. It is in this region that most of the lofty mountain ranges in China are located, including the Kunlun Mountains 崑崙山, Altun Mountains 阿爾金山 and Qilian Mountains 祁連山 in the north, the Bayan Har Mountains 巴顏喀喇山, Tanggula Mountains 唐古喇山 and Gandise Mountains 甘底斯山 in the central area, and the famous Himalayan Mountains 喜馬拉雅山 in the south. To the north, east and southeast of the world's highest plateau, the terrain drops and gradually extends to Step 2, where the other four highlands with mean elevations of 1,000–2,000 m are situated; that is, from north to south, the Inner Mongolia Plateau 內蒙古高原, the Ordos Plateau 鄂爾多斯高原, the Loess Plateau 黃土高原 and the Yunnan-Guizhou Plateau 雲貴高原. Besides mountains and highlands, basins are the third major type of landform in the west. All of the four largest basins in China, the Tarim Basin 塔里木盆地, the Junggar Basin 準噶爾盆地, the Qaidam Basin 柴達木盆地 and the Sichuan Basin 四川盆地, are located in the west and surrounded by mountains and highlands. The very complicated terrain is generally higher in the west and the south, and lower in the east and the north, with gigantic differences in elevation within the region. Amazingly, the world's highest peak — Mount Everest (8,848 m), as well as the lowest lake in China — Ayding Lake 艾丁湖 (–145 m) in the Turpan Basin 吐魯番盆地, can both be found in the west.

The topographical complexities and varieties of the west are not only reflected in the huge differences in elevation, but also in the enormous geomorphic differences among sub-regions and provinces. For example, the southwest is dominated by mountains and highlands, while mountains and basins are most common in the northwest. Located just north of the Qinghai-Tibet Plateau, the world's highest and largest, Xinjiang is largely made up of vast, low-altitude basins featuring extensive deserts. There are tremendous differences in geology and morphology between the Loess Plateau and the Yunnan-Guizhou Plateau, which are, respectively, the most renowned loess and karst landscapes in the world.

Climate

As with landforms, the climate of the west is also tremendously variable. Generally, the west can be divided into three climatic zones. The east and southeast area, mainly controlled by the Indian and Pacific monsoon; the frigid area of the Qinghai-Tibet Plateau; and the inland northwest area, where the aridity is caused by the area's isolation from the ocean and the blocking of atmospheric moisture by the plateau.[6] Due to the large latitudinal stretch and enormous fluctuations in elevation in the region, its climate varies immensely, ranging from tropical to cold temperate and frigid, with arid and frigid climates dominating the largest areas.

The variations in climate are reflected in all elements of the weather throughout the region. Annual mean air temperatures fluctuate from below 0°C in many parts of the Qinghai-Tibet Plateau, the coldest area in China, to over 24°C in southern Guangxi. The mean temperature in the coldest month (January) usually exceeds 15°C along the coast in Guangxi, but never reaches 0°C on the Qinghai-Tibet Plateau and in most of the northwest arid zone (although it can be as low as –20°C in high mountains and in northern Xinjiang). In the hottest month (July), air temperatures are higher in the south and the north (close to 30°C in the southeast corner and as high as 32°C in Turpan 吐鲁番), but remarkably drop to 4–6°C in the central part of the region. Precipitation is the element of weather demonstrating the greatest degree of spatial variation in the west, with higher levels in the southeast and lower ones in the northwest. The Qaidam, Turpan and Tarim Basins are zones of aridity, normally receiving less than 30 mm of precipitation every year. In the southern parts of Guangxi and Yunnan, however, monsoons bring large amounts of rainfall to the region in the wet season, and annual precipitation can surpass 2,000 mm. Corresponding to precipitation, the aridity index, the ratio of potential evaporation over precipitation on an annual basis, clearly exhibits a trend of increase from the southeast to the northwest. In the southern and eastern parts of the Yunnan-Guizhou Plateau, the Sichuan Basin and the Guangxi Basin, this index is less than 0.5. It increases to 1.0–1.5 in the central part of the Yunnan-Guizhou Plateau, western Sichuan, eastern Tibet and the Loess Plateau. Further north and west, the aridity index continues to increase from 3 to over 10 on the Inner Mongolia Plateau and large parts of the Qinghai-Tibet Plateau. In the northwestern desert areas, potential evaporation is many times greater than precipitation, bringing the aridity index in the range of 10 to over 100. Besides air temperature and water availability, other climatic characteristics also differ remarkably across the west. For example, due to high altitude and thin air, Tibet receives the largest amounts of sunlight in China, and Lhasa 拉薩, called the "Sunshine City," has an annual average insolation duration of 3,005 hours, nearly twice that of regions in the same latitude in the east. In Sichuan, Chongqing and Guizhou, however, cloudy weather is very common and annual mean sunshine falls in the range of only 1,200–1,400 hours. Another weather element differing significantly across the region is wind. For example, it is generally much more windy in Xinjiang than in the Sichuan Basin.

Rivers and Lakes

There is a wide variety of drainage systems and surface bodies of water in the west. A towering topography and sufficient supply of runoff make the west, primarily the Qinghai-Tibet Plateau, the largest area for headwaters in the Euro-Asian continent. Since many of the major rivers in China and Southeast Asia have their source in various highlands and mountains in the region, natural conservation and environmental protection in the west have a far-reaching influence on areas hundreds and thousands kilometers downstream. The Yangzi River 長江, the Yellow River 黃河, the Yarlung Zangbo River 雅魯藏布江, Lancang River 瀾滄江 (Mekong River) and Nujiang 怒江 (Salween River) originate in the Qinghai-Tibet Plateau and discharge into the Pacific and Indian Oceans. The Pearl River 珠江, the third-largest river in China, takes its source from the Yunnan-Guizhou Plateau and flows through the Guangxi Basin before entering Guangdong. The Ertix River 額爾齊斯河, the only river in China that enters the Arctic Ocean, rises in the Altay Mountains 阿爾泰山 in northern Xinjiang. In addition to these external rivers, all of the continental rivers in China are located in the west and the two types of drainage basins (external and internal) cover about the same total area of the region. Inland rivers are mainly distributed in five areas, that is, Xinjiang, Qinghai, Inner Mongolia, Hexi 河西 and Qiangtang 羌塘, each of which consists of varying numbers of river systems.

Due to climatic, geologic and geomorphic differences, rivers in the west vary significantly in their hydrologic characteristics. In the southeastern part of the region, river densities are high and runoff is abundant, but streams contain and carry relatively small amounts of sediment. For example, with a dense river network consisting of the mainstream and numerous tributaries of the Yangzi River, Sichuan is called the "province of a thousand rivers." In the northwest, however, due to substantial evaporation and limited inflow from a relatively small number of tributaries, river systems tend to be sparse and lack volume of flow, but the rivers usually contain quite a lot of silt because drainage areas are covered extensively by loose top soils. These differences can be clearly shown by a comparison of the Yangzi and Yellow Rivers. Average annual flow and sediment load at Yichang 宜昌 on the Yangzi River is 960 billion m^3 and 0.53 billion tonnes, respectively, compared to 58 billion m^3 and 1.43 billion tonnes at Sanmenxia 三門峽 on the Yellow River. In other words, the Yellow River discharges only one-seventeenth the amount of water as the Yangzi River, but carries 2.7 times the amount of sediment every year. Internal rivers originate in glaciers on mountains and gradually disappear in piedmonts. Surface runoff does not exist in large parts of these drainage basins, and the zero-flow area of about 1.6 million km^2 always suffers from the most severe shortage of water in China.

There are numerous lakes in the west and they can be divided into three categories. The Qinghai-Tibet Plateau has the largest number of lakes in China, most of which were formed through tectonic movements and glaciation processes. These lakes on high altitudes (over 4,000 m) are generally very deep and occupy a total area of 36,889 km^2; that is, 51.4% of the national total. Salt-water lakes dominate in this area. Some freshwater lakes can be found, linked with external rivers located in the eastern and southern parts of the plateau. Qinghai Lake 青海湖 is the largest salt-water lake in China. On the Yunnan-Guizhou Plateau, tectonic lakes are very common and dissolution lakes also exist. The total area of these freshwater lakes is 1,108 km^2 or 1.5% of the national total. Dianchi 滇池, Erhai 洱海 and Fuxian Lake 撫仙湖 (the deepest lake in China, with a depth of 151.5 m) are some of the major ones in this area. Located in Xinjiang and Inner Mongolia is a third category of lake. This category consists mostly of inland salt-water lakes created by tectonic movements, which occupy a total area of 9,411 km^2 or 13.1% of the national total. With a depth of less than 1 m, Aiding Lake in the Turpan Basin, as noted earlier, represents the lowest elevation in China. Hulun Lake 呼倫湖 in Inner Mongolia and Bosten Lake 博斯騰湖 in Xinjiang are the two largest freshwater lakes in the northwest.

Natural Resources

The west is the region in China that possesses the richest natural resources in great variety and quantity. The east cannot compare to the west, in terms of the hugeness of the latter's farmlands, forests and grasslands. Also highly ranked in the country is the availability of many other resources in the west, such as solar and wind energy, hydropower and a large variety of minerals. The southeastern part of the west (Chongqing, Sichuan, Yunnan, Guizhou and Guangxi) enjoys abundant heat associated with a warm climate all year round. Tibet is richly endowed by plenty of sunlight which, to some extent, makes up for the deficiency of heat on the plateau. Hydropower in the southwest, as well as wind energy in the northwest, is second to none in China. As for mineral resources, ferrous and non-ferrous metals, as well as many nonmetallic minerals are found in large quantities compared with most area of the country. Proven reserves of coal, petroleum and natural gas are high, and prospective reserves are even more promising.

The major problems associated with natural resources in the west are an unbalanced geographical distribution and a lack of advantageous resource combinations. Water availability perfectly demonstrates the two extremes — a great abundance in the southeastern part of the region and a huge deficiency in the northwest. Iron ores are only concentrated in Sichuan and Inner Mongolia and few reserves can be found in other provinces. Most of the non-ferrous metal mines are in Yunnan, Gansu and Guangxi. Inner Mongolia, Shaanxi, Xinjiang and Ningxia possess the majority of coalfields. Petroleum and natural gas reserves are largely located in Xinjiang and Qinghai, and Sichuan also has plenty of natural gas. Except for coal, Ningxia is poor in many important mineral resources. In the west, natural conditions are often harsh, which is unfavourable for the exploitation of mineral resources. Another disadvantage is the remoteness of the region, leading to extra costs for the long-distance transport of raw materials and semi-products.

Land and Water Resources

Numerous mountains and highlands, as well as extensive deserts, introduce enormous difficulties for land use in the west. Of the total area of 810,000 km^2 of desert in China, all but 67,000 km^2, or only 8.3%, are located in the west and predominantly in Xinjiang and Inner Mongolia. The Gobi Desert occupies a total area of 570,000 km^2, spanning the five western provinces of Xinjiang, Inner Mongolia, Gansu, Qinghai and Ningxia. The frigid environment on the immense Qinghai-Tibet Plateau not only seriously restricts agricultural production, but also introduces many difficulties for urban development, road construction and the exploitation of mineral resources, making southern Qinghai and northern Tibet essentially a no-man's land.

Physical environment and economic development determine land-use practices and land-cover patterns in the west. China has a total area of farmland of about 130 million ha (approximately 1.95 billion *mu* 畝, with 1 *mu* equalling 666.7 m^2), of which 49.7 million ha or 38.2% are found in the west (Table 3.7). The per capita area of farmland in the west (2.10 *mu*) is slightly higher than the national figure (1.54 *mu*). However, arable land in the west is quite limited, comprising only 7.34% of the region's territory, much lower than the national average of 13.54%. Large portions of the farmland are hillside fields, and farming on some plots used to grow grain has had to be stopped for conservation purposes. Also, not much land is

Table 3.7 Land and Water Resources of the West

Unit	Farmland (thousand ha)	Forest (thousand ha)	Usable grassland (thousand ha)	Surface water (km^3)	Hydro-power[1] (thousand KW)	Hydro-power[2] (thousand KW)
Inner Mongolia	8,200	19,987	68,025	37	4,825	2,387
Guangxi	4,400	11,440	807	188	21,330	17,510
Chongqing	2,645	2,975	238	51	14,380	7,500
Sichuan	6,624	19,040	13,750	262	142,690	103,460
Guizhou	4,903	7,540	1,696	104	18,745	16,833
Yunnan	6,421	21,790	792	222	150,000	91,660
Tibet	363	12,660	64,667	448	200,560	56,593
Shaanxi	5,140	9,399	3,179	42	12,750	5,510
Gansu	5,025	4,660	12,912	27	17,240	10,690
Qinghai	688	2,436	40,343	62	23,375	20,990
Ningxia	1,269	266	2,468	1	2,120	902
Xinjiang	3,986	6,400	51,602	79	33,550	8,355
Regional total	49,663	118,593	260,478	1,524	641,565	342,570
% of national total	38.2	52.1	97.8	56.2	95.0	90.4

Note: [1] Theoretical capacity; [2] Capacity available for development.
Source: Adopted from Wang Shaowu and Dong Guangrong (eds.), *Zhongguo xibu huanjing yanbian pinggu* (see note 9), Vol. 1, p. 7.

still available for reclamation and cultivation. Therefore, the reserves of farmland in the west are in no way promising.

The west has 118.6 million ha of forest, representing 52.11% of the national total. With a regional average of 12.1% (less than the national average of about 16%), forest coverage varies greatly throughout the west, ranging from less than 5% in the northwest to over 20% in five eastern and southeastern provinces — Guangxi, Yunnan, Sichuan, Shaanxi and Chongqing. Xinjiang (1.57%), Qinghai (2.65%) and Ningxia (4.2%) are the three provinces with the lowest levels of forest coverage in the country. This great disparity is a reflection of the enormous differences in climate across the vast territory of the west. In contrast to the limited forest coverage, grasslands in the west are extensive, especially in Tibet, Inner Mongolia, Xinjiang, Qinghai, Sichuan and Gansu, representing 97.8% of pastureland in China (Table 3.7).

The west as a whole cannot be considered to be lacking in water, since the region possesses over half of the country's water resources (Table 3.7). Corresponding to the geographical distribution of climatic zones, however, water availability divides the region into two highly distinctive humid and arid areas. In the six southwestern provinces, with a total area of 2.574 million km^2 or 37.8% of the entire west, water resources amount to 1,275 km^3 or 83.7% of the regional total. The remaining 16.3% of water resources is distributed widely over a much larger territory in the other six northwestern provinces, where water shortages are conspicuous. As shown in Table 3.7, with over 90% of total national total capacity, the west enjoys exceptional advantages in hydropower. As with the great unevenness in water availability, the distribution of hydropower is also highly unbalanced in the west. Tibet, Yunnan and Sichuan possess over 75% of total regional capacity, but only about 1% can be found in Ningxia and Inner Mongolia.

Energy and Mineral Resources

The west is richly endowed with coal, petroleum, natural gas and a large variety of mineral resources. Of China's total proven coal reserves of 1007.1 billion tonnes (1999 figure), over half are located in the west. Inner Mongolia (200.9 billion tonnes) and Shaanxi (161.8 billion tonnes) are two of the three provinces in China that have over 150 billion tonnes of coal reserves. Other western provinces with abundant resources of coal are Guizhou, Ningxia, Yunnan and Xinjiang. In the west, reserves of oil and gas can be found in all Mesozoic and Cainozoic tectonic basins. The Tarim Basin has the largest terrestrial oil and gas deposits in China, and the largest natural gas fields are located in the Ordos Basin (also known as the Shaanxi-Gansu-Ningxia Basin 陜甘寧盆地). Recently, it has been reported that prospective deposits of petroleum and natural gas in Xinjiang could reach 50 billion tonnes and 13,000 billion m^3, respectively. Prospective reserves of petroleum in the range of 10–14 billion tonnes have been ascertained in the Qaidam Basin. Another major deposit is the Sichuan Basin, where around 20–25% of total national prospective reserves of natural gas have been found.

Both the variety and quantity of metal minerals are large in the west. Most provinces are ranked in the top few positions in various deposits of metal minerals, including Chongqing (strontium, vanadium, molybdenum and barium), Sichuan (titanium, vanadium, silver, iron, zinc, beryllium, elements of the platinum family), Guizhou (magnesium, gallium, rare earth, manganese and antimony), Yunnan (aluminum, zinc, copper, nickel and cobalt), Tibet (chromium and copper), Shaanxi (rhenium, molybdenum, gold, niobium and beryllium), Gansu (nickel, cobalt, copper, chromium and antimony), Qinghai (rubidium and indium), Xinjiang (beryllium, cesium, lead and chromium), Guangxi (manganese, tin, indium and gallium) and Inner Mongolia (rare earth, chromium, aluminum and zinc). Although China has very few extremely large deposits of high-grade iron ore, such reserves would most probably be found in the Tianshan Mountains 天山 in Xinjiang.

There are also plenty of non-metallic mineral resources in the west, notably deposits of phosphorus in Yunnan and Guizhou, pyrite in Inner Mongolia, Sichuan and Yunnan, leopoldite in the Qaidam Basin of Qinghai and Lop Lake (Lop Nor 羅布泊) of Xinjiang, asbestos in Sichuan and the Qaidam Basin, and mica in the Altay Mountains, Sichuan and Inner Mongolia. Due to the complex geological conditions and mountainous landforms in the west, the region is fairly rich in rock ores of important economic value, such as limestone and red earth for making cement, marble and gypsum for construction, and mirabilite, barite and optical crystal for other industrial usages.

Biological Resources

The west enjoys great advantages in biological resources that cannot be matched by other parts of the country. The highly diversified physical landscape, together with the variable climatic conditions across the vast territory, provide a living environment for over 10 thousand species of plants and animals. This enormous biodiversity in the west has tremendous economic, ecological and scientific value. There are many rare species across the region, most of which have been designated for protection as endangered or threatened species. The most famous of these species are the panda, golden monkey, white-lipped deer, chiru, Chinese sturgeon, Chinese dove tree, metasequoia (the world's most ancient species of tree) and the Chinese tulip tree. Southeastern Tibet, western Sichuan and Yunnan form an area with the richest concentration of biological resources. Ancient species have been preserved and new ones have been created due to neotectonic movements in southeastern Tibet. Western Sichuan is an important area, where communities of flora and fauna of southern and northern China mingle together. Highly dense broadleaf evergreen forests, tropical rainforests and monsoon forests are widely distributed in Yunnan, which is an area where numerous tropical and sub-tropical species of plants and animals can be found.

Ecological and Environmental Challenges

The west is a vast and diversified region, where the physical environment is generally less desirable than other parts of China. For reasons of history and policy, economic development in the west has been slow, and its resource advantages have yet to be fully utilized. Although the economy has not been sufficiently developed, the region faces tremendous ecological and environmental challenges from both natural and man-made causes. The major problems to be illustrated reflect ecological degradation and environmental deterioration in the region, including the decreasing complexity, functionality and stability of ecosystems, severe loss of biodiversity and aggravation of natural hazards.

There are four main types of land degradation problem in the west. First, soil erosion is a key issue that has not been brought under control. By 1999, an area of 104.37 million ha had soil erosion in the west (excluding Tibet), representing 62.5% of the national total. Although the spread of soil erosion has been somewhat reduced in recent years, eroded lands still occupy more than half of the territory of several western provinces and are even expanding in some areas. Generally, the west is still the region with the most serious soil erosion in China. Second, over 90% of desertified lands are in the west, and there is a total area of desertification of 162.56 million ha (1999 figure) in Inner Mongolia, Gansu, Qinghai, Ningxia, Xinjiang,

Tibet and Shaanxi. Desertified lands of huge acreage and broad coverage in the region are extremely difficult to restore. Third, while desertification is a devastating problem in the arid northwest, stony desertification is also one of the most prominent issues in the five south-western provinces excluding Tibet. Although the affected areas are relatively small (totalling 7.3 million ha or 5.3% of the land mass in 1999), they tend to be fairly concentrated and cause serious damage to the regional environment. Last, salinization in some areas could have been caused by irrigation from floods and by land reclamation.

Over the years, the amount of arable lands in the west has been increasing at the expense of forests and grasslands. From 1989 to 1999, 69.5% and 22.4% of the newly reclaimed farmland was obtained by converting grasslands and forests, respectively, to farms. Meanwhile, much farmland is abandoned every year because of low productivity, high cost and several other reasons, exacerbating soil erosion by wind and water. Farmland occupies only small areas of the northwestern oases, but consumes and wastes enormous amounts of the precious water resources of the region. In recent decades, there has been a growth in the quantity of forestland, coupled with a reduction in quality. The mix of different types of forest has been evolving in an increasingly less desirable direction. From 1986 to 1999, forest area and coverage in the west (excluding Tibet, Yunnan, Chongqing, and the Xinjiang Production and Construction Corps[7]) grew substantially by 8.27% and 12.75%, but total and unit area timber stocks dropped substantially in the meantime by 18.96% and 25.41%, respectively. During the same period of time, the acreage of economic forest in the west (excluding Tibet, Chongqing, and the Xinjiang Production and Construction Corps) increased considerably by 62.96%, while natural forest and shelter forest experienced shrinkages in area of 14.49% and 51.07%, respectively. Land degradation caused by the exploitation of mineral resources is also serious in the west. By 1999, the accumulated acreage of destroyed land reached 1.81 million ha, of which 16.3%, 8.6% and 8.0% was forest, grassland and farmland, respectively.

Water problems are generally serious and very diversified across the west. Water is largely used for agricultural irrigation, and water saving technologies have been rarely utilized, leading to a massive waste of water resources. In the northwest, the scarcity of water has been a great barrier to regional economic development. Although the southwest is generally endowed by plenty of water, water shortages may still occur in some localities, especially during the dry season, often because of the lack of hydraulic engineering structures. Other major problems include the silting up of channels, the periodic drying up of rivers, the shrinking of lakes, decreases in the level of groundwater and water pollution. Under the influence of global warming, glaciers have melted and the snowline has been receding. Together with the impact of human activity, natural wetlands have been disappearing and lakes are becoming saline or even drying up.

Ecological and environmental problems in the west have been caused by numerous, often very complex, factors. Over the past several decades, air temperatures in the region have become increasingly variable and some areas have experienced reductions in precipitation. Although changes in the regional climate have accelerated the speed and level of ecological degradation, human influences are undoubtedly the most direct and crucial factors, as illustrated by a wide range of conflicts between economic development and natural conservation. Specifically, the limited ecological carrying capacity is not compatible with the extensive mode of economic development. The gradually degrading natural environment is unable to meet the needs of population growth and ever-increasing demands for a better quality of living environment. With ecological degradation and shortages of certain natural resources, conflicts between local areas and the entire region, as well as between short-term and long-term interests, have become increasingly intense. Some examples of land-use activities that are bringing about the rapid degradation of the regional environment include the deforestation and the destruction of grasslands for conversion to farmland, the cultivation of land on steep slopes, the abandonment of farmlands and extensive cultivation. As the source of the Yangzi River, the Yellow River and the Pearl River, the nation's three largest rivers, the west naturally serves as a "protective screen" of great ecological and environmental importance for the eastern and central China. The west is, therefore, a critical region in ensuring China's ecological security, and resource management and environmental protection play a vital strategic role in sustaining the socioeconomic development of the country.

Sustainable Development: The Way to the Future

Advancing Ecological Restoration and Environmental Protection Together with Alleviating Poverty and Generating Income for Peasants

Logging natural forests, cultivating fields on hillsides and planting grain crops on pastureland are important means of subsistence for poor peasants in the west. As major players in regional development, peasants often damage the fragile environment. Once their livelihood is threatened, they will fell trees and cut grasses, often indiscriminately, and turn the forests and grasslands to farms, causing land degradation and environmental hazards. To solve this issue of conflicts between natural conservation and the needs of local peasants for food and clothing, a long-term strategy is to merge environmental protection with income generation for peasants, as well as with the development of the local economy. This is the only way to place regional development, economically, socially and ecologically, on a sustainable track.

Co-ordinating the Development of Infrastructure and a Modern Manufacturing Industry

Infrastructure is generally less developed in the west, and it is surely necessary to change this situation of backwardness. However, the construction of infrastructure must be accompanied by resource exploitation and industrial development. Since the return from large investments in infrastructure is normally low, the large-scale development of infrastructure must be justified by clear objectives to achieve certain social and economic benefits. It is a policy drawback in the west that the transformation and development of manufacturing technologies have been neglected, while the emphasis has largely been placed on the construction of infrastructure. Over the years, this has expanded the gap between east and west in economic development and regional competitiveness. Therefore, the investment policy should be adjusted to somewhat increase financial inputs for manufacturing industries to bring more economic benefits to the region. In other words, infrastructure in the west should be developed gradually in order of priority, while the development of manufacturing should be expedited with special support for existing industries such as the building of heavy machines, production of iron and steel, the making of automobiles and the processing of agricultural products. The concerted development of infrastructure and manufacturing will play a vital role in economic growth in the west.

Simultaneous Promotion of Resource Exploitation and Comprehensive Utilization

The exploitation of resources in the west for processing in the east has been a long-term regional pattern of industrial division in China. This pattern has not changed significantly, even though it has been possible to purchase many raw materials from overseas markets in the past two decades. Therefore, resource exploitation and utilization must proceed jointly. In this way, processing industries can gradually develop while various resources continue to be exported from the west, thus generating more and more financial revenue for the region. There are huge markets for the abundant mineral resources of the west. As long as the environment can be sufficiently protected, advantage can be taken of the cheap electric power available in the region to exploit these resources, which will require large inputs of energy to accomplish in the abundant energy resources of the west as a regional advantage for attracting capital and industrial investment. In summary, the resources of the west should not only be exported directly, but also be used to attract external investment in processing and manufacturing industries.

Preferential Financial Policies to Boost Regional Economic Growth

While more and more state funds have been poured into the west in recent years, financial investment from other sources is still limited and, meanwhile, local capital continues to flow out of the region to the east. How to attract foreign and domestic investment and to keep local funds is a big issue in developing the west. Institutional measures and policy preference must be introduced to attract not only external capital, but also talented people and a skilled work force. In addition to the existing one-to-one economic partnership between coastal and western provinces, the central government should continue to increase financial inputs to the west and make better use of state funds through policy reform. Other measures such as discounts in the interest charged on bank loans, exemptions from agricultural taxes for a certain number of years and more favourable foreign investment policies than those in the coastal areas, will definitely bring great economic benefits to the west.

Top Priority for Education and Human Resources Development

Human resources are the most fundamental force in driving regional development. However, education in the west generally lags behind the rest of the nation. Deficiency in human capital has been a factor limiting economic development. Compared to the more developed areas in the east, people in the west, especially the peasants, generally receive less education. Therefore, greater effort and more resources must be devoted to developing human resources in the region. Success in developing the west will sooner or later be proven to have depended heavily on this investment.

Conclusion

The aim behind the development of China's west is to boost the economy of the region and place national development on a balanced and sustainable track. The economic backwardness of the west has been the result of not only many human factors such as history and policy orientation, but also of a variety of physical and environmental constraints. This chapter summarizes the basic geographical characteristics of the west, some of which are advantageous and others disadvantageous for regional development. Generally, the west is characterized by immensity and diversity in many aspects. Occupying over 70% of the country's vast territory, the west, strategically located in relation to Central Asia and South Asia, is extremely diverse in population as well as in many geographical characteristics such as landform, climate and hydrology. The region is also enormously rich in a large variety of natural resources. This not only clearly underscores the great importance of accelerating economic growth in the west, but also highlights the necessity of adopting development measures suited to local conditions across the region.

In developing the west, numerous difficulties and challenges will be encountered, resulting not only from limitations in the region's natural environment, but also from many irrational land-use activities and misdirected development strategies. The region's generally inland location and isolation from the outside world, an arid and frigid environment in large areas, extensive deserts and predominantly mountainous terrain are all adverse factors for regional development. Making the best use of advantages and bypassing the disadvantages are vital to the success of development efforts. Ecological conservation and environmental protection play a particularly important role. Over the years, many human factors such as population pressure, faulty policies and poverty have caused or aggravated numerous ecological and environmental problems in the west. It has been easy to degrade and damage the fragile environment, but restoring it is by no means easy or simple. The government has made tremendous efforts and committed a great deal of investment to controlling soil erosion and desertification, to developing and managing water resources, and to rehabilitating ecosystems and watersheds. Developing the west on a sustainable path is the only way to simultaneously achieve social, economic and environmental benefits for the region.

Notes

1. Zhao Songqiao, *Physical Geography of China* (Beijing: Science Press, 1986), p. 2.
2. Zhang Dun 張敦 and Li Zhuorong 李灼榮 (eds.), *Zhongguo xiandaihua juezhan xibu* 中國現代化決戰西部 (Decisive Battle in the West for China's Modernization) (Nanning: Guangxi renmin chubanshe 廣西人民出版社, 2000), pp. 1–3.
3. B. Naughton, "The Third Front: Defense Industrialization in the Chinese Interior," *The China Quarterly*, No. 115 (1988), pp. 351–86.
4. Zheng Du 鄭度 et al. (eds.), *Zhongguo xibu diqu ershiyi shiji quyu kechixu fazhan* 中國西部地區21世紀區域可持續發展 (Regional Sustainable Development of China's West in the 21st Century) (Wuhan: Hubei kexue jishu chubanshe 湖北科學技術出版社, 2001), pp. 30–52. In this book, the West is divided into 5 sub-regions excluding the Guangxi Basin because the 10-unit definition of the west (minus Guangxi and Inner Mongolia) is adopted.
5. Zhao Ji 趙濟 and Chen Chuankang 陳傳康 (eds.), *Zhongguo dili* 中國地理 (Geography of China) (Beijing: Gaodeng jiaoyu chubanshe 高等教育出版社, 1999), p. 15.
6. Lu Dadao 陸大道 et al. (eds.), *2000 Zhongguo quyu fazhan baogao — xibu kaifa de jichu, zhengce yu taishi fenxi* 2000 中國區域發展報告 —— 西部開發的基礎，政策與態勢分析 (Regional Development of China, 2000 — A Development Report of the West) (Beijing: Shangwu yinshuguan 商務印書館, 2001), pp. 30–31.
7. Xinjiang Production and Construction Corps was founded in the mid-1950s as military force of the People's Liberation Army. Being a military unit which occupies a large portion of the territory in Xinjiang, however, it has primarily performed agricultural and other economic activities over the past several decades. In order to be self-supporting and self-sufficient, the corps mainly relied on land reclamation and farming practices (on over 50% of farmland in Xinjiang) in the early years. Later, it has become more and more civilian and expanded its activities from agricultural production to industrial manufacturing, commercial and service sectors.

4

Western Development Policy: Changes, Effects and Evaluation

Fan Jie

Introduction

Due to its relatively disadvantageous natural conditions and peripheral location, China's western region has long been a backward part of the country. Since ancient times, this region has been inhabited by many different peoples. As it shares a border with several different countries, "development and stability" in the western region are matters of great significance. In recent years, with the implementation of a national policy for sustainable development, more and more people have realized that the western region plays a critical role in ecological security that is essential for the sustained and healthy development of the eastern and central regions of China.

For centuries, central governments of China have formulated special policies to stimulate development in the western region. These policies were an important driving force in the economic construction and social development of the region. Most recently, since 1999, the Chinese government has adopted the Great Western Region Development Policy. The strategy aims at the co-ordination of regional economic development and the full realization of the four modernizations. A series of policies have been formulated for the development of the western region.

This chapter reviews western development polices in China in various periods, especially in the pre-reform and reform periods. The current strategy of developing the western region will be examined in detail.

Western Development Policy before 1949

In previous centuries, many regimes existed in the area that has come to be known as China's western region. But during many important periods, the western region was under the control of the state power in the Guanzhong Plain 關中平原, especially of regimes headed by what would now be termed the Han nationality 漢族. During a long development history of thousands of years, the policies and measures adopted by various dynasties had a significant impact on the development of the western region, some of which are still valuable for China's ongoing efforts to develop the area. This section reviews various policies adopted over the years, especially in earlier centuries (compare with Chapter 2, Li Xiaojian, et al.).

Water Conservancy and Agricultural Development

In pre-industrial times, agricultural growth was a long-term development objective. Early in the period of the Warring States (475–221 B.C.), the Dujiangyan 都江堰 project in Sichuan 四川 brought lasting prosperity and progress to the Chengdu Plain 成都平原. Starting from the Qin 秦 (221 B.C.–207 A.D.) and Han 漢 (206 B.C.–220 A.D.) dynasties and into the period of the Three Kingdoms (220–265 A.D.), every dynasty adopted policies to settle and increase the population of the Guanzhong Plain, the Loess Plateau, the Yellow River irrigation area in Ningxia 寧夏 and the Chengdu Plain, resulting in the most advanced agricultural region in China at the time.

Meanwhile, the Chinese state also implemented a policy of having garrisons open up wasteland to produce grain and defend the border. People were encouraged to migrate to some frontier areas, especially regions where nomadic peoples roamed. According to *Records of the Historian*, during the reign of Emperor Wu of the Han dynasty 漢武帝 (140–87 B.C.), the emperor dispatched 600,000 troops to the western region, including the Hexi Corridor 河西走廊. As the Hexi Corridor was a dry area, some irrigation works were subsequently constructed for agricultural development. Some advanced farming technology, as well as cattle, were used for the first time in that area. In the Qing 清 dynasty (1644–1911), the Hexi Corridor experienced a period of economic revival. With the implementation of land reclamation policies, the population increased dramatically through migration, which in turn spurred further land reclamation. Agriculture gradually became the main mode of production for the people of the region. Such conditions lasted until 1949, when the People's Republic of China (PRC) was established.

However, because of low productivity and poor knowledge of the environment, the above policies were implemented only for political and economic benefits, regardless of the environmental consequences. The large-scale reclamation of "wasteland" and migration into the Loess Plateau, the Hexi Corridor and Xinjiang 新疆 damaged forests and grasslands, causing serious soil erosion and environmental degradation.

Opening Trade Passageways

In order to extend its influence, consolidate its control of border areas and promote economic and cultural exchanges, the central government based in the Guanzhong Plain adopted measures to open up trade passageways to boost social and economic development in the western region. The Northwest and Southwest Silk Roads were the two most famous trade passageways. The opening of the Northwest Silk Road promoted economic and cultural exchanges between China and Central and Southwest Asia. It also greatly stimulated the economy of the western region in the Han dynasty, making the Hexi Corridor and Xinjiang important areas. During the Sui 隋 (A.D. 581–618) and Tang 唐 (A.D. 618–907) dynasties, the revival of the Silk Road as well as the emergence of a new northern passage of the Silk Road brought another prosperous era to the western region. In the Western Han 西漢 (206 B.C.–8 A.D.) dynasty, Emperor Wu also opened a Southwest Silk Road following the opening of the Northwest Silk Road, which greatly stimulated the development of agriculture, handcrafts, commerce and culture in the southwest region, especially in the state of Shu 蜀國, one of the Three Kingdoms in ancient China.

Promoting Cultural Exchanges

Since the Han dynasty, state of relations between the Chinese central state and the regimes of the Xiongnu 匈奴, Tubo 吐蕃, Nanzhao 南詔, Dali 大理 and Western Xia 西夏 had a great impact on social and economic stability in China. Therefore, every central state in the Guanzhong Plain attempted to consolidate and strengthen its cultural relations with the western region by dispatching envoys, encouraging inter-marriages and non-governmental exchanges through the Silk Road. As a result, the Han people's political, economic and military systems, as well as their culture, construction and spinning technologies were introduced into the western region. At the same time, the Han came into contact and absorbed many elements of the cultures and technology of the non-Han peoples, of which the most remembered today are the religious and artistic influences that came through the Silk Road. Through these exchanges, significant social and economic progress was achieved in the western region.

Developing Friendly Political Relations with the Western Region

In order to consolidate the rule and control of border areas and to stimulate economic development there, in addition to military measures various dynasties sought to develop friendly political relations with the western region. For example, Emperor Wu and subsequent emperors established the prefectures of Jiuquan 酒泉, Wuwei 武威 and Zhangye 張掖 and 35 counties, which were distributed over oases in the Hexi area. During the periods of the Eastern Han 東漢 (A.D. 25–220), the Three Kingdoms and the Jin 晉 dynasty (A.D. 265–420), Loulan 樓蘭 city became an important political, economic and cultural centre. The above measures played a crucial role in the stability and development of the border areas.

Overall Evaluation

In summary, before 1949, every central government stressed the development of that large area now regarded as China's western region, especially those areas inhabited by non-Han peoples. Different measures were adopted based on different situations. The Loess Plateau, where the central power was located, was always the key area of development. In the Hexi Corridor and the Xinjiang region that were links to Central Asia and Europe, the central governments of various dynasties adopted both military and political means of control. Friendly political relations were developed to strengthen political control and to ensure smooth traffic on the trade routes and steady socioeconomic development. Efforts were also made in water conservancy and land reclamation to develop agricultural production. In Tibet, the central government maintained its rule over the area with little participation in the local economy. In the southwest, the central government was engaged mainly in trying to extend its control over that area and in eliminating resistance to its rule. It can be concluded that the effects of various policies and measures mentioned above achieved the expected results of contributing to the peace, stability and defence of the border areas.[1]

Balanced Development Strategy for National Defence and Security, 1949–1972

Since 1949, the economic position of the western region in the national economy has experienced ups and downs, as the central government adopted different macro-regional development policies in different periods with different policy impacts.[2] This is because the upgrading of the industrial structure and the industrialization process in general in the western region has depended heavily on state investment.[3] In the history of the PRC, western development can be divided into four stages in terms of different regional development strategies. These policies and their economic impact will be analyzed one by one in the following sections. This section concentrates on the regional development policy in the period 1949–1972.

During the period 1949–1972, the Chinese government adopted and implemented a regional development policy emphasizing the objective of maintaining national defence and security. The policy was based on the perceived threat of political and military conflicts in the world and between China and the countries that border it. This period can be further divided into two stages: 1949–1963 and 1964–1972. The regional policies in these two stages have the same direction of development but different backgrounds and constraints in implementation.

Development Period Emphasizing Existing Industrial Bases, 1949–1963

In the three-year period of recovery from 1949 to 1952, the government attempted to change the unbalanced economic distribution in the country by relocating some factories to areas close to sources of raw materials. In the First Five-year Plan (1953–1957), it was prescribed that new industrial bases would be built up to change the situation of a regional division of labour. But the utilization, adjustment and expansion of the existing industrial bases were a prerequisite for the establishment of new industrial bases.

According to China's spatial economic structure, and to the characteristics and differences of various regions, the whole country was divided into the coastal area and the interior area. The regional development policy for a balanced economic distribution emphasized the construction of the interior areas. During this period, the state launched a massive programme of construction in the interior area.[4] Among 150 national key construction projects for capital investment, one-third were located in the western region, mainly in Shaanxi 陕西, Sichuan 四川 and Gansu 甘肃 (Table 4.1).[5] Meanwhile, many of the 694 key projects designated and constructed by local governments were also located in the western region. The construction of these projects increased the proportion of national capital investment in the western region.

National economic construction during this period focused on industrialization, especially the development of heavy industries. The construction laid a preliminary foundation of industrialization in the western region, especially the northwest. The region's long-standing dependence on agriculture for development shifted to industrialization, and the gap in economic development between the coastal and interior areas gradually narrowed.

Table 4.1 Regional Distribution of Key Projects in the First Five-year Plan in China

Area	Numbers of projects	Percentage share (%)
The Northeast	56	37.3
The Northwest	33	22.0
The North	27	18.0
The Central-South	18	12.0
The Southwest	11	7.3
The East	5	3.4
Total	150	100.0

Source: Lu and Sit, *1997 Zhongguo quyu fazhan baogao* (see note 4).

However, with a weak economic foundation and backward urban facilities, the interior area did not have a full manufacturing capacity and was not able to provide adequate support for urban residents. Thus, self-contained industrial zones with multiple functions were established. They played a leading role in the upgrading of the industrial structure of the western region and in its economic growth. But due to characteristics of the centrally planned economy, the new enterprises funded mainly by the state gradually lost their vitality. These problems worsened in the 1970s and 1980s.

Large-scale "Third Front" Construction in the Period of Balanced Development

During the period of the Third Five-year Plan (1966–1970), Fourth Five-year Plan (1971–1975) and Fifth Five-year Plan (1975–1980) from 1964 to 1972, the central government made two major decisions on regional development, which were based on a pessimistic assessment of the possibility and urgency of war.[6]

First, much effort was made to implement the Third Front construction to achieve a strategic shift in industrial distribution. In August 1964, then-Chairman Mao Zedong 毛澤東 pointed out in his two speeches that the concentration of factories in large cities and coastal areas was unfavourable from the point of view of defence and that such situation should be changed by relocating some factories to build a strategic rear. In December 1964, prior to the Third Five-year Plan, the proposal was to enhance the construction of the interior areas. The state invested a total of RMB120 billion for the construction of the Third Front. Sichuan, Guizhou 貴州 and the Three Wests (i.e., west of Henan 河南, west of Jiangxi 江西 and west of Hunan 湖南) became key areas for state investment and construction. Panzhihua 攀枝花, Jiuquan 酒泉 and Chongqing 重慶 were important industrial centres for construction.

The relatively backward southwest and northwest regions' share of national capital investment increased significantly from 16.9% in the First Five-year Plan period to 35.1% in the Third Five-year Plan period. In total, the interior area's share of national capital investment reached 66.8%.[7] In the eastern developed areas in the same period, Shanghai only received 3.6% of total state investment, ranking it thirteenth in the country, while Tianjin 天津, another major industrial city in the coastal area, ranked only twenty-first in terms of state investment.

Second, a strategy to develop independent regional industrial systems was adopted. In a national planning meeting in February 1970, it was proposed that zones of economic co-operation with different levels and features would be established. It was decided that, by 1975, the steel output in co-operation zones in Northeast, North, East, South and Southwest China should be increased by over 6 million tonnes. A series of small and medium-sized steel enterprises would be set up in these regions to achieve the target. Many prefectures and counties would construct their own small coal mines, steel mines and steel factories, to form a dispersed system of steel industries of different sizes in different areas.

According to the above strategy, a strong strategic rear would be built in the interior area, with relatively complete economic sectors and co-ordinated development in manufacturing and agriculture. Industrial construction would be dispersed all over the interior area but would be relatively concentrated at the local level. The location of new industrial factories followed the principle of being close to mountains, decentralized and concealed. Some factories were built inside caves. To serve economic development and defence during a possible war, the whole interior region was divided into ten co-operative zones where industries such as metallurgy, defence, machinery, fuel and chemicals would be constructed step by step in each zone. The development of five kinds of small industries was promoted; that is, small steel factories, small machinery factories, small chemical fertilizer factories, small coal pits and small cement factories. Every local government made great efforts in the development and construction of heavy industry, aiming to create an independent and complete economic and industrial structure.[8]

Under the above strategy, the spatial structure of China's economy became more balanced. The location of industries shifted from the northeast and north to Third Front areas. The share of the eastern region in the gross output value of country's industry and agriculture decreased, while those of the central and western regions increased.

Clearly, the Third Front construction facilitated the development of natural resources and opened the interior market to the coastal area. It also strengthened the economy of the western region and its capability for further development. Economic growth in border areas with many minority nationalities ensured the safety of the borders.

However, some serious problems had emerged due to the lack of an overall plan. First, the industry-based economic development came at the cost of local agriculture. Second, the central government's investment concentrated on Third Front construction even as some projects constructed in the 1950s and early 1960s were not in full operation. Progress on many large projects slowed, and some were eventually aborted. Third, some enterprises that had been relocated to the western region also faced numerous difficulties.

For a period of 10 years, the excessive decentralization of industries resulted in a waste of resources and enormous difficulties in economic activities and in the daily life of the staff involved. The large-scale civil and defence manufacturing projects were relatively independent and complete, with little contribution to the local economy. As a result, a typical dual economic structure was formed. The Third Front projects were isolated from the local economy. The construction of an independent and complete industrial system also marked a new trend of duplicating the same industrial structure in various areas all over the country. In the current effort to develop the western region, lessons can be learned from this experience.

First Strategic Adjustment and the Strategy of Developing the Coastal Region

The first strategic adjustment in regional development policy took place from 1973 to 1978, when the strategic focus of economic construction shifted from the interior to the eastern coastal region. In this period, one key focus of economic construction was to introduce foreign equipment and technology. Large-scale projects began to be located in the eastern region.

In the period of economic reform and opening to the outside world, the central government implemented the strategy of coastal development in 1981–1985 and the development strategy of three economic belts, that is, the eastern, central and western belts, in 1986–1992. This was done with the aim of making full use of local advantages to speed up the country's economic growth.

The two strategies above indicated that the coastal areas had become the focus of national development. The policies on finance, tax and revenue, credit and investment also changed. The following changes had a great impact on regional development. First, state investment began to focus on the coastal region and its investment share reached 52.5% in the period of the Seventh Five-year Plan (1986–1990), the highest in the nation. Second, provincial and local governments were empowered to make investment decisions. Third, responsibilities and powers were evenly divided between the central government and local governments. A fiscal policy of "demarcating income and expenditure and being responsible oneself at various levels of government" was adopted. The share of capital raised by local governments in total investment was increased, and local governments came to wield more financial power. Fourth, opening to the outside world became a basic state policy and an important part of the state's economic development strategy. A regional pattern of opening to the outside world was adopted; that is, focusing on the coastal areas first and moving from the coastal areas to the interior according to different stages in national development.

However, as their power over local economies increased, local governments played an ever more important role in regional economic development. The self-financing of local economic projects became an important fact in local economic development, while the financial power of the central government weakened greatly. Due to the advantages of a good economic base, abundant talent, and excellent locational and technological conditions, the coastal region became the most dynamic area of the national economy. The gap between the eastern and western regions increased dramatically.

Nevertheless, the state adopted a policy of compensation and support for the western region, and thereby made positive contributions to the economic development of the western region. The policies that have had a significant impact on the western region are reviewed below.

Policy of Economic and Technological Co-operation

The Sixth Five-year Plan (1981–1985) stipulated that economic and technological co-operation should be carried out. The policy was designed on the basis of previous experience in raw materials co-operation, technological co-operation and economic co-operation. The Seventh Five-year Plan further stipulated that all areas should encourage rational exchanges in capital, raw materials and talent, and develop all kinds of economic and technological co-operation and establish all kinds of joint ventures within the overall national plan. The following principles were taken into consideration: maximizing favourable factors and minimizing unfavourable ones, multiple approaches, mutual benefit and joint development to speed up the rational adjustment of the economic structure and regional distribution.

There were three key aspects in regional co-operation. The first was the joint construction of projects of national importance. The second was the enhancement of co-operation between the eastern coastal areas and the central and western regions of the country. For example, those industries consuming much energy and materials were to be transferred to the central and western regions and old Third Front factories were to be restructured to make full use of their technological and capital advantages. The third was the active promotion and organization of support to backward areas by relatively developed areas to boost economic development in the backward areas.[9]

The implementation of the above policy facilitated the interregional flow of raw materials and promoted complementarity in advantageous industries. Interregional co-operation increased, and the impact on economic development in the western region was positive.

Policy of Regional Compensation

During the periods of the Sixth and Seventh Five-year Plans, the central government improved the regional compensation system by targeting the policies on minority nationalities, poverty alleviation and financial subsidies. In 1979, it began to organize and mobilize developed areas and cities to provide assistance to areas with many minority nationalities. In 1980, it began to implement a policy of providing fixed subsidies to minority areas. The amount of compensation allocated by the central government to areas with many minority nationalities increased by 10% annually from 1980 to 1988.[10] The central government also set up a special fund in 1980 through which RMB54.8 billion was allocated to support economically backward areas. In 1983, the central government established a special "Three West" construction fund. For three years, about RMB200 million annually was available to assist economic construction in the Hexi Corridor area, the Dingxi 定西 area and the Xihaigu 西海固 area of Ningxia 寧夏. The central government also supported various local projects in poverty-stricken areas by providing people working on such projects with grain, cloth and industrial products of medium and low quality. The central government also made use of foreign aid in the construction of many infrastructure and poverty-alleviation projects.[11]

The implementation of the regional compensation policy speeded up the economic development of backward areas. Living conditions and the environment also improved by a large margin.

Policy of Industrial Development and Allocation

In this period, the state's policy towards industry in the western interior areas emphasized the construction of energy and raw material bases. The state implemented a series of coal-electric power projects in Shaanxi 陝西 and Inner Mongolia 內蒙古, many hydropower stations in the upper reaches of the Yellow River 黃河, the main stream and tributaries of the Yangzi River 長江, the main streams of the Nujiang River 怒江, Hongshui River 紅水河 and Lancang River 瀾滄江. The state also constructed some non-ferrous metal bases in Gansu, Yunnan 雲南 and Guangxi 廣西. The construction of the above bases gave strong support to economic growth in these areas.

While the focus of regional development had shifted to the coastal region, the enterprises built during the Third Front period, including those in the western region, were adjusted and reformed. The problems of wrong location, large scale and fragmented distribution were solved. Some growth centres were established to drive regional economic development.[12]

Second Strategic Adjustment and the Co-ordinated Regional Development Strategy

The strategy of developing the coastal region reversed the previous pattern of balanced development. A prosperous coastal industrial development region emerged. The strategy spurred the process of industrialization all over the country, contributing significantly to the growth of the macro economy. However, this unbalanced development strategy caused disequilibrium in the spatial economy. The gap in overall economic strength among the eastern, central and western regions increased significantly. Such an increase in development gap worsened financial conditions in backward areas (Table 4.2). The residents of backward areas had low incomes and living standards. There was also a serious capital shortage for the construction of urban infrastructure, basic industries, and for cultural, educational and public health facilities. Tables 4.3 and 4.4 show that the western region had the least ability to finance local projects for both the SOEs (state-owned enterprises) sector and the local economy. In the meantime, local protectionism once again became rampant. Extraordinarily rapid economic growth put severe ecological and environmental pressure on the eastern and southern coastal areas, the Yangzi River Delta and the interior areas, where large-scale development has occurred.

Taking into account of the above situation, the central government began to prepare for a second adjustment of its macro-regional development strategy in 1992, during the period of the Eighth Five-year Plan (1991–1995). The Ninth Five-year Plan (1996–2000) and the National Long-term Goal Plan for 2010 approved by the fourth session of the Eighth National People's Congress on 17 March 1996 adopted the co-ordinated development policy for the first time. National social and economic development would follow the principle of co-ordinated regional development to gradually reduce the inter-regional gap in development.

With the implementation of the Ninth Five-year Plan, the Chinese government emphasized the development of the interior areas. Various measures were adopted to reduce the gap in inter-regional development.

Table 4.2 Distribution and Growth of Local Financial Income among the Eastern, Central and Western Regions, 1980–1994

Region	1980		1994		Annual growth rate in local financial income 1980–1994 (%)
	Local financial income per capita (RMB)	Share of local financial income in China (%)	Local financial income per capita (RMB)	Share of local financial income in China (%)	
Eastern	55.6	43.9	399.5	53.1	16.6
Central	50.7	34.5	221.6	26.3	13.5
Western	48.8	21.6	278.0	20.6	14.9

Note: The western region does not include Guangxi and Inner Mongolia.
Source: Wang and Li, *Zhongguo diqi shehui jingji fazhan bupingheng wenti yanjiu* (see note 7), pp. 163–67.

Table 4.3 Comparison of the Capacity of Local Financing and Capital Accumulation among the Eastern, Central and Western Regions

(Unit: %)

Region	Share in the total investment in SOEs in the region		Capital share of locally financed projects in total investment	The rate of actual capital accumulation
	Capital raised by local areas	Capital funded by the state budget		
		1993		
Eastern	50.82	8.84	71.13	44.64
Central	41.52	9.69	60.69	33.53
Western	38.59	10.46	57.27	27.18
		1997		
Eastern	50.60	4.88	71.42	n.a.
Central	44.75	7.87	56.93	n.a.
Western	45.10	7.86	59.20	n.a.

Note: The western region does not include Guangxi and Inner Mongolia.
Sources: Wang and Li, *Zhongguo diqi shehui jingji fazhan bupingheng wenti yanjiu* (see note 7), p. 125; Guojia tongjiju 國家統計局, *Zhongguo tongji nianjian 1994* 中國統計年鑑1994 (China Statistical Yearbook 1994) (Beijing, Zhongguo tongji chubanshe 中國統計出版社, 1994); *Zhongguo tongji nianjian 1998.*

Table 4.4 Share of Eastern, Central and Western Regions in Various Investments in China, 1993–1997

(Unit: %)

Region	SOE investment			Non-SOE investment		
	Capital raised by local areas	Capital funded by the state budget	Locally financed projects	Central financed projects	Investment of collectives	Investment of joint ventures and foreign-owned enterprises
			1993			
Eastern	62.52	47.61	61.42	48.53	78.59	83.31
Central	23.31	30.77	23.91	30.15	13.84	10.71
Western	14.17	21.62	14.68	21.32	7.57	5.98
			1997			
Eastern	60.68	45.91	62.61	47.89	74.04	84.29
Central	23.49	32.44	22.08	31.93	17.15	12.76
Western	15.82	21.65	15.31	20.18	6.81	2.95

Note: The western region does not include Guangxi and Inner Mongolia.
Sources: Wang and Li, *Zhongguo diqi shehui jingji fazhan bupingheng wenti yanjiu* (see note 7), p. 126; Guojia tongjiju, *Zhongguo tongji nianjian 1994*; 1998 (see table 4.3).

Efforts were made to deal properly with the following: the relation between making full use of regional advantages and a national overall plan, the relation between the coastal and interior areas, and the relation between economically developed areas and relatively undeveloped areas. The objective was to achieve a rational regional division of labour, mutually complementary advantages and co-ordinated development.[13] Some significant policy adjustments related to the western region are briefly outlined as follows.[14]

The first is to extend the open policy from the coastal areas to areas along rivers and national borders. While continuing to pursue export-oriented economic development in the coastal areas, after 1992 the state extended the open policy to areas along rivers, national borders and central cities in the interior. The state selected 13 cities and towns to be opened to the outside world, and 10 of these were located in the western region. The open areas along rivers were represented by the opening of Shanghai's Pudong 浦東 New District in 1990, Chongqing 重慶 municipality and the area surrounding the planned Three Gorges Dam. In 1992, the state opened all provincial capitals in the interior, excluding Lhasa 拉薩, to the outside world. These interior cities were given the same preferential terms as the coastal open cities, so that they could jumpstart the economies of the interior area.

The second is the construction of infrastructure and basic industries in the western region. Through the implementation of an industrial policy and key regional construction projects, the state invested heavily in the mining of the country's rich natural resources and in the construction of infrastructure. Basic industries, large-scale industrial projects and agricultural and stock-raising bases were built in the western region. The share of the state's investment in large-scale projects increased significantly in the northwest region (Table 4.5). The above measures improved the infrastructure, investment environment and supporting capability of the western region. They facilitated the formation of a series of mainstay industries in the western region.

Table 4.5 Changing Ratio of State Investment to Local Investment for Large-Scale Projects, 1988–1993

Area/years	1988	1992	1993
China	1.32:1.00	0.79:1.00	0.67:1.00
Northwest	1.25:1.00	1.65:1.00	1.43:1.00

Source: Lu and Sit, *1997 Zhongguo quyu fazhan baogao* (see note 4), p. 12.

The third is the support and assistance given to backward areas of the western region. During the Eighth and Ninth Five-year Plans, in addition to the increased investment in infrastructure in the western region, the state also increased the funds it earmarks for poverty-alleviation to improve economic and living conditions in depressed areas where people had difficulty meeting their basic needs, such as food and clothing.

In the meantime, the state introduced some preferential policies for the development of impoverished areas in the west. In 1993, the State Council announced a decision to promote the development of township and village enterprises (TVEs) in the central and western regions. An annual special loan of RMB10 billion was allocated to support such activities in the western region. In 1994, the state announced the Eight-Seven Plan for Poverty Alleviation, meaning that poverty alleviation reached a critical stage. In the same year, the state began to implement a new financial administration system on tax distribution, aiming to strengthen central financial capacity and improve financial transfers to undeveloped areas. The state has also made efforts to increase the central and western regions' share of national policy loans and to encourage more foreign investment in these areas. The state also encouraged the eastern region to give assistance to the central and western regions.

The fourth is the improvement in the organization and co-ordination of various policies. The State Development and Planning Commission and other government departments concerned broke down the bounds of administrative divisions and formulated a development plan for the southwest and northwest regions. The goal is to promote economic co-operation between the eastern and western regions, the joint construction of trans-provincial infrastructure and of the basic industrial projects involving energy and raw materials on a large scale, tap into the regional market and accelerate the trans-regional flow of commodities and production factors. The plan was based on the existing economic situation, the principles of a market economy and natural and geographic conditions.

Several economic passageways were opened up to help the western interior areas develop an export-oriented economy to make use of international markets and resources. Under the guidance of the overall plan and policy of the state, all areas were encouraged to launch multi-field, multi-level and multi-form horizontal economic co-operation projects according to the principles of mutual benefit, risk sharing and each making full use of their own advantages.

With the adoption of the above measures, the gap in economic growth rates between the western and eastern regions has narrowed since the beginning of the 1990s. However, as the state's effort to support the western region is still oriented towards the mining of natural resources, the structural problem inherited from previous efforts to develop the interior areas was yet to be solved.[15]

Current Western Development Policy

Since the implementation of the Ninth Five-year Plan, a buyer's market has emerged in the Chinese economy. Relative over-production and insufficient effective demand have become two serious problems in economic development. On the other hand, increasing regional differences in economic development in recent years, a result of continuous rapid growth in the eastern coastal areas, have not only had a negative impact on national economic development but also caused the public to become sceptical of the principle of common wealth. The latter is a potentially serious threat to the social stability and security of the country. The continuous degradation of the ecological environment in the western region has not only threatened its own economic development and living environment, but also become a major obstacle to the sustainable development of the eastern region and the whole country.[16]

Considering the above situation, the state began to design and implement the Strategy for Great Development of the Western Region. Considering the reality of inadequate development advantages, weak social and economic foundation and the strategic role of the western region in ecological issues and national problems, the new development strategy has the following main objectives: protecting and improving the ecological environment, promoting economic prosperity, enhancing the regional capability for sustainable economic development, restraining the growth in the economic gap between west and east, and reducing the differences in social development, focusing especially on the living standards of farmers. The key long-term tasks have been identified as follows: speeding up the construction of infrastructure, reinforcing the protection and construction of the ecological environment, consolidating the fundamental status of agriculture, restructuring the industrial structure, developing niche tourism, and raising standards in science, education and culture, and improving health services. The state has formulated and implemented a series of policies to serve the above objectives and tasks.[17] Some key policies are discussed below.

Increasing Investment and Financial Support to the Western Region

Due to its own limited accumulation capability and weak attraction to external capital, the western region has suffered from capital shortages for a long time. To solve this problem, the central government has increased the western region's share of bank loans through the state financing facility. The state's policy-oriented loans and other loans provided by international financial organizations and foreign governments have also been directed to the western region as far as possible. Over one-third of the long-term construction treasury bonds issued in the period 1998–2001, RMB510 billion in total, were used in the western region. In 2001, this share was as high as 40%, involving approximately RMB60 billion.

The investment for the key infrastructure construction projects planned by the state has come mainly from state-financed construction funds, other special construction funds, bank loans and foreign capital. The central government also plans to raise special funds for the development of the western region through various ways to support a set of key projects. These key projects include the west-east natural gas transmission project and the west-east electricity transmission project, which will play a significant role in the development of the western region. Priority will also be given to the construction of infrastructure for water conservancy, transportation, energy, the mining and processing of quality natural resources and the development of high-tech industries in the western region.

At the same time, the state has also made great efforts to provide support in the form of extending credit for the construction of railways, main artery roads, key energy projects and agriculture. The state is even extending the number of pay-off years for those infrastructure projects involving large investments and long construction times. Preferential terms of credit are also provided for projects in special agriculture, water-saving agriculture and environmental-friendly agriculture. Many bank loans have been given to selected ecological environmental construction projects. By giving priority to the development of electricity supplies, natural gas, tourism and bio-resources, the state is speeding up the restructuring of the economies and industries of the western region. Analysis based on statistical data for recent years has shown that investment in fixed assets has increased significantly in the western region and that the construction of infrastructure has clearly speeded up. This means that the investment effect of the Western Region Development Strategy has caught on (Table 4.6).

Economic compensation and support are still considered important

Table 4.6 Investment in Fixed Assets in the Eastern, Central and Western Regions, 1999–2001

Indicator	Year	China	Eastern	Central	Western[1]
Investment[2] (RMB billion)	1999	2115	1294	476	345
	2000	2339	1402	543	394
	2001	2640	1588	632	470
Growth rate (%)	1999	5.8	5.6	7.1	5.6
	2000	10.6	8.3	13.8	14.4
	2001	12.8	13.3	16.3	19.3
Average annual growth rate (%)	1999–2000	11.7	10.8	15.1	16.8

Notes: [1] The western region does not include Guangxi and Inner Mongolia.
[2] Investment in fixed assets does not include private investment and investment by urban and rural collectives.

Sources: Guojia fazhan jihua weiyuanhui diqu jingji fazhansi diqu jingji fenxi yu pingjia ketizu 國家發展計劃委員會地區經濟發展司地區經濟分析與評價課題組, *Zhongguo diqu jingji fazhan niandu baogao 2001* 中國地區經濟發展年度報告2001 (Annual Report on the Development of the Regional Economy in China 2001) (Beijing: Zhongguo wujia chubanshe, 2001); Guojia tongjiju, *2001 Zhonghua renmin gongheguo tongji gongbao* 2001年中華人民共和國統計公報 (Statistical Bulletin of PRC 2001).

means of increasing general transfer payments to the western region. The central government has also adopted more favourable policies for the development of agricultural science and technology, the development of water-saving agriculture, the protection of the ecological environment for agriculture, the prevention and control of plant diseases, elimination of pests and the improvement of social security, education, public health and other social services.

With the strengthening of the state's financial capacity, the state has gradually increased the funds allocated for poverty alleviation in depressed areas and in areas with many minority nationalities in the western region. The funds are mainly used to construct infrastructure in poverty-stricken villages, to improve elementary education, vocational technical education and training on the application of suitable advanced technologies.

The state has also made efforts in the protection of natural forests and the conversion of farmland into forests and grasslands. To those peasants whose farmland is converted into forests or grasslands, the state makes appropriate compensation in the form of grain and cash using funds from the state financial facility. The state also plans to subsidize those areas whose financial revenues have been reduced for a very long period due to the grain-to-green conversion. Similarly, the central government plans to support, according to the normal means of making transfer payments, villages and towns with financial difficulties arising from the trial reform of collecting taxes instead of fees.

Improving the Investment Environment in the Western Region

The state has made great efforts to help SOEs in the western region reduce their burdens and restructure, in order to make real improvements in the soft investment environment in the western region. The formation of factor and commodity markets has also been accelerated. The state has adopted active measures to stimulate the development of private enterprises and small business in the western region.

The state also offers preferential tax policies to boost the development of special economic activities and advantageous industries in the western region with potential market demand. Amendments to the "Law on the Regional Autonomy of Minority Nationalities" were approved in the Twentieth Session of the Standing Committee of the Ninth National People's Congress. In order to stimulate the development of autonomous areas with many minority nationalities, domestically funded enterprises can be partly or wholly exempted from profits tax and foreign-funded enterprises from local income tax, with the approval of a provincial government. New enterprises involving transportation, electricity supplies, water conservancy, postal services and broadcasting are partly or wholly exempted from profits tax. The construction of provincial and national highways is partly or wholly exempted from farmland occupancy tax. To attract investors, favourable policies have also been adopted to facilitate the conversion of farmland into forests and grasslands, to speed up the construction of infrastructure and to encourage the prospecting and exploiting of mineral resources.[18]

According to a document "Some Views about Promoting the Development of the Western Region Through Price Levers" issued by the State Development and Planning Commission, the state will implement further price reforms, increasing the share of goods and services that are to be determined by market prices. Independent, flexible and special price systems will be adopted in the railway and air transportation sectors. By changing electricity and water prices and setting reasonable prices for electricity and natural gas through west-east transmission, a price formation system for the production and sale of natural gas, electricity power, petroleum and coal will be established by the state. Using price levers, the state will also enhance the grain-to-green conversion and agricultural restructuring. Through the implementation of the above policies and measures, the state aims to significantly improve the development environment in the western region.

Opening Wider Internally and Internationally to Promote International and Inter-regional Exchange and Co-operation

The state has adopted a policy of market entry in the sectors of agriculture, water conservancy, transportation, energy supply, urban construction, environmental protection, development of mineral resources and tourism. In doing so, it has opened the western region to the outside world to attract non-governmental and foreign investment into the above sectors. The adoption of preferential policies has broadened the channels for using foreign investment.

In the meantime, the central government has also extended the autonomous power of enterprises and reduced threshold requirements for obtaining the right to engage in international trade and in economic and technological co-operation in the western region. Favourable border trade policies have been adopted by the central government to promote the mutual opening of markets and economic co-operation between China and its neighbouring countries. Detailed rules and regulations for the management of foreign-funded enterprises and foreign financial institutions have been issued by the state. These lay down the legal basis for the implementation of related policies in the western region.

With regard to opening up to the domestic market, the state has encouraged various forms of co-operation between enterprises in the western region and those in the central and eastern regions. Foreign direct investment (FDI) has increased slowly in the western region to 2001, although individual provincial units such as Sichuan and Shaanxi have performed relatively better (Table 4.7).

Introducing Trained Personnel and Developing Science and Technology

Considering the shortage of trained personnel and backward status of science, technology and education in the western region, the State Council declared, in its "Notice of Adoption of Several Policies and Measures for the Great Development of Western Region," that favourable policies must be adopted to attract and keep trained personnel and encourage them to set

Table 4.7 Foreign Direct Investment in the Western Region, 1999–2001

Region	Foreign direct investment (US$ million)			Share in China (%)			Annual growth rate (%)		
	1999	2000	2001	1999	2000	2001	1999	2000	2001
China	40,318.71	40,714.81	46,877.59	100	100	100	–11.31	0.98	15.14
Eastern	34,414.62	34,886.49	40,343.61	85.36	85.69	86.06	–10.85	1.37	15.64
Central	3,682.85	3,594.34	4,101.20	9.13	8.83	8.75	–14.93	–2.40	14.10
Western	1,837.35	1,852.06	1,922.19	4.56	4.55	4.10	–21.83	0.80	3.79
Inner Mongolia	64.56	105.68	107.03	0.16	0.26	0.23	–28.91	63.69	1.28
Guangxi	635.12	524.66	384.16	1.58	1.29	0.82	–28.33	–17.39	–26.78
Chongqing	238.93	244.36	256.49	0.59	0.60	0.55	–56.69	2.27	4.96
Sichuan	341.01	436.94	581.88	0.85	1.07	1.24	–8.45	28.13	33.17
Guizhou	40.90	25.01	28.29	0.10	0.06	0.06	–9.81	–38.85	13.11
Yunnan	153.85	128.12	64.57	0.38	0.31	0.14	5.61	–16.72	–49.60
Tibet	n.a.	n.a	n.a	n.a	n.a	n.a	n.a	n.a	n.a
Shaanxi	241.97	288.42	351.74	0.60	0.71	0.75	–19.37	19.20	21.95
Gansu	41.04	62.35	74.39	0.10	0.15	0.16	6.21	51.92	19.31
Qinghai	4.59	n.a	36.49	0.01	n.a	0.08	n.a	n.a	n.a
Ningxia	51.34	17.41	16.80	0.13	0.04	0.04	176.62	–66.09	–3.50
Xinjiang	24.04	19.11	20.35	0.06	0.05	0.04	10.94	–20.51	6.49

Sources: Guojia tongjiju, *Zhongguo tongji nianjian 2000; 2001; 2002* (see table 4.3).

up their own companies to meet the needs of a knowledge economy. The system of science and technology would undergo further reform, gradually increasing the western region's share of science and technology funds, enhancing the region's capability in science and technology and in popularizing and industrializing major scientific and technological achievements. The state would continue to support research institutes and universities in applied and basic research with local characteristics, increase education funding for local compulsory education projects, and enhance the science and cultural training of farmers and rural cadres at the grassroots level. Public health services will also be improved.

General Evaluation and Policy Recommendations for the Development of the Western Region

The policies on western development cover almost every aspect of the western region, indicating the extent of the central government's support for the region. But some obvious problems exist.[19]

First, due to the lack of an overall plan, insight into the long-term effects of these policies is lacking, nor have these policies been implemented systematically. It is recommended that short- and long-term plans be made in advance. At the same time, a plan for the formulation of policies for different periods should be made. The Western Development Office of the State Council should assume the overall task of formulating, disseminating, implementing and supervising various policies and measures.

Second, some policies are not suitable for the western region. Much should be done to reduce and waive some central taxes such as value-added tax. To attract foreign investments, we should open the markets of the western region to the outside world, permitting every form of foreign investment, including mergers and acquisitions. Meanwhile, some feasible suggestions have not been included in the policies issued so far, such as setting up funds for western development and industrial investment, and establishing special industrial and border trading zones.

Third, the new policies show the central government's support for the western region. However, only a frame has been provided with no details. With no real preferential policies, it is not easy to carry out the reforms in the western region, such as the reform of SOEs. Every relevant state department should issue detailed implementation rules as soon as possible, so that each western province can make full use of these policies.

Fourth, these policies and measures do not identify the stages of the development of the western region and are hampered by low manoeuvrability. It is suggested that the government should attempt to attract talented people to the western region by devising attractive industrial, financial, educational, training and open policies.

Fifth, these policies and measures do not consider economic restructuring from a strategic viewpoint and are not sustainable. Economic restructuring can be carried out through three approaches, such as increasing inputs, regrouping, and by a combination of increasing inputs and regrouping. It is suggested that in the short term, at least in the period of the Tenth Five-year Plan (2001–2005), economic restructuring should focus on regrouping to realize a rational distribution of the national economy. Then, in the second period of the development of the western region, inputs can be increased dramatically to develop capital markets and promote the upgrading of the industrial structure, with the aim of achieving sustained and stable economic growth.

Conclusion

The central government has paid much attention to the development of the western region. But the government's economic policies and their effects have changed over the years because of different strategic considerations under changing historical backgrounds.

Before the founding of new China, development in the western region mainly focused on encouraging cultivation, cultural development and commercial activities, as well as strengthening political governance. The application of these policies enhanced social and economic development, promoted national concord, kept the peace in remote areas and the borders security, while also leading to serious environmental degradation.

Between 1949 and the time when a new strategy of developing the western region was adopted, there were three big changes in national policy. First, during the 1950–1970s, China focused on the construction of inland areas for balanced development. In the vast inland areas including the western region, the state made large investments and created the basis for a modern economy. As a result, economic development in the western region accelerated, reducing the east-west gap in economic development. But it also resulted in problems, such as ill-conceived industrial locations and the duplication of the economic structure.

Second, in the reform period up to 1992, for reasons of economic efficiency, the central government adopted a policy of favouring the development of areas with inherent development advantages. Investment and construction focused on the eastern region. At the same time, decision-making powers over investment were increasingly decentralized and handed over to local governments. The financial responsibility system also strengthened local power over economic decisions. The central government's power and influence weakened significantly. Under these circumstances, development in the western region slowed down greatly, due to its weak economic base and poor developmental conditions. The state was unable to change the backward state of the western region and hold back the increasing inter-regional gap in economic development using the previous radical approach. However, the application of some state policies, including economic co-operation between different regions, regional compensation and the construction of energy and materials bases, had a clear impact on development in the western region, especially on the improvement of people's living conditions.

Third, after 1992, considering the increasing gap between different regions, the state turned step by step to a strategy of co-ordinated development. The reform and opening of the western region accelerated. Investment in infrastructure in the western region increased. Poverty alleviation, state support and the east-west co-operation were strengthened. The implementation of these policies helped narrow the development gap between the east and the west, but the difference in the industrial structure became an inherent hurdle, leading to the persistence of the economic gap between east and west.

With the onset of the twenty-first century, the CCP (Chinese Communist Party) and state leaders formulated the western region development strategy. This long-term strategic plan faces many difficulties and obstacles. The relevant laws and regulations are necessary to ensure its implementation. Since 1999, the state has formulated a series of systematic policies aimed at increasing investment, improving the environment, opening up further, attracting talent and developing science, technology and education, etc. All of this has demonstrated the state's support for the western region, and some of the policies have produced good results. However, there are still many problems that must be tackled in the future.

Notes

1. Lan Yong 藍勇, "Zhongguo xibu dakaifa de lishi huigu yu sikao" 中國西部大開發的歷史回顧與思考 (Historical Review and Consideration of Western

Development in China), *Guangming ribao* 光明日報 (Guangming Daily), 4 February 2000.

2. Lu Dadao 陸大道 et al., *2000 Zhongguo quyu fazhan baogao – xibu kaifa de jichu, zhengce yu taishi fenxi* 2000中國區域發展報告 —— 西部開發的基礎政策與態勢分析 (China Regional Development Report 2000 – Foundation, Policy and Situation Analysis of the Development of Western China) (Beijing: Shangwu yinshuguan 商務印書館, 2001).
3. Fan Jie, Cao Zhongxiang and Lü Xin, "On the Industrial Spatial Structure of the Western China," *Progress in Geography*, Vol. 21, No. 4 (2002), pp. 280–301.
4. Lu Dadao and Sit Fung-shuen 薛鳳旋 et al., *1997 Zhongguo quyu fazhan baogao* 1997中國區域發展報告 (China Regional Development Report 1997) (Beijing: Shangwu yinshuguan, 1997).
5. The number of national key construction projects was 156 in the original plan. But 2 projects were double-counted while 4 were not implemented eventually.
6. Lu Dadao, *Zhongguo gongye buju de lilun yu shijian* 中國工業佈局的理論與實踐 (The Theories and Practice of Industrial Location in China) (Beijing: Kexue chubanshe 科學出版社, 1989); Lu Dadao, *Quyu fazhan jiqi kongjian jiegou* 區域發展及其空間結構 (Regional Development and Its Spatial Structure) (Beijing: Kexue chubanshe, 1995).
7. Wang Mengkui 王夢奎 and Li Shantong 李善同 et al., *Zhongguo diqu shehui jingji fazhan bupingheng wenti yanjiu* 中國地區社會經濟發展不平衡問題研究 (A Study on the Issue of Unbalanced Social and Economic Development in China's Regions) (Beijing: Shangwu yinshuguan, 2000).
8. Wei Houkai 魏後凱, *Zhongxibu gongye yu chengshi fazhan* 中西部工業與城市發展 (The Industrial and Urban Development of Central and Western China) (Beijing: Jingji guanli chubanshe 經濟管理出版社, 2000); Bian Gu 邊古, *Zhongguo xibu diqu gongyehua de huigu yu qianzhan* 中國西部地區工業化的回顧與前瞻 (Review and Prospect of Industrialization in the Western Region of China), *Zhongguo gongye jingji* 中國工業經濟 (Industrial Economy of China), No. 4 (2000), pp. 35–42.
9. Lu Dadao, Liu Yi 劉毅 and Fan Jie 樊傑 et al., *1999 Zhongguo quyu fazhan baogao* 1999中國區域發展報告 (China Regional Development Report 1999) (Beijing: Shangwu yinshuguan, 2000).
10. The annual growth was halted since 1988.
11. Wang Yiming 王一鳴 et al., *Zhongguo quyu jingji zhengce yanjiu* 中國區域經濟政策研究 (A Study on the Regional Economic Policies of China) (Beijing: Zhongguo jihua chubanshe 中國計劃出版社, 1998).
12. Guowuyuan fazhan yanjiu zhongxin 國務院發展研究中心, *90 niandai Zhongguo xibu diqu jingji fazhan zhanlüe* 九十年代中國西部地區經濟發展戰略 (The Developmental Strategy of the Western Region in China in the 1990s) (Beijing: Huaxia chubanshe 華夏出版社, 1991).

13. Fan Jie and Lu Dadao et al., *Zhongguo yanhai fada diqu xiandaihua daidong zhanlüe yanjiu* 中國沿海發達地區現代化帶動戰略研究 (Research on the Leading Strategy of the Modernization of Coastal Developed Regions in China) (Beijing: Zhongguo youyi chuban gongsi 中國友誼出版公司, 2001); Fan Jie and Lu Dadao et al., *Zhongguo diqu jingji xietiao fazhan yu quyu jingji hezuo yanjiu* 中國地區經濟協調發展與區域經濟合作研究 (Co-ordinated Growth and Co-operation of Regional Economies in China) (Beijing: Zhongguo youyi chuban gongsi, 2001).
14. Liu Jiang 劉江, *Zhongguo diqu fazhan huigu yu zhanwang* (zonghe juan)中國地區發展回顧與展望 (綜合卷) (Review and Prospect of Regional Development in China (general volume) (Beijing: Zhongguo wujia chubanshe 中國物價出版社, 1999).
15. Liu Weidong 劉衛東, "Jinnian lai quanguo quyu fazhan zhuangtai fenxi pingjia yu leixing huafen" 近年來全國區域發展狀態分析評價與類型劃分 (Analysis, Evaluation and Classification of the Regional Development Status of the Country in Recent Years). In *2000 Zhongguo quyu fazhan baogao*, edited by Lu (see note 2), pp. 238–57.
16. Zhongguo kexueyuan xuebu lianhe bangongshi 中國科學院學部聯合辦公室, *Zhongguo kexueyuan yuanshi zixun baogao* (xibei diqu kechixu fazhan bufen) 中國科學院院士諮詢報告(西北地區可持續發展部分) (Consultancy Report by Academicians of the Chinese Academy of Sciences (on the Sustainable Development of the Northwest Region)), September 1999.
17. Fan Jie, Cao Zhongxiang 曹忠祥 and Zhang Wenzhong 張文忠 et al., "Zhongguo xibu kaifa zhanlüe chuangxin de jingji dilixue lilun jichu" 中國西部開發戰略創新的經濟地理學理論基礎 (The Consideration of the Strategic Innovation of Western Exploitation Based on Theories of Economic Geography), *Dili xuebao* 地理學報 (ACTA Geographica Sinica), Vol. 54, No. 6 (1999), pp. 711–21.
18. With regard to the prospecting and exploiting of mineral resources, the Ministry of Land and Resources of China issued a regulation listing many preferential terms for mining activities in the western region.
19. Du Ping 杜平, Fan Jie et al., *Guojia xinghuo jihua xiangmu: Xibu dakaifa hongguan jingji zhanlüe yanjiu* 國家星火計劃項目：西部大開發宏觀經濟戰略研究 (Project supported by State Star Programme: Research on Macro Economic Strategies for Western Development), March 2002.

5

Infrastructure and the New Economy

Y. M. Yeung, Jin Fengjun and Zeng Guang

The sprawling and vast territory of the western region of China has traditionally suffered from slow growth owing, in no small measure, to the glaring lack of infrastructure which, in itself, has been the result of inadequate public spending. Documentaries of the immediate years after the establishment of a new regime in 1949 showed how the military (largely decommissioned soldiers) contributed to constructing roads, reclaiming land, building towns and other infrastructure, often under very trying circumstances. They made a valiant start in building infrastructure in far-flung territories, notably in Xinjiang and Tibet, which have subsequently benefited a great deal from these early efforts. The learned China scholar Doak Barnett has made an insightful and valuable comparison of many parts of China's west. He noted, with astonishment and admiration, the tremendous strides the country had made in four decades of economic transformation up to the late 1980s.[1] The huge improvements in infrastructure that he observed in many of the western cities he visited may have impressed him, but they were still a far cry from what would be required for "balanced" national development and for launching China's west to a path of sustainable development.

The relationship between infrastructure and development is so crucial that the *World Development Report (WDR) 1994* devoted its annual report to that particular theme.[2] Infrastructure may be taken as an umbrella term for many activities referred to as "social overhead capital," which includes public works (roads, railways, major dams and irrigation works), public utilities (power, telecommunications, piped water, solid waste collection and piped gas) and other transport sectors (urban and inter-urban railways, urban transport, ports, waterways and airports). Obviously, the infrastructure needs of an urban area are different from those of a rural area. Although infrastructure is sometimes liberally interpreted to include social infrastructure, that is, medical and health facilities, the provision of education, social welfare and publicly managed facilities, for this chapter a narrower definition is adopted.

Based on an analysis of many countries, *WDR 1994* revealed that infrastructural capacity is positively correlated with economic output. In other words, as GDP per capita increases, so does the stock of infrastructure. Infrastructure is, literally, the "wheels," if not the engine, of economic activity. The report further generalized:

> The adequacy of infrastructure helps determine one country's success and another's failure — in diversifying production, expanding trade, coping with

> population growth, reducing poverty, or improving environmental conditions. Good infrastructure raises productivity and lowers production costs, but it has to expand fast enough to accommodate growth. The precise linkages between infrastructure and development are still open to debate.[3]

> … infrastructure investment is not sufficient on its own to generate sustained increases in economic growth. The demand for infrastructure services is itself sensitive to economic growth, which is notoriously difficult to predict. The economic impact of infrastructure investment varies not only by sector but also by its design, location, and timeliness.[4]

The report equally emphasized the boundless opportunities that technological changes have created for changing the way infrastructure is provided in almost every sector. Technologies that are clearly more efficient, robust and flexible than earlier methods enable developing countries to "leapfrog" the sectoral transitions experienced by more advanced countries.[5] This is, in fact, an underlying theme of this chapter, which argues that, despite significant progress having been made since the policy of developing the west was promulgated in 1999, what is called for is a speedy transition premised upon the new economy with its new technologies. This will shorten the time needed for sectoral transitions, expand markets for material production, and broaden and intensify human socioeconomic activities. The new economy is characterized by its close relationship with informationalization and globalization and, in the context of China's recent accession to the WTO, is highly germane to the development of infrastructure in the western region.

This chapter is divided into three main parts. The first is a survey of the present status of infrastructural provision in China's western region. The second is a review of the elements of the new economy in relation to infrastructure development, in which infrastructure goals for the region are noted against recent trends. The final part evaluates some proposals on infrastructure in the region and draws a conclusion.

Present Status of Infrastructure Provision

Tilting Policies Towards Rapid Construction

Since the central government's announcement in 1999 of its intention to develop the western region, a series of strategic plans and policies have been gradually formulated in order to strongly support the construction of infrastructure to overcome a traditional obstacle to development. In 2000, central decision-makers passed "The State Council's Notice Related to Certain Policy Measures in the Implementation of Western Development" 《國務院關於實施西部大開發若干政策措施的通知》. In essence, the policy involved increasing the financial resources devoted to the development of infrastructure in the region, raising the proportion of the central government's contribution to construction funds and increasing the number of construction projects in the region. Moreover, the government extended larger amounts in financial transfers and loans from its National Development Bank. In a related measure, agricultural land expropriated for use in the building of national highways was declared tax-exempt. In this way, the process of expropriating land for development purposes was streamlined, guaranteeing that land would be available in a timely manner for construction. At the same time, every effort is being made to encourage foreign investment and to attract talent to the region. In a two-year period from 2000 to 2001, six pieces of legislation were enacted by the central and provincial governments to guarantee financial arrangements and the quality of the infrastructure to be constructed in the western region. In short, technological inputs, planning, legal protection and budgetary spending have been deliberately tilted towards the western region (Table 5.1). Indeed, the World Bank and the Asian Development Bank (ADB) have already lent China almost US$5 million to construct a railway to link the western region with the national transport network.[6]

According to information provided by China's Ministry of Finance and the ADB's 2000 Annual Report, in 1999 alone, the central and provincial governments invested a total of RMB1,100 billion to develop infrastructure. During the Tenth Five-year Plan (2001–2005), investment in infrastructure will account for RMB7,100 billion. In the Eleventh Five-year Plan period, it is expected to reach RMB10,000 billion. According to existing estimates, by 2010, annual investment in infrastructure will be RMB2,300 billion, accounting for 40% of fixed asset investments and 13.4% of GDP, compared with the corresponding figures of 36.8% and 13.1% for 1999.[7] As early as 1998, China had already devoted 70% of its national debt, that is, RMB100 billion, to the construction of infrastructure in the western region in order to accelerate the pace of the area's development.[8]

Present Status and Construction Plans

Transport, water works, energy, communication and the construction of urban infrastructure constitute the major sectors of infrastructure

Table 5.1 Recent Initiatives in Infrastructure Construction in China's Western Region

Water conservancy facilities	Construction of water-storage facilities in the field, drought-resistance and water conservation works, fallowing of arable land and demonstration of water-conserving agriculture.
	Water-conserving technologies in the irrigated regions in the Ordos 河套 region, the Yellow River 黃河 in Ningxia and Inner Mongolia 寧蒙河套, the Guanzhong Plain 關中平原 and the Heihe Basin 黑河流域.
	Area-specific water-conserving technologies to promote anti-seepage, water-supply via pipeline, sprinkling irrigation 噴灌 and trickling irrigation 滴灌.
	Promotion of recycling of industrial water and conservation of domestic water, treatment of polluted water.
	Comprehensive treatment of the Tarim River 塔里木河 and the Hei River and the protection of water resources in the upper reaches of the Yangzi River 長江 and the upper-middle reaches of the Yellow River.
	Construction of irrigation projects in Zipingpu 紫坪鋪 on the Minjiang 岷江, Shapotou 沙坡頭 on the Yellow River, Ni'erji 尼爾基 on the Nenjiang 嫩江 and Bose 百色 on the Youjiang 右江.
	Strengthen the use of irrigated water in agriculture and resolve the shortage of drinking water for people and livestock in rural areas.
Transport facilities	Accelerate the construction of national highway trunk lines, especially the 5 North-South and 7 East-West lines "五縱七橫." By 2010, nine national highway trunk lines will have been constructed, and large and medium-sized cities basically connected by superior highways: Inner Mongolia Evenhot 內蒙古二連浩特 - Yunnan Hekou 雲南河口, Chongqing 重慶 - Guangdong Zhanjiang 廣東湛江, Heilongjiang Suifenhe 黑龍江綏汾河 - Inner Mongolia Manzhouli 內蒙古滿州里, Liaoning Dandong 遼寧丹東 - Tibet Lhasa 西藏拉薩, Shandong Qingdao 山東青島 - Ningxia Yinchuan 寧夏銀川, Jiangsu Lianyungang 江蘇連雲港 - Xinjiang Korgas 新疆霍爾果斯, Shanghai 上海 - Sichuan Chengdu 四川成都, Shanghai - Yunnan Ruili 雲南瑞麗, Hunan Hengyang 湖南衡陽 - Yunnan Kunming 雲南昆明.
	Upgrade and construct eight provincial highways: Lanzhou 蘭州 to Yunnan's Mohan 磨憨, Baotou 包頭 to Beihei 北海, Altay 阿勒泰 to Kunjirap 紅其拉甫, Yinchuan to Wuhan 武漢, Xi'an 西安 to Hefei 合肥, Changsha 長沙 to Chongqing, Xining 西寧 to Korla 庫爾勒, Chengdu to Tibet's Zhangmu 西藏樟木.
	Accelerate key railway lines, Xi'an - Nanjing 南京, Yu-huai 渝懷 (Chongqing 重慶 - Huaihua 懷化) and construct cross-border railroads in the northwest and the southwest.
	Improve and elevate the aviation hubs in Chengdu, Xi'an, Kunming, Lanzhou, Urumqi 烏魯木齊 and Chongqing, accelerate the construction of airports in tourist areas, and plan the construction of a number of feeder airports.
	Priority construction of navigation facilities in the upper reaches of the Yangzi River and the Pearl River 珠江. Waterway passages linking the western and eastern regions to be constructed.

Table 5.1 (Cont'd)

Energy facilities	The Tenth Five-year Plan concentrates on accelerating electricity supply via the southern passageway, constructing a power grid and increasing electricity transmission to Guangdong by 1,000MW. The West-East Power Transmission Project 西電東送 is being given priority in implementation, especially the middle section (The Three Gorges to Yangzi River Delta) and the northern passageway (North Shaanxi, Western Inner Mongolia to Jingjintang 京津唐).
	Construction of the backbone projects in the West-East Gas Pipeline Project 西氣東輸 from the Tarim Basin to Yangzi River Delta, gradually establishing oil and gas production and transmission bases in Qaidam 柴達木, Shaanxi 陝西, Gansu 甘肅, Ningxia 寧夏, Sichuan 四川 and Chongqing.
Communication facilities	Accelerate the construction of the 3 West-East and 1 North-South "三横一縱" broadband transmission networks along the Euro-Asian continental bridge, the Yangzi River, the Guiyang 貴陽 - Kunming network and the Huhhot 呼和浩特 - Nanning 南寧 network.
	Improvement and construction of major transmission networks of optical cable, microwave and satellite communications within provinces and autonomous regions, improving customer access to networks.
	Development of fixed-line telephone networks, especially in rural areas and of mobile phone networks. Improve computer information networks and develop public service information platforms and e-commerce, distance education and tele-medical care.
	Strengthen postal service centres in provincial capitals and transform urban postal network facilities. Upgrade postal delivery speed and services in urban and rural areas.

Source: Western Development Office, National Development Planning Committee.

construction in the western region. Of these, transport occupies the highest priority. To date, the central government has already spent more than RMB100 billion launching dozens of infrastructure projects. Following the completion of these projects, the development environment of the western region will have dramatically improved. Some of the major infrastructure projects with the western region as a focus are:[9]

Three Gorges Project 三峽工程

West-East Gas Pipeline Project 西氣東輸工程
Se-Ning-Lan 澀寧蘭 (Sebei 澀北-Xining 西寧-Lanzhou 蘭州) pipeline 管線

West-East Power Transmission Project 西電東輸工程
Power stations at Longtan 龍灘水電站 and Gongboxia 公伯峽水電站

Bose hydrojunction 百色 (廣西) 水利樞紐

Railways: Qing-Zang 青藏鐵路 (Golmud 格爾木 – Lhasa, 1118 km)
Yu-Huai 渝懷鐵路 (Chongqing – Huaihua 懷化, 625 km)
Ning-Xi 寧西鐵路 (Nanjing 南京 – Xi'an 1,024 km)
Nei-Kun 內昆鐵路 (Neijiang 內江 – Kunming 879 km)
Bao-Xi 包西鐵路 (Baotou – Xi'an, 935 km)
Xi-Kang 西康鐵路 (Xi'an – Ankang 安康, 268 km)

National highway trunk lines

Construction of airports in the western region

Urban infrastructure
Chongqing light rail

Transport and Communications

Prior to the adoption of the strategic policy on the western region, transport and communications facilities in the region were very underdeveloped. However, since the 1990s, central planners have begun to favour the west in terms of policies and capital to accelerate the development of its infrastructure. During the Ninth Five-year Plan, national and provincial governments allocated as much as RMB200 billion for transport development. This represented a threefold increase over the previous three five-year plans. Consequently, transport facilities have improved dramatically.[10]

In 2000, significant gains were made in railway development. The Xi-Kang (Xi'an-Ankang) Railroad was completed ahead of schedule and the Cheng-Kun (Chengdu-Kunming) 成昆鐵路 Line completed its electrification upgrading. In addition, the doubling tracking of the Bao-Lan (Baoji 寶雞-Lanzhou) 寶蘭鐵路 Line and the construction of the Ning-Xi, Qing-Zang and Yu-Huai Lines began. In July 2000, construction started on the Qing-Zang Railroad, with 2007 as the anticipated year of completion. Once completed, it will be the world's highest railway in terms of elevation from sea level.[11] The basic pattern of national railways is fast taking shape. It consists of a network of 8 North-South and 8 East-West "八縱八橫" lines, into which the western region is well integrated (Figure 5.1). By 2000, Shaanxi only had the Bao-Xi (Baotou-Xi'an) Line in the north and Ningxia the Bao-Lan (Baotou-Lanzhou) Line 包蘭鐵路 running through its territory, and Qinghai did not have any railway running through the province at all.

Figure 5.1 National Railway Pattern in China, circa 2000

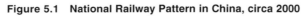

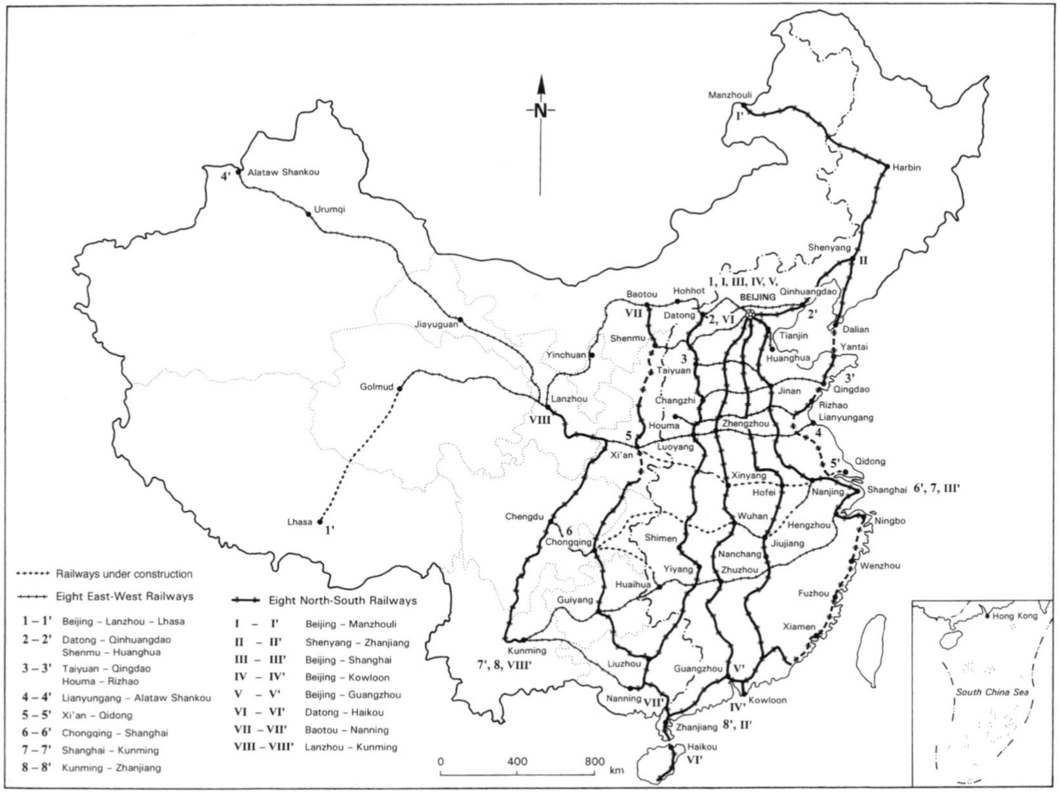

The Southwest was better connected, exhibiting the rudiments of a network but still lacking a driving force. The short, medium and long-term horizon for railway construction targets the years 2000, 2020 and 2050, respectively.[12]

For highway construction, the emphasis has been on constructing new highways to link the western region with the central and eastern regions of the country. Highways occupy a critical position in improving the connectivity and hence, the development potential of the western region. Table 5.1 highlights the national pattern of highways, showing that the western region is still far from well covered. This should be read with Figure 5.2, where the national pattern of 5 North-South and 7 East-West "五縱七橫" trunk lines is shown. The "emptiness" of the west is still striking when the construction of all of the lines will have been completed by 2010. The overarching importance of highways over railways, both nationally and regionally, is clearly revealed in Table 5.2. However, even with the 10 western provincial units, the difference in road connectivity is very large. For example, in 1998, towns in Tibet were the least accessible, such that one-quarter of Tibetan towns could not be reached by road. By contrast, in Sichuan, Yunnan, Shaanxi and Xinjiang, less than 10% of towns and villages were not accessible by road. In 2000, Sichuan was one of the few provinces in China with over 1,000 km of highway.[13] In the western region, highways had a total mileage of more than 30 times that of railways and inland waterways in 1998. Despite the early development of the railway, highways have recently developed much more rapidly because this mode is more flexible in meeting the demands of the terrain and of customers.

Table 5.2 Transport Infrastructure Facilities in China, 1995–1998

Region	National railway coverage (km)		Internal water transport coverage (km)		Highway coverage (km)			
	1995	1998	1995	1998	1995	1998	Of which (1998) classified roads	Of which (1998) high-ways
Eastern	15,905	17,151	58,552	57,971	416,092	461,419	420,251	5,211
Central	25,387	26,646	36,582	31,742	386,190	436,931	366,616	2,351
Western[1]	13,327	13,915	12,615	12,680	354,727	380,124	282,376	1,171

Note: [1] Includes 10 provincial units.

Source: Railway Transport Office, *National Railway Statistical Compendium*, 1990, 1995, 1998; Transport Planning Office, *National Transport Statistical Compendium*, 1990, 1995, 1998 (Quoted in Du Ping et al. See note 11, p. 247).

Figure 5.2 National Highway Pattern in China, circa 2000

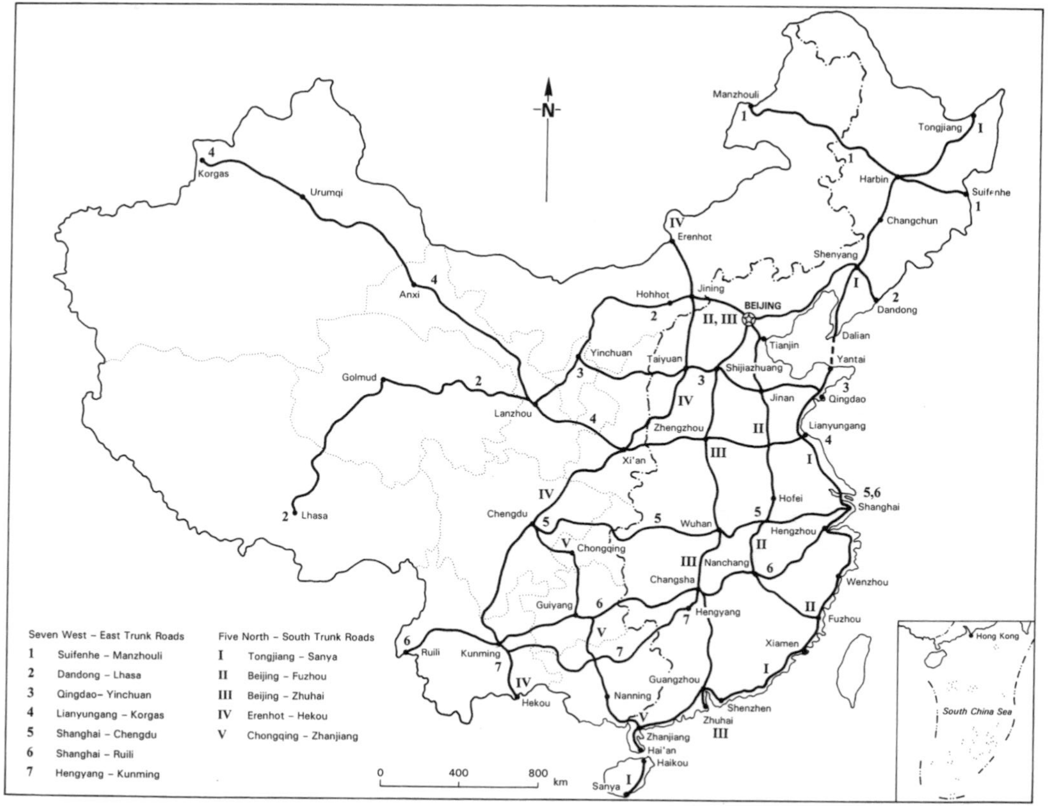

In the period 1950–1980, railways in the west increased nine-fold from 1,189 km to 12,400 km. Meanwhile, in the same period, highways grew from 24,000 km to 283,000 km, representing an 11-fold increase, exceeding the national average. However, in 1980–1995, new railway construction was almost "frozen."[14] In terms of moving cargo, the ratio between railway and highway changed from 2:1 in 1980 to 1:5 in 1989, showing the meteoric rise in the importance of highways. By the end of the 1980s, the division of labour was clear: Railways carried goods for long distances and highways for short distances.[15]

For civil aviation, Urumqi, Xi'an and Kunming have been affirmed as hub airports. Their facilities are being expanded, while feeder airports are also being constructed (Table 5.1). The entire regional pattern of air linkages is being rationalized. In 2000, 18 air routes and feeder airports in the western region were listed as priority areas for development, involving a total investment of RMB7.2 billion. As of the first half of 2002, 11 airport construction projects had been completed, with a total investment of RMB1.34 billion.[16]

In building a new economy in China's western region, communications and telecommunications play a vital role. China is constructing a national network of 8 North-South and 8 East-West "八縱八橫" fibre cables that will greatly assist the development of the western region. At present, information technologies in this area are still at a preliminary stage of development. Based on the informationalization composite index, with the national index at 21, Beijing is 80.87, Shanghai 60.89, Tianjin 天津 42.92 and Guangdong 40.18. The scores for the western region are low, with Chongqing at 27, Sichuan 17.88, Xinjiang 19.26, Qinghai 青海 18.67, Gansu 18.03, Yunnan 15.6, Guizhou 貴州 12.61 and Tibet 10.77.[17] These figures underscore the wide gap between the eastern and western region in the acquisition and development of information technology.

To sum up, the development of transport facilities in western China has been concentrated in Sichuan, Chongqing, Yunnan, Shaanxi and Xinjiang, with 87% of new highway construction in the period 1990–1998 occurring in these provinces. Tibet, Gansu, Ningxia, Qinghai and Guizhou, on the other hand, had a weaker infrastructure base and experienced slower development. Large-scale investment in infrastructure in the western region began only in 1997. Prior to this year, the total level of investment in infrastructure in this region was less than that of the province of Guangdong alone, which has a land area only 1/30 that of the western region.[18]

Irrigated Works

The ecology of the western region is extremely fragile. Water is in short supply in the northwest and water-based infrastructure projects are essential if the ecology is to be protected and sustainable development achieved.

Since 1949, the central government has begun to engage in ecological management, giving labour, material and financial support, especially in respect of the sources of large rivers in the western region. More specifically, since the 1990s, many irrigation projects have been developed. Investment in backbone engineering projects in some river basins, the adoption of drought-resistance technologies, and the large-scale application of water-conservation and ecological regeneration practices are worthy of mention. The region has built a variety of water conservation, diversion and pumping devices, coupled with underground water works in over 200,000 locations. These have gone some way in assuring water supplies for agricultural production and daily life. They have, as well, solved the problem of a drinking water supply for 100 million inhabitants, representing 82% of those in difficulty. The total acreage of land under irrigation has reached 20,752 *mu*. The critical importance of a secure water supply was highlighted by a recent report in a local newspaper that Xi'an was short of water by 38.4% in 2000, and that the problem will worsen to 53% by 2010 and 66.6% by 2030. Consequently, the city has plans to spend RMB8 billion over the next 30 years to build water works to increase and conserve supply, so that future water needs will be satisfied.[19]

On the basis of the real needs of the west, the Ministry of Water Resources has identified key targets in developing water-based infrastructure and water resources. It put forth a guidance note entitled "A Digest for Irrigational Development Planning in the Western Region" 《西部地區水利發展規劃綱要》. Six points were emphasized:

1. Within the period of the Tenth Five-year Plan, solve the problem of drinking water for people and livestock, especially in rural areas.
2. Implement the water-source projects that aim at resolving the problem of water shortages in large urban areas and some agricultural areas. The preliminary work of the South-North Water Diversion Project 南水北調工程 has to be actively followed up.
3. Large-scale water conservancy and conversion projects will be launched in the following irrigated regions: Ningxia-Inner Mongolia Ordos, Guanzhong Plain, Heihe Basin, Tarim River 塔里木河 and Dujiangyan 都江堰. In addition, new irrigation projects will be

constructed, such as Sichuan's Daqiao Dam 大橋水庫, Guizhou's Zunyi 遵義 and Tibet's Manlai 滿拉.

4. Comprehensive water management will take place by developing hydrojunctions at Shapotou on the Yellow River, Ni'erji on the Nenjiang, Zipinpu on the Minjiang and Bose on the Youjiang (Table 5.1).
5. Water and soil conservancy projects will be launched in the Tarim River, Heihe River and the upper reaches of the following rivers: Jinsha River 金沙江, Jialing River 嘉陵江, Nanpan River 南盤江, Beipan River 北盤江 and Hongshui River 紅水河.
6. Flood control and the renovation of dilapidated reservoirs will take place in Chengdu, Nanning 南寧, Wuzhou 梧州, Liuzhou 柳州 and Urumqi.

Energy

Western China is exceptionally well endowed with natural resources. Oil, natural gas, coal and water resources are plentiful. As far as the provision of infrastructure is concerned, natural gas and water deserve special attention because they have bearing on the economic development and environmental sustainability of the country. According to the 2001 *Chinese Statistical Yearbook*, 58% of China's natural gas and 54% of its hydroelectricity are located in the west.

In fact, even without Guangxi and Inner Mongolia, the other 10 western provincial units still account for 80% of China's hydropower potential. As much as 70% of China's water potential is concentrated in the southwest, namely, Yunnan, Guizhou, Sichuan and Tibet, with Sichuan alone accounting for 25%. Among the 10 largest hydropower stations planned for the country, Sichuan accounts for three, which are located at Jinsha River, Yalong River 雅龍江 and Dadu River 大渡河.[20] What is most striking is that, despite the fact that the west possesses over 74% of the country's hydropower potential, only 8% of it has been developed, whereas the east is endowed with only 7% of the potential, and yet 50% has been developed.[21] This imbalance provides a powerful impetus for developing hydropower in the west to transmit to the east.

The West-East Power Transmission Project is grounded on the reciprocal needs and comparative advantages of the east and the west. While the southwest is well endowed in water resources, these have yet to be harnessed to produce electricity for transmission to the economically advanced but environmentally polluted eastern population centres. Therefore, the project can, on the one hand, help bring investment and development to the west and, on the other, allow the east to acquire relatively inexpensive and clean electricity with no adverse effect on the environment. The project has three almost parallel passageways for west-east power transmission. The southern route will transmit power from stations through Nanpan River, Hongshui River, Lancang River 瀾滄江 and Wujiang 烏江 to Guangdong. The middle route will transmit power from the Qingjiang power station 清江水電基地 in the upper and middle reaches of the Yangzi River and the middle and lower reaches of Jinsha River to central and eastern China. The Jinsha River station is the largest in China and is technologically and economically advanced. It will be the most important source of power in the project. The northern route involves the north interconnection grid whereby power generated by the hydro stations in the upper reaches of the Yellow River and the thermal plants in Shaanxi, Shanxi and western Inner Mongolia will be transmitted to northern China, Shandong and northeastern China.[22]

Like the power transmission project, the West-East Gas Pipeline Project is premised on a similar economic logic and on a mutually beneficial regional exchange. The production and consumption share of natural gas in China between 1990 and 1999 both averaged only slightly over 2%, compared with over 73% for coal. This reveals a great potential for developing gas for wider consumption. The severe polluting impact of burning coal in many parts of the country will also, thereby, be reduced. In a broader sense, the project involves transmitting gas produced in the four largest producing areas in the west, namely, Xinjiang, Qinghai, Chuan-Yu (Sichuan-Chongqing) and the Ordos 鄂爾多斯 region, to the Yangzi River Delta area, as well as to Xining, Lanzhou, Beijing, Tianjin, Hunan and Hubei. In all, the project entails four routes of transmission, but the main focus is on the 4,167-km route from the Tarim Basin in Xinjiang to Zhejiang 浙江, Jiangsu 江蘇 and Shanghai. The long route passes through Korla 庫爾勒, Shanshan 鄯善, Hami 哈密, Liuyuan 柳園, Wuwei 武威, Gantang 幹塘, Zhongning 中寧, Jingbian 靖邊, Changzhi 長治, Zhengzhou 鄭州, Huainan 淮南 and Nanjing before reaching Shanghai. The entire route is anticipated to be completed in the near future. The annual amount of gas to be transmitted will be 12 billion m^3 for 30 years. The construction of the pipeline will be an unprecedented engineering feat. The pipeline will cross deserts, the Loess Plateau 黃土高原 and water-rich areas along the Yangzi, and will cross highways 500 times and railways 46 times. Tentatively priced at RMB1.15

to 1.3 per m^3, the gas is competitive with existing fuels.[23] According to North Asia News, China has awarded the construction of the pipeline to Shell, although by March 2001 as many as 19 foreign firms entered the competitive bidding. Consequent upon the successful completion of the project, gas is likely to account for 8% of China's energy supply by 2010, compared with 2.8% in 2000. The project is the centrepiece of China's US$48 billion programme to develop the west.[24]

Push from the New Economy

Since the early 1980s, a battery of technological advances driven by micro-electronics, telecommunications, robotics, biotechnology, nano-technology and new materials have come in rapid succession in developed and a few selected developing countries, so much so that a new era is considered to have arrived. This new age is predicated upon the production, acquisition and transmission of new information, hence the name the Information Age or the New Economy, built around the attributes of high technology and an international division of labour. These changes have rapidly and fundamentally changed the lives of people everywhere, propelled by globalization processes that have intensified during the same period. New information technologies have facilitated the flow of ideas, capital and people across the world with a speed, frequency and magnitude that is unprecedented.[25]

Despite its natural resources, the western region has suffered from slow growth because of its geographical constraints and vast distances to markets. Infrastructure has been too costly to construct and natural resources have not been turned into tangible assets. The new economy, however, offers the opportunity for the west to "leapfrog" sectoral transitions and to capitalize on China's recent entry to the WTO.

In a narrow sense, in the new economy, only mobile objects can be effectively developed. At the risk of over-simplification, development in the world follows two paths: the flow of tangibles (logistics — related to people, goods and energy) and the flow of information (ideas, culture, technology, experience, news, business, capital, etc.). Logistics is the material expression of information and information is the spirit of logistics.[26] Thus, a close relationship exists between logistics and information products. In constructing railways, roads, power networks, gas or oil pipes, housing, offices, restaurants and entertainment facilities, ample consideration must be given to the prospects for applying information technology. Digitized infrastructure provides an excellent platform for highly information-based services. Early forward planning will save time, labour and costs.

Higher-order infrastructure services refer to the wide use of information technologies and time-managed services in transport and communication facilities. Logistics management technologies entail just-in-time, quick response and sustainable applications. Compared with traditional transport and communication infrastructure, higher-order infrastructure does not merely aim at quantitative targets. Rather, through the application of information technologies, logistics technologies and transport technologies mutually reinforce each other in development. Together, they can help firms and regions participate in global competition by reducing transaction costs and shortening the product cycle, giving them a competitive advantage in the market. From the standpoint of manpower, facilities and investment in high technologies, how well is the western region prepared to meet the challenges of the new economy?

According to data provided by the National Bureau of Statistics, in the 1990s, the application/development of postal and telecommunications services in China grew at a phenomenal annual rate of 41%. By 1998, a grid had been laid of 194,000 km fibre cables covering all of China's provincial capitals and over 90% of the country's cities and counties. With the exception of Lhasa, every provincial capital had at least two fibre cables running through it. China possessed over 1 million km of fibre cables for public use in telecommunications. There were satellite earth stations in every province with over 20,000 satellite lines and 60,000 km of digital microwave lines. That year, China also had 32,000 mobile phone stations, extending coverage to 98% of the cities and 90% of the country.[27] Therefore, every part of the country, including the western region, has excellent telecommunications facilities. As for the more distant parts of the west, it may be more appropriate to link enterprises, schools and homes there through wireless networks (mobile phones or satellite dishes).[28]

When the eastern and western regions are compared in terms of enterprise development in high-tech parks, the gap is large. As Table 5.3 shows, the western region had relatively few high-tech parks. Only 9 cities in the west had such a park, 33.3% of the number found in the 11 provinces in the east. As a result, the west absorbed only 31.4% of the employees, 19.3% of the production value, 17.4% of the total income and 2.01% of the export value of the country. Not surprisingly, the west had 5,941 patents approved involving 237 inventions in 1998, compared with 38,076 and 959, respectively, for the east. The number of research institutes in the

Table 5.3 Main Indicators of High-Tech Enterprises in China's Development Zones, 1998

Development zones by region, no. of cities	No. of enter-prises	No. of employees	Total production (RMB million)	Total income (RMB million)	Total export (US$1,000s)
Whole country, 52	16,097	1,740,499	43,336	48,396	8,525,381
Eastern, 27	11,076	827,492	28,081	32,263	7,645,953
Western, 9	2,032	260,020	5,483	5,602	153,676

Source: Fung, *Discussing the Great Development of the West* (see note 29), p. 69.

western region was equivalent to 43.8% of those located in the eastern region, and made up 20.4% of the nation's total.[29] Overall, the western region is not particularly strong in high-tech. However, universities and research institutes in Xi'an, Lanzhou, Chengdu and Chongqing have the potential to incubate strong enterprises, given the appropriate policy support. It is submitted that they could create a Silicon Valley in China and a "virtual park" for IT in the western region.[30] In 2002, Chongqing's Scientific Commission decided to consolidate its support of 23 main research projects, many in the fields of high-tech, in order to more effectively use its resources for technological innovation.[31] In 2001, the region had 997 large-scale enterprises and 1993 medium-sized ones in many sectors of high-tech. The presence of so many high-tech enterprises will cause enterprises to upgrade themselves and speed up their pace of structural change.[32]

With a view to making the best use of the western region's structural characteristics and realizing its transport infrastructure potential, it is submitted that six logistics centres be set up in Xi'an, Lanzhou, Chengdu, Chongqing, Nanning and Urumqi to take advantage of their urban centrality and high technological base. They would be the connecting points to the eastern and central regions and to other logistics centres in neighbouring countries. Six secondary logistics centres can be set up in Hohhot, Yinchuan 銀川, Xining, Lhasa, Kunming and Guiyang 貴陽. Other medium-sized and small cities will also, at suitable levels, develop as logistics distribution points by maximizing their potential in road and rail transport, aviation and pipeline transmission. The objective is to build a three-dimensional and modern logistics framework to link the west with the central and eastern regions of the country.[33]

In order to develop the western region under the new economy, the central government has adopted a policy of "stringing points through lines, developing surfaces along lines" 以線串點，以點帶面. This strategy identifies key cities and urban corridors to invest in infrastructure construction, so that the effects of investment will have a widely felt. On this basis, to support uneven regional development infrastructure construction in the west still requires the devising of suitable policies in its favour, and the establishment of superior spatial structures and infrastructure belts. Table 5.4 summarizes the aims behind the proposed establishment of three main infrastructure corridors in the western region. Planning for infrastructure development is one thing, but overcoming persistent difficulties in an environment that is geographically challenging and only recently attracting investment is another. It is worth remembering the constraints in logistics development as reviewed earlier. Nevertheless, speedy and systematic development of infrastructure, with the full application of new technologies, is the best way for the west to realize the goals China has assigned to it in the new era.

Evaluation and Conclusion

Between 1949 and 1978, the command economy and other factors in China made it possible for resources and attention to be deliberately channelled to the western region. Great progress was made in the construction of infrastructure and transport conditions improved noticeably. However, a vast territory with diverse and often difficult geographical conditions, a sparsely distributed population and high construction costs led to a state of infrastructure development that lagged quite some distance behind that in the eastern region. For example, by the end of 1999, the west possessed only 14,322 km of railways, or 24.7% of the nation's. These railways were unable to form networks, and many areas were not served (Figure 5.1). The carrying capacity of the railways in the west ranged between 1/4 to 1/8 of that in the east. It can even be argued that, because of its vast, sparsely populated areas, transport costs are systemically high for lack of economies of scale. The recent closure of some regional railways in Yunnan is an illustration.

Since the adoption of the open policy in 1978, China has gradually increased her openness to the world, to the latest stage of opening up coastal, riverine and national borders. Since the western region borders on 14 countries, border trade has increased rapidly. However, neighbouring countries cannot match China's rapidly developing eastern coastal region in terms of economic strength, enterprise structure, level of urbanization, infrastructure and economic compatibility. Strategically, it is thus more

Table 5.4 Development Strategies of Three Infrastructure Corridors

Corridors	Strategic development in infrastructure construction	Characteristics and application prospects of infrastructure facilities
Xi'an-Lanzhou-Urumqi	Integrated transport passageways based on railways, high-grade highways, pipelines and air cargo networks. Actively raise levels of culture, education and medical-care facilities. Improve ecological protection and infrastructure. Intensify efforts to prevent desertification along transport routes in drought-prone areas and to improve sand-management facilities.	Support the northwest in national security and energy transmission strategies. Improve Euro-Asian land-bridge transport services, with a view to developing a logistics area serving Asia and Europe. Promote the social development of ethnic minority areas.
Chengdu-Chongqing	Strengthen the construction of urban logistics infrastructure, providing platforms for information networks to spearhead regional logistics development. Raise the level of urban public services, with emphasis on streamlining urban road systems. Develop rail transport routes linking the central and eastern regions and water routes along the Yangzi. Improve the medical and health provisions of villages along these routes.	Further improve existing infrastructure, not only to expand the space for economic activities but also to promote local environmental sustain-ability and popularization of culture. Elevate the status of Chengdu and Chongqing as beachheads in strategically developing the west.
Kunming-Nanning-Guiyang	Construct Kunming as the centre of the southwest air cargo network. Raise the capacity of the southwest land-sea transport passageway and seaports along the Guangxi coast to provide logistics services. Accelerate the construction of irrigation facilities in small river basins, thereby improving the quality of the ecological environment. Plan the construction of a Beihei-Fengsheng-Yinzhou international logistics centre and urban logistics park.	Build a new growth point in logistics enterprises, hence speed up the conversion of natural resources into real material commodities in the southwest specifically and in the west generally. Promote economic development in poverty-stricken areas along transport routes to alleviate poverty.

essential to develop transport links between the west and the east as a matter of priority.

The immediate objective is to develop an efficient and rapid east-west transport system based on railways as the backbone, with equal emphasis on highways to build a network. Water transport, pipelines and aviation should be fully utilized to make use of the special advantages of different transport modes. At present, the west and the east are linked by several railways: Jing-Bao, Bao-Lan, Long-Hai 隴海 (Lanzhou 蘭州-Lianyungang 連雲港), Xiang-Yu 襄渝 (Xiangfan 襄樊-Chongqing), Qian-Gui 黔桂 (Guiyang-Guilin 桂林) and Nan-Kun. Highways that will fully link east and west are still under construction (Figure 5.2). Broadly speaking, the east and the west are linked by two passageways. The northern passageway runs from Jing-Jin-Tang via the Euro-Asian land bridge deep into the northwest of Gansu, Qinghai and Xinjiang. The southern route runs along the Yangzi to the southwest in Chongqing, Sichuan, Guizhou and Yunnan.[34] Also, investment has been increasing in land transport and port expansion in Guangxi, with the aim of constructing a convenient conduit for goods from the southwestern provinces, especially Sichuan, to be exported via the ports in Guangxi in order to develop China's "southwest gateway." In part for this reason, border towns such as Dongxing 東興, Pingxiang 憑祥 and Puzhai 浦寨, and the port of Fangchenggang 防城港 have seen extraordinary growth in recent years[35] (Table 5.4).

Notwithstanding the progress that has been made to date on infrastructure in the western region, its geography, limited capital and traditional management methods have hindered the development of the region. Existing facilities are unable to meet the demands of supporting socioeconomic development in the west. Several problems need special attention.

First, the western region has still to establish its overall comparative advantage. Despite the resources and capital the country has poured into it during recent years, the provision of infrastructure has tended to follow single-project objectives rather than aiming for a collective target. From an overall planning objective, future studies should concentrate on how to maximize multi-sector benefits in new infrastructure construction.

Second, infrastructure construction in the past has characteristically lacked co-ordination in timing, spatial consideration, implementation modes and between different sectors, leading to low investment returns. New provisions should strive for harmonized and inter-connected networks.

Third, transport, energy and communication are sectors that have received relatively more attention and investment. More resources should be devoted to building other types of infrastructure related to ecological protection and disaster prevention.

Fourth, social, economic and management policies are not co-ordinated in the existing infrastructure facilities, resulting in low utilization rates. The low utilization rate of transport and telecommunications facilities is an example. The absence of land use, land supply and urban development plans along highways has hampered comprehensive and rational development.

Apart from these constraints, the western region is still a late developer with certain advantages. It can capitalize on an increasingly globalized and technologically oriented environment by developing new infrastructure that can combine its natural resources with new technologies. Supported by policy and capital, a late developer in the new economy can pick and choose technologies, such that the infrastructure that is built is modern, pro-market and compatible with the natural, economic and social characteristics of the region.

In order to fulfill the government's targets for the region, two pre-requisites should be first achieved. In the first place, the financial arrangements for infrastructure development must be reformed, with the attendant relaxation of government controls, so that multiple channels of investments can be created. The experience of many countries, especially those in the developing world, reveals that, as social investment in infrastructure increased, government policies on financing tended to become more liberal.[36] Prior to 1978, direct government investment in many sectors, including infrastructure, in China's western region reached 50%. In the reform period, notably in the late 1990s, more channels of financing began to be encouraged. Even local governments have raised capital through the issuing of bonds and loans, attracting foreign investment and transferring operating rights. The governments concerned have become more open and infrastructure construction has become more market-oriented, all necessary with China's recent accession to the WTO.

The other condition is the vital importance of modern management methods and technologies, so as to facilitate high utilization rates. Transport and communications facilities are examples. Past infrastructure that did not focus on economic returns suffered from poor management methods and outdated technologies. New construction must, therefore, increase in scale and technological content by focusing attention on a regional division of labour. Through the market mechanism in the distribution of resources, flows of people, capital, goods and information can be effected to promote regional economic development. Both conditions will likewise assist the western region to realize the objectives of economic uplift, social stability and sustainable development.

Notes

1. See A. Doak Barnett, *China's Far West: Four Decades of Change* (Boulder: Westview Press, 1993). As an illustration of the state of minimum construction, it may be noted that, in 1949, the whole northwest did not have an inch of railroad, with the exception of Shaanxi, which had 610 km, and Gansu, which had 52 km, while Qinghai, Ningxia and Xinjiang had none. See Bai Guang 白光 (ed.), *Xibu dakaifa* 西部大開發 (Accelerate the Development of West China) (Beijing: Zhongguo jiancai gongye chubanshe 中國建材工業出版社, 2000), Vol. 3, p. 216.
2. World Bank, *World Development Report 1994* (New York: Oxford University Press, 1994).
3. Ibid., p. 2.
4. Ibid., p. 19.
5. Ibid., p. 35.
6. David Laque, "On Track for a Rail Revolution," *Far Eastern Economic Review*, 18 July 2002, pp. 26–29. The World Bank has openly advised China that future lending from the Bank would focus primarily on its middle and western regions. See Chen Yao 陳耀, *Guojia zhongxibu fazhan zhengce yanjiu* 國家中西部發展政策研究 (Development Policy Studies on the Middle and Western Parts of China) (Beijing: Jingji guanli chubanshe 經濟管理出版社, 2000), p. 226.
7. "2010 nian jichu sheshi niandu zong touzi jiangda 2.3 zhao yuan reminbi" 2010 年基礎設施年度總投資將達2.3兆元人民幣 (Infrastructural Investment will Reach RMB2.3 Trillion in 2010). 雅虎網新聞報導 (Yahoo News Network), 4 April 2002, p. 3.
8. Lu Dadao 陸大道 et al. (eds.), *2000 Zhongguo quyu fazhan baogao — xibu kaifa de jichu, zhengce yu qushi fenxi* 2000 中國區域發展報告 —— 西部開發的基礎、政策與趨勢分析 (Regional Development of China, 2000: A Development Report of the West) (Beijing: Shangwu yinshuguan 商務印書館, 2001), p. 154.
9. The projects listed here may be compared with the "Ten Big Projects" of the West identified elsewhere. The "Ten Big Projects" are: (1) the Xi'an to Hefei section of the Xi'an-Nanjing Railroad; (2) the Chongqing-Huaihua (Yu-Huai) Railroad; (3) western highways, including 17,000 km of the 35,000 km of the 5 North-South and 7 East-West national highways grid; (4) airport construction in Xi'an, Chengdu, Kunming, Xi'an, Lanzhou and Urumqi; (5) an elevated light rail in Chongqing; (6) the East-West Gas Pipeline Project involving the

section from Qaidam Basin 柴達木盆地 in Qinghai and Se-Ning-Lan (Sebei-Xining-Lanzhou), with a total of 953 km; (7) the main irrigation works at Sichuan's Zipingpu and Ningxia's Shapotou; (8) ecological projects of converting cultivated land back to forest and pasture and planting seedlings; (9) a fertilizer project in Qinghai; and (10) support for higher education in infrastructure construction. See Jinlei 金磊 et al., *Xibu kaifa de jingshi* 西部開發的警示 (Warnings on Western Development) (Shenyang: Liaoning kexue chubanshe 遼寧科學出版社, 2000), pp. 339–40.

10. *Zhongguo jiaotong tongji nianjian 2001* 中國交通統計年鑑2001 (China Transport Statistics Yearbook 2001) (Beijing: Zhongguo jiaotong chubanshe 中國交通出版社, 2002), p. 3.
11. Du Ping 杜平 (ed.), *Xitu qujin* 西土取金 (Seeking Gold from the Western Land) (Beijing: Zhongguo yanshi chubanshe 中國言實出版社, 2000), pp. 119–20.
12. Zou Dongtao 鄒東濤 (ed.), *Zhongguo xibu dakaifa quanshu* 中國西部大開發全書 (Complete Volume on the Great Development of Western China) (Beijing: Renmin chubanshe 人民出版社, 2000), Vol. 2, p. 76.
13. Du Ping 杜平 et al., *Xibu kaifa lun* 西部開發論 (Introducing Western Development) (Chongqing: Chongqing chubanshe 重慶出版社, 2000), p. 250.
14. Lu, *Regional Development* (see note 7), pp. 146–47.
15. Bai, *Accelerate the Development* (see note 1), p. 218.
16. *Zhongguo minhang bao* 中國民航報 (China Civil Aviation News), No. 2342, issue 4 (2002), p. 4.
17. Yang Kaizhong 楊開忠 et al. (ed.), *Zhongguo xibu dakaifa zhanlüe* 中國西部大開發戰略 (The Great Development Strategy in China's West) (Guangzhou: Guangdong jiaoyu chubanshe 廣東教育出版社, 2001), p. 310.
18. Lu, *Regional Development* (see note 8), pp. 149–53.
19. Liu Zhengshangyou 劉爭上游 and Feng Qing 馮青 (eds.), *Xibu dakaifa* 西部大開發 (The Great Development of the West) (Beijing: Zhongguo shihua chubanshe 中國石化出版社, 2000), pp. 132–33.
20. See Lu Tiecheng 盧鐵城 and Zhang Zhongyuan 張忠元 (eds.), *Zhongguo xibu tese jingji* 中國西部特色經濟 (Special Characteristics of Western China's Economy) (Chengdu: Sichuan cishu chubanshe 四川辭書出版社, 2000), pp. 48–52; Shi Wanjian 石萬儉, "*Xidian dongsong*" *zhengdang shi* "西電東送"正當時 ("Western Electricity Eastern Bound" at the Right Moment), in *Zhongguo xibu dakaifa* 中國西部大開發 (China's Great Western Development), edited by Guojia jiwei hongguan jingji yanjiuyuan 國家計委宏觀經濟研究院 (Beijing: Zhongguo sanxia chubanshe 中國三峽出版社, 2000), pp. 26–28.
21. Fu Tao'an 傅桃安, *Shishi xibu dakaifa zhanlüe sikao* 實施西部大開發戰略思考 (Thoughts on Implementing the Great Western Development Strategy) (Beijing: Zhongguo shuili shuidian chubanshe 中國水利水電出版社, 2000), pp. 142–43.
22. Zhang Zhiyin 張志銀 et al. (eds.), *Xibu dakaifa touzi shouce* 西部大開發投資

手冊 (Investment Guide to the Great Development of China's Western Region) (Beijing: Jingji kexue chubanshe 經濟科學出版社, 2000), p. 210.

23. Much of this paragraph has been distilled from Chow Chuen-ho and Chau Min-kit, "The West-East Gas Pipeline Plan and Its Relationship to Neighbouring Countries." Unpublished manuscript, Department of Geography, Hong Kong Baptist University, 2001.
24. Le-min Lim, "Exxon to Invest in China's 46 Bin Yuan Gas Pipeline, Shell Says." At http://quote.bloomberg.com.
25. Many books have been written on these important and popular subjects. See, for instance, Fu-chen Lo and Yue-man Yeung (eds.), *Globalization and the World of Large Cities* (Tokyo: United Nations University Press, 1998) and Yue-man Yeung, *Globalization and Networked Societies: Urban-Regional Change in Pacific Asia* (Honolulu: University of Hawaii Press, 2000).
26. This statement is paraphrased from Chen Wei 陳偉 (ed.), *Zoujin xibu* 走進西部 (Initiating Western Development) (Beijing: Huawen chubanshe 華文出版社, 2000), p. 188.
27. Fu, *Thoughts on Implementing* (see note 21), p. 136.
28. Yang, *China's West* (see note 17), p. 112.
29. Feng Zhixun 馮之浚 (ed.), *Lun xibu dakaifa* 論西部大開發 (Discussing the Great Development of the West) (Hangzhou: Zhejiang jiaoyu chubanshe 浙江教育出版社, 2000), pp. 60–70.
30. *Xibu kaifa zhishi duben*《西部開發知識讀本》(ed.), *Xibu dakaifa* 西部大開發 (The Great Development of the West) (Xi'an: Xibei daxue chubanshe 西北大學出版社, 2000), pp. 156–58.
31. "This Year Chongqing Supports 23 Large Science and Technology Projects." At http://www.chinawest.gov.cn/Chinese/doc/XBKJKJ/20020114270.htm.
32. Tuo Wenjuan 脫文娟, *Shui wei xibu tiaoyueshi fazhan zhuru nengliang*? 誰為西部跳躍式發展注入能量？ (Who Will Energize the Western Region's Leapfrog Development?) *New Western Part* (Xi'an), 1 June 2001, pp. 50–51.
33. The proposal here is highly similar to four regional comprehensive information centres to be established in Chongqing, Chengdu, Xi'an and Lanzhou, with secondary centres linked to them covering the west. See Chen Wei, *Initiating Western Development* (see note 26), p. 182. A word of caution is in order here, as it was reported that even post-WTO, it would be difficult to set up a distribution centre in China. The nightmare of logistics afflicts even coastal China, let alone the west. The logistics industry is extremely fragmented, with the average Chinese trucking company owning less than two vehicles! See Ben Dolven, "The Perils of Delivering the Goods," *Far Eastern Economic Review*, 25 July 2002, pp. 28–31.
34. The gist of this section so far is derived and expanded from Yang, *China's West* (see note 17), pp. 304–6.
35. Observations based on field reconnaissance by the first author carried out in

May 2001. See also Chen Shupeng 陳述彭, Y. M. Yeung 楊汝萬 and Lin Hui 林琿 (eds.), *Xin jingji yu Zhongguo xibu fazhan* 新經濟與中國西部發展 (The New Economy and China's Western Development). Hong Kong: Hong Kong Institute of Asia-Pacific Studies, The Chinese University of Hong Kong, 2001.

36. Neil Roger, "Recent Trends in Private Participation in Infrastructure." The World Bank Group Finance, Private Sector and Infrastructure Network, 1999.

6

Education and Skill Training

Shi Peijun, Liu Xuemin and Yang Mingchuan

Introduction

The low levels of education, backwardness in science and technology, and abundant human resources but insufficient human capital are serious constraints to economic and social development in the western region. The national western region development strategy has the urgent task to improve the capacity of science and technology to develop human capital through education.

Twelve provinces, municipalities and autonomous regions in the western region have some common characteristics, such as their relatively fragile ecological environment, large minority population and backward economy compared with the advanced eastern region. There are two basic questions about the western region.

First, some areas in the western region are relatively advanced. Some large and medium-sized cities have a similar degree of modernization as those in the east. However, the difference between urban and rural areas in the western region is certainly greater than the gap between city and country in the eastern region. Thus, the statistical data for provincial units adopted in this chapter mask the difference between urban and rural areas.

Second, the western region is vast in size and can be divided into many "economic areas" that differ from each other. For this reason, it is essential to pay attention to the differences within the western region. Essential data are needed to analyze such "economic areas." But the existing data and research materials are based on "administrative units." Thus, previous research cannot show the differences among "economic areas" and may in fact reduce the relevance of any proposed policy to resolve economic problems in the western region.

At the same time, because information concerning "economic areas" in the above perspective is inadequate, this chapter is based on provincial units in the western region as it is not necessarily the case that doing so will prejudice the results of the research. Data will be obtained according to "administrative units" and some provincial units are analyzed as examples to explain typical issues.

Status of Education, Science and Technology in the Western Region

Low Levels of Education and Inadequate Development of Human Resources

The low levels of education and inadequate development of human resources are important factors restricting economic growth and social development in the western region. It is clear from Table 6.1, which shows the different levels of education per 100,000 persons, that the western region lags behind the national average, with the exception of Shaanxi 陜西 and Xinjiang 新疆 whose averages exceed the nation.

According to national statistics, by the end of 2000, nine-year compulsory education had basically become universal and illiteracy among youth had been eliminated (dubbed, the "two bases"). Over 85% of the population passes the "two bases" assessment. The figure in the advanced eastern region is 100%, while that in the western region is only 71%. Table 6.2 lists the results of the "two bases" assessment in 2000 for different regions of the country.

At present, the average amount of education for children in China is eight years; for the western region, it is less than seven. By the end of 2000, most eastern and central regions had passed the "two bases" assessment, while many provinces in the western region had not. Rates of illiteracy and semi-illiteracy in the western region are higher than the national average. Professional education also lags behind. There are only about 200 colleges and universities in the western region, with a total of about 900,000 students.

Table 6.1 Comparison of Population with Different Educational Attainments Per 100,000 Persons by Region, 2000

Region \ Education	Junior college and above	Senior high/ technical school	Junior high school	Primary school
China	3,611	11,146	33,961	35,701
Inner Mongolia 內蒙古	3,803	13,760	34,798	31,134
Guangxi 廣西	2,389	9,554	32,339	42,176
Chongqing 重慶	2,802	8,596	29,413	43,386
Sichuan 四川	2,470	7,587	29,358	42,960
Guizhou 貴州	1,902	5,626	20,480	43,595
Yunnan 雲南	2,013	6,563	21,233	44,768
Tibet 西藏	1,262	3,395	6,136	30,615
Shaanxi 陜西	4,138	12,246	33,203	34,475
Gansu 甘肅	2,665	9,863	23,925	36,907
Qinghai 青海	3,299	10,431	21,661	30,944
Ningxia 寧夏	3,690	10,910	27,830	31,770
Xinjiang 新疆	5,141	12,089	27,528	37,950

Source: Guojia tongjiju 國家統計局, *Zhongguo tongji nianjian 2001* 中國統計年鑑 2001 (China Statistical Yearbook 2001) (Beijing: Zhongguo tongji chubanshe 中國統計出版社, 2001).

Table 6.2 Situation of the Country and Different Regions Passing the "Two Bases" Assessment, 2000

Region	Population (million)	Percentage of the population passing the "two bases" assessment	Number of units at county level not passing the "two bases" assessment	Number of poor counties at national level not passing the "two bases" assessment
China	1,266	85	524	273
East	416	100	0	0
West	355	71	465	235

Sources: Guojia tongjiju 國家統計局, "2000 nian di wuci quanguo renkou pucha zhuyao shuju gongbao" (dier hao) 2000年第五次全國人口普查主要數據公報(第2號) (The Fifth National Census Data Communiqué, 2000) (No. 2), *Renmin ribao* 人民日報, 3 April 2001; Jiaoyu bu 教育部, "2000 nian quanguo jiaoyu jingfei zhixing qingkuang tongjibiao" 2000年全國教育經費執行情況統計表 (Statistical Table of National Expenditure on Education in 2000), *Zhongguo jiaoyu bao* 中國教育報, 31 December 2001.

After student enrollments were expanded in 1999 and 2000, about 11 million students are now enrolled in some types of post-secondary educational programme in China. Over 5.5 million are studying at colleges and universities. The average enrollment rate of applicants was about 56% in China, even as high as 70% in some eastern provinces. But the enrollment rate in the western region was lower than the national average, with only 40% or less in some provinces. Another example is postgraduate training. There were 300,000 postgraduate students in universities in the whole country, but only 39,000 of them were in the western region. In short, the scope of higher education in the western region does not match its population.[1] Furthermore, the loss of talent through migration is serious. The challenge faced by the western region is real.

Some typical cases in 1999 and 2000 may be described as follows. The enrollment percentage of preschool children in Qinghai was 17.1% lower than the national average. Except for Shaanxi, the corresponding percentage in other provinces of the western region was also lower than the national average. About 10% to 15% of elementary school graduates and about 50% to 65% of junior school graduates did not continue their studies. The illiteracy rate of adult women in the countryside in the western region varied between 17% and 72%. The average educational level of those 15 years old or above was also lower than the national average. The annual dropout rate of elementary school pupils varied from 1.1% to 3.0%, and that of junior school students from 3.4% to 5.6%. The total floor area of junior schools and elementary schools in Xinjiang considered dangerous was about 1.02 million m^2, and in Shaanxi and Ningxia over 300,000 m^2.

The educational level of workers plays an important part in economic development. There is a strong correlation between the education level of workers and productivity. It has been estimated that if the percentage of children enrolled in preschools increases by 0.1% each year, the average GDP per capita will rise by 0.35–0.59%. At the same time, the educational level of workers and their job mobility are closely linked. According to a 1995 study on the nature of the jobs found by laid-off workers and on the quality of the workers for 11 western provinces, those with certain knowledge had an advantage. This means that, if a worker's educational level is higher and if he/she can understand some production technologies, that worker will find it easier to find employment and will have more choices in jobs. But the education level of local workers engaged in agricultural production is low. Table 6.3 shows the difference between the country's educational level and the western region's educational level, indicating the low quality of western workers.

The low level of education has already become a factor restricting the development of the western region. However, investment in education is,

Table 6.3 Percentage of the Population with Various Levels of Education in China and the Western Region, 1999 (Unit: %)

Region	Illiterate or semi-illiterate	Elementary school	Junior high school	Senior high school	Over junior college
China	11.0	33.3	39.9	11.9	3.8
Inner Mongolia	12.7	29.1	36.6	16.4	5.1
Guangxi	8.1	42.5	40.2	8.2	0.9
Chongqing	10.9	44.3	33.2	9.0	2.7
Sichuan	13.4	43.4	33.5	7.5	2.2
Guizhou	22.8	40.7	26.0	7.8	2.7
Yunnan	20.5	47.7	25.3	5.1	1.4
Tibet	67.5	28.5	4.0	0.1	0.0
Shaanxi	14.0	27.4	39.3	15.1	4.2
Gansu	23.6	30.9	31.1	11.3	3.2
Qinghai	29.6	30.1	23.5	11.5	5.3
Ningxia	22.0	26.9	35.1	11.6	4.4
Xinjiang	7.1	32.4	33.4	16.7	10.5

Source: Guojia tongjiju 國家統計局, *Zhongguo tongji nianjian 2000* 中國統計年鑑 2000 (China Statistical Yearbook 2000) (Beijing: Zhongguo tongji chubanshe 中國統計出版社, 2000).

to many decision-makers, not an essential part of the drive to develop the western region.

Less is invested on education in the west than in the eastern region. This explains an even wider difference in the education level of the two regions. Due to its backward education, a phenomenon similar to that seen in many developing countries has occurred in the western region. Human resources are abundant, but human capital is deficient. According to the capital theory, people acquire technical and production knowledge as an outcome of some investment and become human capital. Education plays an important role in the acquisition of knowledge and in the formation of human capital. Due to low education levels in the western region, human resources are insufficiently developed and the formation of human capital lags behind most other areas of the country.

Low Technological Capacity

Research in science and technology is another important factor affecting economic development and is closely related to education. The acquisition of knowledge and the development of technology are critical factors in economic growth and social development.

The western region has fewer technical workers than the eastern region. Table 6.4 reveals the differences in technical workers between selected eastern and western provinces. Migration from west to east has both caused the number of technical workers to grow more slowly in the western region and accelerated their growth in the eastern region.

While examining the subject of scientific research in the western region, we cannot ignore the structure of the development of science and technology there. Four points should be noted about research and the development of science in the western region. First, the west exhibits both strengths and weaknesses in this aspect. Many industrial bases were established in the western region during the years of the centrally planned economy. The western region is strong in the aerospace and nuclear industries. However, as the country moves from a planned to a market economy, these industries are no longer seen as the advantages they once were.

Second, the development of science and research is so slow that it can no longer support economic development. There are many centres of innovation in the western region such as Lanzhou 蘭州, Xi'an 西安 and Chengdu 成都. These cities and their provinces have an advanced military industry, aerospace industry, energy industry, and so on, but few of these

Table 6.4 Comparison of Technical Workers between Some Eastern and Western Provinces, 1998

Region	Population (million)	Number of university students per million population	Number of general technical workers (engineers or above)	Number of general technical workers (engineers or above) per million population
China	1,236.26	2,568	1,489,452	1,200
Eastern Region				
Beijing	12.40	15,813	149,158	12,030
Tianjing	9.53	7,747	41,968	4,400
Shanghai	14.57	10,575	98,130	6,740
Liaoning	41.38	4,547	104,782	2,530
Jiangsu	71.48	3,345	126,305	1,770
Zhejiang	44.35	2,307	35,555	800
Fujiang	32.82	2,379	20,685	630
Shandong	87.85	2,004	93,616	1,070
Guangdong	70.51	2,478	68,770	980
Western Region				
Inner Mongolia	23.26	1,697	17,768	760
Guangxi	46.33	1,523	18,171	390
Chongqing	30.42	2,340	25,453	840
Sichuan	84.30	1,780	91,739	1,090
Guizhou	36.06	1,067	17,116	470
Yunnan	40.94	1,403	19,934	490
Tibet	2.48	1,290	271	110
Shaanxi	35.70	3,902	72,689	2,040
Gansu	24.94	2,032	32,577	1,310
Qinghai	4.96	1,654	5,513	1,110
Ningxia	5.30	2,068	4,851	920
Xinjiang	17.18	2,660	15,758	920

Source: Zhongguo kexueyuan kechixu fazhan yanjuzu 中國科學院可持續發展研究組, *2000 nian Zhongguo kechixu fazhan zhanlüe baogao* 2000 年中國可持續發展戰略報告 (China Strategic Report on Sustainable Development in 2000) (Beijing: Kexue chubanshe 科學出版社, 2000).

industries can contribute directly to the economic development of the region.

The third point is the unbalanced capability in science and research, as well as the uneven distribution of technical workers. Almost all technical workers are employed by provincial and state-owned industries while a few are located in small cities and towns. More than half of the technical workers are located in Lanzhou, Xi'an, Chengdu and Chongqing 重慶. A similar problem has plagued the distribution of personnel. Most workers are employed in the traditional industrial sector, while there are more jobs in the IT industry in the west than people to fill them.

The last point is that there is little investment in science and research. The growth rate of such investment in the western region is lower than that in the eastern region. Over the last 20 years, total government funds, projects and programmes in the western region accounted for only about 10% of that received in the eastern region. Only in 2000 did the government launch the programme "The Development of the Western Region — Action in Science and Research" with an investment of RMB278 million in the western region, especially in Ningxia.[3] Tables 6.5 and 6.6 reveal the low levels of investment in science and technology in the western region.

The "China Regional Innovation Capacity Report 2001" showed that the three leading provinces or municipalities in terms of innovative capacity are Shanghai 上海, Beijing 北京 and Guangdong 廣東, scores of 58.33, 58.27 and 49.68, respectively.[4] Except for Shaanxi, Sichuan and Chongqing, the other provinces in the west have low ranks and scores: Xinjiang (22nd, 19.38), Gansu (23rd, 19.24), Guangxi (24th, 19.06), Yunnan (25th, 18.92), Inner Mongolia (27th, 17.74), Ningxia (28th, 17.48), Guizhou (29th, 16.89), Tibet (30th, 15.69) and Qinghai (31st, 15.01).

Table 6.5 Technology Expenditure by Region, 1999

Region	Technology expenditure amount (RMB billion)	Growth rate %	Expenditure per technical worker (RMB1,000)
Total	118.30	13.6	50
East	78.32	14.4	65
Central	21.63	14.2	33
West	18.37	9.1	36

Source: Kexue jishubu fazhan jihuasi 科學技術部發展計劃司, *2000 niandu keji tongji baogao huibian* (neibu ziliao) 2000年度科技統計報告彙編 (內部資料) (2000 Science and Technology Statistical Report (Internal data)), 2000.

Table 6.6 R&D Expenditure by Region, 1999

Region	R&D expenditure (RMB billion)	Per capita R&D expenditure of R&D personnel (RMB1,000)
Total	58.34	81
East	38.85	99
Central	10.00	57
West	9.50	62

Source: See Table 6.5.

Emigration of Talents from the West

Another reason for the inferior status of science, technology and education in the western region is the emigration of talented people from the area. Since the 1980s, highly skilled people have been moving out at twice the rate of those moving in. The departure of middle-aged professionals is especially serious. During the last few years, more than 35,000 technical workers in science and research left for the eastern and central regions, many of them senior professionals. For example, in November 2001, the provincial government of Zhejiang 浙江 gathered together representatives from 546 local enterprises from its 11 cities and 64 counties in a drive to recruit about 9,300 persons in Shaanxi. They invited 580 persons such as academic experts, entrepreneurs, professors, senior engineers and others who had at least an undergraduate degree. This was the largest recruiting exercise held in Shaanxi by the government of an eastern province.

It has been reported that thousands of graduates of the Chengdu University of Electronic Science and Technology are conducting research in the field of high-tech in Silicon Valley or other places. None of the first batch of students graduating in insurance and accounting from the Southwest University of Finance and Economics remained in China. Also, none of the MBA graduates of this university remained in the western region — all of them either worked in the coastal cities or studied aboard. Lanzhou University has similarly seen the departure of many talented people, including academics and supervisors of doctoral students.[5]

About 91% of the students who graduated from universities in China in 1998 were employed in the eastern region but only 9% worked in the western region. In 1999, only 6.2% of the students who graduated from the universities administrated by various ministries of the central government and located in seven provinces of the eastern region were employed in the western region. About 50.5% of the students who studied in the eastern region were employed in the western region, while 54.5% of the students who studied in the western region were employed in the western region. The percentages for postgraduate students in the western, central and eastern regions were 2.7%, 26.5% and 59.0%, respectively.

As mentioned before, many highly skilled people tend to move out of the western region. Most of these are middle-level or high-level technicians with great capabilities, abundant experience and high achievements. Most of them are young, vigorous and at the peak of their career. It is clear that the talented are flowing from backward regions to developed regions, from the countryside to cities, from mountainous areas to lowland cities, from lower rank departments to higher rank departments. Many of them are professionals in the natural sciences, and are involved in scientific research, R&D and production.

Consequences of Backward Education and Technology

Backward education and technology have had the following negative consequences for the economy and society of the western region.

Backward Technology Retards Economic Development

With modernization and mechanization, science and technology have become crucial elements in the production process. Technology is productivity. Furthermore, the growth of labour productivity depends on the progress of scientific and technological advancement. The growth of the economy and the development of social productivity mainly depend on the increase in labour productivity rather than on an increase in labour force, in working intensity and working time. For example, high-tech industries have the highest labour productivity. In China, the per capita production value of high-tech industries is 5 to 10 times that of traditional industries and 50 to 100 times that of handicraft industries. At the same time, the intensive use of science and technology increases the value of production. On the basis of unit weight, the price ratio of steel is 5, a colour TV, 30, and a computer is as high as 1,000. Thus, backwardness in science and technology will constrain the economic development of the western region.

Above all, a low scientific and technological level also affects the adjustment of the industrial structure. China is at an important stage of structural adjustment. The economic system is in transition from a planned economy to a market economy, and the macroeconomy is moving from scarcity to surplus. Traditional industries are facing the dual pressure of systemic innovation and structural adjustment. In the eastern region, a market economic system has almost been established. Therefore, the eastern region can make structural adjustments rapidly, with the support of more developed technology. In the western region, the market economic system has developed slowly. The region cannot make structural adjustments rapidly. The main reason is that its levels of science and technology are so weak that they cannot contribute to productivity. Thus, the western region is in an inferior position in economic competition. The economic gap between the eastern and the western regions will widen further.

Backward Education has an Impact on Technological and Economic Development

Education has a close relationship with science and technology. The effect of science and technology on economic development is partly realized via modern education. The connection between education and technology has become more and more important with the continuous development and application of new technologies. Modern education is a precondition for technological production, reproduction and application. In the modern era, basic working ability depends on intelligence and knowledge rather than on physical strength. Education is essential to the growth of intelligence and technological development.

Education also has the function of knowledge reproduction. The transmission of heritage and the accumulation of knowledge for reference are the preconditions for the development and reproduction of science and technology. Modern education reinforces the diffusion of the basic sciences, brings past and present knowledge, experiments and technology together, and provides a foundation for the development of new technology.

Backwardness in education has a direct impact on the development of science in the western region. Because of the low educational level of the western region, human resources are insufficiently developed, which seriously restricts economic development. While the coastal region is moving into the age of the knowledge economy, the western region is still at the age of primary production by handwork.

Employment will become more and more difficult with further population growth in the western region. The limited diffusion of knowledge and skills means that there are more unemployed people in the western than in the eastern cities during this stage of structural adjustment. Qinghai has the highest unemployment rate in China. The knowledge and skill of employees who have been laid off are far below what is required by society. In other words, the quality and quantity of human resources cannot match the needs of society. The scarcity of professional talent and the low level of education is affecting the development of every enterprise in the western region.

The backward economy in turn has a negative effect on education and talent. Thus, a vicious circle operates in the western region and in minority areas. It is difficult to express the relationship between education and economic development. Only during the period of sustainable economic development is the role of education clearest. During the initial period of economic development or economic stagnation, education does little to help the economy. However, economic development depends more and more on knowledge and talent. At the same time, social wealth accumulates gradually in places with advanced science and technology. Thus, the lack of knowledge and talent in the western region will have a serious impact on its economic development.

Backward Education, Science and Technology Affect the Progress of Social Development and Civilization

Education plays a role not only in the economy but also in social civilization. The primary task of basic education is to develop civil wisdom, allowing children to know and adapt to society, and acquire the ability to live an independent life in the future. Education aims not only to impart the necessary knowledge but also to cultivate the spirit of civilization, consciousness of citizenship, social conscience, social responsibility and understanding of human rights. Education lets people know the history and cultural tradition of their nation, and cultivates and enhances national integration. By this token, basic education has an "overflow effect." Backwardness in education, science and technology slows down economic development and increases the gap between the east and the west. Students cannot learn new culture and new knowledge, which affects social development and the progress of civilization.

Strategic Considerations on the Development of Education, Science, Technology and Human Resources

Taking a New View of Talent

In the market economy, the principle of resource allocation is that a productive factor moves to the region that offers the highest returns. It is not surprising that many skilled people move to the eastern region due to slow economic growth and low incomes in the western region. Many provinces and companies in the western region have been trying all means to retain their talented people, even refusing to release their personnel documents or using political punishments. But such tactics are rarely effective. Therefore, despite such harassment, many people still leave their jobs.

Every skilled person has an active circle in the field of science and business. Thus, if he or she breaks a promise with anyone in this circle, there will be a negative chain reaction. Local governments in the western region should recognize this rule when they deal with the problem of talent. It is important to use this rule to serve the development of the western region. We should also adopt a new view towards talent. The western region should give up the conventional view of "departmental ownership" and "local ownership" of skilled people. The new view should be that of "working for us without staying with us."

Talented people leave the western region due to its poor environment and relatively backward economy and society. The western region should improve its environment and introduce a new policy to attract those with the desired skills, such as allowing them to keep their original household registration, permitting them to come and go freely, and providing favourable working conditions. It is also important to deal correctly with the relationship between those who are currently employed and those coming from other cities who are attracted by the new policy. The first thing is to make use of the skilled people who are already employed.

A New Policy for Development of Education, Science and Technology

The problem of the brain drain faced by the western region is similar to that of China. In America's Silicon Valley, it is rare that a high-tech company has no Chinese professionals. Providing a good education to Chinese children is a difficult and long process. The U.S. government does not spend much effort on this. However, the U.S. still easily attracts top Chinese talent due to the country's high living standards. The western region of China is no exception. It is not attractive to talented people due to the lack of a creative environment and proper management mechanisms. It cannot attract people from the outside, while skilled people from the west flow to the eastern region via all kinds of channels.

A convenient environment is needed to attract talent. All kinds of specialists are always required for economic development. The east is more attractive to such people than the west, because it is more developed and has more flexible mechanisms of employment. It may take a long time to build an effective mechanism in the west because of its backward economy and insufficient capital. This is disadvantageous to the development of the western region and to the harmonious growth of the national economy.

The competition for talent between the west and the east is an unequal one because their starting points are different. This means that regulation by the central government is needed. On the one hand, the introduction of some management systems depends on the reform of the whole administrative system. On the other hand, the government should also introduce some policies to attract talented people from the eastern and central regions or abroad to participate in the development of the west.

The salary is usually the main source of income for people. It is a critical factor for the development of human resources. Thus, the government should implement a flexible policy of income distribution according to the different needs of skilled people at different stages of the country's economic development. A mechanism favourable to the cultivation and use of talent must be established. Such a policy will bring notable returns in the development of economic and human resources in the western region.

A science and technology system with characteristics of the planned economy constrains the potential of researchers. Thus, reforms to the system should be accelerated. The following measures can be adopted. First, scientific research systems should be set up in various forms. It is necessary to continue to support public research institutes and, at the same time, encourage some research institutes to privatize. For example, some of them can form companies or ally with other corporate groups. Local enterprises should be encouraged to set up scientific research institutes. Second, researchers should be encouraged to focus on innovations in knowledge and technology, especially in those areas that are relevant to the western region. Third, the strategy of high and new technological development should focus on importing and utilizing high and new technology, and developing them selectively to meet the needs of local, domestic and international markets.

Finally, the external resources of science, technology and talents should be utilized. There are many academics, professors, senior engineers and entrepreneurs in the eastern region and even in foreign countries who have come from the western region and will go home periodically. We should make full use of their presence and make it convenient for them to give lectures and talks about technology, information exchanges, investment and trading. They should be encouraged to participate in local programmes on technological innovation.

In summary, the reform of the science and technology system should turn the traditional management of scientific research into a supporting service for scientific research.

Integrating Education and Economic Development

It is important to integrate education and economic development. Educational development is needed to reduce poverty and increase income. It should facilitate long-term economic and social development in the western region. Education should be developed according to the characteristics of the economy, the needs of society and the culture of the western region. It is necessary to comprehensively reform the management system of education as well as the objectives of education, the school management, teaching contents and methods. The link between education and the labour market should also be enhanced. Training should avoid "academicism, scholasticism and aristocratism" to meet the needs of economic and social development. The following suggestions are offered.

First, professional education should adopt a flexible system to reduce the time and costs of training, and to provide the practical technical training most needed by local people. Professional schools should become popular centres of practical technology. Practical scientific knowledge and skills should be emphasized so that students can use what they have learned after graduation and contribute to economic development.

Second, the quality of higher education in the western region should be improved to accelerate the application of science and technology. Higher education run by the state and local people should be expanded and developed to meet the popular demand for higher education.

Third, higher education should be developed in many forms and be open to the market. Cross-regional "open" universities can be developed to achieve economies of scale. The Ministry of Education and the National Broadcasting and Television Bureau should allow the western region to set up "open" universities that involve television, long-distance communication networks, virtual universities via satellites and the Internet. This will allow students in various regions to share educational resources. National libraries and coastal universities should set up digital libraries and provide convenient information and teaching services to the western region. First-class universities in the east should be encouraged to expand the recruitment of students from the western region. The costs can be reimbursed by the government if these students go home to work after graduation. With the help of the central and local governments, a key university should be set up in provinces without a professional college. It is necessary to increase investment in higher education in minority areas and implement a free or partly free education policy.

Finally, it is important to increase investment in the construction of colleges in the western region. Emphasis should be given to the development of main subjects and qualified teachers, and on the construction of infrastructure such as buildings and laboratories, which are sorely needed at present. A series of key laboratories at the state or ministry level, as well as training bases for teaching and research, should be established for key subjects.

Strengthen Central Government Support for Education

Human resources are the most important factor for development. Therefore, the first task in the development of the western region is to develop human resources and education. First, basic education should be developed. The cost of basic education is relatively low, and can be divided into direct cost and opportunity cost. The direct cost is the monetary expenditure on education. Opportunity cost is the income students give up by studying. This cost will increase with the age of the students. The government should invest in and develop basic education in the west because investment in basic education by a family for their children is based on its return, which is beneficial to society as well.

Second, higher education should be developed to meet the needs of economic development in the western region. Since 1978, much progress has been made in this respect. But its development is much slower than in the eastern region. Rapid economic development in the eastern region has provided strong support for education. However, with its limited fiscal revenues, the western region is not able to strongly support the development of education, while non-governmental institutions also give limited support due to a weak economy. Higher education involves "science" and "technology." The former focuses on science education to train researchers while the latter focuses on technology education for students who will engage in economic activities after graduation. In the western region, higher education should focus on educating students in the kinds of technology that are most important to the economic development of the region.

Third, all effort should be made to develop the physical infrastructure for education, both basic education and higher education. The underdevelopment of education in the western region is due largely to its poor infrastructure. In order to develop education in the western region, it is necessary to reconstruct school buildings, increase investment in laboratory construction and update all kinds of teaching equipment.

Fourth, the central government should increase financial support for basic education in the western region. The following are some feasible means. Large and medium coastal cities in the eastern region should be encouraged to help poor children in rural areas of the west to continue their education. Because of a decline in the number of school-age children in the eastern region, much idle equipment can be used to establish schools in poor areas of the west. Undergraduate students should be encouraged to go to the west and provide voluntary support during holiday periods. All junior high school students should be given opportunities to receive senior high school education, senior professional high school education or secondary technical education. Rural professional schools should be established to serve agricultural production and industries in rural areas. The government should support professional technical education in poor areas. In order to implement the programme of mass civil education, the administrative system should be reformed to match the socialist market economy. The operation and distribution of all aid for education received from the central government and from poverty alleviation programmes should be open and lawful.

Finally, training should be strengthened in the western region. Training includes the training of managers, skilled workers, non-skilled workers, etc. Compared with the eastern region, the western region also has the advantage of a cheaper labour force, in addition to abundant natural resources and a stunning environment. Existing and new industries here will benefit from cheaper labour costs compared with the eastern region. Over the past 20 years, rapid economic development in the eastern coastal region has been mainly due to its lower labour costs. With an open environment, enterprises and capital from many countries have been attracted to the eastern region, contributing to its development.

If the western region is to play the same role that the eastern region has played in the past, it must actively adapt to the situation. At the same time, it is very important to strengthen the training of workers in the fields of management, finance, production and marketing, in order to change labour resources into labour capital. With a skilled labour force, more investors will invest in the western region.

Promote the Co-operation with the Eastern Region in Technology and Education

Co-operating with the eastern region in technology and education is important. By making use of the eastern region's advantages in information, capital and technology, the natural resources, and existing technology and capital of the western region can be explored and developed. It is difficult to develop border areas with only a resource advantage. Its multiplier effect is too small and may even result in a structural decline. For the time being, foreign investment in some areas is increasing rapidly, and this is a great opportunity. Co-operation with developed countries in economic and technological areas through foreign direct investment should also be promoted.

The eastern region can also take part in the development of education in the western region. The central and eastern regions should offer their support, such as offering special classes for students from Tibet and Xinjiang and sending volunteers to teach in the western region. More importantly, they can take part directly in education projects in the western region. For example, they can set up branch schools there, promote exchanges among teachers of both regions, take part in science projects such as the construction of science and technology parks in western colleges, train officials and teachers for western schools, transfer excellent leaders to the west, and organize groups of education experts to give lectures regularly. Through co-operation in education, education in the western region can be improved rapidly, while the eastern region can also benefit from many opportunities in the western region.

Concluding Remarks

This chapter has examined various problems and strategies in education, science and technology in the western region. It should be noted that improving the level of science and technology in the western region is not the ultimate objective. The main task is to develop those dimensions in science and technology that can support and promote economic development directly and solve key issues about the environment. The central government should support the construction of infrastructure and provide a good environment for technological development in the western region. The central issue is to find out a way to develop technology to meet the needs of the economy.

The management system and educational system should be reformed. At the same time, special funds should be set up for compulsory education, education programmes for reducing illiteracy, continuing education, vocational education and long-distance education. Suitable policies and capital investment are needed for the western region. A special area of higher education can be designated with preferential open policies. The advantages of the two big higher education bases in the western region (Xi'an and Chengdu) should be fully used to attract investment from inside and outside of China.

Notes

1. Zhang Baoqing 張保慶, "Zai xibu diqu kaifa zhong bixu shizhong zhuyi chongfen fahui jiaoyu de xiandaoxing, quanjuxing, jichuxing zuoyong" 在西部地區開發中必須始終注意充分發揮教育的先導性、全局性、基礎性作用 (Make Full Use of Those Functions of Education including Leadership, Wide Impact and Foundation in the Development of the Western Region), *Zhongguo jiaoyu bao* 中國教育報 (News on China Education), 14 February 2001.
2. Shi Peijun 史培軍 and Zhou Wuguang 周武光, "Xibei diqu kechixu fazhan de jige guanjian wenti" 西北地區可持續發展的幾個關鍵問題 (Several Key Problems in Sustainable Development in the Western Region, *Beijing shifan daxue xuebao* (shehui kexue ban) 北京師範大學學報 (社會科學版) (Journal of Beijing Normal University (Social Science Edition)), No. 5 (2000), pp. 110–17.
3. Kejibu fu xibei wushengqu diaoyanzu 科技部赴西北五省區調研組, "Woguo xibei keji fazhan mianlin de kunnan yu duice" 我國西北科技發展面臨的困難與對策 (The Difficulty of Developing Science and Technology in the Northwestern Region and Countermeasures), *Jingji yaocan* 經濟要參 (Key Economic Reference), Vol. 53 (2002).
4. Zhongguo keji fazhan zhanlüe yanjiu xiaozu 中國科技發展戰略研究小組, *Zhongguo quyu chuangxin nengli baogao 2001* 中國區域創新能力報告2001 (China Regional Innovation Capacity Report 2001) (Beijing: Zhonggong zhongyang dangxiao chubanshe 中共中央黨校出版社, 2001).
5. Guojia jiaoyu fazhan yanjiu zhongxin 國家教育發展研究中心, *2001 nian Zhongguo jiaoyu lüpishu — Zhongguo jiaoyu zhengce niandu fenxi baogao* 2001年中國教育綠皮書 — 中國教育政策年度分析報告 (2001 Green Book of Chinese Education — Annual Report of Chinese Education Policy) (Beijing: Jiaoyu kexue chubanshe 教育科學出版社, 2001).

7

Resource Mobilization

Mao Hanying and Zhang Li

Introduction

The central initiative to develop the western region (hereafter, the region), known as the Western Region Development Strategy (hereafter, the strategy) or the "Go West" programme, is one important component of China's modernization drive in the new millennium, representing a major decision on the part of the Chinese leadership. At the end of 1999, the Central Economic Work Conference made the strategic decision to develop western China, with the goal of transforming the west into a prosperous and advanced region by the middle of the twenty-first century. In 2000, the State Council formulated a number of policies to support the region.[1] The thrust of these policies was to lessen the tangible and intangible obstacles to development in western China. While the central authorities have taken the position that persistent underdevelopment of the region is politically and economically unacceptable,[2] the State Council has recognized that the region needs to create mechanisms to bring together existing and new resources if the central initiative is to be implemented.

The concept of resources can be defined in a very broad sense. Anything that is considered necessary or useful for human beings at a given stage of technology may be referred to as the resources of a region (or nation).[3] In the context of economic development, the term may be more specifically reserved for substances of the physical environment (natural resources), labour, knowledge and entrepreneurial skills (human resources), capital or investment funds (financial resources), and policies and cultural attributes (institutional resources), if these factors can be directly used to generate wealth.

From the point of view of resources, the major advantages of the region are its abundant natural resources, a certain industrial base and relatively strong capabilities in science and technology. It is generally believed, from various sources, that the region is endowed with substantial proven reserves of mineral resources, both in terms of absolute size and relative national share. Some parts of the region are also rich in natural gas and cultural relics. Nonetheless, many resources are still underutilized. The consumer market has its potential, too. Human capital, particularly high-tech personnel, is claimed as another great asset of some provinces in the region. For strategic, rather than economic, reasons, China situated many industrial enterprises and high-tech research bases in inland provinces in the 1950s and 1960s. As a result, most of the industries there have large productive capacities that absorb skilled labour, including science and technology personnel, from other parts of the country. The percentage of senior scientists and technicians working in the region is higher than the national average. Thus, the region can provide many resources and opportunities that are valuable for the country's economic development and can be attractive for investors seeking resources and markets.

Nonetheless, the region remains economically backward, as it has been for the past several decades. It possesses 72% of China's total land area and 28% of its population. The region's share of primary industry in terms of GDP is high and the per capita income is low. Traditional modes of production and animal husbandry prevail. The region today has still done little to open up to the outside world and, thus, has received very little foreign direct investment (FDI). Market awareness is poor, market competitiveness is weak, and the consumer market is underdeveloped.[4] There is little doubt that the region has lagged far behind the eastern provinces in economic development and social progress. This raises concerns about the negative impact of growing regional disparities on economic and social development, particularly following China's entry to the WTO, as the region is perceived to be less likely to benefit in many aspects.[5] The central leadership has, therefore, made the accelerated development of the region a priority in the new century.

Given its status of underdevelopment, the region has to overcome a raft of comparative disadvantages in order to realize the advances envisaged under the strategy. This is to be a long-term, gigantic and capital-intensive programme — one with a timeline of several decades and requiring substantial capital. Policy-makers have to reckon with the challenges of responding to policies that not only address questions of why, but also, more importantly, of how, to develop the region. How best to mobilize resources is at the heart of the strategy, especially when the Chinese economy is still resource-constrained. The Chinese authorities are fully aware of the need for such an emphasis. In addition to the direct allocation of more central funding and financing, the central leadership is going to create a favourable environment to attract investment and talent. As a prerequisite for successful resource mobilization, the State Council has identified the key areas of development and formulated working polices. Following the central circular on policies and measures pertaining to the development of the region, at the implementation level, governments of the region have come up with their plans for preferential treatment for investors.

In this chapter, the question of how to develop the region from the perspective of resource mobilization is addressed. First, the key areas of development set out in the strategy are outlined. This is followed by a discussion of the government's approach to mobilizing resources in the course of carrying out the strategy, based on documents published by various governmental departments and research conducted by Chinese scholars. Finally, the government's approach is assessed, with particular attention paid to their plans to improve the investment environment.

The Key Areas of Development Advocated

In his government work report to the Third Session of the Ninth National People's Congress, Premier Zhu Rongji 朱鎔基 set forth the major objectives for the implementation of the strategy over the next 10 years (2001–2010).[6] The strategy focuses on six areas, as outlined below.

To accelerate the development of infrastructure. Efforts will be made to expand the region's transport network, electric power grids and telecommunications systems, radio and television facilities and to rationally exploit water resources.

To conserve and improve the ecological environment. The strategy will encourage projects to protect natural forests along the upper reaches of the Yangzi River and the upper and middle reaches of the Yellow River. Terraced fields on steep slopes should be returned to forests or pastures at the expense of grain production. Local farmers will be compensated in the form of grain or cash.

To restructure industries with local characteristics. In light of local geography, resources and other conditions, the strategy encourages the different provinces in the region to restructure their industries in such a way as to maximize local comparative advantages. Where possible, the region should capitalize on high- and new-technology industries.

To vigorously improve education, science and technology. The strategy postulates that the workforce in the region will be trained in different fields at different levels of expertise. The strategy also recommends that the region accelerate the translation of scientific and technological advances into productive forces.

To create a favourable investment environment. The strategy envisages China opening up further to the outside world and trying its best to attract foreign capital, technology and managerial expertise. The channels of foreign investment and fund raising will be broadened. Preferential policies such as tax concessions and the extension of loan repayment periods are being formulated to encourage investment. More opportunities will be offered to foreign firms.

To promote east-west co-operation. The strategy sees the more developed eastern and coastal provinces playing an active role and increasing their support to the region in various ways, such as through joint development projects and co-operative efforts for mutual benefit. The government anticipates that advanced enterprises in developed areas will explore new markets and bring advanced management and innovative production styles to less-developed western enterprises. In return, the region will provide markets, energy, and a supply of raw and semi-finished materials that will contribute to the economic restructuring of the eastern region.

In line with the above key areas, the Western Region Development Office (under the State Council) and the State Development Planning Commission launched "Ten Key Projects" in 2000 and another "Twelve Key Projects" in 2001 as a key part of the strategy (Table 7.1). Seven of the above projects focus on transportation, so as to improve distribution networks and boost the investment environment. Work on most of these projects has already started or will be starting very soon. Also, the State Council has designated 10 localities where natural resources, including minerals, metals and energy, will be exploited (Table 7.2). In addition, each province in the region has announced its priority projects. There is no question that the Western Region Development Strategy is a large-scale campaign consisting of many mega-projects.

According to the central government, the strategy will be carried out in three phases. In the first phase (2000–2010), emphasis will be placed on improving the region's infrastructure and ecological environment. During this phase, it is expected that the region's economy will be transformed from one dependent on natural resources to one that is semi-industrialized. The second phase (2011–2030) will be an "acceleration period" characterized by rapid industrialization and urbanization. Modernization will be fully under way in the third phase (2031–2050). By the middle of the twenty-first century, the level of economic prosperity in the region will be closer to that of developed parts of China.

The Government's Approach to Mobilizing Resources

It is understandable that, given the scale of development, a huge amount of resources will be required to implement the strategy. The mega-projects are capital-intensive. To push forward the strategy, the central government has promised to increase the amount of investment earmarked for the region in its budget. When allocating loans from state policy-mandated banks and

Table 7.1 Key Projects under the Western Development Strategy

Area	Project
Transport	*Launched in 2000* • Xi'an 西安-Hefei 合肥 railway (955 km, part of Xi'an-Nanjing 南京 railway) and Yu-Huai 渝懷-Chongqing 重慶 railway (640 km) • Western China highway projects (national highway trunk lines and roads through state-designated poor counties) • Construction and expansion of airport projects, including the following main hubs – Xianyang 咸陽 Airport in Xi'an – Shuangliu 雙流 Airport in Chengdu 成都 – Wujiaba 巫家壩 Airport in Kunming 昆明 – Zhongchuan 中川 Airport in Lanzhou 蘭州 – Urumqi 烏魯木齊 Airport • Chongqing elevated light railway • Natural gas pipeline from Sebei 澀北 (Qaidam 柴達木 Basin) to Xining 西寧 and Lanzhou (953 km) *Launched in 2001* • Qinghai 青海-Tibet 西藏 railway • West-to-east pipeline from Xinjiang 新疆 to the Yangzi River Delta
Water/Environment	*Launched in 2000* • Irrigation centres in Zipinpu 紫坪鋪 (Sichuan 四川) and Shapotou 沙坡頭 (Ningxia 寧夏) • Reforestation, ecological improvements and seedling-growing projects *Launched in 2001* • Longtan 龍灘 hydropower station in Guangxi 廣西 • Hinge water conservancy project in Bose 百色, Guangxi • Nirji 尼爾基 hydro-junction project, Inner Mongolia 內蒙古 • Xiaowan 小灣 hydropower station in Yunnan • Projects to harness the Tarim River 塔里木河 and Hei River 黑河 • Several pivotal construction projects as feature agriculture
Industry	*Launched in 2000* • Qinghai 青海 chemical project for potassium fertilizer 鉀肥 *Launched in 2001* • Construction of electrolytic aluminum • West-east power transmission line
Education	*Launched in 2000* • University infrastructure undertakings *Launched in 2001* • Broadcasting and TV coverage and Telnet education

Sources: *People's Daily*, 28 August 2001; 20 February 2002.

Table 7.2 Ten Designated Localities for Resource Development

Locality	Resource development
• Tarim 塔里木 Basin in Xinjiang	• Energy
• Middle section of the Yellow River	• Energy
• Tianshan Mountains 天山 in Xinjiang and Qilian Mountains 祁連山 in Qinghai and Gansu 甘肅	• Nonferrous metals and energy
• Qaidam Basin in Qinghai	• Energy, chemicals and minerals
• Qinling Mountains 秦嶺 in Shaanxi 陝西	• Nonferrous and rare metals
• Confluence of "Three Rivers" in southwest China	• Nonferrous metals
• Panzhihua 攀枝花 in Sichuan and Guizhou 貴州	• Minerals
• Sichuan 四川 Basin	• Natural gas
• Hongshui River 紅水河 in Guangxi	• Nonferrous and rare metals
• Areas around the Yarlung Zangbo River 雅魯藏布江, Lhasa River 拉薩河 and Nianchu River 年楚河 in Tibet 西藏	• Nonferrous and rare metals

Source: *People's Daily*, 2 April 2002.

concessionary loans from international financial institutions and foreign governments in accordance with lending conditions, Beijing will try to direct as much capital as possible towards projects in the region.[7] In January 2000, the Western Region Development Conference affirmed that central government agencies would manifest their financial support for the region when formulating sector development plans and allocating special funds. Zeng Peiyan 曾培炎, Chairman of the State Development and Planning Commission, announced that in the year 2000, the state would pour 70% of fixed-asset investment and foreign loans into the region. Following a proactive fiscal policy, treasury bonds and capital construction funds in the central fiscal budget used for western development totalled RMB43 billion in 2000. In 2001, investment from budgetary funds and treasury bonds for the region exceeded the level of the previous year.[8] A major proportion of central government funding has been geared towards the construction of infrastructure.

To the extent that the central government can afford to do so, it will offer special subsidies for social security, science and education, health care, family planning, and culture and environmental protection. The central government will be responsible for providing grain or cash allowances relating to the implementation of state-approved projects to convert cultivated land to forests and grasslands, protect natural forests and prevent desertification. The government will also give more financial and credit support to the region by increasing loans and extending loan repayment periods.[9]

The central government's sponsorship of the strategy does not necessarily mean that all investment will come from Beijing. Despite an increase in central inputs, there will be a shortfall in capital financing given the overall amount required for so many mega-projects. With funding problems looming as a bottleneck for the proposed western development, the central government intends to make full use of market forces in implementing the strategy. Local governments are principally responsible for mobilizing the required resources. The central government will provide preferential policies and give greater power to local governments to help them to find their way. The State Development and Planning Commission has recently promulgated a range of preferential policies to lure overseas investors.[10] Highlights of these policies are:

1. In the coming decade, income taxes for certain overseas enterprises in the region will be reduced by 15% as compared to national levels.
2. Overseas investors investing in the sectors of transportation, electric power, water conservation, postal services and TV broadcasts will be exempted from income tax for the first two years. They will also be eligible for a higher depreciation rate and a higher retention rate from the technology development fund.
3. Those investing in government-designated key projects in the region will be exempted from tariffs and import-related value-added tax (VAT) on advanced technological equipment for their own use.
4. Certain sectors including banking, insurance, tourism, accounting, engineering and telecommunications will be open to overseas investors.
5. Foreign-funded projects listed on the Catalogue Guiding Foreign Investment in Industry will enjoy reduced tax rates.
6. Chinese financial institutions will provide more loans to foreign-invested projects.
7. Oil and gas companies in the region will be permitted to attract foreign investment through management right transfers, equity sales, mergers and reorganizations, Sino-foreign joint ventures, the raising of venture capital and other means.
8. Methods of commercial co-operation will be expanded to include build-operate-transfer (BOT) projects, security financing and others.

The central government has acknowledged that the investment environment has to be improved in order to overcome financial constraints to developing the region. The central government has increased the region's share of its fiscal allocations for infrastructure projects. The government has adopted favourable financing, taxation and pricing policies to allow investors to reap reasonable returns. The State Council has granted state-level status to several provincial economic and technology development zones in Xi'an 西安, Chengdu 成都, Chongqing 重慶, Kunming 昆明 and Guiyang 貴陽, meaning that these development zones can offer generous incentives to investors similar to those in special economic zones in the coastal region. The channels of foreign investment and fund raising have also been broadened.

Central leaders have actively promoted the strategy by releasing information on investment opportunities and preferential policies in various national and international conferences as well as on different occasions. President Jiang Zemin 江澤民 recently called for pushing forward western development in a national conference on the large-scale development of China's Western Region.[11] Zeng Peiyan, Chairman of the State Development and Planning Commission, spoke about the strategy at the Sixth World Chinese Entrepreneurs Convention in Nanjing 南京 and at the Fortune Globe Forum 2001 in Hong Kong. The China Western Forum, established in 2000, is intended to be an annual meeting to update and co-ordinate specific policies on the western region. Its first meeting drew top leaders from central government departments, regional governments and the renowned enterprises around the country, as well as many top executives from Fortune 500 companies.

Another important way in which the government is striving to improve the investment environment is by according favourable treatment to the development of human capital. In order to sustain the strategy over the long term, professional and highly skilled manpower must be secured for the western labour market. The central government has already unveiled the training, appointment and recruitment of human resources as well as the development of science and technology as being part of the strategy. Over the past decades, large numbers of highly skilled personnel had been deployed to the region to support the military industries located there. As a matter of personal choice, however, talented people have not been willing to work in the west because material conditions in the region are less attractive than those in more prosperous areas of China. The government has continuously put a great deal of effort into encouraging people with talent and skill to move from more developed areas to the western region. They are allowed to retain their household registration in their place of origin, or they and their family members are entitled to legally reside in urban areas of the region. A proposal has been put forward to raise the salaries of the personnel of government agencies and research institutions in the region to the national average or higher. A hardship allowance will be offered to people working in harsh, remote or frontier areas. Along with monetary incentives, the central government has pledged to provide good working and living conditions to attract and retain people with technical and managerial talent from within the country or overseas.

The central government is also seeking international resources (particularly foreign aid) to train professionals for the region. China has joined with the United Nations Development Programme (UNDP) to provide a high-level training at home and abroad for those professionals already working in the region. According to the China Education and Research Network, during the period 2002–2004, the UNDP will invest US$1 million in the training programme, and domestic funds will also be earmarked to support it.

From the account so far, it is clear that the central government is giving different kinds of support for different kinds of development. The central government has played a leading role in improving infrastructure and protecting the ecological environment, as these two areas are crucial to the development of the west, but seem highly unlikely to be commercially viable in most cases. In other areas, the central government is helping local governments and markets take more initiative through policy inducements instead of directly extending financial aid. Generally speaking, the government's approach to resource mobilization can be described as a market-oriented framework with preferential policies to lure financial and human resources to the region.

Assessing the Government's Approach

Support from the Central Government

The effort to develop the region is not new in the history of People's Republic of China (PRC). In the years immediately following the founding of the PRC, China, fearing imperialist attacks, had relocated its critical defense industries to some provinces of the region.[12] Table 7.3 shows that, in terms of investment policy, China has attached importance to the development of its inland areas. In certain periods, the region received quite a substantial share of centrally allocated resources. For instance, four-fifths of 156 national key projects during the First Five-year Plan were conducted in non-coastal areas. During the 1960s and 1970s, the central and western regions received more investment in construction than did the eastern region (Table 7.3). A sizeable proportion of the resources received had been allocated to Third Front industries, which were largely military-oriented.

While the earlier efforts simply arose out of concerns for national defense, the latest endeavour is aimed at achieving the multiple economic and political objectives outlined in the strategy. For the strategy to succeed, strong and comprehensive support from the central government is required

Table 7.3 Respective Shares of the Eastern and Western Regions in Basic Construction Investment (1953–1999)

(Unit: %)

Period	East	Central and West	Central	West
1953–1957 (First Five-year Plan)	36.9	46.8	28.8	18.0
1958–1962 (Second Five-year Plan)	38.4	56.0	34.0	22.0
1963–1965 (adjustment period)	34.9	58.2	32.7	25.6
1966–1970 (Third Five-year Plan)	26.9	64.7	29.8	34.9
1971–1975 (Fourth Five-year Plan)	35.5	54.4	29.9	24.5
1976–1980 (Fifth Five-year Plan)	42.2	50.0	30.1	19.9
1981–1985 (Sixth Five-year Plan)	47.7	46.5	29.3	17.2
1986–1990 (Seventh Five-year Plan)	51.7	40.2	24.4	15.8
1991–1995 (Eighth Five-year Plan)	54.2	38.2	23.5	14.7
1996	53.0	7.6	23.6	14.0
1997	52.4	39.2	23.7	15.5
1998	52.2	39.2	22.2	17.0
1999	52.1	39.6	22.5	17.1

Source: Yasuo Onishi, "Chinese Economy in the 21st Century and the Strategy for Developing the Western Region," in *China's Western Development Strategy: Issues and Prospects*, edited by Yasuo Onishi (Japan: Institute of Developing Economies, 2001), p. 7.

to lessen both tangible and intangible obstacles to the development of the region. The tangible obstacles include little outside investment, a lack of economic capacity for capital accumulation and development, poorer infrastructure, a more fragile ecosystem, a larger population of poor people, a larger surplus of rural labour and a lower level of social development than the rest of the country. The major intangible obstacles are the business philosophy and non-transparent legal mechanisms that underlie the region's investment environment. Changing ways of thinking and doing things is now officially regarded as crucial to the success of the latest drive to develop the region.[13] The central government is gradually systemizing individual policies on western development into the broad framework of a state strategy. The State Council established in January 2000 the "State Council Leading Group for Western Region Development" chaired by Premier Zhu Rongji. Members of the leading group include all top leaders of the party and heads of the government departments in charge of economic and social affairs (Table 7.4). The line-up demonstrates the unprecedentedly strong support and active involvement of the central government in the strategy. The new development strategy and associated means of resource mobilization are more systematic and comprehensive than before.

With regard to resource mobilization, the government's approach shows the old pattern of government-led regional development in the sense that state investment forms the central pillar, at least in the initial stage. Only when the central government leads the development can the region make its start. The central government has allocated and will continue to allocate a bigger slice of its financial "pie" to the region. But at the same time, a wide variety of preferential fiscal and monetary policies has been proposed to boost investment, indicating the central government's expectation that local governments and markets should become the main players in regional development.

From different points of view, there are good reasons to justify the active role of markets. Institutionally, after two decades of pursuing economic reforms and an open-door policy, China is establishing a so-called socialist market economic system. It is now regarded as desirable for the region to rely primarily on market mechanisms for development. Economically, as the relative weight of the central government's finances in the national economy has declined considerably and the central government's capacity to redistribute income to the least-developed regions is shrinking, the region must recognize that it will need to use market mechanisms to foster its own resource bases for development[14] and that it

Table 7.4 Composition of the Leading Group for Western Development, 2000

Title	Name	Government position
Group leader	Zhu Rongji	Premier
Deputy group leader	Wen Jiabao 溫家寶	Vice Premier
Members	Zeng Peiyan 曾培炎	Chairman of the State Development and Planning Commission
	Li Rongrong 李榮融	Chairman of the State Economic and Trade Commission
	Chen Zhili 陳至立	Minister of Education
	Xu Guanhua 徐冠華	Minister of Science and Technology
	Liu Jibin 劉積斌	Chairman of the Commission of Science, Technology and Industry for National Defense
	Li Demo 李德沫	Chairman of the State Nationalities Affairs Commission
	Xiang Huaicheng 項懷誠	Minister of Finance
	Tian Fengshan 田鳳山	Party Secretary of the Ministry of National Land and Natural Resources
	Fu Zhihuan 傅志寰	Minister of Railways
	Huang Zhendong 黃鎮東	Minister of Transportation
	Wu Jichuan 吳基傳	Minister of Information Technology and Telecommunications Industry
	Wang Shucheng 汪恕誠	Minister of Water Resources
	Du Qinglin 杜青林	Minister of Agriculture
	Sun Jiazheng 孫家正	Minister of Culture
	Dai Xianglong 戴相龍	Governor of the People's Bank of China
	Liu Yunshan 劉雲山	Deputy Head of the Propaganda Department, the Central Commission of the Chinese Communist Party
	Xu Guangchun 徐光春	Director of the State Administration of Radio, Film and Television
	Zhou Shengxian 周生賢	Director of the State Forestry Bureau
	Zhang Xuezhong 張學忠	Minister of Personnel
	Wan Xueyuan 萬學遠	Director of the State Bureau of Foreign Experts
	Wang Guangtao 汪光燾	Minister of Construction
	Shi Guangsheng 石廣生	Minister of Foreign Trade
	Jie Zhenhua 解振華	Director of Environmental Protection Bureau

Source: The home page of the State Council Leading Group for Western Region Development: http://www.chinawest.gov.cn/chinese/frame.htm.

would be unrealistic to expect to receive a large amount of financial assistance from the central government. Politically, the allocation of central investment in the region involves the balancing of different interests so that, in reality, it is the political process that is behind the allocation of pieces of the "central pie" to local governments in the region. Localities usually fight hard to be the recipients of central investment. It is not easy for the central government, with its limited financial resources, to mediate between the interests of local governments. Currently, the criteria and processes for determining the allocation of central funds and projects are decided arbitrarily without explicit laws or regulations.[15] Markets may be more helpful, to some extent, to ease conflicts of interest among governments at all levels.

Effectiveness of Preferential Policies

One may be skeptical about the effectiveness of preferential policies for attracting foreign investment. Preferential treatment as a fund-raising mechanism proved to be highly successful in developing the coastal areas in the early 1980s when China had been closed to the outside world for three decades. By most indications, governments at all levels in the region wish to follow the same road. However, the internal and external circumstances surrounding the region nowadays are quite different from those seen for the coastal areas from the 1980s through the mid-1990s. This is true in terms of such factors as locational advantage, economic structure and growth pattern, supply and demand, provincial relationship, degree of openness and policy environment. How preferential policies can be effective in developing the west seems to be an open question, even if such policies are getting popular everywhere in China. To be effective, preferential measures must be "special" in nature. They would be no longer preferential if everyone could receive similar treatment everywhere, and certainly would become less effective over time. From official figures, we see that there was a rise in FDI, with some fluctuations, in most provinces of the region over the 1990s (Table 7.5). The biggest attractions of the region to foreign investors include the huge and rapidly growing market, the abundance of raw materials and cheap labour. Tax incentives and preferential policies were also one form of attraction. Without detailed information, however, we cannot systematically determine whether this increase has been a result of preferential policies or a consequence of region-specific endowment factors such as raw materials or growing markets.

Table 7.5 Foreign Direct Investment in the Western Region

(Unit: US$1 million)

Year	Inner Mongolia	Guangxi	Chongging	Sichuan	Guizhou	Yunnan	Tibet	Shaanxi	Gansu	Qinghai	Ningxia	Xinjiang
1990	10.64	28.66	—	16.04	4.68	2.61	—	41.91	0.85	—	0.25	5.37
1991	1.66	31.85	—	80.91	14.09	3.51	—	31.76	4.78	—	0.18	0.22
1992	5.20	182.01	—	112.14	19.79	28.75	—	45.53	0.35	0.68	0.35	—
1993	85.26	884.56	—	571.41	42.94	97.02	—	234.30	11.95	3.24	11.90	53.00
1994	40.07	836.33	—	921.74	63.63	65.00	—	238.80	87.76	2.41	7.27	48.30
1995	57.81	672.63	—	541.59	57.03	97.69	—	324.07	63.92	1.64	3.90	54.90
1996	71.86	663.13	—	440.90	31.38	65.37	—	326.09	90.02	1.00	5.55	63.90
1997	73.25	885.79	418.02	228.46	49.77	165.66	—	628.16	41.44	2.47	6.71	24.72
1998	90.82	886.13	431.07	372.48	45.35	145.68	—	300.10	38.64	—	18.56	21.67
1999	64.56	635.12	238.93	341.01	40.90	153.85	—	241.97	41.04	4.59	51.34	24.04
2000	105.68	524.66	244.36	436.94	25.01	128.12	—	288.42	62.35	—	17.41	19.11

Sources: State Statistical Bureau, *China Statistical Yearbook*, various years.

The Chinese authorities firmly believe in a close relationship between the investment environment and foreign investment. Every government involved in western development is making an effort to foster a good environment for investment. This is evident in the fact that both the central and local governments have promulgated, and are continually drawing up, many preferential policies for specific sectors and projects in the region. These policies have focused mainly on offering lucrative incentives such as tax concessions, tariffs exemptions or the repatriation of profits. So far, governments at all levels have made extensive use of incentive policies. The way local governments have mobilized needed resources to achieve their investment goals reflects the fact that the central government has granted localities more independence and autonomy in pursuing development. Nevertheless, the government's effort to create a good investment environment should go beyond the current preferential policies, as the power of such policies remains open to question.

Preferential policies alone may not work as powerfully and effectively to attract foreign investment as is conventionally perceived, partly because investment environment is a very broad concept and contains many elements. Previous empirical studies have shown that inward foreign investment was affected by a host of pull factors of locational endowment, including market size, real costs of production factors, infrastructure, political stability, agglomeration effect and government policies towards FDI.[16] Li and Li have categorized a wide range of factors under hard and soft investment environments. In their view, it is critical that investors understand these factors when assessing risks and making strategic and operational decisions (Table 7.6).[17] The "hard" environment basically refers to the tangible infrastructure and the "soft" environment to intangible factors. Based on multi-factor analysis, Agarwal has argued that the effect of government incentive policies would be eliminated by other factors of the investment environment.[18] By statistically testing the impact of fiscal incentives on the distribution of FDI in less-developed countries, Lim has rejected the hypothesis that more generous fiscal incentives will attract more FDI.[19] He concludes that while incentives in developing countries have become increasingly generous, the overall impact of incentives on FDI has been minimal.

Improving the Investment Environment

As the range of elements related to the investment environment is extensive,

Table 7.6 The Key Elements of the Foreign Investment Environment

Hard environment	Soft environment
• Transportation	• Historical elements
• Telecommunications	• Political background
• Energy supply	• Cultural and social structure
• Public utilities	• Economic regime
• Other infrastructure	• Social security and welfare
• Supply of raw materials and components	• Law and the legal system
• Others	• Human resources
	• Labour relations
	• Government policies and services
	• Business services
	• Others

Source: Modified from Li and Li, *Foreign Investment in China* (see note 16), Table 4.1, p. 85.

a major challenge for governments is how to promote the good ones to overcome capital deficiencies. The hard environment can change very quickly if the relevant authorities have the will to initiate changes and if the necessary capital is made available. By contrast, the soft environment takes much longer to accomplish, as social and political transformations are not a matter of a few years.

In order to attract more investment to the region, the government's endeavours should go beyond the narrow confines of financial and fiscal incentives. Although it will take time to bring the region's hard environment to a level comparable with the developed areas, the central government has made a start by investing in infrastructure (see the discussion above and in Chapter 5). The construction of physical infrastructure is currently at the centre of the central government's investment plan. It is expected that improvements there will be impressive before long. However, many problems in the soft investment environment have been put aside in the strategy, probably because of their political sensitivity. These problems include: an incomplete legal system, the lack of transparency in government policies, non-standardized local charges, inefficient government administration and inconsistent implementation of state policies. No serious suggestions have been offered to deal with these problems in the many proposals to improve the investment environment. Foreign companies often complain about unnecessary institutional costs resulting from long delays in the process of approving licence applications and bureaucratic red tape, as well as the confusion arising from the ill-defined and unpublicized functions and responsibilities of different government departments.[20] Because China is still in the process of transition between systems, both administrative and market forces continue to affect the operations of domestic and foreign companies in China. From the perspective of foreign investors, China still has a very approval-intensive economy and the operating environment of business is still controlled by various bureaucratic mechanisms.[21] Because the administrative role of the government in the economy has not fundamentally declined, government administration and services for business operations must be reformed in order to reduce the institutional costs and risks of investing in the region for foreign and domestic investors. In this regard, the marketization of resource allocations, the building up of a legal infrastructure for market transactions and the further improvement of macro-economic management would be major aspects.

Another aspect of widening the investment base of the region is to promote co-operation between the eastern and western parts of the country. There are sound reasons to promote some forms of regional co-operation. Domestic sources can make up the region's investment shortfall. Prosperous areas of the coast such as Shanghai 上海 and Guangdong 廣東 have the capacity to accelerate western development. The development of the west may benefit the eastern region as well. For instance, improvements to the electrical grid distribution and the construction of more pipelines in the west will alleviate the energy shortages in the east. The environmental and ecological projects in the upper reaches of major rivers in the west will reduce flooding in downstream areas of the east. Better transportation will allow the east to move its products more easily to large and growing consumer markets in the west.

Despite the potential benefits, east-west co-operation cannot be simply based on the market because of the inner laws of economic forces. Market forces tend to drive production factors (financial or human) to areas with high returns. The west's unfavourable physical environment (rough terrain, cold dry weather, remoteness from lucrative urban and international markets, poor infrastructure, and the like) has naturally led to higher production and transaction costs and to poorer economic performance as compared with the more developed east. The west's advantages (relatively rich natural resources, cheap labour and favourable policies) have not been sufficient to offset the region's low capacity in productivity and profit generation. The development experience of many countries has shown that the magic power of the market to reduce regional disparities is only illusory. Production factors, if left to themselves, will not automatically move along the routes the government deems desirable. So far, most of the east's support for western development has been made on charitable rather than on economic grounds. That is to say, the free play of market forces will not lead to sustained east-west co-operation, at least in the foreseeable future. In order to obtain the required amounts of capital to develop the western region, the central government should build a standardized system of interregional fiscal transfers to mitigate profit-making differentials and iron out some of the variations in levels of economic development across regions.

Galvanizing the support of the east to develop the west for purposes of trade is difficult because of institutional constraints to achieving an integrated domestic market. With the decentralization of fiscal responsibility, the effect of administrative boundaries on regional development has intensified and led to ever-increasing market fragmentation. The relationship among local jurisdictions is changing from one of relative isolation and self-sufficiency in the pre-reform period to one of wholesale competition today. Under reforms that decentralized administrative power and expanded local bases of revenue, different regions benefit disproportionately and the political logic of regional co-operation is weak. It has been found that every local bureaucracy seeks to shield its own market from outside competition by establishing all kinds of trade and non-trade barriers. There are many reports about trade wars among regions, especially between the natural-resource-exporting west and the commodity-exporting east.[22] While poor provinces often complain about receiving insufficient support from the central government, more developed provinces frequently perceive any kind of distributive intervention by the central government as an unfair siphoning off of their economic outcomes. Although the central government is no doubt encouraging mutual support between the east and the west, its policy measures are insufficient to cope with regional conflicts. Nor is there co-ordination by the central authorities to ensure east-west co-operation. In the absence of an integrated market within China, it is hard to envisage any commitment from the east to funding the development of the west on the basis of mutual benefit.

Making talent available is one precondition the region has to meet in order to attract substantial inflows of FDI. The pool of talent is largely due to the development of education, which is often perceived as a public good principally determined by government inputs. A region with a larger revenue base can devote more resources to education, but a poor region may not even be able to afford basic education for all. While rich provinces can usually commit regular amounts for the advancement of education, poor provinces have to rely heavily on ad hoc support (such as occasional donations or special funding from the central government or international organizations) to maintain minimum expenditures on basic education. In other words, the poorer the region, the harder it is for local governments fund education. One quantitative study of changing regional disparities in education has revealed that, since the advent of economic reforms, the western region has had much lower levels of public spending in education and in science-related endeavours than the rich coastal region. As a result, the knowledge infrastructure has shrunk and the level of educational attainment in the region lags far behind other parts of the country.[23] If one believes that self-motivated migrants will be attracted to more prosperous regions where the per capita income is expected to be higher, the impoverished western region will face great challenges in luring and keeping professionals and skilled workers because of lower incomes, despite the existence of favourable policies to attract qualified migrants. The shortage of a trained workforce will pose a long-term challenge to the improvement of the region's investment environment and the successful implementation of the strategy. However, this issue seems to have been relatively overlooked in the government's effort to attract FDI. The allocation of more fiscal resources to education, by both the central and local governments, should form a key element of any affirmative policy agenda to promote the development of the west.

Concluding Remarks

Regional development has long been a profound issue in China's modernization. Many scholars and policy-makers believe that, since the late 1970s, China's regional disparities have widened at an unprecedented rate when policies on regional development shifted in orientation from equity in the era of Mao to efficiency in the era of economic reforms. The western region has thus lagged far behind the eastern region in many dimensions of development. Such a situation represents an outright contradiction of socialist values and should supposedly not be tolerated in today's China, where the authorities are seeking to preserve important socialist components of an evolving socio-political system and where equalitarianism is a proof of legitimacy of that system. For reasons of social control, among others, the Chinese authorities cannot afford to overlook the chronic under-development of the country's western region.

The literature on regional development suggests that both a strong desire and capacity on the part of the central government are necessary if regional gaps are to be reduced. The Western Development Strategy is an ambitious top-down effort, representing a new focus in China's regional development in the new century. The central government has shown high expectations, strong leadership and true commitment to the strategy. Financial and institutional support from the central government appears to be more comprehensive for this than for any past programmes. Given its limited resources and the large scale of the strategy, however, the central government has to mobilize alternative resources in order for the strategy to succeed. Resource mobilization forms an important part of the strategy to develop the west.

A number of features underlie the current government's approach to resource mobilization. First, an overwhelming proportion of central government funding is being directed to physical infrastructure, where non-government investment is scarce. Second, in line with the ongoing reform of the Chinese economic system, local governments and markets are expected to play a major role in almost all of the development initiatives. Third, the cornerstone of the government's efforts to mobilize resources is the improvement of the investment environment through preferential policies.

While the government approach is generally pragmatic, there is room for improvement. As discussed earlier, production factors (capital and talent), if subject only to market forces, will not necessarily move to the western region as the government wishes, at least in the initial stage of development. This suggests that resource mobilization cannot be left to *laissez-faire* policies and that the central government must play a significant redistributive role in directing the movement of production factors. To accelerate the development of the west, the region needs to be empowered with the provision of stable, adequate and predictable resources. The core basis of support for the Western Region Development Strategy remains that of financial contributions from the central government. In order to increase its financial commitment to western development on a regular basis, the central government needs to rebuild its extractive capacity and regularize the institutions of interregional fiscal transfers, so that it is able to command a large surplus from the rich provinces and make necessary transfers to the poor areas.

To attract more resources, the governments involved have continuously adopted traditional preferential policies such as tax concessions or other financial incentives as major measures to forge a good investment environment. By reviewing international experiences, we conclude that financial incentives are inadequate to create an investment environment as favourable as that expected by the governments. The heavy focus on preferential treatment for overseas investors undermines the improvement of the soft investment environment that can enhance investment efficiency. Among the many factors of the soft investment environment listed in Table 7.6, good governance in investment activities and the quality of the labour force are particularly important if the region is to enhance its ability to mobilize resources. Good governance ensures the characteristics of transparency, predictability and accountability of the markets that are vital for attracting capital inflows. Given the constraints faced by the region in attracting and retaining professionals and skilled workers, both the central and local governments should pay special attention to educating and training local people. In making interregional fiscal transfers, the central government should earmark special funds for human capital.

The mobilization of domestic resources is an issue that has not received as much attention in the current strategy as the mobilization of FDI. Of course, FDI should play an important role. FDI brings not only financial resources, but many other intangible assets such as management know-how and business best practices. But foreign resources cannot replace domestic resources. While FDI should be continuously pursued, it cannot by itself meet the high investment requirements of the region. Foreign capital can also disappear in an increasingly globalized world. Too much reliance on highly mobile foreign capital to finance the western projects will make the development of the region vulnerable to external shocks. Therefore, effectively tapping domestic resources from rich provinces will be equally important for marshalling the necessary financial resources. The key is for foreign and domestic sources of funding to complement each other.

Notes

1. State Council, *Circular of the State Council on Policies and Measures Pertaining to the Development of the Western Region* (Beijing: China Planning Press, 2000).
2. Hu Angang 胡鞍鋼 (ed.), *Xibu kaifa xinzhanlüe* 西部開發新戰略 (New Strategies for the Western Development) (Beijing: Zhongguo jihua chubanshe 中國計劃出版社, 2001).

3. Brian J. L. Berry, Edgar C. Conkling and D. Michael Ray, *The Global Economy: Resource Use, Locational Choice, and International Trade* (New Jersey: Prentice Hall, 1993).
4. Chen Dong-sheng, "Problems of Economic Development in Inland China and the Strategy for Developing the Western Region," in *China's Western Development Strategy: Issues and Prospects*, edited by Yasuo Onishi (Japan: Institute of Developing Economies, 2001), pp. 31–41.
5. Godfrey Yeung, *Foreign Investment and Socio-economic Development in China: The Case of Dongguan* (New York: Palgrave, 2001).
6. *People's Daily*, 5 March 2000.
7. State Council, *Circular of the State Council* (see note 1).
8. *People's Daily*, 28 August 2001.
9. State Council, *Circular of the State Council* (see note 1).
10. *People's Daily*, 20 September 2001.
11. *People's Daily*, 2 April 2002.
12. Barry Naughton, "The Third Front: Defense Industrialization in Chinese Interior," *China Quarterly*, No. 115 (1988), pp. 351–86.
13. Thomas L. Sims and Jonathan James Schiff, "The Great Western Development Strategy," *The China Business Review*, Vol. 27, No. 6 (2000), pp. 44–49.
14. Xiaobin Zhao and Li Zhang, "Decentralization Reforms and Regional Dilemmas in China: A Review," *International Regional Science Review*, Vol. 22, No. 3 (1999), pp. 251–81.
15. Norihiro Sasaki, "Political Analysis of the Strategy for Developing the Western Region," in *China's Western Development Strategy* (see note 4), pp. 17–30.
16. John H. Dunning, "The Determinants of International Production," *Oxford Economic Papers*, Vol. 25, No. 3 (1973), pp. 289–336; John H. Dunning, "Towards an Eclectic Theory of International Production: Some Empirical Effects," *Journal of International Business*, No. 11 (1980), pp. 9–31; F. R. Root and A. A. Ahmed, "Empirical Determinants of Manufacturing Foreign Investment in Developing Countries," *Economic Development and Cultural Change*, Vol. 27, No. 4 (1979), pp. 751–67; N. J. Glickman and D. P. Woodward, "The Location of Foreign Direct Investment in the United States: Patterns and Determinants," *International Regional Science Review*, Vol. 11, No. 2 (1988), pp. 137–54; Berry, Conkling and Ray, *The Global Economy* (see note 3); Milford B. Green and Rod B. McNaughton (eds.), *The Location of Foreign Direct Investment: Geographic and Business Approaches* (Aldershot, Hants; Hong Kong: Avebury, 1995); Feng Li and Jing Li, *Foreign Investment in China* (Basingstoke: Macmillan Press Ltd., 1999); Yeung, *Foreign Investment* (see note 5).
17. Li and Li, *Foreign Investment in China* (see note 16).
18. J. P. Agarwal, "Determinants of Foreign Investment: A Survey," *Weltwirtschaftliche Archiv*, Vol. 116, No. 4 (1980), pp. 739–73.

19. D. Lim, "Fiscal Incentives and Direct Foreign Investment in Less Developed Countries," *The Journal of Development Studies*, January (1983), pp. 207–12.
20. Michael Du Pont, *Foreign Direct Investment in Transitional Economies: A Case Study of China and Poland* (Basingstoke: Macmillan Press Ltd., 2000).
21. British Consulate-General, Chongqing, *China's Western Development Strategy* (Trade Partners, U.K., 2001).
22. K. Forster, *China's Tea War.* Working paper, No. 91/3, Chinese Economy Research Unit (Adelaide: University of Adelaide, 1991); X. H. Zhang, W. G. Lu and K. L. Sun, *The "Wool War" and the "Cotton Chaos": Fibre Marketing in China.* Working paper, No. 91/14, Chinese Economy Research Unit (Adelaide: University of Adelaide, 1991); A. Watson and C. Findlay, "The 'Wool War' in China," in *Challenges of Economic Reform and Industrial Growth: China's Wool War*, edited by C. Findlay (Australia: Allen and Unwin, 1992), pp. 163–80; Zhao and Zhang, "Decentralization Reforms and Regional Dilemmas in China: A Review" (see note 14).
23. Donggen Wang and Li Zhang, "Knowledge Disparity and Regional Inequality in Post-reform China," *Development and Change* (forthcoming).

8

Urban and Regional Development

Gu Chaolin, Shen Jianfa and Yu Taofang

Introduction

The transition towards a market economy in China after 1978 has reshaped the focus of regional development. Many studies have been conducted on the uneven nature of regional development in China between the inland and coastal regions and among provinces.[1] Relatively speaking, far fewer studies have been conducted on the differences in the urban system between the eastern and western regions.[2] The aim of proposed strategy of developing the western region is to tackle the gap in development between the western and eastern regions that has widened during the reform period. State policy is widely perceived to have contributed to underdevelopment in the western region of China since 1978.

The western region has a weak ecological environment and a poor economic foundation. The region also suffers from a series of ecological, social and economic problems, which are discussed in other chapters of this book. This chapter examines the status and strategies of urban and regional development in the western region.

New Regime of Regional Development in the Reform Period

Uneven spatial development is a fundamental issue in regional studies. There are different theories of balanced and unbalanced regional development.[3] Neoclassical economic growth theory predicts that regional disparities are unlikely to persist while other scholars have argued that regional development will not necessarily converge.[4] More recently, a new endogenous growth theory has introduced the concept of increasing returns into the production function. It emphasizes the impact of externalities generated by capital investment, human capital, technological change due to "learning by doing," "knowledge spillovers" and deliberate innovations from research and development (R&D). The new theory is closely related to the debate on the process of cumulative causation in regional development. But the socio-institutional context of regional development is often ignored.[5] The institutional approach argues that industrial interdependence and ties of proximity and association, as sources of knowledge and learning, are the basis of regional/local advantages.[6]

The changing regime of regional development in post-reform China is a good example of how institutional arrangements, coupled with various geographical, social and economic conditions, have led to underdevelopment in the western region of China.

During the Maoist era, the Chinese government emphasized policies of even regional development.[7] In the period 1949–1978, some coastal industries were transferred to inland provinces, and some new industrial bases were established there. The most dramatic measure was the implementation of the "Third Front" 三線 policy from 1964 to the early 1970s, mainly due to considerations of national defence. However, even regional development in the country did not result from such policies. Zhao argued that the central planning mechanism could hardly be relied upon to achieve regional equalization in economic development.[8] There was no efficient mechanism to do that and there was also a conflict between the goals of economic development and even spatial distribution. Zheng et al. concluded that China's core and periphery situation has persisted for over 40 years since 1949.[9]

The introduction of economic reforms and the open-door policy in China since 1978 have given rise to new forces of spatial polarization. In 1994, China formally declared the adoption of a socialist market system. Since then, constraints on the private economy have gradually been removed.[10] The mechanism of regional development in the reform period was fundamentally different from that of the pre-reform Maoist period. It is appropriate to describe the pre-reform period as a phase of the socialist planning system that used the top-down centralized development approach, and the reform period as a phase of the socialist market system that is using the bottom-up decentralized development approach.[11] In the pre-reform phase of the socialist planning system, the two major goals of regional policy were regional equality and national defence.

In the reform period of the socialist market system, the major goal of regional policy has been economic growth. The existence of a regional division of labour has been recognized and each region has been encouraged to make use of its own factor endowments or comparative advantages. A model of three economic belts and coastal development strategy was proposed, based on the so-called "ladder-step" doctrine in the 1980s.[12] The influence of western theories of regional development has also increased in China. Fan found that since the late 1980s, the growth pole theory has emerged as an alternative to the "ladder-step" doctrine.[13] China's regional development policy in the reform period has clearly focused on the more developed coastal region, especially in the period 1979–1994 when the region adopted various preferential policies.[14] Heralded by the announcement that a socialist market economy was to be established in China, the gap in policy incentives has narrowed since 1994. The Ninth Five-year Plan (1996–2000) made the reduction of inequality between regions a top policy priority. However, the market economy has tended to favour the coastal region. Thus, by the mid-1990s, attention was once again being paid to the development of the inland region,[15] culminating in 1999 in the strategy of developing the western region.

There are two components in the broad development of political economy in China. The first is the economic reforms, by means of which the central planning system is being replaced by market mechanisms. For example, state investment is playing a decreasing role in capital investment for construction.[16] Among the total of RMB1,266 billion in capital investment in China in 2000, only RMB159 billion came from the state's budget, while RMB359 billion was from domestic loans from banks. On the other hand, RMB523 billion was raised by local governments and enterprises; RMB85 billion was foreign investment and RMB140 billion came from other sources. Among the total capital investment of RMB37 billion in Xinjiang 新疆 in 2000, only RMB4 billion was from the state's budget, while RMB19 billion had been raised by local governments and enterprises. The Chinese government has also steadily decentralized and the power of regional and local governments has increased. Local governments, firms and residents have acquired great power and flexibility in the areas of economic management, operation and competition. Such changes have had a great impact on the economy of the western region, with its dependence on state-owned enterprises (SOEs), few township and village enterprises (TVEs) and undeveloped markets.

The second component is the open-door policy that has been most favourable to coastal areas such as Guangdong 廣東. Owing to the proximity between Hong Kong and Guangdong, in particular the Pearl River Delta 珠江三角洲, Guangdong has been the recipient of about half of the total investment from Hong Kong to Mainland China.[17] But the western region has not been able to attract large-scale foreign investment, due to its peripheral location, inconvenience of transportation, weak economic foundation, undeveloped market economy and slow economic reforms. The impact of the open-door policy and foreign investment on the situation of unbalanced regional development cannot be underestimated.

It is clear that the western region currently faces a new regime of regional development based on the market economy and that this regime has so far been unfavourable to the region. This is the key reason why the central government has introduced special policy measures and financial support to stimulate economic development and increase competitiveness in the western region.

Regional Development in the Western Region

As mentioned before, many scholars have argued that central control over financial resources and the economy limited inequality among regions in the pre-reform period, while others argued that regional inequality in China persisted or even increased in the period due to regional autarky and localism.[18] There is also a keen debate on whether regional disparities have grown or been reduced in the reform period. Some have argued that the gap between regions has increased due to the coastal development strategy and the open-door policy, while others have argued that the gap between regions has been reduced, due to the decline of traditional industrial bases, such as Shanghai 上海 and Liaoning 遼寧 and the rise of the coastal provinces of Guangdong, Fujian 福建, Zhejiang 浙江, Jiangsu 江蘇 and Shandong 山東. Part of the difference is due to the use in analyses of different spatial scales, indicators, methods and periods. Regional inequalities in GDP (gross domestic product) per capita, income, industrial output, state capital investment, fiscal revenue and fiscal expenditure have been analyzed, with different findings.[19]

Wei found that the percentage growth in fiscal expenditure was greater in the western region than in the eastern region in the period 1952–1978, while the percentage growth was close in two regions in the period 1978–1991. But in both periods, the percentage growth in national income per capita was smaller in the western region than the eastern region.[20]

The regional gap among the eastern, central and western regions is different from the regional gap among provinces as they refer to two spatial scales. Fujita and Hu conducted a comprehensive study of regional development in China.[21] They found that the regional disparity in GDP per capita between coastal and inland areas increased in the period 1985–1994, especially in the 1990s. They argued that the role of state policy in regional development has been exaggerated in previous studies, as globalization, economic liberalization and production agglomeration are also important factors.

This section attempts to analyze the inequality between the western and eastern regions and among provinces in the western region in 1952–2000, using GDP per capita. GDP data based on constant prices are used because GDP data based on current-year prices tended to significantly affect the regional inequality indicator of GDP per capita, as was found in an earlier study for the period 1978–1994.[22] Population data and GDP data have been collected from various sources to estimate GDP per capita for five years: 1952, 1978, 1982, 1990 and 2000.[23] The year 1952 is the earliest year for which reliable data are available, while 1978 represents the end of the pre-reform period. The years 1982, 1990 and 2000 have been chosen because reliable population data from population censuses are available for those years. The main results are presented in Tables 8.1–8.4.

Considering the pre-reform period 1952–1978, the GDP share of the western region increased from 21.86% to 21.98%, following a similar trend in the eastern region (Table 8.1). The average annual growth rate of GDP in the western and eastern regions was higher than that in the central region in the period 1953–1978 (Table 8.2). However, the western region had the lowest GDP per capita in 1952, just 77.77% of the national average. Its relative level of GDP per capita was further reduced to 76.62% in 1952–1978 due to rapid population growth (Table 8.3). The annual growth rate in GDP per capita in the western region in the period 1953–1978 was only 3.64%, below the national average (Table 8.4). It is clear that a weak

Table 8.1 Share of GDP of Various Regions in China, 1952–2000

(Unit: %)

Region	1952	1978	1982	1990	2000
China	100	100	100	100	100
Eastern	41.68	47.51	47.84	50.82	57.29
Central	36.47	30.51	30.20	28.30	25.58
Western	21.85	21.98	21.96	20.88	17.13
	Share of GDP (Western region = 100)				
Inner Mongolia	7.41	7.56	8.08	8.40	8.41
Guangxi	10.55	12.61	12.74	10.45	12.31
Chongqing	11.58	10.07	10.23	9.59	9.54
Sichuan	28.42	24.73	25.12	23.56	24.08
Guizhou	7.61	6.31	6.58	6.59	5.97
Yunnan	10.65	11.05	11.24	12.25	11.74
Tibet	1.21	0.76	0.89	0.68	0.71
Shaanxi	7.82	9.77	9.38	10.61	9.97
Gansu	6.29	6.50	5.23	6.07	5.90
Qinghai	1.28	2.38	2.05	1.83	1.58
Ningxia	0.80	1.70	1.58	1.78	1.59
Xinjiang	6.39	6.57	6.88	8.20	8.19

Sources: Calculated on the basis of GDP data at constant prices. GDP data in 2000 are from NBS, *China Statistical Yearbook 2001* (see note 16). GDP data in 1952, 1978, 1982 and 1990 at 2000 prices, calculated using the GDP in 2000 and the development index estimated by the authors (see note 23).

Table 8.2 Annual GDP Growth Rates and Relative Annual GDP Growth Rates in Various Regions in China, 1952–2000

(Unit: %)

Region	1953–1978	1979–1990	1991–2000
China	5.87	9.28	11.94
Eastern	6.40	9.90	13.29
Central	5.14	8.60	10.81
Western	5.89	8.82	9.75
Relative annual GDP growth rate (Western region = 100)			
Inner Mongolia	101.42	110.87	100.18
Guangxi	112.35	80.83	118.63
Chongqing	90.40	95.03	99.40
Sichuan	90.40	95.03	102.47
Guizhou	87.09	104.54	88.83
Yunnan	102.57	110.64	95.21
Tibet	68.44	87.65	104.54
Shaanxi	115.45	108.49	93.08
Gansu	102.30	93.06	96.81
Qinghai	143.58	73.44	83.72
Ningxia	152.35	104.77	87.90
Xinjiang	101.92	122.90	99.93

Source: See Table 8.1.

economic foundation in 1952 and rapid population growth during 1952–1978 were key factors for the low GDP per capita in the western region in 1978, although its GDP growth rate was slightly higher than the national average during that period.

It is also interesting to look at the different rates of development within the western region, a subject that has rarely been examined. According to Table 8.1, the GDP shares of Inner Mongolia 內蒙古, Guangxi 廣西, Yunnan 雲南, Shaanxi 陝西, Gansu 甘肅, Qinghai 青海, Ningxia 寧夏 and Xinjiang more or less increased in the pre-reform period 1952–1978. Only four regions, including Chongqing 重慶, Sichuan 四川, Guizhou 貴州 and Tibet 西藏 experienced a decline in their GDP share in China in this period. The annual GDP growth rate in these regions was lower than the average in the western region (Table 8.2).

The GDP per capita in Inner Mongolia, Chongqing, Tibet, Qinghai and Xinjiang were above the average for the western region in 1952 (Table 8.3). By 1978, GDP per capita in these regions, plus Guangxi and Ningxia, was higher than the average for the western region. The relatively high

Table 8.3 Relative Levels of GDP Per Capita of Various Regions in China, 1952–2000

(Unit: %)

Region	1952	1978	1982	1990	2000
China	100	100	100	100	100
Eastern	107.68	126.71	127.54	134.91	147.18
Central	109.86	90.22	89.28	83.62	77.68
Western	77.77	76.62	76.62	73.30	60.87
	Relative GDP per capita (Western region = 100)				
Inner Mongolia	162.73	113.99	120.60	126.04	125.80
Guangxi	85.42	101.87	100.63	79.62	97.43
Chongqing	102.15	105.02	108.79	107.04	109.73
Sichuan	96.60	96.12	99.49	96.80	102.72
Guizhou	80.32	64.55	66.31	65.52	60.13
Yunnan	98.82	98.28	99.38	106.69	97.27
Tibet	165.73	117.52	135.41	99.34	95.65
Shaanxi	80.51	96.64	93.38	103.87	98.29
Gansu	92.87	95.55	76.96	87.43	81.89
Qinghai	124.58	179.11	151.10	132.28	108.56
Ningxia	89.08	131.14	116.59	122.88	100.81
Xinjiang	216.32	146.59	151.40	174.16	151.21

Source: Calculated on the basis of GDP data at constant prices and population data (see note 23).

GDP per capita at constant prices in Qinghai and Xinjiang was consistent with GDP per capita based on the current-year price. In 1952, GDP per capita at the current-year price in Qinghai and Xinjiang was RMB101 and RMB170, respectively, while that in Guizhou was only RMB57. The situation was similar in 1978, when GDP per capita at the current-year price in Qinghai and Xinjiang were RMB426 and RMB317, respectively, while that in Guizhou was only RMB154. According to Table 8.3, it is clear that Qinghai, Ningxia and Xinjiang had a relatively higher level of development in 1978, while Guizhou was less developed within the western region. However, the annual growth rate of GDP per capita was lowest in Tibet and Xinjiang but highest in Qinghai and Ningxia in the period 1952–1978 (Table 8.4). High GDP per capita in Xinjiang in 1978 had much to do with its good economic foundation in 1952, while Qinghai and Ningxia did achieve significant growth in 1952–1978.

With the introduction of economic reforms and the open-door policy in China in 1978, the economic and policy environments have become

Table 8.4 Annual Growth Rates and Relative Annual Growth Rates of GDP Per Capita in Various Regions of China, 1952–2000

(Unit: %)

Region	1953–1978	1979–1990	1991–2000
China	3.70	7.79	10.71
Eastern	4.35	8.36	11.68
Central	2.92	7.11	9.90
Western	3.64	7.39	8.67
Relative annual growth rate of GDP per capita (Western region = 100)			
Inner Mongolia	61.31	112.22	99.76
Guangxi	119.34	70.48	125.55
Chongqing	103.03	102.31	103.11
Sichuan	99.46	100.85	107.46
Guizhou	76.18	101.82	89.28
Yunnan	99.40	109.98	88.48
Tibet	62.63	79.80	95.27
Shaanxi	120.06	108.75	93.11
Gansu	103.12	89.28	91.82
Qinghai	140.02	63.77	75.48
Ningxia	142.65	92.14	75.45
Xinjiang	57.73	121.01	82.42

Source: See Table 8.3.

unfavourable to the western region due to its weak economic foundation and disadvantageous geographical conditions. As shown in Table 8.1, the western region's share of the national GDP declined steadily from 21.98% in 1978 to 20.88% in 1990 and 17.13% in 2000. The drop in the 1990s was the most significant, even though the state replaced its biased coastal development strategy in 1996 with a co-ordinated strategy of regional development. Weak economic competitiveness in an emerging market economy and delayed institutional reform are the main causes of poor economic performance.

However, GDP growth in the western region was still remarkable. Annual GDP growth rates were 8.82% and 9.75% in the periods 1979–1990 and 1991–2000, respectively (Table 8.2). Indeed, the GDP growth rates in the western region in the reform period were much higher than in the pre-reform period. At the same time, they were lower than the national average. As a result, the relative level of GDP per capita in the western region fell from 76.62% of the national average in 1978 to just 60.87% in 2000 (Table 8.3). The growth rates of GDP per capita in the western region were 7.39% and 8.67% in the periods 1979–1990 and 1991–2000, respectively, lower than the national average (Table 8.3). Clearly, the gap in GDP per capita between the western and eastern regions further widened in the reform period.

Within the western region, there were noticeable changes in regional development (Table 8.1). The rising trend of GDP share in the pre-reform period reversed into a declining trend in Guangxi, Gansu, Qinghai and Ningxia in the reform period. The GDP shares of Inner Mongolia, Yunnan, Shaanxi and Xinjiang continued to rise in the period 1979–2000 following rising trends in the pre-reform period. The GDP shares of Chongqing, Sichuan, Guizhou and Tibet declined in both the pre-reform and reform periods. But there was a rebound in Sichuan and Tibet in 1990–2000.

The annual GDP growth rate in Inner Mongolia, Guizhou, Yunnan, Shaanxi, Ningxia and Xinjiang was higher than the average in the western region in the period 1979–1990 (Table 8.2). But only Inner Mongolia, Guangxi, Sichuan and Tibet had a higher GDP growth rate than the average in the western region in 1991–2000. The GDP growth rate was particularly small, below 90% of the average growth rate in the western region, in Guizhou, Qinghai and Ningxia in the 1990s.

As a result, relative GDP per capita improved only in Inner Mongolia, Chongqing, Sichuan and Shaanxi after 1978, while it declined in the remaining provinces in the western region (Table 8.3). The increase in GDP per capita in Chongqing was partly due to its slow population growth in 1979–2000. The annual growth rate of GDP per capita was lower than the regional average in Tibet, Gansu, Qinghai and Ningxia in the whole period 1979–2000 but higher than the regional average in Chongqing and Sichuan (Table 8.4). Inner Mongolia, Guizhou, Yunnan, Shaanxi and Xinjiang had an annual per capita GDP growth rate higher than the regional average in 1979–1990 but lower than the regional average in 1991–2000. On the other hand, Guangxi's annual per capita GDP growth rate was lower than the regional average in 1979–1990 but higher than the regional average in 1991–2000.

The above analysis based on GDP data at constant prices revealed the patterns of regional development in the pre-reform and reform periods. The GDP growth rate in the western region was higher than the national average in the pre-reform period, so that its GDP share increased slightly. But due to rapid population growth, its per capita GDP growth rate was lower than the national average. Thus, the relative level of GDP per capita in the western region, as a percentage of the national average, declined even in the pre-reform period. In the reform period, the growth rates of GDP and GDP per capita in the western region were lower than the national average, due to unfavourable development conditions mentioned before. Thus, the gap in development between the western region and the eastern region further widened during the reform period.

It is important to note that the western region's low level of development in 1952 (22.23% lower than the national average) was largely responsible for its low level of development in 1978, reflecting historical conditions or path-dependency, as its GDP growth rate was actually slightly greater than the national average. But the low rate of economic growth in the reform period further reduced the level of development in the western region (15.75 percentage points lower than the relative level in 1978). Clearly, geographical constraints, historical legacy, regional policies and development processes are four key factors in underdevelopment in the western region.

Inequality within the western region is a complicated issue. In the pre-reform period, relative GDP per capita improved in Guangxi, Chongqing, Shaanxi, Gansu, Qinghai and Ningxia. In the reform period, relative GDP per capita improved in Inner Mongolia, Chongqing, Sichuan, Shaanxi, Gansu and Xinjiang. By 2000, Guizhou and Gansu were the least developed areas, with a GDP per capita of less than 82% of the average for the western region. On the other hand, Xinjiang was the most developed area, with a GDP per capita 51% greater than the average for the western region. The GDP per capita in the remaining provinces was in the range of 90% to 110% of the average for the western region.

Comparative and Competitive Disadvantages in the Western Region

The low level of development in the western region has much to do with its comparative and competitive disadvantages, which are the focus of this section. The environmental and ecological problems in the western region are discussed in detail in Chapter 3.

One myth about the western region is that its territory is huge and there is a relatively large amount of land per capita. State-organized migration for agricultural development in the 1950s and 1960s was largely based on such a promise.[24] The available information shows that, except for some areas, there is little room in the western region for extensive agricultural development, and the region is facing mounting ecological pressures. Table 8.5 presents a set of data to show in a straightforward manner that arable land and grain output on a per capita basis are not adequate in the western region and are below the national average when various factors are taken into consideration.

Using the total population as the base population, arable land per capita in the western region was 0.14 ha, 40% greater than the national average and 100% greater than in the eastern region in 2000. However, because industrialization and urbanization are at much higher levels in the eastern region, direct population pressure on arable land there was not 100% greater than in the western region. Thus, considering the rural population as the base population, arable land per person was 0.18 ha in the western region, compared with a national average of 0.14 ha and an average of 0.10 ha for the eastern region. Different age structures and dependency ratios also had a slight impact on arable land per person. Using the rural labour force as the base population, arable land per person at working age was 0.34 ha in the western region, compared with a national average of 0.27 ha and an average of 0.19 ha for the eastern region.

As a large part of the rural labour force in the eastern region is actually engaged in non-agricultural sectors, arable land per person at working age in rural areas in the eastern region would be much closer to the western region if the agricultural labour force in rural areas were used as the population base. In this case, arable land per person would be 0.45 ha in the western region, 0.32 ha in the eastern region and 0.40 ha for China as a whole in 2000. The western region only had a slight advantage over the eastern region in land resources.

The small cropping index in the western region would further reduce the above advantage. Taking into account of the cropping index, the cropping area per agricultural person at working age in rural areas was only 0.45 ha in the western region, slightly lower than the 0.46 ha for the eastern region and 0.48 ha for China as a whole.

Considering the low grain yields in the western region, it is not surprising that grain output per person in rural areas is quite low in the western region. In 2000, grain output per person, using the total population as the base, was 363 kg in the western region, lower than the national average of 365 kg but greater than the 308 kg for the eastern region. Guangxi, Guizhou, Yunnan, Shaanxi, Gansu and Qinghai were particularly poor. In these regions, grain output per capita in 2000 was only 340 kg, 329 kg, 342 kg, 302 kg, 278 kg and 160 kg, respectively. The western region itself may not have sufficient revenue to buy grain from elsewhere, while the

Table 8.5 Arable Land and Grain Output on a Per Capita Basis in the Western Region and China, 2000

Region	Arable land per person based on the following				Cropping area per agricultural person in rural areas	Grain output per person based on total population	Grain output per agricultural person in rural areas
	Total population	Rural population	Rural labour force	Agricultural labour force in rural areas			
	Ha	Ha	Ha	Ha	Ha	Kg	Kg
China	0.10	0.14	0.27	0.40	0.48	365	1,409
Eastern	0.07	0.10	0.19	0.32	0.46	308	1,507
Central	0.12	0.15	0.30	0.41	0.52	438	1,557
Western	0.14	0.18	0.34	0.45	0.45	363	1,164
Inner Mongolia	0.35	0.60	1.30	1.56	1.13	523	2,369
Guangxi	0.10	0.11	0.21	0.28	0.40	340	982
Chongqing	0.08	0.10	0.18	0.26	0.39	358	1,201
Sichuan	0.08	0.10	0.18	0.26	0.37	405	1,282
Guizhou	0.14	0.16	0.27	0.36	0.34	329	846
Yunnan	0.15	0.19	0.33	0.38	0.35	342	877
Tibet	0.14	0.17	0.36	0.40	0.26	367	1,068
Shaanxi	0.14	0.19	0.38	0.51	0.45	302	1,087
Gansu	0.20	0.25	0.54	0.72	0.54	278	1,023
Qinghai	0.13	0.20	0.40	0.48	0.39	160	581
Ningxia	0.23	0.33	0.64	0.83	0.66	450	1,650
Xinjiang	0.21	0.44	1.13	1.27	1.08	407	2,492

Source: Calculated by the authors based on data from *China Statistical Yearbook 2001* (see note 16).

eastern region may have little difficulty in purchasing sufficient grain from domestic or international markets.

On the other hand, grain output per agricultural person at working age in rural areas, a measure of agricultural labour productivity, was only 1,164 kg in the western region, the lowest among the three regions in China. It was particularly low, less than 1,000 kg, in Guangxi, Guizhou, Yunnan and Qinghai. The low agricultural productivity makes it hard for the western region to move beyond subsistence agriculture for industrialization and urbanization, at least in the initial stage. The region has great difficulty in balancing food supply against population growth. External grain transfers and financial subsidies, as proposed in the strategy to develop the western region, will be very helpful in lifting the region out of the vicious cycle of population growth and underdevelopment.

Poor agricultural production is coupled with structural and competitive disadvantages in the western region. To analyze the structural advantage/disadvantage and competitiveness of the primary, secondary and tertiary sectors in the western region and in China in general, data on GDP per employee for three economic sectors have been calculated for various regions.[25] For China as a whole, GDP per employee was RMB4,450, 36,699 and 21,332 in the primary, secondary and tertiary sectors, respectively, in 2000. GDP per employee was highest in the secondary sector and lowest in the primary sector. This pattern was the same for the western region, where GDP per employee was RMB3,289, 29,278 and 13,024 in the primary, secondary and tertiary sectors, respectively, in 2000.

The level of development in an area depends on the area's structural advantage (a higher proportion of workers in a sector with a higher GDP per employee) as well as competitive advantage (a higher rate of GDP per employee than other areas in the same sector). The GDP per employee in an area can be decomposed into four components; that is, the national average, structural advantage, competitive advantage and a small adjustment item reflecting the interaction between competitive advantage and structural advantage. An area will have an average GDP per employee for the country if its economic structure and economic performance in each sector are identical with those of the national economy. However, an area will have a structural advantage if it specializes in a sector with a higher GDP per employee, such as the secondary sector. An area will have a competitive advantage if its GDP per employee in a sector is higher than the average GDP per employee in the same sector of the country.

Figure 8.1 presents the results of the decomposition analysis. It is clear that the low level of development in the western region was primarily due to the poor competitiveness of its three sectors. GDP per employee in the western region was lower than the national average in each of the three economic sectors. Furthermore, the western region also had a serious structural disadvantage. It had a small share in the secondary sector, which has the highest GDP per employee in economies all over the country. With a few exceptions, such a double disadvantage prevailed in most provincial regions in western China. For example, Guizhou was the poorest province in China with a GDP per employee of only RMB4,856 in 2000. It suffered from a competitive disadvantage of RMB8,434 and a structural disadvantage of RMB4,050. On the other hand, Tibet had a slight positive competitive advantage in the secondary and tertiary sectors. But due to a significant structural disadvantage of RMB5,666 per employee, overall GDP per employee was only RMB9,522 in Tibet, lower than the national average. Xinjiang had a significant competitive advantage in the secondary sector with a high GDP per employee of RMB63,273. As a result, Xinjiang's GDP per employee was RMB20,288, higher than the national average.

The above analysis reveals that, except for Xinjiang, most provincial regions in western China have a low level of development, due to significant

Figure 8.1 GDP per Employee and Its Components in Various Regions in 2000

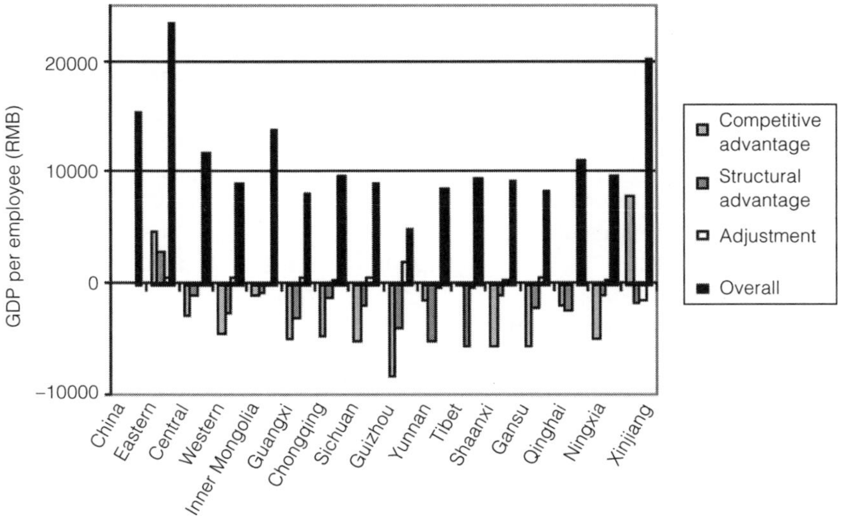

competitive and/or structural disadvantages. Such disadvantages pose a major challenge to the western region.

Urbanization and Urban System

Urbanization is an important process associated with economic development and modernization. Rapid urbanization has taken place in China during the reform period. Under a new model of dual-track urbanization, there has been a rapid increase in the non-agricultural population and temporary population in urban areas, along with rural urbanization.[26] However, urbanization has occurred at a much slower pace in the western region than in the country as a whole.

Among the total population of 355 million in the western region in 2000, 102 million were classified as belonging to the urban population. The western region accounted for 21.9% of China's urban population. Table 8.6 presents some key urban and economic indicators in China in 2000. The level of urbanization, that is, the percentage of the urban population in the total population, was 36.2% in China and as high as 46.1% in the eastern region in 2000. But it was only 28.7% in the western region. Within the western region, the level of urbanization varied from 18.9% in Tibet to as high as 42.7% in Inner Mongolia in 2000. The level of urbanization was over 30% in Chongqing, Shaanxi, Qinghai, Ningxia and Xinjiang, and was close to the national average. However, it was below 30% in the populous provinces of Guangxi, Sichuan, Guizhou, Yunnan and Gansu, each with a

Table 8.6 Key Urban and Economic Indicators in Various Regions of China, 2000

Indicator	Eastern region	Central region	Western region	China
Share of urban population (%)	46.1	33.0	28.7	36.2
Share of rural population (%)	53.9	67.0	71.3	63.8
GDP per capita (RMB)	11,334	5,982	4,687	7,701
Average staff wage (RMB)	11,529	7,440	8,321	9,371
Income per urban resident (RMB)	7,929	5,191	5,642	6,554
Net income per rural resident (RMB)	3,200	2,071	1,691	2,367
Cities per million population[1]	0.57	0.55	0.45	0.53
Cities per million km^2	272	138	24	72

Note: [1] Number of cities refers to year 1999.

Sources: Calculated from data in the *China Statistical Yearbook 2001* (see note 16); *Zhongguo chengshi tongji nianjian 2000* (see note 27).

population of over 25 million. Urbanization has a long way to go in these provinces.

Proportionally speaking, there was only 0.45 of a city for each million inhabitants in the western region, while the figure was 0.57 in the eastern region. In terms of city density, there were only 24 cities per million km^2 in the western region, but 272 cities per million km^2 in the eastern region. Clearly, cities in the western region are sparsely distributed. But it is noticeable that Inner Mongolia, Guangxi, Chongqing, Sichuan, Yunnan and Shaanxi each already had a large urban population of over 10 million in 2000. The challenge of promoting further urbanization is enormous.

GDP per capita was RMB11,334 in the eastern region, but only RMB4,687 in the western region in 2000. The small figure for GDP per capita in the western region has much to do with its low level of urbanization, related to the structural disadvantage found previously. In 2000, the average staff wage and income per urban resident was only slightly lower in the western region than in the eastern region. But the per capita income of urban residents was generally more than twice of that of rural residents. A low level of urbanization means a low GDP per capita for the region as a whole. Furthermore, the net income per rural resident in the western region was only about half of that in the eastern region. Speeding up urbanization in the western region would dramatically reduce the gap in development between the eastern and western regions. This section comprehensively analyzes the urban system in the western region, comparing it with the eastern region.

According to the *Urban Statistical Yearbook of China 2000*,[27] there were 159 cities in the western region and 667 cities in China in 1999. But data on GDP are not available for Lhasa 拉薩市 and Xigaze 日喀則市 in Tibet, Arxan 阿爾山市 in Inner Mongolia and Shihezi 石河子市 in Xinjiang. Of these four cities, only Lhasa is a prefectural-level city and other three are county-level cities. A prefectural-level city is an administrative unit between a provincial and county-level unit in China. The analysis in the chapter excludes the above four cities and is mostly based on the 155 cities in the western region and the 663 cities in the nation as a whole. All of the data refer to urban proper; any county or county-level city under the administration of a prefectural-level city is excluded.

Table 8.7 presents the number of cities of various sizes in the eastern, central and western regions in China in 1999. Cities are divided into six categories according to the size of their non-agricultural population: mega-cities each with a non-agricultural population of over 2 million, super-large

Table 8.7 Distribution of Cities by the Size of the Non-agricultural Population in Urban Proper in Various Regions in China, 1999

City-size (thousand)	2,000+	1,000–2,000	500–1,000	200–500	50–200	0–50	Total
				Number of cities			
China	13	24	49	216	342	23	667
Eastern	7	11	23	96	137	7	281
Central	3	8	22	74	115	5	227
Western	3	5	4	46	90	11	159
Inner Mongolia	0	1	1	6	10	2	20
Guangxi	0	0	2	4	11	2	19
Chongqing	1	0	0	2	2	0	5
Sichuan	1	0	0	13	17	0	31
Guizhou	0	1	0	3	8	1	13
Yunnan	0	1	0	2	11	1	15
Tibet	0	0	0	0	1	1	2
Shaanxi	1	0	0	5	7	0	13
Gansu	0	1	0	2	9	2	14
Qinghai	0	0	1	0	1	1	3
Ningxia	0	0	0	2	3	0	5
Xinjiang	0	1	0	7	10	1	19
			Population required for each city (million)				
China	97	53	26	6	4	55	2
Eastern	70	45	21	5	4	70	2
Central	139	52	19	6	4	83	2
Western	118	71	89	8	4	32	2
Inner Mongolia		24	24	4	2	12	1
Guangxi			22	11	4	22	2
Chongqing	31			15	15		6
Sichuan	83			6	5		3
Guizhou		35		12	4	35	3
Yunnan		43		21	4	43	3
Tibet					3	3	1
Shaanxi	36			7	5		3
Gansu		26		13	3	13	2
Qinghai			5		5	5	2
Ningxia				3	2		1
Xinjiang		19		3	2	19	1

Note: A blank space means that there is no such city in an area.
Source: See Table 8.6.

cities of 1–2 million, large cities of 500–1,000 thousand, medium cities with 200–500 thousand, small cities of 50–200 thousand and tiny cities with a non-agricultural population of less than 50 thousand.

Among the 159 cities in the western region, there were only 3 mega-cities, 5 super-large cities and 4 large cities. The number of super-large cities and large cities was comparatively small. For example, in the western region, only 2.5% of cities were large cities, compared to 8.2% in the eastern region. The absence of large cities means that there are few strong economic centres to drive industrialization and development in the western region.

One important issue of urban development is the relationship between the size of a city and the level of economic development. Table 8.8 presents the data for three regions in China. It is clear that the average GDP per capita, using the total population as a base, generally increases with a city's size, and this regularity holds in the western region as well. The only exception is for tiny cities with a non-agricultural population of less than 50,000. The average GDP per capita in such tiny cities is larger than that in small cities in the western and central regions. This is because the percentage of the non-agricultural population in tiny cities is higher, and in China, the non-agricultural population generally has a higher income than the agricultural population. According to Table 8.8, the percentage of the non-agricultural population was 27.6% for tiny cities, but only 23.5% for small cities in the western region.

Table 8.8 GDP per Capita and Percentage of the Non-agricultural Population in Cities of Various Sizes in China, 1999

City-size (thousand)	2,000+	1,000–2,000	500–1,000	200–500	50–200	0–50	Total
			GDP per capita (RMB)				
China	19,916	17,622	17,113	9,671	7,866	8,122	11,605
Eastern	24,305	21,042	21,144	12,491	10,723	9,226	15,211
Central	15,340	14,223	12,658	7,100	5,660	7,967	8,340
Western	11,933	14,996	11,992	7,024	5,314	5,612	7,851
			Percentage of Non-agricultural Population (%)				
China	70.8	76.2	68.2	37.1	21.2	18.0	41.2
Eastern	78.0	74.1	61.8	34.5	19.4	11.8	41.6
Central	68.2	77.6	75.6	38.8	22.0	27.5	41.5
Western	53.3	79.1	75.2	40.9	23.5	27.6	39.8

Source: Calculated based on data from *Zhongguo chengshi tongji nianjian 2000* (see note 27).

Comparing cities of the same size in the western and eastern regions, the average GDP per capita in the western region was smaller than that in the eastern region. For example, the average per capita GDP in large cities in 1999 was RMB11,992 in the western region, but as high as RMB21,144 in the eastern region. Similarly, the average GDP per capita in small cities was RMB10,723 in the eastern region but only RMB5,314 in the western region. The above gap in GDP per capita between the eastern and western cities is due to different urban economic efficiency and urban competitiveness in the two regions, rather than to the share of the non-agricultural population in the total urban population. Indeed, the percentage of the non-agricultural population in all cities except mega-cities was higher in the western region than in the eastern region. In a word, the western region is behind the eastern region both in state-sponsored and spontaneous urban development. Inefficient SOEs and less-developed TVEs in the western region confirm such a status.

Table 8.9 presents further information on the per capita GDP of provincial units in the western region by city size. It is clear that the level of economic development was highest in cities with a non-agricultural population of over 0.5 million in all western provincial units except Chongqing and Qinghai. Their GDP per capita, over RMB10,000, was close

Table 8.9 GDP per Capita in Cities of Various Sizes in the Western Region, 1999

(Unit: RMB)

City-size (thousand)	2,000+	1,000–2,000	500–1,000	200–500	50–200	0–50	Total
Western region	11,933	14,996	11,992	7,024	5,314	5,612	7,851
Inner Mongolia		12,902	10,346	6,275	7,263	16,911	8,263
Guangxi			15,180	7,503	4,341	9,849	6,896
Chongqing	8,520			5,191	4,857		7,297
Sichuan	18,933			6,379	5,108		7,292
Guizhou		10,192		5,267	3,428	4,757	5,350
Yunnan		22,120		9,512	8,997	6,844	12,137
Shaanxi	13,409			8,599	3,286		8,659
Gansu		12,253		5,256	5,011	4,746	6,933
Qinghai			6,214		14,259	4,995	6,828
Ningxia				10,571	6,023		8,449
Xinjiang		16,197		12,233	5,748	1,942	10,537

Note: Data for Tibet are not available. A blank space means that there is no such city in an area.

Source: See Table 8.8.

to the national average. The least developed were small cities in Shaanxi and Guizhou with a non-agricultural population of 50,000–200,000 and the only tiny city, Artux 阿圖什市, in Xinjiang, which had a GDP per capita of below RMB3,500. Comparing cities in various provincial units in the western region, cities in Yunnan and Xinjiang had the highest GDP per capita in 1999, at over RMB10,000. On average, in the same year, cities in Guizhou had the lowest GDP per capita, at below RMB5,400.

It is useful to examine the structure of the urban system in the western region both in terms of administrative status and population size, as these are widely considered to influence urban development in China's transitional economy, characterized as it is by strong state power and emerging market forces such as agglomeration economies.[28]

In terms of administrative status, there are four kinds of cities in China: provincial level (such as the municipalities of Shanghai, Beijing 北京, Tianjin 天津 and Chongqing), pro-provincial level, prefectural level and county level. Municipalities are directly under the administration of the central government. They are the most powerful of all of the cities in China, and have the legislative power to enact regional laws. The category of pro-provincial cities 副省級市 was introduced in the reform period; the status of such cities is higher than that of a prefectural-level city but lower than that of a municipality. Pro-provincial cities enjoy a certain power of decision-making and economic administration in a province. In national economic plans, they are listed as independent entities, along with provinces. Some of them also have the power to enact regional laws. They have a great deal of power in economic administration, but they are still under the administration of provincial governments. A prefectural-level city can administer, directly or on behalf of its provincial government, other counties or county-level cities. County-level cities are at the bottom of the urban hierarchy. In 1999, there were 4 municipalities, 15 pro-provincial cities, 221 prefecture level cities and 427 county level cities in China (Table 8.10).

In 1999, the eastern region had 3 municipalities and 10 pro-provincial cities while the western region only had 1 municipality and 2 pro-provincial cities. The western region had fewer cities than the eastern region even when the population factor was taken into account. In the eastern region, there was, on average, one municipality for 164 million people and one pro-provincial city for 49 million people. But in the western region, 355 million people were "needed" for one municipality and as many as 178 million people for one pro-provincial city. In the western region, most

Table 8.10 Distribution of Cities by Administrative Status, 1999

Region	Municipality	Pro-provincial city	Prefectural-level city	County-level city	Total
		Number of cities			
China	4	15	221	427	667
Eastern	3	10	85	183	281
Central	0	3	84	140	227
Western	1	2	52	104	159
Inner Mongolia	0	0	5	15	20
Guangxi	0	0	9	10	19
Chongqing	1	0	0	4	5
Sichuan	0	1	13	17	31
Guizhou	0	0	3	10	13
Yunnan	0	0	3	12	15
Tibet	0	0	1	1	2
Shaanxi	0	1	7	5	13
Gansu	0	0	5	9	14
Qinghai	0	0	1	2	3
Ningxia	0	0	3	2	5
Xinjiang	0	0	2	17	19
		Population required for each city (million)			
China	316	84	6	3	2
Eastern	164	49	6	3	2
Central		139	5	3	2
Western	355	178	7	3	2
Inner Mongolia			5	2	1
Guangxi			5	4	2
Chongqing	31			8	6
Sichuan		83	6	5	3
Guizhou			12	4	3
Yunnan			14	4	3
Tibet			3	3	1
Shaanxi		36	5	7	3
Gansu			5	3	2
Qinghai			5	3	2
Ningxia			2	3	1
Xinjiang			10	1	1

Note: A blank space means that there is no such city in an area.
Source: See Table 8.6.

provincial units only had prefectural-level cities. The exception is Chongqing, which is a municipality, and Sichuan and Shaanxi, which each has one pro-provincial city. It is clear that the western region does not have adequate urban centres with pro-provincial status. Such cities should be increased to enhance their administrative and economic power to act as growth poles to develop the western region.

In terms of city-size distribution, it has been mentioned that there are few super-large and large cities in the western region. Table 8.7 also presents the distribution of cities of various sizes in the western provinces and the population "required" for a city of a specific size. In the western region, there was a mega city for 118 million people, a super-large city for 71 million people and a large city for 89 million people. In the eastern region, the number of population "required" is much smaller: 70 million for a mega city, 45 million for a super-large city and 21 million for a large city. In the western region, only Chongqing, Sichuan and Shaanxi each had a mega city, while Inner Mongolia, Guizhou, Yunnan, Gansu and Xinjiang each had a super-large city. Guangxi had two large cities while Qinghai has one large city. On the other hand, Tibet and Ningxia had no large city at all. This may not be a problem as the population of Tibet and Ningxia numbered only about 2.6 and 5.6 million, respectively.

Table 8.11 lists the top 23 western cities with a non-agricultural population of over 0.4 million in 1999, and presents their non-agricultural population, GDP and their rank in the western region and nationally. Among these cities, Chongqing is a municipality while Xi'an 西安 and Chengdu 成都 are pro-provincial cities. The remaining are all prefectural-level cities. They are the key economic centres in the western region. Two were among the top 10 cities and five among the top 20 in terms of non-agricultural population in China. One western city was among the top 10 cities while four western cities were among the top 20 in terms of GDP in China.

Clearly, except for a few cities, economic centres in the western region are relatively weak. There are few large cities with an administrative status at the pro-provincial level. In most cases, each provincial unit only has one large city, not enough to support economic development in its huge hinterland. Due to the long distances between main cities, spatial economic links tend to be weak, further constraining economic development in the western region. Thus, much needs to be done to strengthen the economic competitiveness of these cities to lead economic development effectively in the western region.

Table 8.11 The Non-agricultural Population, GDP and Their Ranks in the Western Region and China of the Top 23 Western Cities with a Non-agricultural Population of over 0.4 Million, 1999

City	Provincial unit	Non-agricultural population			GDP		
		Population (million)	Rank in western region	Rank in China	GDP (RMB billion)	Rank in western region	Rank in China
Chongqing	Chongqing	3.65	1	6	71.8	1	8
Xi'an	Shaanxi	2.44	2	10	51.4	3	16
Chengdu	Sichuan	2.21	3	11	62.5	2	12
Kunming	Yunnan	1.46	4	18	45.6	4	20
Lanzhou	Gansu	1.45	5	20	21.8	7	52
Guiyang	Guizhou	1.36	6	24	18.4	9	58
Urumqi	Xinjiang	1.29	7	26	23.2	5	47
Baotou	Inner Mongolia	1.11	8	32	17.5	10	65
Nanning	Guangxi	0.96	9	39	19.8	8	55
Hohhot	Inner Mongolia	0.78	10	50	10.9	13	121
Liuzhou 柳州	Guangxi	0.78	11	51	13.7	12	91
Xining	Qinghai	0.61	12	62	5.7	35	296
Panzhihua	Sichuan	0.49	13	87	9.2	16	151
Zunyi 遵義	Guizhou	0.48	14	92	6.1	31	269
Xianyang	Shaanxi	0.48	15	95	9.6	15	144
Yinchuan	Ningxia	0.48	16	96	6.8	25	237
Guilin 桂林	Guangxi	0.47	17	97	8.9	18	162
Zigong	Sichuan	0.47	18	98	8.2	19	182
Chifeng 赤峰	Inner Mongolia	0.47	19	99	6.2	28	262
Baoji	Shaanxi	0.46	20	102	8.9	17	160
Mianyang	Sichuan	0.41	21	113	14.2	11	83
Leshan	Sichuan	0.41	22	114	6.3	26	259
Nanchong	Sichuan	0.41	23	115	6.1	32	276

Source: See Table 8.8.

Strategies of Urban and Regional Development

Economic development in China in the reform period has focused on the coastal areas, while the areas along the Yangzi River 長江 have received increasing attention since the opening of Pudong 浦東 in Shanghai in 1990. A T-form spatial strategy has emerged in China. Nevertheless, the most rapid development has taken place in the coastal areas, creating a dominant growth axis in China, while areas in the lower and middle reaches of the

Yangzi River such as Anhui 安徽, Jiangxi 江西, Hubei 湖北, Hunan 湖南 and Chongqing have also begun to develop.

Indeed, open-door policies have been extended to many areas in the central and western regions of China since Deng Xiaoping's 鄧小平 famous tour to southern China in 1992. But being at an initial stage of industrialization, the western region will not catch up with development in the eastern region in next 10 to 20 years. According to current conditions in the western region, a suitable regional development strategy would be a "nodes and axes-based development model" combined with a "network-based development model."

There are two main reasons for this. First, an important cause of underdevelopment in the western region is that the cities there are small and sparsely distributed. The western region should make full use of the strategy to develop the western region and of preferential policies to select and support some cities with favourable conditions. These cities will be developed as growth poles to lead economic development in the region. Development corridors will also emerge along these cities according to the "nodes and axes-based development model." Second, in the highly urbanized areas, a "network-based development model" will be adopted to enhance the linkages and division of labour between urban and rural areas and among various cities. Transport and telecommunications infrastructure will be constructed to facilitate such network-based development.

Regarding urban development in the western region, some suggestions are proposed as follows.[29] First, it is essential to follow the mechanism of urban development that has been extensively studied by various scholars. Spatial urban models that are suitable for conditions in the western region, in terms of population, economy and ecological environment, should be promoted. Second, it is important to make use of the existing cities and resource bases that are being developed. Third, an urban development model of "focusing on growth poles, combining nodes and axes" should be adopted to consolidate and develop a series of secondary cities in the western region that can serve their hinterland effectively. This means a strategy of concentrated development based on the concept of growth poles. Fourth, a series of new cities and towns should be established along key development axes of railways, expressways and rivers, as well as at important inland border crossing areas and areas where major mining and resource development projects will take place.

There are two primary national growth axes involving the western region. First, the Yangzi River axis is an economic belt extending from Shanghai in the east to Panzhihua 攀枝花 in Sichuan in the west. It is 100–

200 km wide from north to south. The agriculture in this belt is relatively developed and there are advanced manufacturing bases and high-tech parks. There are three big urban clusters along this axis: the Yangzi River Delta urban cluster with Shanghai as the centre, the urban cluster at the middle reaches of Yangzi River with Wuhan 武漢 as the centre, and the Cheng-Yu 成渝 urban cluster with Chongqing and Chengdu as the two poles. The key development area in this axis under the strategy of developing the western region is the Cheng-Yu economic region, while the secondary development areas in this axis are those surrounding medium-sized cities located along the Yangzi River.

Second, the Euro-Asian continental bridge 歐亞大陸橋 axis refers to the 100 to 150 km wide belt, in which industries and cities are concentrated, extending from Lianyungang 連雲港 in Jiangsu in the east to the Alashan Pass 阿拉山口 in Xinjiang in the west. The axis involves several provincial units in the western region such as Shaanxi, Gansu, Ningxia, Qinghai and Xinjiang. The important national east-west artery in this economic belt connects with major railways in Europe. The focus of western region development in this belt is on infrastructure and ecological construction. Major construction projects involving railways, highways, airports, optical-fibre cables and gas pipelines are planned.[30] These infrastructure and ecological construction projects will facilitate the mining and development of energy and raw materials, and improve the investment environment in the western region.

The development of the Euro-Asian continental axis should adopt the "nodes and axes-based development model." The Long-Hai 隴海 (Lanzhou 蘭州-Lianyungang) and Lan-Xin 蘭新 (Lanzhou-Xinjiang) railways, parallel expressways and major transport lines will be the axes while provincial capital cities and regional cities will be the nodes connected by these axes. The economic strength of provincial capital cities such as Lanzhou, Xi'an and regional cities should be fully utilized to extend the development from "nodes" to "lines" and then to "areas" to construct the Euro-Asian continental axis. Indeed, the Guanzhong economic region 關中經濟區 and the Hexi corridor economic region 河西走廊經濟區 are currently taking shape. These regions and their central cities, such as Xi'an and Lanzhou, will play a leading role in the development of the western region. Some important national bases will be constructed in the western region for the following products: cotton and livestock, petroleum chemicals, and energy and non-ferrous metals.

On the basis of national growth axes, urban development axes, urban agglomeration areas and urban clusters will emerge in the western region. "One vertical and two horizontal urban development axes" are planned to link central cities and major cities in major economic areas in the western region. These axes are along trunk transport corridors.

The vertical urban developmental axis is along the main railways in the western region. The Bao-Lan 包蘭 (Baotou 包頭-Lanzhou), Bao-Cheng 寶成 (Baoji 寶雞-Chengdu) and Cheng-Kun 成昆 (Chengdu-Kunming 昆明) railways include the 18 major cities of Baotou, Linhe 臨河, Wuhai 烏海, Yinchuan 銀川, Qingtongxia 青銅峽, Wuzhong 吳忠, Lanzhou, Tianshui 天水, Baoji, Guangyuan 廣元, Mianyang 綿陽, Deyang 德陽, Guanghan 廣漢, Chengdu, Neijiang 內江, Emeishan 峨眉山, Xichang 西昌 and Kunming.

One of the two horizontal urban development axes includes the five cities of Dukou 渡口, Yibin 宜賓, Luzhou 瀘州, Chongqing and Wanzhou 萬州 along the Yangzi River, and links the southwestern region with the eastern region.[31] The second horizontal urban development axis includes the following 16 cities along the Long-Hai and Lan-Xin railways: Shihezi, Kuitun 奎屯, Changji 昌吉, Urumqi 烏魯木齊, Hami 哈密, Yumen 玉門, Jiuquan 酒泉, Zhangye 張掖, Wuwei 武威, Lanzhou, Tianshui, Baoji, Xianyang 咸陽, Xi'an, Weinan 渭南 and Lingbao 靈寶. This axis links the northwestern region and the eastern region and joins the vertical urban development axis in the middle. It has become the most important east-west transport artery, with both ends open to foreign countries.

Two urban agglomeration areas will play important roles in the western region. The first urban agglomeration area is in the Sichuan basin with Chongqing as the centre. Other cities include Chengdu, Nanchong 南充, Leshan 樂山, Mianyang, Yibin 宜賓, Zigong 自貢, Neijiang, Deyang, Luzhou and Ziyang 資陽. This southwestern urban agglomeration area is supported by the Cheng-Yu 成渝 (Chengdu-Chongqing) railway and expressways. Chongqing should aim to become a modern international city to link the western region and the outside world. The second is the Guanzhong 關中 urban agglomeration area with Xi'an as the centre. Other cities include Baoji, Xianyang, Weinan 渭南 and Tongchuan 銅川. This agglomeration area is supported by the Long-Hai railway and national trunk roads. It will become an important urban agglomeration area in the northwest of China.

Other than the above urban agglomeration areas, the western region will foster seven urban clusters according to their natural, social and economic conditions. The first is the urban cluster in the south of Guangxi. The existing cities in this cluster include Nanning 南寧, Beihai 北海, Qinzhou

欽州, Fangchenggang 防城港 and Dongxing 東興. Measures should be taken to increase the economic strength of Nanning city in the future. The service industry and investment environment in the cities along border frontiers and rivers should be improved and their "gate" role for international trade and economic co-operation should be enhanced.

The second urban cluster is in central Guizhou. This cluster includes several cities, Kaili 凱里, Duyun 都匀, Guiyang 貴陽, Qingzhen 清鎮 and Anshun 安順. Transport infrastructure will be strengthened to increase the overall transport capacity in this cluster. Tourist routes will be organized and promoted to stimulate the development of tourism in this area.

The third urban cluster is in eastern Yunnan and includes the cities of Qujing 曲靖, Kunming, Yuxi 玉溪 and Chuxiong 楚雄. By developing tourism and special industries, this urban cluster will become the leading economic base of the whole province.

The fourth urban cluster is in the central part of Inner Mongolia and includes the cities of Hohhot 呼和浩特 and Baotou. Urban development in this area should not neglect ecological conservation and environment protection.

The fifth urban cluster is in the upper reaches of the Yellow River in Ningxia and Inner Mongolia and includes the cities of Wuhai, Shizuishan 石嘴山, Yinchuan, Wuzhong, Qingtongxia and Lingwu 靈武. Industrial restructuring is a major focus in this urban cluster. Environmental protection is also very important.

The sixth urban cluster is in the Gansu-Qinghai region, including the cities of Baiyin 白銀, Lanzhou and Xining 西寧. The emphasis in development is on making full use of the talent and technology advantages of these old industrial bases to implement industrial restructuring and protect the environment.

The seventh urban cluster is north of the Tianshan Mountain 天山 in Xinjiang and includes the cities of Turpan 吐魯番, Urumqi, Fukang 阜康, Changji, Shihezi, Kuitun, Wusu 烏蘇 and Karamay 克拉瑪依. According to the unique characteristics of various cities, attention will be paid to the spatial division of labour, inter-city co-operation and environmental protection.

To consolidate and foster the urban agglomeration areas and urban clusters mentioned above, it is necessary to speed up the development of central cities in the western region. One key factor of success in the development of the western region is whether several modern central cities can be constructed in each province to lead its economic development.

Historically, the growth of central cities in the western region has been closely related to the country's programme of western development. During the 1960s and 1970s, the "Third Front" construction in the western region speeded up urban development in Chongqing and in provincial capitals such as Chengdu, Xi'an, Kunming, Lanzhou, Guiyang, Urumqi, Xining, Yinchuan and Lhasa. Some new cities such as Panzhihua, Mianyang and Deyang also experienced rapid development during that period. Among these cities, Chongqing, Chengdu and Xi'an have already become important metropolitan areas while Kunming and Urumqi are also becoming important central cities in the frontier areas.

Central cities play an important supporting role in the development of the western region. Urban clusters of different scales, levels and functions can only be fostered by speeding up the construction and development of various regional central cities, which can also promote the development of medium and small cities in surrounding areas in the western region. This is an important measure for enhancing economic dynamism and achieving rapid socioeconomic development in the western region. These cities can be divided into the following four kinds according to their role in the development of the western region.

The first kind is the central cities of the whole western region, including Xi'an and Chongqing. These core cities should become international cities assuming a leading role in development. The second kind is regional central cities such as Chengdu, Lanzhou, Urumqi and Kunming. They should become important bases for R&D and technical innovation for industrial development in China. The third kind is provincial central cities, including the capital cities of various provinces such as Hohhot, Yinchuan, Xining, Nanning and Guiyang and other important cities such as Baotou. As central cities at the provincial level, these cities with unique characteristics play a leading role in the social and economic development of their provinces. The fourth kind is local central cities within a province or serving a cross-border area of two or more provinces. Most such cities are prefectural-level cities. They are socioeconomic centres with strong spreading effects to their hinterlands.

Overall, the urban system in the western region is currently relatively weak. The urban agglomeration areas in the Sichuan basin and the Guanzhong area are the most influential. The capital cities in Tibet, Ningxia and Qinghai are relatively weak and greater effort should be made to develop them. These areas also have few regional centres at the prefectural level. Each of them should develop three or four regional central cities. On the other hand, the size of the capital cities in Shaanxi, Gansu, Guizhou, Guangxi and Xinjiang should be controlled, but the urban infrastructure and built-up environment should be further improved. Those cities with population of 0.25–0.50 million should be expanded to become sub-regional centres. In the southwestern region, Yunnan, Tibet, Guizhou, Guangxi and Sichuan should be key areas for further urbanization.

Finally, it is also useful to explore the focus of urban economic development in major cities, as urban economy is the foundation of urban growth and development. Two key economic sectors are considered here.

The first is modern Chinese medicine. Some cities in Sichuan, Shaanxi and Yunnan are well known for their advanced R&D in Chinese medicine. The Chengdu University of Chinese Medicine 成都中醫藥大學 is the most important training centre. The results of research carried out at that university in such areas as Taiji 太極 and Di'ao 地奧 have been successfully applied to produce medical products. As Chinese medicine becomes more and more popular inside and outside of China, these western cities should make use of their advantage to become centres of modern Chinese medicine, both in research and manufacturing. Further efforts should be made to develop health foods, functional foods[32] and cosmetics that are based on the raw materials of Chinese medicine. Attention should also be paid to the production, promotion and marketing of Chinese medicine.

The second key economic sector is high-tech industry. As a legacy of the Maoist development strategy, strong research capabilities are located in some western cities such as Xi'an, Chengdu and Mianyang. The construction of the state-designated Chengdu high-tech industrial development zone and the Mianyang science and technology zone is under way. The Chengdu high-tech industrial development zone will focus on the development of electronic information and Chinese medicine. The Mianyang science and technology zone can make full use of advanced defence-related industry and technologies, enhancing its linkages to the local economy. The electronic information sector can be another focus.

High-tech industrial zones have also been established in Xi'an, Baoji and Yangling 楊凌. The development of project centres for software design and development is being speeded up in the Guanzhong high-tech industrial development belt. There is also a proposal to develop a technological park in the northern part of the Chongqing high-tech industrial development zone to develop high-tech industries and modern manufacturing.

Conclusion

This chapter has discussed the changing regime of regional development and its implications for the development of China's western region. The status and strategies of urban and regional development have been examined. The analyses in this chapter have revealed patterns of regional development in the pre-reform and reform period. The GDP growth rate in the western region has been found to be higher than the national average in the pre-reform period. However, due to rapid population growth, the relative level of GDP per capita in the western region declined in the pre-reform period. Due to path-dependency, the region's low level of development in 1952 was largely responsible for its low level of development in 1978. In the reform period, the development gap between the western and eastern regions widened further.

Inequality within the western region is a complicated issue. In the pre-reform period, relative GDP per capita improved in Guangxi, Chongqing, Shaanxi, Gansu, Qinghai and Ningxia. In the reform period, relative GDP per capita improved in Inner Mongolia, Chongqing, Sichuan, Shaanxi, Gansu and Xinjiang. By 2000, Guizhou and Gansu were the least developed areas while Xinjiang was the most developed area in the western region.

The comparative and competitive disadvantages of the western region have also been analyzed. It was found that arable land and grain output on a per capita basis are not adequate in the western region when various factors are taken into consideration. Decomposition analysis reveals that most provincial regions in western China had a low level of development due to significant competitive and/or structural disadvantages.

Except for a few cities, the urban system in the western region is relatively weak. There are few large cities with an administrative status at the pro-provincial level. In most cases, each provincial unit only has one large city. This is not adequate to support economic development in its huge hinterland. The urban agglomeration areas in the Sichuan basin and the Guanzhong area are the most influential. Regional central cities should be developed in the western region to act as growth poles for regional development.

In accordance with conditions in the western region, a suitable regional development strategy would adopt a mixed development model, based on the "nodes and axes-based development model" and "network-based development model." National growth axes, urban developmental axes, urban agglomeration areas and urban clusters have been outlined as a broad strategy for urban and regional development in the western region.

Acknowledgements

This chapter was based on research funded by the National Natural Sciences Foundation of China (NSF Grant 40271043) and a Direct Research Grant from The Chinese University of Hong Kong, project code 2020764.

Notes

1. C. C. Fan, "Uneven Development and Beyond: Regional Development Theory in Post-Mao China," *International Journal of Urban and Regional Research*, Vol. 21, No. 4 (1997), pp. 620–39; Y. H. D. Wei, "Investment and Regional Development in Post-Mao China," *GeoJournal*, Vol. 51 (2001), pp. 169–79; L. G. Ying, "China's Changing Regional Disparities during the Reform Period," *Economic Geography*, Vol. 75, No. 1 (1999), pp. 59–70.
2. Lu Dadao 陸大道 et al., *2000 Zhongguo quyu fazhan baogao — xibu kaifa de jichu, zhengce yu taishi fenxi* 2000中國區域發展報告 —— 西部開發的基礎、政策與態勢分析 (China Regional Development Report 2000 — Foundation, Policy and Situation Analysis of the Development of Western China) (Beijing: Shangwu yinshuguan 商務印書館, 2001), pp. 163–74; Jianfa Shen, "The Urbanization Gaps among the Eastern, Central and Western Regions: An Analysis of the Contemporary Chinese Urban System," paper presented at the Hong Kong Geography Day Seminar, 3 November 2001, Hong Kong.
3. Chaolin Gu, Jianfa Shen, Kwan-yiu Wong and Feng Zhen, "Regional Polarization under the Socialist-market System since 1978 — A Case Study of Guangdong Province in South China," *Environment and Planning A*, Vol. 33, No. 1 (2001), pp. 97–119.
4. J. C. Williamson, "Regional Inequalities and the Process of National Development," *Economic Development and Cultural Change*, Vol. 13 (1965), pp. 1–84; F. Perroux, "Economic Space: Theory and Applications," *Quarterly Journal of Economics*, Vol. 64 (1950), pp. 89–104; G. Myrdal, *Economic Theory and Underdeveloped Regions* (London: Duckworth, 1957); J. Friedmann, *A General Theory of Polarized Development* (Los Angeles: UCLA Press, 1969).
5. P. Krugman, *Development, Geography and Economic Theory* (London: MIT Press, 1995); R. Martin and P. Sunley, "Slow Convergence? The New Endogenous Growth Theory and Regional Development," *Economic Geography*, Vol. 74, No. 3 (1998), pp. 201–27.
6. A. Amin, "An Institutional Perspective on Regional Economic Development," *International Journal of Urban and Regional Research*, Vol. 23, No. (1999), pp. 365–78; A. Amin and N. Thrift, "Institutional Issues for the European Regions: From Markets and Plans to Socioeconomics and Powers of Association," *Economy and Society*, Vol. 24, No. 1 (1995), pp. 41–66;

P. Cooke and K. Morgan, *The Associational Economy: Firms, Regions and Innovation* (Oxford: Oxford University Press, 1998).

7. C. C. Fan, "Of Belts and Ladders: State Policy and Uneven Regional Development in Post-Mao China," *Annals of the Association of American Geographers,* Vol. 85, No. 3 (1995), pp. 421–49; Gu, Shen, Wong and Zhen, "Regional Polarization" (see note 3).
8. S. X. Zhao, "Spatial Disparities and Economic Development in China, 1953–92: A Comparative Study," *Development and Change*, Vol. 27 (1996), pp. 131–63.
9. Kaizhao Zheng, Qing Li and Shuchang Qi, "The Core and Periphery Analysis of China's Regional Economics," in *China's Regional Economic Development*, edited by R. C. K. Chan, T. Hsueh and C. Luk (Hong Kong: Hong Kong Institute of Asia-Pacific Studies, The Chinese University of Hong Kong, 1996), pp. 205–28.
10. A. G. Walder, "The Decline of Communist Power: Elements of a Theory of Institutional Change," *Theory and Society*, Vol. 23 (1994), pp. 297–323; J. Oi, "The Role of the Local State in China's Transitional Economy," *China Quarterly*, No. 144 (1995), pp. 1132–49; S. S. Han and C. W. Pannell, "The Geography of Privatization in China," *Economic Geography*, Vol. 75, No. 3 (1999), pp. 272–96.
11. Fan, "Of Belts and Ladders" (see note 7).
12. Ibid.
13. Ibid.
14. J. Shen and Y. M. Yeung, "Free Trade Zones in China: Review and Prospect," Occasional Paper No. 122 (Hong Kong: Hong Kong Institute of Asia-Pacific Studies, The Chinese University of Hong Kong, 2002), pp. 1–36.
15. Fan, "Uneven Development and Beyond" (see note 1).
16. National Bureau of Statistics (NBS) (ed.), *China Statistical Yearbook 2001* (Beijing: China Statistics Press, 2001), p. 164.
17. Y. M. Yeung and D. K. Y. Chu (eds.), *Guangdong: Survey of a Province Undergoing Rapid Change* (Hong Kong: The Chinese University Press, 1998); J. Shen, "Urban and Regional Development in Post-reform China: The Case of Zhujiang Delta," *Progress in Planning*, Vol. 57, No. 2 (2002), pp. 91–140; K. Y. Wong and J. Shen (eds.), *Resource Management, Urbanization and Governance in Hong Kong and the Zhujiang Delta* (Hong Kong: The Chinese University Press, 2002).
18. For a detailed review, see Y. D. Wei, "Regional Inequality in China," *Progress in Human Geography*, Vol. 23, No. 1 (1999), pp. 48–58.
19. Wei, "Investment and Regional Development in Post-Mao China" (see note 1); Ying, "China's Changing Regional Disparities during the Reform Period" (see note 1); Zhao, "Spatial Disparities and Economic Development in China" (see note 8).

20. Y. H. Wei, 1996, "Fiscal Systems and Uneven Regional Development in China, 1978–1991," *Geoforum*, Vol. 27, No. 3 (1996), pp. 329–44.
21. M. Fujita and D. Hu, "Regional Disparity in China 1985–1994: The Effects of Globalization and Economic Liberalization," *The Annals of Regional Science*, Vol. 35, No. 3 (2001), pp. 3–37.
22. S. Wang and A. Hu, *The Political Economy of Uneven Development: The Case of China* (Armonk, New York: M. E. Sharpe, 1999).
23. Provincial population data in 1952 and 1978 are from Department of Comprehensive Statistics of NBS (DSC), *Comprehensive Statistical Data and Materials on 50 Years of New China* (Beijing: China Statistics Press, 1999). The population data for Chongqing in 1952 and 1978 are estimated as the difference of the total population in Sichuan and Chongqing, and the population in Sichuan from the above DSC book. The population figure for Tibet in 1952 is from Sun Huaiyang 孫懷陽 and Cheng Xianmin 程賢敏 (eds.), *Zhongguo Zangzu renkou yu shehui* 中國藏族人口與社會 (Population and Society of Tibetans in China) (Beijing: Zhongguo zangxue chubanshe 中國藏學出版社, 1999), p. 179. Provincial population in 1982, 1990 and 2000 are from Guojia tongjiju renkou he shehui keji tongjisi 國家統計局人口和社會科技統計司 (ed.), *Zhongguo renkou tongji nianjian 2001* 中國人口統計年鑑2001 (China Population Statistics Yearbook 2001) (Beijing: Zhongguo tongji chubanshe 中國統計出版社, 2001), p. 53. Provincial GDP development indexes for 1953–1978, 1979–1982 and 1983–1990 were estimated using data from the above DSC book. GDP development indexes for Chongqing for 1953–1978, 1979–1982 and 1983–1990 use the data of Sichuan. GDP development indexes for Hainan 海南 for 1953–1978 use the figures of Guangdong. The GDP development index for Tibet for 1953–1978 is the development index of the total output value of agriculture and industry in 1959–1978 from Guojia tongjiju zonghesi 國家統計局綜合司, *Quanguo gesheng zizhiqu zhixiashi lishi tongji ziliao huibian 1949–1989* 全國各省自治區直轄市歷史統計資料匯編1949–1989 (Comprehensive Statistical Data 1949–1989) (Beijing: China Statistics Press, 1990). Provincial development indexes in 1991–2000 are estimated using development indexes for 1991–1998 from the above DSC book and the development index for 1999 and 2000 from NBS, *China Statistical Yearbook 2001* (see note 16), pp. 51 and 56. Finally, the GDP data in 2000 are from NBS, *China Statistical Yearbook 2001* (see note 16). GDP data in 1952, 1978, 1982 and 1990 at 2000 prices are calculated using the GDP in 2000 and the development indexes estimated above.
24. See Chapter 9 of this book for details.
25. GDP per capita is commonly used when studying an economy. But population data are rarely broken down to economic sectors. Thus, GDP per employee is used in this analysis.
26. J. Shen, K. Y. Wong and Z. Feng, "State Sponsored and Spontaneous

Urbanization in the Pearl River Delta of South China, 1980–1998," *Urban Geography*, Vol. 23, No. 7 (2002), pp. 674–94; L. J. C. Ma and C. S Lin, "Development of Towns in China: A Case Study of Guangdong Province," *Population and Development Review*, Vol. 19, No. 3 (1993), pp. 583–606; J. Shen, "A Study of the Temporary Population in Chinese Cities," *Habitat International*, Vol. 26 (2002), pp. 363–77.

27. Guojia tongjiju chengshi shehui jingji diaocha zongdui 國家統計局城市社會經濟調查總隊 (ed.), *Zhongguo chengshi tongji nianjian 2000* 中國城市統計年鑑 2000 (Urban Statistical Yearbook of China 2000) (Beijing: Zhongguo tongji chubanshe, 2001).
28. See L. J. C. Ma, "Urban Transformation in China, 1949–2000: A Review and Research Agenda," *Environment and Planning A*, Vol. 33 (2001), pp. 1545–69; Zhang Tingwei, "Urban Development and a Socialist Pro-growth Coalition in Shanghai," *Urban Affairs Review*, Vol. 37, No. 4 (2002), pp. 475–99; C. Gu and J. Shen, "Transformation of Urban Socio-spatial Structure in Socialist Market Economies: The Case of Beijing," *Habitat International*, Vol. 27, No. 1 (2003), pp. 107–22; C. Pannell, "China's Continuing Urban Transition," *Environment and Planning A*, Vol. 34 (2002), pp. 1571–89; John R. Logan (ed.), *The New Chinese City: Globalization and Market Reform* (Oxford: Blackwell Publishers, 2002).
29. Gu Chaolin, Zhang Qin 張勤, Cai Jianming 蔡建明, Niu Yafei 牛亞飛 and Sun Ying 孫櫻 (eds.), *Jingji quanqiuhua yu Zhongguo chengshi fazhan* 經濟全球化與中國城市發展 (Economic Globalization and Chinese Urban Development) (Beijing: Shangwu yinshuguan, 2000); Office of the Leading Group for Western Region Development of the State Council (ed.), *The Overall Plan of Western Region Development and Related Policy Measures* (Beijing: China Planning Press, 2002).
30. See Chapter 5.
31. Along the middle and lower reaches of the Yangzi River, there are 21 other cities including Yichang 宜昌, Yidu 宜都, Zhijiang 枝江, Shishou 石首, Yueyang 岳陽, Wuhan 武漢, Huanggang 黃崗, Ezhou 鄂州, Huangshi 黃石, Jiujiang 九江, Anqing 安慶, Tongling 銅陵, Wuhu 蕪湖, Maanshan 馬鞍山, Nanjing 南京, Zhenjiang 鎮江, Yangzhong 揚中, Jiangyin 江陰, Nantong 南通, Shanghai and Changshu 常熟.
32. Functional food means food that has a favourable effect on the human body.

9

Population Distribution and Growth

Shen Jianfa and Wang Guixin

Introduction

The huge size of China's population has long been considered a fundamental obstacle to the country's development and modernization.[1] The population issue has attracted considerable attention from both Chinese and foreign scholars as well as from the Chinese government and international communities. The main debates have focused on whether there is a negative relationship between population growth and development, and whether and how China should implement a strict family planning policy.[2] One key measure adopted by the Chinese government is to remove local officials from their posts if the implementation of family planning in their jurisdiction fails according to the "one vote" criterion. Under this criterion, local officials are deemed not satisfactory if they fail in family planning (one vote) no matter what other achievements they may have achieved. Thus, although the state's family planning policy emphasizes education and voluntarism, some local officials have used harsh measures to enforce the policy, especially in the early 1980s. Such cases have been declared illegal and reported by both the Chinese and foreign media.[3]

On the other hand, the existence of more than one hundred million surplus labourers in China does suggest that the country needs to control its population growth to relieve pressures on food supply and employment.[4] A slowing population growth with a total fertility rate (TFR) of below two since the early 1990s, plus sustained grain output at about 500 million tonnes a year in the period 1996–1999, contributed to achieving a balance in food demand and supply for the country as a whole. Despite an improved food supply situation, the state has remained firm on continuing family planning by formally passing a law on population and family planning in 2001. The law stipulates that citizens have the obligation to practise family planning. Those couples who give birth to only one child will be rewarded while those who do not abide with family planning regulations are required to pay a social raising fee for extra children.[5] Such a state policy is not to be regarded as simply following the classical Malthusian view or Nelson's concept of the low-level equilibrium trap.[6] Given certain limits to economic growth and capital investment, a slowly growing population is better than a rapidly growing one for improving human resources and capital stock per capita. Thus, population control is not only necessary if a country is to escape the "Malthusian trap" but also useful by allowing it to take a faster track towards development and modernization.

In the post-reform period, economic development in the western region of China has lagged behind that of the coastal provinces. Population pressure and its constraints on steady economic development are most obvious in a region in which many of China's minority nationalities and a large impoverished population are concentrated.[7] The existence of this large impoverished population was surely the main reason why the Chinese government launched its "Western Region Development Strategy" in 1999. Employing many financial and policy measures, the objective of the strategy is to raise the level of development in the region as well as to strike a balance between the population and the ecological environment.[8]

This chapter examines the demographic aspects of the western region that are considered one of the many factors behind its underdevelopment. A good understanding of the situation regarding the region's population is also essential for social, economic and spatial planning for the western region. The chapter attempts to assess the different situations on population among the eastern, central and western regions as well as among provincial regions in the western region, the dynamics of minority populations, and the issue of migration to the western region. A thorough analysis of population distribution and growth, and of the population of minority nationalities will be conducted in the following two sections. The issue of migration to and from the western region will then be examined in the final section.

Population Distribution and Growth

One major feature of China's western region is its huge area in comparison with the size of its population. The western region has an area of 6.87 million km^2, accounting for 71.54% of China's total, while the eastern and central regions only account for 11.07% and 17.39%, respectively. The population of the western region makes up around 28% of China's total, while the eastern and central regions make up about 39% and 33%, respectively. These percentages were quite stable throughout the period 1952–2000 (Figure 9.1). As a result, with 51.7 persons per km^2, the western region had the country's lowest population density, much lower than the 465.0 persons per km^2 in the eastern region and the 131.9 persons per km^2 for China as a whole in 2000. The low population density of the western region sometimes leads to the mistaken perception that it can support many migrants from the eastern region. The reality is that it is an indication of the western region's small population carrying capacity per unit of area.

Detailed population changes in 3 regions and 12 provincial units in the

Figure 9.1 Distribution of Population among Three Regions in China, 1952–2000 (%)

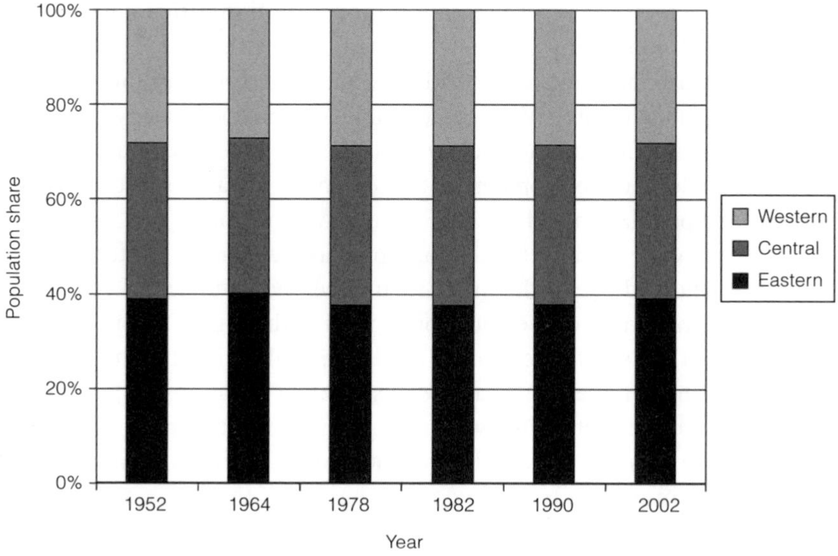

Source: See Table 9.1.

western region are presented in Tables 9.1 and 9.2. The population data for 1964, 1982, 1990 and 2000 are based on four population censuses in these years. Those for 1952 and 1978 are from official population statistics.[9] The population data from the first population census in 1953 cannot be used due to some provincial boundary changes. The year 1952 is the earliest for which comparable population data are available after the founding of the People's Republic of China (PRC). According to Tables 9.1 and 9.2, in the period 1952–2000, the total population in the western region increased from 157.3 million to 355.3 million, while the total population in China increased from 574.8 million to 1,265.8 million. The population in the western region increased by 82.91% in the period 1952–1982 and by 23.48% in the period 1982–2000. Comparing population trends in the western and eastern regions, there was one significant change after 1982. In 1952–1982, population growth was faster in the western region than in the eastern region, possibly due to high fertility rates in the western region. In 1982–2000, the population trend was reversed due to net migration from the west to the east, a finding that is consistent with the patterns of economic development in these two regions.

Table 9.1 Population in Selected Years, 1952–2000

(Unit: millions)

Region	1952	1964	1978	1982	1990	2000
China[1]	574.8	694.6	962.6	1,008.2	1,133.7	1,265.8
Eastern[2]	216.7	276.6	359.4	376.6	425.8	491.3
Central[3]	185.9	227.3	324.1	339.6	382.7	415.6
Western	157.3	187.3	274.9	287.7	322.0	355.3
Inner Mongolia	7.2	12.3	18.2	19.3	21.5	23.8
Guangxi	19.4	23.2	34.0	36.4	42.2	44.9
Chongqing[4]	n.a.	n.a.	n.a.	27.1	28.9	30.9
Sichuan[5]	64.1	68.0	97.1	72.7	78.4	83.3
Guizhou	14.9	17.1	26.9	28.6	32.4	35.3
Yunnan	17.0	20.5	30.9	32.6	37.0	42.9
Tibet	1.2	1.3	1.8	1.9	2.2	2.6
Shaanxi	15.3	20.8	27.8	28.9	32.9	36.1
Gansu	10.7	12.6	18.7	19.6	22.4	25.6
Qinghai	1.6	2.2	3.7	3.9	4.5	5.2
Ningxia	1.4	2.1	3.6	3.9	4.7	5.6
Xinjiang	4.7	7.3	12.3	13.1	15.2	19.3

Notes: [1] Regional populations do not add up to the national total, as the army is only included in the national total.

[2] The eastern region includes: Beijing 北京, Tianjin 天津, Hebei 河北, Liaoning 遼寧, Shanghai, Jiangsu, Zhejiang, Fujian 福建, Shandong and Guangdong.

[3] The central region includes: Shanxi 山西, Jilin 吉林, Heilongjiang 黑龍江, Anhui 安徽, Jiangxi, Henan, Hubei and Hunan 湖南.

[4] Data for Chongqing are not available for 1952, 1964 and 1978.

[5] Figures for Sichuan for 1952, 1964 and 1978 include both Sichuan and Chongqing.

Source: See note 9.

Population growth appears to differ significantly among various provincial units in the western region. In 1952–1982, the populations of Inner Mongolia 內蒙古, Qinghai 青海, Ningxia 寧夏 and Xinjiang 新疆 increased by over 140% while in Sichuan 四川 the population only increased by 55.53%, lower than China's average, due to net out-migration. In 1982–2000, the populations of Chongqing 重慶 and Sichuan increased by less than 15%, while those of Yunnan 雲南, Tibet 西藏, Gansu 甘肅, Qinghai, Ningxia and Xinjiang increased by over 30%. It is clear that the population in many areas in the western region continued to grow faster than the average for the nation, although population growth in the entire western region was slower than China as a whole in 1982–2000.

Another major feature of the western region is that the population is

Table 9.2 Percentage of Population Growth and Population Density, 1952–2000

Region	Percentage of population growth (%)		Population density (Persons per km²)			
	1952–1982	1982–2000	1952	1964	1982	2000
China	75.40	25.55	59.9	72.4	105.0	131.9
Eastern	73.76	30.47	204.0	260.4	354.5	462.5
Central	82.72	22.39	111.3	136.2	203.4	249.0
Western	82.91	23.48	22.9	27.3	41.9	51.7
Inner Mongolia	169.13	23.30	6.1	10.4	16.3	20.1
Guangxi	87.44	23.26	82.3	98.3	154.3	190.2
Chongqing[1]	n.a.	14.19	n.a.	n.a.	328.4	375.0
Sichuan[2]	55.53	14.65	113.0	119.9	149.8	171.7
Guizhou	91.61	23.47	84.7	97.4	162.2	200.3
Yunnan	92.04	31.74	43.0	51.9	82.6	108.8
Tibet	64.35	38.62	0.9	1.0	1.5	2.1
Shaanxi	89.14	24.74	74.3	101.0	140.6	175.3
Gansu	83.76	30.91	23.5	27.8	43.1	56.4
Qinghai	142.24	32.82	2.2	3.0	5.4	7.2
Ningxia	174.65	44.10	27.4	40.7	75.3	108.5
Xinjiang	181.29	47.17	2.8	4.4	7.9	11.7

Notes: [1] Data before 1982 for Chongqing are not available.
[2] Figures for Sichuan for years before 1982 include both Sichuan and Chongqing.

Source: Calculated by the authors based on the population data in Table 9.1 and data on land area from *Zhongguo renkou tongji nianjian 2001* (see note 9), p. 40.

unevenly distributed. In the year 2000, Tibet, Qinghai and Ningxia only had 2.6, 5.2 and 5.6 million people, respectively. The population in each of these three regions is smaller than that of a large city such as Shanghai 上海 and Shenzhen 深圳. The numbers for other provincial regions ranged from 19.3 million in Xinjiang to 83.3 million in Sichuan. Population density also differs within the western region (Table 9.2 and Figure 9.2). In 2000, Guangxi 廣西, Chongqing, Sichuan, Guizhou 貴州 and Shaanxi 陝西 had more residents than the national average of 131.9 persons per km^2. But Inner Mongolia and Xinjiang had fewer than 21 persons per km^2, and the figures were as low as 2.1 persons per km^2 in Tibet and 7.2 persons per km^2 in Qinghai in the same year. Needless to say, population density increased in all provincial regions along with population growth in 1952–2000. For example, population density in Inner Mongolia more than tripled from 6.1 to 20.1 persons per km^2 during the period.

It may be much clearer to compare the annual population growth rates

Figure 9.2 Population Densities in Western China in 2000 (persons per km²)

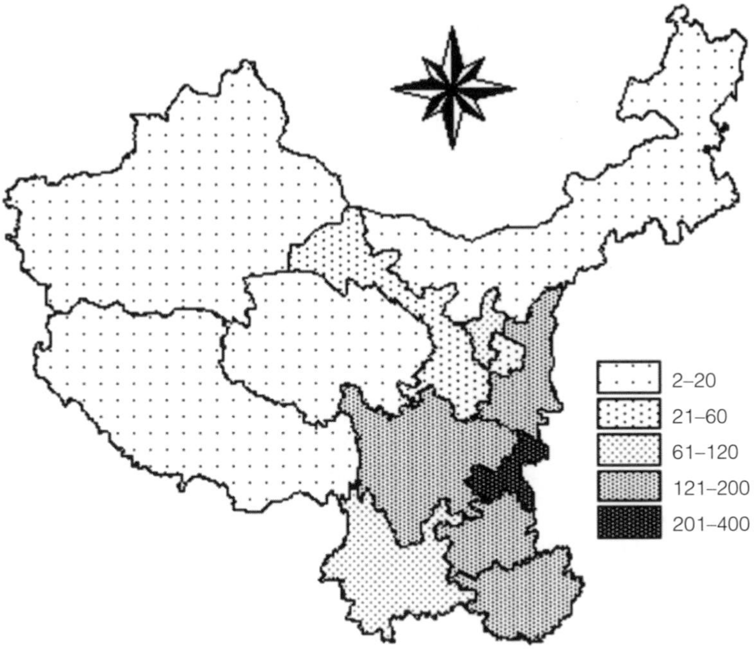

Source: See Table 9.2.

among various periods that are shown in Table 9.3. Growth rates in the periods 1952–1964 and 1964–1978 were calculated to show the dynamics of population in the pre-reform period. For China as a whole, the annual population growth rate increased from 1.66% in 1952–1964 to a peak of 2.28% in 1964–1978. The famine in 1959–1961 and the subsequent baby boom can explain the change in the rate of population growth in these two periods. The growth rate then declined to only 1.07% in the period 1990–2000, reflecting sustained family planning efforts in China, as mentioned before. The trends in three regions and in the provincial units in the western region were generally consistent with the national trend. The annual population growth rate of the western region as a whole was higher than the national average in 1964–1982, but below the national average in 1952–1964 despite in-migration, as well as in 1982–2000 due to out-migration. However, annual population growth rates in Inner Mongolia, Shaanxi, Qinghai, Ningxia and Xinjiang were well over the national average in 1952–

Table 9.3 Annual Population Growth Rates in Various Periods

(Unit: %)

Region	1952–1964	1964–1978	1964–1982	1982–1990	1990–2000	1982–2000
China	1.66	2.28	2.09	1.48	1.07	1.25
Eastern	2.14	1.82	1.73	1.55	1.39	1.46
Central	1.77	2.48	2.25	1.50	0.80	1.11
Western	1.53	2.68	2.41	1.42	0.96	1.16
Inner Mongolia	4.84	2.73	2.51	1.35	0.99	1.15
Guangxi	1.55	2.68	2.54	1.87	0.59	1.15
Chongqing[1]	n.a.	n.a.	n.a.	0.81	0.66	0.73
Sichuan[2]	0.51	2.48	2.15	0.95	0.59	0.75
Guizhou	1.23	3.15	2.88	1.59	0.82	1.16
Yunnan	1.65	2.89	2.62	1.61	1.44	1.51
Tibet	0.73	2.51	2.32	1.89	1.72	1.80
Shaanxi	2.71	2.03	1.85	1.63	0.89	1.21
Gansu	1.49	2.74	2.46	1.69	1.32	1.48
Qinghai	2.55	3.72	3.36	1.68	1.47	1.56
Ningxia	3.50	3.67	3.47	2.24	1.84	2.01
Xinjiang	3.96	3.71	3.32	1.86	2.34	2.13

Notes: [1] Data for Chongqing are not available for periods before 1982.
[2] Figures for Sichuan for periods before 1982 include both Sichuan and Chongqing.

Source: Calculated by the authors based on the data in Table 9.1.

1964 due to significant state-planned in-migration programmes. Various regions had a low rate of population growth at different times. The annual population growth rate in Shaanxi was already below the national average in 1964–1982. It was also below the national average in Inner Mongolia, Chongqing and Sichuan in 1982–2000. But it was below the national average in Guangxi and Guizhou only in the 1990s. In Yunnan, Tibet, Gansu, Qinghai, Ningxia and Xinjiang, annual population growth rates were over the national average in 1964–2000, indicating increasing population pressure due to high fertility rates but limited out-migration.

Population dynamics are best described using conventional indicators such as the rate of natural increase, TFR and life expectancy, as shown in Table 9.4. As only limited results of the most recent population census conducted in 2000 have been released so far, data on TFR and life expectancy have to rely on the results calculated from the 1995 One Percent Population Sampling Survey and the 1990 Census, respectively. These data should be

Table 9.4 Rate of Natural Population Growth, TFR and Life Expectancy

Region	Natural growth rate (One per thousand)			TFR	Life expectancy in 1990 (Year)	
	1978	1990	1999	1995	At birth	At age of 60
China	13.28	14.27	6.86	1.46	68.55	16.90
Eastern	12.56	12.64	5.32	1.30	71.12	17.50
Central	13.69	16.24	6.95	1.41	68.21	16.38
Western	13.74	14.09	8.76	1.70	65.75	16.77
Inner Mongolia	13.30	13.98	7.24	1.44	65.68	14.07
Guangxi	18.90	13.60	8.03	1.82	68.72	18.51
Chongqing[1]	n.a.	n.a.	4.96	n.a.	n.a.	n.a.
Sichuan	8.10	11.45	6.78	1.45	66.33	16.76
Guizhou	21.24	15.19	14.24	2.23	64.29	17.30
Yunnan	21.44	15.68	11.66	1.96	63.49	20.35
Tibet	14.20	16.43	15.80	2.97	59.64	16.34
Shaanxi	10.32	16.96	6.13	1.54	67.40	15.41
Gansu	12.20	14.48	9.17	1.80	67.24	15.36
Qinghai	19.49	16.87	13.90	1.86	60.57	14.49
Ningxia	23.00	18.82	12.32	1.86	66.94	15.81
Xinjiang	14.86	18.62	11.80	1.67	62.59	18.12

Note: [1] Chongqing was designated as a city with provincial status in 1997 and its data were included in Sichuan before 1997.

Sources: *Zhongguo renkou tongji nianjian 2001* (see note 9), p. 214; *Comprehensive Statistical Data and Materials on 50 Years of New China* (see note 9), p. 112; Guojia tongjiju renkou yu jiuye tongji si (ed.), *Zhongguo renkou tongji nianjian 1995* 中國人口統計年鑑1995 (*China Population Statistics Yearbook 1995*) (Beijing: Zhongguo tongji chubanshe, 1995), pp. 232–327; *Zhongguo renkou tongji nianjian 1997* 中國人口統計年鑑1997, p. 203.

adequate to indicate the magnitude of regional differences in TFR and life expectations. The TFR in 1995 and the rate of natural increase in 1999 were significantly correlated at the 0.01 level, with a correlation coefficient of 0.805 based on the data for 11 provincial units in the western region. TFR measures the average number of children that a couple would have in a lifetime, based on the level of fertility level in a particular year. According to Table 9.4, the TFR of the western region was 1.70, higher than the figure of 1.30 in the eastern region and 1.46 for the country as a whole. Thus, levels of fertility in the western region remain high, especially in Guizhou and Tibet where the TFRs were 2.23 and 2.97, respectively. Nevertheless, it is encouraging to see that the TFR is below 2 even in the western region, as family planning has been implemented in most areas and among minority nationalities with large populations. The issue of minority nationalities will be discussed in detail in the next section.

Life expectancy measures the expected length of a person's life based on the level of mortality in a particular year. Table 9.4 presents both life expectations at birth and at the age of 60 years. The two measures were significantly correlated at the 0.01 level, with a correlation coefficient of 0.972 based on the data for 11 provincial units in the western region. Generally, life expectancy was shorter in the western region than the national average, indicating a higher mortality level associated with poor material well-being and medical services. Life expectancy was shortest, at 59.64 years, in Tibet. Qinghai and Xinjiang also had relatively short life expectancies of 60.57 and 62.59 years, respectively, in 1990. The effect of development levels on life expectancy is clear.

The Changing Population of Minority Nationalities

The Chinese population consists of Han Chinese (*Hanzu* 漢族) and 55 other minority nationalities (*shaoshu minzu* 少數民族).[10] A minority nationality is defined as a group of people who share a common territory, bodily structure, language, religion, customs and livelihood. Some minority nationalities such as Bouyei 布依 and Tujia 土家 are entirely within China while others such as the Mongolians and Koreans have counterparts living in independent nations such as Mongolia, South Korea and North Korea. Ever since the founding of the PRC in 1949, the official state policy has been to ensure equality and harmony among Han and minority nationalities. Great efforts have been made to identify and recognize minority nationalities. Among the total of 55, 38 were identified in the period 1953–1954, 15 in 1954–1964 and 2 more in 1964–1982.[11]

One major feature of the western region of China is its concentration of minority nationalities, which has raised the issue of separatist activities, especially in Xinjiang and Tibet.[12] Some foreign comments about China's attitude towards Xinjiang and Tibet are misinformed. Earlier claims that China's firm position on Tibet was motivated by a desire for Tibet's natural resources have been dismissed, as the central government has transferred large amounts of capital and goods into Tibet in the past decades. China's concern with national integration and security has been considered more important in explaining China's policy on minority areas.[13] One scholar commented that the minorities received better treatment under the CCP

(Chinese Communist Party) than under Guomindang 國民黨.[14] In terms of the national economy, subsidies to the ethnic minority areas have outweighed income from those areas from production, taxation and other sources.[15] One major policy measure regarding minority nationalities is the designation of autonomous areas. At the provincial level, there are 5 autonomous regions, namely, Inner Mongolia, Guangxi, Tibet, Ningxia and Xinjiang, all located in the western region. In the remaining 6 provinces of the western region, there are 22 autonomous prefectures and 62 autonomous counties.[16] By the constitution of PRC, these autonomous areas have been granted much greater legislative and administrative powers to administer their affairs than have other areas. The governor of an autonomous area is required by law to be a member of the relevant minority nationality. Due to special incentives and more relaxed family planning policies for minority nationalities, many people who once hid their minority background have applied to gain the status of minority nationality.[17] Such reclassifications have had a substantial impact on the population growth rate of minority nationalities.[18]

According to the recent population census of 2000, the total population of minority nationalities amounted to 106.43 million, accounting for 8.41% of China's total population. Of the minority nationalities, 71.63% were concentrated in the western region, while 14.11% and 14.25% were found in the eastern and central regions of China, respectively. Figure 9.3 presents their distribution among the provincial regions of western China. The general pattern is clear that the population of minority nationalities is concentrated in Guangxi, Guizhou, Yunnan and Xinjiang. Each of these provinces has a minority population of over 10 million, and each accounts for over 10% of the total minority population in China. Inner Mongolia and Sichuan had about 4–5 million minority nationalities each in 2000. Chongqing, Tibet, Gansu, Qinghai and Ningxia had about 2 million. The population of minority nationalities was least in Shaanxi in the western region, with only 0.18 million in the year 2000.

However, the percentage of minority nationalities in an area also depends on the size of the Han population. Table 9.5 and Figure 9.4 present the percentages of minority nationalities in various regions in China. The share of minority nationalities in the total population varies among the provincial regions of western China. In 2000, it accounted for 94% in Tibet, nearly 60% in Xinjiang, 46% in Qinghai, 31–40% in Guangxi, Guizhou, Yunnan and Ningxia, but less than 11% in Chongqing, Sichuan, Shaanxi and Gansu. As will be shown later, the growth rate of minority nationalities

Figure 9.3 Population of Minority Nationalities in Western Region, 1964–2000 (million)

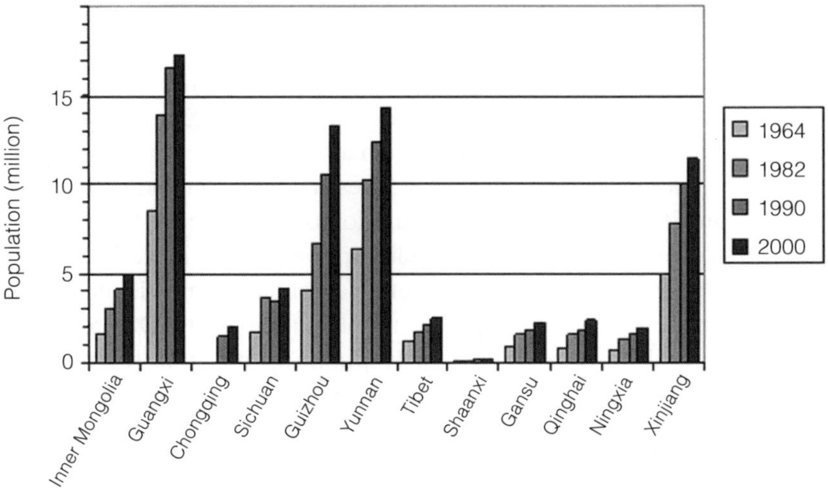

Note: Data for Chongqing in 1964 and 1982 are included in Sichuan.
Source: *China's Ethnic Statistical Yearbook 2000* (see note 16), pp. 433–44.

is generally greater than the Han population. Thus, the percentage of minority nationalities is increasing in most areas. For China as a whole, the figure rose from 5.76% in 1964 to 8.41% in 2000. In the western region, the figure also increased from 16.54% in 1964 to 21.54% in 2000. The exceptions are Tibet and Xinjiang, where minority nationalities as a percentage of the population declined from 68.07% to 59.61% and from 97.10% to 93.65%, respectively, in the period 1964–1982, due to the in-migration of the Han population. In the period 1982–1990, some Han people clearly left Xinjiang and Tibet, as the Han population declined from 5.28 to 5.19 million in Xinjiang and from 0.12 to 0.08 million in Tibet, possibly due to more flexible state policies allowing them to return to the coastal region. In 1990–2000, when many Han people moved to Xinjiang and Tibet to engage in business and trade, the size of the Han population reached the level recorded in 1982. Clearly, state policies and increasing mobility in an emerging market economy are having an important impact on the migration of the Han population to and from western China.

In the period 1964–2000, the populations of minority nationalities and Han experienced different growth rates in various regions (Table 9.6). For

Table 9.5 Percentage of Minority Nationalities in the Total Population of Various Regions in China, 1964–2000

(Unit: %)

Region	1964	1982	1990	2000
China	5.76	6.68	8.04	8.41
Eastern	1.56	1.67	2.83	3.07
Central	2.03	2.52	3.40	3.66
Western	16.54	17.93	20.50	21.54
Inner Mongolia	13.02	15.55	19.42	20.75
Guangxi	36.87	38.26	39.24	38.34
Chongqing[1]	n.a.	n.a.	5.13	6.41
Sichuan	2.54	3.67	4.35	4.98
Guizhou	23.39	23.38	32.43	37.84
Yunnan	31.22	31.57	33.41	33.42
Tibet	97.10	93.65	96.18	93.89
Shaanxi	0.45	0.46	0.48	0.50
Gansu	7.56	7.95	8.30	8.70
Qinghai	38.57	39.38	42.14	45.56
Ningxia	30.82	31.90	33.27	34.52
Xinjiang	68.07	59.61	65.73	59.38

Note: [1] Data for Chongqing in 1964 and 1982 are included in Sichuan.
Sources: Calculated from the data in Table 9.1 and the data from *Zhongguo renkou tongji nianjian 2001* (see note 9), pp. 34 and 60; *China's Ethnic Statistical Yearbook 2000* (see note 16), pp. 433–34.

China as a whole, the minority population grew faster than the Han population in all three periods: 1964–1982, 1982–1990 and 1990–2000. This was also true in the western region. For example, the annual growth rates of the Han and minority populations were 1.03% and 1.51% nationally, 0.83% and 1.44% in the western region in 1990–2000. The faster growth of the minority nationalities is related to both a higher fertility rate and the reclassification and inheritance of nationality status. The situation of fertility will be examined later in this section. As mentioned before, many people prefer to acquire the status of minority nationality to be eligible for special privileges under state policy. For example, members of minority nationalities are given preference in job recruitment by state enterprises and in promotion in government. Family planning policy is also more relaxed for minority nationalities. Thus, even the children of inter-nationality couples prefer to take on minority status. These reclassifications and inter-nationality marriages (which we will dub "social changes") contributed 56% of the

Figure 9.4 Percentage of Minority Nationalities in Total Population in 2000 (%)

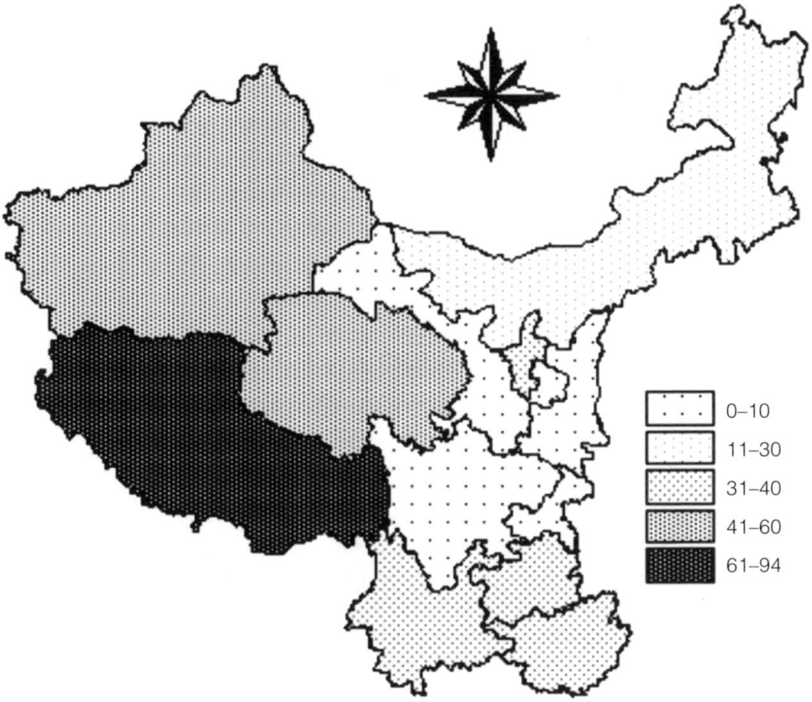

Source: See Table 9.5.

total population growth of minority nationalities in 1982–1990. The contribution of social changes to population growth was significant among 11 minority nationalities, involving over 1 million people in 1990, and was responsible for the following growth percentages for the following groups: 90.94% for Manchu 满, 23.88% for Hui 回, 61.28% for Miao 苗, 17.54% for Yi 彝, 88.97% for Tujia, 64.39% for Mongolian, 26.67% for Bouyei, 80.37% for Dong 侗, 73.33% for Yao 瑶, 68.18% for Bai 白 and 31.58% for Dai 傣.[19]

Most studies have examined the distribution of the population of minority nationalities in various regions of China. It is also of great significance to examine the distribution of individual minority nationalities. Detailed data from the 2000 Census have not been released. The 1990 Census provides the most recent and reliable information. Table 9.7 lists the distribution of 18 minority nationalities in the western region, each with a

Table 9.6 Annual Growth Rates of Minority and Han Populations in Various Regions in China, 1964–2000

(Unit: %)

Region	Minority population			Han population		
	1964–1982	1982–1990	1990–2000	1964–1982	1982–1990	1990–2000
China	2.93	3.87	1.51	2.04	1.29	1.03
Eastern	2.13	8.48	2.19	1.72	1.40	1.37
Central	3.50	5.35	1.54	2.23	1.39	0.78
Western	2.87	3.13	1.44	2.32	1.01	0.83
Inner Mongolia	3.53	4.21	1.64	2.34	0.76	0.83
Guangxi	2.75	2.20	0.36	2.41	1.67	0.73
Chongqing[1]	n.a.	n.a.	2.86	n.a.	n.a.	0.53
Sichuan	4.26	3.68	1.92	2.08	0.79	0.53
Guizhou	2.87	5.83	2.34	2.88	0.01	0.01
Yunnan	2.68	2.33	1.45	2.59	1.26	1.44
Tibet	2.12	2.23	1.49	6.89	–4.39	6.45
Shaanxi	1.95	2.04	1.37	1.85	1.62	0.89
Gansu	2.74	2.25	1.78	2.44	1.64	1.28
Qinghai	3.48	2.55	2.24	3.29	1.09	0.87
Ningxia	3.67	2.78	2.20	3.38	1.98	1.65
Xinjiang	2.56	3.11	1.34	4.67	–0.21	4.04

Note: [1] Data for Chongqing in 1964–1990 are included in Sichuan.
Source: See Table 9.5.

population of over 1 million in 1990. These 18 main minority nationalities accounted for 93.78% of the total population of minority nationalities in China, for 92.89% in the whole western region and for 80–100% in each of the 12 provinces of western China.

Two main points are clear according to Table 9.7. First, 14 out of the 18 main minority nationalities, except for the Manchu, Tujia, Korean 朝鮮 and Li 黎, were concentrated in the western region with different degrees of concentration. The Zhuang 壯, Uygur 維吾爾, Yi, Tibetan, Bouyei, Bai, Hani 哈尼, Kazak 哈薩克 and Dai nationalities were highly concentrated in the western region, accounting for over 90% of their total population in China. Over 70% of the Miao, Mongolian and Yao nationalities were also concentrated in the western region, while about 58–68% of the Hui and Dong nationalities were found in the western region.

Second, most minority nationalities were also concentrated in a few

Table 9.7 Populations of Main Minority Nationalities in China and Their Percentage Distribution in the Western Region in 1990

Region	Zhuang	Manchu	Hui	Miao	Uygur	Yi	Tujia	Mongolian	Tibetan
China (million)	15.56	9.85	8.61	7.38	7.21	6.58	5.73	4.80	4.59
Percentage (%)									
Western	98.23	5.86	58.70	74.87	99.82	99.77	37.28	76.38	99.72
Inner Mongolia	0.01	**4.68**	2.24	0.01	0.00	0.01	0.01	**70.38**	0.02
Guangxi	**91.38**[1]	0.06	0.32	5.78	0.00	0.11	0.04	0.02	0.00
Sichuan[2]	0.03	0.12	1.26	7.23	0.00	**27.17**	**18.80**	0.57	**23.68**
Guizhou	0.25	0.17	1.48	**49.66**	0.00	**10.75**	**18.26**	0.50	0.01
Yunnan	6.50	0.07	6.06	**12.13**	0.00	**61.72**	0.04	0.27	2.42
Tibet	0.00	0.00	0.03	0.00	0.00	0.00	0.00	0.00	**45.65**
Shaanxi	0.01	0.14	1.53	0.01	0.01	0.00	0.01	0.06	0.03
Gansu	0.01	0.17	**12.72**	0.00	0.01	0.00	0.01	0.17	7.99
Qinghai	0.00	0.09	7.43	0.01	0.00	0.00	0.01	1.49	**19.86**
Ningxia	0.00	0.17	**17.71**	0.00	0.00	0.00	0.01	0.05	0.00
Xinjiang	0.04	0.19	7.93	0.04	**99.79**	0.01	0.09	2.87	0.05

Notes: [1] The bold figures in the table indicate major areas of concentration of individual minority nationalities.
[2] Data for Chongqing are included in Sichuan.

Source: Guowuyuan renkou pucha bangongshi 國務院人口普查辦公室, Guojia tongjiju renkou tongjisi (eds.), *Zhongguo 1990 nian renkou pucha ziliao diyice* 中國1990人口普查資料第一冊 (Tabulations on the 1990 Population Census of the People's Republic of China, Vol. 1) (Beijing: Zhongguo tongji chubanshe, 1993), pp. 300–8.

provinces. Thus, nine main minority nationalities, namely, the Zhuang, Uygur, Mongolian, Bouyei, Yao, Bai, Hani, Kazak and Dai were concentrated in one province, each accounting for 60–100% of their total population in China. Only small proportions of the Manchu, Korean and Li nationalities were found in the western region, but each of them was also concentrated in a single province, the Manchu and Korean in Inner Mongolia and the Li in Guizhou. In addition, each of the four main minority nationalities of Hui, Miao, Dong and Tujia was concentrated in only two provinces, although the western region only accounts for 37.28% of the Tujia population. The two main minority nationalities of Yi and Tibetan were each also concentrated in three provinces. Even in these cases, the geographical areas in which minority nationalities were concentrated were mostly contiguous, broken only administratively by the provincial

Table 9.7 Populations of Main Minority Nationalities in China and Their Percentage Distribution in the Western Region in 1990 (*continued*)

Region	Bouyei	Dong	Yao	Korean	Bai	Hani	Li	Kazak	Dai	Total
China (Million)	2.55	2.51	2.14	1.92	1.60	1.25	1.11	1.11	1.03	85.52
Percentage (%)										
Western	99.47	67.48	71.69	1.40	92.22	99.68	7.70	99.95	99.58	71.69
Inner Mongolia	0.00	0.01	0.01	**1.15**	0.01	0.00	0.01	0.00	0.00	4.75
Guangxi	0.46	**11.46**	**62.12**	0.01	0.02	0.00	0.28	0.00	0.03	**19.08**
Sichuan	0.29	0.11	0.02	0.03	0.46	0.09	0.02	0.01	0.55	5.45
Guizhou	**97.35**	**55.80**	1.43	0.01	7.72	0.01	**7.30**	0.00	0.04	**11.39**
Yunnan	1.34	0.06	8.08	0.01	**83.95**	**99.56**	0.06	0.00	**98.95**	**12.20**
Tibet	0.00	0.00	0.00	0.00	0.01	0.00	0.00	0.00	0.00	2.46
Shaanxi	0.01	0.01	0.00	0.06	0.02	0.00	0.00	0.01	0.00	0.18
Gansu	0.00	0.00	0.00	0.03	0.01	0.00	0.00	0.28	0.00	1.75
Qinghai	0.00	0.00	0.00	0.02	0.01	0.00	0.00	0.05	0.00	1.91
Ningxia	0.00	0.00	0.00	0.02	0.00	0.00	0.00	0.00	0.00	1.81
Xinjiang	0.02	0.03	0.02	0.05	0.02	0.00	0.01	**99.60**	0.00	**10.71**

boundaries. Such spatial concentrations of the minority population makes it easy to design area-specific policies for development; however, the isolation of such population groups makes socioeconomic integration more difficult to achieve.

The population dynamics and composition of Han and minority nationalities are likely to be different from each other due to their particular social and cultural traditions, stages of economic development and the different state policies that apply to them. Although it remains debatable whether poverty and a low level of development are major causes of a high level of fertility,[20] the state's preferential family planning policy for minority nationalities surely has a significant impact on the growth of their populations.

The state's family planning policy for minority nationalities has undergone a change from encouraging high fertility to family planning, although in a much more relaxed manner than for the Han population.[21] Soon after 1949, the state's policy was to encourage high fertility to increase the populations of minority nationalities that had experienced stagnancy or decline due to poverty before 1949. When the Central Committee of CCP issued a document on controlling population growth in China in March

1955, the minority population was exempted from family planning policies. However, family planning has been widely introduced since the early 1970s in China, while the most restrictive "one-child policy" was introduced in 1979. By 1982, when a census was conducted, it was found that the population of minority nationalities grew much faster than that of the country as a whole. The minority population increased from 5.76% of China's total population in 1964 to 6.68% in 1982. By 1981, the TFR of minority nationalities was 4.23, much greater than the national average of 2.61.

Thus, starting from 1982, government documents began to emphasize the need for family planning among minority nationalities, although such a shift probably began even before that year. The official policy was announced in the No. 7 document of the Central Committee of the CCP in April 1984. The document suggested for the first time that a suitable family planning policy was needed for the minority nationalities. For a minority nationality with a population of less than 10 million, each couple would be allowed to have two children. Some couples could have three children in special cases, but no couple should have more than that number. The exact regulations were to be made by the People's Congress and government of each province or autonomous region, subject to the approval of the higher level People's Congress and government.[22] By 1994, except for some rural areas in Tibet, all autonomous areas had implemented a family planning policy that was characterized as "more relaxed than that for the Han population and different among various minority nationalities in different areas" ("*shidang fangkuan*" 適當放寬, "*qubie duidai*" 區别對待).

Table 9.8 presents the key limits on the number of children a minority could have in various provincial regions under different conditions. Most family planning regulations for minority nationalities have been established by the People's Congresses at the provincial level. In Sichuan, the People's Congresses in three autonomous prefectures made their own regulations. Most regulations set different quotas for urban and rural areas and for normal and exceptional cases. In exceptional cases, couples may be granted the permission to have another child, a policy that has also been practised for the Han population. In Xinjiang, for example, a rural couple may have three children under normal circumstances. But a rural couple may have four children under the following three exceptional conditions. First, some of the first three children are disabled, as certified by an expert family planning team in a prefecture. Second, there is no boy among the first three children. Third, a remarried couple only has three children in total.

Other special conditions have also been attached to some regulations

Table 9.8 Family Planning Regulations for Minority Nationalities in Various Provincial Regions after 1982

Region	Year	Urban		Rural		Other special conditions
		N	E	N	E	
Inner Mongolia	1990	2		2		No limit on the Daur 達斡爾, Ewenki 鄂溫克 and Oroqen 鄂倫春 nationalities; a rural Mongolian couple may have three children
Guangxi	1988	1		1		For a minority nationality with a national population of less than 10 million, two children per couple in rural areas. This concession is limited to 10 minority nationalities in urban areas
Sichuan	1987	2		2	3	A policy similar to that for the Han population applies to the non-agricultural population in areas outside of the three autonomous prefectures
Guizhou	1987	2		2	3	In urban areas, both wife and husband must be members of minority nationalities to be eligible for the relaxed policy
Yunnan	1990	1		1	2	In a border county/city, a couple may be permitted to have one more child in urban or rural areas
Tibet	1992	2	3	3 preferred	No limit	Non-local Han and other nationalities are allowed to have two children only under special conditions
Shaanxi	1991	2		2		
Gansu	1989	1		1		Rural couples except those in densely populated areas may have two children. Rural couples in remote areas and those belonging to the Baoan 保安, Dongxiang 東鄉 and Yugur 裕固 nationalities may have three children. Urban couples in remote areas may have two children
Qinghai	1992	2		2		A couple in animal husbandry areas may have three children
Ningxia	1990	2		2		In eight counties, rural couples may have three children
Xinjiang	1992	2	3	3	4	A couple of minority nationalities with a total national population of less than 50,000 may have an additional child

Notes: N: Normal cases; E: Exceptional cases.
Source: Deng, *Zhongguo shaoshu minzu renkou zhengce yanjiu* (see note 11), pp. 59–73.

so that some minority nationalities with a small population are exempted from family planning or given more concessions. Consideration is also given to couples living in less densely populated areas, border areas, areas in which animal husbandry is a way of life, and some specific areas. Thus, the limit on the number of children that a couple may have varies with provinces and circumstances. In most provinces, minority couples are allowed to have two children. The family regulations in Guangxi, Yunnan and Gansu are the most restrictive, as a couple is allowed to have one child in most cases, although many rural couples are also allowed to have two children. Regulations are less strict in Xinjiang, where an urban or rural couple is allowed to have two or three children under normal conditions, and three or four children under exceptional circumstances. The regulations for Tibet, announced in 1992, are the least restrictive. Rural Tibetan couples are encouraged to have only three children, but no real limit is set. Discrepancies between a formal regulation and its implementation may occur, as in Tibet. Goldstein et al. reported that birth limits were extended to rural Tibet in 1984, and fines and penalties were introduced in the 1990s.[23] They also found surprisingly rapid voluntary adoption of birth control methods in the 1990s due to several factors: the division of rural land on a one-time basis, the pressures of competition in migrant labour markets and poverty. Their study revealed the danger of using refugee reports and anecdotal evidence, which often present a horrific picture of birth control in Tibet, to interpret highly politicized situations.

It is noted that most provincial family planning regulations were issued in the period 1987–1992. Before the issuing of formal regulations, temporary regulations that may have set similar or more relaxed limits on the number of children a couple was permitted to have were adopted in some provinces.[24] The formal regulations issued later tend to be stricter as family planning among minority nationalities became more established. For example, an earlier resolution of the government of the Guangxi Autonomous Region, issued in 1985, allowed many urban and rural couples to have two children and the couples of some minority nationalities to have three children. The formal family planning regulation, issued in 1988, tightened the scope of those allowed to have two children and prohibited all couples from having three children.

It can be expected that the implementation of family planning among minority nationalities would have had some impact on their fertility levels and population growth rates. The most recent and reliable data on the fertility and mortality levels of minority nationalities are from the 1990 Census.

The available data shown in Figures 9.5 and 9.6 are on the figures on the minority population of China as a whole, rather than western China only. However, as the majority of the minority population is concentrated in the western region, the data would be representative of minority nationalities in the western region with the exception of the Manchu, Tujia, Korean and Li nationalities whose main areas of concentration are elsewhere.

According to Figure 9.5, there was a significant decline in TFR among minority nationalities in the period 1981–1989, as family planning began to be implemented among them. The TFR of minority nationalities as a whole declined by 31.37%, from 4.24 in 1981 to 2.91 in 1989. Such a decline was much greater than the 10.76% for Han population and the 12.26% of the country as a whole in the same period. The TFR gap between the Han population and minority nationalities was effectively closed from 1.73 to 0.67 in the period 1981–1989. This is because the Han population already reached a low TFR of 2.51 in 1981, as family planning was implemented widely among them in the 1970s. Almost all minority nationalities experienced a similar decline in TFR in the 1980s. Those with a higher TFR at the beginning of the period experienced a greater decline in TFR. For example, in 1981–1989, the TFR of the Zhuang population

Figure 9.5 Total Fertility Rates of Various Populations in China, 1982–1989

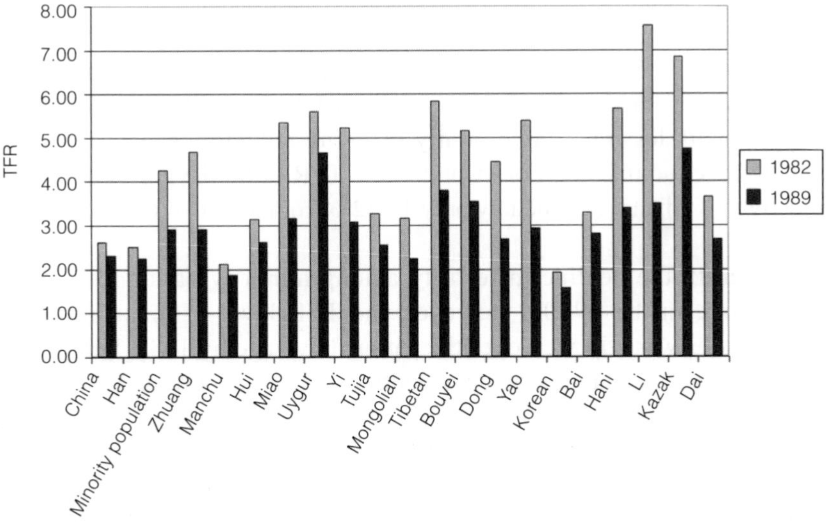

Source: Deng, *Zhongguo shaoshu minzu renkou zhengce yanjiu* (see note 11), p.103.

Figure 9.6 Infant Mortality Rate and Life Expectancy at Birth of Various Populations in China in 1990

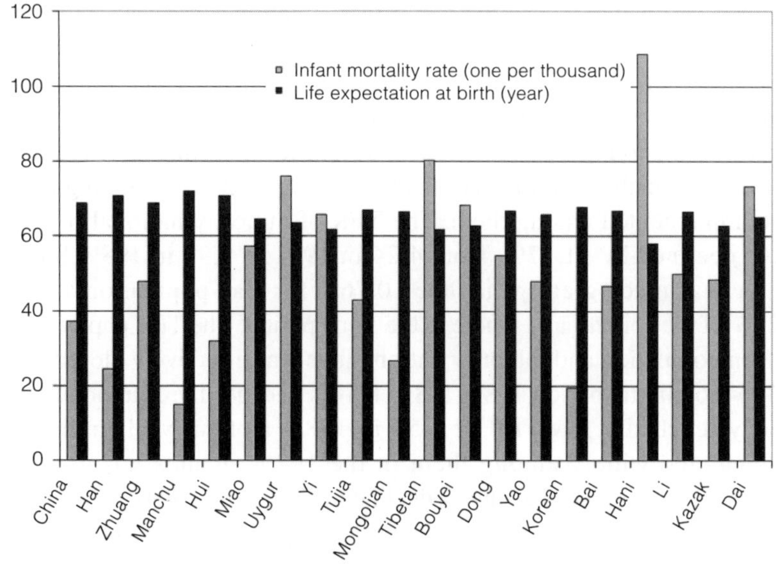

Sources: Guojia tongjiju renkou yu jiuye tongjisi (ed.), *Zhongguo renkou tongji nianjian 1995* (Beijing: Zhongguo tongji chubanshe, 1995), p. 232; Zhang and Huang, *Zhongguo shaoshu minzu renkou diaocha yanjiu* (see note 10), p. 336; Cai, *Renkou lüpishu 2000 nian* (see note 1), p. 213.

declined by 37.69% from 4.67 to 2.91, while the TFR of the Mongolian population declined by 29.11% from 3.16 to 2.24. The minority population in areas with less restrictive family planning regulations experienced a smaller decline in TFR. For example, the TFR of the Uygur population, mostly in Xinjiang, declined by only 16.82% from 5.59 to 4.65 in the same period.

Overall, the decline in fertility among minority nationalities was impressive in the 1980s. However, the TFR level of most minority nationalities was still well over the national average by 1989, being over three among the eight minority nationalities — the Miao, Uygur, Yi, Tibetan, Bouyei, Hani, Li and Kazak — whose population was over 1 million in 1990. With the exception of the Li, these nationalities were concentrated in the western region. The higher fertility level led to a faster population growth of minority nationalities. According to Table 9.9, in the period 1982–1990, the annual growth rate of minority population was 3.87%, greater than the

Table 9.9 Annual Population Growth Rates and Composition of Various Populations in China

Indicator	Annual population growth rate 1982–1990 (%)	Percentage of population by age groups in 1990 (%)			Gender ratio in 1990	Percentage of illiterate and semi-illiterate aged 15+ in 1990 (%)	
		0–14	15–64	65+		Males	Females
China	1.48	27.69	66.74	5.57	106.04	12.98	31.93
Han	1.29	27.13	67.20	5.67	106.12	12.38	31.15
Minority population	3.87	34.06	61.51	4.43	105.14	20.52	41.73
Zhuang	1.88	33.64	61.17	5.19	104.27	9.67	32.85
Manchu	10.34	30.78	65.11	4.11	109.46	7.35	15.93
Hui	2.19	31.99	63.50	4.51	103.21	23.72	42.72
Miao	4.82	34.82	61.08	4.10	107.87	26.25	58.74
Uygur	2.37	39.42	55.81	4.77	104.47	24.49	28.77
Yi	2.34	35.36	60.59	4.05	103.60	35.04	64.83
Tujia	8.78	29.56	65.55	4.89	110.63	14.72	37.04
Mongolian	4.28	35.82	61.10	3.08	103.27	12.63	23.19
Tibetan	2.21	35.86	59.33	4.81	97.64	55.71	82.40
Bouyei	2.30	33.74	61.41	4.85	103.40	24.30	61.68
Dong	7.06	32.22	63.55	4.23	112.23	15.12	43.64
Yao	5.13	36.68	59.16	4.16	109.10	17.71	43.27
Korean	1.07	24.74	70.67	4.59	98.07	2.68	11.13
Bai	4.31	32.49	62.70	4.81	102.84	14.64	46.10
Hani	2.12	36.66	59.46	3.88	104.32	45.50	75.90
Li	2.83	38.93	57.20	3.87	103.05	17.98	39.13
Kazak	2.35	42.92	54.44	2.64	104.92	9.09	15.78
Dai	2.50	33.61	61.92	4.47	99.47	31.04	53.18

Sources: Deng, *Zhongguo shaoshu minzu renkou zhengce yanjiu* (see note 11), p. 215; Guowuyuan renkou pucha bangongshi, Guojia tongjiju renkou tongjisi (eds.), *Zhongguo 1990 nian renkou pucha ziliao diyice* (Beijing: Zhongguo tongji chubanshe, 1993), pp. 380–412 and 736–37; Zhang and Huang, *Zhongguo shaoshu minzu renkou diaocha yanjiu* (see note 10), p. 302.

1.29% of the Han population. The Miao, Mongolian, Dong, Yao and Bai populations grew by over 4% a year in the same period, although social change also contributed significantly to their growth as mentioned before. The Manchus and Tujias also had high growth rates, but the majority of their population was not in the western region.

Life expectancy at birth and the rate of infant mortality are two common measures of the mortality level as well as quality of life. As shown in Figure 9.6, the life expectancy of most minority nationalities was generally a few years lower than the national average, consistent with their low level of economic development. For example, in 1990, the life expectancy of the Bouyei nationality was 62.73 years while the national average was 69.55 years. Meanwhile, the life expectancy of the Hani nationality was the lowest at 57.94 years. That for the Uygur and Tibetan populations was 63.43 and 61.66 years, respectively.

However, the infant mortality rate of minority nationalities seems to be much higher than the national average and varies widely among various populations. This is likely related to the much poorer medical facilities and services in poor areas with large minority populations. The infant mortality rate was 37.0 per thousand for the country as a whole and 24.4 per thousand for the Han population. But it was as high as 108.4 per thousand for the Hani population, although it was also as low as 26.6 per thousand for the Mongolian population. The infant mortality rates of the Uygur and Tibetan populations were 75.8 and 80.1 per thousand, respectively, in 1990. Great efforts are needed to stimulate development and improve health conditions in areas with large ethnic populations.

The relatively high fertility and mortality levels have had an important impact on the age structure of the population of minority nationalities. Under such demographic conditions, the minority population had a high proportion of young people (aged 0–14 years) and a low proportion of elderly (aged 65 years and over). According to Table 9.9, in 1990, the proportion of the young was 34.06% for minority nationalities as a whole, higher than the 27.13% for the Han population. On the other hand, the proportion of the elderly was only 4.43% for minority nationalities as a whole, compared with 5.67% for the Han population. In terms of gender ratio, that is, the number of males per one hundred females, there was little difference between the Han population and minority nationalities as a whole. However, the gender ratio of the Dong population was as high as 112.23, while that of the Tibetan population was as low as 97.64. One explanation for the low gender ratio of the Tibetan population is its low gender ratio before the 1960s.[25] Indeed, it was only 94.19 in 1952, reflecting the particular social conditions of old Tibet. A high infant mortality rate for boys in particular and the eruption of frequent small-scale wars and conflicts contributed to a small male population before 1949, while female infanticide was rare.[26] Since the 1970s, the gender ratio in Tibet has increased, to over 97 by 1990. As for the Dong population, the male-biased reclassification of nationality status, which was popular in the 1980s, and gender differences in infant mortality were two plausible reasons for their high gender ratio.[27]

An examination of the social and economic characteristics of minority nationalities is also important for a better understanding of the problems of population and development that face them. Generally, despite significant improvements in the past few decades, minority nationalities have a low level of urbanization and the majority still engages in agriculture or animal husbandry, activities associated with a low level of development. Only the situation of education levels will be examined briefly here. It has been well recognized that the minority nationalities have a generally low level of education. Table 9.9 also presents the percentage of illiterate and semi-illiterate people aged 15 years and over in various nationalities in 1990. In 1990, the percentage of illiterate and semi-illiterate among males for minority nationalities as a whole was as high as 20.52%. By contrast, the figure for the Han population was 12.38%, and for the entire country it was 12.98%. The situation was even worse for women, although both Hans and non-Hans neglected the education of women.[28] The percentage of illiterate and semi-illiterate among females for minority nationalities as a whole was as high as 41.73%, in contrast to 31.15% for the Han population and 31.93% for the entire country in the same year. The problem was the most serious in Tibet. In 1990, its percentage of illiterate and semi-illiterate population was as high as 55.71% for males and 82.40% for females. Clearly, much needs to be done to improve education for minority nationalities. Many studies have already pointed out that investing in human resources is the first step in dismantling the vicious cycle of poverty and under-development.[29]

Migration to and from the Western Region

The previous sections have examined the growth and distribution of the total population and minority population in the western region. Migration to and from the western region has also been an issue debated both inside and outside of China. In the period 1949–1978, the direction of regional migration was generally from the central and eastern regions to the western region.[30] Some scholars in the 1980s believed that there was much potential for migration to the west because of the region's low population density and large amounts of land and resources.[31] Some estimated that 60 or 70 million migrants could be moved to the northwest. Nevertheless, some previous studies had already revealed that the direction of regional migration was from the western and central regions to the eastern region in the post-reform period, due to strong pull factors in the coastal region.[32] This section provides an overview of migration patterns in the pre-reform and post-reform periods. The relationship between population and development is then examined.

Up to 1980, the main source of data for migration would be the records of household registration. But, according to this data source, for the country as a whole, in-migration generally exceeded out-migration. This indicates that some instances of out-migration were not recorded, as international migration was minimal at the time. For example, the number of net migrants was 1.11 million, or 7.2% of total out-migrants in 1975.[33] This degree of data error should be borne in mind when evaluating migration data such as that shown in Table 9.10. Generally, net migration to the western region took place mainly in the 1950s and 1960s. In 1960, the western region had 1.708 million net migrants. Inner Mongolia, Shaanxi and Xinjiang were the main destinations, receiving net numbers of 1.060, 0.260 and 0.288 million people, respectively, in that year. Net migration to the western region declined to less than 0.210 million a year after the early 1970s. It was estimated that net migration to Inner Mongolia was about 5 million in the period 1954–1984.[34] To Qinghai and Ningxia, it was about 1–2 million each and to Xinjiang it was about 3 million in the same period. In the pre-

Table 9.10 Net Migration to Western China, 1955–1980

(Unit: thousands)

Region	1955	1960	1965	1970	1975	1980
Western	759	1,708	740	−173	205	156
Inner Mongolia	200	1,060	35	−173	−26	−54
Guangxi	72	9	23	39	47	105
Sichuan	192	121	137	99	66	10
Guizhou	−7	−131	64	184	4	−14
Yunnan	−37	−2	127	n.a.	41	34
Tibet	n.a.	n.a.	n.a.	n.a.	3	3
Shaanxi	168	260	−15	−3	8	30
Gansu	76	−12	118	−394	13	−3
Qinghai	22	61	18	20	8	−3
Ningxia	10	54	33	5	14	21
Xinjiang	63	288	200	50	27	27

Note: Data on Chongqing are included in Sichuan.
Source: *Zhongguo renkou tongji nianjian 1990* (see note 9), pp. 622–38.

reform period, the main form of migration was organized migration by the state.[35] Technical staff, officials, scientists and their dependents were moved from industrial cities on the coast to the northwest and southwest as well as to the northeast, north and central regions of China to built up old and new industrial cities according to the state's plans. Similarly, some demobilized soldiers and urban youth were also moved to Xinjiang, Inner Mongolia, Guangxi and Yunnan in the western region as well as to Guangdong 廣東 and Jiangxi 江西 to construct state-owned farms. There was also spontaneous rural migration, mainly to China's northeast region.

The case of Xinjiang may illustrate the dynamics of migration in the pre-reform period.[36] Xinjiang's population increased from 4.33 million to 13.08 million in the period 1949–1982. It was estimated that the net migration was 2.90 million, accounting for 33% of the total population increase in this period. The most significant migration took place in 1957–1960, when Xinjiang gained 1.07 million people. The main migration stream consisted of the organized migration of educated youths, demobilized soldiers and some spontaneous migrants. For example, the state mobilized 0.3 million educated youths to migrate to Xinjiang in 1958–1962 in order to support the construction of the border areas. In this regard, the most notable move was the establishment of the Xinjiang Production and Construction Corps (*Shengchan jianshe bingtuan* 生產建設兵團) in 1954, made up of demobilized soldiers who had previously been stationed in Xinjiang. It was established to be a backup for the military but also to engage in agriculture, mining and industrial production in peacetime. Other educated youths and migrants also joined this special organization in subsequent years. The population of this organization increased from 0.18 million in 1954 to 0.72 million in 1960, 1.69 million in 1968 and 2.20 million in 1979. The population stabilized in the reform period, at 2.22 million in 1985.

Similar to Xinjiang, there was also much migration to Qinghai in the pre-reform period.[37] There was a net migration of 0.60 million in the period 1954–1985, equivalent to 17.33% of the total population in 1985. But large-scale migration mostly took place in the 1950s. Indeed, net migration reached 0.75 million in the period 1954–1959. This was followed by net out-migration of 0.57 million in 1960–1963 due to the agricultural and economic failures resulting from the Great Leap Forward. Adjustment policies were introduced in 1962 so that migration to Qinghai was on a small scale. The net migration was 0.43 million in the period 1964–1985, about 20,000 a year.

Organized migration to Qinghai in this period was related to economic construction in the province. For example, to implement the policy of "Third Front" construction introduced in 1966, 24 large industrial enterprises were relocated there from 1966–1970, mainly from coastal areas such as Shanghai and Beijing 北京. About 90% of these enterprises relied on the staff that were relocated along with them. Accordingly, it was estimated that 50,000 workers and 70,000 dependents moved into the province during that period. Much migration had also been induced by the construction of the Longyangxia 龍羊峽 hydropower station in the 1970s and 1980s. This was a key project of the state, with a power-generating capacity of 1.28 million kw. The hydropower station had 28,000 employees and a total population of about 50,000, 80% of whom were migrants from other provinces.

In 1956, the state mobilized and sponsored 69,728 people in 14,416 households to move to Qinghai. However, the organized migration to Qinghai for land and agricultural development in the 1950s was largely a failure.[38] Most households soon returned to their hometown due to the difficulties of adapting to the local environment and lifestyle. In 1958, the state's migration strategy changed to focus on youths. About 0.12 million youths were mobilized from Henan 河南 to Qinghai in the period 1958–1960. But many left Qinghai in the same period. By 1960, only 53,055 young migrants were left in the youth farms. Production in these farms was so poor that the output was just sufficient to provide seeds for farming, leaving nothing to feed the migrants. In 1965, a new strategy of migration, establishing agricultural construction army divisions, was introduced. Among the total population of 10,000, over 7,000 youths were recruited from Shandong 山東 and 1,200 youths from Xining 西寧 whose hometown was Shandong, while others were demobilized soldiers. Once again, this project was a failure. The army division was again unable to feed itself, and the state had to supply it with 4,720 tonnes of grain a year. Eventually, members of the army division had to be relocated to Shandong in 1980–1983, when more liberal polices on migration were adopted in the reform period. Thus, by the beginning of the reform period, almost all of those who had been moved to Qinghai to work on agricultural and land development had left the region. This is an important lesson for the state in dealing with the issue of migration in the twenty-first century.

There were also two special streams of migration to Qinghai in the pre-reform period.[39] The first was the settlement of demobilized soldiers. In 1956, about 5,000 army officers stationed in North China were demobilized and relocated to work in Qinghai, together with their 9,000 dependents. Another 5,000 army officers who had been stationed in Qinghai previously were also asked to settle in the province following demobilization. The second migration stream was that of criminals from 14 provincial regions who were sentenced to serve in the labour reform camps set up in the province by the state. Most offenders decided to stay in Qinghai when they were released.

In the reform period, migration to the western region was reversed.[40] According to the data from 1990 Census and from the 1995 One Percent Population Sampling Survey shown in Table 9.11, the western region lost 1.544 and 1.533 million people in 1985–1990 and 1990–1995, respectively. In 1985–1990, most provinces, except for Qinghai, Ningxia and Xinjiang, lost people through migration, with a significant loss of 0.874 million in

Table 9.11 Migration to the Western Region in 1985–1990 and 1990–1995

(Unit: thousands)

Region	1985–1990			1990–1995		
	In-migration	Out-migration	Net migration	In-migration	Out-migration	Net migration
China	11,007	11,007	0	10,384	10,384	0
Eastern	6,028	3,660	2,368	6,759	2,730	4,029
Central	2,648	3,472	–824	1,528	4,024	–2,496
Western	2,331	3,875	–1,544	2,097	3,630	–1,533
Inner Mongolia	254	303	–49	268	242	26
Guangxi	142	589	–446	117	540	–423
Sichuan	439	1,313	–874	385	1,419	–1,035
Guizhou	190	313	–123	148	391	–243
Yunnan	249	277	–28	201	236	–34
Tibet	n.a.	n.a.	n.a.	35	27	7
Shaanxi	310	362	–53	159	257	–99
Gansu	197	281	-84	136	244	–109
Qinghai	115	102	13	50	75	–24
Ningxia	92	57	35	48	53	–5
Xinjiang	342	277	64	551	146	405

Notes: Data on Chongqing are included in Sichuan; international migration is excluded.

Sources: Guowuyuan renkou pucha bangongshi, Guojia tongjiju renkou tongjisi (eds.), *Zhongguo 1990 nian renkou pucha ziliao diyice* (Beijing: Zhongguo tongji chubanshe, 1993), pp. 152–331; Quanguo renkou chouyang diaocha bangongshi 全國人口抽樣調查辦公室 (ed.), *1995 quanguo 1% renkou chouyang diaocha ziliao* 1995全國1%人口抽樣調查資料 (Tabulations of China 1% Population Sample Survey 1995) (Beijing: Zhongguo tongji chubanshe, 1997), pp. 558–617.

Sichuan and 0.446 million in Guangxi. It was found that much migration to Xinjiang was due to employment and the carrying out of small businesses. In addition to labour migration, migration due to marriage was also an important reason for leaving the western region. For example, due to marriage, a net number of over 100,000 people moved from Sichuan to Jiangsu 江蘇 and Hubei 湖北 in 1985–1990.[41] In 1990–1995, many provinces continued to lose population through migration. Sichuan and Guangxi had a significant loss of 1.035 million and 0.423 million, respectively. There was a small net migration to Inner Mongolia and Tibet. But net migration to Xinjiang became very significant, reaching 0.405 million. Contrary to the previous period, migration to Xinjiang in the reform period was mostly spontaneous, as people from developed regions such as Jiangsu and Zhejiang 浙江 were attracted to areas operated by the Xinjiang Production and Construction Corps along the second Euro-Asian railway corridor and to the cotton and petroleum mining areas.[42] Many such migrants were tradesmen and members of construction teams from rural areas in the coastal region seeking business and income opportunities in the western region in China's emerging market economy.[43]

The overall reversion in the direction of migration to and from the western region has three main causes. First, much migration was organized by the state in the pre-reform period. Many were reluctant migrants who wanted to return to the eastern region if possible.[44] Second, there has been a significant change in the migration regime in China. In the reform period, the state is very much concerned with economic development and less interested in sponsoring migration to border regions for purposes of defence.[45] The state policy towards migrants also has become more liberal. Since the early 1980s, migrants previously relocated to the border regions have been allowed to return to the eastern region. Third, the focus of the regional development strategy shifted to the coastal areas, especially in the period 1978–1994. The coastal areas experienced dramatic economic growth before and after 1994[46] due to a combination of favourable polices, a good economic foundation, a coastal location and significant amounts of foreign investment. The economic opportunities available there have attracted waves of migrants from the western region, notably from Sichuan and Guangxi to Guangdong.[47]

The previous analysis of migration revealed that migration to the western region in the pre-reform period mainly occurred under the auspices of the state. Migration out of the western region was mainly a spontaneous choice because of the emergence of economic and job opportunities in an emerging market economy in the post-reform period. Although a few provinces still experienced net migration, such as Xinjiang, out-migration was the rule in the post-reform period. The loss of skilled labourers and professionals has no doubt had a significant negative impact on the economy of the western region. To some extent, skilled technical and professional people are much needed in the western region. Nevertheless, it is clear that there is no economic and ecological foundation for large-scale labour migration from the eastern and central regions to the western region.[48]

Conclusion

This chapter has examined the demographic aspects behind the under-development of the western region. The key findings can be summarized as follows.

First, rates of fertility and migration have had a significant impact on population growth in the western region. In the period 1952–1982, population growth was faster in the western region than the eastern region due to a high fertility rate and net migration in the western region. In the period 1982–2000, the population trend was reversed, due to net migration from the western region to the eastern region. Fertility levels in the western region have remained high, especially in Guizhou and Tibet. But it is encouraging that, even there, the TFR has fallen to below two.

Second, the concentration of minority nationalities is a major feature of the western region. A higher growth rate for the minority population than for the Han population, due to a higher fertility level and to the reclassification and inheritance of nationality status, has resulted in a further concentration. The state's family planning policy for minority nationalities has undergone a change from encouraging high fertility in the 1950s to family planning, especially after 1982, although it is still much more relaxed than for Han population.

Third, the life expectancy of minority nationalities has generally been lower than the national average, while infant mortality rate has been much higher and has varied widely among various populations. This has been due to a very low level of development and to poor medical facilities and services in poor areas with large minority populations. Minority nationalities have also had a low level of education. A high proportion of the population was illiterate and semi-illiterate in 1990, especially the women.

Fourth, in 1949–1978, the direction of regional migration was generally from the central and eastern regions to the western region. Organized migration by the state was a defining feature of migration in the pre-reform period. In the reform period, the direction of migration was reversed. Three main causes for such a reversal were identified. First, the organized migration of the pre-reform period produced many reluctant migrants who strove to return to the eastern region. Second, migration in China changed as the state liberalized its policy towards migrants. Finally, the dramatic economic growth in the coastal areas in the post-reform period has attracted migrants from the western region. The loss of skilled labourers and professionals has undoubtedly had a significant impact on the economy of the western region.

Other chapters in this book will identify the potential for ecological conservation and economic development and the measures needed to achieve these goals. From the perspective of population and development, a combination of family planning, education and training, and migration policies will greatly facilitate the development of the western region, bringing prosperity to its people. It should be emphasized that a family planning policy may not be seen as a passive response that simply follows the classical Malthusian view or Nelson's concept of the low-level equilibrium trap. A slowly growing population would be able to do better to improve human resources and capital stock per capita than a rapidly growing one. Therefore, family planning is not only necessary if the country is to escape the "Malthusian trap" but also useful for taking a society towards a faster track of development and modernization.

Acknowledgement

The chapter is based on research funded by a direct grant from The Chinese University of Hong Kong, project code 2020764.

Notes

1. Tian Xueyuan 田雪原, *Daguo zhinan — dangdai Zhongguo de renkou wenti* 大國之難 — 當代中國的人口問題 (Challenge of a Big Country: Population Problems in Contemporary China) (Beijing: Jinri Zhongguo chubanshe 今日中國出版社, 1997); J. Shen, "China's Future Population and Development Challenges," *The Geographical Journal*, Vol. 164, No. 1 (1998), pp. 32–40; Cai Fang 蔡昉 (ed.), *Renkou lüpishu 2000 nian: Zhongguo renkou wenti baogao — nongcun renkou wenti jiqi zhili* 人口綠皮書2000年：中國人口問題報告 — 農村人口問題及其治理 (Green Paper on Population in 2000: A Report on China's Population Problem — Problem and Solution of the Rural Population) (Beijing: Shehui kexue wenxian chubanshe 社會科學文獻出版社, 2000).

2. Tien H. Yuan, *China's Strategic Demographic Initiative* (New York: Praeger, 1991); S. Greenhalgh, "Shifts in China's Population Policy: 1984–86 Views from the Central, Provincial, and Local Levels," *Population and Development Review*, Vol. 12 (1986), pp. 491–516; Y. Zeng, P. Tu, B. Gu, L. Xu, B. Li and Y. Li, "Causes and Implications of the Recent Increase in the Reported Sex Ratio at Birth in China," *Population and Development Review*, No. 19 (1993), pp. 283–302; Ansley J. Coale and J. Banister, "Five Decades of Missing Females in China," *Demography*, Vol. 31, No. 3 (1994), pp. 459–69.
3. J. Z. Lee and F. Wang, *One Quarter of Humanity: Malthusian Mythology and Chinese Realities, 1700–2000* (Cambridge: Harvard University Press, 1999), p. 95; J. Banister, *China's Changing Population* (Stanford: Stanford University Press, 1987); K. Hardee-Cleaveland and J. Banister, "Fertility Policy and Implementation in China, 1986–88," *Population and Development Review*, Vol. 14 (1988), pp. 245–86.
4. J. R. Taylor and J. Banister, "China: Surplus Rural Labour and Migration," *Asia-Pacific Population Journal*, Vol. 4. No. 4 (1989), pp. 3–20; and J. Shen and Nigel A. Spence, "Trends in Labour Supply and the Future of Employment in China," *Environment and Planning C: Government and Policy*, Vol. 13 (1995), pp. 361–77; Lester Russell Brown, *Who Will Feed China? Wake-up Call for a Small Planet* (New York: W. W. Norton & Co., 1995); G. Smil, "Who Will Feed China?" *The China Quarterly*, No. 143 (1995), pp. 801–13; J. Shen, "Modelling National or Regional Grain Supply and Food Balance in China," *Environment and Planning A*, Vol. 32 (2000), pp. 539–57.
5. Zhonghua Renmin Gongheguo renkou yu jihua shengyufa 中華人民共和國人口與計劃生育法 (Population and Family Planning Law of PRC), passed by the 25th meeting of the Standing Committee of the 9th National People's Congress, China, on 12 December 2001. Similarly, in March 2000, The Central Committee of the CCP and the State Council announced a decision entitled "Guanyu jiaqiang renkou yu jihua shengyu gongzuo wending di shengyu shuiping de jueding" 關於加強人口與計劃生育工作穩定低生育水平的決定 (Resolution on Enhancing Family Planning and Stabilizing the Low Fertility Rate).
6. T. R. Malthus, *An Essay on the Principle of Population* (Cambridge: Cambridge University Press, 1989); R. R. Nelson, "A Theory of the Low-Level Equilibrium Trap," *American Economic Review*, Vol. 46 (1956), pp. 894–908.
7. See R. D. Hill, "People, Land, and an Equilibrium Trap: Guizhou Province, China," *Pacific Viewpoint*, Vol. 34, No. 1 (1993), pp. 1–24; J. Shen, "Population Growth, Ecological Degradation and Construction in the Western Region of China," *Journal of Contemporary China*, Vol. 13, No. 39 (2004), forthcoming; Li Honggui 李宏規 and Yang Shengwan 楊勝萬, "Zhongguo xibu de renkou yu fazhan wenti" 中國西部的人口與發展問題 (The Issues of Population and

Development in the West of China), *Renkou yu jingji* 人口與經濟 (Population and Economics), No. 3 (2001), pp. 3–6.

8. Lu Dadao 陸大道 et al., *2000 Zhongguo quyu fazhan baogao — xibu kaifa de jichu, zhengce yu taishi fenxi* 2000中國區域發展報告 —— 西部開發的基礎政策與態勢分析 (Regional Development of China, 2000 — Foundation, Policy and Situation Analysis of the Development of Western China) (Beijing: Shangwu yinshuguan 商務印書館, 2001); Hu Angang 胡鞍鋼 (ed.), *Diqu yu fazhan: Xibu kaifa xinzhanlüe* 地區與發展：西部開發新戰略 (Regions and Development: New Strategies for the Development of the Western Region) (Beijing: Zhongguo jihua chubanshe 中國計劃出版社, 2001); Chen Shupeng 陳述彭, Yeung Yue-man and Lin Hui (eds.), *Xinjingji yu Zhongguo xibu kaifa* 新經濟與中國西部開發 (The New Economy and China's Western Development) (Hong Kong: Hong Kong Institute of Asia-Pacific Studies, The Chinese University of Hong Kong, 2001).
9. National Bureau of Statistics (NBS) (ed.), *China Statistical Yearbook 2001* (Beijing: China Statistics Press), pp. 93 and 99; Guojia tongjiju renkou tongjisi 國家統計局人口統計司 (ed.), *Zhongguo renkou tongji nianjian 1990* 中國人口統計年鑑1990 (China Population Statistics Yearbook 1990) (Beijing: Kexue jishu wenxian chubanshe 科學技術文獻出版社, 1991), pp. 42–43; Guojia tongjiju renkou he shehui keji tongjisi 國家統計局人口和社會科技統計司 (ed.), *Zhongguo renkou tongji nianjian 2001* 中國人口統計年鑑2001 (China Population Statistics Yearbook 2001) (Beijing: Zhongguo tongji chubanshe 中國統計出版社, 2001), p. 53; Department of Comprehensive Statistics of National Bureau of Statistics, *Comprehensive Statistical Data and Materials on 50 Years of New China* (Beijing: China Statistics Press, 1999), p. 112; Sun Huaiyang 孫懷陽 and Cheng Xianmin 程賢敏 (eds.), *Zhongguo Zangzu renkou yu shehui* 中國藏族人口與社會 (Population and Society of Tibetans in China) (Beijing: Zhongguo zangxue chubanshe 中國藏學出版社, 1999), p. 179.
10. The study of minority nationalities in China has increased significantly since the early 1990s, aided by the release of population census data in 1982 and 1990. For example, Tian Xueyuan (ed.), *Zhongguo ge shengqu shaoshu minzu renkou* 中國各省區少數民族人口 (Population of Ethnic Nationalities in Provinces and Regions in China) (Beijng: Zhongguo renkou chubanshe 中國人口出版社, 1998); Zhang Tianlu 張天路 and Huang Rongqing 黃榮清 (eds.), *Zhongguo shaoshu minzu renkou diaocha yanjiu* 中國少數民族人口調查研究 (An Investigation of the Population of Ethnic Nationalities in China) (Beijing: Gaodeng jiaoyu chubanshe 高等教育出版社, 1996).
11. Deng Hongbi 鄧宏碧 (ed.), *Zhongguo shaoshu minzu renkou zhengce yanjiu* 中國少數民族人口政策研究 (A Study on the Population Policy on Ethnic Nationalities in China) (Chongqing: Chongqing chubanshe 重慶出版社, 1998), p. 2; Information Office of the State Council of PRC, *National Minorities Policy and Its Practice in China*, Beijing, 1999.

12. C. Mackerras, *China's Minorities: Integration and Modernization in the Twentieth Century* (Hong Kong: Oxford University Press, 1994), pp. 5 and 167–97.
13. I. G. Cook and G. Murray, *China's Third Revolution: Tensions in the Transition Towards a Post-Communist China* (Richmond, Surrey: Curzon Press, 2001), pp. 120–47; Shakya Tsering, *The Dragon in the Land of Snows: A History of Modern Tibet since 1947* (London: Pimlico, 1999), p. 92.
14. Mackerras, *China's Minorities* (see note 12), p. 140.
15. Ibid., p. 201.
16. Economic and Development Department, State Ethnic Affairs Commission and Department of Integrated Statistics, NBS (eds.), *China's Ethnic Statistical Yearbook 2000* (Beijing: Ethnic Publishing House, 2000), pp. 373–82.
17. See B. Sautman, "Preferential Policies for Ethnic Minorities in China: The Case of Xinjiang," in *Nationalism and Ethnoregional Identities in China*, edited by W. Safran (London: Frank Cass Publishers, 1998), pp. 86–118.
18. Deng, *Zhongguo shaoshu minzu renkou zhengce yanjiu* (see note 11), p. 4; Zhang and Huang, *Zhongguo shaoshu minzu renkou diaocha yanjiu* (see note 10), pp. 363–70.
19. Zhang and Huang, *Zhongguo shaoshu minzu renkou diaocha yanjiu* (see note 10), p. 366.
20. Chen Yiping 陳義平, "Xibu kaifa cunzai renkou wenti ma?" 西部開發存在人口問題嗎？(Are there any Population Problems in the Development of the West of China?), *Renkou yanjiu* 人口研究 (Population Research), Vol. 24, No. 4 (2000), pp. 51–55.
21. Deng, *Zhongguo shaoshu minzu renkou zhengce yanjiu* (see note 11), pp. 52–59.
22. Ibid., p. 3.
23. M. C. Goldstein, B. Jiao, C. M. Beall and P. Tsering, "Fertility and Family Planning in Rural Tibet," *The China Journal*, No. 47 (2002), pp. 19–39.
24. Deng, *Zhongguo shaoshu minzu renkou zhengce yanjiu* (see note 11), p. 64.
25. Sun and Cheng (eds.), *Zhongguo zangzu renkou yu shehui* (see note 9), pp. 209–17.
26. Mackerras, *China's Minorities* (see note 12), pp. 133 and 245–48.
27. See Yan Tianhua 嚴田華, *Guizhou shaoshu minzu renkou fazhan yu wenti yanjiu* 貴州少數民族人口發展與問題研究 (A Study on the Development and Problems of the Population of Minority Nationalities in Guizhou) (Beijing: Zhongguo renkou chubanshe, 1995), pp. 75–77; Zhang Tianlu, *Minzu renkou xue* 民族人口學 (Demographic Study of Nationalities) (Beijing: Zhongguo renkou chubanshe, 1998), pp. 252–59.
28. Zhang and Huang, *Zhongguo shaoshu minzu renkou diaocha yanjiu* (see note 10), pp. 380–97.
29. M. P. Todaro, *Economic Development* (New York: Longman, 1997), pp. 378–

416; Liu Jiaqiang 劉家強, "Xibu kaifa zhong de renkou huanjing fenxi" 西部開發中的人口環境分析 (An Analysis of the Population Environment in the Western Development), *Renkou yanjiu*, Vol. 24, No. 4 (2000), pp. 46–50.

30. J. Shen, "China's Economic Reform and Its Impact on Migration Processes," *Migration Unit Research Paper 10* (1996), pp. 1–25, Department of Geography, University of Wales Swansea; G. Clarke, "The Movement of Population to the West of China: Tibet and Qinghai," in *Migration: The Asian Experience*, edited by J. Brown and R. Foot (New York: St. Martin's Press, 1994), pp. 221–57.
31. Tian Fang 田方 and Zhang Dongliang 張東亮 (eds.), *Zhongguo renkou qianyi xintan* 中國人口遷移新探 (A New Exploration of Population Migration in China) (Beijing: Zhishi chubanshe 知識出版社, 1989), pp. 196–214; Tian Fang and Lin Fatang 林發棠 (eds.), *Zhongguo renkou qianyi* 中國人口遷移 (Population Migration in China) (Beijing: Zhishi chubanshe, 1986), pp. 106–33.
32. J. Shen, "Internal Migration and Regional Population Dynamics in China," *Progress in Planning*, Vol. 45, No. 3 (1996), pp. 123–88; J. Shen and N. A. Spence, "Modelling Regional Population Growth in China," *Mathematical Population Studies*, Vol. 6, No. 3 (1997), pp. 241–74.
33. Guojia tongjiju, *Zhongguo renkou tongji nianjian 1990* (see note 9), pp. 622–38.
34. Tian and Zhang, *Zhongguo renkou qianyi xintan* (see note 31), pp. 6 and 198–99.
35. Tian and Lin, *Zhongguo renkou qianyi* (see note 31), pp. 289–91; Shen, "China's Economic Reform" (see note 30).
36. Tian and Zhang, *Zhongguo renkou qianyi xintan* (see note 31), pp. 196–214.
37. Ibid., pp. 214–35.
38. Ibid.
39. Ibid.
40. Shen, "China's Economic Reform" (see note 30); J. Shen, "Modelling Regional Migration in China: Estimation and Decomposition," *Environment and Planning A*, Vol. 31 (1999), pp. 1223–38.
41. Wang Guixin 王桂新, *Zhongguo renkou fenbu yu quyu jingji fazhan* 中國人口分佈與區域經濟發展 (Population Distribution and Regional Economic Development in China) (Shanghai: Huadong shifan daxue chubanshe 華東師範大學出版社, 1997), pp. 345–52.
42. R. Iredale, N. Bilik and W. Su (eds.), *Contemporary Minority Migration, Education and Ethnicity in China* (Cheltenham: Edward Elgar, 2001), p. 175.
43. Tian and Lin, *Zhongguo renkou qianyi* (see note 31), p. 77.
44. See the case of Qinghai, for example. Tian and Zhang, *Zhongguo renkou qianyi xintan* (see note 31), pp. 214–315.
45. See Cook and Murray, *China's Third Revolution* (see note 13), p. 79.

46. The Chinese government switched to a strategy of balanced regional development in 1994.
47. Shen, "Urban and Regional Development in Post-reform China" (see note 32); J. Shen, "A Study of the Temporary Population in Chinese Cities," *Habitat International*, Vol. 26 (2002), pp. 363–77; Eva Poon, "Non-hukou Migration to the Pearl River Delta, South China, 1990–1995," *Occasional Paper 145* (2000), pp. 1–30, Department of Geography, The Chinese University of Hong Kong; Eva Poon, *A Study of Non-hukou Migration in the Pearl River Delta of China in the 1990s*, M.Phil. Thesis (2000), The Chinese University of Hong Kong.
48. Shen, "Population Growth, Ecological Degradation and Construction in the Western Region of China" (see note 7).

10

Xinjiang

Chau Kwai-cheong

Introduction

The Xinjiang 新疆 Uygur 維吾爾 Autonomous Region lies in northwestern China, between the latitude 32°22'–49°33'N and longitude 73°21'–96°21'E. With an area of 1.66 million km^2, it makes up roughly one-sixth of the total land area of China. Of China's provinces and autonomous regions, it is the largest and has the longest boundary line. It shares 5,600 km of frontier with Mongolia in the northeast; Russia, Kazakhstan, Kyrgyzstan and Tajkistan in the west; and Afghanistan, Pakistan and India in the southwest. Xinjiang shares internal borders with Gansu 甘肅 and Qinghai 青海 to the southeast and Tibet 西藏 to the south (Figure 10.1). Xinjiang was liberated in 1949 and the Xinjiang Autonomous Region was formally established on 1 October 1955, with 5 autonomous prefectures and 6 autonomous counties in the following months. To date, there are altogether 85 counties and cities.

The total population of Xinjiang is 16.9 million, of which minority nationalities comprise over 10 million. As a major ethnic group in Xinjiang, the Uygur nationality has the largest population of 7.9 million. Most of the minority nationalities believe in Islam, making Xinjiang one of the main areas where Chinese Muslims reside. The common languages within the autonomous region are Uygur and Chinese.

The autonomous region is characterized by a typical continental climate, with abundant sunshine but scanty rainfall. Mean annual temperatures range from 10°–15°C in the south and 5°–8°C in the north. The diurnal range of temperature in the whole region is above 12–16°C. The mean annual precipitation is 145 mm, which is low compared to an average evaporation of 2,000–2,500 mm. Precipitation increases from below 10 mm in the Turpan Basin 吐魯番盆地 to 400–600 mm in the mountainous areas. Topographically, the Junggar Basin 準噶爾盆地 and the Tarim Basin 塔里木盆地 are sandwiched between the three mountain ranges of the Altay 阿爾泰 in the north, the Tianshan 天山 in the middle and the Kunlun 崑崙 in the south. Xinjiang has a diverse topography of mountains (27.5%), deserts (22.4%), undulating hills (21.8%), Gobi deserts (28.2%) and oases (4.3%). The population density averages 8.6 persons per km^2, reaching 400 persons per km^2 in the oases.[1] Overall, the bio-physical environment of South Xinjiang is harsher than that of North Xinjiang, yet the Tarim Basin in the south is the most developed region.

Xinjiang has rich natural resources, including oil, natural gas, minerals, forests and steppelands. With plenty of sunshine and irrigation water from

Figure 10.1 Xinjiang in Its Geographical Setting

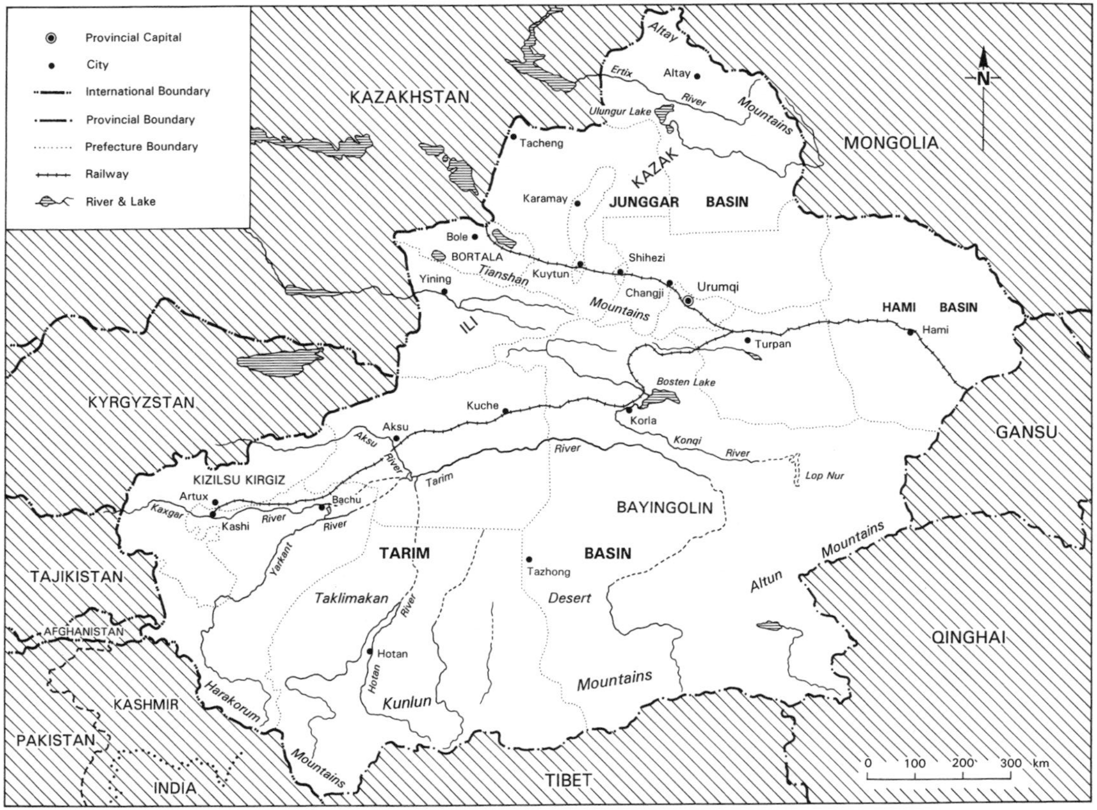

snowmelt, the autonomous region is also famous for cotton growing and rapeseed production. Crop agriculture was initiated in 1954 and resulted in the establishment of man-made oases and enterprises in otherwise inhospitable desert lands. In 2001, the gross domestic production reached RMB148.5 billion, a figure 42 times higher than that in 1952. Per capita income had increased from RMB166 to RMB7,913 during the same period.

Xinjiang is an ecologically fragile region, and the Tarim Basin is the area most vulnerable to the impact of development. After decades of over-exploitation of the water and land resources, Xinjiang in general is suffering from serious problems of land degradation. In China's western development programme, the autonomous region is earmarked as the production base of cotton, oil and natural gas for the country. The best cotton in China is grown in the Tarim Basin, yet there is stiff competition in this product in domestic and international markets. Adjustments are needed to boost productivity and improve quality, especially after China's entry to the World Trade Organization (WTO). Likewise, Xinjiang has a large reserve of oil and natural gas, rendering it a powerhouse of the country. As natural gas is a cleaner energy than oil, it will be exported to Shanghai 上海 and the Yangzi Delta 長江三角洲 region via a 4,200-km pipeline. This will lessen China's reliance on coal and help clean up atmospheric pollution in cities. The objectives of this chapter are threefold: (1) to examine the sustainability of growing cotton in Xinjiang; (2) to examine the causes of environmental degradation in Xinjiang with special reference to the rehabilitation of the Tarim Basin; and (3) to examine the potential use of Xinjiang's natural gas to ameliorate atmospheric pollution in eastern China.

Cotton as a Kind of "White Gold" in Xinjiang

Cotton is a fibre, feed and food crop. As a fibre crop, it is noted for its versatility, appearance, performance and natural comfort, hence the name nature's wonder fibre. The crop belongs to the genus of *Gossypium* of the family Malvaceae. It originated in Africa and Asia and on the west coast of America. The original short-fibred cotton has been domesticated for approximately 4,000 years. In China, the long-staple cotton (up to 35 mm) is only grown in Xinjiang, where there are 11 production bases including Turpan, Bachu 巴楚 and Aksu 阿克蘇. The Uygurs used to grow cotton as a cash crop around the upper reaches of the Tarim River and agriculture was established by Xinjiang Production and Construction Corps. In the 1950s, the growing areas were further expanded to the lower reaches, the Manas Valley and the Turpan Hami Basin 吐哈盆地.[2]

The crop grows best in warm arid climates with long hours of sunshine and a great range in diurnal temperatures. Cool temperatures of below 20°C can have an adverse effect on the maturing of the fibres, so cotton is grown in the summer on irrigated oases that are surrounded by poplars. The crop requires deep soil with a reaction pH of about 6, and medium-to-high levels of nitrogen, potassium and phosphorus, of which the local soils are unfortunately deficient.[3] These elements are added in the form of combined fertilizers that are not easily leached from the soil under conditions of low rainfall. Cotton is resistant to salt, hence the halomorphic soils in Xinjiang have no effects on its growth. With a favourable growing environment, Xinjiang cotton ranks highest in per capita yield, output and quality in China. Indeed, the location quotient of cotton in Xinjiang is 20 times higher than that in eastern and central China.[4]

The textile industries of China account for 25% of the country's total export value. This sector employs 9 million workers in addition to the 55 million growers. Although cotton occupies 2–3% of the country's total cultivated area, it contributes 7–10% of the total value of agriculture. China was the world's largest importer of cotton in 1994–1995, but in 1998–1999 was the world's fourth-largest exporter. In the period 1993–2000, China produced about 20% of the total amount of cotton in the world. This is partly due to the fact that China's average cotton yields are the highest in the world as a result of intensive management, averaging 943 kg per ha in 1998–1999, compared to the world average of 584 kg per ha.

Nowadays, China's cotton for export is mainly produced in Xinjiang. Eastern and central China used to produce more than 70% of China's cotton yarn in the 1980s. To promote the growing of cotton in Xinjiang, the government granted price subsidies to the region at the end of 1998. This resulted in a rapid increase in exports of cotton to US$237 million, or a 90.3% increase in earnings for raw cotton exports in 2000 over 1999. Exports of cotton yarn and fabrics increased by 23% to US$215 million during the same period. Today, 70% of Xinjiang's cotton is grown in the Tarim Basin and the remaining 30% in the Manas Valley and Turpan Hami Basin.[5]

The growing importance of cotton in Xinjiang is also related to its declining importance in other parts of China. Cotton production in the country is quite fragmented, being grown mainly by individual families after the abolition of the commune system in 1984.[6] The 43 million growers today are located in the Yangzi Valley and in the Yellow River and Huaihe

Valleys 黃淮流域. To improve the scale of production and level of modernization, the base of production gradually shifted from eastern and central China to Xinjiang, where a plentiful amount of land, more cotton resources and cheaper labour are to be found.[7] In 2000, Xinjiang had a total of 1.12 million ha of cultivated land sown to cotton, accounting for 27.3% of the national total. Its cotton output reached 1.5 million tonnes or 34.5% of the national total. Indeed, the best-quality cotton in terms of grade is produced in Xinjiang, although its sugar content is sometimes excessive due to the effect of marked diurnal differences in temperature.

It is estimated that the cost of the fertilizer and insecticides needed to grow cotton is at least 25% higher than for other crops. The need for frequent applications of these farm inputs and other crop management practices tie cotton growers to the farms more so than other crops. Although this reduces opportunities for off-farm employment, it helps to stabilize rural to urban migration, which is a sensitive issue in Xinjiang.

Xinjiang has a competitive edge over the Yangzi Valley and the Yellow River and Huaihe Valleys in cotton production. The Tarim and Junggar Basins have abundant water, land, light and heat resources. People build ditches to irrigate the reclaimed lands and surround the land with red willow shrubbery, jujube trees and white poplars, typical of an agroforestry production system.[8] These man-made oases, mostly found in the Tarim Basin, are like pearls in the deserts. They are fed by melted snow from the mountains. The agricultural production system of the Xinjiang Production and Construction Corps established in the 1950s resulted in a systematic expansion of the cotton-growing areas. There is no shortage of labour and, in the harvesting season, extra labour is imported from Qinghai, Gansu and Sichuan 四川.

Eastern and central China have a long history of cotton growing. Since the end of the 1980s, cotton production has decreased due to a decline in yield and acreage. The decline in yield of 15–30% was mainly caused by bollworm infestation, accounting for a direct loss of about US$630 million in 1992 and 1993. Xinjiang has a shorter history of cotton growing, hence the problem of pest infestation is less severe compared to other parts of China.

Cotton growers in eastern and central China were discouraged by the low procurement price compared to vegetables and fruits. There was a tendency to shift production from relatively favourable areas towards marginal lands. For instance, the area of land in Hebei 河北 devoted to the growing of cotton decreased from 0.67 million ha before 1990 to 0.2 million ha after 1990. Conversely, the cotton-growing area in Xinjiang increased by 20% during the same period and reached 0.73 million ha in 1997. Since 1993, Xinjiang has become the nation's number one cotton producer and the issue now is whether or not that growth can continue.[9]

Although cotton accounts for 65% of the income of farmers in Xinjiang, the expansion of cotton fields has led to an imbalance of the ecosystem and a decline in the quality of cotton. Cotton is a cross-pollination crop; it is essential to seal off the production area. For instance, the important colourful variety, widely promoted in Xinjiang, must be sealed off from white cotton, or cross-pollination will lead to a decline in genetic purity. Unfortunately, the proportion of cotton fields in areas suitable for cotton growth has reached 60–75%, which is too high to maintain an ecological balance. Continuous cropping has led to a problem of insect infestation, not to mention a growing demand for water for irrigation. The indiscriminate use of chemical fertilizers, up to 800 kg per ha, and insecticides has resulted in polluted soils and contaminated water.[10] In particular, there has been a hardening and structural breakdown of the soil aggregates. This will further aggravate the problems of water supply and ecosystem imbalance in the Tarim Basin.

Xinjiang has been earmarked as China's major cotton production base in the programme to develop the western region. In view of Xinjiang's relatively fragile ecological environment, it is unwise to expand the cotton growing areas.[11] Instead, priority should be given to the growing of high-quality cotton that is competitive in domestic and international markets.[12] Considerable success has been achieved in terms of selecting seeds, pricking out sprouts, using plastic sheets to assist growth, employing water-saving irrigation methods and disease control. This is, however, not adequate because overseas countries such as the United States have made breakthroughs in the use of genetic engineering to boost cotton production.

Transgenic cotton is a variety of cotton that has been genetically altered by the addition of foreign genetic material (DNA) from another variety. In 1998, 48.6% of the cotton produced in the U.S. was made up of genetically modified varieties that are either resistant to herbicides, insects or a combination of both. China lags far behind in this technology, and the first two Bt varieties were only released in 1996 by the Chinese Academy of Agricultural Science. The acreage of Bt cotton (*Guokang* variety) increased slowly from 667 ha in 1997 to 13,300 ha in 1998. Institutional and policy constraints have since remained problematic to the rapid expansion of Bt cotton in Xinjiang.[13] These include inadequate investment in R&D, lack of incentives for plant breeders and scientists, and an outdated institutional framework to disseminate the new technologies.

Future cotton production in Xinjiang, as in other parts of China, is expected to depend on the debate on whether fibre production should be reduced in favour of an expansion in food production. There has always been a strong bias towards the production of foods, such as wheat, rice and corn, over cotton. Indeed, Xinjiang also excels in the production of cash crops, including fruits, rapeseed oil and beetroot.

Although guaranteed procurement at guaranteed prices is essential to maintaining the incomes of farmers and social stability, this income-stabilizing effect of cotton production is declining. This is because cotton prices are likely to decline and fluctuate more in the future, especially after China's entry to the WTO in 2001. China had immediately opened up an import quota of 743,000 tonnes in the first year of its membership in the WTO, rising to 894,000 tonnes within four years compared to just 50,000 tonnes in 1999.[14] Within four years, imports will make up more than 22% of China's current annual consumption of 4 million tonnes. The impact of the WTO on China's cotton production is clearly going to be negative, and local output is going to fall. Most of the reduction will take place in central China, where land and labour costs have been inflated by the proximity of the area to Shanghai. The imported cotton will increase if domestic prices of cotton rise even slightly from those in the international market. Also, competition will escalate once foreigners are allowed to directly engage in cotton purchasing, processing and business operations. At the national level, almost 5 million cotton farmers are expected to lose their jobs within seven years of entry into the WTO. Within a few years of joining the WTO, China's annual output will likely stabilize to around 3 to 3.5 million tonnes. Cotton production in Xinjiang will likely be steady because China has strategically converted the autonomous region into a base for the production of cotton in its western development programme. An important priority is to improve the competitiveness of the cotton production.

Several adjustments are needed if cotton production in Xinjiang is to remain competitive in both domestic and international markets. UNEP has proposed to improve the cotton breeding programme, encourage the formation of co-operatives, maintain a balance between supply and demand, and avoid fluctuations.[15] It is equally important to secure an adequate supply of irrigation water, which is fast shrinking in the autonomous region. Xinjiang's reserve of underground water is the fourth largest in China, yet the effectiveness of irrigation is low as a result of outdated irrigation methods and a high evaporation rate. Environmentalists are already calling for a halt in the expansion of agriculture, including cotton farms, to preserve water resources.[16] Xinjiang requires a more professional breed of cotton farmers, along with a larger scale of production. Cotton growers looking to switch production to other farm products such as fruits may face the same problems, as WTO rules also boost imports in other crops. Innovative measures are needed to upgrade irrigation and mechanization and to integrate farm management. Hopefully, this will cut down the cost of production from around US$0.9 a pound to US$0.5 a pound in the near future.

Xinjiang cotton costs more to produce and takes longer to transport from the production areas to the cotton mills in eastern China. In 1999, China liberalized the cotton trade to make the cotton sector fully market-oriented. Besides reforms in procurement prices and offering incentives to mills to use Xinjiang cotton for export products, cotton growers were given limited rights to sell cotton to buyers other than the government's Cotton and Jute Bureau. These changes came more than a decade after similar reforms for grains and oilseeds, and this immediately sparked off a price war between cotton-producing provinces. Each province has been trying to keep control of local markets for their own cotton in the face of lower-priced cotton from Xinjiang.[17] The lower procurement prices as a result of trade liberalization have made the cotton produced by other provinces competitive with that of Xinjiang. The chief financial incentive to encourage mills to use Xinjiang cotton is the offering of a partial rebate on the value-added tax on Xinjiang cotton if the textile products are exported.

Despite the abovementioned uncertainties in cotton prices and trade, Xinjiang will remain the most important cotton-producing area in China. This trend will become more important as China's agricultural economy shifts away from that of a planned economy. The establishment of a price band rather than fixed prices for cotton, and granting farmers more discretion over planting decisions are two important steps to make cotton production more sensitive to market forces. At the international level, it is essential to develop standards for grading cotton and to understand the universal cotton contract standards to facilitate imports and exports, otherwise China will continue to suffer in the cotton trade.[18] Farmers need to lower their costs of production to make domestic cotton competitive in the world market. One way of doing this is to expand the scale of production through mechanization and the promotion of transgenic cotton. This will not be possible without a comprehensive rehabilitation of the ecological environment of the Tarim Basin, where most of the cotton farms are located.

Tarim River Basin Rehabilitation

China has accorded top priority in its Tenth Five-year Plan (2001–2005) to rehabilitate the degraded riparian forest ecosystem of the Tarim River Basin. With an investment of RMB10.7 billion, the project constitutes part of the country's western development programme launched in 1999. It is also an ambitious project representing the first of this kind ever undertaken by mankind. The project is necessitated by a compelling need to halt environmental deterioration in the Tarim Basin which, as mentioned, is the most important economic region in Xinjiang. Much has been said in the literature about the fragile ecological environment of the western region of China.[19] While Xinjiang is no exception in this regard, the Tarim Basin is ecologically the most sensitive to pressures from development. The crux of the problem is land degradation in an already fragile ecological environment as a result of unwise resource exploitation by an expanding population. The major problems confronting the Tarim Basin include the interruption of river flow, soil salinization and alkalization, shrinkage of biological resources and desertification.[20] It is also an excellent example of the interrelationship between rational planning, resource management and sustainability.

With a length of 1,321 km, the Tarim River is the longest inland river in China and the fifth longest in the world, after the Volga, Syr Darya, Amu and Ural. It is located in the northern part of the Taklimakan Desert 塔克拉瑪干沙漠, which is the largest moving desert in China (Figure 10.2). As the mother river of Xinjiang, the catchment covers an area of 1.02 million km^2, with a population of 8.26 million or 47% of Xinjiang's total. The Tarim Basin is thus the most important part of the Xinjiang Uygur Autonomous Region. It was an early centre of the civilization of western China and a stopping point on the ancient Silk Road. The area has an annual precipitation of 50 mm, but the evaporation rate is as high as 2,000–3,000 mm. The Taklimakan Desert in the Tarim Basin is dominated by moving sand dunes and a sparse vegetation cover, hence the ecological environment is inferior to the Junggar Basin in the north. Desertification is a prevailing problem and the effect of sandstorms can be felt as far as eastern China. The number of dusty days has increased from 39.5 to 75.9 between the 1970s and 1981–1993.[21]

The Tarim River has changed its course many times in history. It was once fed by six tributaries, including the Konqi 紅旗河, Weigan 渭干河, Kaxgar 喀什葛爾河, Yarkant 葉爾羌河, Hotan 河田河 and Aksu 阿克蘇河

Figure 10.2 The Tarim Basin

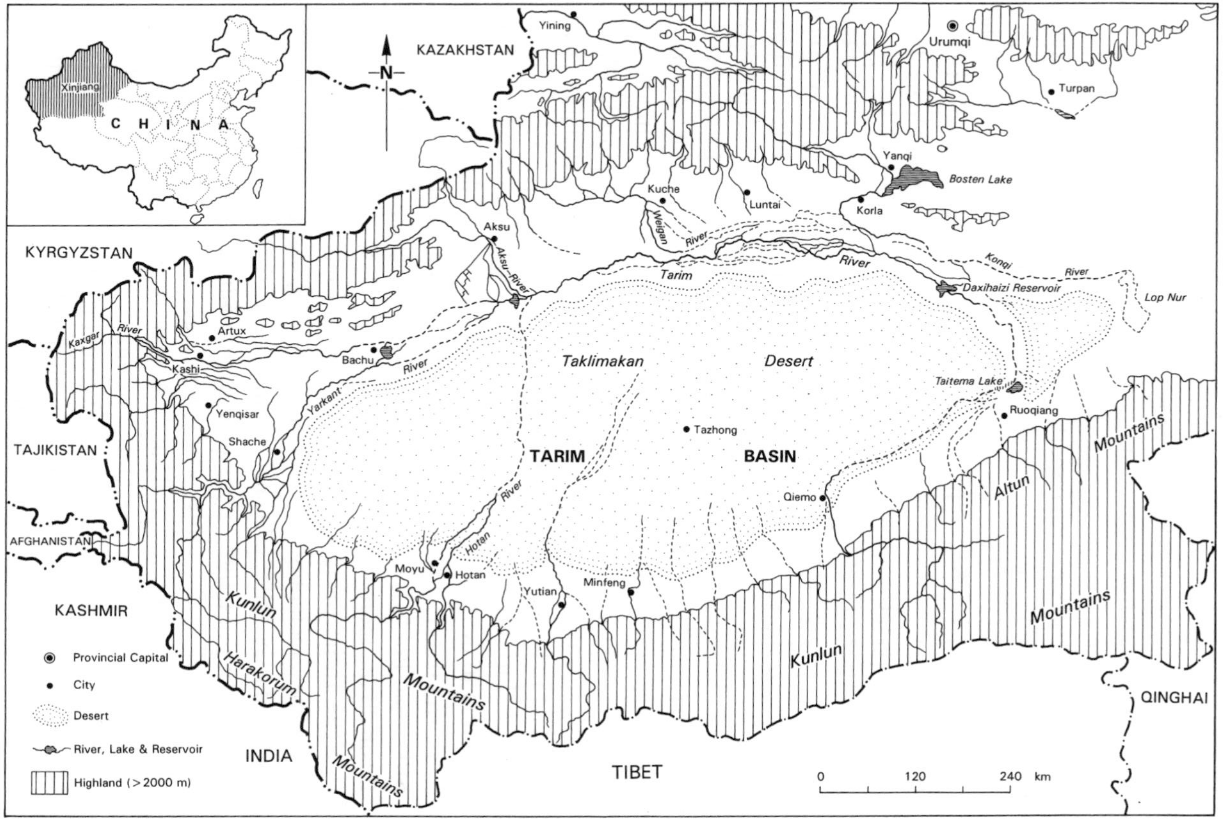

Rivers. Today, it is mainly replenished by the Aksu and Hotan and, in periods of flooding, by the Yarkant because of a lowering of the water table as a result of overgrazing and over-cultivation in the past. In the last 50 years, the majority of the water-harnessing projects in South Xinjiang have been implemented in the Tarim Basin. The farmers of the Tarim Basin produce 80% of Xinjiang's cotton or one-sixth of China's total. Grain, fruits, rapeseed oil, silk and wool are also important agricultural products in this region. It is Xinjiang's home of fruit, cotton, song and dance.

The mountain ranges bordering the Tarim Basin contain abundant snowmelt water, which runs into the desert, feeding oases and tributaries before emptying into the Tarim River. Farming was traditionally confined to oases along the river valleys but, during the last 50 years, water diversion and irrigation initiatives have permitted the expansion of agriculture to otherwise uncultivable land. Many reservoirs were built to supply irrigation water to feed the man-made oases; they are mostly shallow and have a large surface area. The loss from evaporation and seepage accounts for up to 50% or 2 billion m^3 of the stored water.[22] Since the 1990s, excessive pumping has led to a progressive decline in water from 3.2 billion m^3 in the upper reaches of the Tarim River to 1.8 billion m^3 in the middle reaches and 0.24 billion m^3 in the lower reaches.[23] Since 1972, the 320-km long section downstream from the Daxihaizi Reservoir has virtually dried up, resulting in the shrinking of Taitema Lake 台特瑪湖.[24]

The Tarim Basin is expected to keep developing, as a result of China's ambition to develop the west, the opening up of the desert highway, the discovery of oil and natural gas as well as the unceasing attraction the old Silk Road holds for tourists. This makes the rehabilitation of the Tarim Basin all the more necessary.

The Tarim Basin is ecologically fragile and made up of a mosaic of landscapes, including gobi and sandy deserts, basins, marshes, oases, salt lakes and river valleys. In ancient times, because the region never had more than a small population engaged in nomadic and subsistence farming activities, its sustainability was maintained. The population amounted to 0.21 million in the Western Han 西漢 dynasty and increased progressively to 1.78 million in the late Qing 清 dynasty and to 3.0 million in 1949[25] (Table 10.1). Drastic changes have occurred since the 1950s with the establishment of the autonomous region and the deployment of the army corps to Xinjiang. The problem of irrational land use was most critical from the 1950s to 1990s, during which over-cultivation occurred along the entire Tarim River valley. Agricultural lands increased from roughly

Table 10.1 Population Changes in the Tarim Basin

Year	Population (million)
200 B.C.	0.21
1900	1.78
1949	3.00
1995	3.51

Source: Song et al. (see note 25).

33,000 ha in the 1980s to 53,000 ha in early 2000. These man-made oases constitute about 20% of the total oasis agriculture in the desert region. The river valleys of the major tributaries were likewise deforested and converted to farmland, resulting in a reduced flow into the Tarim River. This problem is particularly critical in the Konqi, Weigan and Kaxgar Rivers, the flow of which has either been reduced or is becoming intermittent.

Open ditch or flood irrigation is widely practised in the Tarim Basin, which is not viable under the prevailing conditions of high evaporation. Excessive salts brought by irrigation water deposit and accumulate on the surface of the soil; they increase the osmotic potential of crops and destabilize the structure of the soil. Excessive pumping reduces the volume of water flowing downstream, causing trees to die and resulting in a loss of habitats and wildlife with conservation value. For instance, construction of the Daxihaizi Reservoir 大西海子水庫 lowered the water table by 4–5 m in the 1970s to 12 m in early 2000, resulting in the almost complete eradication of the poplars (*Populus euphratica*) endemic to Xinjiang[26] (Table 10.2). These changes have been speeding up the process of desertification, especially when the winter season is warmer and shorter than the average year. Winds blowing from Siberia pick up the loose particles of sand from the dried-up riverbeds and deposit them downwind. Sandstorms of different magnitudes are then initiated, causing respiratory diseases, the silting up of waterways and roadways and the closure of airport. Between the 1950s

Table 10.2 Changes in the Area Covered by Poplars in the Tarim Basin, 1950s–1990s

(Unit: km^2)

Year	Upper reaches	Middle reaches	Lower reaches	Total
1950s	23,000	17,580	5,400	45,980
1970s	5,820	10,020	1,640	17,840
1990s	11,730	11,650	660	24,000

Source: Gao and Fan (see note 26).

and 1990s, the area covered by poplars declined by 4,740 km^2 and desertified land expanded by 12,300 km^2. Protecting the ecological environment of the lower Tarim River is crucial to the sustainability of Korla 庫爾勒 and Turpan. Geographically, the green corridor dominated by poplars acts as an effective buffer between the Kumtag Desert 庫吾克塔格沙漠 in the north and Taklimakan Desert in the south. Sandstorm particles originating from the Taklimakan Desert can be filtered by this green corridor, preventing the amalgamation of the two deserts and offering protection to the cities downwind. While several sections of the national highway 218 are already under threat, the planned railway between Xinjiang and Qinghai is scheduled to pass through this green corridor.[27]

The nature of the problem at the middle reaches of the Tarim River is different. While water is pumped excessively at the upper reaches to support oasis agriculture, a large proportion of the water at the middle reaches is wasted in seepage and evaporation. The section is braided, wide, shallow and vulnerable to disturbance by nomads. It is estimated that as much as 1.6 billion m^3 of water is consumed by a population of less than 10,000 in the region.[28]

Owing to reduced flow from the tributaries, the salt content of the river water increased from 1.28 g per litre in the 1960 to 4.0 g per litre in early 1980 and 7.8 g per litre in 1998. Salts desalinized in the upper reaches during land reclamation are discharged downstream, spreading the environmental problem. In the desert region, quality irrigation water should contain less than 500 ppm of dissolved salts.[29]

Like other parts of China, the price of water in Xinjiang is low and unsustainable. It cost the user merely RMB0.006 per m^3 in 1997, which is one-quarter the average cost of supplying the water. Slack administrative control over the resource and inadequate penalties for its misuse do not help the situation.

The authorities have rightly adopted a total watershed management strategy for rehabilitating the Tarim River Basin. It involves a close collaboration between the forestry, agriculture and husbandry departments and major stakeholders.[30] Greater emphasis is placed on stabilizing the ecosystem than on developing agriculture and the economy. Recognizing the importance of oasis agriculture in the region, especially along the river valleys, shelterbelts consisting of poplars and *Tamarix spp.* are being planted to conserve water resources and protect the soil. Oases, sparsely vegetated areas and arid areas are being preserved to prevent the further encroachment of farmlands.

There are three objectives in this rehabilitation programme, namely, restoration of river flows, the rehabilitation of the ecosystem and halting desertification. Water is diverted from Bosten Lake 博斯騰湖, located 530 km to the north, to restore the flow of the river between Daxihaizi Reservoir and Taitema Lake. It is hoped that this will raise the level of the water, restore the poplars and recreate the aquatic habitats. This is an ambitious project because it is expensive in terms of energy to pump the water. In addition, ecological rehabilitation is a slow process, more of an art than a science. To date, three diversions have been attempted, in 2000 and 2001, each with a capacity of roughly 320 million m^3.[31] The water level has risen by 3 m, and more diversions are anticipated in the future to restore 13,000 km^2 of poplars and to annually supply 0.35 billion m^3 of water to Lake Taitema.[32] Since 1976, about 169 million m^3 of water annually has also been diverted from the Konqi River to the Tarim River, which has contributed to the drying up of Lop Nor 羅布泊.

Rehabilitating the ecosystem of the Tarim Basin is an arduous task. The unplanned reclamation of wastelands, undue pumping of water and deforestation are strictly prohibited. In particular, a massive reforestation programme is under way to rehabilitate the tributaries, especially the Yarkant River and Hotan River, to improve the stability of the ecosystem, protect water resources and safeguard the supply of water to the Tarim River. Reservoirs will be built in mountainous areas to replace those in the lowlands. The efficiency of irrigation will be enhanced to improve agricultural yields by covering irrigation trenches with plastic microfilm, lining canals with concrete and practising drip irrigation. Agroforestry involving the planting of woody species, such as poplars, in a checkerboard layout to protect the crops is a common and effective measure to improve yields and increase income. The rational use of underground water has implemented and, since 1997, the price of water has been raised from the average cost of supply of RMB0.02–0.03 per m^3 to RMB0.18 per m^3.

Halting desertification in Xinjiang is essential to rehabilitating the degraded landscape. There is no quick solution to the problem when an ever-increasing population is constantly putting pressure on land use. Rational land-use planning in the entire basin can put a brake on the encroachment of the desert. This should be accompanied by the balanced use of water among the agricultural, industrial and domestic sectors. Since 2002, the local government has initiated a massive programme to convert unproductive cultivated lands to forests and grasslands. Regarded as the sixth reforestation project in China, the responsibility rests with the corps in Xinjiang.[33] This is made possible by subsidizing the farmers, who are willing to participate in the conversion programme, with cash and grain. In Xinjiang, as in other parts of northern China, the subsidy per ha of farmland converted is equivalent to RMB300 and 1,500 kg of grain a year. The subsidy is to last for two years for the conversion to grasslands and five years for the conversion of forests.[34] As stated in the regulations governing this programme, in order to rehabilitate the fragile ecological environment, a conservation forest is preferable to an economic forest.

The rehabilitation of the Tarim Basin is an ongoing project, the scale of which is unprecedented in the history of China. While other river rehabilitation projects in China focus on pollution control and channel improvement, this one deals with ecological rehabilitation and integrated water resources planning. Many of the benefits brought about by this project are easily recognizable, yet hidden problems may only appear in future. For instance, the continuous pumping of water from Bosten Lake and Konqi River can have a significant impact on the ecological environment of these bodies of water. The conversion of unsustainable farmlands to forests and grasslands is largely acceptable to the farmers because China has had an 8–9% grain surplus in the last six years.[35] The situation could be reversed if grain production were to suffer from outbreaks of pests and other natural hazards. The government will have to give more cash subsidies to the farmers instead of supplementing it with grain. Nevertheless, the Tarim Basin rehabilitation project is a good example of the interrelationships between population, resources and environment. The government has rightly recognized that the sustainability of Xinjiang's development hinges on the successful rehabilitation of the Tarim Basin.

Natural Gas as a Clean Energy for China

Xinjiang has abundant reserves of petroleum and natural gas, making it the powerhouse of China. In terms of the competitive advantages of these two commodities, Xinjiang ranks first in China.[36] Oil cities complete with refinery facilities have emerged in the region of the oilfields, the largest being Karamay 克拉瑪依 in the Junggar Basin. However, it is natural gas that has the potential to change the country's energy structure amid the growing awareness of environmental protection in the twenty-first century. During 2000–2002, the consumption of coal in China dropped by 15% without affecting production. Beijing will host the summer Olympics in 2008 and, besides efforts invested in preventing the outbreak of contagious diseases such as Severe Acute Respiratory Syndrome (SARS), China certainly wants to impress visitors with a clean environment. Unfortunately, many of the coastal cities suffer from atmospheric pollution, in large part due to the use of coal. The 4,200-km natural gas pipeline between the Tarim Basin and Shanghai can be an answer to the problem. It is being accorded top priority in China's Tenth Five-year Plan.

China has the largest reserves of coal in the world, estimated at 1,007.1 billion tonnes.[37] The country has a long history of coal use, and energy consumption increased 5.1% annually from the 1980s to the 1990s. Coal accounted for 75% of commercial energy production during the same period. Although the percentage of coal in China's overall energy consumption dropped to 72.9% in 2000, it is nearly three times higher than the world average (Table 10.3). On the other hand, China uses less petroleum, nuclear energy and natural gas than the world average. China's heavy reliance on coal is both a result of the country's huge reserves and of its past policy of self-reliance. This has had a tremendous impact on the environment and overall productivity of the country.

Coal combustion produces two major pollutants, namely, sulfur dioxide and nitrogen oxide. They dissolve in rainwater to form acid rain or acid precipitation because the acid can also be present in snow, ice, sleet, fog and smog. Acidified water with a pH of below 5.6 is classified as acid rain. Sulfur dioxide generated from the burning of coal accounted for 89% of total pollutants and total emissions in 1997. Sulphur dioxide amounted to 23.5 million tonnes, being higher from the industrial sector than for the domestic sector. Acid rain occurs mainly in areas south of the Yangzi River, east of the Qinghai-Tibet Plateau and the Sichuan Basin, representing 30% of the total land area of China[38] (Table 10.4). Forty-three out of 84 cities monitored yielded a rainfall of pH <5.6, among which Changsha 長沙, Zunyi 遵義, Hangzhou 杭州 and Yibin 宜賓 had a pH <4.5. In 2000, the United Nations has officially labelled China the world's third acid rain centre, after the eastern U.S. and central Europe.

Table 10.3 Energy Composition in China and the World (Unit: %)

Country \ Type	Coal	Petroleum	Nuclear	Natural gas
China	72.9	22.5	2.5	2.1
World	26.2	40.0	10.0	23.8

Source: Liang (see note 37).

Table 10.4 Acid Rain in China

Area	Average pH	Frequency of occurrence, %
Central China	<5.0	>70
Southwest China	<5.0	70
South China	<5.0	50
North China	<5.5	20

Source: State Environmental Protection Agency (see note 38).

Of the 10 cities in the world hit hardest by atmospheric pollution (the aggregate of SO_2, CO_2, CH_4 and RSP), 7 are found in China. They include Taiyuan 大原, Beijing 北京, Urumqi 烏魯木齊, Lanzhou 蘭州, Chongqing 重慶, Ji'nan 濟南 and Shijiazhuang 石家莊.[39] Acid rain reduces the output of grain, vegetables and fruits, and damages forests and buildings. It is hazardous to the health of human beings and wildlife. Economic losses from acid rain and sulfur dioxide pollution approached 2% of GDP in 1995. China has adopted many measures to combat this problem, including closing down coal mines with a sulfur content greater than 3%, providing coal washing facilities, desulfurizing and relocating power plants away from large and medium-sized cities. However, these measures are not entirely effective because coal is not a clean energy. The rich reserves of natural gas in Xinjiang may help to restructure China's energy budget.

The systematic prospecting of petroleum and natural gas in Xinjiang is accorded top priority by the central government. Natural gas consists of methane, the combustion of which releases energy, carbon dioxide and water. Carbon dioxide is less hazardous to the environment than sulfur dioxide and nitrogen oxide, hence natural gas is a cleaner energy than petroleum and coal. The reserves of usable natural gas in China are estimated at 1,370 billion m^3, which ranks China nineteenth in the world. About 32.4% of the known reserves are in the Tarim Basin (494.1 billion m^3) and the Junggar Basin (57.6 billion m^3). One of the latest discoveries is the rich reserve in the Kuche 庫車 region, north of the Tarim Basin. The Kela Gas Field 克拉油田 No. 2 in Kuche alone has an estimated reserve of 251 billion m^3, which is rated as the best natural gas field ever discovered in China (Table 10.5).

According to forecasts, there will be a growing demand for natural gas in eastern China in the next decade (Table 10.6). Eastern China is the most developed region of the country, and it relies on coal as the principal source of energy. It is China's strategy to use more natural gas, hydroelectric power and nuclear energy. Contracts were signed with Indonesia and Australia to

Table 10.5 Kela Gas Field No. 2 in Kuche, Xinjiang

Estimated reserve, billion m^3	251
Richness, billion m^3/km^2	5.3
Average thickness, m	154.1
Pressure, Mpa	74.6
Purity, % CH_4	97
Daily production, million m^3/day	8.1

Source: Liang (see note 37).

Table 10.6 Forecast of the Demand for Natural Gas in Eastern China, 2000–2015

Region \ Year	2000	2005	2010	2015
China (billion m^3)	28.7	67.0	116	188
East China (billion m^3)	12.9	40.1	78.2	129.2
Percentage of total	15	60	67.4	68.7

Note: Eastern China includes the northeast region, Bohai region, Yangzi Delta and the southeast coastal region.
Source: Liang (see note 37).

import natural gas from these countries in 2002. Despite this, the major source of supply has to come from its domestic reserves and Xinjiang is targeted as a base for the production of natural gas. The pipeline linking the Tarim Basin (Kuche Gas Field No. 2) with Shanghai is being built in 2001–2003 at a total cost of RMB120 billion. It traverses Gansu, the Ningxia 寧夏 Hui Autonomous Region, Shaanxi 陝西, Shanxi 山西, Henan 河南, Anhui 安徽 and Jiangsu 江蘇. The amount of gas delivered via the 1.1-m diameter duct will increase progressively from 4 billion m^3 in 2003 to a maximum of 12 billion m^3 in 2005 and thereafter. The pipeline has a life expectancy of 30 years and there are already plans to include supplies from the Junggar Basin, Tazhong 塔中 and the Hami Basin 哈密盆地 (see also Chapter 5).

The project itself will bring an annual revenue of RMB1 billion to Xinjiang and create many jobs.[40] This will speed up economic development in Xinjiang and help consolidate the autonomous region as a base for the production of energy in China. According to forecasts, for every cubic metre of natural gas consumed in eastern China, there will be an additional investment of RMB5–8 million on ancillary facilities to boost internal spending. Annually, the energy derived from 12 billion m^3 of natural gas can substitute for 4.7 million tonnes of coal. This will reduce the emissions of 29.7 million tonnes of carbon dioxide, 1.1 million tonnes of RSP, 0.12 million tonnes of nitrogen oxide and 0.18 million tonnes of sulfur dioxide.

Conclusion

Xinjiang is an autonomous region with diverse topographies, cultures and natural resources but an ecologically fragile environment. In China's western development programme, it is earmarked as a production base of cotton, oil, natural gas and rapeseed. Cotton is the backbone of the textile industry, which accounts for 20% of the total value of China's exports and 50% of Xinjiang's agricultural output. While Xinjiang is endowed with rich cotton resources, it has become China's biggest producer since 1993. There has been a gradual increase in cultivated lands devoted to the growing of cotton since the establishment of the corps production system in the 1950s, mainly on reclaimed oases in the Manas Valley, Turpan Hami Basin and lower reaches of the Tarim Basin. Cotton is a big consumer of water and the open trench irrigation system in Xinjiang further reduces the efficiency of its use. Apart from the need to liberalize the cotton trade and improve the quality of cotton, the government needs to exercise care in controlling the acreage of the crop because over expansion will likely deplete the water resources. This problem occurred in the then USSR in the mid- to late-1960s, when the excessive pumping of water for cotton irrigation dried up lakes and caused irreversible salinization of the land.

Likewise, oil and natural gas will bring wealth to Xinjiang and help restructure China's energy programme, which is being accorded top priority in the nation's strategic development in the twenty-first century. However, the environmental problems arising from their prospecting, drilling, refining and delivery should not be underestimated. Ill-planned prospecting and drilling is being carried out at close proximity to tourist attractions and oases, not to mention the construction of the nation's first highway in the Taklimakan Desert to back up this industry. In view of the rich reserves of natural gas and oil in Xinjiang, careful planning is needed to optimize their use, otherwise the present environmental problems in eastern China would simply be externalized to the autonomous region.

Indeed, Xinjiang is characterized by an ecologically fragile environment, the most vulnerable area being the densely populated Tarim Basin. Many of the environmental problems including the shrinking of water resources, salinization and desertification are man-made, resulting from the over-exploitation of the region's natural resources in the past. When land becomes degraded, more is reclaimed to meet the needs of an ever-increasing population. A vicious circle of land degradation is initiated, which is comparable to the rest of China, including the impact of the leftist policies of the past. It is crucial to prevent similar problems from occurring in unaffected lands and to rehabilitate the degraded landscapes through rational planning, capital inputs, legislation and law enforcement. The rehabilitation of the riparian ecosystem of the Tarim Basin is an ambitious project aimed at the long-term sustainability of Xinjiang, the scale of which is unprecedented in the history of mankind. The issues are complicated, involving the restoration of river flows, ecological restoration, land-use planning, water pricing, the revolution of irrigation technology, and the like. It requires the close co-operation of different government departments and stakeholders, yet this is easier said than done. Commitment from the central government is crucial to the success of this rehabilitation project, which should be viewed as an extension of China's Three Norths Afforestation Project launched in 1987. Many of the environmental problems now confronting China will not be resolved until this Green Great Wall has been successfully completed. Xinjiang is not only home to fruits, song and dance, but its sustainable development is also closely linked to the well-being of the whole nation.

Notes

1. Dong Peide 董培德, "Xinjiang nongye kechixu fazhan zhanlüe tantao" 新疆農業可持續發展戰略探討 (A Discussion on a Sustainable Development Strategy for Agriculture in Xinjiang), in *Zhongguo nongye kechixu fazhan yanjiu* 中國農業可持續發展研究 (A Study on the Sustainable Development of Agriculture in China), edited by Zhongguo nongxue hui 中國農學會 (China Agricultural Association) (Beijing: Zhongguo nongye keji chubanshe 中國農業科技出版社, 1998), pp. 176–78.
2. Ni Tianlin 倪天麟, Hai Reti 海熱提, Tu Erxun 涂爾遜 and Ye Wenhu 葉文虎, "Xinjiang mianqu di huafen jiqi fazhan qianli yuce" 新疆棉區的劃分及其發展潛力預測 (The Division and Forecast of the Scale of Development of the Cotton Growing Areas of Xinjiang), *Jingji dili* 經濟地理 (Economic Geography), Vol. 20, No. 4 (2000), pp. 89–93; Jiang Fengqing 姜逢青 and Tian Changyan 田長彥, "Xinjiang dianxing diqu zhuyao nongye ziyuan liyong xiaolü fenxi" 新疆典型地區主要農業資源利用效率分析 (An Analysis of the Efficiency of Agricultural Resource Utilization in Representative Regions of Xinjiang), *Ziyuan kexue* 資源科學 (Resource Science), Vol. 23, No. 2 (2001), pp. 65–69.

3. C. Li and O. Sun, *Soils of China* (Beijing: Kexue chubanshe 科學出版社, 1990), p. 873; S. M. Brown, M. Bader, S. Culpepper, R. Davis, G. Harris, P. Roberts and D. Sgurley, *2000 Cotton Production Guide*. At http://www.griffin.peachnet.edu/caes/cotton/2000/p_guide.htm.
4. Yang Kaizhong 楊開忠 et al., *Zhongguo xibu dakaifa zhanlüe* 中國西部大開發戰略 (A Strategy for China's Western Development) (Guangzhou: Guangdong jiaoyu chubanshe 廣東教育出版社, 2001), p. 390.
5. Gong Tianliang 公天亮 and Fan Yali 樊亞利, "Xinjiang mianye fazhan qianjing fenxi yu zhengce xuanze" 新疆棉業發展前景分析與政策選擇 (An Analysis of the Development Prospects and Policy Choices of Xinjiang's Cotton Manufacturing Industry), in *Mianhua jiage liutong tizhi ji Xinjiang mianye yanjiu* (di jiu zhang) 棉花價格流通體制及新疆棉業研究（第九章） (The Circulation System of Cotton Prices and a Study of Xinjiang's Cotton Manufacturing Industry, Chapter 9) (Xinjiang: Xinjiang keji weisheng chubanshe 新疆科技衛生出版社, 1999), pp. 190–207.
6. World Bank, *China 2020* (Washington D.C., 1997), p. 161; Qiu Jianjun 邱建軍 and He Jun 禾軍, "Qiantan Zhongguo mianhua shengchan jiegou tiaozheng yu jidi jianshe" 淺談中國棉花生產結構調整與基地建設 (An Introduction to Structural Adjustments in the Cotton Manufacturing Industry in China and to Infrastructure on the Site), *Zhongguo mianhua* 中國棉花 (China's Cotton), Vol. 27, No. 11 (2000), pp. 2–4.
7. Bureau of Cotton and Jute 2001, *Production of China's Cotton.* At http://www.cncotton.com/cotton/e_cview/production.asp.
8. A. Young, *Agroforestry for Soil Conservation* (Wallingford, U.K.: CAB International, 1989), p. 276.
9. H. Colby, *Is Self-Sufficiency in the Cards for China's Cotton?* Agricultural Outlook Forum, 1996. At http://usda.mannlib.cornell.edu/reports/waobr/aof/aof96/whcolby.asc; Hai Reti, Tu Erxun, Ni Tianlin, Han Delin 韓德麟, Zeng Jing 曾靜 and Lei Jun 雷軍, "Shilun Xinjiang mianhua shengchan jiqi kechixu fazhan" 試論新疆棉花生產及其可持續發展 (A Discussion on Xinjiang's Cotton Manufacturing Industry and Its Sustainable Development), *Zhongguo mianhua*, Vol. 27, No. 4 (2000), pp. 6–9.
10. Wang Yongxing 王永興, "Xinjiang shengtai huanjing xianzhuang, fazhan qushi he baohu" 新疆生態環境現狀、發展趨勢和保護 (The Current Situation, Developing Trends and Protection of Xinjiang's Ecological Environment), in *Xibu shengtai* 西部生態 (Western Ecology), edited by Xi Guojin 奚國金 and Zhang Jiazhen 張家楨 (Beijing: Zhonggong zhongyang dangxiao chubanshe 中共中央黨校出版社, 2001), pp. 121–48.
11. Xiong Jingming 熊景明, "Xinjiang 'lüse zoulang' yu shengchan jianshe bingtuan" 新疆「綠色走廊」與生產建設兵團 (Xinjiang's "Green Corridor" and the Production and Construction Group) (2001). At http://www.usc.cuhk.edu.hk/wk.asp.

12. Sheng Chengfa 盛承發, "Quanguo mianhua dahuisheng zhishi ji dangqian duice jianyi" 全國棉花大回升之勢及當前對策建議 (An Upswing in Cotton Production and Some Suggestions with Regard to the Current Situation), *Nongye xiandaihua yanjiu* 農業現代化研究 (Research on Agricultural Modernization), Vol. 22, No. 1 (2001), pp. 2–5.
13. Y. Song, "Introduction of Transgenic Cotton in China," *Biotechnology and Development Monitor*, No. 37 (1999), pp. 14–17.
14. C. E. Hanrahan, *Agriculture and China's Accession to the World Trade Organization* (2000). At http://www.cnie.org/nle/inter-3.html.
15. UNEP, *Integrated Assessment of Trade Liberalization and Trade-Related Policies — A Country Study on the Cotton Sector in China* (New York: United Nations, 2002), p. 66.
16. Li Liping 李立平, Ma Qiong 馬瓊 and Han Lu 韓路, "Fazhan Nanjiang xiandaihua zhimianye di duice" 發展南疆現代化植棉業的對策 (A Strategy to Develop Modernized Cotton Cultivation in Southern Xinjiang), *Nongye xiandaihua yanjiu*, Vol. 21, No. 4 (2000), pp. 1–4.
17. American Embassy, *Cotton* (1998). At http://www.cotstat.com/cotstat/Adobe%20…nnuals%2098/China%20Annual%20June98.htm.
18. Lu Feng 盧鋒, "Woguo mianhua duiwai maoyi weihe 'jianmai guimai'? — Mianhua jiage ganyu, gongqiu bodong yu maoyi xiaolü de guanxi" 我國棉花對外貿易為何「賤賣貴買」— 棉花價格干預, 供求波動與貿易效率的關係 (Why does China's Cotton Trade Buy Dear and Sell Cheap — Price Regulation, Market Fluctuation and Trade Performance: A Case Study on the Chinese Cotton Policy)(2000). At http://ccer.pku.edu.cn/workingpaper/paper/c2000003.doc.
19. Zhu Junfeng 朱俊鳳 and Zhu Zhenda 朱震達, *Zhongguo shamohua fangzhi* 中國沙漠化防治 (Combatting Desertification in China) (Beijing: Zhongguo linye chubanche 中國林業出版社, 1999), p. 495; Hu Angang 胡鞍鋼, *Diqu yu fazhan: Xibu kaifa xinzhanlüe* 地區與發展：西部開發新戰略 (Regions and Development: New Strategies for the Development of the Western Region) (Beijing: Zhongguo jihua chubanshe 中國計劃出版社, 2001), p. 376.
20. Wang (see note 10).
21. Ibid.
22. Deng Shengming 鄧盛明, Chen Xiaojun 陳曉軍 and Zhu Xiangmin 祝向民, "Talimuhe liuyu shuiziyuan he shengtai huanjing wenti jiqi duice silu" 塔里木河流域水資源和生態環境問題及其對策思路 (Water Resources and Ecological Problems in the Tarim River Basin and Some Thoughts on Corresponding Strategy), in *Lüse songge* 綠色頌歌 (A Green Carol), edited by Jiang Xuguang 蔣旭光 (Beijing: Zhongguo shuili shuidian chubanshe 中國水利水電出版社, 2001), pp. 175–82.
23. Wang (see note 10).
24. Guojia huanjing baohuju ziran baohusi 國家環境保護局自然保護司 (ed.),

Zhongguo shengtai wenti baogao 中國生態問題報告 (A Report on China's Ecological Problems) (Beijing: Zhongguo huanjing kexue chubanshe 中國環境科學出版社, 2000), p. 129; Qian Zhengying 錢正英, *Duiyu Talimuhe liuyu zhili de chubu renshi* 對於塔里木河流域治理的初步認識 (A Preliminary Understanding on Conserving the Tarim River Basin) (2000). At http://www.chinawater.net.cn/CWR_Journal/200001/02.html.

25. Song Yudong 宋郁東, Fan Zili 樊自立 and Lei Zhidong 雷志棟, *Zhongguo Talimuhe shuiziyuan yu shengtai huanjing wenti* 中國塔里木河水資源與生態環境問題 (Water Resources and Ecological Environment Problems in China's Tarim River Basin) (Urumqi: Xinjiang renmin chubanshe 新疆人民出版社, 2000), pp. 166–98.
26. Gao Qianzhao 高前兆 and Fan Zili, "Talimuhe liuyu di huanjing zhili yu shuitu baochi shengtai jianshe" 塔里木河流域的環境治理與水土保持生態建設 (Environmental Protection and Water and Soil Conservation Facilities in the Tarim River Basin), *Shuitu baochi xuebao* 水土保持學報 (Journal of Water and Soil Conservation), Vol. 16, No. 1 (2002), pp. 11–12.
27. Wang (see note 10).
28. Ibid.
29. Li and Sun (see note 3).
30. Gao and Fan (see note 26).
31. Ministry of Water Resources, *The Implementation of State Bond-Financed Water Projects* (2001). At http://www.china.org.cn/e-news/news01-1220.htm.
32. Ren Ming 任明, "Guowuyuan pizhun Talimuhe liuyu zonghe zhili fang'an" 國務院批准塔里木河流域綜合治理方案 (The Proposal on Comprehensive Conservation Works in the Tarim River Basin was Approved by the State Council), in *Lüse songge* (see note 22), pp. 98–101.
33. Zhang Hongwen 張鴻文, *Tuigenghuanlin gongcheng jinzhan shunli chuxian chengxiao* 退耕還林工程進展順利初顯成效 (The Project to Turn Farmland into Forest and Grassland Demonstrated Effectiveness) (2002). At wysiwyg://29/http://www.peopledaily.com.cn/GB/huanbao/55/20021226/895825.html.
34. Xinhuashe 新華社, *Tuigenghuanlin tiaoli* 退耕還林條例 (Regulation on Turning Farmland into Forests and Grasslands) (2002). At http://www.peopledaily.com.cn/GB/huanbao/55/20021225/895611.html.
35. Hu (see note 19).
36. Ibid.
37. Liang Digang 梁狄剛, *"Xiqidongshu" gongcheng — Zhongguo xibu dakaifa di xumu* (wei fabiao baogao) 「西氣東輸」工程 — 中國西部大開發的序幕 (未發表報告) (The West-East Power Transmission Project: A Prelude of Western Development in China) (an unpublished report, 2000).
38. State Environmental Protection Agency, Chinese Academy of Sciences, *The Atlas of Population, Environment and Sustainable Development of China* (Beijing: Kexue chubanshe, 2000), p. 251.

39. Liang (see note 37).
40. *Guowuyuan xinwenban fabiao "Xinjiang di lishi yu fazhan" baipishu (2002)* 國務院新聞辦發表「新疆的歷史與發展」白皮書 (2002) (State Council's White Paper on "The History and Development of Xinjiang," 2002). At wysiwyg://104/http://www.peopledaily.com.cn/GB/shizheng/20030526/1000677.html.

11

Gansu

Fang Chuanglin and Gary M. C. Shiu

Introduction

Ever since China embarked on economic reform and pursued an open-door policy in 1978, its economy has experienced phenomenal growth. From 1986 to 1990, China's GDP grew an average of 7.9% annually. Economic growth accelerated especially after 1992, when the then paramount leader Deng Xiaoping visited southern China. Between 1991 and 1995, the national economy grew at an average annual rate of 12%. Despite the Asian financial crisis that erupted in late 1997, the Chinese economy still managed to attain a respectable average annual growth rate of 8.1% between 1996 and 2001.[1]

The high rate of economic growth achieved by China as a nation, however, masks the diverse performances of its provinces. While coastal provinces have gained tremendously during the reform period, other inland provinces have been left behind.[2] In a bid to rectify regional economic inequalities, China has mapped out a strategy to jump-start the development of its hinterland in the west.[3]

This chapter on Gansu 甘肅 is organized as follows. In the first section, an overview of Gansu's economic conditions is provided. Problems that are hindering the further development of Gansu's economy are also identified. We then examine what kind of development strategy should be adopted in guiding the province in searching for ways to develop more quickly, with the benefit of hindsight drawn from China's own economic reforms since 1978. To reinforce our argument with regard to development strategy, a detailed case study is presented of Gansu's potential in developing its tourism industry. The final section is a concluding section.

Gansu's Economic Landscape

Overview

Situated in the hinterland of northwestern China, Gansu extends from the border with Mongolia in the north to China's geographic centre in the south. It has a total area of 455,000 km^2 and a population of 25 million. The province is made up of 14 prefectures and cities (Figure 11.1). They in turn include 87 counties, towns and districts. With a population of 2.7 million, Lanzhou 蘭州 is the provincial capital and the second-largest city in northwestern China. A city with a history of over 2,000 years, Lanzhou's strategic location made it a key junction in the ancient Silk Road. In addition to being a centre of commerce and trade in northwestern China, Lanzhou has long been renowned as a hub of transportation and communications. In

Figure 11.1 Gansu in Its Geographical Setting

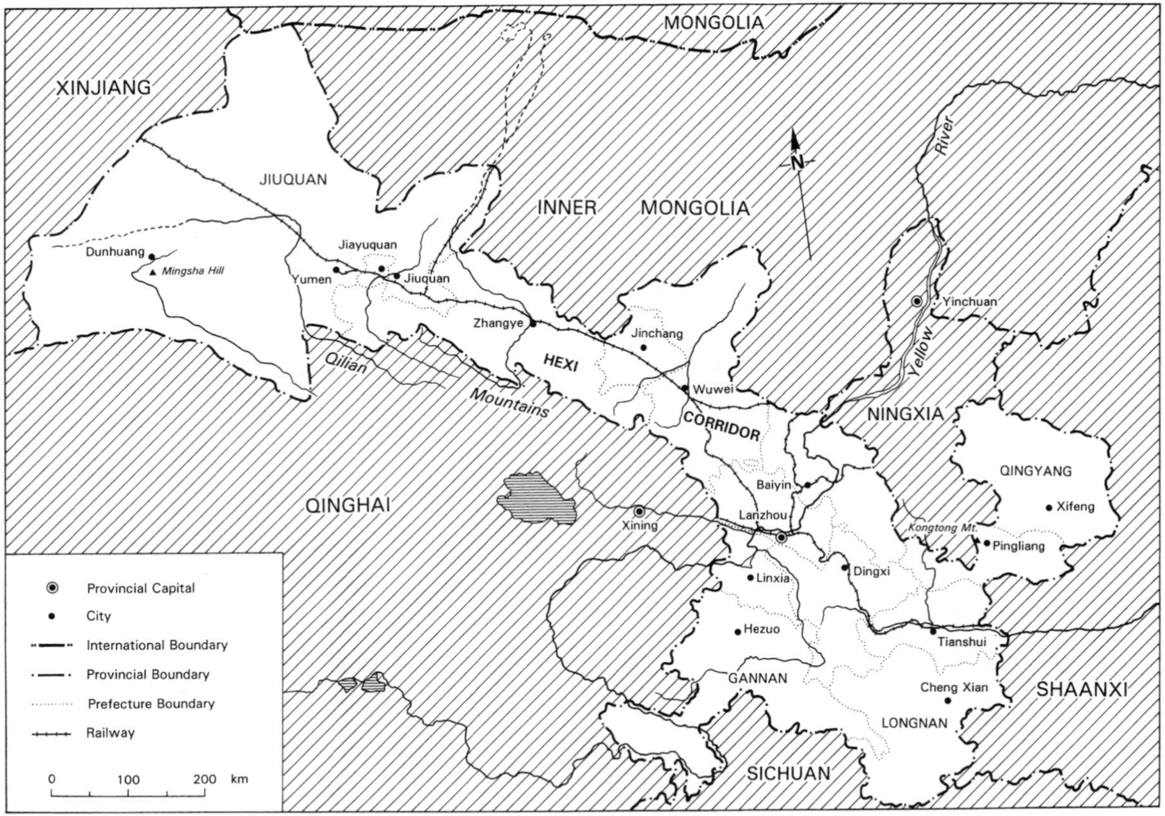

1992, Lanzhou was designated by the State Council as an inland open city with the same preferential policies as those of the coastal open cities, and given provincial-level administrative power in economic management. Other important cities in Gansu include Dunhuang 敦煌, Jiayuguan 嘉峪關, Tianshui 天水 and Jinchang 金昌.

More than 3 million ha of Gansu's total land area are cultivated. Grasslands and forests occupy 16.6 and 4.3 million ha, respectively. Standing timber reserves amounts to 200 million m^3. In addition, there are 1 million ha of uncultivated land suitable for use in agriculture, and another 6.7 million ha that could be turned into forests. More than 4 million ha of mountain slopes could be used for animal husbandry.

The province also has a variety of minerals. Around 3,000 deposits of 145 kinds of minerals have been found in the province, including nickel, cobalt, platinum, selenium, casting clay and finishing serpentine, among others. Such an abundance of mineral resources has made Gansu one of China's most important bases for the production of non-ferrous metals such as copper, aluminum, nickel, lead and zinc. In addition, the scale of the exploitation of Jinchang's copper and nickel mines ranks the second in the world.

Water resources are limited in Gansu. Those found in the province are mainly dispersed in nine river systems along the Yellow, Yangzi and inland river drainage basins. With a hydropower potential of 17.24 million kw, Gansu ranks ninth in the country in terms of hydropower potential. Thus far, 29 hydropower stations have been built with an installed generating capacity of 3 million kw and an annual output of more than 23 billion kwh.[4]

Despite Gansu's abundance in natural resources, the province's potential is far from being fully exploited. The next section provides a sketch of the province's current economic conditions through an examination of some of its more important economic indicators.

Current Economic Conditions

Despite more than two decades of reform, Gansu's economic development still trails that of many of the provinces located in the coastal region. Even when compared with the national economy as a whole, Gansu does not fare much better, as Table 11.1 illustrates.[5]

In 2001, Gansu's GDP amounted to RMB107.3 billion, up 9.4% from the previous year. With value added at RMB48.1 billion, the secondary sector still accounted for the lion's share of provincial GDP at 44.8%, an

Table 11.1 Comparative Growth Performance of GDP by Industry, 2000

Indicator	1952–2000 average annual growth rate (%)		
	China	Gansu	Growth differential
GDP	7.68	6.49	–1.19
Primary industry	3.27	2.52	–0.75
Secondary industry	11.24	10.17	–1.07
Tertiary industry	7.66	8.29	+0.63

Source: All data used for calculations are from Guojia tongjiju 國家統計局 (ed.), *Zhongguo tongji nianjian 2001* 中國統計年鑑2001 (China Statistical Yearbook 2001) (Beijing: Zhongguo tongji chubanshe 中國統計出版社, 2001).

increase of 0.1% from 2000. The service sector with value added at RMB38.5 billion occupied second place at 35.9%, while agriculture accounted for the remainder at 19.3%. While the share of the service sector in the province's GDP rose from 35.6% in 2000 to 35.9% in 2001, the share of agricultural sector dropped from 19.7% to 19.3%. Half-year numbers for 2002 showed that provincial GDP grew by 9.3% at about RMB43 billion.

Industrial value added for Gansu stood at RMB31.65 billion in 2001, up 11.51% from 2000. Of the total, state-owned and state-holding industrial enterprises accounted for the majority portion of industrial value added at about 69%. In terms of the industrial value added of light and heavy industry, the former had a share of 15% while the latter accounted for 85% in 2001.

In terms of fixed asset investment, the figure for 2001 was RMB50.54 billion. The state sector again played an important role, accounting for 83% of the total amount. The remaining portion of fixed investment came from urban and rural collectives as well as private investment, with the share of the former at 6% and the latter at 11%.

With regard to foreign trade, total trade amounted to US$779 million in 2001, an increase of 36.76% from the previous year. Of the total, exports stood at US$476 million, while imports totalled US$303 million. In terms of foreign direct investment (FDI), contractual foreign investment in 2001 amounted to US$0.16 billion, up 33.3% from the previous year. Foreign investment utilized during the year stood at US$0.074 billion, an increase of 11.6% from 2000. Thus, the export sector is relatively small in Gansu, where exports only made up 3.7% of provincial GDP in 2001. In that same year, exports accounted for 23% of national GDP.

A glance at the data reveals that the strong involvement of the state-owned sector in the local economy continued despite two decades of economic reform. This is especially so in the heavy industrial sectors.

Foreign participation in local economic activities is also limited. The non-state sector, in contrast to some coastal areas such as Wenzhou 溫州, has only a small role to play in Gansu's economy. These characteristics of the province's economy, which will be examined in detail in the next section, indeed act as roadblocks to further development.

Current Problems with Gansu's Economic Structure

Despite the considerable amount of natural resources found in Gansu, the legacy of central planning continues to constrain economic development. An examination of this legacy is the main focus of this section.[6]

The State-owned Sector Continues to Predominate

Similar to other provinces in China's western region, the state sector still plays an important role in Gansu's economy. In 2001, the share of the industrial value added generated by state-owned industrial enterprises amounted to 56% for the country as a whole, while the figure for Gansu was 77%. In 2000, the proportion of urban employees working in the state sector accounted for 68% of the total, while the proportion was only about 38% for the country as a whole. Li and Wang estimated that the non-state sector accounted for less than a quarter of Gansu's GDP in 2000 (24.3%).[7] The preceding information indicates that Gansu has to step up its efforts to both diversify its industrial ownership structure and encourage the development of its non-state sector.

Structural Imbalance

The legacy of the Third Front Construction has left Gansu and many other places in western China with an economy in which heavy industry predominates. In 2001, light industry accounted for 40% of China's total industrial value added for all state-owned and non-state-owned industrial enterprises. The rest was accounted for by heavy industry. Gansu's light industry, by contrast, only accounted for 15% of the same measure for the province.

A hallmark of a mature economy is that its service sector should occupy a larger share of the economy, while the manufacturing and agricultural sectors shrink in importance. In the U.S., for example, the service sector accounted for 77% of GDP in 2000.[8] Similarly, the share of the service sector in Hong Kong's GDP in the same year was 86%.[9] Although Gansu has come a long way in developing its service sector since reforms were launched in 1978, this sector still amounted to only 35.8% of provincial GDP in 2001.[10]

Another problem confronting Gansu in further developing its economy is its dependence on the agricultural sector. The agricultural sector's share of GDP in China's economy shrank to 15.2% in 2001 from 28% in 1978. In 2001, Gansu's agricultural sector stood at 19% of provincial GDP. In developing countries like China, the main challenge that a large agricultural sector poses to policy-makers in their effort to further promote economic growth is the problem of surplus labour. Job growth in the urban area cannot adequately absorb all of the labour released from the agricultural sector resulting from improvements in agricultural productivity following the introduction of the household responsibility system. Cai estimated that in 1990, surplus rural labour in Gansu amounted to 2.7 million.[11] Thus, how to generate enough jobs in Gansu in order to address the problem of surplus labour should occupy the attention of the province's officials for some time to come.

Limited Role of Foreign Trade and Foreign Direct Investment

A characteristic that is common to all places in China's western region is the fact that foreign investors play only a small role in their respective local economies. Table 11.2 shows that foreign involvement in selected local economies in the western region stayed low even in 2001, more than two decades after China began opening up to the world.

A glance at Table 11.2 reveals that in terms of the limited role played by foreign investors in the local economy, Gansu is no different from other provinces. In 2000, there were 826 foreign-funded enterprises in Gansu, up 8.8% from 1999. However, these enterprises accounted for only 0.4% of the national total in that same year.

The same pattern exists in terms of sources of funding for fixed asset investment. Funding derived from foreign sources accounted for only 2% of total fixed investment in Gansu in 2001, whereas the same share at the national level came to 8%. The low level of foreign involvement in Gansu's local economy has had adverse consequences for its economic development, as studies on FDI have time and again shown the multifaceted benefits that such investments can bring.[12]

Insufficient Supply of Human Capital

The insufficient supply of human capital serves as yet another obstacle to

Table 11.2 Foreign Involvement in the Economies of Gansu and Selected Provincial Units, 2001

Provincial unit	Foreign trade as % of local GDP	Foreign trade as % of national total	FDI as % of national total
Sichuan	6.28	0.66	1.36
Guizhou	6.65	0.17	0.10
Yunnan	8.56	0.42	0.31
Tibet	N.A.	0.02	N.A.
Shaanxi	11.90	0.52	0.93
Gansu	7.00	0.18	0.20
Qinghai	6.87	0.05	0.21
Ningxia	17.48	0.12	0.09
Xinjiang	13.21	0.46	0.13

Note: Nominal GDP figures are used, and FDI includes both contracted and actual FDI. N.A. means not available.

Source: Calculated with raw data from Guojia tongjiju, *Zhongguo tongji zhaiyao 2002* 中國統計摘要2002 (China Statistical Abstract 2002) (Beijing: Zhongguo tongji chubanshe, 2002).

the province's development. At the forefront of this issue is the problem of illiteracy in Gansu. Gansu compares unfavourably even with the 12 provincial units within China's western region, with an illiteracy rate of 14.34% in 2000, higher than Guangxi 廣西, Inner Mongolia 內蒙古, Sichuan 四川, Chongqing 重慶, Yunnan 雲南, Guizhou 貴州, Xinjiang 新疆, Shaanxi 陝西 and its close neighbour, Ningxia 寧夏.[13]

In terms of educational attainment per 100,000 persons, Gansu does not fare much better, as Table 11.3 illustrates. If the 12 provinces in the western region are divided into two groups with the sixth place serving as a dividing line, Gansu is the only province, with the exception of Tibet, to consistently rank at or below this level in the different indicators of educational attainment.

Now that we have a broad overview of Gansu's economic problems, the next question that needs to be answered by policy-makers is what kinds of policies does Gansu need to pursue in order to promote economic growth?

Economic Restructuring

What Kind of Development Strategy Should Gansu Adopt?

Soon after the founding of PRC in 1949, in a bid to catch up with economically advanced countries, China pursued a strategy that relied on the

Table 11.3 Educational Attainment in the Western Region, 2000 (persons per 100,000 people)

Region	Junior college	Senior secondary/ secondary technical school	Junior secondary school	Primary school
National	3,611	11,146	33,961	35,701
Inner Mongolia	3,803 (3)	13,760 (1)	34,768 (1)	31,134 (10)
Guangxi	2,389 (9)	9,554 (7)	32,339 (3)	42,176 (5)
Chongqing	2,802 (6)	8,596 (8)	29,413 (4)	43,386 (3)
Sichuan	2,470 (8)	7,587 (9)	29,358 (5)	42,960 (4)
Guizhou	1,902 (11)	5,626 (11)	20,408 (11)	43,595 (2)
Yunnan	2,013 (10)	6,563 (10)	21,233 (9)	44,768 (1)
Tibet	1,262 (12)	3,395 (12)	6,136 (12)	30,615 (12)
Shaanxi	4,138 (2)	12,246 (2)	33,203 (2)	34,475 (8)
Gansu	2,665 (7)	9,863 (6)	23,925 (8)	36,907 (7)
Qinghai	3,299 (5)	10,431 (5)	21,661 (10)	30,944 (11)
Ningxia	3,690 (4)	10,910 (4)	27,830 (6)	31,770 (9)
Xinjiang	5,141 (1)	12,089 (3)	27,528 (7)	37,950 (6)

Note: The number in parentheses is the ranking of each province within a particular category in the western region.

Source: All data used below are from Guojia tongjiju (ed.), *Zhongguo tongji nianjian 2001* (see note 5).

development of heavy industry. Lin characterized such a development strategy as "comparative-advantage-defying" (CAD).[14] A mismatch between natural/human resources and patterns of industrial development always develops under such a strategy, as developing countries like China usually have abundant labour and/or natural resources, but are short on the capital required by heavy industry. To alleviate such a mismatch, a system of administrative allocation was used to replace the market system. Such a system persisted for more than two decades in China, with disastrous economic results.

Following the introduction of economic reforms in China and the opening up of the country in 1978, the development of heavy industry ceased to be a national priority. Since then, China has followed what is known as the "comparative-advantage-following" (CAF) strategy. With the shift in development strategy from one that defied comparative advantages to one that fully utilized them, rapid economic growth resulted.

What, then, are the main drivers under the CAF development strategy that have helped China to create a record of impressive economic growth? Numerous studies on the sources of China's economic growth have been undertaken in the past. We need no more than distill the factors that are commonly identified in these studies as key to China's stellar economic performance in the past two decades or so.[15] Among the myriad factors, three stand out: the rise of the non-state sector, the country's engagement in international trade/economic openness and the accumulation of human capital. The importance of these three factors lies not only in their ability to account for China's economic growth, but also in their contribution to the regional inequalities that accompanied the reforms.[16] The implication is, therefore, that policy-makers should take these three factors into account when formulating their policies for promoting growth in China's western region. To provide a more concrete example of how economic restructuring in the province can be achieved under the guidance of the CAD development strategy, we will use Gansu's tourism industry as an example.

Several factors have prompted us to choose the tourism industry for closer scrutiny. Foremost, of course, are the rich tourism resources available in the province, which allow Gansu to enjoy a comparative advantage in the tourism industry. Second, facing serious environmental challenges, Gansu has to focus on developing industries that will help it to achieve the twin objectives of development and environmental protection. Tourism, especially eco-tourism, is one such industry. In order to cope with surplus agricultural labour and with the increasing number of unemployed people resulting from the continued restructuring of state industries, it is imperative for the province to promote labour-intensive industries. Once again, tourism meets that requirement. Finally, the rising popularity of Gansu as a tourism destination among both foreign and domestic visitors serves to underline its vast potential for further development.

Gansu is Well Endowed with Tourist Attractions

Presently, Gansu has 2 outstanding state-designated tourism cities, 4 outstanding state-level historical and cultural cities, 23 relics sites under state-level protection and a group of tourism resorts, forest parks and nature reserves.[17] Among the famous tourist sites in the province, doubtless the most famous are areas like Dunhuang that used to be part of the Silk Road, with their rich historical and cultural relics. Other spots attractive to tourists include four national forest parks and the Jiayuguan section of the Great Wall 長城. We will now go on to provide a brief sketch of two places among many others in Gansu that offer a combination of historic, cultural and scenic attributes that serve as the main draw for visitors. The two spots are Pingliang 平涼 and Dunhuang.

A 1,600-year-old city, Pingliang is located at the point at which Shaanxi, Gansu and Ningxia converge. In terms of sites that would be of interest to tourists, the city has 465 ancient cultural ruins, 55 ancient tombs, 12 ancient town ruins, 8 ancient grottoes, 5 ancient pagodas and more than 1,000 cultural relics. The jewel in the crown of tourist attractions in this city is doubtless the Kongtong Mountain 崆峒山, located 11 km west from the city centre. The mountain has a peak elevation of 2,123 m, a relative elevation of 673 m and a touring area of 14 km^2. The site has long been famous for its scenic beauty, including its towering pines and cypresses, verdant bushes, strangely shaped peaks and jagged rocks of grotesque shapes. A legend relating to Kongtong has it that emperor Huang Di 黃帝, the legendary first unifier of the Chinese nation, came to the mountain to learn Taoist doctrines from the Taoist sage Guangchengzi 廣成子. The other tourist attractions the city has to offer include the Jingchuan Hot Springs 涇川溫泉, the Wangmugong Mountain 王母宮山, Liuhu Park 柳湖公園 and others.[18]

The local government has made ceaseless efforts to improve the city's ability to draw tourists. For instance, the city government plans to spend RMB32 million in 2002 alone to improve urban conditions. The construction of the Kongtong Mountain scenic zone, with a size of 83.59 km^2, is one of its latest efforts to draw more visitors. Thus far, about 17% of the Kongtong Mountain zone has been completed and is in operation. The zone promises to offer better tourism facilities to the mountain's visitors. The local government has also invested heavily in the city's infrastructure in recent years, building the roads, hotels, and sewage and garbage disposal facilities that are crucial to promoting tourism. In 2001, the city received more than 590,000 domestic and foreign visitors and earned RMB171 million from tourism.[19]

Located at the western end of the Hexi corridor 河西走廊 in Gansu, Dunhuang used to be one of the most important stops on the ancient Silk Road connecting China with West Asia and Europe. Visitors, both local and foreign, flock to Dunhuang because it houses some of the greatest examples of Buddhist art in the world: the Mogao Grottoes 莫高窟, better known as the Thousand Buddha Caves 千佛洞. Located about 25 km southeast of Dunhuang, Dunhuang's Mogao Grottoes were carved out of the rocks that stretch for about 1,600 m along the eastern side of the Mingsha Hill 鳴沙山. The total number of grottoes at the site exceeds 400. In them are over 2,000 sculptures and 45,000 m^2 of murals.[20] Existing records from a Tang 唐 dynasty inscription traces the history of the very first cave in the Mogao Grottoes back to A.D. 366. In 1987, the United Nations Educational,

Scientific and Cultural Organizations (UNESCO) included the Mogao Grottoes in the World Heritage List.[21] Other tourist attractions in Dunhuang include the Mingsha Hill (also known as Singing Sand Hill 沙角山), the Yueya Spring 月牙泉, the Yang Pass 陽關, Yumen Pass 玉門關 and other spots.

In 2000, the city continued to draw in more than 600,000 domestic and foreign visitors, and earned RMB220 million from tourism.[22] Also, the city government decided to build a new tourism economic zone to further boost the city's attractiveness to visitors. Yitang Lake 伊塘湖, located 15 km from the Mogao Grottoes, is the chosen location of the new zone. The new zone is expected to cover an area of 5 km^2, and the first phase of construction will cost RMB800 million. The city government has also formulated preferential policies to attract both local and foreign investors to become involved in the development of the zone.[23] In 2000, work began on the expansion of the Dunhuang Airport, which was completed in August 2002. Dunhuang's airport is now equipped with a new runway that is 2,800 m long and 48 m wide, and able to accommodate 20 flights a day. At the cost of RMB320 million, it will enable larger-sized aircrafts like Boeing 737 to land there and allow the city to accommodate a greater number of tourists.[24]

Environmental Protection and Eco-tourism

Gansu faces considerable challenges in finding development polices that will not only stimulate the economy but also help to preserve the environment. Take soil erosion as an example. Recent reports indicate that in Gansu, 21,900 km^2 of land are suffering from soil erosion, accounting for more than half of the total amount of eroded land along the Yangzi River.[25] Other environmental problems include, but are not limited to, desertification and deforestation.

This is where developing the tourism industry, especially eco-tourism, fits in, as an essential goal of eco-tourism is to minimize the adverse impact of tourism. The global demand for eco-tourism is on the rise, especially among tourists from developed nations. For instance, recent research has shown that 85% of all German tourists would like to have an environmentally correct holiday.[26] Hence, given Gansu's environmental situation, encouraging the development of the tourism industry, especially its more environmentally friendly variant, is one way of attaining the twin objectives of further developing the local economy while preserving the environment.

Tourism as a Labour-intensive Industry with a High Multiplier Effect

The ongoing restructuring of state-owned industries will inevitably swell the pool of unemployed workers in Gansu. In addition, as mentioned above, there is a large army of surplus labour from the province's agricultural sector.

However, heavy industries dominate Gansu's industrial structure. Such an industrial structure has a limited capacity to absorb labour, as heavy industry is more dependent on inputs of capital than of labour. To generate more jobs, the promotion of labour-intensive industries should thus be high on the agenda of provincial policy-makers. Tourism is one such industry. As a service sector industry, tourism has a large demand for labour relative to capital. Furthermore, the tourism industry's capacity to absorb labour spills over to other sectors as well. In other words, it has a large multiplier effect. For example, when tourists visit a site, they will not only spend money on hotels and local tours; taxi drivers, restaurants and other related businesses will all also benefit from the arrival of tourists. Indeed, using data from Yunnan, Wen and Tisdell provided a rough estimate of the multiplier effect of China's tourism industry.[27] In Yunnan, at least, it was found that each RMB spent on tourism helped to generate RMB1.5 in further expenditures.

Visitors to Gansu are on the Rise

On the demand side, Gansu has made great strides in drawing visitors since 1978. In 1979, only about 2,400 foreign visitors came to Gansu, earning the province US$200,000 in tourist income.[28] In 2001, more than 200,000 foreign tourists visited the province, and tourist income rose to US$45 million. To forecast the future growth of international tourists in Gansu, we generated a trend line for international tourist arrivals based on a linear regression.[29] The trend analysis allows us to predict that, if the current trend continues, 244,727 and 288,653 international tourists are expected to visit the province in 2010 and 2015, respectively.

With the rising income of Chinese people, especially urban residents, domestic tourism has been flourishing as well. In 2000, more than 7.3 million domestic tourists visited the province. Between 1995 and 2000, domestic tourists spent about RMB6.5 billion during their stay in Gansu, with double-digit annual growth rate at 48.4%.[30] While the absence of statistics prevents us from doing a trend analysis for domestic tourists similar to the one above, it is still safe to suggest that the continuous growth of the Chinese economy will certainly provide Chinese people with both the means and the time to travel within the country. Domestic tourism in Gansu will inevitably benefit as a consequence.

Despite the availability of rich tourism resources in Gansu and the increasing popularity of the province among visitors, the province's tourism industry trails that of its coastal counterparts. For instance, both in terms of the number of international tourist arrivals and the number of days they spent in the province, Gansu did not place in the top 10 of China's provinces in 2001. More alarming is the fact that Gansu's tourism industry is not performing that well even in relation to other places in China's western region, such as Yunnan and Guangxi 廣西, which were among the top 10. The overall performance in tourism for the western region in 2001 is shown in Table 11.4 below. What accounts for the unsatisfactory performance of Gansu's tourism industry? It is to this topic that we now turn.

Table 11.4 Performance Indicators of International Tourism in the Western Region, 2001

Provincial unit	Tourist arrivals (1,000)	Tourism income (US$1,000)
Inner Mongolia	399.9 (19)	137,400 (19)
Guangxi	1,267.2 (7)	300,630 (11)
Chongqing	313.3 (22)	163,410 (17)
Sichuan	574.8 (14)	165,790 (16)
Guizhou	205.5 (26)	68,730 (26)
Yunnan	1,131.3 (8)	367,010 (9)
Tibet	127.1 (29)	46,380 (28)
Shaanxi	759.2 (10)	308,710 (10)
Gansu	222.6 (25)	44,810 (29)
Qinghai	39.7 (30)	9,020 (30)
Ningxia	8.7 (31)	2,730 (31)
Xinjiang	273.0 (23)	98,560 (23)

Note: National ranking in parentheses.
Source: Data from Zhongguo lüyouwang 中國旅遊網, *2001 nian gediqu guoji lüyou (waihui) shouru* 2001年各地區國際旅遊 (外匯) 收入 (International Tourism Receipts by Locality 2001) and *2001 nian gediqu jiedai rujing lüyouzhe qingkuang* 2001年各地區接待入境旅遊者情況 (International Tourists by Locality 2001), available on China National Tourism Administration website at http://www.cnta.com/tongjibanlan/2002/7.htm and http://www.http://www.cnta.com/tongjibanlan/2002/8.htm.

Factors Hindering the Development of Tourism in Gansu

Not surprisingly, the same three factors that have been identified above as critical components of a CAF development strategy do not have an important role to play in the province's tourism industry. The result is not only the under-exploitation of Gansu's comparative advantage in tourism, but the under-performance of the industry as well.

Education

Despite the growth of the tourism industry in China since economic reforms, people in the industry are unsatisfied with their recruits in terms of their service attitude, skill level and language ability, which fall short of what international travellers expect. Employers in the sector sense that the low-quality education and training that their employees have received are the main reasons for their lackluster performance. What, then, accounts for the poor education and training of those employees?

Lam and Xiao have identified a number of factors that may help explain the inadequacy of current tourism education in providing the skills and knowledge that students need.[31] First of all, graduates from educational institutions in the tourism industry have little, if any, hands-on experiences/practical knowledge in the field because internships are lacking at hotels and other related business entities. Curricula in tourism education are outdated, with insufficient attention being paid to tourism-related subjects such as training in hotel facilities, the management of services and the management of tourist attractions. Insufficient funding from the government also constrains efforts to improve the quality of tourism education. Without enough funding, high-quality tourism educators will not be interested in joining the field of education. In addition to all of these reasons, which apply equally across China, the western region also faces a shortage of training and educational facilities for tourism that coastal provinces do not similarly confront, as illustrated by Table 11.5 (see also Chapter 6, Shi Peijun et al.).

Even within the western region, educational institutes for tourism are not evenly distributed. In 2000, for instance, Gansu only accounted for 9% and 6%, respectively, of the total number of institutes of higher education and secondary and vocational schools found in China's western region.[32] As human capital plays an extremely important role in raising labour productivity, and the effect of such productivity will be more obvious in labour-intensive industries like tourism, if the province is serious about

Table 11.5 Distribution of Tourism Schools and Colleges, 2001

Types of tourism schools and colleges	Western region	Coastal region
Number of institutes of higher education as % of national total[1]	22 %	46 %
Number of secondary and vocational schools as % of national total[2]	23 %	50 %

Notes: [1] Tourism colleges and ordinary institutes of higher education with tourism departments.
[2] Secondary tourism professional schools, vocational tourism high schools, tourism classes at other secondary professional schools, vocational high schools and technical schools.

Source: Raw data obtained from Zhongguo lüyouwang, *2001 nian quanguo lüyou jiaoyu tongji qingkuang* 2001年全國旅遊教育統計情況 (China Tourism Education Statistics 2001), available on the China National Tourism Association website, accessible at http://www.cnta.com/24-jypx/2002/6-2.htm.

developing tourism into a pillar industry, the rapid development of such educational institutes in tourism should be Gansu's top priority.

The Inefficiency of State-owned Operators and the Limited Amount of Foreign Investment in Gansu's Tourism Industry

Due to limitations to the data, our focus will solely be on the performance of the hotel business.[33] State-ownership predominates in Gansu's hotel sector, just as in the province's industrial sector mentioned above. In 2000, the country had a total of 10,481 hotels, of which 63% were state-owned. In sharp contrast, Gansu had 94 hotels in the same year, 98% of them owned by the state. The same pattern characterizes the number of foreign-funded hotels in the same period. Foreign-funded hotels, 833 in all, accounted for 8% of the total number of hotels in the country.[34] Gansu, meanwhile, had only two foreign-funded hotels, and their share in the province's total was a miniscule 2%.

In terms of efficiency, the economic indicators of the province's state-owned and foreign-funded hotels show that the performance of the former trails that of the latter. While foreign-funded hotels generated, on average, RMB20.16 million of revenue per establishment in 2000, their state-owned counterparts only generated RMB5.35 million each.[35] In terms of labour productivity, again the foreign-funded hotels fared much better than the state-owned ones. In the foreign-funded enterprises, each employee helped to generate RMB70,100 on average, more than 1.6 times the RMB42,400 at state-owned ones in the same period.

Low Quality of Service

In a service sector like tourism, the quality of the services offered matters a great deal. The quality of service in the tourist industry does not seem to have improved in tandem with the rapid development of the sector as a whole. Studies on the services found in China's hotels, for example, have shown that they are far below international standards.[36] A recent study, based on survey data, has indicated that hotels are not doing a good job of meeting the expectations of tourists.[37] In addition, the managers and senior staff of the hotels surveyed in the study tended to perceive the quality of the services delivered to be higher than perceived by the tourists themselves. This finding is worrisome because it will be impossible for hotel operators to address the issue of quality without first recognizing that the problem exists. Bearing in mind that the survey was conducted in more economically advanced places (Beijing, Shanghai and Guangzhou), it is not hard to imagine that the situation is far worse in Gansu, where the education for employees in the tourism industry is underdeveloped and state-owned hotels still predominate.

How to Transform Gansu's Tourism Industry into a Pillar Industry?

In order to best utilize Gansu's comparative advantage in tourism, it is imperative for the province to rectify the weaknesses that are dragging down the growth of its tourism industry. To help speed up growth in this sector, the government must encourage the development of the three factors of nurturing human capital in the sector, opening the sector further to non-state enterprises and encouraging foreigners to invest in Gansu's tourism industry.

Nurturing Human Capital

As discussed above, there is a general shortage of talent in the province as a whole, not just in its tourism industry. To rectify that situation, more resources have to be dedicated to education. However, the biggest problem confronting Gansu in its bid to promote education is funding.[38] Despite the fact that education accounted for 4% of the province's GDP in 1999, about two percentage points higher than at the national level, this is still not enough, given the low level of education attained the province's population. Therefore, besides the traditional approach of having the government finance education, the province should also pursue other sources of funding to support education. The broadening of funding sources has already begun to occur at the national level. For example, while the government accounts for only 68% of the total amount of funding dedicated to education at the national level, the figure is 81% in Gansu in 1999.[39] International organizations, like the United Nations Development Programme and the World Bank, as well as international non-governmental groups like World Vision, should be actively pursued in order to diversify sources of support in the funding of education.[40] Domestic funding from non-state sources should also be explored. Indeed, in some parts of Gansu, non-state-run schools have already emerged. It has been reported that in Lanzhou, the province's capital, schools run by communities, enterprises and even individuals have flourished. Currently, there are about 100 such schools in the city, serving 25,000 students.[41]

Furthermore, advances in computer technology and communications should be utilized to provide new forms of education. Long-distance education programmes are a case in point. The central government, for instance, has launched a distance-learning project in 14 places in China's central and western region, with an investment of RMB80 million. The main benefit of promoting long-distance education in the western region is that it circumvents the severe shortage of teachers there.[42] In addition, it seems to be a more economical way to deliver education than the more traditional method.

Leveraging on China's WTO Membership to Encourage Foreign Involvement in Gansu's Tourism Industry

The absence of foreign capital in Gansu's tourism industry is apparent. One of the things that Gansu can do to promote foreign participation in the sector is for the province to leverage on the market entry commitments for foreign investors that the country made when China was admitted into the World Trade Organization (WTO) in late 2001. Under the WTO agreement, China plans to allow foreign investors to hold a controlling stake in joint-venture travel agencies before the end of 2003 and to set up wholly foreign-owned travel agencies by the end of 2005. There have also been reports that the watchdog of the industry, China National Tourism Administration, intends to allow the timetable to be moved up, and to permit such joint ventures to be formed in early 2003 on a trial basis.[43] The Gansu government should try its best to have the province chosen as the site for such a trial. Indeed, this same strategy can be applied for other sectors. For instance, under the WTO agreement, foreign banks will be allowed to conduct any businesses of their choice five years from 2001.[44] Again, the province could lobby to become the test site for this measure.

Furthermore, to attract foreign investors, the provincial government can introduce policies that are not available elsewhere. It seems that such policies are being considered. Recently, the provincial government announced a package of 53 preferential policies covering such areas as market access, the equal treatment of domestic and foreign enterprises, investment, taxation and land use. Some of the incentives are not being offered in other places in China. To promote foreign participation in the province's tourism industry, similar specific sector-wise policies can be formulated as well.

Encouraging the Development of the Non-state Sector

Probably the most urgent task facing the provincial government in its bid to promote the development of the non-state sector is to nurture a market-friendly environment. The government should ensure that all laws and regulations are observed and property rights enforced. Indeed, the evidence suggests that violations of various economic laws and regulations are prevalent in the province. In 2000, there were more than 30,000 such cases of violation in Gansu, a jump of more than 50 times compared to 1995.[45] Another obstacle to the growth of the non-state sector is the scant amount of bank lending that this sector is able to obtain from the financial system.[46] As long as state-owned banks continue to dominate the financial sector and non-state financial institutions are slow to emerge, this situation is likely to persist.[47]

Therefore, our suggestion is that Gansu lobby the central government to let it become the site for allowing foreign financial firms to conduct RMB business ahead of other places. If that materializes, a new source of funding should exist to allow cash-strapped firms to expand and grow in spite of the domestic banking sector's bias towards state firms. The provincial government should also remove administrative barriers and eradicate the illegal fees and charges that are hindering the development of Gansu's non-state sector. These suggestions to help the non-state sector grow are applicable not only to the tourism industry, but are equally relevant to other industries.

Further Tasks to be Accomplished

In addition to the strengthening of the three factors mentioned above, other tasks have to be undertaken by the provincial government if foreign investors are to be persuaded to invest in Gansu's tourism industry. Improving the province's infrastructure is one of those tasks. There are already signs that this is happening. It has been reported that from 2001 onwards, the provincial government will devote RMB50 million each year to the construction of facilities geared towards tourism. Plans also include transforming Lanzhou's Zhongchuan Airport 蘭州中川機場 into an international airport, and expanding the Jiayuguan and Qingyang 慶陽 airports. In addition, five military airports in the province are also being upgraded to enable them to accommodate both military and civilian flights.[48] On policies that will promote tourism more directly, the provincial government plans to set up a tourism centre, three tour zones and six key tourist routes within the next five years, starting from 2001.[49]

The policy recommendations presented above in the context of Gansu's tourism industry have a wider applicability. The abundance of natural scenic spots in the province is only one area where Gansu enjoys a comparative advantage. At the conceptual level, a CAF-development strategy can be applied in any industry as long as the industry in question indeed enjoys comparative advantages relative to others.[50] Hence, with suitable adjustments for local differences, the strategy should also be applicable to other areas of China's western region.[51]

Conclusion

One of the important lessons from China's phenomenal economic growth since 1978 is the importance of choosing an appropriate development strategy. In the case of China, impressive growth occurred after the country switched from a development strategy that defied comparative advantages to one that respects it. Comparative advantage alone is not enough, however. With the latter strategy, certain vehicles are still required through which a nation's/province's comparative advantage can best be utilized. Three factors have been found to be the main vehicles through which China's comparative advantages are exploited. In addition, local conditions also have to be taken into account when development policies are formulated.

In this chapter, it was found that the relatively minor role played by those three factors helped account for Gansu's inability to enjoy a faster rate of growth, despite the abundance of certain resources in the province. Not only does this analytical result hold for the provincial economy as a whole, it is also the case at the industry level. A thorough examination of Gansu's tourism industry also reveals that those same three factors play a pivotal role at the micro level. Policy recommendations have been provided on the nurturing of those factors in the case of Gansu in general and its tourism industry in particular.

Notes

1. Guojia tongjiju 國家統計局 (ed.), *Zhongguo tongji zhaiyao 2002* 中國統計摘要2002 (China Statistical Abstracts 2002) (Beijing: Zhongguo tongji chubanshe 中國統計出版社, 2002).
2. It is important to qualify this statement as even inland provinces have grown in absolute terms in the reform period, although they have fallen behind their coastal counterparts in relative terms.
3. The studies that have emerged of late on China's efforts to develop its western region have been voluminous. Some recent publications in English include Lai Hongyi, "China's Western Development Program: Its Rationale, Implementation, and Prospects," *Modern China*, Vol. 28, No. 4 (2002), pp. 432–66; Tian Xiaowen, *China's Drive to Develop Its Western Region (I): Why Turn to This Region Now?* East Asia Institute Background Brief, No. 71 (2000) (National University of Singapore) and *China's Drive to Develop Its Western Region (II): Priorities in Development*. East Asia Institute Background Brief, No. 72 (2000) (National University of Singapore); and Yasuo Onishi, *China's Western Development Strategy* (Tokyo: Institute of Developing Economies, 2001).
4. For further information on Gansu's geographical conditions, see Fang Chuanglin 方創琳, "Xibu kaifa de qianyan zhendi — Gansusheng" 西部開發的前沿陣地 — 甘肅省 (Gansu: The Frontier of Western Development), 2002 (unpublished manuscript, Institute of Geographical Sciences and Natural Resources Research, Chinese Academy of Science) and *Gansu xiangtu dili* 甘肅鄉土地理 (Gansu's Local Geography) (Lanzhou 蘭州: Gansu jiaoyu chubanshe: 甘肅教育出版社, 1994).
5. Guojia tongjiju (ed.), *Zhongguo tongji nianjian 2001* 中國統計年鑑2001 (China Statistical Yearbook 2001) (Beijing: Zhongguo tongji chubanshe 2001); Gansu tongjiju 甘肅統計局 (ed.), *2001 Gansusheng guomin jingji he shehui fazhan tongji gongbao* 2001 甘肅省國民經濟和社會發展統計公報 (2001 Gansu's National Economic and Social Development Statistical Communique). At http://www.gs.stats.gov.cn and Guojia tongjiju (ed.), *Zhongguo tongji zhaiyao 2002* (see note 1).

6. Gansu tongjiju (ed.), *2001 Gansusheng guomin jingji* (see note 5).
7. See Li Jufen 李菊芬 and Huang Peng 黃鵬, "Gansusheng fei gongyouzhi jingji fazhan zhuangkuang fenxi" 甘肅省非公有制經濟發展狀況分析 (An Analysis of Current Conditions and Economic Development in Gansu's Non-state Sector), *Shengqing ziwen* 省情咨文 (Consultation Papers on Provincial Conditions), No. 2 (2002). At http://210.72.51.4/kys/wsyd/show.asp?year=2002&month=2&filename=3.htm.
8. Bureau of Economic Analysis, Commerce Department, U.S. government website, at http://www.bea.gov/bea/dn2/gposhr.htm.
9. Census and Statistics Department. *Gross Domestic Product 2002: 2nd Quarter* (Hong Kong: HKSAR Printing Department, 2002).
10. Despite the relatively small size of Gansu's service sector compared with other mature economies, its share in the local economy was still larger than that for the Chinese economy as a whole in 2001.
11. See Cai Fang 蔡昉, *Zhongguo liudong renkou wenti* 中國流動人口問題 (China's Floating Population Problem) (Zhengzhou 鄭州: Henan renmin chubanshe 河南人民出版社, 2000).
12. See Jiang Xiaojuan 江小娟 and Li Rui 李蕊, "FDI dui Zhongguo gongye zengzhang he jishu jinbu de gongxian" FDI 對中國工業增長和技術進步的貢獻 (The Contribution of FDI to China's Industrial Growth and Technical Progress), *Zhongguo gongye jingji* 中國工業經濟 (China's Industrial Economy), No. 7 (July 2002), pp. 5–15.
13. Guojia tongjiju (ed.), *Zhongguo tongji nianjian 2001* (see note 5).
14. See Justin Lin 林毅夫, "Development Strategy, Viability, and Economic Convergence," *Economic Development and Cultural Change*, Vol. 55, No. 2 (2003), pp. 277–308; also Justin Lin, Cai Fang and Li Zhou 李周, *Zhongguo de qiji: Fazhan zhanlüe yu jingji gaige* (zengdingban) 中國的奇蹟：發展戰略與經濟改革 (增訂版) (The China Miracle: Development Strategy and Economic Reform) (revised edition) (Shanghai: Shanghai renmin chubanshe 上海人民出版社, 1999).
15. Works explaining China's economic growth since the launching of reforms are numerous. Representative ones include Joseph Chai, *China: Transition to a Market Economy* (New York: Oxford University Press, 1997); Jun Ma, *The Chinese Economy in the 1990s* (New York: St. Martin's Press, 2000); Barry Naughton, *Growing Out of the Plan* (Cambridge and New York: Cambridge University Press, 1995); and Yingyi Qian, "How Reform Worked in China, 2002," U.C. Berkeley Working Paper. At http://elsa.berkeley.edu/~yqian/how%20reform%20worked%20in%20china.pdf.
16. While the effects of the differential accumulation of human capital across China in generating spatial inequality may be obvious, the same may not be true of openness (including the influx and associated spatial dispersion of FDI) and of the emergence of the private sector. Based on regression analysis,

Wei found that about 90% of the differential rate of growth between the coastal and inland regions is accounted for by the uneven distribution of foreign direct investment. See Wei Houkai 魏後凱, "Waishang zhijie touzi dui Zhongguo quyu jingji zengzhang de yingxiang" 外商直接投資對中國區域經濟增長的影響 (Effect of Foreign Direct Investment on Regional Economic Growth in China), *Jingji yanjiu* 經濟研究 (Economic Research), No. 4 (2002), pp. 19–26. Chen and Feng showed that the higher concentration of non-state firms found in the coastal region compared to the inland region might have caused the divergence in growth observed in the two regions. See Chen Baizhu and Feng Yi, "Determinants of Economic Growth in China: Private Enterprise, Education, and Openness," *China Economic Review*, No. 11 (2000), pp. 1–15.

17. See *Inland Province Invests Heavily in Tourism*. At http://211.147.20.14/chinagate/focus/west/news/i102/20010703in.html.
18. For more information about tourist attractions in Gansu, see Gao Hailong 高海龍 (ed.), *Sichou zhilu Gansu duan lüyou zhinan* 絲綢之路甘肅段旅遊指南 (Travel Guide along the Silk Road in Gansu) (Lanzhou: Gansu renmin chubanshe 甘肅人民出版社, 1992).
19. See Ma Lie, "Ancient Gansu City Attracts Visitors" on *China Daily* Internet edition at http://www1.chinadaily.com.cn/cndy/2002-05-08/68419.html.
20. See Gao, *Sichou zhilu Gansu duan lüyou zhinan* (see note 18).
21. See "Backgrounder: Famous Dunhuang Mogao Grottoes" on *People's Daily* Internet edition at http://english.peopledaily.com.cn/200003/29/eng20000329R105.html.
22. See "China Dunhuang International Cultural, Tourism Festival Opens" on *People's Daily* Internet edition at http://english.peopledaily.com.cn/200108/29/eng20010829_78704.html.
23. See "Dunhuang in NW China to Build New Tourism Economic Zone" on *People's Daily* Internet edition at http://fpeng.peopledaily.com.cn/200005/24/eng20000524_41539.html.
24. The airport can now handle about 300,000 visitors. See "Expanded Dunhuang Airport Operational" on *People's Daily* Internet edition at http://english.peopledaily.com.cn/200208/19/eng20020819_101685.shtml.
25. See "Gansu Water Conservation Scheme Pays Off." At http://211.147.20.14/chinagate/focus/west/news/i001/20020222gansu.html.
26. See "Eco-tourism." At http://www.touristguides.org.uk/hklectures.html.
27. See Julie Wen and Clement Tisdell, *Tourism and China's Development* (Singapore: World Scientific, 2001).
28. Guojia tongjiju (ed.), *Zhongguo tongji nianjian 2001* and *Zhongguo tongji zhaiyao 2002* (see note 5).
29. The regression is a linear one with the functional form $y=a+bx$, where y is the number of international tourist arrivals from 1979 to 2001 and x is the year.

The coefficient of the regression is 8,785 and the value of the R-square is 0.84.

30. See "Inland Province Invests Heavily in Tourism." At http://211.147.20.14/chinagate/focus/west/news/i012/20010703in.html.
31. See Terry Lam and Xiao Honggen, "Challenges and Constraints of Hospitality and Tourism Education in China," *International Journal of Contemporary Hospitality Management*, Vol. 12, No. 5 (2000), pp. 291–95.
32. Calculation based on raw data from Guojia lüyouju 國家旅遊局 (ed.), *Zhongguo lüyou tongji nianjian 2001* (fuben) 中國旅遊統計年鑑 2001 (副本) (The Yearbook of China Tourism Statistics 2001 (Supplement)) (Beijing: Zhongguo lüyou chubanshe 中國旅遊出版社, 2001).
33. Zhongguo lüyou nianjian bianji weiyuanhui 中國旅遊年鑑編輯委員會, *Zhongguo lüyou nianjian 2001* 中國旅遊年鑑 2001 (The Yearbook of China Tourism 2001) (Beijing: Zhongguo lüyou chubanshe, 2001) and Guojia lüyouju, *Zhongguo lüyou tongji nianjian 2001* (see note 32).
34. Here, foreign-funded hotels include those funded by investors from Hong Kong, Macau and Taiwan.
35. Guojia lüyouju, *Zhongguo lüyou tongji nianjian 2001* (see note 32).
36. See Cai Liping and Robert Woods, "China's Tourism Service Failure," *The Cornell Hotel and Restaurant Administration Quarterly*, Vol. 34, No. 4 (1993), pp. 30–39.
37. See Nelson Tsang and Qu Hailin, "Service Quality in China's Hotel Industry: A Perspective from Tourists and Hotel Managers," *International Journal of Contemporary Hospitality Management*, Vol. 12, No. 5 (2000), pp. 316–26.
38. See Zhang et al., "China's International Tourism Development: Present and Future," *International Journal of Contemporary Hospitality Management,* Vol. 12, No. 5 (2000), pp. 282–90.
39. 1999 is the latest year for which statistics on education funding are available, as reported in NBS 2001 (see note 5).
40. The United Nations Development Programme (UNDP) will spend US$1 million to support training programmes in China's western region between 2002 and 2004. See "China Joins Hands with UNDP to Train Professionals in the West." At http://211.147.20.14/chinagate/focus/west/news/i007/20020116coop.html.
41. See "Non-government-run Schools Booming in Northwest China City." At http://211.14.20.14/chinagate/focus/west/news/i007/20010617such.html.
42. See "Computerized Teaching Networks Aid Education in Central, Western Areas" on the *China Daily* website at http://search.chinadaily.com.cn/isearch/i_textinfo.exe?dbname=cndy_printedition&listid=5704&selectword=COMPUTERIZED%20TEACHING%20NETWORKS%20AID%20EDUCATION.

43. See "China Opens Door to Foreign Travel Agencies" at the Hong Kong Trade Development Council website at http://www.tdctrade.com/alert/ch0201c.htm.
44. See Karby Leggett, "Foreign Influx Stands to Benefit China Banks," *Asian Wall Street Journal*, 27 August 2002.
45. See Li Jufen and Wang Peng, "Gansusheng fei gongyouzhi jingji fazhan zhuangkuang fenxi" (see note 7).
46. See Ross Garnaut et al., *Private Enterprise in China* (Canberra and Beijing: Asia Pacific Press, 2001).
47. A stock market listing is not a viable option, either. Thus far, almost all of the firms listed on China's stock exchanges are state-owned ones.
48. See "Inland Province Invests Heavily in Tourism." At http://www.chinavista.com/travel/travelnews/en/tc0703-3.html.
49. See "Gansu Province to Develop Tourism Industry." At http://www.chinawest.gov.cn/english/asp/showinfo.asp?name= 200103070010.
50. For more on how to develop the industrial and agricultural sectors in Gansu, where they enjoy comparative advantages, see Zhang Xusheng 張緒勝 (ed.), *Xibu dakaifa: Jiyu, tiaozhan, jueze* 西部大開發：機遇，挑戰，抉擇 (Development of China's Western Region: Opportunities, Challenges and Choices) (Beijing: Jingji guanli chubanshe 經濟管理出版社, 2001), and *Xibu dakaifa: Gansu gongye zenmeban* 西部大開發：甘肅工業怎麼辦 (Development of China's Western Region: What is to be Done with Gansu's Industry) (Beijing: Jingji guanli chubanshe, 2001).
51. See also Fang Chuanglin 方創琳, *Quyu fazhan zhanlüe lun* 區域發展戰略論 (Introduction to Regional Development Strategy) (Beijing: Kexue chubanshe 科學出版社, 2002).

12

Qinghai

Li Tongsheng and Liu Xiaoming

Standing in the northwestern part of the Qinghai-Tibet Plateau 青藏高原 in China's west, Qinghai 青海 is named after the largest salt lake — Qinghai Lake 青海湖 — in China. Located in the hinterland of Eurasia, its topography varies from area to area, with an average altitude of over 3,000 m above sea level. It is the source of the Yangzi River 長江, the Yellow River 黃河 and Lancang (known as the Mekong to the West) River 瀾滄江, and thus is called the "source of the rivers" and the "watertower of China." The land is sprawling, rich with natural resources, populated by minority peoples and militarily strategic.

A Sketch of the Province

The Geographical Background

Qinghai has an area of 721,120 km^2, accounting for one-thirteenth of China's total area. It has a high altitude terrain and its topography is complex, with a more elevated western portion, lower east, higher southern and northern portion and lower middle. The major mountain ranges are the Qilian 祁連山脈, Bayan Har 巴顏喀拉山脈, Kunlun 崑崙山脈 and Tanggula 唐古拉山脈, making up the basic framework of the province. The province can be divided into three regions: the high-altitude Qilian-Altun region 祈連山–阿爾金山山地 in the north, the Yellow River Valley 黃河谷地 and Huangshui Valley 湟水谷地 in the middle and the high-altitude Qingnan Plateau 青南高原 in the south (Figure 12.1).[1]

Qinghai is characterized by its continental and plateau climates. High altitudes, low temperatures, little rainfall, long hours of sunshine, great differences among regions, long winters and cool summers are its typical characteristics. The living conditions in Qinghai are very harsh because of the bitter cold, strong winds, heavy snowfalls and frequent drought, hail and frost. Due to natural and man-made reasons, the ecological problems of soil erosion, desertification, degradation of grasslands and shrinkage of lakes are striking, making the ecology very vulnerable. Qinghai is the source of three large rivers, so its natural environment is of national importance.

Qinghai had only 5.18 million inhabitants in 2000. The average population density is 7.2 persons/km^2, but the population is very unevenly distributed — sparse in the west and dense in the east. The areas of Xining 西寧 and Haidong 海東 take up only 2.84% of the total area, but their populations account for 67.2% of the provincial total, with a density of 146 persons/km^2. The area west to the Riyue Mountain 日月山 comprises

Figure 12.1 Qinghai in Its Geographical Setting

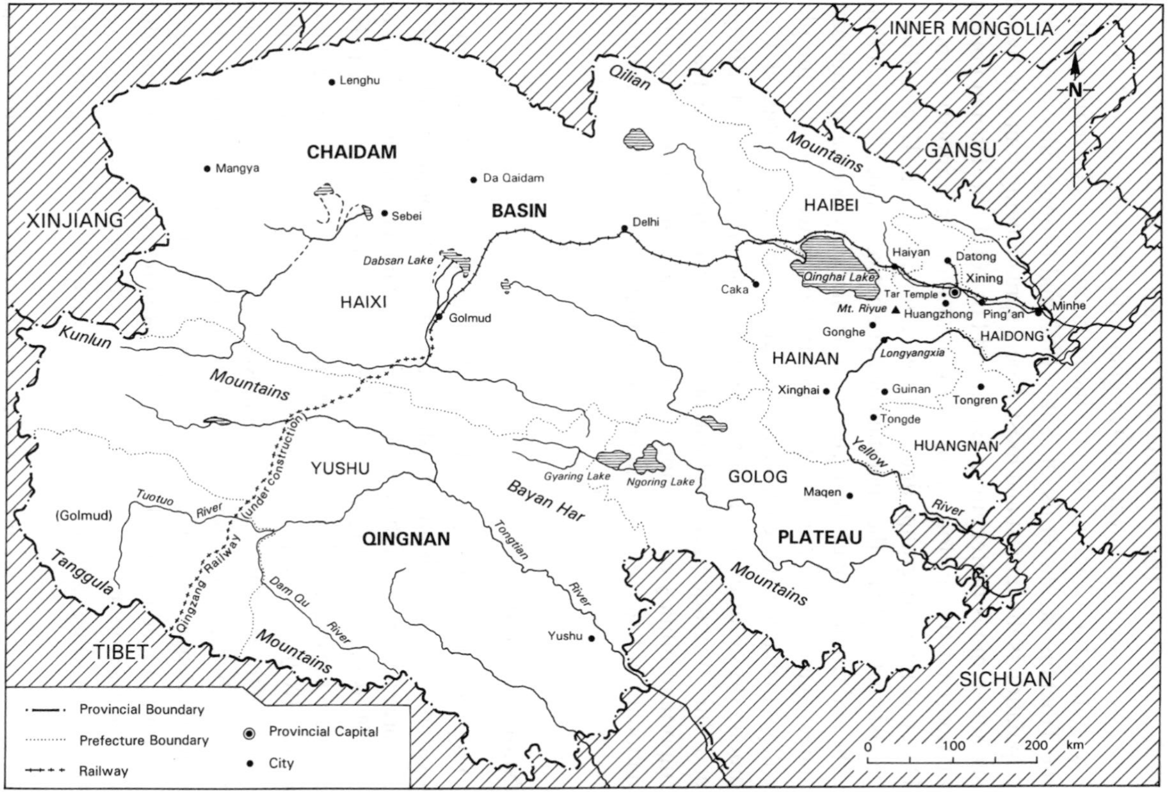

97.16% of the total area, but contains only 32.8% of the province's population, with a density of 2–3 persons/km^2. In many places in Golmud 格爾木 and in the Haixi Region 海西洲, there are no residents.

There are 43 minorities in Qinghai with a population of 2.18 million, accounting for 42.1% of the province's population. The major groups are the Tibetans 藏, the Huis 回, Salas 撒拉 and Mongolians 蒙古. Tibetan population is the largest and most widely spread, being found in five of the six autonomous prefectures.[2] By the end of 2000, the Tibetan population numbered 1.05 million, comprising 48.8% of the minority population. Different minority groups find common cultural bonds in Tibetan Buddhism and Islam. Qinghai is the important passage between Tibet 西藏 and Xinjiang 新疆 and China proper. Historically, it has not only been a springboard for states located in China proper to expand to the west and for the plateau nations to march to the east, but also an area of both co-operation and conflict among the cultures of China proper and those of the Tibetan, Mongolian and Hui.[3] Its unique geographical position means that Qinghai plays a very important military and economic role; and the co-existence there of many nationalities that are also found beyond China's borders makes the province politically sensitive as well.

Natural Resources

Qinghai is rich in various kinds of natural resources. Among them, hydropower, minerals and grasslands are the most prominent. The particular resource advantage of the province is its huge mineral deposits. Liu Zaixing 劉再興 used the total resource reserve and average reserve per person to measure the degree of richness of natural resources of various provinces in China. By this measure, the 9 provinces of the western region ranked in the top 12 in the country.[4] Table 12.1 shows Qinghai holding the very top rank. Qinghai has a good combination of natural resources, which is ideal for comprehensive development. Huge energy industries can be developed using hydropower, coal and oil. The smelting of non-ferrous metals, production of construction materials and heavy-duty chemical engineering bases can be built to take advantage of the province's rich energy and mineral resources.

Even as most resource markets in China are approaching saturation, some resources in Qinghai are rare and can meet special needs. Chen Dongsheng 陳棟生 and others[5] divided the mineral resources into four classes, based on whether known reserves can meet the needs of economic

Table 12.1 The Ranking of Nine Western Provinces by Richness of Natural Resources

Province	Total natural resources		Per capita natural resources		Total richness advantage in natural resources	
	Rank	Advantage index	Rank	Advantage index	Rank	Total richness degree
Qinghai	1	1.1609	3	3.3231	2	1.9641
Tibet	3	1.0920	1	7.0307	1	2.7708
Xinjiang	4	1.0805	4	1.9495	4	1.4514
Yunnan	5	1.0345	6	1.5984	5	1.2859
Guizhou	7	0.9080	8	1.2109	8	1.0486
Sichuan	8	0.8966	11	0.9956	10	0.9448
Ningxia	10	0.8046	7	1.2663	9	1.0094
Shaanxi	11	0.7816	10	1.0408	11	0.9015
Gansu	12	0.7816	12	0.7144	12	0.7472

Source: Writing Committee, *Xibu dakaifa zhishi duben* 西部大開發知識讀本 (Manual on the Development of the West) (Xi'an: Xibei daxue chubanshe 西北大學出版社, 2000), p. 13.

development (Table 12.2). It is clear that oil, gas, gold, boron, chrome metals of the platinum family, etc., are in high demand in the country.

Although rich in natural resources, Qinghai is constrained by a series of factors. Its peripheral location, poor transportation, harsh natural conditions, low economic development and capital shortages have led to high production costs, low efficiency and serious damage to the resources. Qinghai should take advantage of the policy of developing the west and rely on the use of science and technology to improve the quality and efficiency of the development of its resources, so that its resource advantage can be turned into an economic one.

A Unique Transport Passage

Historically, the economy in Qinghai grew very slowly and communication with the outside was difficult. Recently, with the changes in the international political economy, the Chinese government has extended the open policy to areas along the country's rivers and borders. Qinghai lies at a hub and its prospects are, therefore, very outstanding. Currently, the strategy of developing the west has entered the phase of implementation, and the central government has increased its financial support to Qinghai and other provinces in the west to speed up the construction of infrastructure. The

Table 12.2 Meeting the Demand for Minerals Resources in China

Degree to which demand can be satisfied	Mineral types	Reserve conditions
Highest degree. Can meet the needs of the present and of economic development in the near future. Can be exported.	Coal, tungsten, stannum, copper, antimony, titanium, rare soil metals, graphite fluorite, barite, gesso kaoline, diatormite, silicon, natrium, materials for concrete, materials for glass, marble, granite, etc.	Abundant resources, rich reserves. Nationwide advantage.
High degree. Can meet the needs of the present and near future.	Iron, manganese, aluminum, plumbum zinc, nickel, sulfur, uranium asbestos meerschaum, etc.	Fairly rich in resources, rather plentiful reserves.
Low degree. Can meet the needs of the present but not of the future.	Oil, natural gas, copper aururn, silver boron, top grade gems, etc.	Not enough discovered or for exploitation, but certain potential reserves.
Lowest degree. Cannot meet the needs of development. Imports are required every year.	Chrome metals of the platinum family.	Little discovered. Nationwide shortage.

Source: See Table 12.1, p. 14.

most ambitious of the projects, the west-east gas transmission project and the Qing-Zang 青藏 (Qinghai-Tibet) Railway project, have been launched.

The Qinghai-Tibet Railway, totalling 1,963 km, starts from Xining and ends in Lhasa 拉薩. The section from Xining to Golmud has been completed and the construction of the section from Golmud to Lhasa, totalling 1,118 km, has begun. Because 600 km of the route runs through terrain that is frozen year-round and over 960 km of it is above the altitude of 4,000 m above sea level, the engineering work is extremely difficult. When completed, the Qinghai-Tibet Railway will be the longest plateau railway at the highest altitude in the world. The construction of the Qinghai-Tibet Railway will greatly help develop the resources and economy of the areas in Qinghai through which it passes. Being the most important passage connecting China proper and Tibet, it will further strengthen the province's role as a hub.

The west-east gas transmission project aims to pipe gas from the west to the energy-short Yangzi River Delta area 長江三角洲地區 in the eastern part of China. Gas reserves in the Chaidam Basin 柴達木盆地 are remarkable, with a confirmed reserve of 147.2 billion m^3. Thus, Qinghai enjoys the advantages of having natural resources and being a passageway. The importance of the project to Qinghai lies in the fact that it can turn its resource advantage to a real economic one. This will be a new starting point for economic growth in the area, which will greatly change local patterns of energy consumption but protect the ecological environment. The exploitation of gas resources will also stimulate the development of related industries and enhance the development of ethnic societies and economies.

Development History and Policy Evolution in Qinghai from the End of the Qing Dynasty to 1949: A Period of Germination

The Foreign Industrial Movement 洋務運動 that started in the late nineteenth century aiming to learn and adopt foreign technology was a government-supported modern industrial movement. The effort had an impact on the development of regional industries in China, including the northwest. Based on the conditions of the northwest — a large territory, expansive grasslands, developed animal husbandry and rich mineral resources — the local officers, in an effort spearheaded by the renowned Qing dynasty military leader and official, Zuo Zongtang 左宗堂, started a series of energy, mining, leather-making, match and resource industries which were spin-offs of military industries and which also marked the beginning of civil industry in the region.

After the founding of Guomindang 國民黨 government, a policy of developing and building the northwest was formulated in 1928, for reasons of regional development and social stability. A field survey was conducted and a schedule for development was drawn up. For a variety of reasons, the schedule was not put into practice although public interest was aroused.

At that time, Qinghai's economy was very backward. The relations of production resembled slavery and the economy was solely focused on farming and animal husbandry. Industry was at its infancy. Except for a few small shops — the so-called industry at that time in Xining and in the nearby areas to the east — not a single factory had been set up in the extensive grasslands. All of the activities in farming and animal husbandry were done by hand, with very low rates of efficiency.

1949 to 1978: Setting the Foundation for Socioeconomic Development

After 1949, based on the assessment that the economy was overly concentrated in the coastal areas, the state adopted the policies of balanced regional development, strengthening national security and locating production close to sources of raw materials and areas of consumption. At the same time, the state conceived the aim of restricting the development of the coastal areas and expanding the development of the interior areas. From 1949 to 1978, momentous changes took place in the socioeconomic development of Qinghai.

From 1950 to 1957, according to the national plan and to local conditions, the local government focused on developing animal husbandry and agro-industry. Grain production was raised to a level at which the province became self-supporting and local industry developed to meet the needs of the local people and economy. At the same time, Qinghai's authorities began to develop the Chaidam Basin, particularly by constructing roads, after ordering that a survey be carried out.

From 1958 to 1962, during the period of the "Great Leap Forward" 大躍進, the economic development that was being pursued in Qinghai was neither proper nor practical. The steel industry and related service industries expanded excessively. Too much land was ploughed for farming, resulting in the serious destruction of the ecological environment. Contrary to naive expectations, grain output dropped and the cattle population also fell sharply.

From 1963 to 1965, the local government adopted the policy of "adjustment, consolidation, substantiation and improvement." The province concentrated on strengthening farming and light industry, and reduced the scale of heavy industry. Farming developed while some factories and mines were closed down and a portion of the urban population was sent to the countryside to farm. Qinghai's economy was adjusted. It improved shortly afterwards and gradually began to progress.

From 1966 to 1978, during the period of "Cultural Revolution" 文化大革命, the ratio between farming and industry became unbalanced again. Too many factories were set up to prepare for war. Heavy industry expanded greatly while light industry declined, resulting in the shortage of commodities. In agriculture, although the output of grain increased, production of other crops decreased. However, some economic achievements were realized. A group of mechanic, metallurgical, fertilizer and textile enterprises was set up, laying a foundation for modern industry in the province.

Development since 1978

In 1978, China entered a new era of economic reform and opening to the outside world. In such an environment, the most urgent problem for Qinghai was to speed up development to emerge from backwardness.

After 10 years of hard work from 1978, Qinghai's economy developed significantly. The four major industries of hydropower, oil and gas, salt production and non-ferrous metal production progressed greatly. At the same time, metallurgy, medicine, the manufacturing of construction materials and the processing of agricultural and animal husbandry products had begun to develop. The development of resources was making healthy progress, and a group of national projects was established, setting the foundation for further development in the province.

In 1988, the province began an economic strategy of reform and opening up, fighting poverty and developing resources. Xining became an open city and a group of test areas for reform was set up, such as the minority reform area in Golmud, the resource development area in Chaidam, the Kunlun economic development area, the minority economic construction area in Minhe 民和 county and the economic development area in Datong 大通. The local government set up many middle- and small-sized enterprises in resource development. It pooled its financial resources and launched a group of large projects, such as the Longyangxia 龍羊峽 hydropower station, the Black Spring 黑泉 Reservoir, the 0.3 million-tonne extension project of the Qinghai cement factory, the Dagan'gou 大干溝 hydropower station in Golmud, the Ping'an 平安 copper foil factory and the extension of Qilian asbestos factory, etc. Especially notable were the installation of four sets of generators at the Lijiaxia 李家峽 hydropower station, the laying out of gas pipes from Sebei 澀北 to Golmud, the second phase of the Qinghai aluminum factory and the second phase of the Minhe magnesium factory. The extension at the Mangya 茫崖 asbestos factory and the laying out of optical cables in Lanxi 蘭西 improved basic conditions at the energy and communication industries in Qinghai and brought general development to a new level. In 2000, the province's GDP reached RMB26.359 billion. Total investment reached RMB15.114 billion and the average income per person was RMB2,225.

Since 1978, Qinghai has made significant progress, both economically and socially. However, its economy still lags behind that of provinces in the east and the gap is still increasing.

Developing Qinghai with New Policies and Measures

The rapidly growing difference between the development in the east and that in the west has strong implications for social stability, national solidarity and the healthy development of the national economy. The central authorities decided that the time had come to narrow the differences. Thus, the policy of developing the west was adopted in 1999.

To make full use of this new opportunity, the government of Qinghai has adopted a strategy focusing on economic construction by meeting market demands and speeding up the construction of infrastructure. It has strengthened the protection of the ecological environment, the regulation of the industrial structure and has promoted economic and social development to benefit all minorities. In particular, it has been trying its best in the following aspects.

First, it will pool its financial resources to develop transport, communications, electricity and hydroelectric resources, farming and grasslands, education, culture, broadcasting and TV. Second, it will improve the ecological environment. During the period of the Tenth Five-year Plan and up to 2015, large-scale ecological protection projects will be carried out in the Yangzi River source area, the Yellow River area, the Qinghai Lake area, the eastern drought-prone area, the Longyangxia Reservoir area and the Chaidam Basin area. Third, the government will work to adjust the province's economic structure. It will adjust the farming and manufacturing industries, refine animal husbandry, speed up the development of the Salt Lake, and of the hydropower, oil, gas and non-ferrous and rare metal industries, and develop its mineral industries (sodium, magnesium, potassium, lithium, strontium and boron) to gradually make Qinghai a national base for the production of potassium fertilizer, metal lithium and strontium carbonate. Fourth, the government will invest in education. It will enhance basic education, actively develop minority education and higher education, and speed up training for modern enterprises to raise the cultural and scientific knowledge of the workers.

According to the Tenth Five-year Plan and the Perspective Target of 2010 of Qinghai, the province's GDP will reach RMB66 billion and the average income per capita will be RMB11,480 by 2010. The ratio comprised by the primary, secondary and tertiary industries will evolve from 18:48:34 in 2000 to 10:59:31 in 2010.

At present, some major projects have already been launched, such as construction of the section from Golmud to Lhasa of the Qinghai-Tibet Railway, the expressway from Xining to Lanzhou 蘭州, the gas pipeline from Golmud to Xining to Lanzhou and the pilot project of returning farmland to grassland.

Resources and Economic Development

Present Situation

Qinghai enjoys the advantage of having rich resources and a comprehensive industrial system. Some factors, however, are restricting its development.

The low level of economic development and primary structure of industry. Since 1949, especially since 1978, Qinghai has experienced rapid development. Until now, however, its level of economic development is still rather low as measured by modern industrial and economic indices. In 2000, at RMB26.359 billion, Qinghai's GDP accounted for 0.3% of the national total, while its average GDP per capita was only 69.1% of the national average (Table 12.3).

According to its industry and manpower structure (Tables 12.3 and 12.4), industrialization is at a rather low level. Its industrial structure is in a "two, three, one" form, meaning in order of importance, secondary, tertiary and primary industry, while its employment structure is typically in a "one, three, two" form, meaning, again, in order of importance, primary, tertiary and secondary industry. It can be concluded that Qinghai's industrial structure is still dominated by farming and animal husbandry.

Single industrial structure. Industrial output in Qinghai is rather limited, and the majority of the industrial structure is owned by the central or provincial authorities. After years of development, an industrial system has been established. However, the focus is only on resource development and efficiency is very low.

Table 12.3 A Comparison between the National Industrial Structure and that of Qinghai, 2000

Region	GDP (RMB billion)				Average GDP per capita (RMB)
	Total	1st industry	2nd industry	3rd industry	
China	8,940.36	1,421.20	4,548.78	2,970.38	7,078
Qinghai	26.36	3.85	11.40	11.11	5,087

Source: *Statistical Yearbook of China, 2001.*

Table 12.4 A Comparison between Employment Nationally and in Qinghai, 2000

Region	Total (1,000)	1st Industry	2nd industry	3rd industry	Ratio
China	711,500	355,750	16,009	195,660	50.0:22.5:27.5
Qinghai	2,386	1,453	319	614	60.9:13.4:25.7

Source: *Statistical Yearbook of China, 2001.*

Output in farming is very small. In 2000, farming and animal husbandry made up 43.6% and 53.5%, respectively, of agricultural output. Although farming and animal husbandry are traditional economic activities, their development has been slow. Today, animal husbandry is still in the form of free grazing and a herdsman measures his wealth by how many animals he owns. This has led to overgrazing, with a negative impact on the environment and a poor outlook for sustainable development.

Perspectives on Special Industries

Considering the characteristics of a small population, vast territory, a poor economy and rich resources, Qinghai has adopted a strategy of reform, poverty alleviation, and of developing its resources for economic growth. The core of the strategy is to maximize the advantage of its natural resources by establishing a resource-based economic structure to speed up development.

Establishing a large agricultural system. Qinghai needs to make full use of the diversity of its agricultural resources and of the advantages of its energy and biological resources to establish an overarching agricultural system. Farmland is limited in the province. The main farming areas are in the valleys (especially the He-Huang Valley 河湟谷地), while the border areas are suitable for both farming and animal husbandry. The improvement of the system should begin with market reforms and be based on local conditions in different areas. Farming and animal husbandry should be integrated. With the goal of stabilizing present amounts of farmland, efforts should be made to adjust the agricultural structure, reduce the production of highland barley and turn to the development of feed grains and high plateau economic produce to develop house-feeding animal husbandry. In the future, Qinghai should reform its production system, help its people change their traditional ideas of wealth and animal husbandry methods, build up commercialized animal husbandry areas and expand industrialization.[7]

Developing special energy mines and building production bases. Qinghai is rich in energy resources, which are found in relatively concentrated locations and in a fairly good combination. According to Qinghai's development plans, the following bases will be built by 2010. First, a major national oil and gas mining and engineering base and a salt production base will be constructed in the Chaidam Basin. Second, a comprehensive industrial base for steel, non-ferrous metals, mechanical and electric equipment, construction materials, and the processing of farm and animal husbandry products will be established in the He-Huang Valley. Third, a huge hydropower station at the lower reaches of the Longyangxia River will be constructed. It will become a major national base for the production of electricity. Meanwhile, making use of its rich supply of electricity, Qinghai will develop its own energy consuming metallurgical industry.

Developing the tourism industry. Qinghai has many and varied attractions for tourists. In 2000, it received 32,600 foreign visitors, and generated an income of US$7 million from this source. In the future, it should develop its tourism industry by developing top tourist spots, such as a high plateau lake and a bird island around Qinghai Lake. Also, a scientific survey and expedition site at the original areas of major rivers and Tibetan Buddhism centre at Tar Temple 塔爾寺 should be developed for tourism. The facilities in these areas should be designed and built with environmental protection in mind, and measures taken to ensure that tourism is developed in a sustainable way.

Protection of the Natural Environment

Qinghai is characterized by its backwardness, harsh living conditions, frequent natural disasters, an unstable ecological environment and serious environmental problems. As China's three major rivers originate in Qinghai, the state of Qinghai's environment has implications not only for the local people, but for ecological safety and sustainable development in the areas downstream from these rivers as well. Thus, the ecological environment in Qinghai is of national strategic importance.

Major Ecological Problems

Desertification. A total of 125,240 km^2 of land in Qinghai suffers from desertification, comprising 14.1% of the province's total land area and 8.4% of all land suffering from desertification in China. Such land is mainly located in the Chaidam Basin, the Yangzi River source area, the Yellow River source area, around Qinghai Lake and the Gonghe 共和 Valley. Because of natural and man-made factors, desertification is still expanding. From 1959 to 2000, the annual rate of desertification in Qinghai was 1.6%.

Soil erosion. In 2000, the province had 0.364 million km^2 of eroded land, making up 50.4% of the Qinghai's total land area. The loss of soil along the Yellow River is occurring over an area of 98,000 km^2, with 88.14 million tonnes of soil and sand washed into the river annually. The largest area of eroded land, comprising 0.106 million km^2, is found along the Yangzi River, with an annual loss of 12.32 million tonnes of soil and sand. The eroded areas of other parts of the province amount to 0.16 million km^2, representing 44.0% of Qinghai's total eroded area.

Shrinking of ice valleys and reduction of frozen land. The majority of Qinghai's ice valleys are shrinking. The annual rates of shrinkage at the Yangzi River source area and at the Tuotuo River 沱沱河 and Damqu River 當曲河 areas from 1961 to 1986 was 8.25 m and 9.0 m, respectively. The tip of the Gangjiaquba 崗加曲巴 ice valley at Geladaindong 各拉丹冬 retreated at least 500 m from 1970 to 1990, with an annual retreat of 25 m. Since the late 1970s, the Qinghai-Tibet Plateau has been experiencing warmer temperatures, especially during the winter, resulting in the reduction of frozen land. This reduction has changed the growing environment of plants, directly influencing and restricting the plant growth and further speeding up the retreat of the grasslands.

Shrinking lakes and wetlands. The shrinking of the lakes is evident by the reduction in lake areas, the inward flowing of rivers and salinization. Chibuzhang Lake 赤布張湖 previously had an area of 600 km^2 has now become a string of four small lakes, while Wulanwutuo 烏蘭烏托 Lake has been cut into five small lakes. Salinization is now a common phenomenon, with many lakes having become salt fields. Water levels in Qinghai Lake have fallen and salt levels are rising daily. In the Yangzi River source area, plants have stopped growing on many of marshlands and wetlands on the slopes and, in some spots, dry black earth can be seen. The marsh area in the Yellow River source area shrank from 3,895.2 km^2 in the late 1980s to 3,247.5 km^2 by the end of the 1990s, with a total reduction of 647.7 km^2 and an annual reduction of 58.9 km^2.

Deterioration of the grasslands. The deterioration seen by the expansion of grassy marshlands, the desertification of the grasslands, the growth of poisonous wild grasses and epidemics of rats, all of which have reduced the productivity of the grasslands. It has been found that, from 1986 to 1999, the degraded area of grassland increased by 25,260 km^2 and grass production fell by one-third to one-half, while the sheep population fell by 5.528 million.

Serious loss of biological species. Driven by economic interests, people have illegally slaughtered many wild animals and have dug up or destroyed many valuable plants and grasses. The result has been a serious reduction in the numbers of many species, some of them rare or endangered. Examples of victims are the Tibet antelopes, which once roamed the grasslands in large numbers, and Chinese ephedra and dahuang 大黃, which are rare ingredients in Chinese medicine. The situation is especially serious in the Yangzi River source area.

Frequent natural disasters. First, unusually severe snowstorms buffeted Golog 果洛 and Yüshu 玉樹 in the winter of 1997–1998, bringing snow with an average height of 30 cm and a maximum of 42 cm. As a result, 0.17 million herdsmen were severely affected. Over 7,300 people suffered from frostbite and over 0.30 million animals died of cold. Second, an unusual number of sandstorms affected the Wudaoliang 五道梁 and Tuotuo River areas in the Yangzi River source area, with an annual average of 14.7 and 13.7 days, respectively. Third, the abnormally warm climate that the province has been experiencing in the past decade has brought devastating droughts to Qinghai. This has resulted in the deaths of many animals, who have been unable to adapt themselves to the hot weather.

Countermeasures

The protection and reconstruction of the ecological environment are the basis for the implementation of resource development and the premise of economic development. Qinghai has to follow the principle of sustainable development, enforcing protection, reinforcing administration and actively engaging in restoration. Measures need to be taken to launch some ecological engineering projects that are vital to the whole province and even to the whole country. The province has plans for projects to turn farmland into grasslands and forests according to local conditions, to protect the soil by planting trees that can nourish sources of water, to protect grass at areas of water sources, to combat desertification, to kill rats and harmful insects, and to protect wild animals and plants to build up a proper ecological framework for agriculture and animal husbandry.

In a vast province, ecological problems differ from one place to another. Hence, measures to attack the problem should suit local conditions. The Chaidam Basin is dry all year round with little rainfall and few plants. In addition to serious desertification, overgrazing has worn out much of the natural grassland. In this case, coal mining should be encouraged and the development of gas, solar energy and wind energy be broadly carried out to protect desert plants and man-made forests. The remaining primary desert forests and plants should be strictly protected and some areas should be designated natural protection zones. As many trees as possible should be planted to protect farmland and halt desertification. The number of cattle needs to be controlled to preserve the grasslands. In fact, man-made feed bases should be actively built to reduce the pressure on the grasslands. After meeting ecological needs, water resources can be properly developed and utilized. Oasis agriculture can be actively pursued. As far as the salt industry is concerned, development should go with protection.

The Qingnan Plateau, the source of the Yangzi River, the Yellow River and Lancang River, is characterized by a high altitude, thin atmosphere, diverse plant and animal life, fragile ecology and harsh climate. This area has been designated as a national natural protection zone. The following work has to be done. Administration of the region should be strengthened. Attention should be paid to monitoring, planning and scientific research in the zone. Governments should relocate people currently living in the area, and assist them in settling into new homes.

Prior to 1949, the Qinghai Lake area was an area where animal husbandry had been traditionally practised. After 1949, large tracts of grassland were turned to farmland. Because of the backward economy and overgrazing, the area of grassland was drastically reduced. In addition, both a change in climate and the practice of irrigation lowered water level in the Lake, leading to a deterioration in water quality. Ecologically, the area should develop both farming and animal husbandry. The present area of grassland should be protected, the full potential of the arable land should be developed, stable bases for grain and oil production should be set up, fish stocks in Qinghai Lake should be further protected and developed, and the management and construction of the protected zone of Qinghai Lake — Bird Island — should be strengthened.

The area of the Southeast Plateau is the province's most densely populated and is where most of the grain, oil, fruits and vegetables in Qinghai are produced. The area is experiencing several major ecological problems. The population has been increasing too rapidly. Soil erosion is serious and the agricultural ecology is in serious imbalance. Due to natural and man-made reasons, the Huangshui 湟水 is shrinking. The municipal environment is seriously polluted. Thus, the province has to make good use of the valley areas, both utilize and conserve the land and improve land of medium and low productivity; properly adjust the structure of agriculture and raise the share made up by animal husbandry and forestry; properly manage small river areas and strengthen soil protection; and increase investment to strengthen the treatment of polluted urban water and raise the environmental quality of urban areas.[8]

Construction of Infrastructure

The Present Situation and Problems

In the years immediately following 1949, there was no railway in Qinghai. The province had only 472 km of highway and communications was backward, seriously hindering the economic development of the province. From 1952, the state began to consider the issue of transportation and communications seriously, and invested a considerable amount of manpower, money and materials. Since 1978, in particular, the construction of infrastructure in Qinghai has speeded up.

Highways. Due to Qinghai's complex topography, transportation mainly depends on highways, the construction of which has been most rapid. By the end of 2000, there were 18,679 km of highways and an initial network of 5 national and 28 provincial highways. However, some problems exist. First, highway lines in Qinghai are few and density is low. In 2000, the province ranked 26th nationally in terms of highway mileage, with an average density of 2.58 km/100 km^2, which is far below the national average of 14.5 km/100 km^2. Second, the highways are concentrated in the eastern part of the province, while transportation in other parts is rather poor, seriously hindering local economic development. Third, the quality of Qinghai's highways is generally poor. In addition, because of the province's high altitude and complex topography, the roads are subject to a great deal of wear and tear, making them difficult to travel on.

Railways. By the end of 2000, there were over 1,100 km of railway in the province. In addition to the Lan-Qing 蘭青 (Lanzhou-Qinghai) and Qing-Zang (Qinghai-Tibet) Railways, there were four other lines: Hai-Hu 海湖, Ning-Da 寧大 (Xining 西寧-Datong 大通), Cetan 柴達爾 and Caka 茶卡. Railway transportation is important for cultural, political and economic exchanges between Qinghai and other provinces. It has not only changed the culture and economy of isolated and backward areas, but also helped in the development of resources in the Chaidam Basin and the province in general. Yet, there is only one railway that crosses the province to the outside, which is far from enough for the vast territory and the strategic position of the province. Also, population density in the province is far below the national average. In the near future, with the completion of the Golmud-Lhasa portion of the Qinghai-Tibet line, the major railway lines will reach all parts of the province.

Aviation and Pipe Construction. Much progress has been made in the areas of aviation and in the construction of pipelines in Qinghai. Caojiabao 曹家堡 Airport was built in Xining in 1991 and Golmud Airport is currently being extended. Both will greatly improve the province's connections with the outside world. Three pipe systems have been built, an oil pipeline from Golmud to Lhasa and a gas pipeline from Sebei Gas Field to Golmud and Dunhuang 敦煌.

Communications. From 1978, given the state's policies on the improvement of communications, the province speeded up construction at different levels and enhanced its communications capabilities. In 2000, the value of communications services reached RMB650 million, an increase of 33% from 1999. Investment in communications totalled RMB2,454 million in 2000. By the end of 2000, there were 0.38 million fixed telephone lines for households, 0.09 million mobile telephones and 0.04 million long-distance telephone service subscribers in the province, with a coverage of 7.5 telephones per 100 persons. In most villages and towns, telephone services are available and a stable, reliable and highly efficient communications network has been built.[9]

Strategic Projects

The construction of infrastructure is a key to the development of the west. Qinghai is determined to invest more in the construction of communications networks, the generating of electricity, the development of resources and irrigation. In 2000, investment in transportation reached RMB3,700 million, and the figure will increase gradually. At present, the Xining-Lanzhou expressway is under construction. From 2000 to 2005, all state and provincial highways will be reoriented to reach every town and every county. From 2005 to 2015, first-class highways from Xining to Machangheng 馬場恒, to Huangzhong 湟中, to Datong and to Huangyuan 湟源 will be built. By 2020, highway construction will meet the basic needs of socioeconomic development and, by 2050, transportation will be basically modernized.

Railways. At present, the Golmud to Lhasa portion of the Qinghai-Tibet Railway, a major national project, is under construction and is projected to be completed by 2005. Within the next 20–25 years, the Xining to Golmud portion of the Qinghai-Tibet Railway will be upgraded, and a new line from Golmud to Korla 庫爾勒 along the Qing-Xin 青新 (Qinghai-Xinjiang) Highway will be built.

Pipe transportation. The 868 km-long pipeline project form Sebei to Xining, part of the west-east gas transmission project 西氣東輸工程, is under construction. The completion of the above project will contribute to resource utilization, economic development and social progress in the Xining area.

Communications. Networks of public data, intelligence, support and management will gradually set up to match national levels of technology, service and quality. At the same time, auxiliary facilities in pastoral areas will be strengthened so that poor communications and isolation will belong to the past. In addition, radio broadcasts and TV coverage will be extended to cover every village.

Urban and Regional Development

Urban Development

In 1949, there was only 1 city, Xining, and 19 county towns with a total of 0.1 million inhabitants, accounting for 7% of Qinghai's population. Tremendous changes have taken place since then. By 2000, there were 3 cities, 60 towns, the equivalent of 19 county towns, 49 ordinary towns and 2 industrial towns, with a total area of 0.16 million km^2 and a built-up area of 300 km^2. The level of urbanization has reached 27%.[10] Towns have emerged in the western and southern parts of the province, and towns have changed in function from administrative to economic. The facilities in the towns are being improved, making the towns important in the socioeconomic development of the province. At present, an urban system centred on Xining is gradually taking shape. According to their functions in local political and economic activities, the cities and towns of Qinghai can be divided into five types (Table 12.5).

Qinghai's economic development and urbanization are at an early stage. Except for Xining and its surrounding area, the cities and towns in the province are few and small, with poor facilities. As those cities are mainly for administration and their economic base is weak, they have little influence on the areas of farming and animal husbandry. Several strategies have been advanced to spur the urbanization of Qinghai, as briefly mentioned below.

The province should become a base for the development of the west. The eastern part of the province has good natural conditions, rich human

Table 12.5 Types of Major Cities and Towns in Qinghai

Category	Major cities and towns	Functions
Comprehensive	Xining. Six regional capitals and Haidong 海東 prefecture	Multi-faceted
Centre of farming and manufacturing	Towns in Haidong area and some small towns in Hainan 海南, Haibei 海北 and some animal husbandry areas	Trading, distribution and manufacturing of farming products
Administration	All the counties in Yüshu 玉樹 and Golog 果洛 regions, Henan 河南 and Zekog 澤庫 in the Huangnan 黃南 region, Tongde 同德 and Xinghai 興海 in the Hainan 海南 region	Administration
Industrial	Qiaotou 橋頭 Town in Datong County, Mangya 茫崖, Lenghu 冷湖, Dachaidan 大柴旦, Huatugou 花土溝 and Caka in the Haixi 海西 region, the hot-water-mining area in Gangca 剛察 County and Longyangxia 龍羊峽 in Gonghe 共和 County	Resource development
Others	Golmud City, Huangzhong Town and Longwu 隆務 Town, etc.	Transport and tourism

Source: See Table 12.1.

resources, a fairly good industrial foundation and basic infrastructure. The impact of investment is better than in the western and southern parts. The eastern region should therefore be developed first, with the help from Xining.[11] Xining is the centre of the province's political, economic and cultural activities. It possesses an efficient communications network and offers favourable investment conditions. In the future, the province has to do its best to develop information technology and strengthen the reform of the traditional industries in which it excels (the manufacturing of machinery and animal husbandry products). At the same time, Xining can develop its basic chemical industry to utilize the salt from the lake in the Chaidam Basin. In addition, Xining has to speed up its own urban construction, perfect its comprehensive urban functions, further develop its commerce and trade, and actively develop its markets for production materials, technology, manpower, finance and information to strengthen its influence over the surrounding areas.

After years of construction, the industrial foundations of the areas of Datong, Ping'an, Huangzhong (Lushar 魯沙爾), Duoba 多巴, Ledu 樂都 and Minhe around Xining are fairly satisfactory. These places possess utilizable land and transportation links with Xining. With Xining, these towns can group up to form an economic centre. For instance, Tar Temple in Huangzhong can spur the tourism industry of the entire region. Datong has a reasonably sound heavy industrial foundation, but its structure is not ideal. Thus, the fragmented structure should be adjusted and reasonably centralized to form an industrial group.

The resources and industrial towns centred on Golmud should be further developed. To facilitate the development strategy of the Chaidam Basin, favourable financial and policy considerations should be given to the city of Golmud to enhance the development of the basin as a whole. Golmud should develop a chemical industry to maximize its favourable location in air transportation, strengthen its urban functions and develop trade, commerce, social services, culture, scientific research and education in the basin. The mining and industrial areas in the basin should be developed to form an independent town system centred on Golmud and Delhi 德令哈.

The construction of towns in areas of animal husbandry should be strengthened. The local administration mainly serves the herdsmen and the animal husbandry industry. Urban development should focus on commerce, trade, culture and technology. In the animal husbandry counties, urban functions should enhance the modernization of husbandry and the processing of animal husbandry products.

Regional Development

The urgent objective of regional development is to gradually rationalize the industrial structure and human resources.[12] With its vast land and sparse population, the province has to focus its limited manpower, material and financial resources on the relatively less-developed areas and stimulate the development to these areas with the assistance of the more-developed areas so as to boost the economy of the whole province. It has to speed up the development of the resources in which it has a comparative advantage and improve the industrial structure for sustainable growth. Regional development should focus on the major development area along the Lanzhou-Qinghai and Qinghai-Tibet Railway lines, and from Minhe in the east to Haidong, Xining and Chaidam to the west. In addition, the valley area in Haidong and Xining should become an investment area, with concentrated efforts to develop the autonomous prefectures of Hainan 海南 and Haibei 海北.

According to geographical conditions and levels of economic development, Qinghai can be divided into four regions: the east, the Chaidam Basin, the animal husbandry area around the Lake and Qinghai's high plateau animal husbandry region.[13]

The eastern region. This consists of Xining city, Haidong prefecture, Tongren 同仁 and Jainca 尖扎 counties in the Huangnan 黃南 Tibetan autonomous prefecture, counties in the Hainan Tibetan autonomous prefecture and Menyuan 門源 Hui autonomous county in the Haibei Tibetan Autonomous prefecture. The eastern region contains much land suitable for farming, animal husbandry and forestry, and has rich water resources, manpower, developed transportation links. It is the industrial centre of the province. Its metallurgical, textile and machinery industries are quite outstanding. It is also a major farming area, a base of production for grains, oil, vegetables, fruits and melons. A transportation industry based on railways and highways is being formed in this area, making the circulation of goods easier and economic connections with other provinces closer. At present, the area is strengthening its urban infrastructure and improving its urban functions to enable it to play a leading role in the economic development of the province. At the same time, relying on its rich natural resources, it is doing its best to develop its raw material industry and manufacturing, and build up commercial grain and by-products industries to enhance the economic development of the whole area.

Chaidam Basin. The Chaidam Basin is comprised of Golmud city, the two counties of Ulan 烏蘭 and Dulan 都蘭 in the Haixi 海西 Mongolian and Tibetan autonomous prefecture and the three towns of Dachaidam 大柴旦, Lenghu 冷湖 and Mangya, with a population of 0.3 million. It is rich in land resources. Its area of 0.3 million km^2 unbroken by mountains is suitable for farming if transportation is developed. The temperature differences here are large and there are long hours of sunshine, providing good potential for farming. The area is short of water and suffers from frequent sandstorms and salinization, which restrict agricultural development. Irrigation, however, should be carried out and the planting of protective forests planned. It is rich in mineral and energy resources, especially in salt, gas and oil, with remarkable development potential. Here also lies the largest potassium production base in the country, as well as one of the sources of gas to be transported to the east.[14] At present, its salt and oil/gas resources are being fully developed to build Golmud into a petro-chemical base. The development of the following industries is being speeded up to act as new sources of economic growth: salt chemical engineering, construction materials, coal mining and gold mining. Furthermore, oasis agriculture and bases for the growing of grain and the processing of grain by-products are being developed, while efforts are being made to protect natural resources and the ecological environment.

Animal Husbandry Area around the Lake. This area consists of the counties of Qilian, Gangca and Haiyan 海晏 in the Haibai Tibetan autonomous prefecture, the counties of Gonghe, Tongde 同德, Xinghai 興海 and Guinan 貴南 in the Hainan Tibetan autonomous prefecture and Tianjun 天峻 county in the Haixi Mongolian-Tibetan autonomous prefecture, with an area of 97,345 km^2. Here, the grasslands are extensive, accounting for over 80% of the total arable land of 26.7 million km^2 in the province, and the water resources are rich. The area is the province's most important base for animal husbandry with a unique advantage, considering Qinghai as one of the five largest stockbreeding areas in China.[15] In addition, the area has certain farming and planting bases, which have been growing fairly quickly. They are fairly close to the manufacturing bases and to markets in Xining, and convenient transportation links are available. At present, work has started on the "four supporting projects" 四配套 — namely, the settlement of herdsmen, the protection of the grasslands by encircling them, the planning of grass and the feeding of cattle under the cover of a roof — to carry out the modernization of animal husbandry. To integrate farming and animal husbandry, the region is carrying out the comprehensive development of agriculture and is speeding up the construction of oil crops bases. It is also developing local resource advantages. Haibei is mainly developing its coal and asbestos industries and speeding up the development of water resources in the Datong River. In Hainan, the copper and tourism industries are being developed, relying on the resources of Qinghai Lake and Longyangxia. In the future, the animal husbandry advantage of the Lake area should be fully developed into a commercial animal husbandry with high yields, good quality and a high level of efficiency. Water energy, non-ferrous metals, and coal and construction materials industries are to be developed in the area according to local conditions.

Qinghai Plateau Husbandry Area. This area is made up of two Tibetan autonomous prefectures: Yüshu and Golog, Zekog 澤庫 county in the Huangnan Tibetan autonomous prefecture, the Henan 河南 Mongolian autonomous county and the town of Tanggula, with an area of 339,963 km^2. The area has a large Tibetan population of over 0.4 million, with an average population density of 1.2 persons/km^2, the lowest density in the province. Being the main portion of the Qinghai-Tibet Plateau, the high altitude and low-oxygen atmosphere make the area a very harsh one for the survival of human beings. It is the source of the Yangzi River, the Yellow

River and the Lancang River, and therefore has immense ecological importance. With grasslands of 200,000 km^2, accounting for 58% of the total in the province, it has historically been an important area for animal husbandry.

In the future, the disaster-prevention efforts represented by the four supporting projects should be strengthened, the local advantage of gold should be fully explored and the local character and tourism be developed to ensure steady economic growth.

Notes

1. Shi Keming 史克明 (ed.), *Qinghaisheng jingji dili* 青海省經濟地理 (Economic Geography of Qinghai) (Beijing: Xinhua chubanshe 新華出版社, 1988), p. 3.
2. Hu Yongke 胡永科 (ed.), *Zhongguo xibu gailan — Qinghai* 中國西部概覽 —— 青海 (A General View of China's West — Qinghai) (Beijing: Minzu chubanshe 民族出版社, 2000), p. 7.
3. Wang Lücang 王綠倉 and Shi Peiji 石培基, "Ganchuanqing minzu jiaojie quyu chengzhen tixi de jiben tezheng ji beijing fengxi" 甘川青民族交接區域城鎮體系的基本特徵及背景分析 (The Features and Background of Urban Systems in the Areas of Gansu, Sichuan and Qinghai), *Renwen dili* 人文地理 (Human Geography), No. 3 (2000), pp. 25–28.
4. Liu Zaixing 劉再興, *Zhongguo quyu jingji* 中國區域經濟 (Regional Economies of China) (Beijing: Zhongguo wujia chubanshe 中國物價出版社, 1993).
5. Chen Dongsheng 陳棟生 (ed.), *Xibu jingji jueqi zhilu* 西部經濟崛起之路 (A Road to Developing the Economy of the Western Region) (Shanghai: Shanghai yuandong chubanshe 上海遠東出版社, 1996).
6. See note 3.
7. Wu Hao 吳豪, Yu Xiaogan 虞孝感 and Mei Jieren 梅潔人, "Qinghaisheng shengtai huanjing ruogan wenti jiqi duice cuoshi" 青海省生態環境若干問題及其對策措施 (Major Eco-environmental Problems in Qinghai and the Corresponding Countermeasures), *Dilixue yu guotu yanjiu* 地理學與國土研究 (Geography and Territorial Research), No. 3 (2001), pp. 58–62.
8. See note 2.
9. Ibid.
10. See note 1.
11. Zhuo Macuo 卓瑪措 and Liu Fenggui 劉豐貴,"Cong kechixu fazhan lun quyu kaifa — yi Qinghai quyu kaifa weili" 從可持續發展論區域開發 —— 以青海區域開發為例 (Discuss Regional Development with Sustainable Development — Qinghai as an Example), *Jingji dili* 經濟地理 (Economic Geography), No. 3 (2000), pp. 26–29.
12. Zhang Yaosheng 張耀生, Zhao Xinquan 趙新全 and Zhou Xingmin 周興民,

"Qinghaisheng caodi xumuye kechixu fazhan zhanlüe yu duice" 青海省草地畜牧業可持續發展戰略與對策 (Strategy and Countermeasure for Sustainable Development of Animal Husbandry in Qinghai), *Ziran ziyuan xuebao* 自然資源學報 (Journal of Natural Resources), No. 4 (2000), pp. 328–34.

13. Lu Dadao 陸大道 (ed.), *2000 nian Zhongguo quyu fazhan baogao* 2000年中國區域發展報告 (China's Regional Development Report in 2000) (Beijing: Shangwu yinshuguan 商務印書館, 2000).
14. Zhang et al., "Qinghaisheng caodi" (see note 12).
15. Ibid.
16. Zhu Lidong 朱麗東, "Qinghai shengtai lüyou fazhan gouxiang" 青海生態旅遊發展構想 (The Concept of Developing Ecological Tourism in Qinghai), *Jingji dili*, No. 4 (2000), pp. 118–21.

13

Ningxia

Hu Xia

In China, a unified country with multiple nationalities, the Hui 回 nationality numbers nearly 10 million, making it the third largest among the minority nationalities, following closely after the Zang 藏 and Manchu 滿. The Hui are found in every province, municipality and autonomous region in the country, but most live in compact communities in northwestern China, especially in the Ningxia Hui Autonomous Region 寧夏回族自治區 (hereafter called Ning 寧 for short). Deemed the "home" of all Huis, this is one of the five autonomous regions in China, and is also the only provincial-level Hui autonomous locality. Since the Huis believe in Islam, Muslims from various countries pay great attention to the role of Ningxia in western region development.[1]

General Background

Geographic Environment

The Ningxia Hui Autonomous Region is an inland region located in north-central China, but it is usually referred to as being in northwestern China.[2] Eastern Ningxia borders on Shaanxi 陝西, western and northern Ningxia on the Inner Mongolia 內蒙古 Autonomous Region and southern Ningxia on Gansu 甘肅 (Figure 13.1). Ningxia has an area of 64,400 km^2. It is narrow from north to south, and has higher altitudes in the south than in the north. Notable regions from north to south include the Helan Mountain 賀蘭山, the Ningxia Hetao Area 寧夏河套地區, the Loess Plateau 黃土高原 and the Liupan Mountain 六盤山, etc., with an average elevation of 1,090–2,000 m above sea level.

In terms of human geography, the whole region can be divided into three agricultural zones, namely, the northern plain, the middle drought-prone, sandy belt and the southern loess wolds. The water channelled from the Yellow River irrigates the Ningxia's northern region. This northern region lies in the middle reaches of the Yellow River and has a high population density and relatively advanced agriculture. Therefore, this area has been described as "lush southern-type fields north of the Great Wall." The middle region is large with a small population. The people here are mainly engaged in animal husbandry. During the last few years, as many as 70,000 ha of land has come under irrigation, benefiting from the water channelled from the Yellow River. The people in the southern region of Ningxia devote themselves to working the land under a dry climate. The climate of the southern region is drought-prone and windy. The surface of the earth has abundant loose materials such as gravel, sand and loess. Hence,

Figure 13.1 Ningxia in Its Geographical Setting

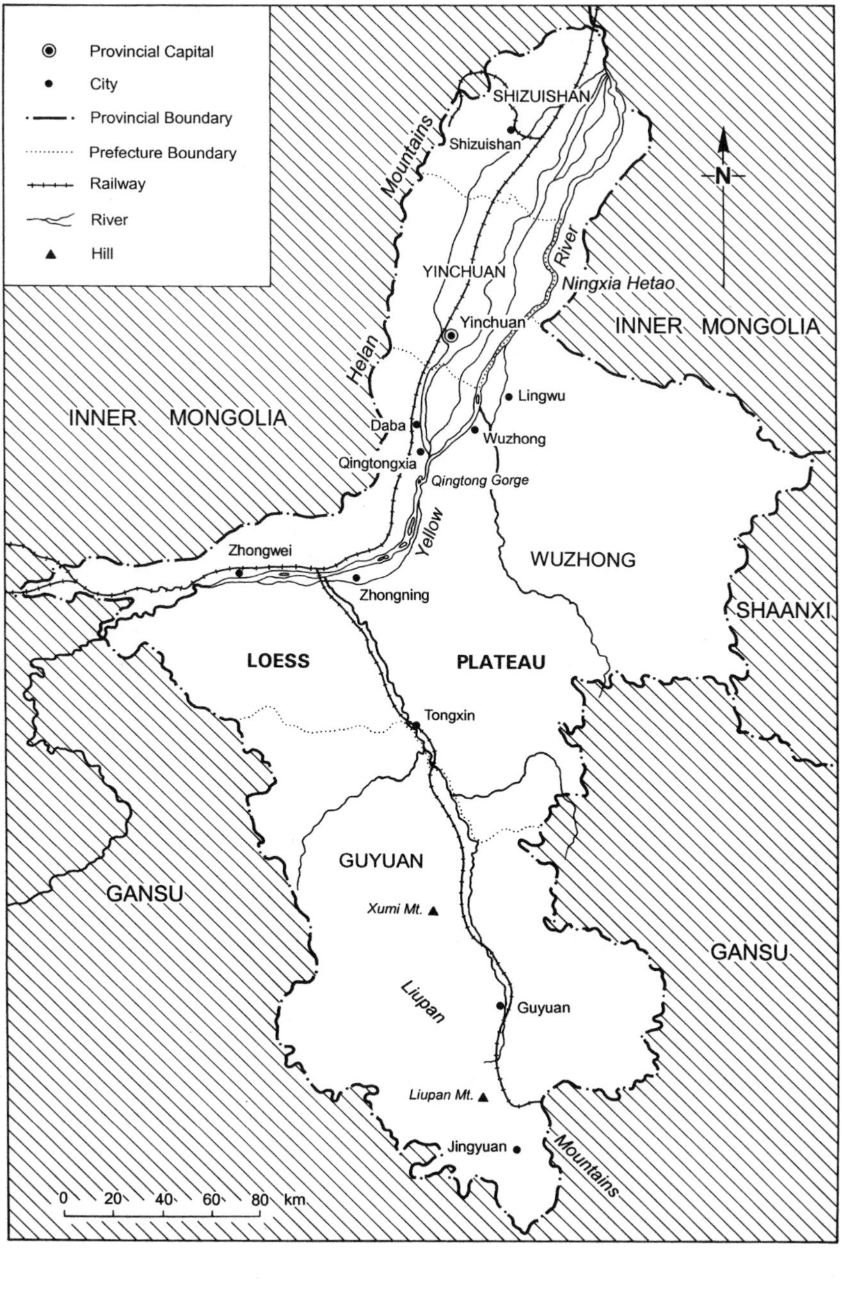

soil erosion is serious and natural disasters frequently occur in this area. The area is well known for its poverty within China. The major river within the boundaries of Ningxia is the Yellow River, running 397 km through 13 counties and cities of Ningxia.

Climate

Lying in the inner portion of northwestern China, Ningxia has a typical continental semi-moist and semi-arid climate, with late springs, short summers, early autumns and long winters. The region has long hours of sunshine, averaging 2,000–3,000 per year, and strong solar radiation, with an annual total of 123 to 149 therm per cm^2, ranking it first in the country on both counts. There are 100–162 frost-free days in a year. In most areas, the annual average temperature is between 5°C and 9°C. The average temperature in January, the coldest month in a year, is below –8°C, and temperatures can drop below –22°C. It is above 20°C in the summer, and the temperature may exceed 30°C occasionally for a short period. Temperatures vary greatly between day and night, with a general difference of 12°C to 15°C, which accounts for the high quality of the fruits and beets produced in the region. Precipitation is low in Ningxia, amounting to 200 to 700 mm per year. Most of the precipitation falls between June and September, but the annual total evaporation reaches 1,000 to 2,400 mm. "Nine drought years in ten years" is a saying that well describes the reality of the southern area.

Major Resources

Although small in area, Ningxia is rich in resources. About 50 kinds of mineral resources have been found, notably coal and gypsum. Coal reserves are estimated at 31.3 billion tonnes, and the average per capita reserves are estimated to be about 7,000 tonnes in Ningxia, ranking the region sixth in the country. The coal is of fine quality and buried in the shallow earth, so the cost of mining is low. In particular, the smoke-free coal of Rujigou 汝箕溝 Mine, also called "Taixi coal" 太西煤, is characterized by a low ash content, low concentrations of phosphorus and a high quantity of heat, and has sold well in more than 10 countries and regions, including in Europe and North America. Electric power is a very good example of Ningxia's advantage in energy resources. Ningxia's total annual production of electric energy is 15.03 billion kilowatt-hours, with an average per capita production of over 2,000 kilowatt-hours, ranking it second among the provinces and autonomous regions in the country.

As for agriculture, the present total area of cultivated land is 1,267,000 ha and the average per capita is about 0.23 ha, again ranking Ningxia second in the country. The autonomous region has 400,000 ha of irrigated land. In addition, it has more than 667,000 ha of uncultivated land suitable for farming, 133,000 ha of which is land suitable for aquaculture, and 56,000 ha water surface. The Ningxia Plain teems with rice and wheat, and is a commercial grain production base for northwestern China. Cash crops are grown as well, such as fruits, beet, rape, etc. These crops are harvested once a year. The mountainous area of southern Ningxia, which is experiencing serious soil erosion, is much less agriculturally productive. Wheat and buckwheat are the main crops, while cash crops include flax, hemp, etc. In average grain production per capita, Ningxia ranks fifth in the country. There are 3 million ha grassland, accounting for 58.2% of Ningxia's total area, and the total number of large domestic animals in the autonomous region is 921,000.

Helan Mountain and Liupan Mountain are full of trees, mainly pine, oak, birch, poplar, etc., which are harvested for timber. A variety of plants for medicinal uses and wild fauna are also found there. There are five local products for which Ningxia is especially known both nationally and abroad, namely, "Red, Yellow, Blue, White and Black" wolfberries, licorice roots, Helan stone 賀蘭石 (a special clay stone), fur and black moss.[3]

Nationalities, Population and Administrative Divisions

According to official statistics of 2001, there are 35 nationalities in Ningxia, including the Hui, Han 漢, Manchu, Mongol 蒙古. The Huis numbered 1,910,101, accounting for 34.46% of Ningxia's total population of 5,543,214 and about 1/5 of China's Hui population.[4] The autonomous region has three cities at the prefectural level under its jurisdiction, namely, Yinchuan 銀川, Shizuishan 石咀山, Wuzhong 吳忠 and one prefecture, Guyuan 固原. The city of Yinchuan, capital of the autonomous region, is the political, economic and cultural centre of Ningxia. It is also a city of great historical interest, having once been the capital of Western Xia 西夏 Kingdom. With an area of 51,800 km^2 and a population of 1,009,000, Yinchuan is an important centre for the eastern part of northwestern China, and is also a bridgehead for western development. The population of the southern mountainous area was 2,384,000, comprising 43% of the total population. Of these, 1,182,000 were Huis, making up 49.6% of the local population. In Jingyuan 涇源, the population is 97% Hui. Farming and husbandry are the local people's means of livelihood, with 90% of the people in this locality engaged in that occupation.[5]

Historical Evolution

Ningxia has a long history dating back 30,000 years when human beings first set foot there.[6] In the Spring and Autumn Period (770–476 B.C.) and the Warring States Period (475–221 B.C.), peoples such as the Qiang 羌, Rong 戎 and Xiongnu 匈奴 lived here. Since the third century, when the emperor of the state of Qin 秦 conquered competing states to create a unified Chinese empire, troops have been stationed in Ningxia. They worked on building what is now known as the Great Wall of China, constructed the Qin Canal and started the practice of channelling water from the Yellow River into fields for irrigation. In the Han and Tang 唐 dynasties, this area was further developed, and Ningxia eventually became an important route on the Silk Road. The forefathers of the Hui came to China from Arabia and Persia. Some of them arrived in Ningxia, engaged in business, and stayed. In 1038, The Dangxiang 黨項 people established the Daxia Kingdom 大夏國 here, called Western Xia in history, making Xingqing Fu 興慶府 (an ancient administrative division, today's Yinchuan) its capital. Villages inhabited by the forefathers of the Huis were already in existence. In 1227, the Yuan 元 dynasty conquered the Western Xia and established Ningxia Fu Road 寧夏府路, the origin of Ningxia, as a place name. During this period, a large number of Muslims from various countries in Central Asia moved into Ningxia. Some were stationed in agricultural garrisons set up to grow food for the soldiers, and some engaged in trade. They intermarried with the Uigurs, Mongolians and Han, and became the Hui, the main residents of the area. In the Ming 明 dynasty, Ningxia Fu Road was replaced by Ningxia Wei 寧夏衛 (an ancient administrative division) and, in the Qing 清 dynasty, by Ningxia Fu 寧夏府. Shortly after the Guomindang 國民黨 established its regime, Ningxia Fu was replaced by Shuofang Dao 朔方道 (another administrative division). In 1929, Ningxia was established. When the Red Army marched into southern Ningxia, Soviet governments were set up all over the region. Later in October 1936, the Hui Autonomous Government of Yuhai County 預海縣 was founded in Tongxin 同心 under the leadership of the Chinese Communist Party (CCP). This was the first autonomous locality for minority nationalities in China,[7] and also the first attempt by the CCP to follow a policy of autonomous nationalities. In 1949, after the founding of the People's Republic of China, Ningxia was abolished and some parts of Ningxia like the Alxa Banner 阿拉善旗 (an administrative division used only by minority nationalities such as the Manchu and Hui) were merged into the Inner Mongolia Autonomous Region, with the rest becoming part of Gansu. On 25 October 1958, the Ningxia Hui Autonomous Region was established, amalgamating the Wuzhong Hui Autonomous Region (formerly under the jurisdiction of Gansu), the Guyuan Hui Autonomous Region and the countries and cities adjacent to these regions. Over the past 44 years, great improvements have been made in every field. Especially after the implementation of policy on western development, the region has taken on a new look of common prosperity and advancement for all nationalities.

Review of Social and Economic Development

For reasons of history, geography and transport, Ningxia's economy used to be very backward. Since the founding of Ningxia Hui Autonomous Region, and particularly since the introduction of reforms and the open-door policy, Ningxia people have been concentrating on economic development. As a result, the region has been experiencing growing prosperity and living standards have improved.

Gross Production and Rising Rural and Urban Living Standards

In 2000, Ningxia's GDP reached RMB26.56 billion, among the lowest of the western provinces. Its economic structure has gradually been rationalized, as can be seen in Table 13.1, with the proportions of the production made up by primary, secondary and tertiary industries being 17.30%, 45.20% and 37.50%, respectively, in 2000. Its per capita GDP ranked third among the western provinces.

With the economic development of Ningxia and the increase in urban and rural incomes, living standards have improved. In 2000, the per capita disposable income of urban dwellers reached RMB4,912, an increase of 9.8% over 1999. Per capita net income in rural areas amounted to RMB1,724.3. The average wage level of employees was RMB8,681, up by 14.9%. Housing has also improved. Public welfare has developed steadily as well. In 2000, state-subsidized housing in the whole region totalled 11 and rest homes 180, with a staff of 568.

Table 13.1 Changes in Economic Structure and Per Capita GDP, 1960–2000

(Units: million RMB; %)

Year	GDP (million RMB)	Primary industry		Secondary industry		Tertiary industry		Per capita GDP (RMB)
		GDP	Ratio	GDP	Ratio	GDP	Ratio	
1960	480	152	31.70	199	41.50	129	26.80	227
1970	652	207	31.75	271	41.56	174	26.69	241
1980	1,596	426	26.69	727	45.55	473	27.76	433
1990	6,484	1,684	25.97	2,534	39.08	2,266	34.95	1,393
2000	26,557	4,595	17.30	12,004	45.20	9,958	37.50	4,839

Source: *Ningxia tongji nianjian 2001* (see note 1).

Agriculture and Industry

Agriculture and the Rural Economy

Agriculture is an industry in which Ningxia has traditionally held an advantage, and which has played an essential role in the region's economic development. Since the adoption of the reform and open-door policy, Ningxia's agriculture has developed rapidly and productivity has increased substantially.

Two main factors have contributed to the notable agricultural achievements. One is the implementation of policies that have proved to be very effective; the other is the introduction of science and technology. Ningxia has been actively involved in introducing and disseminating a series of new technologies and in devising and improving a series of new products. In 2001, the grain output of the whole region reached 2.748 million tonnes, an increase of 8.7% over 2000. Per capita grain output exceeded 200 kg and per capita sugar output was greater than 50 kg. As a matter of fact, every year an average of 0.7 million tonnes of grain is exported to other provinces and areas. Various types of forest have been planted in the whole region, according to different conditions in mountainous areas, sandy areas and low-lying lands. Specifically, in mountainous areas, soil erosion in an area of 5,500 km^2 has been controlled through an ecological forestry project aimed at conserving the soil and controlling the water sources. In sandy areas, local people have made full use of sand as a resource by planting adaptable crops, a practice which has effectively curbed desertification. Finally, in lowland areas, the major task has been to construct shelterbelts.

Animal husbandry has developed rapidly in Ningxia and has become an important source of growth in its rural economy. In 2001, the total output of meat amounted to 0.21 million tonnes, milk 0.21 million tonnes and eggs 0.087 million tonnes. Today, Ningxia has become one of the 10 bases for stockbreeding in China.

Fish production, an important branch of agriculture in Ningxia, has increased steadily. The area of Ningxia covered by water is 499,000 ha, of which 23,000 ha is cultivatable water area, constituting 90% of the irrigated areas along the Yellow River. More than 20 major types of fish are raised, such as crucian, carp, catfish, weever, pomfret, crab, shrimp and frog, with an annual output of 30,000 tonnes, ranking Ningxia first in northwestern China.

The emerging township and village enterprises have developed quite rapidly, with food processing, non-metal mining and black metal smelting and rolling the mainstay industries. Over 100 major products are produced, such as ferro-alloys, metallic natrium, calcium carbide, coke, plaster, coal, dehydrated food, blankets, amylum, beverages, and so on. The township enterprises are playing an important role in readjusting Ningxia's economic structure.

Generally, Ningxia's agricultural and rural economy has undergone three transitions so far. One is a transformation from unitary farming to comprehensive agriculture; another is from straight agriculture production to the all-round development of its rural economy; the last is from traditional rural to modern productivity.

Industry

Ningxia has made outstanding achievements in industry. First, enterprises have been enlarged in size and economic strength has been enhanced. The gross industrial output value in 2001 reached RMB29.39 billion. It was largely the result of production in the electric power, coal, paper-making, chemical and mechanical industries. These traditional pillar industries have been effectively adjusted, upgraded and invigorated, promoting the development of the whole economy.

Second, some emerging and high-tech industries have developed rapidly in Ningxia and have become competitive in domestic and overseas markets. In 2001, the growth rate of the non-ferrous metal, electric machinery, and instrument and meter industries was 15.7%, 16.3% and 19.1%, respectively. The high-tech industry accounted for 11% of the value-added of industry as a whole. A great number of large enterprises, big groups and listed companies have prominently expanded and are at the forefront of Ningxia's economic development and foreign trade. For example, in Ningxia's non-ferrous metal smeltery, over 90% of the products can be described as using high-tech, and Ningxia has one of the three largest tantalum and columbium companies in the world.

Third, the structure of industry is inclined towards heavy industry and this industrial advantage has further strengthened. When the Ningxia Hui Autonomous Region was founded, light industry dominated the regional economy. After 40 years of development, Ningxia has developed six pillar industries, namely, chemistry, machinery, metallurgy, electric power, petroleum and coal, which together comprise over 80% of Ningxia's total industrial output. Feature products have been further developed; over 50 kinds of products related to coal, chemical engineering, machinery and non-ferrous metals enjoy a high reputation in the domestic market and have entered the international market.

Fourth, the chemical industry in Ningxia is another newly emerging and lucrative industry. The total value of the output from this industry accounts for 18.4% of Ningxia's whole industry. The annual production capacity and output quality of the Ningxia Chemical Factory 寧夏化工廠, the Ningxia Natrium Manufactory 寧夏製鈉廠 and the Yinchuan Fine Chemicals Factory 銀川精細化工廠 lead China and even Asia.

Ningxia's industrial development has been accompanied by an increase in the number of scientific and technological personnel, improved production facilities and a general increase in the level of knowledge of science and technology as well. These developments, in turn, have led to the continuous innovation of industrial products. Therefore, a virtuous circle has been formed, laying a solid foundation for Ningxia's industrial development in the new millennium, under the strategy of developing the west.

Construction of Infrastructure

Regional transportation within Ningxia includes railway, highway, aviation and river transport. The Bao-Lan Railway (from Baotou 包頭 to Lanzhou 蘭州) and the Bao-Zhong Railway (from Baoji 寶雞 to Zhongwei 中衛), which link Ningxia with two main railways, Jing-Bao 京包 Railway (Beijing 北京-Baotou) and Longhai 隴海 Railway (Lianyungang 連雲港-Lanzhou 蘭州), lead to the Euro-Asian Transcontinental Bridge. There is another local special railway from Lingwu 靈武 to Daba 大壩. All of these constitute Ningxia's railway transport system. The railway mileage within Ningxia is

850 km. With Yinchuan as the centre, 12 national and provincial highways as the skeleton, county highways as the veins, the Ningxia highway network extends in all directions, connects urban and rural areas and covers 10,171 km. In recent years, Ningxia's aviation transport has expanded and many airlines now offer connections to major large cities such as Beijing, Shanghai 上海, Guangzhou 廣州, Xi'an 西安, Chengdu 成都, Urumqi 烏魯木齊, Wuhan 武漢 and Hangzhou 杭州. The total air mileage represented by these services adds up to 16,823 km. The newly built Yinchuan Hedong 銀川河東 Airport, 4D class, was opened in September 1997. River transportation in Ningxia depends mainly on the Yellow River, which runs 397 km within its territory. Finally, some expressways are planned for construction.

Ningxia has gradually modernized its equipment in postal services and telecommunications. A cable transmission network has been formed. It connects Xi'an, Lanzhou, Urumqi, Beijing and Hohhot 呼和浩特 with trunk cables and consists of a microwave network, digital data network and mobile phone network. There are more than 700,000 phones in urban areas. Phone coverage in Ningxia ranks first among the western provinces, far above the national average. Automatic roaming mobile phone services with 900 aura and 139 global service have national and international links, making it possible for messages to be quickly transmitted to 14 countries and regions and for direct calls to be made to 243 countries and regions. This means that Ningxia's overall telecommunications capability has reached the national advanced level. Postal services have also been expanded. Many businesses have been opened, involving such services as stamp collecting, post-savings, express delivery, international exchanges and e-mailing.

Foreign Trade and Tourism

Although Ningxia's foreign trade started late and at a low level, it has developed rapidly. According to Customs statistics, in 2000, the total value of Ningxia's exports and imports was US$0.443 billion, an increase of 39.3% over 1999. Specifically, the exports were US$0.327 billion, up by 32.2% and imports were US$0.116 billion, up 64%. By 2000, actual foreign investment reached US$90.90 million and 42 new project agreements had been signed. By the end of 2000, there were 408 joint ventures and foreign-funded firms in Ningxia. Ningxia's export market has expanded from Hong Kong, Macao, Taiwan, Southeast Asia and Japan to include Europe, North America, the Middle East, Australia and Africa.

With its long history, unique geographical features and many minority cultures, Ningxia has much to offer the tourist. Tourism is now being promoted and has become another new driving force in Ningxia's regional economy. In 2000, Ningxia received 2.437 million visitors and total tourism income reached RMB0.93 billion. Tourists from Hong Kong, Macau, Taiwan and foreign countries totalled 7,807, and the foreign exchange earned from tourism amounted to US$2.72 million.

Development of Human Resources

In the 44 years since the Ningxia Autonomous Region was founded, great strides have been made in education, science research and public health. A large number of leaders of various nationalities including Hui and Han have been cultivated, providing talent pool for the development of western China. At present, there are 115 research institutions, 140,063 researchers, 5 colleges and universities, 793 vocational schools, 433 middle schools and 3,267 primary schools. Ninety-seven percent of children of school age are receiving an education. In terms of minority education, there are 97 primary schools, 17 middle schools and 1 vocational school exclusively for Hui students. Special classes are also offered for Hui students in three middle schools and in Ningxia University. Favourable policies are being implemented to improve minority education and to increase the proportion of newly enrolled minority students. At present, minority education in Ningxia is flourishing as never before.

Unity of Peoples

Since the founding of a new China in 1949, and especially since the establishment of the Ningxia Hui Autonomous Region in 1958, all of the nationalities in Ningxia including the Han and Hui have trusted, respected, helped and co-operated with each other, and have shared benefits and met challenges together.[8] In the course of advancing the construction of material and cultural civilization, a socialist relationship of equality, unity and mutual benefit has been formed and has developed among the Hui, the Han and others. The implementation of the country's nationality policies has been remarkably successful.

First, this can be seen from the legalization of a new socialist national relationship. A series of laws and regulations have been introduced by the Standing Committee of National People's Congress of Ningxia.[9] The principle of national equality is exhibited by respecting the habits, customs and religious beliefs of minority nationalities. Respecting the habits, customs and religious beliefs of the Hui nationality is a prerequisite to ensuring equality and unity among different peoples. The government of the Ningxia Autonomous Region issues and implements "several rules about respecting the habits and customs of minority nationalities" and the local authorities of Yinchuan has issued "interim rules to manage Muslim food." Under the guidance of these policies, people have gradually cultivated the ethos of respecting the customs of other nationalities. In the autonomous region, Party and government organizations at all levels strictly implement the religious policy of the CCP. There are more than 3,000 mosques and more than 5,000 imams in the whole region. The religious authorities organize Muslim groups to make their pilgrimage to Mecca every year. Moreover, the Ningxia Institute of Islam and the Tongxin Arabic Language School 同心阿拉伯語學校, which are important bases for cultivating qualified religious and Arabic-speaking personnel, have been set up.

These institutions also devote a great deal of effort to train minority cadres and to foster unity and progress. In this case, it is certain that the economy and society of the whole region will develop smoothly and that people of all nationalities will share the prosperity and the fruits of development together.

Comparative Advantages in Economic Development and the Problem of Regional Imbalance

The strategy of developing the western region as advanced by the central government provides a rare opportunity to develop Ningxia in a sustainable manner. Generally, Ningxia's major advantages are as follows.[10]

Geographical Advantage

As mentioned before, Ningxia is geographically located in north-central China, although it is administratively classified as one of the northwestern provinces. Ningxia's position itself as the "beachhead" in western development constitutes one of its advantages. In fact, Yinchuan, together with Lanzhou and Chengdu, can serve as one of the three "beachheads" in western development for two reasons. First, Ningxia was once part of the north line of the well-known ancient Silk Road and acted as the key communications route from the northwest to China proper in history. Second, Yinchuan (together with Zhongwei) connects northern China to northwestern China. The Bao-Zhong Railway, Bao-Lan Railway and Zhong-Tai 中太 Railway (Zhongwei-Taiyuan 太原) have greatly strengthened Yinchuan's role in communications by providing convenient and direct connections with China's northern areas. In addition, Yinchuan (together with Zhongwei) is directly connected to Gansu and Xinjiang through the Lan-Xin 蘭新 (Lanzhou-Xinjiang 新疆) Railway, and to the southwestern part of the country through the Bao-Zhong and Bao-Cheng 寶成 Railways (Baoji-Chengdu).

Resource Advantages

Ningxia offers the following resource advantages. First, it has a large agricultural advantage and potential because there are still thousands of hectares of uncultivated land in Ningxia's irrigated areas. With the strategic focus of national economic development gradually moving west, 7 of the 11 counties in the irrigated areas have been listed as National Commodity Grain Bases and another 4 as National Cattle and Sheep Exemplary Counties. A number of major internationally funded projects, including World Bank projects, are well under way and some large and medium-sized enterprises have also begun to become involved in the agricultural sector. Promoted by those major projects and programmes, the irrigated areas along the Yellow River have expanded to 6.67 million ha. Great efforts are being made to turn this resource advantage into an economic advantage, and the six industries of grain, milk, fur, grape wine, bio-medicine, fruits and vegetables are being fostered and developed.

Second, Ningxia has formed an industrial system focusing on the following industries: coal, electric power, metals, machines, chemicals, textiles, paper-making and food. A significant basis has been laid in the energy industry, with four large and medium-sized coal mines and five power plants. The building materials industry is well developed, producing electrolysis aluminum, iron alloys, carbon products, magnesium, cement, etc. The Qingtongxia Aluminum Factory 青銅峽鋁廠 will be built as China's largest manufacturer of electrolysis aluminum. The machine industry, one of Ningxia's traditional strengths, leads China in the production of digital machine tools, automation meters, bearings, material experimental machines, etc. The petroleum and chemical industries are Ningxia's new technology industries. Ningxia's chemical plant utilizes natural gas from the gas fields in Shaanxi, Gansu and Ningxia and has expanded by acquiring a second set of large fertilizer-processing equipment with a yearly production capacity of 1 million tonnes. The plant has become one of the largest fertilizer manufacturers in China, ranking 27th nationwide. The Yinchuan rubber plant is the country's largest tyre manufacturer for the aviation industry. The Ningxia non-ferrous metal smeltery tops China and ranks third in the world in the production of metal. It also leads China and ranks third in the world in the production of tantalum and niobium-related products.[11]

Tourism is also an important resource. Ningxia boasts a large number of interesting sights, among which are the Western Xia relics, sand slopes, sand lakes, the rock caves on Xumi Mountain 須彌山 and the rock frescos on Helan Mountain.

Ethnic and Religious Advantage

Ethnic groups and religions represent an important part of life in the autonomous region. If well guided, they may become another advantage for Ningxia. The Huis in Ningxia make up a major part of the Huis in the country. The Huis in other areas are particularly attached to Ningxia and look to the region and support it, either through the provinces and regions where they work and live or simply as individuals and in the enterprises with which they are associated. The Huis are Muslims and have close relations with Muslims in other countries. If the CCP's policy on ethnic groups and religions can be well implemented, religions may also be adaptable to socialism and serve western development. Since the founding of the Ningxia Hui Autonomous Region, Islamic countries, regions and the World Islamic Bank have given financial support to Ningxia. For instance, the construction of the dormitory buildings of the Ningxia School of Islamic Teaching and of the Tongxin Arabic Language School were both funded by them. Ningxia carries out intensive economic and cultural exchanges with Saudi Arabia, Egypt, Turkey, Malaysia and Central Asian countries. It has held exhibitions in some countries, which have promoted its foreign trade. Yinchuan has established a sister-city relationship with Bishkek, the capital of Kyrgyzstan, Islamic countries and regions are a potentially large market for Ningxia's exports. Moreover, Ningxia will be able to attract foreign investment if relevant policies are formulated and implemented properly.

However, compared with other areas in China, Ningxia's economy is still relatively undeveloped.[12] In addition to different natural conditions,

Table 13.2 Main Indicators of Imbalance in Economic Development between Southern and Northern Ningxia

Indicators \ Area	Northern	Southern	The autonomous region
Per capita farm area (ha)	0.14	0.39	0.23
Per capita agricultural production (RMB)	2,368.1	764.1	1,416.8
Per capita grain production (kg)	638.4	230.8	460.5
Crop growing area (ha)	421,771	602,312	1,024,083
Percentage in the whole region (%)	41.2	58.8	100
Gross agricultural production (thousand RMB)	3,646,630	1,052,420	4,699,050
Percentage in the whole region (%)	77.6	22.4	100
Average per capita net income of peasant households (RMB)	2,700.71	987.37	1,724.30
Consumption expenditure (RMB)	1,938.85	906.27	1,417.13
Ratio of consumption to income (%)	71.8	91.8	82.2
Population growth rate (‰)	9.95	14.44	11.92
Non-agricultural population (person)	1,353,172	239,096	1,529,268
Percentage in local population (%)	42.8	10.0	28.7

Source: See Table 13.1.

the disparities between the northern and southern parts of Ningxia are traceable to historical, social and economic conditions in the two areas.

The imbalance in economic development between the northern and southern parts of the autonomous region is reflected clearly in Table 13.2.

1. Although the farming area per capita in the south is greater than in the north, the grain yield per capita is only 230.8 kg a year and the value of agricultural production is less than one-third that in the north. What is more, all of these outcomes have been solely the result of the reclamation of new land.
2. Land under cultivation in the south accounts for 58.8% of all cultivated land in the autonomous region, but the south accounts for only 22.4% of the value of agricultural production.
3. The income of an average southern farming family is only one-third that of a northern farmer. More than 90% of the annual income of a farming family in the south goes towards living expenses, with little left for capital investment. The average annual income of RMB906.27 can only secure survival for a farmer who depends only on agriculture for a living.

4. Population growth is a significant factor contributing to under-development. Natural population growth in Ningxia reached 11.92‰ in 2000, higher than the average for western China. The situation in southern Ningxia was even worse, with natural population growth reaching 14.44‰ in 2000. Such a high rate of increase slows down development in the already over-populated southern mountainous area.
5. The proportion of the non-agriculture population, an indication of urbanization, is not high in Ningxia, and there is a great gap between the north and the south. At only 10%, the level of urbanization in the south is much lower than in the north.

The imbalance between the northern and southern areas of Ningxia is, therefore, a crucial problem in the autonomous region's economic development.

Ecological Environment under Population Pressure

Superficially, one may attribute the large gap in development between the north and the south to the differences in natural conditions in the two areas. However, a closer examination would reveal more basic reasons. Both the dramatic population growth and the unscientific approach to production have destroyed the ecological environment, particularly in the south, and a degraded environment leads to low productivity. To survive, local residents have to reclaim more lands, even if such land is not arable. Reclamation then leads to further degradation of the environment. This vicious circle has kept the local area underdeveloped for a long time.

As Table 13.3 shows, the population in the southern mountainous area of Ningxia has been growing very rapidly in the past decades. The population in 2001 was three to five times larger than in 1949. There are several reasons for this consistently high rate of population growth.

Historical reasons and a moderate family planning policy. Historically, most local residents in the southern mountainous area are Muslims. The local population was once dramatically reduced because of wars. For a long time, the local people believed that only by increasing population could they become prosperous. On the other hand, the local family planning policy has been very moderate, even after a strict family planning policy was implemented in the rest of the country. According to the rules, a local farming family can have three children, and it is a very common phenomenon in Ningxia.

Table 13.3 Population Changes in Eight Counties in Mountainous Areas, Southern Ningxia

(Unit: person)

Year / County	1949	1959	1969	1979	1989	1999	2000	2000/1949
Guyuan (固原)	138,400	186,700	248,700	338,400	434,687	516,706	507,874	3.67
Haiyuan (海原)	67,601	110,546	157,174	218,476	296,019	370,734	364,240	5.39
Xiji (西吉)	89,142	157,193	208,211	281,476	366,671	454,021	452,477	5.08
Longde (隆德)	89,478	105,371	132,154	152,419	181,106	216,658	216,954	2.42
Jingyuan (涇源)	26,914	45,941	55,910	74,925	91,256	112,167	81,888	3.04
Pengyang (彭陽)	68,090	92,030	122,703	168,553	213,155	248,793	245,095	3.60
Yanchi (鹽池)	26,940	53,939	81,285	111,108	136,658	152,213	152,117	5.65
Tongxin (同心)	28,104	90,705	131,885	189,624	268,377	258,387	363,630	12.94

Sources: *Forty Years of Ningxia*; *Ningxia tongji nianjian, 2001* (see note 1).

Marrying too early and giving birth at short intervals. Traditionally, having no offspring is regarded as a serious violation of the filial piety held dear by the local people. According to convention, the local legal age of marriage is set at two years below (males 20 and females 18) that of other areas in the country. However, some under-aged couples are still getting married. Marrying and giving birth too early is very popular in the local area and some families illegally have more than three children. All of this puts further pressure on the ecological environment in the southern mountainous area.

Promotion of economic benefit. The prevailing mode of economic production often determines a family's notion of the value of bearing children. Often, people believe that having more children means having a larger labour force in the future. In fact, the expense of an additional child is very low from birth to 16 years old. However, the contribution a child will make to the family in the coming decades after he becomes an adult is considerable. There is another direct reason. After China carried out the "contract responsibility system" reform, in which each household's income is linked to its output, the family became the basic working unit. The number of men is a crucial factor determining the income of a family, especially in the southern mountainous area, where productivity is comparatively low.

Overgrazing under Population Pressure

Planting and grazing are the traditional modes of production in the southern mountainous area. To support a larger population, people have to enlarge their scale of production, including increasing stocks of sheep and converting grassland to farmland. However, overgrazing causes desertification, which in turn leads to a sharp decrease in pasturage. To survive, the sheep have to gnaw even the roots of the grass and the grazing season is brought forward. The grasslands are unable to recover, the sheep are reduced to starvation and the problem of desertification becomes ever more serious.

Land Abuse under Population Pressure

Bringing more land under cultivation by reclaiming forests and grassland is the traditional way to support a fast-growing population. However, grain yields in the southern area are low and unsteady, owing to the unscientific approach to agriculture as briefly outlined below.

Breakdown of the rotational system. With the growth of the population, rotation has given way to continuous cultivation. Agricultural productivity has decreased since the farmland's natural fertility recovery process is halted.

Insufficiency of manure. Straw and manure are used as fuel instead of as organic fertilizer. The decrease in the fertility of the farmland has reduced grain yields. In addition, the cultivation of forest and grasslands has exacerbated water loss and soil erosion.

Relying too much on nature. In the southern mountainous area, rainfall from autumn to spring is critical for agricultural production in the coming year. Low yields are a result of the fact that the area is hit by drought nine years out of ten.

All the above agricultural practices have aggravated ecological problems in the southern mountainous area of Ningxia. To improve the situation, the government has been carrying out an emigration programme since 1983 to alleviate the pressure of population on the environment. Up to 2001, as many as 480,000 inhabitants have left the area. At the same time, more water conservancy projects have been constructed, improving the arid land by irrigation. The agricultural structure has also been adjusted and the production style has changed from herding to feeding to reduce the destruction of grazing. Trees were planted while felling was forbidden to improve ecological conditions in small drainage areas.

After the implementation of the western development strategy, under the support of favourable government policies, much farmland has been converted back to forests. Although time is needed to evaluate the economic and the ecological outcomes of the strategy of western development, one thing is certain, the development of Ningxia has been accelerated. In this, no other approach can be taken except to simultaneously solve the three problems of the deterioration of the ecological environment, over-population and poverty because they are closely connected.

In spite of the above favourable conditions, Ningxia is facing many challenges. First, it would be unwise to totally depend on the central government to develop Ningxia. Its own advantages and potential should be made to come into full play while the central government is expanding investment in this region. Local people should be educated to be largely self-reliant in their efforts to combat poverty instead of counting wholly on outside assistance. Concern should also be shown to disadvantaged urban people. Second, much attention should be paid to education in developing the economy because education serves as the basis for economic development. There will be no rapid economic progress without high-quality talent. Third, the party's policy on ethnic groups and religions should continue to be strictly implemented, as reform and development will not be possible without social stability. Ethnic and religious work can never be ignored because of the stress on economic development. Fourth, attention should be paid on balancing development between the north and the south. Further efforts should be made to relieve poverty and promote education in the southern mountainous areas. Fifth, importance should be attached to maintaining an ecological balance and returning farmlands to forests and grasslands. Sixth, the dissemination of information should be strengthened and exchanges at home and abroad should be enhanced. Both Ningxia and the outside world need to get to know more about each other through all possible means. Finally, the growth of private and jointly-owned firms should be greatly encouraged so that they can play a bigger role in Ningxia's development.

In addition to the support for western development extended by the central government in the form of funds, human resources and materials, the party committee and government of Ningxia have issued a number of official documents in order to maintain the favourable situation of social stability and economic openness that is necessary for development. These include "Some Proposals on Promoting Science and Technology Enterprises" issued in 1996, "A Document on Continuing to Support the Development of Energy-Consuming Industries" issued in 1999 and "Regulations on Encouraging Foreign Investment" issued in 2000, etc. Those documents serve as a guarantee for Ningxia's continuous development.

Summary and Conclusion

The Ningxia Hui Autonomous Region is the main base of the Hui nationality in the northwest. The region's advantages of a unique culture and natural resources provide it with favourable conditions for the development of its society and economy. However, for historical, geographical, communications and other reasons, Ningxia's economy has lagged behind other provinces.

Within Ningxia, the economic gap between the north and the south is a problem that constrains the region's overall development. In order to accelerate the socioeconomic development of Ningxia, several development strategies should be pursued as early as possible. First, it is vital to improve the fragile ecological environment. Second, economic productivity should be and can be improved. Third, reducing the heavy pressure of population should be viewed as a priority. Fourth, promoting science and education is a basic and long-term approach to socioeconomic uplift. Only when these strategies are properly pursued can the problems besetting Ningxia be solved. Ningxia will then be able to make use of its potential advantages to reduce the gap between the south and the north, and even the gap between Ningxia and other provinces. The government and people are dedicated to making a new Ningxia with a sustainable environment, a safe society, united nationalities and common wealth. Such is the spirit and real significance of western development — to create a collective goal and dream, and to mobilize all societal, financial and institutional resources for their realization.

Notes

1. In this chapter, except for statistics in 2001 quoted from "The 2001 Regional Economic Situation and the 2002 Regulating Suggestions" issued on 25 January 2002, all other data quoted are from Ningxia Huizu zizhiqu tongjiju 寧夏回族自治區統計局 (ed.), *Ningxia tongji nianjian 2001* 寧夏統計年鑑2001

(Ningxia Statistical Yearbook 2001) (Beijing: Zhongguo tongji chubanshe 中國統計出版社, 2001).

2. Ningxia gaikuang bianxiezu 寧夏概況編寫組 (ed.), *Ningxia Huizu zizhiqu gaikuang* 寧夏回族自治區概況 (A Survey of the Ningxia Hui Autonomous Region) (Yinchuan: Ningxia renmin chubanshe 寧夏人民出版社, 1986). The next two sub-sections are also based on the same data source.
3. *Ningxia techan fengwei zhinan* 寧夏特產風味指南 (Guide to Ningxia's Specialties) (Yinchuan: Ningxia renmin chubanshe, 1985).
4. *Ningxia tongji nianjian 2001* (see note 1).
5. Ibid.
6. Zhong Kan 鐘侃 (ed.), *Ningxia gudai lishi jinian* 寧夏古代歷史紀年 (Ningxia's Ancient History) (Yinchuan: Ningxia renmin chubanshe, 1988); Wu Zhongli 吳忠禮 (ed.), *Ningxia jindai lishi jinian* 寧夏近代歷史紀年 (Ningxia's Modern History) (Yinchuan: Ningxia renmin chubanshe, 1987); Ningxia jiaotongting bianxiezu 寧夏交通廳編寫組 (ed.), *Ningxia jiaotongshi* 寧夏交通史 (History of Ningxia's Transport) (Yinchuan: Ningxia renmin chubanshe, 1988).
7. See also Qiu Shusen 邱樹森 (ed.), *Zhongguo Huizu da cidian* 中國回族大詞典 (Dictionary of China's Hui Nationality) (Nanjing: Jiangsu guojia chubanshe 江蘇國家出版社, 1992), p. 142.
8. Liu Baojun 劉寶俊 (ed.), *Ningxia Hui Han tuanjie sishinian* 寧夏回漢團結四十年 (Forty Years of Hui-Han Unity in Ningxia) (Yinchuan: Ningxia renmin chubanshe, 1999).
9. A sample of these laws and regulations are: "Supplementary Regulations on the Marriage Laws of the PRC 中華人民共和國婚姻法的補充規定," "The Detailed Rules of the Electoral Law 各級人民代表大會選舉法細則," "Regulations on Family Planning 寧夏回族自治區計劃生育條例" and "Regulations on Compulsory Education 寧夏回族自治區義務教育條例."
10. Ma Hanwen 馬漢文 (ed.), *Zhongguo xibu gaikuang: Ningxia* 中國西部概況：寧夏 (A Survey of Western China: Ningxia) (Beijing: Minzu chubanshe 民族出版社, 2000).
11. Hu Zhenhua 胡振華 (ed.), *Zhongguo Huizu* 中國回族 (China's Hui Nationality) (Yinchuan: Ningxia renmin chubanshe, 1993).
12. Jiang Guojin 姜國金 and Zhang Jiazhen 張家楨 (eds.), *Xibu shengtai* 西部生態 (Ecology of the West) (Beijing: Zhonggong zhongyang dangxiao chubanshe 中共中央黨校出版社, 2001).

14

Shaanxi

Zhao Rong and Zheng Guo

Population, Environment and Natural Resources

Shaanxi 陜西, abbreviated as Shaan 陜 or Qin 秦, is located in the northwest region of China. It is physically located in the centre of the country. An inland province along the middle reaches of the Yellow River and a gateway to northwestern China, Shaanxi links the western part of the nation with its east, and its north with its south. Prior to the Song 宋 dynasty (960–1279), Shaanxi was the political and cultural centre of China and led the whole country in economic and urban development. Although no longer the centre of China in anything but geography, this advantage has brought some development opportunities to the province. After the foundation of the People's Republic of China (PRC), the central government planned a series of key national construction projects in Shaanxi due to its central location. In the context of the current drive to develop China's western region, the fact that Shaanxi is situated between the developed and backward regions in China means that it has the potential to utilize the resources and markets of the two regions.

Administratively, Shaanxi consists of one prefecture, Shangluo 商洛 and the nine cities of Xi'an 西安, Baoji 寶雞, Xianyang 咸陽, Tongchuan 銅川, Weinan 渭南, Hanzhong 漢中, Ankang 安康, Yulin 榆林 and Yan'an 延安 (Figure 14.1). The above administrative units, in turn, administer 103 counties and districts, and 2,019 townships. The economic indicators of major cities are presented in Table 14.1.

Table 14.1 Economic Indicators of Major Cities and Prefectures, 2000

Cities	Population (thousand)	GDP (RMB billion)	Total value of industrial output (RMB billion)	Retail sales (RMB billion)
Xi'an	6,745	60.9	36.9	29.8
Xianyang	4,795	21.1	17.8	4.8
Baoji	3,567	16.8	12.4	5.2
Weinan	5,220	16.4	9.1	3.9
Hanzhong	3,649	13.8	6.7	3.9
Yan'an	1,939	7.9	6.0	1.9
Tongchuan	825	3.9	2.9	1.3
Ankang	2,671	7.8	2.0	2.3
Yulin	3,208	7.9	2.3	2.5
Shangluo	2,392	5.6	1.7	1.5

Sources: Guojia tongjijiu 國家統計局, *2001 Shaanxi tongji nianjian* 2001陜西統計年鑑 (Statistical Yearbook of Shaanxi, 2001) (Beijing: Zhongguo tongji chubanshe 中國統計出版社, 2001).

Figure 14.1 Shaanxi in Its Geographical Setting

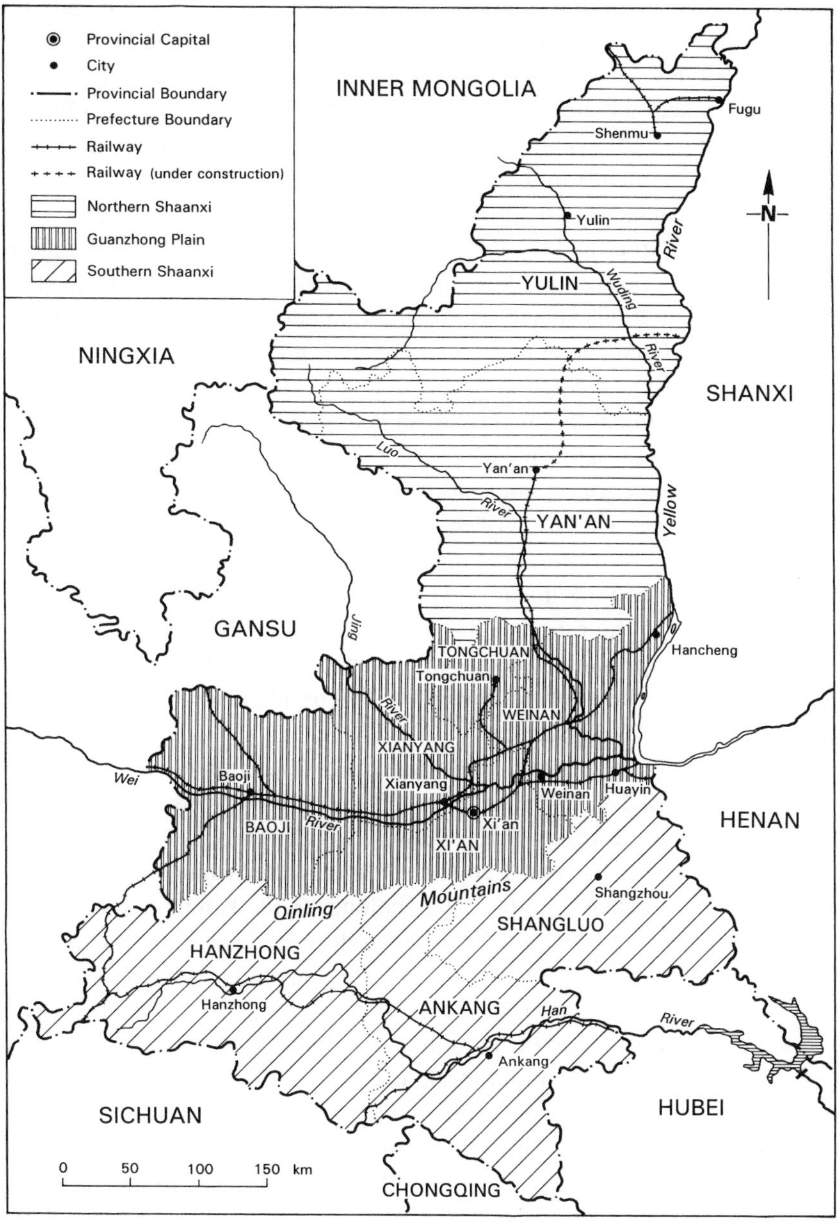

Shaanxi has an area of 205,600 km^2, accounting for 2.1% of the national total. The province extends 1,000 km from the north to the south and 360 km from the west to the east. The whole province can be divided into three natural regions from the north to the south: the northern Shaanxi Plateau, the central Shaanxi Plain or the Guanzhong Plain 關中平原, and the Qinling 秦嶺 and Bashan 巴山 ranges. The Guanzhong Plain, a low-lying area, lies between two highlands in the north and the south.

In 2001, Shaanxi had a population of 36.44 million. Of these, 33% reside in urban areas and 99.4% are of Han 漢 nationality. The population density was 174 persons per km^2, and the natural rate of increase was 0.76 per thousand in 2000. Shaanxi's population is unevenly distributed. Over half live in the Guanzhong Plain, which makes up only 26.94% of the total area of the province. Such an uneven distribution is a reflection of the different environmental, geographic and economic conditions that prevail in different parts of the province.

Shaanxi has a continental monsoon climate, with great differences between the north and south of the Qinling range. From the north to the south, there are three different climate zones: the temperate zone, the warm temperate zone and the northern sub-tropical zone. The average annual temperature is in the range of 8–16°C, low in the north and high in the south. The average annual precipitation ranges from 300 mm to 700 mm, decreasing from the north to the south. The number of frost-free days is between 150 to 270 days a year.

The Qinling range, with an altitude of 1,000–3,000 m and extending from east to west, divides major rivers. The area to the north of the Qinling range belongs to the Yellow River system, which comprises the Wei River 渭河, the Jing River 涇河, the Luo River 洛河 and the Wuding River 無定河. The area to the south of Qinling range belongs to the Yangzi River system, comprising the Han River 漢江 and the Jialing River 嘉陵江. The annual water flow in the whole province is 438 billion m^3 and its total hydropower capacity is over 14 million kw.[1]

Centuries ago, Shaanxi was endowed with lush grass and dense forests and was known as the Natural Storehouse and the Green Sea on Land. But over the course of many dynasties, due to severe desertification, war and soil erosion, the land was gradually destroyed. Today, the image of Shaanxi is that of the Loess Plateau, crisscrossed by gullies. The Yan'an and Yulin areas have been the most heavily affected by the erosion taking place in the upper reaches of the Yellow River, where more than 100 million tonnes of silt is washed down annually.

A project called "Beautifying the Mountains and Rivers of Northern Shaanxi" has recently been launched. The project focuses on the ecological environment, especially on soil erosion, and concentrates on the areas that are often hit by sandstorms. These include places along the Great Wall, the Loess Plateau, the gullies in northern Shaanxi and areas north of the Wei River, the Guanzhong Plain, and the Qinling and Dabashan 大巴山 mountain areas. The aim is to achieve sustainable economic and social development so that, after several decades of effort, Shaanxi will again become a land with green mountains, clean water, blue sky and wealthy people.

Shaanxi is a national energy resources base and a centre for the nation's heavy chemical industry. Abundant reserves of coal, natural gas and petroleum are found in the northern part of the province. Shenmu 神木 and Fugu 府穀 are major production bases of quality fine coal in China with a total reserve of over 160 billion tonnes. Shaanxi has proven reserves of natural gas of 200 billion m^3. It is also rich in metal and non-metal mineral resources. The province ranks third nationally in reserves of 27 of the 91 kinds of mineral resources that are found there. On the basis of 81 mineral varieties with proven reserves, the total potential value of Shaanxi's mineral resources is RMB8,837 billion, ranking it fourth in China. Calculating the potential value per capita, the figure is RMB242,501, ranking it sixth in the country. Calculated per km^2 of area, it is RMB42.98 million, ranking Shaanxi second nationally.

Shaanxi has 59,300 km^2 of forest in the mountainous areas of Qinling, Dabashan, Guanshan 關山, Huanglong 黃龍 and Qiaoshan 樵山, covering 28.8% of the area of the province. Over 750 species of wild vertebrates are found in Shaanxi, of which 79 are rare. It is also home to 12 species of animals and birds that are under state protection including the giant panda, the snub-nosed monkey and the clouded leopard. There are over 3,300 species of wild plants, 37 of them rare. Some 800 species of medicinal plants, such as sea-buckthorn and gynostemma pentaphylla 絞股藍, are of great economic value. The province is the country's top producer of raw lacquer, which is of a high quality. Its traditional exports include dates 大棗, walnut meat and tung oil.[2]

In the next three sections, this chapter will examine the situation in Shaanxi in terms of infrastructure, science and technology; economic conditions; and development opportunities and strategies.

Infrastructure, Science and Technology

Development of Infrastructure

Infrastructure is a precondition for regional economic development, and Shaanxi's has improved a great deal in the past 50 years. There are currently several major railways linking Shaanxi with other provinces: Longhai 隴海 (Lanzhou 蘭州-Lianyungang 連雲港), Bao-Cheng 寶成 (Baoji-Chengdu 成都), Yang-An 陽安 (Yangpingguan 陽平關-Ankang), Bao-Zhong 寶中 (Baoji-Zhongwei 中衛), Shen-Shuo 神朔 (Shenmu-Shuozhou 朔州), Xi-Yan 西延 (Xi'an-Yan'an) and Xi-Kang 西康 (Xi'an-Ankang). The cargo railway station in Xi'an handles 36 million tonnes of cargoes annually and is one of the top stations in China. Xi'an is the hub of highway transportation in the province. Major highways include the following: Xi'an-Lintong 臨潼, Xi'an-Baoji 寶雞, Xi'an-Tongguan 潼關, Xi'an-Tongchuan 銅川. Xi'an's Xianyang International Airport has over 95 routes to major cities in China, including Hong Kong and Macao, and routes to international destinations such as Japan, Thailand, Singapore, South Korea, Saudi Arabia and European countries.

The province's telecommunications infrastructure has also been upgraded. By the end of 2000, the numbers of fixed-line telephone subscribers, pager users and mobile phone users reached 3.5 million, 1.5 million and 1.5 million, respectively. In addition to 9 main optic-fibre trunks totalling 7,319 km in length, Shaanxi's telecommunications network is supplemented with satellite systems and inter-exchange stations.[3]

However, there are still many problems in the province's infrastructure. First, infrastructure in Shaanxi is less developed than in eastern provinces. Moreover, the gap in terms of both total investment and per capita investment in infrastructure is widening. Second, the development of infrastructure within Shaanxi itself is also uneven. The Guanzhong Plain has a good communications system. Infrastructure in the southern and northern areas of Shaanxi, however, cannot meet the needs of energy resources exploitation and regional development. Third, infrastructural development in Shaanxi is not systematic. For example, communications between the northern and the southern parts of the province is not convenient. The central government is attempting to accelerate the development of western China by building new railway lines, including the Xi'an-Hefei 合肥 line and the Baoji-Lanzhou line, and a new highway between Xi'an and Hanzhong. To further improve overall accessibility to the province, the provincial government will invest a total of RMB52.3 billion in the construction of roads and highways during the period of the Tenth Five-year Plan. A total of 4,000 km of new roads will be constructed by the end of 2005, for a total of 48,000 km. During the same period, a number of domestic airports (in Hanzhong, Ankang, Yan'an and Yulin) will be renovated and expanded to improve air transportation in the province.[4]

Science and Technology

Shaanxi ranks third in China in terms of overall research and development (R&D) capability after Beijing 北京 and Shanghai 上海. It contains over 2,000 research institutes of science and technology, 50 of which are recognized as leading research institutes in the country. It also hosts 10 key national laboratories and 50 specialized laboratories administrated by various government agencies. The province's research capabilities are particularly strong in defence, space and agricultural technologies. Output from the high-tech industry reached RMB10.2 billion in 2000.

But there are several obvious problems in the development of science and technology in Shaanxi. First, although Shaanxi is rich in natural resources, the research being conducted in the province does not match well with the needs of resources development, since little of it is related to natural resources. Thus, the province's researchers cannot help to transform Shaanxi's resources into products of high-added value. Shaanxi is currently only a supplier of primary energy resources in China. If Shaanxi is to develop, such a situation must change.

Second, Shaanxi's achievements in science and technology are not matched by the number of entrepreneurs in the province. Entrepreneurs play an important role in transforming advantages in science and technology into economic advantages. Yet, because they are in very short supply, only a small number of innovations in science and technology results in marketable products.

Third, due to its low level of development, Shaanxi is short of capital. This constrains the development of science and technology to a certain extent. However, attracted by abundant capital in southern China, many research institutes in Shaanxi are now collaborating with enterprises in the south. Thus, Shaanxi is becoming a research base for southern China.

Fourth, the development of science and technology faces an institutional problem. Because Shaanxi's institutes of science and technology were set up during the First and Second Five-year Plan periods and the Third-Front period, their development has been led by plan for many years. Being administered and operated by the central government, many have difficulties meeting the needs of a socialist market economy, and are handicapped in their further development.

To accelerate development of high-tech industries in the period of the Tenth Five-year Plan, five research and production bases will be established, focusing on the following sectors: digital electrical appliances, computer and network products, mobile telecommunications, electronic accessories and parts, and electronic products. To enhance the development of a computer software industry, the provincial government, in co-operation with research institutes in Xi'an Jiaotong University 西安交通大學, the Northwest Polytechnic University 西北工業大學 and Northwest University 西北大學, will establish a software park in the Xi'an High-tech Industrial Development Zone (XDZ). Currently, with over 1,000 servers, Xi'an is the largest Internet data centre in northwestern China. An investment of RMB5 million is planned to spur the development of the IT industry.[5]

Economic Conditions

Shaanxi has a long and splendid history, although it is a relatively backward area today. Shaanxi was one of the cradles of the Chinese nation and its long civilization. One million years ago, the Lantian Ape Man 藍田猿人 roamed this land. Six thousand years ago, the Banpo 半坡 primitive man lived in Shaanxi, and one of their villages has been excavated. The tomb of the Xuanyuan Emperor 黃帝, highly respected by all Chinese, is located in Huangling 黃陵 county, north of Xi'an. The Shaanxi government, on behalf of the state, holds a public ceremony there each year.

Before the tenth century, Shaanxi was the political, economic and cultural centre of China. Xi'an served as the capital of 14 dynasties in the past 1,100 years, including the Zhou 周, the Qin 秦, the Han 漢, the Sui 隋 and the Tang 唐. In the period of the Han and the Tang dynasties, the capital city of Chang'an 長安 (present-day Xi'an) was the starting point of the Silk Road. It was an international commercial and trade centre and the meeting place between western and eastern cultures.

Shaanxi was also significant during the Chinese revolution in the twentieth century. The small city of Yan'an played a key role in modern Chinese history as the headquarters of the Chinese Communist Party (CCP) during the 1930s and 1940s. In 1935, the Red Army reached Yan'an after the famous Long March. In the period from 1935 to 1949, Shaanxi was the base of the Chinese Communists.[6]

Shaanxi has been one of China's most important industrial bases since the founding of the PRC in 1949. During the periods of the Three-year Renovation (1949–1952), the First Five-year Plan (1953–1957), the Second Five-year Plan (1958–1962) and the Third-Front Construction (1964–1972), the central government and Shaanxi government built many large industrial and infrastructure projects. Among the total of 156 national key projects, 24 were situated in Shaanxi during the 1950s. In the 1960s to 1970s, a number of factories were moved to Shaanxi from the coastal areas, which spurred urban and economic development in the province. After the Fifth Five-year Plan (1975–1980), however, the emphasis of the regional development in China moved to the eastern and southern regions, and Shaanxi became a backward region in China.

The large projects implemented in the early years still play an important role in the province. But several problems exist. First, these projects were led by government plans. Their operations and management were under the control of the central and provincial governments. Under the system of central planning, these factories had no independent decision-making power. Following the economic reforms of recent years, these factories have found it difficult to compete in a market economy. Second, these factories are not well integrated with the local economy. These factories were built under a planned economy for the purpose of serving the whole country rather than the local economy. Thus, these factories had only loose relations with the local economy and were unable to do much to stimulate local development. Many factories in the defence industry were distributed in mountainous areas. They contributed almost nothing to the local economy.

During the reform period, Shaanxi has established new types of enterprises. Shaanxi has formed a complete, strong and modern industrial system, contributing to the economic development of the province. The rate of economic growth in Shaanxi has been higher than the national average for five consecutive years. Among all of the provinces, municipalities and autonomous regions of Mainland China, Shaanxi ranked 18th, 19th, 21st and 24th in number of enterprises, value of fixed assets, sales revenue and profit, respectively. Key economic indicators of Shaanxi are presented in Table 14.2.

Agriculture, the machinery and electronic industries, tourism and the defence industry are important to the development of Shaanxi. The Shaanxi government has identified them as the backbone industries of the province.

Table 14.2 Key Economic Indicators of Shaanxi, 2000

Economic indicators	Value	Growth rate (%)
Gross domestic product (RMB billion)	166.09	9.0[1]
– primary industry	27.91	4.5
– secondary industry	73.19	9.7
– tertiary industry	64.99	10.3
Per capita GDP (RMB)	4,549	8.3
Disposable income per capita (RMB)		
– urban	5,124	10.1
– rural	1,470	1.0
Investment in fixed assets (RMB billion)	52.9	10.7
Retail sales (RMB billion)	60.8	9.1
Export (US$ billion)	1.3	30.3
Import (US$ billion)	1.1	0.2
Foreign direct investment (US$ billion)	0.3	

Note: [1] In real terms.
Source: Guojia tongjijiu, *2001 Shaanxi tongji nianjian* (see Table 14.1).

Shaanxi is an important agricultural area in China. The province has 3.36 million ha of arable land and 3.53 million ha of grassland. Rice is one of its major food crops, accounting for 80% of the total planting area. Other major crops include wheat, corn, sweet potatos and fruits. In 2000, the output of apples in Shaanxi was the largest in China, accounting for one-fifth of the total output of the country.

Shaanxi's machinery and electronic industries play an important role in the national economy, producing passenger planes, cargo planes, digital exchange switches, ultra-high voltage transmission equipment, heavy-duty trucks, automatic industrial meters, electronic devices, precision machine tools, petroleum instruments, precision rolling mills, engineering machines, colour TV tubes, radar equipment, navigation equipment, computers, and telecommunications and broadcasting equipment. The medical, chemical, construction materials, tobacco and food industries have also developed rapidly, as has light industry. The energy industry has a great potential for development, involving coal, petroleum, natural gas and electric power generation.

Shaanxi has become one of the largest production bases for the defence industry in China. During the 1960s, under the project of the Third-Front Construction, China built many ordnance factories in inland areas. They were set up to prepare for an expected war with the Guomindang 國民黨, whose forces had fled to Taiwan in 1949. Because of this legacy, there are

132 companies in the defence industry in Shaanxi. Approximately 30 of them are special research institutes in the space, aircraft, nuclear, electronics and weapons industries. While the most sophisticated technologies are directly controlled by the People's Liberation Army (PLA) and the central government, other factories in the defence industry have been brought under the umbrella of the Shaanxi Commission of Science, Technology and Industry for National Defence run by civilians. Many factories in Shaanxi have operated at a loss in the past few years, as their products are out-of-date. It is inevitable that the old factories in the defence industry will face many difficulties as the reform of state-owned enterprises (SOEs) continues. Under the "Military-to-Civilian" initiative, many military enterprises in Shaanxi have used their technology and production capacities to develop and produce products for commercial purposes. Successful examples include the Xi'an Aircraft Co., Xi'an-Volvo Automobiles and the Shaanxi Changling Refrigerator Co.[7]

The tourism industry is a special and backbone industry of Shaanxi. Due to its long and glorious history, Shaanxi has much to offer culturally and historically. There are 35,750 historical sites in the region, with 55 designated at the state level and 372 at the provincial level. There are at least 56,000 historical relics, 3,526 deemed to be of first-class at the state level and 123 of other classes at the state level. The province ranks first nationally in density of cultural sites and in the quantity and grade of cultural relics. Thus, Shaanxi is known as the natural history museum of China, with a complete array of historical sites representative of various historical periods.

Shaanxi has become a favourite destination for both domestic and foreign tourists. There has been considerable growth in the tourism industry in recent years. In 2000, 712,800 international tourists visited the region, generating a revenue of US$280 million, an increase of 3.7% over 1999. The Shaanxi government invested heavily to develop the tourism industry. The tourism industry can propel the western region into developing an advanced service sector.

The development of the retail sector is very impressive. In 2000, retail sales of consumer goods in Shaanxi increased by 9.1%, reaching RMB 60.8 billion. Major department stores and shopping centres in Shaanxi include the Xi'an Minsheng Group 西安民生集團 and the Xi'an Jiefang Department Store 西安解放百貨大樓. Their total sales were RMB859 million and RMB725 million in 1999, respectively. They were among the top 50 department stores in terms of sales value in the country. Chain stores and supermarkets have also expanded rapidly in the province. In 2000, the sales revenue of the Shaanxi Haixing Supermarket 陜西海星連鎖超級市場, with a total of 46 outlets, was RMB179 million, ranking it 34th among all supermarket chains in China.

Although Shaanxi is an inland province, its economy is also increasingly linked with the global economy. In 2000, Shaanxi's exports increased sharply by 30.3%, reaching US$1.3 billion. Exports of electrical products/machinery and garments soared by 49% and 69%, respectively. The province's major items of export included textiles, garments, machinery, electronic components and devices and medicinal raw materials. Its major export markets were Hong Kong, Japan, Malaysia, Singapore and Iran. Hong Kong was Shaanxi's largest trading partner. The total value of goods exported to Hong Kong reached US$208 million in 1999, up 17.7% from the previous year. Imports increased slightly by 0.2% to US$1.1 billion in 2000. Major imported items included synthetic fibres, machinery, chemicals and raw materials in pharmacy, electronic equipment and instruments, and ferrous and non-ferrous metals. Major sources of import were Japan, Hong Kong, the U.S., Germany and the U.K.

By the end of 2000, there were 2,357 foreign-invested enterprises (FIEs) in Shaanxi, with an accumulated investment of US$4.5 billion. Transnational corporations such as Philips, Coca-Cola, Mitsubishi Electric Power Products, Inc. and Siemens have established joint ventures in Shaanxi. But Hong Kong is the largest source of overseas investment in Shaanxi. Total investment from Hong Kong reached US$1.45 billion in Xi'an by the end of 2000, accounting for 52% of all overseas investment in the city.

To stimulate the development of the central and western regions of China, the State Council has granted additional tax incentives to FIEs in China. Since January 2001, FIEs in the central and western regions have been granted an incentive tax rate of 15% for another three years on top of the existing incentive policy; that is, an exemption from profit taxes for the first two years of operation and a tax rate of 50% of the normal level for three years thereafter. The tax rate will be further reduced to 10% if an enterprise exports over 70% of its total output each year.

Development Strategies and Government Plans

Development Strategies

While various provinces are struggling to find their role in the Go-West programme, Shaanxi seems to have been very clear about its role from the very beginning. It is the "bridgehead" to the western region. It is where the state cranks the engine of the go-west strategy. In fact, the west development programme officially started when President Jiang Zemin 江澤民 declared at a meeting in Xi'an in June 1999 that the state would look westward in the next few decades. As mentioned in the beginning of the chapter, Shaanxi has a sound geographical and economic position in China. Its bid to become the bridgehead to the western region means that it faces the challenging task of unleashing its economic potential. To achieve such an objective, the province will concentrate its efforts on developing and improving its infrastructure and environment. It will further adjust its economic system and open up more to the outside world.

Shaanxi has adopted overall strategies of economic development that are "giving priority to the development of education, rejuvenating the local economy by means of science and technology, and stimulating resource exploitation for rapid economic growth by adhering to the opening policy." By opening up to the outside world and making full use of its resource, technology and cultural advantages, Shaanxi aims to build "a highly developed economy with technology-intensive industries and famous tourist attractions."[8] Some of the key measures to be taken include:

1. Making efforts to build a technology-intensive base of resources;
2. Taking effective measures to improve the management of capital and to speed up the re-capitalization process;
3. Using market advantages to attract overseas investors to help upgrade and update the products of its large and medium-sized state enterprises; and
4. Generating incremental returns by liquidizing its current stock of assets for industrial restructuring.

Regional Development

Shaanxi is divided into three economic regions. Table 14.3 presents the basic information. The Guanzhong region had a per capita GDP of RMB4,093 in 2000 and was more developed than the southern and northern regions, which had a per capita GDP of about RMB2,300. The Shaanxi government has decided to focus first on developing the Guanzhong area, although it will also endeavour to accelerate the pace of opening up the northern and southern regions.

Table 14.3 Basic Information on the Three Economic Regions, 2000

Region	Guanzhong	Southern region	Northern region
Administrative units	Xi'an, Baoji, Weinan, Tongchuan, Xianyang	Hanzhong, Shangluo, Ankang	Yan'an, Yulin
Population (million)	21.5	9.0	5.2
Area (km^2)	55,384	69,929	80,290
GDP per capita (RMB)	4,093	2,333	2,327
GDP (RMB billion)	88.0	21.0	12.1
Gross agricultural output value (RMB billion)	28.1	12.4	6.0
Gross industrial output value (RMB billion)	96.4	9.3	12.7

Source: Guojia tongjijiu, *2001 Shaanxi tongji nianjian* (See Table 14.1).

The general idea and goal for regional economic growth is to emphasize the development of the central region and strengthen its overall capacity, and to accelerate the development of northern and southern Shaanxi. Efforts will be focused on the construction of the economic centre of Xi'an, the economic belt along the Great Wall and the economic belt along the Han River. Co-ordinated development policies will be adopted by giving priority to investments in the south and north of Shaanxi for energy exploration and infrastructure construction. Foreign investment in the south and north of Shaanxi will be encouraged by favourable polices. Efforts will be made to gradually transfer primary processing and labour-intensive industries to these areas. The export of surplus labour from northern and southern Shaanxi will also be speeded up. Developed areas and government departments will continue to be encouraged and organized to support the southern and northern regions. The focus of development in the three regions is discussed as follows.

The central region will concentrate on developing the mechanical engineering, electronics and high-tech industries. Much effort should be made to develop the textile, food, pharmaceutical, metallurgical, chemical, building materials and energy industries. Great efforts should also be made to develop the finance, technology and service industries. It is important to increase the production of agricultural and non-staple products, including cereals, cotton, oils, fruits, vegetables, meat, eggs and milk. The objective of the central region is to become a highly modernized comprehensive economic zone in northwestern China and in the whole country.

Efforts will be made to speed up the construction and development of Xi'an into an economic centre. It is necessary to accelerate the construction of urban infrastructure, strengthen the city's pillar industries of electronics, machinery and tourism by making full use of its advantages, and actively develop the tertiary industry and increase its overall economic capacity. It is important to follow the conventions of international business practices to turn Xi'an into a centre of finance, commerce, trade, science, technology, information and tourism for the western region of China. Such a development will stimulate the economic development of the whole province.

The southern region will focus on river navigation and the construction of cascaded power stations along the Han River to stimulate the development of mineral, biological and hydropower resources and develop the metallurgical, forest product processing, hydropower and mechanical industries. Efforts will also be made to develop the silk, food, pharmaceutical and building materials industries and enhance the development of agriculture and of tertiary industries. The objective is to make the region a provincial production base of raw materials, hydropower and special forest products. An important task is to build an industrial corridor along the Han River for potential integration with the Yangzi River 長江 economic circle.

The northern region will make full use of its abundant energy resources and preferential policies for development to develop coal, power, petroleum and natural gas industries. It will become an important national base of energy sources and of the heavy chemical industry. Attention should be given to infrastructure construction, agriculture production and the development of the chemical, building materials and tertiary industries. In addition, it is important to develop industries processing agricultural products including tobacco, fruits and fur. A coal, power and natural gas development belt along the Great Wall and the Zichang 子長-Yan'an-Huangling petroleum, coal and power development belt will be developed.

In the implementation in the province of the above regional economic development strategy, priority will be given to the planning of resource development and infrastructure construction projects in the northern and southern regions. Preferential policies will be adopted to introduce overseas investment to these regions for the joint development of resources. Some processing industries involving primary resources which are labour-intensive will be moved to the northern and southern regions to absorb the local surplus labour.[9]

Five Big Preferential Development Programmes in Shaanxi

The central government has selected five big preferential development programmes to spearhead the national strategy of developing the western region, using the following principles. First, the preferential programmes should have superior competitiveness in the western region of China. They should also be consistent with national and provincial industrial policies and regional development policies. Second, the preferential programmes should have a great catalytic impact on economic development, facilitating social development in Shaanxi. Third, they should improve the overall investment environment of Shaanxi. Fourth, they should play a key role in the whole of northwestern China and promote its development. The five programmes that have been selected are: the project to beautify the mountains and rivers of northern Shaanxi 陝北山川秀美工程, the construction of the Yanliang Aircraft Town 閻良航天城, the Yangling Agricultural Town 楊凌農科城, the Yulin Energy Base 榆林國家級能源基地 and the Guanzhong High-tech Development Belt 關中高新技術產業帶.

Project to Beautify the Mountains and Rivers of Northern Shaanxi. The programme covers 45 counties with an area of 108,000 km^2 in northern Shaanxi and the Weibei Plateau 渭北高原. This is an area with serious soil erosion. For half a century, particularly after the 1980s, the people of northern Shaanxi have been battling soil erosion and desertification. Altogether, there are 2.1 million ha of forest, 250,000 ha of grasslands and 32,000 km^2 of controlled areas with severe soil erosion. In 1997, an important meeting was held in northern Shaanxi. At that meeting, state officials stressed that controlling soil erosion and national economic and social development were of equal importance; it was decided that greater efforts should be made to control soil erosion and protect the viability of the forests and rivers of northern Shaanxi. The programme will bring immense social and ecological benefits to the area.

Construction of Yanliang Aircraft Town. Yanliang district, 45 km from Xi'an, is China's most important base for aircraft research, production and testing. It has processed and produced aircraft parts and vertical tails for American, French, Italian and Canadian aircraft companies. In 1997, the state invested US$1.2 billion to build an aircraft assembly line in Yanliang to produce 100-seat passenger planes, jointly developed by China, the Euro Airbus Group, Italy, Singapore and seven other countries. This programme will not only promote the development of China's aviation industry but also foster the development of the raw materials, electronic instruments

Figure 14.2 Cities and the Three Major Regions of Shaanxi

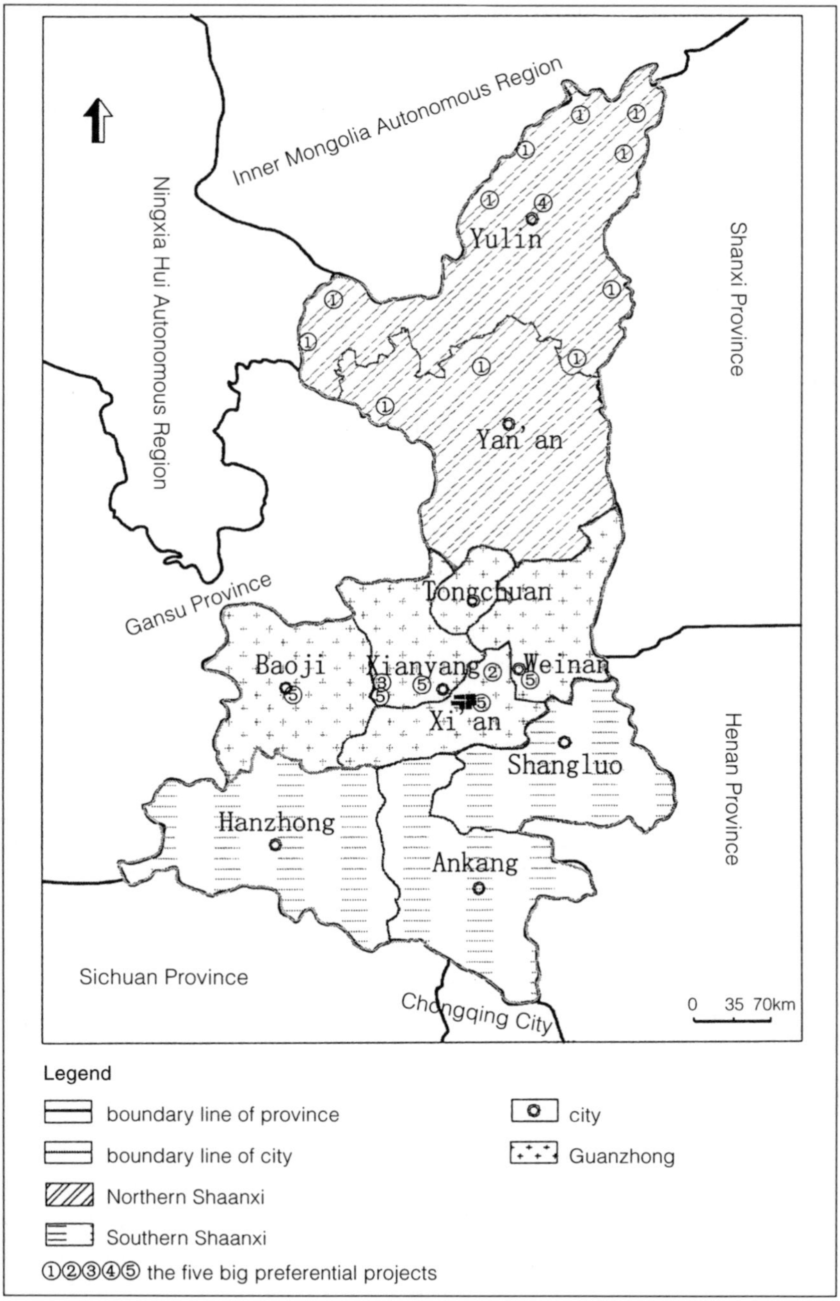

and machinery industries as well as improving modern management in Shaanxi. Yanliang aims to become "China's Seattle" in the twenty-first century.

Construction of the Yangling High-tech Agricultural Demonstration Zone (Yangling HTADZ). Yangling district, 90 km from Xi'an, is China's biggest agricultural base. The Longhai Railway and the Xi'an-Baoji Expressway pass through the district. The Northwest Agricultural University 西北農業大學 and 11 other agricultural and forestry research institutes at the ministerial level, as well as a group of modern national key laboratories, are located in the district. There are over 4,000 technicians and scientists engaged in agriculture, forestry, irrigation and 70 other research fields. Over 5,000 scientific achievements have resulted in economic benefits of RMB200 billion.

In 1997, the state decided to jointly establish the first national agricultural high-tech model zone in the district with the province and other relevant ministries of the central government. The high-tech zone has an area of 21 km^2, including a science park, an industrial park, an international co-operation park, a modern comprehensive agricultural park, a dozen testing and popularization bases and five multi-functional parks. Teaching, research, production and trade are conducted within the zone. The state also decided to establish several national key laboratories and research and development centres to promote research on wheat, non-irrigated farmland techniques, water-saving irrigation techniques, research on water and soil conservation, as well as the conversion of scientific achievements for practical applications. The zone aims to develop improved varieties of crops, safe insecticides, biological medicines, chemical forestry products and processed farm products. Efforts are being made to strengthen international co-operation and to introduce, utilize and popularize new agricultural techniques.

Construction of the Yulin Energy Base. Yulin, situated in the northern tip of Shaanxi, is rich in mineral resources. Approximately 40 varieties of 8 kinds of mineral resources have been discovered in the area. Total coal reserves amount to 142 billion tonnes. The coal is of high heating quality, but of extremely low sulphur, phosphorus and ash content. A field with rich natural gas resources has been discovered in northern Shaanxi with a reserve of 300 billion m^3. Newly discovered and proven petroleum reserves total 300 million tonnes and 25 million tonnes, respectively. Proven reserves of rock salt, kaolin and bauxite exceed 100 million tonnes, 680 million tonnes and 23.19 million tonnes, respectively. The rich resources of coal, petroleum, salt and natural gas provide favourable conditions for the construction of this energy base.

Three larger enterprise groups have been set up to develop energy resources in the area. Shenhua Group 神華集團 is engaged in developing the Shenfu Coal Field 神府煤田 which has an annual production capacity of over 100 million tonnes. With an investment of RMB90 billion, it is a large-scale project, second only to the Three Gorges Project. China's Natural Gas Corporation 中國天然氣公司 engages in the development of natural gas. Its total annual output capacity reached 3 billion m^3 by 2000. China's Huaneng Group 中國華能集團 engages in the construction of large-scale thermal power plants. It plans to have an electricity generating capacity in northern Shaanxi of 4.5 million kw. Total investment in the programme reached RMB3 billion by the end of 2001.

Construction of the Guanzhong High-tech Development Belt. The Guanzhong Plain is home to 600,000 professionals in over 40 universities and colleges, 340 research institutes, and 300 defence and civilian enterprises. To take advantage of the abundant expertise in science and technology and to speed up the conversion of scientific achievements to applications, Shaanxi has decided to establish the Guanzhong High-tech Development Belt. The fact that the new Euro-Asian Continental Bridge passes through the Guanzhong Plain makes the area even more accessible and viable. Within the belt are the state-level Xi'an, Baoji and Yangling high-tech zones and the provincial-level Weinan and Xianyang high-tech zones. The belt is estimated to have 1.44 million m^2 of completed floor space. There are 2,500 enterprises in the belt, of which 580 are high-tech enterprises and 300 are FIEs, private enterprises and joint ventures. In 1997, the total revenue from technology, industry and trade was over RMB20 billion. Four incubating centres with a total floor space of 22,000 m^2 have nurtured 204 enterprises. The Xi'an Enterprise Service Centre was named China's International Enterprise Incubator by the State Science and Technology Commission in 1997.[10]

The Xi'an High-tech Development Zone was established in 1988 as a national high-tech zone. The zone has a newly constructed area of 10 km^2 and a planned area of 29.15 km^2. Within the zone are over 22 universities and colleges, 49 research institutes above the city level, and 20 large and medium-sized enterprises. The zone also contains 5 industrial parks, which are home to 18 corporate groups, 2 transnational corporations and 496 approved projects involving a total investment of RMB7.34 billion. Its total revenue from technology, science and trade exceeded RMB10 billion in

1997. Currently, enterprises in the zone with annual revenues from technology, science and trade of over RMB10 million number 70, while there are 12 enterprises with annual revenues of over RMB100 million each.

Five pillar industries have taken shape in the zone. The first is the electronic telecommunications industry with Datang Telecommunications Corporation 大唐電信 as the principal enterprise. The second is the energy-saving refrigeration industry, led by the Qing'an Freezer Factory 慶安製冷設備公司. The third is the information and computer industry, at the forefront of which is the Xi'an Haixing Group 西安海星集團. The fourth is the machinery and electric industry led by the Brothers Corporation. The fifth is the new materials industry led by Xi'an Tongrui Group 西安通瑞集團. Some 288 foreign enterprises and joint ventures involving 20 countries and regions have invested a total of US$500 million in the zone, while foreign investors have committed US$300 million. The Brothers Corporation from Japan, MEMC from the U.S., Philips Company from the Netherlands, Canada's North Electric Corporation and other world famous companies have invested in Xi'an.

The Baoji High-tech Development Zone is a national high-tech zone approved by the state in 1992, focusing on the development of electronics, machinery and new materials. There are 67 enterprises in the zone, 31 of which are high-tech enterprises. In 1997, revenues from technology, science and trade totalled RMB2 billion and exports were valued at US$4.7 million.

The Xianyang High-tech Development Zone is in fact an electronics town with a complete set of electronic sectors. Its output value accounts for half of Shaanxi's electronics industry. The various enterprises in the zone are engaged in electronic information, optical machinery, biological engineering, new medicines, colour TV tubes, deflection coils and deflecting cores and copper-clad plates.

The Weinan High-tech Development Experimental Zone was initiated in June 1992. Three functional parks have been established in this zone, including a high-tech creative park hosting knowledge-intensive research institutes and enterprise service centres, a high-tech industrial park, and a high-tech popularization park focusing on the restructuring of key enterprises within the zone. Its fine chemicals industry takes a leading position in the Guanzhong Development Belt. There are 104 scientific development enterprises in this zone, and their annual revenues totalled RMB74 million in 1997.

According to the Five Big Preferential Programmes discussed above,

20 priority projects, involving over 260 sub-projects, have been identified as the focus of the efforts to accelerate the development of the local economy in Shaanxi. These projects fall into four broad categories, according to their nature and to the timing of their construction. Projects in the first category will reinforce the region's agricultural foundations and strengthen its infrastructure. They include such projects as water and power supply, highways and telecommunications. The second category involves basic industrial projects to speed up the development of natural resources. The projects in the third category focus on new and high-tech industries to facilitate technology transfers and the expansion of businesses in industries with competitive advantages. The fourth category focuses on projects co-ordinating social development with economic development.

Conclusion

Shaanxi once had a glorious past, but its development has lagged behind that of other coastal regions in the early years of reform period. But Shaanxi's future seems hopeful. It has a good location and fine economic foundations in the western region. The implementation of the strategy to develop the west offers an unprecedented opportunity for Shaanxi to enter another splendid era. The objective and main programmes of development are clear in Shaanxi. Whether they can be successfully achieved depends on the ability and efforts of the people and the government of Shaanxi and of others.

After the completion of the 20 priority projects mentioned above, Shaanxi will have created a good investment environment in the early twenty-first century. Its industrial mix and distribution will be optimized. The province's economic strength will greatly increase. Shaanxi will become an important producer of energy and raw materials in the country and an important base for its machinery, electronics, pharmaceutical, non-ferrous metals and petrochemical industries. With the full integration of the tourism, science, technology, education and high-tech industries, Shaanxi will play an important role in China's northwest.

Notes

1. Tang Haibin 唐海彬 (ed.), *Shaanxisheng jingji dili* 陝西省經濟地理 (Economic Geography of Shaanxi) (Beijing: Xinhua chubanshe 新華出版社, 1988), pp. 5–26.
2. Zhang Zhiliang 張志良 and Zhang Tao 張濤, "Zhongguo xibei diqu renkou,

ziyuan, huanjing wenti ji kechixu fazhan" 中國西北地區人口、資源、環境問題及可持續發展 (Population, Resources, Environment and Sustainable Development in Northwest China), *Ganhanqu ziyuan yu huanjing* 乾旱區資源與環境 (Journal of Arid Land Resources and Environment), No. 2 (1997), pp. 1–5.

3. He Gongding 何公定, "Shaanxi quyu jingji fazhan zhanlüe xuanze — jiakuai gonglu jiaotong jianshe" 陝西區域經濟發展戰略選擇 —— 加快公路交通建設 (A Choice of Strategy for Shaanxi's Regional Economic Development — Speeding up Highway Construction), *Xi'an gonglu jiaotong daxue xuebao* 西安公路交通大學學報 (Journal of Xi'an Highway University), No. 4 (2000), pp. 71–73.
4. Fan Shaoyan 范少言 and Chen Zongxing 陳宗興, "Shaanxi jiaotong kechixu fazhan zhanlüe de fenxi" 陝西交通可持續發展戰略的分析 (Analysis of a Sustainable Development Strategy for the Transportation System in Shaanxi), *Jingji dili* 經濟地理 (Economic Geography), Vol. 19, No. 6 (1999), pp. 110–13.
5. He Liancheng 何煉成, "Xibei jingji kaifa de guoqu, xianzai yu weilai" 西北經濟開發的過去、現在與未來 (The Past, Present and Future of the Economic Development of Northwest China) (Xi'an: Shaanxi renmin chubanshe 陝西人民出版社, 1997), pp. 113–18.
6. Ibid.
7. Zhao Rong 趙榮, "Guanzhong zhongxin juluo diyu jiegou de xingcheng yu yanbian" 關中中心聚落地域結構的形成與演變 (The Formation and Evolution of the Regional Structure of Settlements in Guanzhong), *Renwen dili* 人文地理 (Human Geography), No. 1 (1995), pp. 56–64.
8. Li Zongzhi 李宗植, "Xibei diqu zai dakaifa zhong tiaozheng chanye jiegou de sikao" 西北地區在大開發中調整產業結構的思考 (Reflections on the Readjustment of the Industrial Structure in Northwest China in the Large-Scale Development of the Western Region), *Zhongyang minzu daxue xuebao* (*zhexue shehui kexueban*) 中央民族大學學報 (哲學社會科學版) (Journal of Central University of Nationalities (Philosophy and Social Sciences)), No. 4 (2000), pp. 33–36.
9. Guo Xiaodong 郭曉東 and Wang Shaohua 王少華, "Xibei diqu jingji fazhan zhanlüe gousi" 西北地區經濟發展戰略構思 (The Conception of the Economic Development Strategy in Northwest China), *Gansu jiaoyu xueyuan xuebao (zirankexue ban)* 甘肅教育學院學報 (自然科學版) (Journal of Gansu Education College (Natural Sciences)), No. 4 (2000), pp. 55–59.
10. Li Jingwen 李京文, *Zouxiang 21 shiji de Zhongguo quyu jingji* 走向21世紀的中國區域經濟 (Chinese Regional Economy in the 21st Century) (Nanning: Guangxi renmin chubanshe 廣西人民出版社, 1999), pp. 223–24.
11. Duan Hanming 段漢明, "Da Xi'an de kuangjia yu fazhan jizhi" 大西安的框架與發展機制 (The Structure and Development Mechanism of the Municipality of Xi'an), *Chengshi guihua* 城市規劃 (City Plan), No. 12 (2001), pp. 23–24.

15

Inner Mongolia

Wang Jing'ai and Yang Mingchuan

Introduction

The Inner Mongolia 內蒙古 Autonomous Region is located in China's northern frontier[1] (Figure 15.1). It shares a long border of 4,421 km with Mongolia 蒙古 in the north and Russia in the northeast. Its neighbours in China include Heilongjiang 黑龍江, Jilin 吉林, Liaoning 遼寧, Hebei 河北, Shanxi 山西, Shaanxi 陝西, Ningxia 寧夏 and Gansu 甘肅. Its territory spans 2,400 km from east to west and 1,700 km from north to south, with a total area of 1.18 million km^2. Inner Mongolia is China's third largest province or region and accounts for 12.3% of the country's total area. It had a population of 23.7 million in 2000, comprising 1.83% of the China's population.[2] There are 49 nationalities residing in the region, including the Mongolian 蒙, Han 漢, Hui 回, Man 滿, Dahan'er 達翰爾, Korean 朝鮮, Ewenke 鄂溫克 and Elunchun 鄂倫春. Inner Mongolia has 12 prefecture-level cities and 101 counties. The Autonomous Region's capital is located in Hohhot 呼和浩特.

Inner Mongolia Autonomous Region was founded on 1 May 1947, with Ulanhot 烏蘭浩特 as its capital. This was the first time that an autonomous region had been established for the Mongolians in China. In 1664, the government of the new Qing 清 dynasty, using desert and wilderness as a boundary, demarcated the area north of the desert as "Outer Mongolia" and the area south of the desert as "Inner Mongolia." Inner Mongolia was placed directly under the jurisdiction of the Lifan 理藩 Council, a central body that handled affairs relating to non-Han peoples of the north, and the non-Han peoples were organized under a system of Leagues 盟-Banners 旗 system. Since the founding of the People's Republic of China (PRC) in 1949, the area administrated by Inner Mongolia has changed many times. Thus, it is important to note the difference between "the small Inner Mongolian territory" and "the large Inner Mongolian territory." The former does not include Hulun Buir 呼倫貝爾, Hinggan 興安, Chifeng 赤峰, Tongliao 通遼 in the east and Alxa 阿拉善 in the west, while the latter refers to the current administrative division used since 1979. The administrative division at present includes 12 prefectural-level cities and leagues, namely, the cities of Hohhot, Baotou 包頭, Wuhai 烏海, Chifeng, Tongliao and Dongsheng 東勝, and the leagues of Hulun Buir, Hinggan, Xilin Gol 錫林郭勒, Ulan Qab 烏蘭察布, Bayannur 巴彥淖爾 and Alxa. In terms of economic regions in China, Inner Mongolia once belonged to the Northeast Economic Region 東北經濟區, North China Economic Region 華北經濟區 and Northwest Economic Region 西北經濟區, respectively.[3] Inner Mongolia is not only a

Figure 15.1 Inner Mongolia in Its Geographical Setting

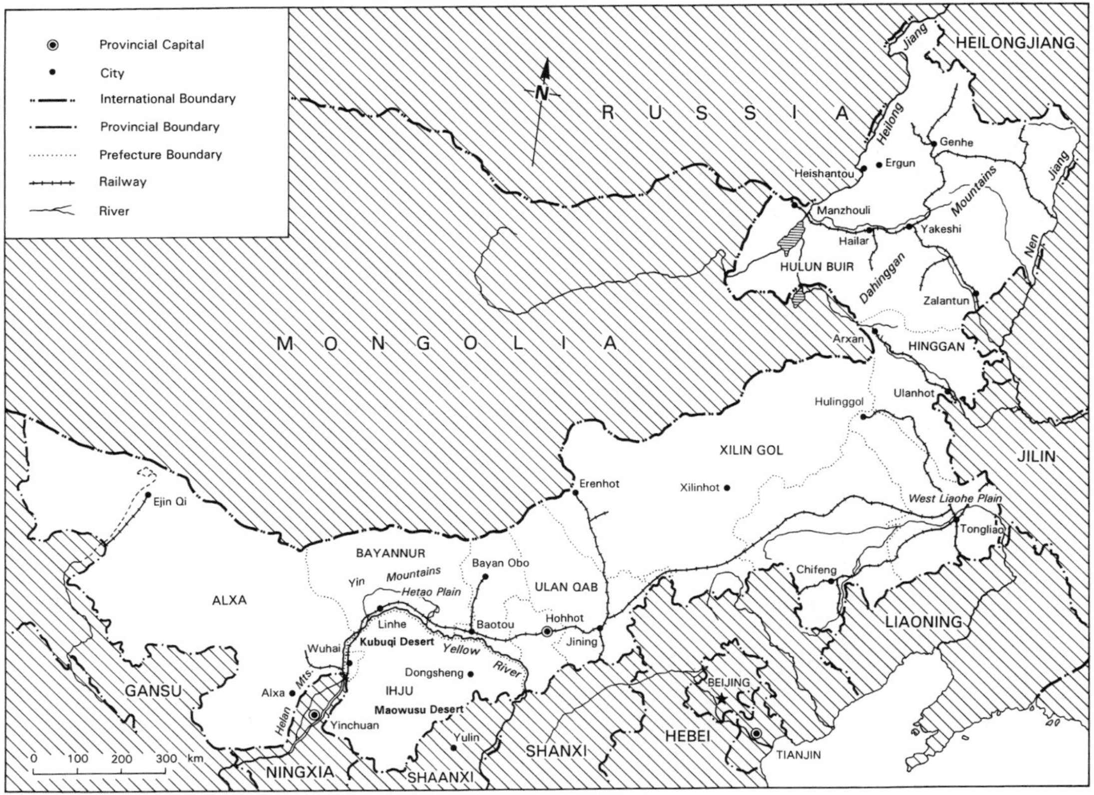

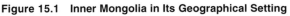

base of energy resources but also a base for commercial animal husbandry in China. It is a region with mixed farming and grazing. While it has a fragile natural environment, which will require care and attention, in the development of the western region, Inner Mongolia plays an important part due to its various advantages.

Locational advantage. Inner Mongolia stretches over the "Three Northern Regions" (*Sanbei* 三北) and adjoins eight provinces. The central and eastern areas of Inner Mongolia are part of the Economic Circle surrounding Bohai 環渤海經濟圈. Relying on the Bao-Lan 包蘭 Railway (Baotou-Lanzhou 蘭州), the "Golden Triangle" 金三角 in western Inner Mongolia is part of the Western Economic Zone of Longhai 隴海, Lanzhou and Xinjiang 新疆 (西隴海蘭新經濟帶), which is a key zone in the development of the western region. In the north, Inner Mongolia shares a border with Mongolia and Russia and has 18 border crossings, such as Manzhouli 滿洲里 and Erenhot 二連浩特. Therefore, in the economic development of China, Inner Mongolia is not only an important link between east and west, but also a frontier that opens to other countries in the north.

Resource advantage. The saying "Forest in the east and iron in the west, farming in the south and grazing in the north, plus coal all over the area" (*donglin xitie, nanliang beimu, biandi shi mei* 東林西鐵，南糧北牧，遍地是煤) is a lively description of the resource advantages of Inner Mongolia. Through 50 years of development and construction, Inner Mongolia has become an important production base for livestock and energy in China. Inner Mongolia has 86.66 million ha of grasslands, the most in the country. Inner Mongolia also has 8.20 million ha of farmland and the farmland per capita is three times that of the national average. The region has 18.66 million ha of forests, the second most in the country. Inner Mongolia is one of the largest producers of livestock products such as wool, leather, beef, mutton and milk. It is the largest producer of wool and cashmere in the country. With abundant resources for farming and grazing, there has been much progress in the industrialization of farming and grazing and in the processing of farming and grazing products. Several famous enterprises and well-known brands such as Yili 伊利, Luwang 鹿王, Shiqi 仕奇 and Caoyuan Xingfa 草原興發 have emerged.

Policy advantage. Inner Mongolia has done well in maintaining a safe frontier, harmony between nationalities and a stable polity for a long time. In accordance with the constitution and law for autonomous regions, the state has granted many favourable policies to Inner Mongolia. In the new century, Inner Mongolia has been designated as one of the 12 provinces to implement the strategy of the development of the western region. This will have a great impact on the development of Inner Mongolia in the future.

Environment and Economic Development

Inner Mongolia has a mixed distribution of mountains, plateaus and basins. The Dahinggan Mountain 大興安嶺 in the east, the Yin Mountain 陰山 in the centre and the Helan Mountain 賀蘭山 in the west separate the Inner Mongolia Plateau from the Northeast Plain, the Jibei Mountains 冀北山地 and the Ordos Plateau 鄂爾多斯高原. They form not only a boundary between the grassland ecosystem and forest-grassland shrub-grassland ecosystem, but also a boundary between the inland and open drainage areas. The area northwest of the mountains belongs to the inland drainage area, where the grasslands have become seriously degraded due to desertification and overgrazing. The area in the northeast belongs to the open drainage area, where the problem is the alternate erosion of wind and water.

The Inner Mongolia Plateau lies northwest of the above boundary and is a wide inland plateau extending from northeast to southwest. Its altitude declines slowly from south to north and west to east, and the average altitude is above 1,000 m. Sediments of the Quaternary period cover the Inner Mongolia Plateau and often form sandy land due to wind erosion and the overgrazing of the grasslands. This affects the productivity of the grasslands.

In addition to the mountains and plateaus, there are also the West Liaohe Plain 西遼河平原, the Hetao Plain 河套平原 and other plains. These plains are important production bases of grain, cotton and oil. They are also core areas of urbanization and industrialization.

Most areas of Inner Mongolia enjoy a temperate continental monsoon climate with little and uneven precipitation and clear seasons. Inner Mongolia can be divided into four dry-wet zones (*ganshi didai* 乾濕地帶): moist, semi-moist, arid and semi-arid, with precipitation decreasing from 500 mm to 50 mm from east to west, but evaporation increasing from 1,000 mm to 3,000 mm. Inner Mongolia can also be divided into three temperature zones: warm temperate, temperate and cold temperate. The average air temperature in January changes from –10°C to –30°C from south to north and in July from 27°C to 16°C from south to north. It is obvious that these temperatures are all lower than areas in the same latitude. There are clear seasonal changes, and the range in temperature in a year is 34°C to 36°C. The region lies at the end of the monsoon area and at the frontier of the anticyclones from Mongolia. The combination of unstable precipitation, mountainous topography, loess and sand has led to an ecological environment that is vulnerable and sensitive to global changes in climate. The strengthening of the ecological environment is very important for the sustainability of agriculture in Inner Mongolia.

Great changes have taken place to the land cover due to human activity, especially to the highlands covered with loess, where the former forests and grasslands have been replaced by barren or dry land. In mountainous areas, most of the virgin forests have been destroyed. Such virgin forests only exist north of the Dahinggan Mountain. Large forested areas have been degraded and become shrubbery. Some areas have even lost their vegetation cover and become bare land. The grass of the Inner Mongolia Plateau has degraded severely due to overgrazing and has been replaced in some areas by drift sand or alkaline soil. The forest coverage is only 5% in the broad, loess highland, 1.7% in the Ordos Plateau, less than 1% in the Inner Mongolia Plateau and over 50% in the Dahinggan Mountain.

Inner Mongolia is relatively deficient in surface water. There is a volume of 23.5 billion m^3 of water from the middle reaches of the Yellow River and 44 billion m^3 in the inland drainage area. River systems such as Heilongjiang 黑龍江, Nenjiang 嫩江, West Liaohe, Luanhe 灤河 and Haihe 海河 are the main water resources, especially for the eastern Inner Mongolia. The water resources of Inner Mongolia only account for 1.5% of the total in China, an important factor restricting the distribution of agricultural, manufacturing and mining activities.

According to the Fifth Population Census in 2000, the population of Inner Mongolia reached 23.7 million, which was an increase of 10.71% from 21.5 million in 1990. But its population density was 20 persons per km^2, only one-fifth of the national average. Most of the population resides in the areas of farmland and mixed farmland and grassland. Few live in north of the Hulinhe 霍林河-Yulin 榆林 of Huhuanyong 胡煥庸 Line, but many south of the Line.[4] Mongolians account for 16% of the total population of Inner Mongolia. Seventy percent of the total Mongolian population in China is in Inner Mongolia, and about four-fifths are concentrated in three leagues and two cities in eastern Inner Mongolia. Although the Mongolian share of the population is not large, the influence of Mongolian culture is extensive. Regional differences among the Mongolian grazing culture, the mixed Mongolian and Han culture, and the Han farming culture are very clear (Table 15.1). Land use is an important factor behind such differences.

Grasslands make up 86.66 million ha, the largest of any type of area in the region. Of this, 68.06 million ha can be utilized, accounting for 60% of

Table 15.1 Comparison of Cultures in Inner Mongolia

Culture		Mongolian grazing culture in the north	Mongolian and Han mixed culture in the central area	Han culture in the south
Land use	Management	Coarse natural grazing	Half raising in shed, grazing and dry land farming	Raising in shed, grazing and irrigated and dry land farming
	Land-use share (%)	Grassland >80, farmland <5	Farmland: 5–15, grassland: 35–55	Farmland >25
Tribes	Share of Tribe area (%)	<0.5, scattering like speckles	0.5–3, scattering like flyspecks	>3, speck and net street
	Density (Tribes per 100 km^2)	5–15	15–35	>35
	Architecture style	Mongolian house, round roof	Arched roof	Hill-like or inclined roof
Diet		Milk tea, parched sugar, with salt	Boiling tea, parched sugar, with salt	Making tea, without salt
Head scarf of man		Cloth belt around head with a knot on the side	Towel around head with a knot in the front	Towel around head with a knot behind
Language		Speak Mongolian, understand Chinese	Speak Chinese, understand Mongolian	Chinese

Note: The Land-use data is for 1987.

the total area of Inner Mongolia. About half of the grasslands are in the central and eastern parts of the Inner Mongolia Plateau. Forests occupy an area of 18.66 million ha, accounting for 13.9% of total forests in China. The forest coverage is 14.82%. Most forests are concentrated in the Dahinggan Mountain. The area of farmland is 8.20 million ha, comprising 6.31% of the total in China. The farmland per capita is 0.36 ha, the largest in the country, although the quality of the farmland is poor. Fluctuations in precipitation have a great impact on land use, and land-use changes often take place in the mixed zone. The main land-use problems in the region include the rough management of natural grasslands and dry lands, and lower and unstable land productivity and improper control of land use, resulting in serious land degradation.

Inner Mongolia has undergone several periods since its founding. Agriculture and animal husbandry dominated the economy in the period of recovery (1947–1952) during which the ratio of primary, secondary and tertiary industries was 71.05:11.27:17.68. In the period of the First Five-year Plan, more local industries were established and the corresponding ratio of the three industries was 53.1:23.7:23.2. In the Great Leap Forward (*dayuejin* 大躍進) and national economic adjustment period, raw materials and livestock product processing became the major industries and the ratio of three industries became 43.0:34.1:22.9. During the period of the Cultural Revolution, heavy industry was emphasized. The ratio of three industries was 32.7:45.5:21.8. In the reform period, the economy has been growing at a rate of 9% a year. Agriculture and animal husbandry have been transformed from being part of a self-sufficient and half-self-sufficient economy into a modern commercial economy. Industry has also developed, as have the areas of transportation, postal services and telecommunications, real estate and social services. In 2000, the ratio of the three industries was 23.37: 40.38:36.25. In the period 1952–2000, GDP per capita increased from RMB173 to 5,872[5] (Table 15.2). Due to differences in natural environment, resource conditions, regional policies and development histories, there are clear regional differences between leagues and cities in Inner Mongolia (Table 15.3).

The main objectives on the economic and social development of Inner Mongolia in the Tenth Five-year Plan are as follows. Economically, GDP will increase by 9% a year and reach RMB215 billion by 2005 (at year 2000 prices). GDP per capita will be RMB8,650 in 2005. The GDP of primary industry will increase by 4% a year, secondary industry by 10% and tertiary industry by 12%. The ratio of the three industries will become 20:41:39 by 2005. Total investment in fixed assets will increase by 12%

Table 15.2 Inner Mongolia's GDP and Per Capita GDP, 1949–2000

Year		1952	1955	1957	1960	1965	1970
GDP (RMB billion)		1.22	1.75	2.13	3.56	3.54	3.92
As a percentage of national GDP (%)		1.79	1.92	1.99	2.44	2.06	1.74
Per capita GDP (RMB)		173	213	232	325	275	263
As a percentage of national per capita GDP (%)		145.38	142.00	138.10	149.08	114.58	95.64
Year	1975	1978	1980	1985	1990	1995	2000
GDP (RMB billion)	4.86	5.80	6.84	16.38	31.92	83.28	140.08
As a percentage of national GDP (%)	1.62	1.60	1.51	1.83	1.72	1.42	1.57
Per capita GDP (RMB)	280	317	361	809	1,478	3,639	5,872
As a percentage of national per capita GDP (%)	85.63	83.64	78.48	94.62	90.45	74.97	82.96

Note: The figures given are quoted in current year prices.

Sources: Data for 1949–1995 are from *Huihuang de Neimenggu 1947–1999* (see note 5), and for 2000 are from *Neimenggu tongji nianjian 2001* (see note 2).

Table 15.3 Uneven Economic Development in Inner Mongolia, 2000

Indicator	Unit	Hohhot	Baotou	Wuhai	Chifeng	Tongliao	Hulun Buir	Xingan	Xilin Gol	Ulan Qab	Dongsheng	Bayannur	Alxa
GDP	RMB billion	17.91	22.84	3.84	16.08	14.88	15.70	6.14	6.92	9.17	15.01	11.11	2.18
GDP per capita	RMB	848	11,186	9,543	3,559	4,834	5,748	3,804	7,432	3,380	11,505	6,518	10,590
Gross output value of industry and agriculture	RMB billion	24.77	40.15	3.66	19.20	19.62	11.48	7.54	7.70	13.57	20.15	11.25	1.86
Total revenue of local government	RMB billion	2.02	2.73	0.40	1.27	0.91	1.57	0.52	0.63	0.77	1.57	0.73	0.25
Retail sales of consumer goods	RMB billion	6.91	8.76	1.24	7.31	4.50	5.53	2.53	2.63	2.57	2.75	3.22	0.43
Cash income per capita in urban areas	RMB	7,584	7,517	6,658	6,199	5,779	6,884	6,005	7,109	6,529	7,951	6,194	9,134

Note: Hohhot, Baotou, Wuhai, Chifeng, Tongliao and Dongsheng are cities. Others are leagues.

Source: *Neimenggu tongji nianjian 2001* (see note 2), pp. 550, 556, 563, 574, 579, 588.

annually. Total retail sales of consumer goods will increase by 11% a year and exports will increase by over 11% a year. Government revenues will increase at an annual rate of 10% and reach RMB25 billion by 2005. The disposable income per capita of urban residents will increase by more than 7% a year and that of peasants by more than 6% each year. The floor space per capita of urban residents will reach 22 m^2 in 2005. The share of R&D expenditure in GDP will rise to 1.5%, and the proportion of the population receiving nine-year compulsory education will rise to 85% for each county. Seventy-five percent of graduates from junior schools will enter high schools and 14% of youths will receive higher education. By the end of 2005, people in Inner Mongolia will enjoy a good standard of living. Achieving these objectives will depend on the success of various industries.

A Base for Grassland Animal Husbandry

Inner Mongolia is the most important animal husbandry base in China. It has the greatest extent of natural pasture in China. Pastureland accounts for 74.6% of the total area of Inner Mongolia. Inner Mongolia raises the following portions of China's total livestock: one-tenth of herbivorous domestic animals, one-sixth of horses, one-eighth of sheep, two-fifths of camels and one-seventh of milch cows in China. It produces the following amounts of China's total: one-third of thin wools, one-third of goat hair, one-half of camel hair, one-tenth of mutton, one-seventh of horse meat, one-half of camel meat and one-tenth of "green milk" (milk raised without pollution). As a base for animal husbandry, Inner Mongolia is very close to markets in northeastern China and northern China, especially Beijing and Tianjin. With the application of science and technology in animal husbandry and the development of a commercial economy, the traditional animal husbandry of Inner Mongolia is undergoing a process of industrialization. The specialization and regionalization of livestock production bases and export bases are emerging with the rise of famous enterprises. This section examines these developments.

Natural Grasslands and Livestock Groups

Inner Mongolia has the main part of the temperate grasslands in China and the main meadow resources in northern China. The grasslands also form an ecological barrier. From east to west, the grasslands become dryer and dryer and change from forest grasslands to steppe and desert steppe[6] (Table

Table 15.4 Main Characters of the Inner Mongolian Grasslands

Character \ Type	Meadow-steppes	Steppes	Desert steppes
Representative formation	Stipa *baicalensis* steppe	Stipa *grandis* steppe	Stipa *klemenzii* steppe
Symbolic synusia	Mesic herbaceous	Xeric cespitose meadow-grass	Xeric half-shrub
Dominant soil	Chernozem	Castanozem	Brown soil
Degree of cover (%)	40–75	20–40	10–15
Area biomass (dry weight, kg/ha)	2,000±	800–1,000	200±
Livestock	Cow, horse, sheep	Sheep, cow, horse, goat	Sheep, camel, goat

Source: Li Bo et al., *Zhongguo beifang caodi*; Wu Jinghua, "Caoyuan shengtai jingji" (see note 6).

15.4). There are significant annual variations in rainfall in the Inner Mongolian grasslands. As a result, the growth of grass is very unstable. In general, grass yields can decline by 20–50% in the east and about 33% in the west during drought years.

The grasslands and the ecological system of animal husbandry are sensitive to the factor of climate.[7] Due to seasonal changes in climate and meadow, the livestock is generally strong in summer, fat in autumn, thin in winter and weak in spring. Milk yields peak in July and August. Achieving ecological security is vital for the sustainable development of animal husbandry in Inner Mongolia.

The Economy of Animal Husbandry

Animal husbandry is the economic foundation of Inner Mongolia. In 2000, Inner Mongolia produced 1.434 million tonnes of meat, 0.83 million tonnes of fresh milk, 65,000 tonnes of wool, 3,815 tonnes of goat hair and 73 million head of livestock, respectively. The production value of animal husbandry was RMB11.24 billion, accounting for 37.8% of the total production value of agriculture.

Since 1978, livestock numbers in the grazing area and agriculture-grazing area have increased by 80%, the output of meat increased 5 times and the output of fresh milk 7.3 times. A number of livestock bases have been set up. Thirty counties have over a million head of livestock each, accounting for 60% of all of the livestock in Inner Mongolia. The following numbers of counties each produces the following quantities of products: 33 counties each producing over 3,000 tonnes of mutton, 21 counties over 3,000 tonnes of beef, about 19 counties over 10,000 tonnes of fresh milk, 27 counties more than 1,000 tonnes of wool and 25 counties each producing over 50 tonnes of cashmere. These counties accounted for 75%, 65%, 76%, 63% and 79% of the total output of various products in Inner Mongolia. With the development of the animal husbandry economy, grasslands increased by 3.46 million ha in 1999, 2 million ha more than the increase in the Eighth Five-year Plan period. The above developments indicate that traditional animal husbandry in Mongolia is becoming modernized.

Compared with other western provinces of China such as Xinjiang and Qinghai 青海, Inner Mongolia's advantage in animal husbandry is the region's proximity to the markets of northeastern China, Beijing and Tianjin. Fresh products can be sent to these markets in time and even to Southeast Asia and neighbouring countries. Compared with the eastern provinces of China, the green food of Inner Mongolia has an advantage and is favoured by urban customers.

The Industrialization of Animal Husbandry

With good resources of grasslands, a locational advantage and a market advantage, Inner Mongolia has established a number of companies and products such as the Ordos brand of cashmere clothing and the Yili brand of dairy products that are famous in China.

Since 1949, Inner Mongolia has been a national cashmere-spinning base and the region's woolen products are famous in China. Ordos Cashmere Ltd., the largest cashmere processing corporation in the world and the top brand in the cashmere spinning industry in China, was named the King of Cashmere Products in China by the 50th World Statistics Conference. In 2000, among 100 large and medium-sized companies in Inner Mongolia, Ordos Cashmere Ltd. ranked ninth in terms of total capital and seventh in terms of total output value. It ranked seventh in sales income for industrial products, third in revenue and second in profit. Wool and cashmere are two products in which Inner Mongolia has an advantage. Recently, the new cashmere brand Luwang is becoming famous. In 1993, the Shiqi Business Suit Ltd., which uses wool as its main material, ranked first among the nation's top 10 brands. This is called the Shiqi phenomenon in China. In 2000, Shiqi Business Suit Ltd. ranked ninth in profits among the top 100 large and medium-sized companies in Inner Mongolia.

Mongolians in the grassland have various kinds of traditional food including white food, red food, tea and flour. White food, also called milk foods (*chaganyide* 査幹伊德 in Mongolian), refers to the products made from the milk of cows, sheep, camels and horses. Mongolians regard white as a symbol of purity, luck and sublimity. They serve milk to guests to show their respect. Examples of milk foods include fresh milk, sour milk, fermented milk drink, milk tea, cream, cheese, butter, and so on. Taking advantage of the quantity and quality of Inner Mongolia's livestock products, Inner Mongolia Yili Industry Ltd., whose profit ranked first among companies in the same industry in China in 1999, introduced its Yili dairy product series and its brand in 2000 and was designated a key company by the government. In 2000, among 100 large and medium-sized companies in Inner Mongolia, Yili Industry Ltd. ranked twenty-sixth in terms of total capital, eighth in total industrial output, eighth in sales of industrial products, fifth in total revenue and fourth in total profit.[8] Red food, also called meat foods (*wulanyide* 烏蘭伊德 in Mongolian), refers to the meat products of cows, sheep, and so on. The demand for Yili's frozen products, especially swilling and boiled dumplings, exceeds supply showing a new development in Mongolia's red food culture. People recognize that making use of new technology in the production of livestock products and improving quality and profit under a multi-market brand strategy are very important. Some new companies such as Mengniu 蒙牛 and Caoyuan Xingfa are growing rapidly.

In 1998, some scholars, including Li Bo 李博 and Shi Peijun 史培軍, completed a report on the industrialization of animal husbandry in Inner Mongolia's farming-pastoral zone (*nongmu jiaocuodai* 農牧交錯帶).[9] This is a first step in the industrialization of animal husbandry in Inner Mongolia, an important project in the development of China's west.

The farming-pastoral zone of Inner Mongolia has great potential in animal husbandry and is an important area in Inner Mongolia.[10] Its development will stimulate the development of the region. Five aspects are considered in the regional distribution of industrialization in animal husbandry (Figure 15.2). First, 70% of the total population of this zone lives in poverty. Considering its high population density and low income per capita, eliminating poverty with the help of the industrialization of animal husbandry is a pressing matter. Second, the ecology of the farming-pastoral zone is fragile. Long-term dry cultivation has resulted in serious land degradation and low crop yields. The commercial return from farming is lower than that from animal husbandry. The industrialization of animal

Figure 15.2 Regional Distribution of Animal Husbandry Industry in Inner Mongolia

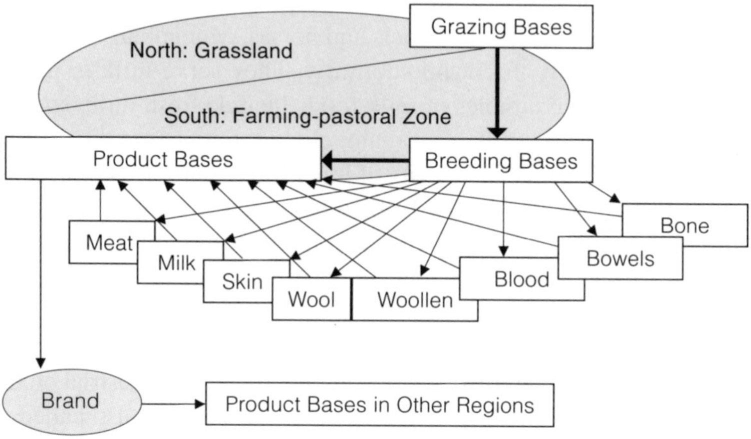

husbandry should be strengthened to improve the people's standard of living. Third, as there is more surplus labour and more fallow land and grassland in the farming-pastoral zone than in the agricultural area, several processing bases whose main raw materials are livestock products can be set up. Fourth, the industrialization of animal husbandry, with both the advantages of farming and pasturing, can not only help control the degradation of the environment but also propel the farming-pastoral zone towards rapid development. Fifth, such industrialization will turn a resource advantage into production and market advantages.

In essence, there are three levels to the strategy of animal husbandry projects in Inner Mongolia's farming-pastoral zone (Figure 15.3). First, on the fundamental level, ecological construction will safeguard the sustainable development of industrialization. Ecological construction should not only follow natural principles but also bring economic benefits. The increase of grass and livestock should be combined with improved quality and profit. Second, on the adjustment of land use and the construction of a forage grass base, more attention should be paid to achieving a high output from the land, limiting cultivation and the realization of sufficiency in the supply of basic foodstuffs in order to provide a stable material base for project implementation. Third, on the key issue of nurturing companies, a famous brand strategy should be implemented. Famous products should be combined with companies, companies with a production base and a base

Figure 15.3 Strategy and Measures of Animal Husbandry Project in the Farming-pastoral Zone of Inner Mongolia

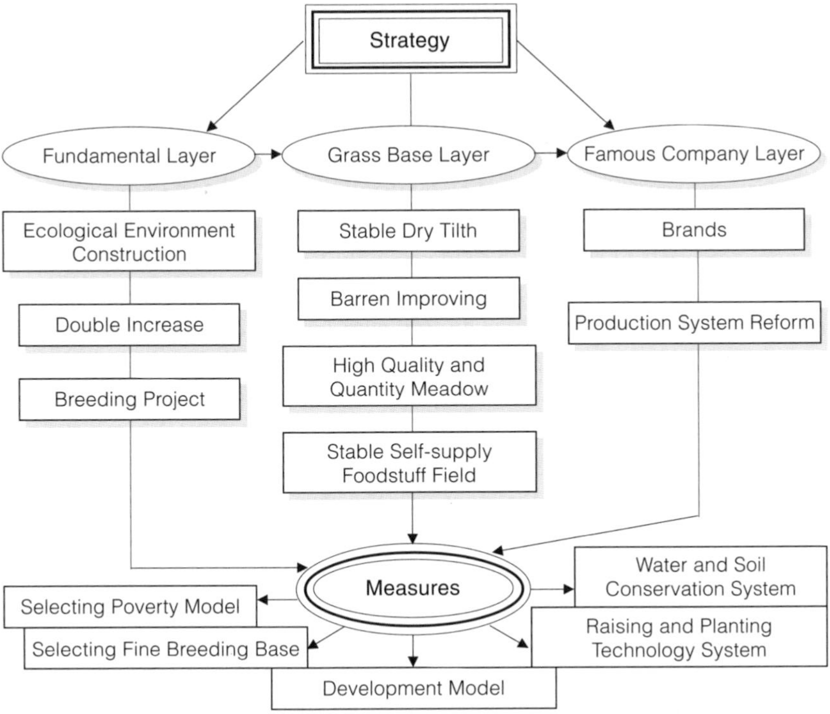

with producing families so as to formulate a trade-industry-agriculture chain. In this strategy, the key objective is to increase the value of livestock and agricultural products. The main measures of industrialization include the construction of model areas, the selection of grass and livestock, the regeneration of the environment, modern production technology, the construction of breeding bases, and so forth.

An Energy Resources Base

Inner Mongolia is an important base for energy resources in China as it has rich minerals such as coal, non-ferrous metals, rare-earth metals and non-metal resources. Its regional advantage of connecting east and west and its mainstay industries of coal, electric power, rare-earth metals, machinery and chemicals are also important.

Advantage of Mineral Resources

Of more than 140 kinds of mineral resources found in the world, 128 have been found in Inner Mongolia. Of 83 kinds with proven reserves, the region's national rankings are as follows: 42 kinds are among the top 10, 22 kinds are among top 3 and 7 kinds are ranked first. Inner Mongolia's coal lies in a concentration strip of mines in northern China and its reserves are extremely rich, accounting for one-quarter of the national total of proven reserves, the second largest in the country. The main part of China's world-class oil and gas field is situated in the Ordos Basin of Inner Mongolia. The region's reserves of rare-earth oxide account for 90% of the country's total and rank first in both the country and the world. The potential value of minerals in Inner Mongolia, excluding petroleum and natural gas, is RMB 13,000 billion, ranking the region third in the country.[11] A shortage of water in the region complicates the exploitation of minerals and the construction of the electric power and raw materials industries. Despite this, conditions for exploitation are relatively good. The main energy resources and minerals are concentrated in or near the main area of agriculture. Many metal minerals are located near coal deposits and the ladder-like exploitation of the Yellow River 黃河 means that it is possible to take advantage of both power and water. All of these factors are favourable for the construction of a resource industry in Inner Mongolia.

Inner Mongolia can be divided into eight areas for minerals:[12] the Ordos resource area (refined coal, Glauber's salt and alkali resources); the resource area along the railway between Baotou and Bayan Obo 白雲鄂博 (iron, rare metals and rare-earth resources); the Hailar 海拉爾 resource area (coal and non-ferrous metal resources); the Tongliao resource area (silicon sand and non-ferrous metals); the Chifeng resource area (non-ferrous metals, precious metals and coal resources); the Xilin Gol-Jining and Erenhot resource area (coal, petroleum, natural alkalis and fluor resources); the Langshan 狼山-Chaertaishan 查爾泰山 resource area (non-ferrous metal resources); and the Wuhai resource area (salt and limestone resources).

Advantage of Industries

The advantages possessed by local industries indicate that such industries should take a leading place in the national or regional economy, and that they should have a greater development potential and be extremely competitive. Considering the comparative advantages of the region from a macro viewpoint, the energy resources industry and other industries in Inner

Mongolia are leading industries in the country and are forces driving the regional economy.[13]

In 2000, among Inner Mongolia's top 100 large or medium-sized enterprises in terms of total assets, 25% were in the electricity power industry, 11% in coal, oil and gas, 7% in steel, aluminum and rare earth, 7% in the chemical industry, 5% in machinery production.[14] In total, 55% were from these industries. Of the top 100 large or medium-sized enterprises in gross output value, 14% were in the electricity power industry, 21% in coal, oil and gas, 6% in steel, aluminum and rare earth, 18% in the chemical industry and 5% in machinery production. In total, 64% were from these industries. Among the top 100 large or medium-sized enterprises in terms of profit, the electrical power industry occupied 10%, coal, oil and gas 9%, steel, aluminum and rare earth 9%, the chemical industry 17% and machinery production 2%. In total, 47% were from these industries.

Some industrial products of Inner Mongolia that occupy a leading place in the country include: steel, rolled steel and timber (first place), raw coal, pig iron and raw salt (second place), electricity generation (third place), edible vegetable oil and beer (fourth place), as well as flat glass and sugar (fifth place).[15] All of this shows that in energy resources, Inner Mongolia has a great advantage in both the western region and in the country.

In 2001, Inner Mongolia produced 18.63 million tonnes of raw coal, 7.08 million tonnes of washing coal, 850 thousand tonnes of crude oil, 0.7 billion m^3 of natural gas, 4.76 million tonnes of pig iron, 4.54 million tonnes of steel and 3.88 million tonnes of finished steel. The industry of energy resources in Inner Mongolia builds upon the resource advantage, market-orientation and transformation of coal to electric power and coal to oil and lustration coal. The transformation of coal and charcoal to power will be accelerated and the transfer of coal and electric power from the west to the east will be carried out. At the end of the Tenth Five-year Plan, electric power generation (*dianli zhuangji* 電力裝機) will reach a capacity of 13 million kw. Meanwhile, there is a reserve of wind energy of about 0.31 billion kw, accounting for one-fifth of the total in the country. Inner Mongolia lies in the pivotal belt of the electric networks of northeastern, northern and northwestern China, where there are wide grasslands, smooth terrain and good conditions for geological engineering. All of this is convenient for the construction of large-sized power plants and electric networks to deliver electricity to the "Three Northern Regions."

The emphasis of the metallurgy industry is for the Baotou Steel Plant to eliminate the backward technology of open-hearth steel (*ping liangang*

平煉鋼) to save energy. The non-ferrous metals industry needs to strengthen mineral exploration, develop large-scale smelting and in-depth processing, and implement intensive management. The machinery industry should make use of the advantages of the weapons industry, improve the quality of its products and try to construct a national production base for heavy automobiles in Baotou. The chemical industry should introduce advanced technology, produce products with a high value-added and high-tech content, and actively develop the petroleum and coal chemical industries based on the consolidation and expansion of the salt-alkali chemical industry. The refined chemical industry using castor, mealie and bitter ginseng as raw materials should be developed and expanded with advanced technology.

The development of a high-tech industry and the ability of science and technology to keep coming up with new innovations are not only goals in the adjustment and optimization of the current industrial structure, but also directions in which the industrial economy should be developed in the future. During the course of the Tenth Five-year Plan, high-tech industries such as rare earth, bio-tech and new materials should be main focus. The rare earth industry should emphasize refining and in-depth processing, optimize advanced products, energetically develop middle-range products, and extensively study lower products to accelerate the application and marketing of rare earth products. Through the efforts of scientific researchers, Inner Mongolia will become the biggest base in the country for the scientific research, production and export of rare earth products.

The Second-largest Coal Reserves in China

Resources of coal and charcoal in Inner Mongolia are abundant and the potential is tremendous. At the end of 1998, proven reserves of coal and charcoal were about 225.6 billion tonnes and accounted for 22% of the country's total. Thus far, 318 coalfields have been found, covering an area of 120,000 km^2. Four coalmines in Inner Mongolia (the Yimin River 伊敏河, Hulin River, Yuanbao Hill 元寶山 and Junggar 準噶爾) are among the five largest strip coalmines in China. About 97% of the coal for power is concentrated in the central and western parts of the region. Lignite is mainly found in the east. The energy resources industry in Inner Mongolia has tremendous potential to develop. In the long term, three lignite bases (the Yimin River, Hulin River, Yuanbao Hill) in the eastern part of Inner Mongolia can transmit electric power to three provinces in the northeast. Dalad 達拉特, Togtoh 托克托, Fengzhen 豐鎮, Haibowan 海渤灣 and Junggar in the central and western parts of Inner Mongolia can transmit electric power to Beijing and Tianjin. Copper, lead, zinc, tungsten, stannum, and so on, are also plentiful in Inner Mongolia. The large reserves, concentrated distribution and the presence of over a dozen kinds of associated elements, such as aurum, argentine, molybdenum, sulphur, and so forth, make integrated exploitation viable. The abundant coal resources provide a plentiful amount of energy for the smelting of non-ferrous metals. Inner Mongolia's energy resources industry offers clear advantages, particularly in the areas of coal, charcoal and electric power, and the heavy chemical industry, with emphasis on non-ferrous metals, rare earth and coal.

The large coalfield called the Black Golden Triangle (*Wujin Sanjiao* 烏金三角) is situated in the contiguous areas of Shanxi, Shaanxi and Inner Mongolia. It has an area of about 69,000 km^2 and spans 16 counties. There is tremendous potential for the coal and electric power industries to be developed in this area. Coal has been proven to be present in area of about 30,000 km^2 and the reserves of coal are estimated to be about 250.5 billion tonnes, accounting for 26.3% of China's total. The coal in this area is of generally high quality being low in ash (<10%), phosphorus (0.03–0.06%), and sulphur (<0.7%) and a middle-to-high heat-generating capacity (6,000–7,000 kcal/kg). Most coal beds are suitable for opencast mining on a large scale, so that the cost of construction and production is low. This area lies along the Yellow River and much water and land is available for the construction of power stations.

Due to the advantages mentioned above, a few giant power stations or a series of power stations can be built along both banks of the Yellow River in the contiguous areas of Shanxi, Shaanxi and Inner Mongolia to produce five or six times more electric power than in Shanxi, to be transited to the east. The biggest environmental problem in the construction of an energy resource base is water and soil erosion. The area has the most severe water and soil erosion in the country and both processes, as well as wind erosion, will certainly be accelerated by operating opencast mining on a large scale. Thus, the task of land recovery and protection is going to be a very challenging one.

The greatest problem in the development of Inner Mongolia's energy resources is the shortage of water and poor transportation. Most parts of Inner Mongolia are located in semi-arid areas and the distribution of water resources is uneven. The Yellow River passes through this area and brings much water for development, but its flow is unstable. In the last decade, incidences in which the Yellow River has dried up have increased. This is a serious threat to the water supply required to develop energy resources. Water consumption is increasing in industry, agriculture and household use, particularly as the population increases. The supply of a sufficient amount of water for all purposes cannot be guaranteed. In order to solve the problem, the water conservancy project of Wanjiazhai 萬家寨 is being built along the Yellow River. It will be the third biggest water conservancy project in the country, after the Sanxia 三峽 Reservoir in the Yangzi River 長江 and the Xiaolangdi 小浪底 Reservoir in the Yellow River.

There is a big difference in the spatial distribution of energy resources in China between the north and the south and between the west and the east. The difference becomes greater due to disparities in regional economic development. Coal is transported from the north to the south and from the west to the east. The coal is transported mainly by train. But inadequate railway capacity is affecting the development of the coalfields. Improvements in this area are currently being made. In the meantime, electric power and coal chemical industry bases will be built to transform raw coal into electricity to be transmitted to other areas through electric networks, or into coal gas to be transmitted through pipelines. In this way, the serious problem of transportation will be solved.

Inner Mongolia has adopted a strategy of resource transformation by aiming to make use of rich resources, such as timber, iron and coal. The strategy of resource transformation is to attract talent, technology and capital from within and outside the country to increase current levels of productivity and to turn the region's resource advantage into a market advantage. The essence of transforming a closed economy to an open one depends on several factors. First, the construction of a national base of energy resources, especially the establishment of large coal mines such as Dongsheng 東勝 and Junggar, will power the development of local industries in Inner Mongolia. Second, the scarcity of capital is a critical factor hindering resource transformation. Resource exploitation through joint ventures, or financing by loans and the stock market, may promote transformation. Third, Inner Mongolia should formulate favourable policies to attract capital, technology and talents, and establish enterprises serving both domestic and international markets.[16]

Border Trade

The Inner Mongolia Autonomous Region shares a 3,193 km border with Mongolia and a 1,010 km border with Russia. Manzhouli and Erenhot, two important border towns of the Eurasia land bridge, are located in Inner Mongolia. Besides, Inner Mongolia is located within the Bohai Bay economic circle, the Northeast Asia economic circle and the Central Asia economic circle. Thus, it is an important point of connection, both domestically and internationally, which is significant for the opening up and development of its economy. Preferential policies to minority areas can also be used to stimulate the opening up and internationalization of Inner Mongolia's economy.

Border Towns and Trade

The open belt along the border (*yanbian kaifangdai* 沿邊開放帶) of Inner Mongolia refers to 18 banners and cities and to the Hulun Buir League, which border on Mongolia and Russia. The basic tasks relating to the open belt are as follows: the frontier open towns (*bianjing kaifang kouan* 邊境開放口岸) are to act as "windows" and "channels" to the outside world; the transportation system is to function as a link to inland areas; development along the railway and the resource development zone are to be the engines powering the regional economy; trade with Mongolia, Russia, other CIS (Commonwealth of Independent States) countries and Eastern European countries is to be facilitated; resource exploitation and the economic development of the open belt is to be speeded up and, finally, the full opening up of Inner Mongolia is to be promoted.

Inner Mongolia has three first-class trading towns along its border with Russia, namely, Manzhouli, Heishantou 黑山頭 and Shiwei 室韋, as well as two second-class trading towns, Hulieyetu 胡列也吐 and Erka 二卡. Six leagues and 15 banners (or cities) in Inner Mongolia border on 6 provinces and 26 counties of Mongolia. Besides Erenhot, three other frontier trading towns have recently been opened: Arihashate 阿日哈沙特 of the Xin Barag Right 新巴爾虎右 banner, Zhuengadabuqi 珠恩嘎達布其 of the Eastern Ujimqin 東烏珠穆沁 banner, Ganqimaodao 甘其毛道 of the Central Urad 烏拉特 banner. There are four other second-class trading towns: Ceke 策克 of the Ejin 額濟納 banner of the Alxa League, Ebuduge 額布都格 of the Xin Barag Left 新巴爾虎左 banner of the Hulun Buir League, Arxan 阿爾山 of the Hinggan League, Mandula 滿都拉 of the Ulan Qab League. Together, the above towns make up a system of border trading towns to open Inner Mongolia up to the outside world. In the 50-year history of the Autonomous Region, the number of trading towns has increased from 1 to 18.[17] In 1983, border trade between China and Russia was restored. The Russian border trade merchants mainly came from Siberia. In 1983, the export and import trade with Russia (the Soviet Union) amounted to only 2.73 million Swiss francs. When Inner Mongolia's border trade with Mongolia began in 1985, the value of this barter trade amounted to only 0.63 million Swiss francs.

In Inner Mongolia's border trade, the export goods are mainly meat, agricultural and animal husbandry products, textiles, clothing, home appliances, small machines and tools used in animal husbandry, building materials and daily consumer goods. The imported goods mainly consist of chemical fertilizers, lumber, steel products, cement, industrial chemicals, combines, passenger vehicles and trucks. Inner Mongolia also has extensive economic and technological links with nearby countries on a trade and barter basis. It exports labour services, has contracted to carry out many overseas projects, and has set up joint ventures and solely owned enterprises overseas. The region sends many kinds of technical and management personnel to work on co-operative projects such as planting vegetables and processing food to serve the needs of construction at home, earn foreign exchange, increase the country's international influence, and achieve social and economic benefits. Since the founding of the Autonomous Region, the annual volume of freight transportation and the number of people crossing through border towns have increased 6.4 times and 131 times, respectively.

The frontier areas of Inner Mongolia are flat and wide, and transportation is easy. Mongolians in both China and Mongolia belong to the same ethnic group and share the same language and culture. This makes for a frontier environment that is conducive to trade and other economic activities. Since 1994, the annual value of China's border trade has been over US$10 billion. This is of enormous benefit to economic development and to the construction of border defense in the frontier areas. With China's entry into the WTO (World Trade Organization), border trade will become a regular trade category.[18] Inner Mongolia will make full use of Russia's advantages in energy, raw materials and technology, to reform its old enterprises, wisely use the resources of agriculture and animal husbandry to earn foreign exchange and, simultaneously, develop co-operative economic and technological links. Besides border trade, Inner Mongolia can also vigorously develop cross-border tourism. Measures can be taken to strengthen the infrastructure for tourism, increase the production of tourist goods, and increase the number of tourist routes and programmes.

Manzhouli

The city of Manzhouli is located west of Inner Mongolia's Hulun Buir prairie. It is near the Russian border, less than 10 km from Russia's Zabaykalsk. Manzhouli is also close to northeastern China's heavy industry base and to grain-producing provinces. Domestically, it links with the Beijing-Tianjin area of northern China. Internationally, it faces Siberia, one of the richest areas of Russia, and through Siberia is linked with various CIS countries and with Europe. It is on the most important and convenient land route between Europe and Asia. Compared with other Asian and Pacific harbours, there are obvious advantages in distance, time and cost in freight transportation. Construction of the town of Manzhouli began in 1903, and Manzhouli was officially opened in 1907 as a trading town. It has more than 90 years' history as a national first-class trading town.[19]

The city of Manzhouli has both rail and road networks. The railway has a wide track that can connect with the Russian railway system. Imported cargos change trains in the Manzhouli station while exported cargoes change trains in the railway town of Zabaykalsk. Manzhouli is the biggest railway city in China with an annual handling capacity of over 5 million tonnes. There are two aspects to its cargo services. The first is to undertake international transportation for imports and exports. The Manzhouli Foreign Shipment Company is the only company to undertake international containerized land transportation in China. The second is domestic freight transportation. In 1989, the State Council approved the establishment of a road network for Manzhouli, to connect with Russia. The Hou Baikal Sike Company, with annual handling capacity over 200,000 tonnes, was given the licence to handle these operations. The poor backward frontier town of Manzhouli has become a prosperous "window of Asia."

In 2001, the volume of Manzhouli's import and export trade reached 7.3 million tonnes. The total value of this trade was US$1.939 billion, of which imports constituted US$1.735 billion and exports US$0.204 billion.[20] Manzhouli's fiscal revenues increased from RMB35 million in 1991 to RMB240 million in 2001. Manzhouli started to attract direct capital investments in 1995, receiving RMB45 million that year. In 2001, the figure was RMB47 million. In February 1990, Manzhouli introduced one-day tours to Russia and three-day tours to Chita 赤塔. An additional 17,000 tourists were attracted to the area by the end of 1991. In 2001, border tourism attracted over 300,000 tourists, 388% times the number in 1992. The income from tourism reached US$0.162 billion.

Since 1988, Manzhouli has hosted many import-export trade fairs. Overseas merchants come from Russia and other CIS countries, the U.S., France, Japan, Korea and Australia. Merchants also come from over 30 provinces, autonomous regions, municipalities and special economic zones of China. The goods that are imported include not only steel products, cement, chemical fertilizers and timber, but also discarded tanks, airplanes, internal combustion engines, helicopters, electrolytic copper, engines and heavy transport machines. There are also some joint venture projects involving vegetables plantations, food processing plants, department stores, electronic computer assembly factories, automobile assembly factories and the construction of transport facilities. Led by border trade, Manzhouli has become a major inland city of China.

Erenhot

Erenhot lies in the Xilin Gol area of Inner Mongolia, only 9 km from Dzamiïn Üüd in Mongolia. Erenhot's location is very important because it is the only railway city that opens to Mongolia. It is 830 km to Beijing and 860 km to Ulaan Baatar. The Jining-Erenhot railway line is 1,141 km shorter than the Binzhou 濱州 line and is the shortcut to Ulaan Baatar, Moscow and other countries in Eastern Europe. The Jining-Erenhot line is linked with Tianjin harbour through the Beijing-Baotou line and Beijing-Shandong 山東 line and is the best link between Europe and Asia. The Erenhot railway town was established initially in 1956. The State Council approved the development of a barter trade with Mongolia in 1986 and with Russia in 1991. As an open border city, Erenhot has been empowered to develop border trade. Because Mongolia has a large stock of waste metals, leather and timber, and is eager to exchange them for daily consumer goods, the border trade has become very active. Since 1995, the mode of Inner Mongolia's border trade has changed from barter to cash.

During the period of the Ninth Five-year Plan, Erenhot has expanded imports and exports, and improved its ability to speed up economic development. The total value of Erenhot's imports and exports reached US$403.84 million in 2001, 2.8 times more than that in 1995.[21] Imports were US$331.85 million, while exports reached US$72.09 million. The total volume of imports and exports in 2001 was 2.12 million tonnes, 3.2 times more than in 1995. International passengers going through Erenhot numbered 580,000. In recent years, Erenhot's imports have mainly consisted of copper powder, timber, crude oil and steel, some of them from Russia via Mongolia. The Mongolian demand for textiles, daily consumer goods and food has also greatly increased.

To facilitate border trade, Erenhot has invested RMB4.3 million to improve its railway transportation facilities and RMB20 million to improve the highway transportation as well as urban business and residential conditions and dining services.

Land Degradation and Ecological Construction

The key regions in the National Planning for Ecological Environment Construction include the upper and middle reaches of the Yellow River, and the sand-blown areas and grasslands that cover most of Inner Mongolia.[22] In the development of western China, the construction of the ecological environment is one of three key tasks.[23] On the one hand, Inner Mongolia is a special area where land degradation is the most serious in China. Its ecological security and the construction of an ecologically sound environment have become key issues for sustainable regional development. This is particularly the case with the development in Inner Mongolia of a large national base for the energy and chemical industries, the expansion of pasturelands, the growth of agriculture and of the population.[24]

Land Degradation

In the loess hill area of Inner Mongolia, the most serious water and soil erosion area in China,[25] the soil erosion modules reach 8,000–10,000 $t/km^2 \cdot a$ (per annum). In the Maowusu 毛烏素 sand dune and sandy loess area, the most serious desertification area, the soil erosion modulus reaches 7,000–9,000 $t/km^2 \cdot a$. The grass in the farming-pastoral zone in Inner Mongolia is seriously degraded and the salination of the Hetao Plain is the most serious in China. The area north of the Dahinggan Mountain in Inner Mongolia is the most serious area of ice erosion in eastern China; the average erosion modulus is about 500 $t/km^2 \cdot a$. Within Inner Mongolia, 40% of the land is experiencing water and soil erosion, and 30% desertification. In addition, 60% of the grasslands are seriously degraded.

Previously stationary sand dunes have begun to move, mainly the Maowusu, Kubuqi 庫布齊, Hunshandake 渾善達克, Keerqin 科爾沁 and Hulun Buir dunes. The retreating of ancient sand, including underlying ancient dunes and quicksand that are emerging to the surface, is occurring mainly in the area north of the Yin Mountain. The sand comes mainly from the sandy loess area north of the Loess Plateau. The dunes that are moving forward to cover the surrounding land are mainly from the desert in the west or near all kinds of quicksand. A wind erosion study was conducted of an area of 743,600 km^2, accounting for 64.6% of the total area in Inner Mongolia. It concluded that wind desertification is serious. It also discovered that area of salinized land is about 35,000 km^2, located mainly in plains or billabongs where there is much evaporation, especially in irrigated areas. Salination is most serious in the Hetao Plain where 70–80% of the land is affected. It is also serious in the Tumd Plain 土默特平原 and the West Liaohe Plain.

In Inner Mongolia, there is widespread degradation of the grasslands. There is a lot of grasslands in the agricultural and pasturing areas. The area of degradation adds up to 21 million ha and accounts for 39.7% of the region's usable grasslands. The area of degraded pastureland is 12.69 million ha (Table 15.5).

Land degradation results from both the activities of nature and man. There are three main natural factors. First is the physiognomy of the earth and its physical instability. Soil brought by the wind and broad loess causes much instability of materials on the earth's surface. Salt and alkaline soils are ubiquitous. Second is various external forces and unstable precipitation. Inner Mongolia is in a transitional belt from the eastern monsoon area to the dry area of the northwest. There are regional differences in external forces, such as wind erosion in the northwest, water erosion in the southeast and ice erosion in the north. Third is the climate change. Records of precipitation in the north show a dry trend in the whole region, which is mainly caused by the degradation of the grasslands.[26] Warming not only accelerates evaporation from the soil but also changes the atmosphere, affecting the distribution of precipitation in some areas. The regional climate becomes drier which accelerates the degradation of the grasslands, wind

Table 15.5 Degradation of Pastures in the Inner Mongolian Grasslands

Pasture area	Degradation		Share with more serious degradation (%)
	Area (km^2)	Percentage of land (%)	
Hulun Buir	15,161	17.86	41.34
East of Xilin Gol	26,728	32.53	46.16
West of Xilin Gol	33,555	41.46	57.06
Ulan Qab	31,955	34.07	32.53
Ordos	23,316	35.94	62.00

Source: Zhao Ji, *Zhongguo dili* 中國地理 (Geography of China) (Beijing: Kexue chubanshe, 1992).

erosion and desertification.[27] Therefore, in windy areas, desertification tends to occur in areas where sand is brought by the wind and where the area is full of sandy soil. In wet areas, water and soil degradation tends to occur on slopes, especially on hills covered by loess. A water transition belt is often associated with an unstable slope belt and a belt of unstable soil. Therefore, the farming-pastoral zone at the end of the monsoon area is the most sensitive to land degradation.

There are three main human factors. First, agriculture has changed the natural land cover and the reflection of sunlight from the earth's surface. Second, irrational land use such as unwise reclamation, overgrazing, deforestation and illegal harvesting of medicinal plants will destroy the vegetation, reduce the productivity of the land and weaken the ability of the surface to resist erosion. Third, poverty and population pressure is a cause of land degradation. Comparatively speaking, Inner Mongolia is a poor area of China. The Huhuanyong Line, the population boundary between the west and the east, runs through Inner Mongolia's farming-pastoral zone. It indicates that population density is lower in the west and higher in the east. The line also shows the influence and pressure of population on land. Compared with the agricultural and pastoral zones, reclamation in the farming-pastoral zone is intensive.

Sustainable Development of the Grasslands and the Farming-pastoral Zone

The farming-pastoral zone in northern China is a transitional belt between the agricultural and pasturing area. In general, it is a semi-arid area with an annual precipitation of 250–500 mm. The zone runs through provinces but the main part of it is in Inner Mongolia.

The farming-pastoral zone is the area with the most unstable environment and land use in China. The planting of cereal crops accelerated the degradation of the land. This zone is one of the most degraded areas in the world, comparable to the tropical grasslands of the Sahara in Africa. The land in the zone is considered to be marginal and it is not easily managed. Although there is a large amount of land per capita and the development of the grasslands holds a certain potential for grain production, it is difficult to arrange the land-use structure and ensure sustainable development at all levels. The key problem of land degradation in the zone is the relationship between variations in precipitation, farming area and livestock capacity. Different combinations of natural and human factors produce different results. Abundant precipitation, a limited farming area and low livestock capacity can cause the land to recover. By contrast, low levels of precipitation, a large farming area and high livestock capacity will result in degradation.

Zhang Xinshi 張新時 has argued that ecology-production paradigms for both economic development and ecological security should be set up according to physical ecological systems. Examples are the three circles paradigm (*sanquan moshi* 三圈模式) of the Maowusu dune in the Ordos Plateau of Inner Mongolia and mountain-basin paradigm (*shanpen moshi* 山盆模式) in Xinjiang. The choice of an ecology-production paradigm (*shengtai-shengchan moshi* 生態生產模式) for a region requires extensive field observations. It is also necessary to consider the recovery and rebuilding of the ecological system to its natural status, the optimal proportion of agriculture, forestry and pasturing, the critical degree of soil erosion and vegetation coverage, and the adjustment of land use to achieve not only economic objectives, but also ecological security.

In the broad western region, large areas of natural grasslands on plateaus and mountains have been reclaimed for farming. As a result, the remaining natural meadow is located in areas with precipitation of less than 300 mm or in areas with an altitude above 3,000 m. In fact, the meadows in deserts and desert steppe areas are not suitable for grazing. The development of large areas of ecologically sensitive land has greatly harmed the region's environment. It has been argued that current spatial land-use patterns in every ecologically sensitive area should be adjusted. The area of production should be reduced while the protected area should be increased. The Chinese government has recently advocated the planting of trees and grass to replace farms in mountainous areas with little rainfall, the restoration of swamps and the planting of grass in natural meadows and the prohibition of grazing in those areas. Recently, an efficient and secure land-use paradigm of a small production area and large protected area (*xiaomianji gao shengchan, damianji gao shengtai* 小面積搞生產，大面積搞生態) has been implemented and has met with success.[28] For example, in lower valleys or basins with low water tables in the Xilin Gol grasslands of Inner Mongolia, the grass output in a small forage grass base is about a hundred times the output of a big natural meadow on a high plain or an undulating high plain.

Ecological Barriers in Northeast and North China

Relationship between wind erosion, desertification in Inner Mongolia and

Sandy weather in north and northeast China. In Inner Mongolia, there are eight deserts and dunes, with a total area of about 200,000 km^2. In the spring and winter, the northwest wind prevails and vegetation is scant. Wind erosion and desertification becomes worse and sandstorms often occur. The sand in the air drifts from west to east, causing sandstorms in northern and northeastern China.[29] Since the slopes of the Dahinggan and Yin Mountains in Inner Mongolia face windward, sand can be brought over the mountain by wind. Wind erosion and desertification become even worse when there is little vegetation cover.

Relationship between water and soil erosion in western China and water resource security in eastern China. Due to China's topography, where altitudes are high in the west and low in the east, most of the country's rivers flow from west to east. For example, the Yangzi and Yellow Rivers originate in the Tibetan Plateau, and the Heilongjiang, Liaohe, Luanhe, Haihe and Zhujiang 珠江 originate in plateaus or mountains in western China. Therefore, western China is an important area for water resources. The Dahinggan, Yin and Helan Mountains, and the hills in Inner Mongolia, are the source of the Heilongjiang, the Nenjiang and the Liaohe in the northeast and the Luanhe, the Yongdinghe 永定河 and the upper and middle reaches of the Yellow River in the north. The areas of forest and grass bear directly on water and soil erosion and flooding. Water and soil erosion near the west can cause silting in river channels and lakes in the east, as well as floods.

The ecological barrier of eastern China. Except for Alxa, all areas in Inner Mongolia belong to the near west.[30] The region, also called the starvation land belt, poverty belt and ecological crisis belt, is the most severely degraded belt of land in China. Slopes, surface soils, precipitation and land use are all unstable. There are many nationalities in the area engaged in a mixture of agriculture and animal husbandry. The key to preventing land degradation, eliminating disasters, increasing income and developing in a sustainable manner is to protect and increase the vegetation cover. At the edge of the region, mountains join the eastern region. Air and water flows from the west bring wind, sand and floods to the east. This threatens ecological security and affects sustainable development. The reconstruction of the region's ecology can lead to the formation of a green shield to maintain water sources and clean air, control the eastward movement of wind and sand, reduce water and soil erosion and relieve flooding.

In the development of western China, the reconstruction of the region's ecology is not only a basic demand for ecological security in the region itself but also an important guarantee of the environmental security of eastern

China. The development of the east can stimulate the development of the near west. According to an estimate by Chen Zhongxin 陳仲新 and Zhang Xinshi, the total ecological value of China was RMB7,783 billion in 1994.[31] Of the top 10 provinces, 7 provinces were in the west. Inner Mongolia ranked third, with a total ecological value of RMB773 billion. Thus, the ecological construction is an important part of China's socioeconomic system. Economic tools of ecological value should be used to harmonize the relationship between human and nature.

Reconstructing the region's ecology. The reconstruction of Inner Mongolia's ecology is of the greatest priority. First of all, the deterioration of the environment must be controlled. Comprehensive planning should be conducted. Key areas of focus should include the areas of water and soil erosion in the upper and middle reaches of the Yellow River, the Inner Mongolia sand source regions around Beijing and Tianjin, the Dahinggan Mountain natural forest regions, the Hulun Buir and Xilin Gol grasslands and natural closed regions in Alxa. The eight key projects include the construction and protection of the ecological system of the grasslands, protection of natural forest resources, planting forests and grass to replace farming, sand barriers, focusing ecological reconstruction on key counties, constructing a green corridor and water and soil conservation. The construction of natural sanctuaries should be strengthened. The rehabilitation of 6.67 million ha of land suffering from desertification is planned. All kinds of ecological construction policies should be improved and implemented gradually. People should be mobilized to plant forests and grass. In the areas where forests and grass will replace farming, the people should be assured that these measures will improve their standard of living. Technology should be used widely to support ecological construction. Various measures should be adjusted to fit local conditions. Finally, the protection of the environment should be enforced by law.

Conclusion

Based on Inner Mongolia's development history, resources, environment and socioeconomic characteristics, the following three conclusions can be drawn:

First, Inner Mongolia is an important link between the east and the west. Inner Mongolia borders on two foreign countries, stretches over the "Three Northern Regions" and adjoins eight provinces.

Second, Inner Mongolia has a resource advantage in animal husbandry and energy production. The region is the most important base for animal husbandry in China and is also close to eastern China. With advances in science and technology and the development of the commercial economy, the traditional animal husbandry of Inner Mongolia has been modernized. Inner Mongolia is gradually becoming an industrial base for livestock products and an export base, led by famous enterprises in China. The Animal Husbandry Industrialization Project and the trade-industry-agriculture integration model in the farming-pastoral zone of Inner Mongolia will stimulate the overall development of the region. Inner Mongolia is an important base for energy resources in China. Its mainstay industries include coal, electric power, rare-earth metals, machinery and chemical industries. In the Tenth Five-year Plan, the emphasis for Inner Mongolia will be on the adjustment of the region's economic structure, especially on strengthening agriculture and animal husbandry. The service industry, information industry, urbanization and the national economy will also be advanced.

Third, land degradation in Inner Mongolia is among the most serious in the country. Its farming-pastoral zone has the most unstable environment and land use in China. Key issues include the study and forecasting of environmental changes and controlling reclamation and livestock under a feasible agricultural policy. It is time to develop a regional ecology-production paradigm to adjust land-use patterns. The desert and dunes of Inner Mongolia are the cause of sandstorms. The Dahinggan, Yin and Helan Mountains and hills in Inner Mongolia are the sources of the rivers that flow to northern and northeastern China. The condition of the forest and grass in the area has a direct bearing on water and soil erosion and flooding. The wetlands and grasslands on the plateaus urgently need to be protected and the vegetation coverage of mountains and hills needs to be increased to ensure supplies of freshwater and a secure environment for eastern China. According to the Tenth Five-year Plan of Inner Mongolia, the reconstruction of the region's ecology is the key to the development of the west. The worsening trend of environmental destruction must be brought under control. This is crucial if the objectives of the Tenth Five-year Plan of Inner Mongolia are to be achieved.

Notes

1. Minzhengbu 民政部, Zhongguo renmin jiefangjun zongcanmoubu cehuiju 中

國人民解放軍總參謀部測繪局, *Zhonghua Renmin Gongheguo zhengqu biaozhun diming tuji* 中華人民共和國政區標準地名圖集 (Atlas of Standard Administrative Units in China) (Beijing: Xingqiu chubanshe 星球出版社, 2000).

2. Neimenggu zizhiqu tongjiju 內蒙古自治區統計局, *Neimenggu tongji nianjian 2001* 內蒙古統計年鑑2001 (Inner Mongolia Statistical Yearbook 2001) (Beijing: Zhongguo tongji chubanshe 中國統計出版社, 2001).
3. Yang Wuyang 楊吾揚 and Liang Jinshe 梁進社, "Zhongguo de shida jingjiqu tantao" 中國的十大經濟區探討 (Discussion of the Ten Major Economic Regions in China), *Jingji dili* 經濟地理 (Economic Geography), Vol. 12, No. 3 (1992), pp. 14–20.
4. Wang Jing'ai 王靜愛, "Zhongguo renkou fenbu yu kechixu fazhan moshi xuanze" 中國人口分佈與可持續發展模式選擇 (China's Population Distribution and Choice of Sustainable Development Pattern), *Beijing shifan daxue xuebao (shehui kexue ban)* 北京師範大學學報 (社會科學版) (Journal of Beijing Normal University (Social Science Edition)), No. 2 (1998), pp. 72–80.
5. Neimenggu zizhiqu tongjiju, *Huihuang de Neimenggu 1947–1999* 輝煌的內蒙古1947–1999 (Brilliant Inner Mongolia 1947–1999) (Beijing: Zhongguo tongji chubanshe, 1999).
6. Li Bo 李博, *Zhongguo beifang caodi xumuye dongtai jiance yanjiu (yi)* 中國北方草地畜牧業動態監測研究 (一) (Dynamic Monitoring and Research of Grasslands Animal Husbandry in Northern China) (Beijing: Zhongguo nongye chubanshe 中國農業出版社, 1993); Wu Jinghua 吳精華, "Caoyuan shengtai jingji he Neimenggu xumuye" 草原生態經濟和內蒙古畜牧業 (Ecological Economy of Grasslands and Animal Husbandry in Inner Mongolia), *Zhongguo caodi* 中國草地 (Grasslands of China), No. 4 (1983), pp. 10–15.
7. Wu Honglin 武弘麟. "Lishishang Zhongguo beifang nongmu jiaocuodai tudi liyong yanbian guocheng" 歷史上中國北方農牧交錯帶土地利用演變過程 (Variations in Land-use Patterns in the Agro-pastoral Zone in Northern China), *Shuitu baochi yanjiu* 水土保持研究 (Research on Soil and Water Conservation), Vol. 6, No. 4 (1999), pp. 91–99.
8. See note 2.
9. Li Bo, Shi Peijun 史培軍, *Neimenggu nongmu jiaocuodai shishi xumuye chanyehua gongcheng zongti lunzheng baogao (neibu)* 內蒙古農牧交錯帶實施畜牧業產業化工程總體論證報告 (內部) (Report of Overall Demonstration of the Implementation of the Industrialization of Animal Husbandry in the Farming-pastoral Zone in Inner Mongolia), 1998.
10. Wang Jing'ai, Xu Xia 徐霞 and Liu Peifang 劉培芳, "Zhongguo beifang nongmu jiaocuodai tudi liyong yu renkou fuhe yanjiu" 中國北方農牧交錯帶土地利用與人口負荷研究 (Land Use and Land-carrying Capacity in Agriculture and Animal Husbandry in Northern China), *Ziyuan kexue* 資源科學 (Resource Science), Vol. 21, No. 5 (1999), pp. 19–24.
11. See note 5.

12. Neimenggu dangwei bangongting zonghe diaoyanchu 內蒙古黨委辦公廳綜合調研處, Neimenggu jingji jishu kaifa zixun zhongxin 內蒙古經濟技術開發諮詢中心, *Neimenggu kaifa kaifang zhinan* 內蒙古開發開放指南 (A Guide of Development and Opening Up of Inner Mongolia) (Hohhot: Neimenggu renmin chubanshe 內蒙古人民出版社, 1992).
13. Zhang Zelu 張澤魯, Wu You 吳優 and Wang Yanghong 汪陽紅, *Buju meng* 佈局夢 (Locational Dream) (Beijing: Dangdai Zhongguo chubanshe 當代中國出版社, 1994).
14. See note 2.
15. Guojia tongjiju, *Zhongguo tongji nianjian 1999* 中國統計年鑑1999 (China Statistical Yearbook 1999) (Beijing: Zhongguo tongji chubanshe, 1999).
16. Zhongguo kexueyuan guoqing fenxi xiaozu 中國科學院國情分析小組, *Liangzhong ziyuan, liangge shichang—goujian Zhongguo ziyuan anquan baozhang tixi yanjiu* 兩種資源，兩個市場 —— 構建中國資源安全保障體系研究 (Two Kinds of Resources, Two Kinds of Markets — Research on Establishing a Security System for Resources in China) (Tianjin: Tianjin renmin chubanshe 天津人民出版社, 2001).
17. See note 5.
18. Mo Dong 莫董, *Jiaru shimao yiweizhe shenme* 加入世貿意味著什麼 (Implications of Entering the WTO) (Beijing: Zhongguo chengshi chubanshe 中國城市出版社, 1999).
19. Tang Xiaoguang 唐曉光 and Zhao Yi 趙毅, *Zhongguo kouan gailan* 中國口岸概覽 (Outline of Open Trading Cities in China) (Beijing: Jingji guanli chubanshe 經濟管理出版社, 1992).
20. Manzhoulishi tongjiju 滿洲里市統計局, *Guanyu 2001 nian guomin jingji he shehui fazhan de tongji gongbao* 關於2001年國民經濟和社會發展的統計公報 (Statistical Bulletin of the National Economy and Social Development in 2001).
21. Erenhot xinxiwang 二連浩特信息網, *Eren gailan — jingji maoyi qingkuang* 二連概覽 —— 經濟貿易情況 (A Summary of Erenhot — Economy and Trade).
22. Guojia jiwei 國家計委, *Quanguo shengtai huanjing jianshe guihua* 全國生態環境建設規劃 (National Planning for the Reconstruction of the Ecological Environment) (7 November 1998), *Guangming ribao* 光明日報, 7 January 1999.
23. Zhongguo kexueyuan kechixu fazhan yanjiuzu 中國科學院可持續發展研究組, *2000 nian Zhongguo kechixu fazhan zhanlüe baogao* 2000年中國可持續發展戰略報告 (Report of Sustainable Development Strategy of China in 2000) (Beijing: Kexue chubanshe, 2000).
24. Liu Yanhua 劉燕華 and Li Xiubin 李秀彬, *Cuiruo shengtai huanjing kechixu fazhan* 脆弱生態環境可持續發展 (Sustainable Development of Vulnerable Ecological Environments) (Beijing: Shangwu yinshuguan, 2001); Shi Peijun, Zhang Hong 張宏 and Wang Ping 王平, "Woguo fangsha zhisha de quyu moshi" 我國防沙治沙的區域模式 (The Regional Patterns for Combating and Controlling Sand in Afflicted Areas in China), *Ziran zaihai xuebao* 自然災害學報 (Journal

of Natural Disasters), Vol. 9, No. 3 (2000), pp. 1–7; Sun Jinzhu 孫金鑄 and Chen Shan 陳山, *Neimenggu shengtai huanjing yujing yu zhengzhi duice* 內蒙古生態環境預警與整治對策 (Warnings on the Ecological Environment of Inner Mongolia and Measures to Counter the Problems) (Hohhot: Neimenggu renmin chubanshe, 1994).

25. Shi Peijun, Hu Tao 胡濤 and Wang Jing'ai, *Neimenggu ziran zaihai xitong yanjiu* 內蒙古自然災害系統研究 (Research on the Natural Disaster System of Inner Mongolia) (Beijing: Haiyang chubanshe 海洋出版社, 1992); Zhao Yu 趙羽, Jin Zhengping 金爭平 and Shi Peijun, *Neimenggu turang qinshi yanjiu* 內蒙古土壤侵蝕研究 (Research on Soil Erosion in Inner Mongolia) (Beijing: Kexue chubanshe, 1989).
26. Shi Yafeng 施雅鳳 and Zhang Xiangsong 張祥松, "Qihou bianhua dui xibei ganhanqu dibiaoshui ziyuan de yingxiang he weilai qushi" 氣候變化對西北乾旱區地表水資源的影響和未來趨勢 (Influence of Climate Change on Surface Water in Drought-Stricken Areas in the Northwest and Future Trends), *Zhongguo kexue (B)* 中國科學 (B輯) (Science in China (B)), Vol. 25, No. 9 (1995), pp. 968–77; Li Jiusheng 李久生, "Beifang diqu ganhan bianhua qushi fenxi" 北方地區乾旱變化趨勢分析 (Temporal Variation of Droughts in Northern Parts of China), *Ganhanqu nongye yanjiu* 乾旱區農業研究 (Agricultural Research in the Arid Areas), Vol. 19, No. 3 (2001), pp. 42–51.
27. Shi Yafeng, "Quanqiu biannuan yingxiang xia Zhongguo ziran zaihai de fazhan qushi" 全球變暖影響下中國自然災害的發展趨勢 (Features and Tendency of Global Warming and Its Implications for China), *Ziran zaihai xuebao*, Vol. 5, No. 2 (1996), pp. 1–10.
28. Shi Peijun, Song Changqing 宋長青 and Jing Guifei 景貴飛, "Jiaqiang woguo tudi liyong/fugai bianhua jiqi dui shengtai huanjing anquan yingxiang de yanjiu" 加強我國土地利用/覆蓋變化及其對生態環境安全影響的研究 (Strengthening the Study of Land Use/Cover Changes and Its Impact on Environmental Security), *Diqiu kexue jinzhan* 地球科學進展 (Advance in Earth Sciences), Vol. 17, No. 2 (2002), pp. 161–68.
29. Wang Jing'ai, Xu Wei 徐偉 and Shi Peijun, "2000 nian Zhongguo fengsha zaihai de shikong geju yu weixianxing pingjia" 2000年中國風沙災害的時空格局與危險性評價 (Spatio-temperal Pattern and Risk Assessment of Wind Erosion in China in 2000), *Ziran zaihai xuebao*, Vol. 10, No. 4 (2001), pp. 1–7.
30. Wang Jing'ai, "Zhongguo 'xibuqu' fanwei jiqi nongye kechixu fazhan moshi de tantao" 中國"西部區"範圍及其農業可持續發展模式的探討 (A Definition of China's Western Region and a Sustainable Development Paradigm for Agriculture in that Area), *Beijing shifan daxue xuebao (renwen shehui kexueban)* 北京師範大學學報 (人文社會科學版) (Humanities and Social Sciences Edition), No. 3 (2000), pp. 116–23.
31. Chen Zhongxin 陳仲新 and Zhang Xinshi 張新時, "Zhongguo shengtai xitong xiaoyi de jiazhi" 中國生態系統效益的價值 (The Value of the Ecosystem in

China), *Kexue tongbao* 科學通報 (Chinese Science Bulletin), Vol. 45, No. 1 (2000), pp. 17–22.

16

Sichuan

Liu Qingquan and Gary M. C. Shiu

Introduction

The province of Sichuan 四川, located in southwestern China along the upper reaches of the Yangzi River 長江, is one of China's landlocked inland provinces. Bordering the municipality of Chongqing 重慶 to the east, the provinces of Yunnan 雲南 and Guizhou 貴州 to the south, Tibet 西藏 to the west and the provinces of Shaanxi 陝西, Gansu 甘肅 and Qinghai 青海 to the north, it is a bridge between two large regions of China, the northwest and the southwest. The province occupies a total area of 484,100 km^2, comprising 7.1% of the total area of western China and about 5% of the total area of the country, placing it fifth in area after Xinjiang 新疆, Tibet, Inner Mongolia 內蒙古 and Qinghai. At the end of 2001, it had a population of 86.40 million, accounting for 6.8% of China's total population, trailing only Henan 河南 and Shandong 山東. The province governs 18 prefectural-level cities, 3 autonomous prefectures, a total of 40 urban districts, 14 county-level cities, 123 counties and 3 autonomous counties. Chengdu 成都 is the provincial capital.

The most important feature of Sichuan's natural environment is the difference in altitude between the western and eastern parts of the province. The west is a high, extensive mountain plateau, while the east is a typical basin surrounded by mountains of medium height, with a depression at its centre — the Sichuan Basin 四川盆地. The different landscapes characterizing the two regions in turn give rise to different natural environments and socioeconomic conditions.

The Sichuan Basin is characterized by a moist monsoon-influenced central subtropical climate with four clearly defined seasons, average temperatures of 16°–18°C and a frost-free period ranging from 290 to 350 days. As the Qinba Mountains 秦巴山 to the north of the basin act as a barrier against cold air flows, normal temperatures during the coldest month average between 5°C and 8°C. This is 3°–5°C higher than the middle and lower reaches of the Yangzi River at the same latitude. The winters are warm enough to permit the survival of economically valuable trees such as longans and lychees, which grow well in the Yangzi River valley. Because of such favourable environmental conditions, the overwhelming majority of the province's population (92%) is concentrated in the Sichuan Basin, making it the heartland of the province and the most developed part of Sichuan.

The western plateau mountain region, which includes the three autonomous prefectures of Garze 甘孜, Aba 阿壩 and Liangshan 涼山 and

Figure 16.1 Sichuan in Its Geographical Setting

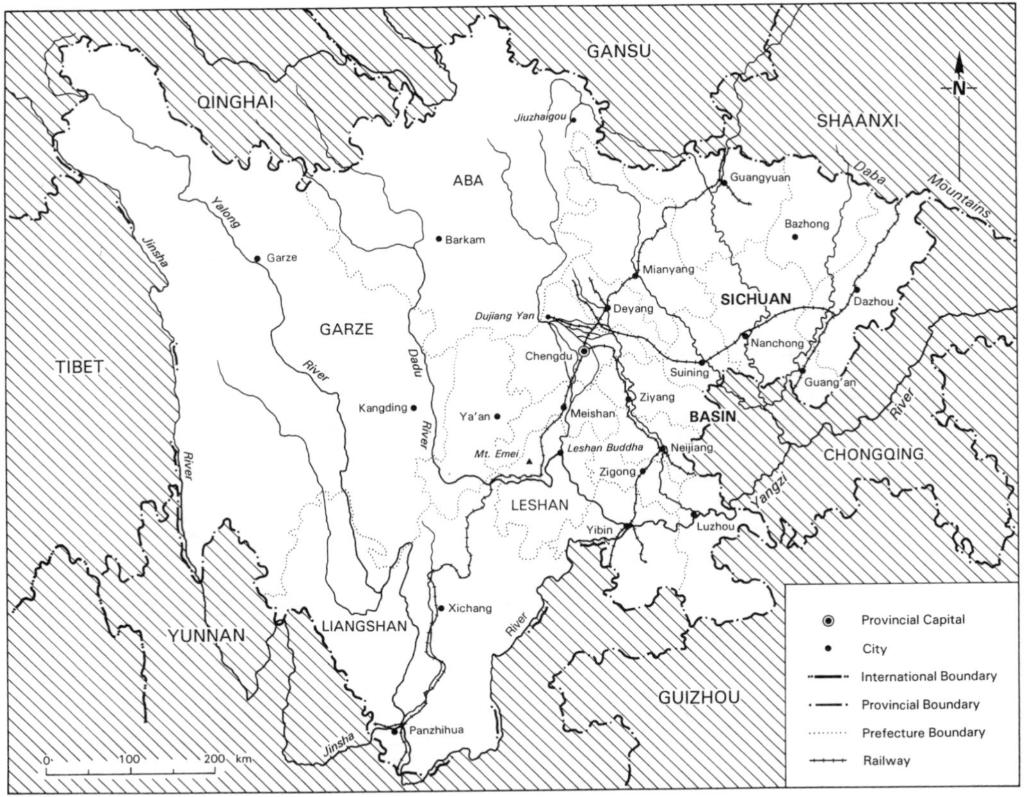

Panzhihua City 攀枝花市, can roughly be divided into two parts; namely, the northwest Sichuan high mountain plateau 川西北高山高原 and the southwest Sichuan mountain region 川西南山地. Water and grass on the plateau are plentiful, making it a fine natural pasture land.

Located in south-central China, Sichuan is the bridge between the northwest and the southwest, and is also one of the easterly provinces of western China. With the advent of communication networks and expressways, its inaccessibility will soon become a thing of the past. The Chongqing-Huaihua 懷化 and Chongqing-Suining 遂寧 high-speed railway lines (140 km/hr) will be completed by 2005 and provide high-speed services to the southern ports of Zhanjiang 湛江 and Beihai 北海. The east-west high speed railway line linking Shanghai 上海 and Chengdu along the Yangzi will also be completed within five years, reducing the travel time between the two cities to 28 hours. The Baoji 寶雞-Chengdu 成都 electric railway running northwards has been newly double-tracked to reach Yangpingguan 陽平關 in Luoyang 洛陽, Shaanxi. From here, it connects to the Ankang 安康-Yangpingguan and Ankang-Xi'an 西安 railway lines, making communication with the northwest much more convenient. Opened to traffic in 2002, the Neijiang 內江-Kunming 昆明 electric railway line provides access to the Guangxi 廣西 port city of Beihai via Shuicheng 水城 and Pan County 盤縣, and connects with the Nanning 南寧-Kunming railway line. With the construction of highways, the expansion of air routes and the development of fibre optic communication networks, the geographical constraints on the province's development are gradually diminishing. Sichuan is thus well positioned to capture trade opportunities with the countries of Southeast Asia, South Asia, the Middle East and North Africa that are opening up with China's entry to the WTO and the signing of a free trade framework with ASEAN.

The discussion above helps pinpoint the broad contour of Sichuan in terms of its geographical location. In the next section, we move on to examine the abundance of resources that nature has bestowed on the province. Following this is a description of economic development in Sichuan since the founding of the PRC in 1949, and then a discussion of the problems currently preventing the province from fully mobilizing its resources for development. Also examined are the ways in which the province can deal with such problems and realize its potential for growth. The final section concludes.

Sichuan's Main Endowments

Land

Sichuan's abundant natural resources provide an important material basis for the realization of the strategic objective of developing western China. They are varied, plentiful and regionally concentrated. In many kinds of resources, Sichuan ranks highly not only in western China, but also nationally.

Although Sichuan's land area only accounts for 7.1% of the total for western China, land actually under cultivation comes to 6.37 million ha, accounting for 20% of the total cultivated land area in western China. Sichuan has 11.72 million ha forested area, accounting for 20.8% of western China's forested area. It has a stock of 1,465 million m^3 of lumber, comprising 26.2% of the stock of western China, making it one of China's three largest forestry bases. The plateau grasslands in western Sichuan are extensive, with a wide expanse of grass-covered mountains and hills. There are currently 13.76 million ha of pastureland, accounting for 28.4% of the total area of the province. Well aware of the importance of pursuing economic development without neglecting the environment, Sichuan was the first province in the country to ban the felling of natural forests and to endeavour to return farmland to forest in 1998.[1]

Water

Sichuan has 254.75 billion m^3 of water resources, with an average of 526,200 m^3/km^2, making it one of the provinces of China with an abundance of water. Sichuan alone accounts for 25% of the nation's hydropower resources. By contrast, Zhejiang 浙江, Jiangsu 江蘇, Anhui 安徽 and Shanghai in China's eastern seaboard, while economically advanced, together have only 1.8% of China's hydropower resources.[2] The province has a theoretical reserve of 142.69 million kw, a technically developable capacity of 103.46 million kw, and potential annual generating capacity of 567 billion kwh, in all of which Sichuan ranks first in China. There are close to 20 locations in Sichuan that are suitable for the construction of mega hydropower stations with a capacity of more than 1 million kw.

The province's hydropower resources are mainly concentrated around the "Three Rivers" 三江 — Jinsha River 金沙江, Yalong River 雅礱江 and the Dadu River 大渡河 in the western mountain region. This area has a technically developable capacity of 82.7 million kw, accounting for 80% of the province's technically developable capacity. The 10.34 million kw of hydropower resources which have already been or are currently being developed only account for 10% of the province's technically developable capacity, far below the national average utilization rate of 18% of developable capacity. The development potential of hydropower remains large.

Mineral Resources

Sichuan has abundant and varied mineral resources. Some 132 types of metallic and non-metallic minerals have been found in the province and significant reserves of 90 types have been verified, making Sichuan one of the provinces with the largest number of varieties of verified mineral reserves. Reserves of 46 varieties rank in the top 5 nationally, of which titanium, vanadium, cobalt, sulfur, fused crystals, optical fluorspar and vein quartz used in glass-making rank first nationally; reserves of lithium, cadmium, rare earths, glauberite, mined salt, iodine, garnet, mica, the cement ingredient mudstone and fluxed limestone rank second nationally; and reserves of iron, platinum, beryllium and limestone used in cement rank third nationally.

Flora and Fauna Resources

Sichuan is one of the provinces with the most abundant wild flora and fauna resources. The province has more than 230 families, more than 1,600 genera and more than 10,000 species of higher-order plants, accounting for 66%, 48% and 37%, respectively, of totals in the country. The 670 species of ferns found in the province rank Sichuan second nationally, after Yunnan. In addition, the 88 species of gymnosperms and the 8,453 species of angiosperms found in the province rank Sichuan first and second, respectively, in the nation.

Of Sichuan's flora resources, about 4,100 species are usable or pharmaceutically important. Among these, the traditional Chinese medicine resources are especially varied. In addition to being plentiful, they are of high quality and have a long history of being gathered and cultivated. Hence, Sichuan's traditional Chinese medicine resources enjoy a good reputation, both domestically and abroad. Other flora resources that can be found in Sichuan include, but are not limited to, about 300 species of oil-bearing plants, more than 200 species of aromatic oil bearing plants, more than 100 varieties of fruit and beverage-producing plants and more than 200 varieties of fibre-producing plants. The 101 species of state-protected rare and endangered plants that are available in the province include, but are not limited to, cathaya argyrophylla, davidia involucrata (dove tree) and alsophila spinulosa (spiny alsophila). They account for 29.8% of the total number of third-grade protected plants nationwide.

The varieties of fauna in Sichuan are very numerous as well. There are 1,154 species of vertebrate animals, accounting for 39% of the total number of species of such animals nationwide. Mammals account for 185 species, birds 571, fish 232, amphibians 89 and reptiles 77. A total of 142 species of key protected rare species of animals are found in the province, accounting for 39% of the national total. The availability of such diversity makes Sichuan one of China's, and indeed the world's, most valuable gene pools of living organisms.

Tourism Resources

Sichuan is also one of the provinces with the most abundant tourism resources in the nation, with its complex and varied natural environment, long cultural history and rich minority cultures. There are 9 key state-level scenic or historical areas, 44 provincial level scenic or historical areas and 150 municipal or county-level scenic or historical areas. Among these, Huanglong Temple 黃龍寺, which has been called "the earthly paradise" 人間仙境, and the "fairyland" 童話世界 of Jiuzhaikou 九寨溝, have been listed as World Natural Heritage Sites by the United Nations Educational, Scientific and Cultural Organization (UNESCO). There is also Mt. Emei 峨嵋山, known as the "greatest beauty under heaven" 天下秀; the Jianmen Shu Trail 劍門蜀道, known as the "most impassable under heaven" 天下險; and Mt. Qingcheng 青城山, known as the "most secluded under heaven" 天下幽.

The province boasts 7 national historically or culturally important cities, 24 provincial-level, historically or culturally important cities and 22 historically or culturally important towns. In addition, there are 40 key nationally protected cultural relics and more than 200 provincial-level protected cultural relics. One of the best known among these is the Leshan Buddha 樂山大佛, one of the largest Buddhas in the world. Furthermore, there are 12 state-designated natural reserves and 38 provincially designated natural reserves responsible for protecting such rare animals and plants as the giant panda, golden monkey, takin, cathaya argyrophylla, and katsura tree among others. Set up in 1963, Wolong Nature Reserve 卧龍自然保護區, with its primary aim of preserving the giant panda, has been designated by the United Nations as an International Wildlife Reserve. Additionally, Sichuan is home to 11 state-designated and 50 provincially-designated forest parks, which help to preserve the natural environment.

Abundant Supply of Labour

Sichuan's population of 86.40 million at the end of 2001 ranks it the third most populous in the country and the first in western China, accounting for 22.8% of the total population of this region. Its population density of 178.1 persons/km^2 sets it above the national average of 132.9 persons/km^2, ranking it third in western China behind Chongqing and Guangxi. However, its population distribution is uneven, with 92% of the population concentrated in the eastern basin, where the largest concentrations are found in the Chengdu Plain 成都平原 and in the hilly areas at the centre of the basin. In these areas, the population density reaches more than 700 persons/km^2, among the densest in China.

By contrast, the population of the three prefectures and one city in the west accounts for only 8% of the population of the province, of which three-quarters is concentrated in the city of Panzhihua and in the prefecture of Liangshan 涼山州. According to an early collation of the results of the fifth national population census conducted in 2000, Sichuan's urban population only accounts for 26.7% of its entire population, with rural dwellers comprising the rest. Not only does the province's level of urbanization trail far behind the national average of 36.2%, but Sichuan also ranks in the bottom half, in the eighth place, among the 12 provinces and municipalities of western China.

Sichuan has a large labour pool, with a total labour force of 54.60 million persons in 2000, or 64.9% of the province's total population. Of the 44.36 million persons with employment, 59.6% were engaged in primary industries, 14.5% in secondary industries and 25.9% in tertiary industries. Due to an imbalance between population and available cultivated land, rural areas have a large surplus of labour. Some of the surplus labourers have moved elsewhere to look for jobs. Between 1996 and 2000, about 50 million migrant workers from the province had sent home more than RMB100 billion.[3]

Sichuan's Economic Landscape

Major Developments before China's Reform in 1978

Since 1949, Sichuan's economy has undergone tremendous changes. The province has been transformed from a backward autarkic agricultural economy to one in which industry occupies an increasingly important role. A major break from a past focused on agriculture occurred between 1965 and 1971, during China's "Third Front" industrialization drive.[4] Within that period, Sichuan became one of the main beneficiaries of the central government's drive to speed up industrial development in places that were safe from foreign attack. Vast amounts of manpower and other resources were dedicated to western China in order to undertake large-scale "Third Front" construction projects in that region. Between 1966 and 1970, 13% of total national investment was devoted to Sichuan. Investment in capital construction between the years 1966 and 1975 was more than double the capital construction investment of the preceding 16 years. The Chengdu-Kunming, Sichuan 四川-Guizhou 貴州 and Xiangfan 襄樊-Chongqing 重慶 railway lines were completed during that period. Other major accomplishments included, but were not limited to, the establishment of numerous large and medium-sized enterprises, especially those in defense-related industries and scientific research institutes. Notwithstanding the flaws embedded in the guiding ideology of the "Third Front" industrial drive and the legacies of the latter that still haunt current development efforts in Sichuan, the whole episode certainly helped to lay the foundation to make the province one of China's most important bases for heavy industry.

Major Developments since 1978

Since the commencement of reforms and the opening to the outside world, China's development strategy has undergone important adjustments.[5] The development of China's eastern seaboard before the rest of the country became national policy. As a consequence of this new development strategy, western China, including Sichuan, supplied a steady stream of raw materials and unskilled labour to facilitate the realization of coastal development. In addition, thriving eastern China has also attracted large numbers of scientific researchers and graduates of tertiary educational institutions to migrate to the east.

Since reforms began in 1978, substantial economic progress has been achieved in Sichuan. Between 1992 and 1997, the average annual GDP

Table 16.1 Comparison of Sichuan and Western China in Key Economic Indicators, 2001

Indicators	Sichuan	Western China	Sichuan's percentage in western China	Sichuan's ranking in western China
Nominal GDP (RMB billion)	442	1,824	24	1
Per capita GDP (RMB/person)	5,250	5,043[1]	NA	7
Gross output value of farming, forestry, animal husbandry and fishing (current prices, RMB billion)	147	597	25	1
Gross industrial output value (RMB billion)	231	1,077	21	1
Fixed asset investment (RMB billion)	162	716	23	1
Local government revenues (RMB billion)	27	130	21	1
Local government expenditure (RMB billion)	59	342	17	1
Total retail sales of consumer goods (RMB billion)	168	659	26	1
Exports (US$ billion)	1.6	9.0	18	1
Imports (US$ billion)	1.5	7.8	19	1
Number of foreign-funded enterprises	3,678	15,606	24	1
Actual foreign direct investment (US$ billion)	0.5	1.9	26	1

Note: [1] Average of the 12 provinces and municipalities.
Source: Raw data from Guojia tongjiju (ed.), *Zhongguo tongji nianjian 2002* (see note 8).

growth rate was in the double digits, at 11%. In the following five years, the growth was slower, at 8.2%.[6] In 2001, Sichuan's GDP reached RMB 442.176 billion, 7.4 times the figure for 1978. The province's national ranking in terms of GDP fell from sixth in 1978 to tenth currently. Among the 12 provinces and municipalities comprising western China, Sichuan nevertheless continued to rank first, with a GDP 4.1 times larger than Guizhou, 2.1 times larger than Yunnan and 2.4 times larger than Shaanxi in 2001. Such economic might makes Sichuan the most economically powerful province in this part of China.

Since 1978, Sichuan has come a long way in developing its industrial sector as well. Industrial value added surpassed agricultural value added for the first time in 1992, and the goal of doubling industrial value added was achieved in 1997. Comparing Sichuan with China and selected coastal provinces, however, a relatively large gap remains in terms of the role of industry in the economy. In 2001, industrial value added accounted for an average of 44% of GDP nationally, 46% in Zhejiang, 43% in Shanghai, 45% in Jiangsu and 45% in Guangdong 廣東, but only 32% in Sichuan.

While there is no denying that Sichuan's record of development since 1978 is impressive, the province has to overcome several challenges in order to advance further. It is to an examination of these challenges that we now turn.

Obstacles Hindering Sichuan's Current Economic Development

Imbalance among Agriculture, Industry and the Service Sectors

Compared with developed regions, the proportions of secondary and tertiary industries in the industrial mix in Sichuan are relatively small, whereas that of primary industries is large. In 2001, the primary, secondary and tertiary industries accounted for 15.2%, 51.2% and 33.6%, respectively, of the national economy in terms of GDP, whereas the make-up in Sichuan during the same year was 22.2%, 39.7% and 38.1%, respectively. The province's slowness in developing secondary industry limits its ability to provide off-farm jobs to the surplus labourers in the agricultural sector.[7] Without such off-farm opportunities to relieve the pressure of excess labour on the land, productivity in the primary industry has a limited chance of improving. Furthermore, it is always economically risky for an economy to rely heavily on one sector alone as its major driver of growth. This risk is especially large when that industry is agriculture, because of its vulnerability to non-human factors that are mostly absent in other industries.

Biases in the Industrial Structure towards Heavy Industry

The importance of secondary industry in an economy is an important indicator of the extent of industrialization. Sichuan trails the national economy in industrial development. The province's industrial value added only surpassed that of agriculture in 1992. In the 1990s, the share of industrial value added in the provincial GDP stayed below 40%. In 2001, it stood at only 32%. Such a share was much lower than that of coastal

Table 16.2 Sichuan's GDP Share by Industries, Selected Years

(Unit: %)

	GDP	Primary industry	Secondary industry	Tertiary industry
1992	100	31.6	37.5	30.9
1995	100	29.0	39.2	31.9
1997	100	27.7	39.0	33.3
1999	100	25.4	38.9	35.8
2001	100	22.2	39.7	38.1

Source: Sichuan tongjiju (ed.), *Sichuan tongji nianjian* 2002 (see note 6).

provinces and municipalities. The picture looks similar when one examines the same issue from the perspective of the province's share in the nation's gross industrial output value. In short, Sichuan's share has witnessed a year-on-year decline. In 1978, Sichuan's gross industrial output value accounted for 3.72% of the national total, but this declined to 3.51% by 1990. The share dropped further to 3.05% in 1997. In 2001, according to the new statistical reporting method (in which only state-owned industries and non-state-owned industries with sales revenues exceeding RMB5 million are included in reporting gross industrial output value), Sichuan's share plummeted to 2.42%. Also suffering from the province's diminishing share in national industrial output was its national ranking in this measure, which dropped six positions from its 1978 ranking.[8]

One of the important reasons for the diminishing role Sichuan plays in national industrial production is the irrational internal structure of the province's industry. For many years, Sichuan has had an industrial sector dominated by heavy industry, a legacy of the "Third Front" industrial drive referred to earlier. Much of Sichuan's industry developed as a result of "Third Front" construction during the Third (1966–1970) and Fourth Five-year Plans (1971–1975). In the 1990s, the ratio of heavy industry exceeded that of light industry in the province's gross industrial output value, at 55%. In 2001, that ratio stood at 51%. Not only were the machines and equipment in the heavy industrial sector outdated, the sector was also disadvantaged by post-reform national policies that were biased against heavy industry compared to light industry.[9] Since 1978, given China's gradualist approach to reform, the prices of heavy industrial products that are mainly inputs for further production continue to remain under state control, while those of light industrial goods have been liberalized. The large role played by heavy industry in the province's industrial structure undoubtedly places it in a

Table 16.3 Components of Gross Industrial Output Value in Sichuan, 1993–2001

(Unit: %)

	Gross industrial output value	Light industrial output value	Heavy industrial output value
1993	100	39.2	60.8
1994	100	42.0	58.0
1995	100	44.2	55.8
1996	100	47.5	52.5
1997	100	49.8	50.2
1998	100	51.3	48.7
1999	100	50.2	49.8
2000	100	50.3	49.7
2001	100	49.0	51.0

Sources: Sichuan tongjiju, *Sichuan tongji nianjian 2002* (see note 6) and Ren Jie, *Zhongguo xibu gailan: Sichuan* (see note 15).

disadvantaged position compared with eastern China, where the share of light industry in the industrial structure is large.[10]

Neglect of Light Industries

Sichuan's market potential, especially its consumer goods market, is huge because of its vast population. Between 1996 and 2000, total retail sales of consumer goods grew at an annual rate of 10.2%, much faster than the growth in GDP. In 2001, total retail sales of consumer goods reached RMB168.04 billion, an increase of 10.3% over the preceding year and accounting for 25.6% of total retail sales of consumer goods in western China, ranking Sichuan first in the region. During the same five-year period, the per capita disposal income of urban residents and per capita net income of farmers in Sichuan grew at an annual rate of 8% and 10.5%, respectively. In 2001, they stood at RMB6,360 and RMB1,987, respectively. The figure for the former ranked Sichuan fourth in western China behind Chongqing, Guangxi and Xinjiang, while the latter ranked Sichuan first in the region.

However, Sichuan has failed to benefit much from this large consumer market because of the aforementioned bias in its industrial structure, in which heavy industry predominates. Indeed, at present, locally made products account for a modest 30% of the total available in Sichuan. Hence, while the demand for light industrial goods is large, local light industries are not yet in place to benefit from this. In 2001, for instance, four coastal provinces (Guangdong, Shandong 山東, Jiangsu and Zhejiang), combined with Shanghai, accounted for the lion's share of China's gross industrial output value in light industry, at 62%. The same measure was only 2.4% for Sichuan.[11] Hence, the stunted development of light industry in the province means that there is a large inflow of non-local products, with the associated profits accruing to non-local businesses instead of to local ones.

A Large State-owned Sector versus an Underdeveloped Private Sector

In terms of ownership structure, the state-owned sector continues to account for a prominent role in the provincial economy, while the private sector remains underdeveloped. This dominance of the state-owned sector in the provincial economy has a negative effect on growth, as the private sector is a major driver of progress among coastal provinces.[12] In 2001, state-owned enterprises in Sichuan accounted for 58.5% of the province's gross output value, whereas the equivalent figures were 15% for Zhejiang, 23% for Guangdong and 30% for Fujian 福建. The same pattern persists if we examine the figures on investment. While 45% of funding for fixed asset investment came from state-owned units in Sichuan, they accounted for only 35% in Zhejiang, 35% in Guangdong and 37% in Fujian. It is thus not surprising that the development of the province's private sector was far below the national average. Between 1996 and 2000, during the Ninth Five-year Plan (1996–2000), while the average annual growth rate of the private sector was 33.5% nationally, the same figure for Sichuan was only 20%.[13]

As a large number of state-owned enterprises were established during the "Third Front" era, they are strongly influenced by the traditional planning system. Not only are they not as nimble as private firms in seizing business opportunities, they are heavily indebted and suffer from poor management. Consequently, state-owned firms are finding it difficult to adapt to a changing socioeconomic environment and their contribution to Sichuan's industrial value added is limited. In addition, the slow development of the non-state-owned part of the economy further hampers economic growth in the province.

From the Current Predicament to the Way Forward

The promulgation of the central government's western development strategy offers Sichuan a unique historical opportunity to accelerate its development.

Devising policies in order to taking advantage of the opportunities provided by this strategy should be high on the provincial government's agenda. What follows is an outline of what needs to be done in order for Sichuan to make the best use of the central government's policy of developing the western region.

Improving the Agricultural Sector

Agriculture is the foundation of Sichuan's economic development and social stability. Given its current importance in the provincial economy, improving the sector should be high on the provincial agenda. To accomplish this objective, structural adjustments have to be made to the province's agricultural sector. In addition, such adjustments must be effected in close connection with increasing the harvests of farmers.

The adjustment of the agricultural structure requires that improvements be made in three areas. The first is improving the quality of agricultural products. Whether in crop cultivation or in animal husbandry, efforts must be concentrated on developing quality local products. Second, reducing the proportion accounted for by crop cultivation while accelerating the development of animal husbandry, aquaculture and forestry will help to upgrade the agricultural sector. Third, efforts should be made to help farmers seek off-farm opportunities outside of the province. In 2000, remittances from migrant workers to the province totalled RMB21 billion. This may be the only way in the short run to alleviate poverty among farmers living in localities that are not easily accessible. According to survey data from one county in the province, remittances from migrant workers amounted to 20% of that county's GDP in 2000.[14] Fourth, to best utilize the differential strengths and advantages found in different localities within the province, agricultural production practised in each locality should be tailored to local conditions. Finally, to help absorb the surplus labour in the agricultural sector, it is imperative that the province increase the importance of light industry in its economy. Estimates of the province's surplus farm labour range from 14 million to 19 million.[15] Because of its labour-intensive mode of production, light industry will help generate far more job opportunities for such workers than heavy industry.

Adjustment in the Industrial Sector

Accelerating industrial development is another key area of reform. There is no denying that in the past, especially during the "Third Front" era, industry contributed greatly to Sichuan's development. But the opening up of China in 1978 ushered in an economic environment significantly different from that in the past, which was characterized by central planning and the suppression of the market. Industries that developed in the earlier period are no longer viable under the new market-based economic system. Hence, to revive Sichuan's industrial sector, several steps have to be taken.

First, enterprises have to learn how to play by the rules of the market economy and to discard old habits formed under the era of central planning. Whether in the process of developing new products or contemplating the purchase of a new piece of equipment, market prices should be the main consideration in reaching the final decision. Second, policies need to be in place that will facilitate the entry and exit of state-owned industries. The restructuring of large state-owned enterprises is of paramount importance. Small and medium-sized state-owned enterprises must be deregulated and invigorated through reorganization, alliances, mergers, lease arrangements, contracted operation arrangements, use of the co-operative joint stock system and even their outright sale. Third, emphasis must be placed on the development of a few pillar industries that can best utilize the province's resource endowments. Five such industries are identified: hydropower, electronic information, mechanical metallurgy, pharmaceuticals/chemicals, tourism and foodstuffs/beverages.[16]

Raising the proportion taken up by light industry in industrial output is another important aspect of the province's efforts at industrial restructuring. The small proportion accounted for by light industry is one of the major weaknesses of Sichuan's industry. Accordingly, in the long term, Sichuan must redouble its efforts to lower the share of heavy industry in its industrial sector while raising that of light industry. Such a task is rendered more urgent, given the large consumer market in Sichuan and its current reliance on goods made elsewhere in supplying the local market, as mentioned above. With such a vast unexploited local market for light industrial goods, Sichuan enjoys an advantage that may not be available to other western provinces. Local light industrial firms would have a ready market just around the corner without being constrained by the transportation bottlenecks that pose one of the biggest obstacles to the development of such industries in western China.

Further Development of the Service Sector

The development potential for tertiary industry in Sichuan, currently underdeveloped, is huge. As one of the province's pillar industries, tourism should occupy the centre stage in the province's efforts to build up its service industries. Not only has nature bestowed Sichuan with a vast amount of tourism resources, the spillover effects from the tourism industry proper to other related industries will help jump-start the province's other service industries.

Despite the province's comparative advantage in tourism, income derived from tourism is presently low and comprises only a small proportion of national tourism revenue. Sichuan's tourism revenues are simply not commensurate with its tourism resources. In 2001, 574,800 foreign tourists visited the province and the income derived from such travellers totalled US$166 million, placing Sichuan only fourteenth and sixteenth nationally for these categories. The performance of the province's tourism industry compared unfavourably with the neighbouring provinces of Yunnan and Shaanxi.

If Sichuan is to convert its advantages in tourism resources into industrial strengths, it first has to strengthen its management of tourism and raise the level and quality of its services. Second, it has to fully utilize local resources by concentrating its efforts on developing tourism products with local flavour and cultural content. Third, it has to put a vast amount of effort in promoting tourism through various means, in order to effectively publicize Sichuan's tourist sites. The government can also promote tourism by continuously striving to make the province more accessible to visitors. Thus, investment in infrastructure is a must. More projects like the Jiuzhai 九寨-Huanglong 黃龍 airport linking two of the China's most popular tourists spots, to be completed in September 2003, should be high on the development agenda.[17] Developing Sichuan into an important province for tourism will enable the tourist industry to become another pillar industry for the province.

Facilitating the Development of the Private Sector

Since the commencement of reforms in the late 1970s, the development of the private sector has made important progress, given its low base at the time. Although the rapid development of the non-state sector has injected new life and vitality into Sichuan's economic development, the sector remains relatively small when compared to regions outside the province. With the exception of such well-known firms such as the New Hope Group 希望集團, Top Software 托普軟件, Dingtian Electronics 鼎天電子, the Diao Group 地奥公司, Zhonghui Pharmaceuticals 中匯製葯, Enwei

Pharmaceuticals 恩威製葯 and Dutong Garment 都通製衣, most enterprises are small in size, equipped with outdated technology and equipment, and uncompetitive in terms of product quality, among other weaknesses.

The main obstacle to the development of the private sector is the discriminatory government policies that confront private firms. A vast web of restrictions exists that specifically applies to private firms, but not to their state-owned counterparts. Without a change in government policy, the private sector simply would not be able to thrive. What the government can do in this regard is to lift all such discriminatory controls and take a more positive attitude towards private firms.

Better Utilization of Sichuan's Technological Strengths

In more than 50 years since 1949, Sichuan's science and technology sector has experienced unprecedented development. Despite the many faults exhibited by the "Third Front" industrial drive, one benign outcome has resulted from this episode of development: The foundation of a strong scientific research establishment was built during that period. Concomitantly, a large talent pool has been nurtured in Sichuan in comparison with other places in western China. The province boasts 43 universities and 184 state-owned science and technology research institutes, with a total of 37,690 scientists and engineers.[18] A recent comparative study on the competitiveness of the talent available in 200 Chinese cities conducted by the Chinese Academy of Social Sciences 中國社會科學院 ranked Chengdu seventh.[19]

Since the 1980s, high-tech enterprises in sectors like information technology and biotechnology have sprung up at a rapid pace. The development has received an extra boosting under Sichuan's "science and education to make Sichuan prosperous" development strategy, in which heavy emphasis is being placed on developing high-tech industries. Because of such groundwork and favourable policies, Sichuan's high-tech industries have been able to develop relatively quickly. Chengdu High-Tech Industries Development Zone 成都高新技術開發區 and Mianyang High-Tech Industries Development Zone 綿陽高新技術開發區 have become important bases for the development of the province's technological sector. To maximize the benefits from clustering, the building of an inter-city high-tech industrial belt around the three cities of Chengdu, Mianyang and the city in between, Deyang 德陽, is also being planned. These three places have strong capabilities in areas like bio-engineering, new materials, medical products and electronics, among others. In 2001, their GDP alone accounted for almost half of the province's GDP, at 48%.[20] The high-tech output value of the industrial belt is expected to reach RMB100 billion by 2005, accounting for a quarter of the industrial output value of the economic circle around the Chengdu Plain.[21]

Although foreign direct investment (FDI) in Sichuan, similar to other places in western China, trails that of the coastal region, the technological strength of the province still serves as a magnet in attracting foreign investors. A number of internationally renowned IT companies such as Microsoft, Cisco, Intel and IBM have already decided to invest in Sichuan. Indeed, Motorola has established a research and development centre for mobile telecommunications network in Chengdu, with an investment of about US$10 million.[22]

However, traditional industries still account for a large proportion of Sichuan's industries. Their machines are outdated and the quality of their products remains low. One challenge lying ahead for the province is to mobilize the technological capability it already has to upgrade the traditional industries. Doing so will also extend the market for the existing high-tech industries in the province. The key to reforming traditional industries is the widespread application of advanced technologies in such areas as electronic information and computer-aid manufacturing in the operation of firms in such industries. It is hoped that, with the help of the latest technologies, not only will the firms become more efficient in their operations, but the quality of their products will also improve.

Exploiting Global Opportunities after China's Entry to the WTO

Known as the "land of herbal medicine," Sichuan is richly endowed with herbs, as has been mentioned above. About 5,000 kinds of plants used in traditional Chinese medicine are found in the province. About 66,000 ha of land are devoted to the cultivation of such plants, with an annual output of 100,000 tonnes.[23] The talent available in this area is abundant as well. About 1.7 million people, including researchers, are involved in this sector in Sichuan.[24] One of the four largest traditional Chinese medicine colleges, the Chengdu University of Traditional Chinese Medicine 成都中醫葯大學, has accumulated a vast store of experience in modernizing Chinese medication, in addition to nurturing talent in the field. Between 1990 and 1998, the output value of the province's traditional Chinese medicine industry increased from RMB0.08 billion to 3.86 billion.[25] In 2001, the output value of traditional Chinese medicine stood at RMB5.23 billion, placing Sichuan second in the country. The province's strength in this area got another boosting when the Ministry of Science and Technology 中華人民共和國科學技術部 chose Chengdu to be the location for the first state-level Modernized Science and Technology Industry Base for Traditional Chinese Medicine 中藥現代化科技產業基地 in 1999.[26] It is thus not surprising that traditional Chinese medicine has been designated by the province as one of its pillar industries.

At present, the province already occupies a large share of the domestic market for traditional Chinese medicine. In 1999, of the RMB32.7 billion in sales registered by the national traditional Chinese medicine industry, Sichuan alone accounted for about 12%, with sales at RMB3.94 billion.[27] While there certainly is room for Sichuan's traditional Chinese medicine industry to grow domestically, the market potential is even greater in the global market. Between 1998 and 2000, the Chinese pharmaceutical industry accounted for a mere 3–5% of the US$15–16 billion of the global market for herbal drugs.[28] With trade barriers lifted, now that China has become a full member of the WTO, the growth potential for the traditional Chinese medicine industry is enormous. It is also expected that the demand for natural drugs, of which traditional Chinese medicine is one, will grow further as people become aware of the toxic side effects of Western synthetic medicines.[29] With its strength in scientific personnel and long history in developing traditional Chinese medicine, together with its rich endowments of herbal plants, the province is well positioned to tap into the world market for herbal drugs.

However, to realize its full potential, Sichuan's traditional Chinese medicine industry has to overcome two major obstacles, both of which may be alleviated by China's membership in the WTO. At present, most traditional Chinese medicine is only available in herb form. Users of such medicine have to boil it before consuming it. This inconvenience doubtless discourages many people from using traditional Chinese medicine. But to make traditional Chinese medicine more convenient to use, the active ingredients in the herbs must first be isolated. Vast amounts of capital have to be poured into research activities in order to make this happen. However, most of the firms in Sichuan's traditional Chinese medicine industry are small and will not be able to fund such research activities.[30] These two bottlenecks can be overcome by the liberalization that will result from becoming a member of the WTO. Sichuan should enlist the help of foreign investors to transform and upgrade its traditional Chinese medicine industry.

With both technical expertise and ample funds, multinational firms would certainly be interested in partnering with Chinese firms to exploit the large global market in traditional Chinese medicine.

Reaping the Benefits from the ASEAN-China Free Trade Area

The further engagement of China in the world trading system witnessed another milestone in November 2001. During the Fifth ASEAN-China Summit, held in 2001 in Brunei, Premier Zhu Rongji and other ASEAN leaders concluded an agreement to establish an ASEAN-China Free Trade Area (ASEAN-China FTA) in 10 years.[31] Hence, by 2010, China, together with other members of ASEAN, will form a free trade area with a combined total population of 1.7 billion, a combined GDP of about US$2 trillion and a bilateral trade volume of US$1.23 trillion.[32] By then, the average duty within the ASEAN-China FTA will be below 5%, or even non-existent, while internal trade and investment barriers will be eliminated.[33] The formation of the ASEAN-China FTA is thus expected to lift exports to China originating from ASEAN members by 48%, while they in turn will increase imports from China by 55%.[34] Furthermore, the GDP of ASEAN countries and China is expected to increase by 0.3% and 1%, respectively.[35] In 2001, the trade volume between China and ASEAN reached US$41.6 billion, up from US$8 billion a decade ago in 1991.[36] Of the 2001 figure, exports from ASEAN to China amounted to US$23 billion while ASEAN's imports from China were valued at US$19 billion.[37] This made China the sixth largest trading partner of ASEAN countries, while ASEAN countries in turn formed China's fifth largest trading partner after the United States, Hong Kong, Japan and European Union.[38]

Sichuan, among other provinces in China's west, will certainly receive a larger share of the gains derived from the free trade pact, given its geographical proximity to the ASEAN countries. In 2001, exports from Sichuan to Southeast Asian countries amounted to US$0.22 billion, accounting for about 14% of the provincial total. Assuming that exports to other countries remain unchanged, the free trade pact will raise Sichuan's exports to Southeast Asian countries from the current level to US$0.34 billion in 2010. Exports to Southeast Asian countries will then account for about a quarter of total provincial exports, at 22%.[39] Investment flows from Southeast Asian countries into Sichuan have been equally impressive. By 2001, the cumulative contractual investment in the province from Singapore, Thailand, Malaysia, Indonesia and Philippines amounted to US$380 million,

US$136 million, US$63 million, US$20 million and US$10 million, respectively.[40] Certainly, with the conclusion of the free trade pact, further room for trade and economic integration between Sichuan and its Southeast Asian neighbours exists. To reap the most benefits out of the pact, the provincial government should take the lead in playing the role of a facilitator in promoting further economic integration between the province and the countries of ASEAN.

Conclusion

The twin forces of development (globalization and technological change) have opened up unprecedented growth opportunities for developing economies to catch up with their developed counterparts. How best to capitalize on those opportunities has become a top priority for each developing nation. Similar challenges are also facing Sichuan as a province undergoing rapid transformation. Fortunately, with the policy support of the central government under its recently promulgated western development strategy, Sichuan is well positioned to take advantage of the development opportunities unleashed by those twin forces.

On the one hand, China's newly earned membership in the WTO and the recently announced plan to form a FTA with ASEAN will certainly expedite the integration of the provincial economy with that of the global market. An expected increase in foreign investment, together with the management expertise that comes with it, will act as a potent force in helping the province to upgrade its outdated industrial structure. More importantly, Sichuan's vicinity to Southeast Asian countries means that it can obtain a lion's share of the benefits from the China-ASEAN free trade pact. On the other hand, the availability of a strong technical work force, combined with many fine universities and research institutions, places the province in a favourable position to gain from the emerging knowledge economy.

The current economic structure of Sichuan, however, is inadequate to allow the province to leverage on its strength to capture the growth opportunities thrown open by the twin forces of development. Effecting the strategic adjustment of the province's economic structure is thus a key to determining whether Sichuan can effectively respond to those opportunities. In this adjustment process, reliance has to be placed on markets to provide guidance on how the province's resources and their potential can best be deployed. Some suggestions as to what this adjustment entails are provided in this chapter. Last, to sustain the fruits of the successful restructuring of Sichuan's economy, the expertise and knowledge of provincial government officials must be upgraded as well. Training the officials to make them familiar with issues that they have not encountered before, such as the resolution of disputes under the WTO, thus becomes essential. Well aware of this need, the provincial government has planned to send over 1.7 million officials back to school over a five-year period, starting in 2003. With all of the pieces needed to project the province onto a higher growth path falling into place, it will only be a matter of time before Sichuan can become a growth pole in western China.

Notes

1. See "Sichuan Aims to Become the Best in the West." At http://www.chinavista.com/business/ciec/en/ciec20011126.html#en0006.
2. See "The West Prepares to Send Hydropower to the East." At http://www.china.org.cn/english/156.htm.
3. See "Migrant Labourers from Sichuan Earn 100 Billion *yuan* in Five Years." At http://fpeng.peopledaily.com.cn/200106/29/eng20010629_73842.html.
4. For more on the "Third Front" industrial drive, see Barry Naughton, "The Third Front: Defence Industrialization in the Chinese Interior," *China Quarterly*, No. 115, September (1988), pp. 351–86.
5. On China's development strategy before and after the country began to open up and reform in 1978, see Justin Lin, Cai Fang and Li Zhou, *The China Miracle: Development Strategy and Economic Reform*, revised edition (The Chinese University Press, 2003).
6. The growth rate is for nominal GDP. The data are from Sichuan tongjiju 四川統計局 (ed.), *Sichuan tongji nianjian 2002* 四川統計年鑑2002 (Sichuan Statistical Yearbook 2002) (Beijing: Zhongguo tongji chubanshe 中國統計出版社, 2002).
7. Primary industry is used interchangeably here with the agricultural sector, as the latter forms the major component of the former.
8. The data are from Guojia tongjiju 國家統計局 (ed.), *Zhongguo tongji nianjian 2002* 中國統計年鑑2002 (China Statistical Yearbook 2002) (Beijing: Zhongguo tongji chubanshe, 2002).
9. This is especially the case for sectors such as energy supply and raw materials, which occupy important roles in Sichuan's heavy industrial sector.
10. See Chen Yao 陳耀, *Guojia zhongxibu fazhan zhengce yanjiu* 國家中西部發展政策研究 (An Investigation into the Nation's Central and Western Development Policy) (Beijing: Jingji guanli chubanshe 經濟管理出版社, 2000), pp. 98–99.
11. The data are from Zhongguo qinggongye lianhehui 中國輕工業聯合會 (ed.),

Zhongguo qinggongye nianjian 2002 中國輕工業年鑑2002 (China's Light Industry Yearbook 2002) (Beijing: Zhongguo qinggongye nianjianshe, 中國輕工業年鑑社, 2002).

12. On more about the important role played by the private sector, see Ross Garnaut, Song Ligang, Yang Yao and Wang Xiaolu, *Private Enterprise in China* (Canberra: Asia Pacific Press, 2001).
13. Data from Zhonghua quanguo gongshang lianhehui, Zhongguo min(si)ying jingji yanjiuhui 中華全國工商聯合會，中國民(私)營經濟研究會 (eds.), *Zhongguo siying jingji nainjian 2000–2001* 中國私營經濟年鑑 2000–2001 (Yearbook of China's Private Economy 2000–2001) (Beijing: Zhongguo gongshang lianhehui chubanshe 中國工商聯合會出版社, 2003).
14. See "Migrant Labourers from Sichuan Earn 100 Billion *yuan* in Five Years" (see note 3).
15. See Cai Fang 蔡昉, *Zhongguo liudong renkou wenti* 中國流動人口問題 (China's Floating Population Problem) (Zhengzhou: Henan renmin chubanshe 河南人民出版社, 2000); Ren Jie 任杰 (ed.), *Zhongguo xibu gailan: Sichuan* 中國西部概覽：四川 (An Overview of China's Western Region: Sichuan) (Beijing: Minzu chubanshe 民族出版社, 2000).
16. See "Sichuan Aims to Become the Best in the West" (see note 1).
17. The airport costs RMB777 million to build. See "Future Airport Connects Southwest China Tourist Areas." At http://211.147.20.14/chinagate/focus/west/news/i012/20020325future.html.
18. See "Market Profiles on Chinese Cities and Provinces: Sichuan." At http://www.tdctrade.com/mktprof/china/sichuan.htm.
19. See "Zhongguo chengshi jingzhengli baogao: Chengdu rencai jingzhengli quanguo diqi 中國城市競爭力報告：成都人才競爭力全國第七 (Report on the Competitiveness of Chinese Cities: Chengdu Stands 7th Nationwide in terms of Competitiveness of Talents). At http://www.west.gov.cn/jjsc/20030417091444.htm.
20. The data are from Sichuan tongjiju (ed.), *Sichuan tongji nianjian 2002* (see note 6).
21. See "Sichuan to Build Hi-tech Industrial Belt." At http://211.147.20.14/chinagate/focus/west/news/i006/20000424inv.html.
22. See "Market Profiles on Chinese Cities and Provinces: Sichuan" (see note 18).
23. See "Sichuan Becomes the Largest Traditional Chinese Medicine Base." At http://english.peopledaily.com.cn/200211/05/eng20021105_106264.shtml.
24. See Liu Xun 劉迅, "Sichuan zhongyiyao fazhan hangye fenxi baogao (1) 四川中醫葯發展行業分析報告(一)" (Analytical Report on the Development of Sichuan's Traditional Chinese Medicine Industry, Part 1). At http://www.sinowin.org/reports_detail.asp?id=55.
25. Ibid.

26. See "Market Profiles on Chinese Cities and Provinces: Sichuan" (see note 18).
27. See Liu Xun, *Sichuan zhongyiyao fazhan hangye fenxi baogao* (1) (see note 24).
28. See Godfrey Yeung, "The Implications of WTO Accession on the Pharmaceutical Industry in China," *Journal of Contemporary China*, Vol. 11 (2002), pp. 473–93.
29. See "Analysis: The Chinese Pharmaceutical Industry." At http://www.friendnet.com/news/02112306.html.
30. Of the approximately 300 firms in the industry, over 200 have an annual output value of less than RMB10 million. See Liu Xun, *Sichuan zhongyiyao fazhan hangye fenxi baogao* (1) (see note 24).
31. Members of ASEAN include Brunei, Cambodia, Indonesia, Laos, Malaysia, Myanmar, the Philippines, Singapore, Thailand and Vietnam.
32. See Huang Kwei Bo, "The China-ASEAN Free Trade Area: Background, Framework and Political Implications." At http://www.dsis.org.tw/peaceforum/papers/2002-02/APE0202001e.htm.
33. See "ASEAN-China FTA Benefits both Sides." At http://www.china.org.cn/english/FR/30000.htm.
34. See Yi Xiaozhun, "The China-ASEAN Free Trade Area Envisioned." At http://www.ecdc.net.cn/newindex/chinese/page/sitemap/focus/proceedings/englishg/part%20two/17.htm.
35. See Li Dachang, "Embrace the Opportunity of Setting Up the China-ASEAN Free Trade Area, and Strengthen Trade and Economic Co-operation between Sichuan and ASEAN." At http://ecdc.net.cn/newindex/chinese/page/sitemap/focus/proceedings/englishg/part%20two/10.htm.
36. See John Wong and Sara Chan, "China-ASEAN Free Trade Area Arrangement: Opportunities and Challenges." At http://www.ecdc.net.cn/newindex/chinese/pages/sitemap/focus/proceedings/english/part%20two/08.htm.
37. See Chana Kanaratanadilok, "ASEAN-China Trade and Economic Co-operation." At http://www.ecdc.net.cn/newindex/chinese/page/sitemap/focus/proceedings/english/part%20two/04.htm.
38. See "China-ASEAN Summit Eyes Free Trade." At http://www.china.org.cn/english/BAT/44349.htm.
39. See Yi Xiaozhun, "The China-ASEAN Free Trade Area Envisioned" (see note 34).
40. See Li Dachang, "Embrace the Opportunity of Setting Up the China-ASEAN Free Trade Area, and Strengthen Trade and Economic Co-operation between Sichuan and ASEAN" (see note 35).

17

Chongqing

Chen Yue, Chen Caiti and Lin Hui

Introduction

Chongqing 重慶 is the only municipality in western China that is under the direct administration of the central government. It is a relatively developed city in southwestern China with a long history of over 3,000 years. Its population of 31 million consists of over 50 nationalities, such as the Han 漢, Miao 苗 and Tujia 土家. The city has four major characteristics. First, it extends over a huge area of 82,400 km^2. Its territory and population are larger than some provinces in China and even some countries in the world. Second, the city has a dual economy of industry and agriculture. It is one of the six old industrial bases in China and is a centre for the automobile, natural gas, chemical, armaments and instruments industries. It is also a major agricultural base and its large rural area accounts for 80% of the total area of the municipality. Third, it is rich in natural resources such as natural gas, hydropower, plants and animals. Over 40 types of mineral resources have been found and mined. Fourth, it occupies a strategic location between the western and central regions of China. It is expected that Chongqing will play a very important role in the programme of developing western China.[1] This chapter will examine the historic evolution, future economic development and construction of urban infrastructure in Chongqing.

Emergence and Consolidation of a Regional Economic Centre

Chongqing is an important economic centre, a land and water transportation hub, and an inland trading port serving the upper reaches of the Yangzi River 長江. In 1986, Chongqing was designated a national historical and cultural city by the State Council. On 14 March 1997, it was designated a municipality under the direct administration of the central government. Events in the following periods have contributed to the development of Chongqing as a regional economic centre.

The Opening of Chongqing as an International Trading Port

On 31 March 1890, the "Special Treaty of Yantai 煙臺" was signed in Beijing between China and the United Kingdom. Under this pact, Chongqing was designated an international trading port. One year later, the Chongqing Customs was established. Foreign businessmen began to set up many companies in Chongqing to serve as bases for direct import and export. The arrival of foreign capital transformed Chongqing's economy. From

1891 to 1911, the city underwent a period of significant development. New industries emerged and commerce flourished, further stimulating the development of financial services and river transportation. With the opening of a large number of banks in Chongqing, the financial centre of Sichuan 四川 shifted from Chengdu 成都 to Chongqing.

Chongqing as a Temporary Capital during the War against Japanese Invasion

Japan invaded China on a large scale after July 1937, and soon occupied North China and many coastal areas. On 20 November 1937, the Guomindang (GMD) 國民黨 government declared that the national capital would be moved to Chongqing. Less than two years later, on 5 May 1939, Chongqing was designated a municipality. It formally became the nation's temporary capital on 6 March 1940. During the period of the war against the Japanese invasion, many public and private enterprises in the eastern coastal areas were moved to Chongqing. Many new factories were also established to meet the needs of the war. In 1940, the number of enterprises in Chongqing reached 1,690 and the number of workers and staff about 100,000, accounting for one-third of those in the region controlled by the GMD. An industrial system was established, consisting mainly of weaponry, mechanical, chemical, iron and steel, textile and food industries. This was the period of rapid economic development in Chongqing. The city became the national political, economic, cultural and transportation centre. After the war, when these activities shifted back to eastern China, Chongqing's economy experienced a decline.

The Construction of a "Third Front"

From 1949 to 1978, along with the changing political situation and policies in China, Chongqing went through unexpected turns in its economic development. In particular, the move to construct a "Third Front" had the most important impact on Chongqing's economic development. During this period, many industries were moved from the coastal region to Chongqing, significantly increasing the scale of production and the level of technology in the city. A solid foundation was built for Chongqing to be the economic centre of the upper reaches of the Yangzi River.

First, a strong defence industry was established. Second, the city's industrial and economic structure and its geographic distribution were improved. A relatively complete industrial system was established, consisting mainly of the following industries: metallurgy, machinery, electronics, instruments, chemicals, building materials, textiles, energy and transportation. Third, Chongqing's strength in science and technology was enhanced with the concentration of talented people in the city. Fourth, Chongqing became a hub for land and river transport in the upper reaches of the Yangzi River. Fifth, the urban layout was improved.

However, the construction of the "Third Front" was not well planned, as it had been initiated hurriedly in preparation for a possible war. It was also affected by the 10-year turmoil of the Great Proletarian Cultural Revolution. These events generated a series of negative effects, such as an irrational investment structure, the fragmentation of industrial locations and an over-reliance on enterprises to provide social services.

Reform and Opening

In December 1978, the central committee of Chinese Communist Party (CCP) adopted a strategy to focus on socialist construction towards modernization. Following this new strategy, Chongqing entered another period of economic development through reform and opening.

From 1979 to 1982, Chongqing adopted a number of major measures to adjust its economic structure. First, the agricultural base was consolidated and investment in agriculture was increased to stimulate the development of the rural commercial economy. Second, investment was concentrated on the textile industry and on other light industries so as to effectively increase consumer goods. Third, the scale of capital construction was reduced to increase economic efficiency. Fourth, enterprises in the defence industry, built during the period of the construction of the "Third Front," were relocated and restructured. Fifth, the construction of urban infrastructure was speeded up. By 1982, these measures had produced a positive impact on the economy.

From 1983 to 1990, China began a comprehensive reform of the urban economic system. Chongqing was selected in 1983 by the central government to undergo a series of experimental micro and macro reforms in city management.

First, a system treating the city as an independent unit in the national plan was adopted, with Chongqing given the status of a provincial unit. There were also reforms in urban macro-economic administration to unleash the economic potential of the city. The management of provincial enterprises was transferred to a lower level. Chongqing's financial power was increased through reforms in the banking system, in wage regulation and in management systems.

Second, the enterprise system was reformed to revitalize enterprises. Enterprises received more decision-making power and a greater share of the profits. A manager responsibility system was introduced and experiments were made in the renting, contracting and sharing of enterprises. A system of taxation was introduced to replace the system of collecting profits from enterprises.

Third, the trading system was reformed. The wholesale system was overhauled and trading centres were established. The management of medium and small commercial enterprises was relaxed. Reforms were also made to the system of rural supply and sales co-operatives and that of international trade. The goods supply system was reformed to increase the share of market procurement. A "dual track price system," meaning a planned price and a market price system, was applied to major commodities and enterprises with the power to sell some of their products.

Fourth, the new system of "city leading counties," that a city put some counties under its administration, was introduced to accelerate the integration of urban and rural areas. The economic and administrative power of a county government was expanded. Economic and technological co-operation between urban and rural areas was enhanced. Much support was given to the rural township and village enterprises (TVEs).

Fifth, the defence industry went through experimental reforms to enhance its link with civil enterprises.

Sixth, the management system of science and technology was also reformed. The system of allocating operating funds from the government was changed to a contract system of funding research. Science and technology markets were explored to promote technology transfers and commercialization. A system of open bidding for key research projects was implemented.

After 10 years of reform, Chongqing's economic strength and integrated urban services were significantly enhanced. This was the city's most prosperous period since 1949.

The second stage of the national plan to realize the strategic goal of socialist modernization came in the period of 1991–2000. The Eighth Five-year Plan (1991–1995) was aimed at the development of Chongqing into an early modern city in the upper reaches of the Yangzi River, with a rational industrial structure, relatively advanced science and technology, fully urban functions, and a healthy and harmonious social environment. Chongqing itself also designed a 10-year plan for economic and social development. The following measures were adopted.

First, the systems of management, pricing, distribution and labour recruitment in trading and retail enterprises were fully relaxed.

Second, the autonomous power of industrial enterprises in management, pricing, distribution, labour recruitment and technological upgrading was greatly enhanced through reforms.

Third, the ownership structure of state-owned enterprises (SOEs) was adjusted and improved. This included adjusting the structure of SOE assets, reducing the share of SOEs in manufacturing and enhancing the controlling power of SOEs in the economy. Meanwhile, foreign-invested and non-public enterprises were actively supported.

Fourth, changes were made to the social security system. The previous special government arrangement for retirement benefits was reformed. An integrated social security system was established, increasing the number of beneficiaries. Housing reforms were also introduced. Housing benefits in Chongqing were replaced with a housing provident fund and a system of guaranteeing funds and cash allowances. Medical insurance began to be introduced in the city. A system to protect the minimum living standards of urban residents was also established.

After 10 years, Chongqing had developed significantly (Table 17.1). From 1990 to 2000, the city's gross domestic product (GDP) grew from RMB29.8 billion to RMB158.9 billion.

Designation as a Municipality and the Development of the Western Region

On 18 June 1997, Chongqing municipality was founded. Forty-three districts/counties/county-level cities (reduced to 40 after adjustment) were placed under its administration. Two years later, the central government launched the strategy to develop the western region. As the only centrally administered municipality in western China and one with the best economic base, Chongqing is expected to play a key role in the implementation of the strategy. Indeed, Chongqing has made use of this great opportunity to develop its economy. The nation's Ninth Five-year Plan (1996–2000) has been successfully completed. Its main achievements are as follows.[2]

First, there has been a steady growth in GDP, with annual growth rates of 7.5%, 8.5% and 9.0% in 1999, 2000 and 2001, respectively. The GDP

Table 17.1 Main Economic Indicators of Chongqing, 1990–2000

(Unit: RMB Billion)

Indicators	1990	1995	1998	1999	2000
GDP	29.841	100.947	142.926	147.971	158.934
Primary industry	9.958	26.152	29.867	28.428	28.300
Secondary industry	11.853	42.719	58.538	60.439	65.751
Tertiary sector	8.030	32.076	54.521	59.104	64.883
Capital investment in fixed assets	6.931	27.097	49.815	56.287	65.581
Local financial revenues	n.a.	4.577	8.580	8.989	10.446
Local financial expenditures	n.a.	6.622	13.595	16.237	20.246

Source: *Chongqing jingji nianjian 2001* (see note 2).

growth rate in Chongqing in 1999 was lower than the national average of 9.0%. But it was greater than the national average of 8.1% and 7.3% in 2000 and 2001, respectively. Second, economic restructuring was speeded up. A new and improved economic structure has been created based on the automobile, chemical, building materials, food and tourism industries. Third, great progress has been made in the reform of SOEs and the objective of overcoming major difficulties has been achieved. Fourth, financial support for poverty alleviation has been increased. Some 20 counties designated as impoverished areas have climbed out of poverty. Fifth, initial progress has been made in resettling the population and urban enterprises in the area of the Three Gorges Reservoir. Sixth, the ecological environment has improved. Seventh, the investment environment has improved with further opening to the outside world. Eighth, an initial municipal administrative system has been established.

Development Opportunities

Current Economic Condition

This section provides a brief overview of the economic performance of the city in 2001, the fifth year following the designation of Chongqing as a municipality. First, there was a high economic growth rate and the industrial structure was improved. The city's GDP increased by 9%, reaching RMB175 billion in 2001. GDP per capita was RMB5,655. The industrial structure of primary, secondary and tertiary sectors changed from a ratio of 17.8:41.3: 40.9 in 2000 to 16.7:41.5:41.8 in 2001, with the share of the primary sector declining.

Second, the rural economy underwent further reforms. The output of grain declined because of serious crop diseases and a pest infestation during the summer, and a serious drought in the fall. But due to further rural economic reforms and an improved agricultural structure, the value of agricultural output still increased by 2.2%, reaching RMB29.3 billion in 2001. There was a significant expansion in TVEs. Their value-added increased by 18.1%, reaching RMB27.38 billion, their gross income by 18.3%, to RMB109.13 billion, and their profits by 16.8%, to RMB3.78 billion. The amount of tax contributed by TVEs also increased by 24.3%, to RMB3.08 billion.

Third, industrial output and profits increased. In 2001, Chongqing's industrial GDP increased by 11.2%, reaching RMB57.7 billion. For the first time, the gross output of major state and non-state-owned industrial enterprises (MEs), with a sale revenue of over RMB5 million each, increased by 14.3%, to RMB106.2 billion. Chongqing's industry also did well in terms of R&D. The GDP related to new products by MEs increased by 10.5%, to RMB21.43, accounting for 20.2% of the industrial output. Exports also increased by 15.8%, to RMB5.80 billion, accounting for 5.5% of the total sales of industrial enterprises. Profits also increased, along with rapid industrial growth. The integrated indicator of economic efficiency increased by 6.8%, reaching 92.4%. The profit of MEs increased by 55.4%, to RMB 2.18 billion. The profits of the top 50 enterprises increased by 4%, to a total of RMB2.26 billion.

Fourth, investment remained a major factor of economic growth in Chongqing. Total investment increased by 22.3%. Investment in infrastructure and economic projects increased by 24.9% and accounted for 40.9% of total investment. Investment in technical upgrading increased by 17.4% and real estate investment increased by 40.9%. As a whole, investment contributed to over 70% of Chongqing's economic growth.

Fifth, consumer expenditure increased along with an increase in the price index. Retail sales of consumer goods increased by 8.7%, reaching RMB69.93 billion in 2001. The fall in the consumer price index in the previous three years was halted, increasing by 1.7% in 2001 for urban consumers.

Sixth, exports and foreign investment increased. Total imports and exports increased by 2.7%, reaching US$1.83 billion. Exports increased by 10.8 %, to US$1.10 billion, while imports decreased by 7.5%, reaching US$0.73 billion. Electronic products and machines made up 61.7% of total exports. Meanwhile, exports of motorcycles and their accessories increased by 27.5%, reaching US$0.51 billion. Chongqing became one of the 10 largest export bases for electronic products and machines in China. Exports of high-tech products also increased by 12.2%, to comprise 12.1% of total exports.

Stimulated by economic globalization, by the strategy to develop the western region and by the improvement in the investment environment, foreign investment in Chongqing increased by 22.9% to total US$0.42 billion in 2001. Of this figure, US$0.26 billion was direct investment, which increased by 5%. A total of 191 contracts for foreign investment projects were signed in 2001. Domestic investment from outside the city reached RMB4.64 billion, with RMB3.11 billion from the eastern region, RMB0.35 billion from the central region and RMB1.18 billion from the western region.

Seventh, the income of urban and rural residents increased steadily. The salaries of employees in government and public institutions were raised in 2001. Due to steady growth in the manufacturing sector, the income of urban residents increased by 7.1%, reaching RMB6,721. That of rural residents increased by 4.2%, to RMB1,971. Meanwhile, perhaps due to a weak stock market, residents saved more: bank savings increased by 21.3%, reaching RMB131.12 billion in 2001.

Eighth, due to tax reforms and improvements in the economic efficiency of the industrial economy, the fiscal revenues of the city government increased by 21%, to reach RMB12.64 billion. But due to increases in spending on education, social welfare and salaries for employees of government and public institutions, local fiscal expenditures increased by 22.6%, to RMB25.59 billion, resulting in an increase in the fiscal deficit.

Ninth, good progress was made in resettling residents of the Three Gorges Reservoir Area. In 2001, 56,100 residents were moved to other provinces while 121,000 were settled locally. A total of 3.8 million m^2 of residential buildings were constructed. Approximately 25 towns were relocated in 2001 for a total of 40. As many as 210 enterprises in the area were also moved. The total cost of the resettlement project was RMB5.02 billion in 2001.

Significant achievements were made in ecological construction and environmental protection. Some 2.39 million ha of natural forest were protected and 45,333 ha of farming land were converted to forests or pastureland. Measures were taken to reduce soil erosion in an area of 2,800 km^2. The quality of the environment improved. The frequency with which air quality reached of over level two in the city proper increased from

51.1% in 2000 to 56.7% in 2001. All surface water now meets minimum quality standards. Average noise in the city proper was 55.9 db and 70% of the industrial waste is now reused.[3]

The Development Environment of Chongqing

Chongqing has a favourable environment for development. It is centrally located between eastern and western China and is rich in natural resources, water resources, hydropower resources and human resources. In addition, the status of the new municipality is a huge advantage.[4] As a municipality, Chongqing can more easily obtain support from the central government. The municipal government operates more efficiently and effectively than before. The previous four-tiered framework of province, prefecture, county and township has become a three-tiered framework of city, county and township. The ratio of the population to government employees in Chongqing is 50:1, while that in western China as a whole is 20:1 and the national average is 30:1. The Chongqing government is authorized to allocate resources within the city. Chongqing has not only an integrated industrial system and a skilled workforce, but also an extensive rural area. It has plenty of surplus rural labour and a potentially large rural market to sustain economic development. The city has also become more attractive to skilled and professionally talented people. In the past few years, thousands of Ph.D. and master's degree holders and other professionals have come from all over the country to Chongqing, contributing much to its development.

Second, the strategy of developing the western region offers a great opportunity to the city. The central government has granted the western region many preferential policies. Many large projects have been approved for construction with much inflow of capital investment. As the only municipality in the western region, Chongqing is included in these preferential policies. To attract more capital investment, technology and talented people, to speed up socioeconomic development and develop the city into the economic centre of the upper reaches of the Yangzi River, Chongqing has adopted 50 preferential measures, which were announced in the document "Some Preferential Measures for the Implementation of the Western Region Development Strategy in Chongqing." These measures deal with taxation, finance, loans, land and resource development, talent, research and innovation. They provide a good soft environment for the economic development of Chongqing.

Third, China's entry to the World Trade Organization (WTO) and subsequent changes in the macro-environment mean that the impact on Chongqing will come from at least three aspects: the direct impact of WTO rules; the overall adjustment of national policies; and the indirect impact of the policies and measures adopted by the coastal areas.[5] These will have positive and negative effects on Chongqing. Some positive effects may include the following:

1. An increase in exports as enterprises take advantage of favourable trading conditions;
2. An inflow of domestic and foreign capital;
3. The upgrading of industries;
4. An increase in the share of the private sector in the economy;
5. The speeding up of the formation of a market economy and the development of a unified regional market; and
6. Improvements to the industrial structure.

Some of the negative effects may include:

1. The decline or closure of some industries, such as the chemical, pharmaceutical industry and mining industries;
2. The worsening of the problem of an insufficient number of high-level, skilled labour and a surplus of unskilled labour. The number of talented people leaving the city may increase; and
3. The need to restructure Chongqing's industry due to the shifting of industries to advanced areas and the catching up of less-advanced areas.

Development Goals and Planning in the Twenty-first Century

Development Goals

With a sound economic foundation and favourable development environment as outlined in the previous section, it is expected that in the next 10 years, Chongqing's economy will grow more quickly than the national average by two to three percentage points. Such a high economic growth rate will enable Chongqing to become an economic centre in the upper reaches of the Yangzi River and an international metropolis. According to the development experiences of metropolises in China and abroad, the municipal government of Chongqing has proposed the following development goals for the city.[6]

In 2001–2005, Chongqing will invest heavily in the construction of infrastructure, with a focus on transport. Many large-scale projects will be implemented to build Chongqing into a hub for transport, information and communication. An integrated transportation system composed of expressways, waterways and airways will be built to provide rapid and convenient transport services. A system to develop and utilize information resources and an infrastructure project called "Digital Chongqing" will be launched. The construction of "Chongqing digital port" will be completed and Chongqing will become the communications hub and information centre of the upper reaches of the Yangzi River.

In 2006–2010, Chongqing will focus on adjusting its industrial structure in the broad sense. First, to improve agriculture and increase the income of peasants, the Chongqing government will adopt four strategic measures to speed up the development of agricultural processing industries, rural industrialization and rural urbanization, including the application of science and technology in agriculture, integrated processing and development, urbanization and sustainable development. Specialized agriculture and a green industry will emerge in Chongqing.

Second, the government will speed up industrial restructuring via technological upgrading to improve the comprehensive competitiveness and profitability of industry and commerce. The motorcycle, chemical, food and building industries will be greatly expanded. Three new and high-tech industries of information engineering, bioengineering and the manufacturing of environmental protection equipment will be established. At the same time, the existing, traditional industries such as the metallurgical, machinery and light industries will be upgraded.

Third, the tertiary sector will be expanded to include a variety of services, service quality will be improved and urban services strengthened. The tourism and real estate industries will be nurtured for economic growth. Chain shops, logistics services and e-commerce will be consolidated.

Through the development of urban infrastructure and the expansion of urban functions, the aim is to double Chongqing's GDP in the period 2000–2010, to reach RMB500 billion by 2010.

In 2011–2015, the distribution of capital and resources will be adjusted to concentrate on specific areas. The development of such areas as finance, insurance, the circulation of money, loans, trading, logistics, technology, information and land resources will be speeded up. Finance, information technology and land resources will play an important role in the modern economy. Both domestic and foreign capital and resources will be fully utilized to facilitate economic development and consolidate Chongqing as an important economic centre.

In 2016–2020, the focus will be on the management and modernization of the city to improve its comprehensive competitiveness so that Chongqing will become a well-developed metropolis. Its level of urbanization, main economic indicators and the living standards of its residents will reach the level of medium-developed countries. The city's GDP will double in the period 2010–2020, reaching RMB1,000 billion. Three economic zones will emerge: a metropolitan economic zone based on the concept of "three centres, two hubs and one-base" in the upper reaches of the Yangzi River,[7] an economic corridor in Yuxi 渝西 (western Chongqing) consisting of dense urban industry zones, and an ecological zone in the "Three Gorges Reservoir Area" focused on green industries, the ecological economy and tourism. Chongqing will become a garden city with rivers and mountains. Given more years of development, the aim is for Chongqing to eventually become an international metropolis.

Different forces will drive economic development in the next 20 years. In the first stage of 2001–2005, economic growth will be driven by capital investment. In 2001, capital investment contributed over 70% to economic growth and this will continue in the near future. In the second stage of 2006–2010, capital investment and consumption will be the main driving forces. The adjustments to the industrial structure will have been completed, resulting in a significant increase in the comprehensive competitiveness of industry and commerce. Residents will enjoy higher living standards. The contribution of consumption to economic growth will increase. In the third stage of 2011–2015, capital investment, consumption and production will emerge as three driving forces. After 15 years of development, the agglomeration of finance, insurance, trade, transportation, logistics and land use will have been greatly enhanced, and able to make a much greater contribution to economic growth. In the fourth stage of 2016–2020, exports will become the fourth driving force of the economy. Exports are expected to contribute approximately 20% to GDP growth in Chongqing.

Outline Planning of Three Economic Zones

The 40 districts, county-level cities and counties in Chongqing are divided into 3 economic zones (Figure 17.1). The metropolitan economic zone is

Figure 17.1 Chongqing in Its Geographical Setting

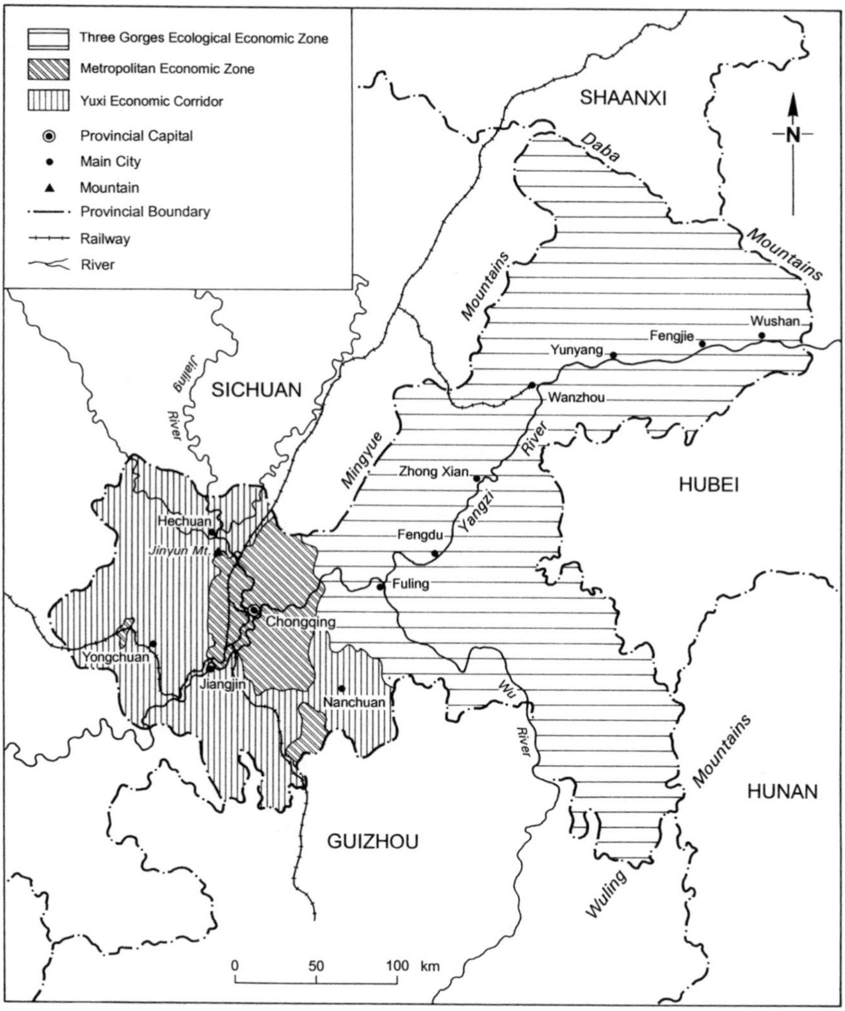

located between the Jinyun Mountain 縉雲山 and the Mingyue Mountain 明月山 where the Yangzi and Jialing Rivers 嘉陵江 meet. It consists of 9 districts. The Yuxi economic corridor extends along several transport lines and includes the Cheng-Yu 成渝 (Chengdu-Chongqing), Yu-Qian 渝黔 (Chongqing-Guizhou), Sui-Yu 遂渝 (Suining 遂寧-Chongqing) and Yu-He 渝合 (Chongqing-Hefei 合肥) lines. It circles the western part of the metropolitan economic zone. This zone consists of 2 districts, 4 county-level cities and 6 counties. The ecological-economic zone of the Three Gorges Reservoir Area covers the Three Gorges area and parts of Wuling Mountain 武陵山 and Daba Mountain 大巴山. It lies to the east of the metropolitan economic zone, and consists of 3 districts and 16 counties.

It has been proposed that the 3 economic zones be developed according to the different natural, economic and social conditions prevailing in the different zones. The following development strategies have accordingly been proposed:

The developed metropolitan economic zone has a good economic foundation and advantages and should play a leading role in achieving modernization ahead of the other zones. This zone leads Chongqing in various indicators, such as in level of economic development, economic reform, institutional innovation, social civilization and tax contributions. As urban competitiveness is enhanced, this zone will become the core of the economic centre in the upper reaches of the Yangzi River. It will try to catch up with the level of development in eastern China and to be the first area to achieve the goals of development and modernization in the western region.

The Yuxi economic corridor is an important part of the Cheng-Yu economic corridor. It has a good economic base for rapid industrialization and urbanization, which will facilitate the integration of the urban and rural areas. The following main measures will be adopted. Competitive industries based in specialist industrial parks will be expanded. The transformation from traditional agriculture to modern agriculture will be speeded up. The development of commerce, suburban tourism and other services will be speeded up to form a dense suburban industrial belt. Some satellite towns and their functions will be further developed. An urban zone consisting of medium and small cities will emerge between the two large cities of Chengdu and Chongqing.

The Three Gorges ecological-economic zone has good access to the main waterways and transportation links. It is also rich in natural resources. It has the advantage of having been granted the benefits from special policies for migration, poverty alleviation and areas with a large minority population. The zone provides long-term support for the economic development of the whole city. The main policy measures include: speeding up the construction of infrastructure to increase urban capacity; accelerating the development of science, technology and education to drive economic development;

accelerating the development of rich resources to form a special industrial structure and to consolidate economic strength; enhancing the protection and construction of the ecological environment to achieve sustainable development.

The construction of three economic zones and the economic centre of the upper reaches of the Yangzi River will start in the Tenth Five-year Plan (2001–2005). With the implementation of the strategy to develop the western region, a total of RMB294.3 billion will be invested in 186 major projects, including 38 industrial parks, each with an investment of RMB30 million. Some 121 projects are already under construction, with a total investment of RMB179.1 billion. Some 25 new projects with a total investment of RMB98.6 billion will soon begin construction and preparation on 40 new projects with an investment of RMB16.6 billion will be made in the period of the Tenth Five-year Plan. Some 62 projects (including 15 industrial parks) with a total investment of RMB68.2 billion are located in the developed metropolitan economic zone. Also, 50 projects (including 16 industrial parks) with a total investment of RMB41.8 billion are in the Yuxi economic corridor. Some 57 projects (including 7 industrial parks) with a total investment of RMB90.3 billion are in the Three Gorges ecological-economic zone. There are 17 significant projects involving 3 economic zones with a total investment of RMB94.0 billion.

The 3 economic zones will be developed according to a node-axis model. The developed metropolitan economic zone will be the node, the Hu-Rong 滬蓉 (Shanghai 上海-Chengdu) expressway and the Yangzi River the main axes, and other main highways the secondary axes. The node and axes will lead the development of the eastern and western wings of the metropolitan area. A network-based development will emerge on the basis of a super large city, several regional central cities and small cities. Urban and rural areas will also be integrated.

In the developed metropolitan economic zone, the main urban area is the inner core and development will extend towards the outer metropolitan ring. In the Yuxi economic corridor, the development will take place in a belt form along three axes, the Cheng-Yu expressway/railway, the Yu-Qian expressway/railway and the Yu-He expressway/Sui-Yu railway. In the Three Gorges ecological economic zone, the development will proceed along two lines to include the Hu-Rong expressway and Three Gorges waterway, and the Yu-Huai 渝懷 (Chongqing-Huaihua 懷化) railway and 319 national highway. Four nodes — Wanzhou 萬州, Changshou 長壽, Fuling 涪陵 and Qianjiang 黔江 — will play an important role in this zone.

Enhancing Three Leading High-tech Industries

Information engineering, biological and medical engineering and the environmental protection industry have been identified as the three leading high-tech industries to be nurtured and enhanced in the period of the Tenth Five-year Plan.

On information engineering, the following measures will be taken. The construction of an information infrastructure and Internet exchange centres will be speeded up. On the basis of the national backbone information network, a high-speed, broadband network platform will be constructed for the Chongqing digital port. The capacity of the first-class long-distance communication lines from Wuhan 武漢 to Chongqing, from Xi'an 西安 to Chongqing and from Chengdu to Chongqing will be increased as part of the national optical fibre communication network. Attempts will be made to persuade the state to construct first-class communication lines from Chongqing to Changsha 長沙 via Huaihua and from Chongqing to Kunming 昆明 via Bijie 畢節. The capacity of the second-class communication lines will also be increased. The communication network in the Three Gorges area and remote villages will be improved. The communication network, broadcasting and TV network and computer networks will be integrated. The construction of a broadband multimedia network and high-speed broadband interfaces will be speeded up. The quality, reliability and security of the network will be enhanced. The coverage of network services and sharing of information resources will be extended.

The optical-electronic project will be launched in Chongqing to develop and produce optical-electronic components, optical transmission equipment and optical-electronic consumer products. The development of 3G mobile communication equipment and mobile phones will be speeded up. The development of special micro-electronic integrated circuits (IC) will be a key focus. Great effort will be put into developing software design and information services.

The following are five key projects in the Tenth Five-year Plan. The first is the optical-electronic industry. The construction of an optical-electronic park in the northern part of Chongqing will be speeded up. The investment environment will be improved to attract domestic and foreign investors. The industry will focus on five key kinds of products: optical communication products and equipment, image processing products, optical-machinery-electronic integrated products, optical-electronic materials and instruments, and optical storage products. The construction of the Chongqing research centre and training centre on optical-electronic engineering will be accelerated.

The second key project is the special IC industry. The production scale of new communication IC products will be increased. Domestic and foreign investors are encouraged to come to Chongqing to develop a special IC R&D base.

The third is the micro-electric machine system (MEMS) industry. A MEMS research centre will be established to improve the technology of the whole industry. A MEMS production base will be formed with the support of the state.

The fourth key project is the construction of a Chongqing digital port and the project to build a "Digital Chongqing." The construction of a high-speed, broadband, large-capacity, multi-media information network and data platform will be speeded up. Domestic network companies are encouraged to participate in the construction of the urban network and broadband network under fair competition. On the basis of the Chongqing Geographical and Spatial Information System, a technical system that can achieve automatic data collection, dynamic monitoring and decision-making support will be developed using geographic information systems (GIS), global positioning systems (GPS), remote sensing (RS), network, multimedia, virtual reality (VR) and other technologies.

The fifth key project is the software industry. The city will strengthen the construction of infrastructure for the software industry and aim to establish a national software park. A software development centre and software evaluation and testing centre will be set up. A number of large software enterprise groups will be nurtured to develop embedded software and application systems, production support software and management software.

Biological and medical engineering is another leading industry in Chongqing. Following the progress in the human genome project and the national genome project on biological resources, efforts will be made to apply the research findings to the functional genome related to serious diseases and special biological resources. A human gene antibody base will be established gradually. The development of new western and Chinese medicines and their industrial production will be promoted. The development of biological materials for medical purposes will be speeded up. An industrial manufacturing base of medical instruments and large equipment will be established.

Techniques of culturing plant tissue, genetic breeding and genetic modification will be used to speed up the growth of wood and grass resources and to develop new kinds of mushrooms. The production scale of Chinese traditional medicine and natural flavours will be expanded. They will be processed with the help of high technology. Special products will be produced for foreign and domestic markets. The biological technologies will also be used widely in agricultural production. The industrialization process of agriculture will be encouraged using different combinations of methods, such as "technology + company + farmer + market," that is, a combination of various factors and "agricultural production based on business orders."

The following are four key projects of the Tenth Five-year Plan. The first is biological medicine and new medicine, mainly for treating diseases related to tumours, the heart, brain and blood vessels. The development of genetic medicine, nucleic acid medicine and synthetic multi-Tai medicine will be the focus in biological medicine. The development of products and the registering of the intellectual property rights to these products will be the focus in chemical medicine. The city's capacity and strength in the research and development of new medicines and in the medicine industry generally will be integrated to turn Chongqing into base for the biological and medical industries in southwestern China.

The second key project in the Tenth Five-year Plan is the new medical instruments industry. High-intensity super-sound focusing on tumour treatment systems, infrared hot imaging diagnostic systems, mixed biological and man-made liver treatment systems, non-wound weak laser blood irradiation treatment instruments, and new multi-contact eye-electric physiological testing and diagnostic systems will be developed.

The third is the creation of a modern base for Chinese traditional medicine in the Three Gorges area. Taking advantage of the rich resources in the region, a large and intensive planting base with an area of 66,666 ha will be established to produce Chinese medicine such as Huanglian 黄連, Qinghaosu 青蒿素, Banxia 半夏, Tianmendong 天門冬 and Shihu 石斛. New and advanced multi-functional refining, filtering, extracting and vaporizing technologies and equipment will be used to produce fine Chinese traditional medicine. Strong industrial groups in Chinese traditional medicine will be developed by upgrading existing enterprises. A modern project centre on Chinese medicine will be established.

The fourth key project in the Tenth Five-year Plan is the model project of transforming rich resources to economic gains in the Three Gorges area. New and high technologies will be used to resolve key issues in the planting and processing of special plants. A high-tech support system will be developed to promote the economic utilization of special resources. An ecological economic zone with an area of 66,666 ha will be developed as a seedling and production base of wood and grass flavours. Next, a seedling base will be established for the new kind of vegetable oil, "Yuhuang No. 1" 渝黃一號, for which the intellectual property rights have been registered. The scale of its refining and processing will be expanded. Third, the technology of mulberry planting and silkworm breeding will be improved. A production base of 66,666 ha will be established. Fourth, efforts will be made to improve the growth of poplar trees, which already grow quickly. The poplar trees will be planted in an area of 66,666 ha supported by advanced technology. Foreign investment will be attracted for the establishment of paper production factories to form a tree-paper production chain. Finally, the planting and processing of the Shigelan 施格蘭 orange will be further expanded to form a production base for quality fruits for the domestic and world markets.

The environmental protection industry is the third leading industry in Chongqing. The state's support for the ecological construction of the Three Gorges area and the protection of water resources provides a good opportunity to develop the industry. The development of environmental protection technologies and equipment sets will be emphasized, such as desulphurization technology for coal-fired power stations, technology to treat urban sewage and waste, and clean liquefied petroleum gas (LPG) technology for motor-vehicles. A number of enterprise groups will be cultivated to engage comprehensively in the development of environmental protection technology, equipment manufacturing, engineering design, construction and operation. A number of model environmental protection projects will be implemented in the Three Gorges area. Various environmental protection services will be provided. Chongqing will become a national base for environmental protection.

The Tenth Five-year Plan will focus on model projects in developing an environmental protection industry. The emphasis will be on the innovation of new technologies and on the domestic manufacture of environmental protection equipment. These projects are as follows. The first is the development of an industry based on flue gas desulphurization (FGD) technology for power stations. The advanced FGD technology using humid limestone/gesso will be imported from developed countries. Key FGD technologies and equipment will then be developed with full project design and equipment manufacturing capabilities for coal-fired power stations with a capacity of 20–30 megawatts.

The second model project in the environmental projection industry is the development of an industry based on the technology to treat urban sewage. Using Chongqing's powerful equipment manufacturing capability, a whole set of waste water treatment equipment will be developed and manufactured in co-operation with environmental protection enterprises in eastern China, using waste water treatment technologies for which the intellectual property rights have been registered. Many environmental protection enterprises will emerge with improved capability in the areas of project design, equipment supply and the construction of sewage processing plants.

The third model project is the development of an industry based on the treatment technology of urban waste. Advanced waste treatment technology will be imported for adaptation. New burning technologies and equipment will be developed to dispose urban waste. A model waste-burning plant, with the capacity of disposing over 1,000 tonnes of waste per day, will be built in the main urban proper, to provide technical support, equipment supply and project construction for the waste disposal of the Three Gorges area.

The fourth model project in the environmental protection industry is the clean LPG project for motor-vehicles. Chongqing has developed technologies for refitting LPG cars, LPG compression and for manufacturing strong lightweight gas cylinders using enhanced intertwined carbonic acid fibres. These technologies will be used to manufacture the relevant LPG equipment to upgrade the fuel systems of vehicles in Chongqing and other parts of China. More LPG gas stations will be constructed in the city.

The fifth is the development of an environmental protection industry park in Chongqing. Under the guidance of the government, the park will operate according to market rules, where enterprises will play a key role. Both domestic and international investors are welcome to invest in the park with their capital, projects and technology. This park will be developed as a symbolic project of the "Chongqing base of the national environmental protection industry."

The Construction of Urban Infrastructure in Chongqing

The overall goals of infrastructure construction in Chongqing in the period of the Tenth Five-year Plan are as follows: the easy movement of urban traffic; the construction of a rapid urban public transport system; enhancing the construction of infrastructure and the capacity for environmental protection; increasing the urban coverage of forests and green areas so that Chongqing will gradually become a garden city with mountain and water area; increasing water supplies; improving water quality; and strengthening the ability to handle geological disasters to ensure urban safety. The key projects to be implemented in the construction of infrastructure are as follows.[8]

The Green Mountain, Clean Water and Fresh Air Project

The project will be implemented to improve the quality of the urban ecological environment. Efforts will be made to control water pollution in the Three Gorges area, control acid rain and build an urban green belt. Based on the principle of both ecological protection and pollution mitigation, comprehensive measures will be taken to protect the environment. A number of key projects to protect the urban environment will be implemented to improve air quality and water quality of the sections of the Yangzi, Jialing and Wu Rivers 烏江 in the main urban area. The construction of environmental monitoring and information networks will be enhanced to provide technical support to the government for its decision-making.

In the Green Mountain, Clean Water and Fresh Air Project, the first issue is the treatment of urban sewage. During the period of the Tenth Five-year Plan, the emphasis will be on the construction of drains in the main urban area, supported by a loan from the World Bank, and on the construction of sewage treatment plants in urban districts and counties in the Three Gorges area and other regional urban centres. The plan is to establish 30 sewage treatment plants for urban areas and sewage treatment facilities for 30 key towns in the Three Gorges area. Some 777 km of class-one pipes will be laid to collect sewage. The treatment capacity of urban sewage will reach 2.22 million tonnes a day. Some 60% of urban sewage will be treated, while 90% of the sewage in the Three Gorges area will be treated. The water quality of Yangzi and Jialing Rivers will be protected to ensure a clean water supply for the urban areas.

The urban sewage and drainage systems will be improved steadily according to the principles of "comprehensive planning and implementation by stages" and "the pipe network having priority over sewage treatment." The new drainage system should consist of independent sub-systems to divert water. The small river basins in the urban area should be improved one by one. Ten tributaries are the key areas in the Tenth Five-year Plan, including the Taohuaxi 桃花溪, Qingshuixi 清水溪 and Xiaozihe 孝子河.

About 80% of these tributaries will function properly after undergoing improvements.

The second issue is the mitigation of urban air pollution. The monitoring of sources of industrial pollution will be enhanced. The sources of pollutants capable of being inhaled will be eliminated. The use of clean energy such as LPG will be promoted. FGD projects will be implemented. Zones of control against SO_2, generated by coal burning, will be designated. New types of LPG vehicles will be developed.

During the period of the Tenth Five-year Plan, the focus will be the Sino-Japan joint project on model cities in the environment. Chongqing is one of the cities in the project. The urban air quality will be improved by upgrading the natural gas supply system in the main urban area, replacing coal with natural gas for medium- and small-sized boilers and restaurant boilers, implementing the 200 megawatt FGD project in the Chongqing power plant (the western plant) and the furnace gas FGD project in Chongqing Steelworks, promoting LPG vehicles and implementing the dust treatment project in the main urban area. The city will try attain the national second-class standard in air quality by 2005.

The third issue is the treatment of urban garbage. The pollution from urban garbage and sewage will be controlled. Classified collection, transportation, treatment and renewal by using garbage bags to collect urban waste will be widely promoted. Comprehensive treatment plants will be established in every district and county to ensure that urban garbage becomes harmless. Furthermore, urban garbage will also be recycled and its volume reduced. In the period of the Tenth Five-year Plan, the emphasis will be the construction of the Changshengqiao 長生橋 Garbage Treatment Plant and other plants in the districts, counties and regional central cities of the Three Gorges area, supported by a loan from the World Bank. About 26 garbage treatment plants in the urban area and treatment facilities for 30 key small towns will be constructed. The daily garbage processing capacity will reach 8,800 tonnes, and by 2005 over 70% of urban garbage will become harmless after treatment. The garbage collection and transportation system will also be consolidated.

The fourth issue is the construction of a green city and urban gardens. The city aims to become an ecological metropolis by expanding and improving the urban green area from the perspective of the whole city. Considering that Chongqing has many mountains and rivers, the scale of tree planting and the forest coverage will be increased, along with the construction of a forest shelter project for the Yangzi River. Environmental conservation projects will also be launched. The urban green system will be consolidated and the greening of suburban areas will be improved to form a large urban green system. The strategic project of a "Garden City based on Mountains and Rivers" for the main urban area will be started. It will focus on the construction of the Nanshan 南山 Botanical Garden, the Tieshanping 鐵山坪 Wooded Park, the Hongen 鴻恩 Temple Park, the Longtou 龍頭 Temple Park, the Jiangbei 江北 Ecological Park and Huaxi 花溪 Park. Non-public investment will be attracted for the construction of several theme parks. By 2005, there will be eight "garden urban areas based on mountains and rivers." The urban green area will have increased by 30 km^2 and the forest coverage will reach 25%. The public green area will be 4,199 ha and the green area per person will be 4 m^2 and 5 m^2 in the main urban area.

The Urban Transport Project

The "half-hour trip within the urban area" and "priority on public transport" project will be started. The construction of urban roads and a public transport system will be speeded up. Regarding the construction of a general transport system in the main urban area, the major tasks are to construct rapid urban transport routes and an urban mass transit rail system, in addition to a basic road network and transport facilities. The development of public transport will be given priority and a public transport system for both passengers and goods will be established to serve the needs of the majority in transportation. An advanced, safe, effective, convenient and economical urban transport system will be established in due course.

First, the construction of an urban road system will be speeded up so that it will be possible to move from one place to another in the main urban area within half an hour. During the period of the Tenth Five-year Plan, the construction of the transport system in the urban area will follow the principles of "high standard, high level and high starting point." The construction of new roads and the upgrading of old ones will be integrated. The ring road in the main urban area will be improved and the number of grid roads, especially the north-south trunk roads, will be increased. More exits and diversion routes will be built in congested areas. At the same time, the construction of a road network in the new northern area, the high-tech industrial development zone, and the economic and technology development zone will be accelerated. By the end of the Tenth Five-year Plan, the total length of all roads in the city will reach 4,059 km. The road density will reach 7 km per km^2 and the road area for each person will be 5.84 m^2.

Second, the construction of an urban rapid transit light rail system will be accelerated. The elevated light rail section from Jiaochangkou 較場口 to Xinshancun 新山村 will be completed. The first phase of the light rail project from Ertang 二塘 in Nan'an 南岸 district to Jiangbei airport will be launched and completed before 2010 to form a "+" type rail transport network. External investment will be attracted to start the underground rail project from Chaotianmen 朝天門 to Shapingba 沙坪壩.

Third, the construction of urban public transport system will be enhanced. During the period of the Tenth Five-year Plan, the main tasks are as follows. Large public buses will gradually replace medium-sized buses in the urban area. The number of taxi will be increased. The public bus service will be improved with an optimal combination of bus routes with fixed bus stops, bus routes and frequencies. Private investment in the public transport system will be encouraged through tending procedures.

The Clean Water Supply Project

The construction of urban water supply facilities will be speeded up through the "clean water supply project." During the Tenth Five-year Plan, the water quality and the capacity of water supply facilities will be improved to meet the demand for fresh water for residential and commercial use. The management of water supplies will be improved to reduce the cost of supplying water. An integrated water supply system for both urban and rural areas will be established. The institutional framework of water supply will be reformed to ensure sound construction, management and capital returns. According to the geographical conditions of Chongqing, both combined and independent urban water supply systems will be adopted. Efforts will be made to solve water supply problems in the new northern area, the high-tech industrial development zone, and the economic and technology development zone. The city's water supply company will be encouraged to grow with policy support and through market competition. Old and dilapidated water supply plants will be gradually closed down. Water supply plants owned by various companies will be transferred gradually to the water supply company of the city.

During the period of the Tenth Five-year Plan, the construction of the first phase of the Fengshouba 豐收壩 Water Plant with a supply capacity of 200,000 tonnes per day and the expansion of the Beipei 北碚 Water Plant with a supply capacity of 50,000 tonnes per day will be completed. The water distribution system related to these plants will also be constructed. The clean water pipe network, 497 km long, in the urban proper will be upgraded. About 68 km of main pipes will be constructed in the new northern area (21 km), and in the Jiangbei, Nan'an, Yuzhong 渝中 and Shapingba districts. Six old water plants with a supply capacity of 325,000 tonnes per day will be upgraded. At the same time, new water supply facilities will be constructed for cities such as Wanzhou, Fuling and Qianjiang. A 150,000-tonne water supply project and its distribution system will be constructed for the Three Gorges area. By 2005, the water supply capacity will be increased by 400,000 tonnes per day. The water supply problem in the urban area will be completely solved. A pilot water supply system for direct drinking water will be installed in some districts to meet the demand for high-quality water. The coverage of urban water supply will reach 98.1% in Chongqing.

Summary

Chongqing was designated an international trading port under the "Special Treaty of Yantai" signed in 1890 in Beijing between China and the United Kingdom. From 1891 to 1911, Chongqing experienced a period of significant development. In March 1940, during the war against Japanese invasion, it became the nation's temporary capital, and the city entered a second period of rapid economic development. From 1949 to 1978, with changing politics and policies in China, Chongqing experienced unexpected turns in its economic development. The construction of the "Third Front" laid a solid economic foundation for Chongqing.

Chongqing entered another period of economic development through reform and opening after 1978. The central government selected it to try out an experiment in reform in February 1983. A series of micro and macro reforms in city management were implemented and significant development resulted.

On 18 June 1997, Chongqing municipality was founded. In 1999, the central government launched the strategy to develop the western region. As the only municipality in western China and possessing the best economic base in the region, Chongqing is expected to play a key role in the implementation of the strategy.

With a sound economic foundation and favourable development environment, Chongqing's economy will achieve rapid growth in the next

10 years. It will become an economic centre in the upper reaches of the Yangzi River and an international metropolis. The chapter outlined detailed plans for three economic zones and three leading industries including information engineering, biological and medical engineering, and the environmental protection industry.

On the construction of infrastructure in Chongqing, the overall goals for the city in the period of the Tenth Five-year Plan are as follows: the easy movement of urban traffic; a rapid urban public transport system; enhancing environmental protection; increasing the urban coverage of forests and green areas; increasing water supplies; improving water quality; and strengthening the ability to handle geological disasters to ensure urban safety. Many key projects will be implemented to achieve these goals.

Notes

1. Chongqingshi chengshi zongti guihua xiubian lingdao xiaozu 重慶市城市總體規劃修編領導小組 and Chongqingshi guihua sheji yanjiuyuan 重慶市規劃設計研究院, *Chongqingshi chengzhen tixi guihua zhuanti baogao* (shangce) 重慶市城鎮體系規劃專題報告 (上冊) (Special Report on the Planning of the Urban System of Chongqing (Volume 1) (March, 2000).
2. Chongqingshi renmin zhengfu bangongting 重慶市人民政府辦公廳 (ed.), *Chongqing jingji nianjian 2001* 重慶經濟年鑑2001 (Chongqing Economic Yearbook 2001) (Chongqing: Chongqing chubanshe 重慶出版社, 2001).
3. Chongqing tongjiju 重慶統計局, *2001 nian Chongqingshi guomin jingji he shehui fazhan tongji gongbao* 2001年重慶市國民經濟和社會發展統計公報 (The Statistics Bulletin of the National Economy and Social Development of Chongqing in 2001), 1 March 2002.
4. Huang Qifan 黃奇帆, "Chongqing zhixiashi de zhanlüe yiyi, fazhan mubiao ji zhanlüe cuoshi" 重慶直轄市的戰略意義、發展目標及戰略措施 (The Strategic Significance, Development Goals and Strategic Measures of Chongqing as a Municipality). Speech in the Working Conference on Chongqing's Economy by the Vice-Mayor (April 2002).
5. Chongqing shehui kexueyuan 重慶社會科學院 and Chongqingshi renmin zhengfu fazhan yanjiu zhongxin 重慶市人民政府發展研究中心 (eds.), *2002 nian jingji shehui xingshi fenxi yu yuce* (Chongqing lanpishu) 2002年經濟社會形勢分析與預測(重慶藍皮書) (An Analysis and Predictions on the Economy and Society in 2002 (Chongqing Blue Book)) (Chongqing: Chongqing chubanshe, 2002).
6. Huang Qifan, "Chongqing zhixiashi" (see note 4).
7. The three centres are: a centre for commerce and trading, a financial centre and a centre for science, technology, culture and information. The two hubs are: a

transport hub and communications hub. One base refers to a modern industrial base with the support of high technology.

8. Chongqingshi jihua fazhan weiyuanhui 重慶市計劃發展委員會 (ed.), *Chongqing: Xinshiji kaiju fanglüe* 重慶：新世紀開局方略 (Chongqing: The General Plan for the Beginning of the New Century) (Chongqing: Chongqing chubanshe, 2002).

18

Guangxi

Huang Yefang and Shen Jianfa

Introduction

Guangxi 廣西 occupies a unique position in the recent drive to develop China's western region. It is among the least developed of China's coastal provinces. However, it is not the least developed among the 12 provincial units of western China. With a population of 47.51 million in 2000, it is the second-most populous in the western region. A high proportion of its population is made up of minority peoples, and it is one of the four autonomous regions in China.[1] Guangxi is also the only region in the west that has direct access to the sea. It is one of China's border regions, sharing a long land and sea border with Vietnam. In contrast to other arid, inland provinces in western China, it has abundant water, agricultural and mineral resources. In all respects, Guangxi is one of the most favourable regions in China, with all kinds of geographical and natural advantages.

However, with a few exceptions, the economy of the Guangxi Autonomous Region has been neglected for many years, especially during the period of the planned economy. The implementation of economic reforms and the open-door policy in Guangxi has seemed to be "one step behind" that of other provinces in China, especially in the 1980s. However, an acceleration in economic reforms and the booming border trade with Vietnam have been key factors behind its economic development since the early 1990s. The state's decision to construct a sea passage in Guangxi for the whole southwest region in 1992 has been an important stimulus, leading to the construction of seaports, railways and highways. The implementation of the state's strategy to develop China's west is expected to further broaden opportunities in Guangxi in the twenty-first century. Nevertheless, Guangxi's industrialization, urbanization and economy remain weak and uncompetitive. Although Guangxi and Guangdong 廣東 share a similar natural environment and geographical setting, and both were under-developed at the outset of the period of reform and opening in 1978, the gap between the two has been widening over time. Thus, Guangxi presents an interesting case for a thorough examination of the links between resources, development, urbanization, economic reforms and state policy, and domestic trade and globalization in a developing region, within the context of a transitional economy in China.

There have been very few studies on Guangxi, especially in English. Most studies on urban and regional development in China have focused on either China as a whole or on well-developed regions such as Guangdong and Jiangsu 江蘇. Hendrischke has made an interesting study on Guangxi focusing on the relations between Guangxi and the central government, the process of reforms and the socioeconomic changes in the region. Hendrischke and Brantly also examined the rising border trade with Vietnam.[2] However, no detailed examination has been made on the changing relations between urbanization and development in Guangxi, although in 1990 Ye considered the strategies of cities in Guangxi.[3]

This chapter will thoroughly survey urban and regional development in Guangxi in the context of the drive to develop the western region of China and open up to the outside world.[4] The region's population, resources and environment are first briefly examined, to provide a background to the development path facing Guangxi. Then, the gap in development between Guangxi and the country as a whole is analyzed to complement previous studies based on all of the provinces of China. Issues of urbanization and regional development are analyzed, followed by a consideration of the opportunities and challenges faced by Guangxi in a globalizing world.

Population, Resource Endowments and Geo-political Advantages

Continuous population growth has been common all over China since the foundation of the PRC in 1949. Guangxi is no exception. Its population increased from 18.75 million in 1950 to 34.03 million by 1978 and 47.51 million by 2000.[5] Given a territory of 236.7 thousand km^2, Guangxi's population density increased by 81.49% in the period 1950–1978 and 39.61% in the period 1978–2000, reaching 201 persons per km^2 in 2000, the third highest in western China, after Chongqing 重慶 and Guizhou 貴州.

Another main feature of Guangxi's population is that it is, to a considerable degree, constituted of minority peoples. This fact has been a key factor in the decision-making of the central government in matters related to Guangxi, whether economic, social, political or regional. There are 37 ethnic nationalities in Guangxi, 12 of which are aboriginal and 25 of which are peoples who have migrated from elsewhere.[6] In the period 1978–2000, the minority population increased from 12.72 million to 18.09 million. Its share of Guangxi's total population increased from 37.39% to 38.08% in the same period. In total numbers, Guangxi has the largest minority population among all of the provinces and regions of China, while its proportion of minority population in its total population is the fourth-largest after Tibet 西藏, Xinjiang 新疆 and Qinghai 青海. The largest minority nationality in Guangxi is the Zhuang 壯; with a population of 15.53 million, they accounted for 32.69% of the autonomous region's total population in 2000. The Han 漢 population, 29.42 million in total, was still the largest, accounting for 61.92% of the total population of Guangxi.

The quality of human resources is a major problem in Guangxi, due to an inadequate provision of education. Only 2.4% of the population had received a tertiary education, lower than the national average of 3.6% in 2000.[7] On the other hand, it is encouraging that the illiterate population has decreased from 4.48 million to 1.70 million in the period 1990–2000. In 2000, the illiterate population was 3.79%, lower than the national average of 6.72% in 2000. Clearly, more educational opportunities need to be provided, from the elementary to the university levels, so that people are better prepared for the on-going development and urbanization.

Guangxi has a favourable natural environment. As much as 41.3% of its territory was covered by forests in 2000. The region's subtropical climate has made Guangxi the largest producer of sugarcane in China. In 2000, it produced 29.38 million tonnes of sugarcane, accounting for 43.02% of the national total. However, about 68% of the land is hilly, including the 18.4% that is composed of rocky hills. This means that arable land in the region is limited. There were 4.41 million ha of arable land in Guangxi in 2000. But arable land per capita was only 0.098 ha, lower than the average of 0.140 ha in the western region and the national average of 0.103 ha. As a result, Guangxi has not been able to achieve self-sufficiency in grain production, resulting in poverty and hardship for a region heavily reliant on agriculture. Grain output per capita was 318 kg in 1978 and 340 kg in 2000. Guangxi's grain output per capita was about the same as the national average of 317 kg in the year 1978, when the whole country was struggling with food supply. By 2000, Guangxi's grain output per capita was below the national average of 365 kg.[8] As the country as a whole has produced a sufficient amount of grain since 1996, it is not necessary for Guangxi to achieve self-sufficiency in grain production. Indeed, its agriculture should specialize in sugarcane and subtropical fruits, to take advantage of the region's favourable climate for the growing of such products.

Unlike other provincial regions in western China, Guangxi is rich in water resources. Annual rainfall is in the range of 730–2,541 mm. In 2000, it received 146 billion m^3, leading to floods. More facilities to fight against floods, and against the droughts that sometimes occur, resulting from the region's hilly topography, need to be constructed. The most significant natural resource in Guangxi is water energy, which theoretically amounts to 21.33 million kw.[9] It is estimated that 17.52 million kw of water energy can be utilized. As many as 856 hydropower stations, each with a capacity of more than 500 kw, can be constructed. The total capacity would be 15.62 million kw, producing 78.8 billion kwh of electricity a year. In 2000, about 20% of water energy was utilized. In that year, hydropower stations generated 16.89 billion kwh of electricity, accounting for 58.42% of the total electricity generated in Guangxi. Of the total amount of energy consumed in Guangxi in 2000, 20.5% was provided by hydropower stations.

One major project in the strategy to develop the western region is to transfer the electricity generated there to the eastern region, including Shanghai. The development of water energy in Guangxi is part of the project. One section of the Hongshui 紅水 River, 1,050 km long, is particularly rich in water energy, as its water level drops by 756.5 m over this section. Five of a planned total of 10 hydropower stations, with a total capacity of more than 11.05 million kw, have been constructed there since 1978.[10] In late 2001, construction commenced on one of the biggest of the hydropower stations, Longtan 龍灘, with a capacity of 4.3–5.4 million kw. Preparations for the construction of another two are underway.

Guangxi is also rich in mineral resources, especially in non-ferrous metals. Guangxi is among the top 10 provincial regions in recoverable reserves of 52 kinds of minerals in China. It has the largest reserves of 15 kinds of minerals, such as tin ore, and ranks among the top six in the country in reserves of another 27 kinds of minerals, such as aluminum ore. Some of its mineral resources, such as aluminum ore and tin ore, are highly concentrated in one site (67.5% and 78%, respectively), facilitating large-scale exploration. Guangxi is also endowed with the country's best and largest reserves of limestone, the main raw material in the production of cement.[11]

A beautiful landscape is another valuable resource of Guangxi, especially in the present period when tourism has become an important economic sector.[12] Karst topography is typified in Guilin 桂林, one of China's most famous attractions to tourists from home and abroad. The cultures of minority nationalities, the nature reserves and coastal resorts are all also quite appealing. In 2000, Guangxi attracted 1.23 million tourists from Hong Kong, Macao, Taiwan and foreign countries, the most among the 12 regions in western China. It also attracted 39.01 million domestic tourists in 2000.

With a coastal location, a border shared with Vietnam and a large population of minority nationalities, Guangxi is geo-politically important.

Because of its large minority population, Guangxi has enjoyed a highly autonomous status as a Zhuang Autonomous Region since 1958. By law, the governor of Guangxi must be a member of the Zhuang nationality. Ethnic minorities are allocated more seats in the People's Congress and its Standing Committee of Guangxi than their proportionate share. Guangxi is also empowered to make its own laws related to political elections, society, economy, education, labour protection and the environment. Special attention is paid to the education and training of the minority population. About 0.37 million people from minority nationality groups are appointed government officials of various ranks. If teachers, scientists and technical personnel who are members of minority nationalities are included, the total in Guangxi is over 1.5 million. The open-door policy has been implemented in Guangxi since 1984, because of its location as part of the coastal region.[13] The inclusion of Guangxi as part of western China is largely due to its special status as an autonomous region.

Guangxi's coastal location is also a major asset. First, the region has direct access to the sea via its own seaports, while other provincial regions in western China have no such advantage. Second, the region has the potential to become a major sea passage for the great southwest region, which includes Sichuan 四川, Chongqing, Guizhou, Yunnan 雲南 and Tibet. The issue will be further examined later in this chapter.

Finally, sharing a 1,020-km long border with a foreign country, Vietnam, gives Guangxi another major advantage in the age of globalization. There is a huge potential for economic co-operation and trade between China and Vietnam. Guangxi is well positioned to benefit from increasing trading between the two countries. The growth of the border trade has been a significant phenomenon since the early 1990s.

Clearly, Guangxi has significant geo-political advantages and rich natural resources. If they can be fully utilized, urbanization and development will proceed rapidly. Currently, Guangxi's economy is relatively weak, and much reform has yet to be carried out to achieve the region's development potential. The next section will assess the changes in the gap in development between Guangxi and the rest of the country since 1978.

Development Gap between Guangxi and China

Guangxi has been a less advanced peripheral provincial region in China for a long time, both before and after 1949.[14] The region's industrial foundation was laid mainly during the period from the late 1960s to the early 1970s, when China implemented the "Third Front" policy. Although as a coastal provincial region, Guangxi has been given incentive open policies since 1984, real progress in economic reform, opening up and economic development only took place after 1992. As mentioned before, Guangxi's position in the western region and in China is quite unique, both geographically and economically. Guangxi provides an excellent case for a thorough examination of balanced and unbalanced development, internally and externally. This section will first analyze the issue externally, by focusing on the development gaps among Guangxi, Guangdong and the country as a whole.

A major issue in regional studies is whether and why the gap in the level of development between different areas is narrowing or widening, especially in the long-term convergence in per capita incomes among sub-national regions and among countries. Changing regional development policies and unbalanced regional development at the provincial and intra-provincial levels in China have been the focus of many studies.[15] Two kinds of convergence have been identified in the expanding literature. First, "σ convergence" occurs if the variance of relative per capita income decreases, which means that the gap between the more and less developed areas has been reduced. Second, a "β-convergence" occurs if there is a negative correlation between the regional growth rate and the level of per capita income at the beginning of the period, meaning that the less developed areas are growing faster than the more developed areas. Most studies on regional convergence are concerned with a spatial system of multiple regions and the result is indicative of the overall trend in the system. Due to the nature of complex spatial systems, it is possible that some less developed regions may become even less developed, although the whole spatial system may show evidence of "convergence" in per capita income. This section will adopt a simplified approach and attempt to assess whether the gaps in GDP per capita between Guangxi and China and between Guangxi and Guangdong have been narrowed or widened. Other than China, Guangdong is also used as a benchmark as Guangdong and Guangxi are neighbouring coastal provinces in South China, and both had a lower level of development in 1978.

Two sets of GDP per capita data for Guangxi, Guangdong and China for the period 1978–2000 have been obtained from official statistical yearbooks.[16] GDP per capita at current year prices are available. But such data on GDP are not comparable over time, especially for the same province. Thus, the second set of GDP per capita, at prices fixed at the levels prevailing in 2000, has been calculated based on data on the indexes of GDP per capita, available from the official yearbooks. The relative GDP per capita of Guangxi is its GDP per capita expressed as a percentage of the GDP per capita in China or in Guangdong. The relative GDP per capita of Guangdong is also defined for comparative purposes and is its GDP per capita as percentage of the GDP per capita in China. An increase (or decrease) in the relative GDP per capita of a region over (or below) 100% indicates an increasing gap in income between the two regions concerned, while an increase (or decrease) in the relative GDP per capita below (or over) 100% of a region indicates a decreasing gap in income, that is, an "σ convergence."

Table 18.1 presents the relative GDP per capita at the current year prices and at the prices fixed in 2000, respectively. The results using the first data set based on GDP per capita at current year prices are first considered. Using China's average GDP per capita as a benchmark, Guangxi's relative GDP per capita remained remarkably stable in the range of 55–68% over the period 1978–2000 (Figure 18.1). This means that Guangxi remained a less developed region during the whole period and that its situation neither worsened nor improved during that period. There were two short periods when relative GDP per capital increased. The first was the early 1980s, due

Table 18.1 Development Gaps in Terms of Relative GDP per capita among Guangxi, Guangdong and China, 1978–2000

	Current year prices			Fixed prices of the year 2000		
	Guangxi		Guangdong	Guangxi		Guangdong
Year	Percentage of China	Percentage of Guangdong	Percentage of China	Percentage of China	Percentage of Guangdong	Percentage of China
1978	59.37	60.98	97.36	69.99	76.83	91.10
1980	60.43	57.92	104.35	67.89	68.69	98.85
1982	67.30	56.10	119.96	71.13	68.19	104.31
1985	55.09	45.95	119.88	59.48	56.72	104.85
1986	54.92	44.95	122.18	58.04	53.39	108.71
1989	61.31	40.18	152.58	52.62	42.10	124.99
1990	65.24	42.02	155.26	54.11	40.76	132.78
1992	65.15	39.06	166.81	57.70	38.35	150.46
1994	68.19	39.37	173.21	60.98	36.03	169.24
1995	68.07	38.89	175.01	61.37	35.01	175.28
2000	61.02	33.52	182.04	61.02	33.52	182.04

Source: See Note 16.

Figure 18.1 GDP per capita of Guangxi as Percentage of GDP per capita in Guangdong and China based on the Current Year Price, 1978–2000 (%)

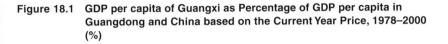

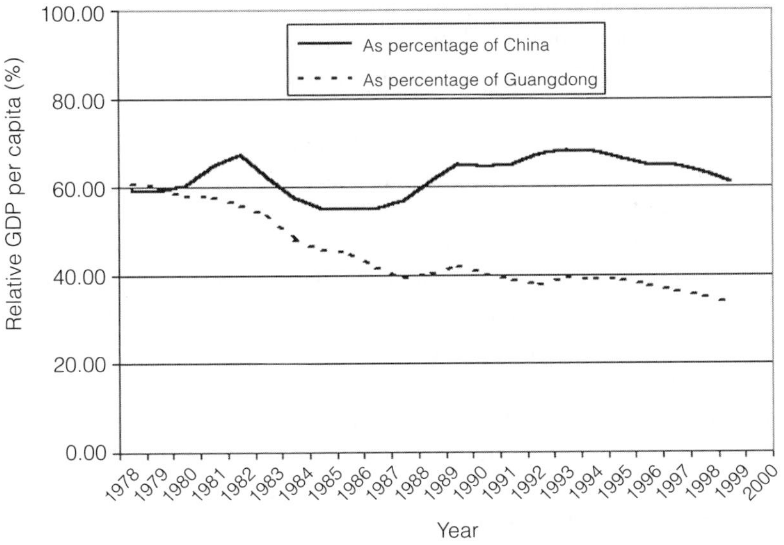

Source: See Table 18.1.

to rising prices of agricultural goods in the early years of reform. The second was after 1992, because the economic boom associated with the designation of Guangxi as a sea passage for greater Southwest China and the southern tour of senior leader, Deng Xiaoping 鄧小平.

However, when the data on GDP per capita based on fixed prices are used, Guangxi's relative GDP per capita, using China's average as benchmark, declined significantly, especially in the early 1980s. Based on prices in 2000, Guangxi's GDP per capita was RMB888 in 1978, about 70% of China's average of RMB1,269. By 1989, Guangxi's GDP per capita was RMB1,548, about 53% of China's average of RMB2,942. The short boom in Guangxi after 1992 restored its GDP per capita to 60% of China's average. It is clear that in the early 1980s, rising prices in agricultural products helped to compensate for slow economic growth in real terms, producing a stable and even improving nominal relative GDP per capita in that period. Changing prices in the reform period have had a significant impact on the trend of relative GDP per capita in Guangxi. The existence of the "convergence" or "divergence" trend in the gap of GDP per capita can be tested statistically using a linear regression of the relative GDP per capita of Guangxi against time. The results show that the regression coefficients of relative GDP per capita of Guangxi in terms of China with time are significant at the 0.05 level, and are 0.286 and –0.382 for cases of current year prices and fixed prices, respectively, indicating opposite "convergence" and "divergence" trends when two different data sets are used.

However, if Guangdong is used as benchmark, the relative GDP per capita in Guangxi declined dramatically, irrespective of whether the data used was based on current year prices or fixed prices. When current year prices were used, the relative GDP per capita of Guangxi as a percentage of the GDP per capita in Guangdong declined from 60.98% in 1978 to 33.52% in 2000. When fixed prices were used, the relative GDP per capita of Guangxi in terms of Guangdong declined even more dramatically, from 76.83% in 1978 to 33.52% in 2000. Statistical analysis reveals that the regression coefficients of relative GDP per capita of Guangxi using Guangdong as benchmark are significant at the 0.05 level and are –1.193 and –2.114 for the two data sets, respectively, indicating a consistent trend of "divergence," that is, an increasing gap in GDP per capita between Guangxi and Guangdong.

Indeed, the GDP per capita in both Guangxi and Guangdong in 1978 was below the national average. By 2000, the GDP per capita in Guangxi was just one-third that in Guangdong. Obviously, the widening gap between Guangxi and Guangdong is largely due to the extraordinary economic growth in Guangdong, driven by a number of favourable factors including the "one-step ahead" policy and reforms, geographical proximity to Hong Kong and Macao, massive investment from Hong Kong, vibrant township and village enterprises (TVEs), local initiatives and bottom-up forces.[17] As a result, Guangdong's relative GDP per capita as a percentage of national average increased from below 100% in 1978 to 182.04% in 2000. Clearly, the gap in income per capita between Guangdong and China as a whole has widened in the period 1978–2000. This is also confirmed by statistical analysis. The regression coefficients of relative GDP per capita of Guangdong using China as benchmark are significant at the 0.05 level and are 4.237 and 4.887 for the two data sets, respectively, indicating a consistent trend of "divergence."[18]

The "β-convergence" can be assessed by comparing the annual growth rates of GDP per capita in Guangxi, Guangdong and China.[19] It was found that the annual growth rate of GDP per capita in Guangxi was only 7.53%, smaller than that in China (8.22%) and Guangdong (11.03%) for the period 1978–2000. Thus, a "β-convergence" did not occur between Guangxi and China and between Guangxi and Guangdong. However, a "β-convergence" occurred between Guangdong and China in the early 1980s, as Guangdong initially had a smaller GDP per capita in 1977 but its GDP per capita grew faster than that of China.

Urbanization and Regional Development

Urbanization has been an important process of socioeconomic transformation in post-reform China.[20] Advanced regions are generally associated with a high level of urbanization; that is, the percentage of urban population relative to total population. According to the 2000 Population Census, the level of urbanization was 36.2% for China as a whole, 46.1% for the eastern region, but only 28.7% for the western region. The level of urbanization in Guangxi was 28.2%, behind the average levels in the western region and China.[21] Does this mean that the urbanization process in Guangxi has been slow in the reform period? How has the economic restructuring process, especially marketization, the reform and privatization of the state-owned enterprises (SOEs), affected urban growth? What are the strengths and weaknesses of the urban system in Guangxi? This section will attempt to assess these issues and also examine the patterns of regional development in Guangxi, where cities play the role of economic centres.

To trace the urbanization process, a systematic data set on urban population is essential. However, the data on the urban population of China as a whole have been subject to frequent adjustments as a result of changes in the definition of urban population.[22] The time-series data for a provincial region like Guangxi are even more confusing. The recent statistical yearbook of Guangxi reported that 35.75 million out of a total population of 47.51 million were urban in the year 2000.[23] Such urban population data are not very useful as they are based on the areas, including counties, under the administration of cities. This chapter will use the population in the urban districts (*shiqu* 市區) of cities as the definition of urban population.

There were only 6 cities, Nanning 南寧, Liuzhou 柳州, Guilin, Wuzhou 梧州, Beihai 北海 and Pingxiang 憑祥 in Guangxi in the period 1958–1978. A total of 13 new cities have been designated in Guangxi since 1978. Figure 18.2 presents the cities and economic regions of Guangxi. Guangxi's urban population increased from 1.86 million to 14.01 million in the period 1978–2000. The percentage of the urban population in the total population

Figure 18.2 Cities and Economic Regions in Guangxi

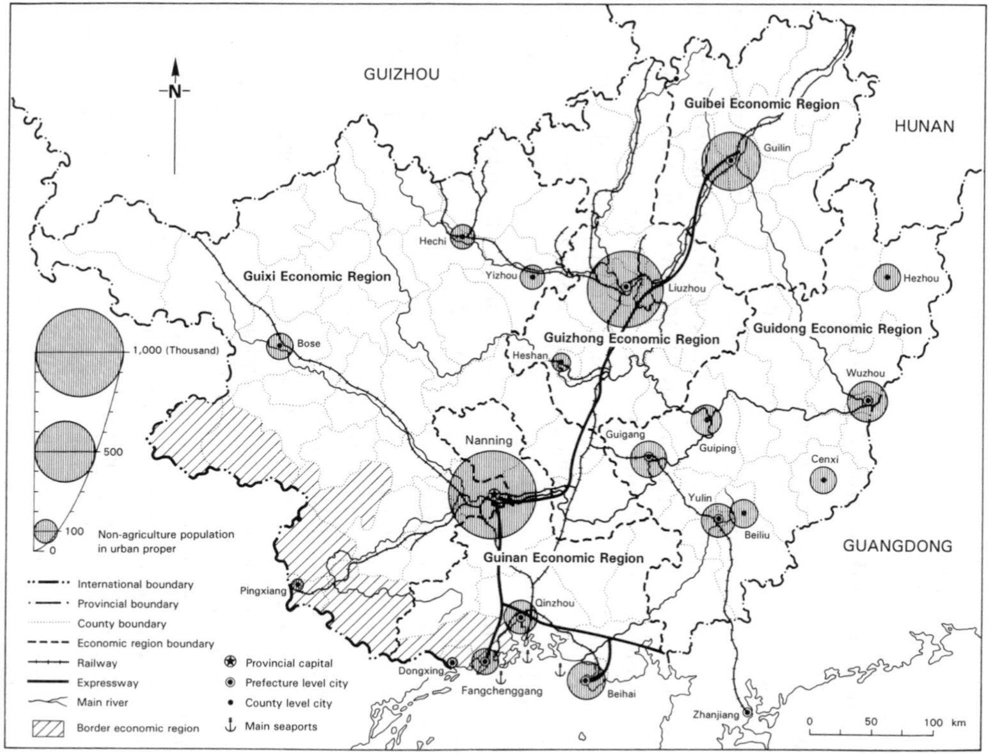

Source: See Table 18.5 for data on the non-agricultural population in various cities.

increased from 5.47% to 29.49% in the same period and is shown in Figure 18.3. The percentage of the urban population, 29.49% in 2000, is only slightly higher than the figure of 28.2% given in the population census of the same year.

According to China's household registration system (*hukou* 戶口), the nation's population is divided into agricultural and non-agricultural. The non-agricultural population, mostly found in cities, is entitled to many social and welfare benefits from the government.[24] As the majority of the non-agricultural population are urban residents, the size of the non-agricultural population is also a useful indicator of urbanization. Indeed, the urban non-agricultural population was the most common and strictest definition of urban population before the population census of 1982.[25] According to the official *hukou* statistics, the non-agricultural population increased from 3.60 million in 1978 to 8.26 million in 2000. The percentage of the non-agricultural population in the total population increased from 10.58% to

Figure 18.3 Percentage of the Urban Population in Guangxi, 1978–2000

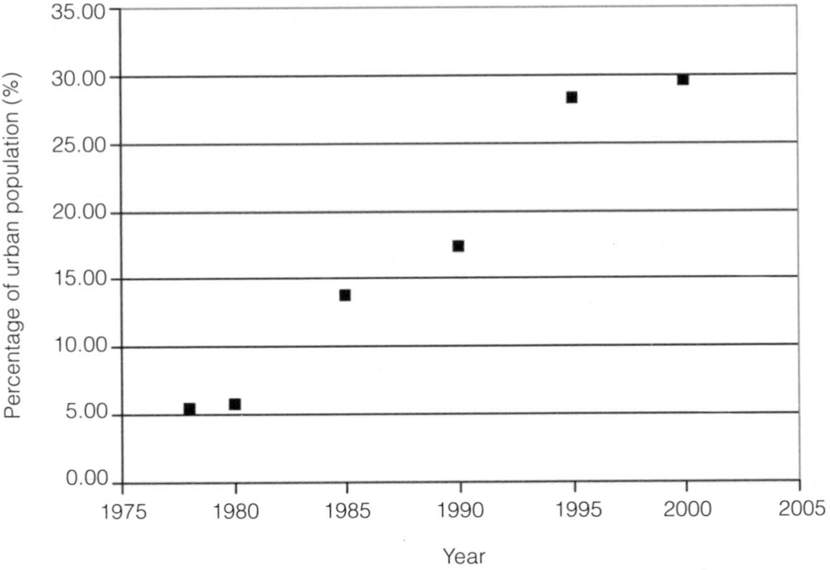

Sources: Calculated from data in *Guangxi tongji nianjian 2001* (see note 5), pp. 39, 173, 377–416; Guojia tongjiju chengshi shehui jingji diaocha zongdui (ed.), *Xin Zhongguo chengshi wushi nian* 新中國城市五十年 (Cities in New China Over 50 Years) (Beijing: Xinhua chubanshe 新華出版社, 1999), p. 40.

17.39% in the same period, as shown in Figure 18.4. It is clear that there has been significant expansion in the urban population and the non-agricultural population in Guangxi. The percentage of the urban population grew faster than the percentage of the non-agricultural population as the designation of new cities, especially the county-level cities, included a substantial proportion of people engaged in agriculture. For example, the city of Guiping 桂平 was designated as a county-level city in 1994 and its percentage of non-agricultural population was only 9.70% in 2000, the lowest in Guangxi.

Urbanization is closely related to industrialization and the transition from rural to urban employment. Thus, it is useful to examine the changes in employment in urban and rural Guangxi in detail to shed light on the process of urbanization and development. Due to continuing population growth, the labour force expanded from 15.50 million in 1980 to 25.66 million in 2000, producing mounting pressure on employment and urbanization in Guangxi. Urban employment increased from 2.50 million to 4.21 million in the period 1980–2000. But urban growth was not rapid

Figure 18.4 Percentage of the Non-agricultural Population in Guangxi, 1978–2000

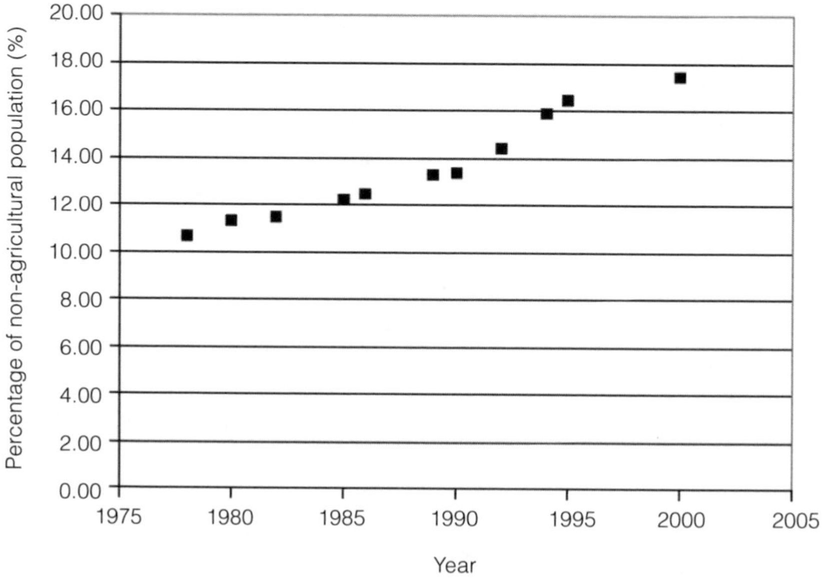

Source: Calculated from data in *Guangxi tongji nianjian 2001* (see note 5), pp. 39–40.

enough to accommodate population growth. Thus, rural employment continued to expand from 13.00 million to 21.45 million in the same period. As a result, as shown in Table 18.2, the shares of urban and rural employment were stable in the period 1980–2000.

Economic reform and marketization brought important changes in urban employment. As shown in Table 18.2, the percentage of those employed by SOEs declined from 83.20% to 59.66% in the period 1980–2000. Similarly, the share of employees in collectives also declined from 16.00% to 7.84% in the same period. According to the results of employment growth analysis, seen in Table 18.3, such reductions in employment in SOEs and collectives took place in the 1990s, when economic reform in Guangxi really began.[26] During the period 1990–2000, the number of SOE employees declined by 3.09% while that in collectives declined by 35.29%. For the period 1980–2000 as a whole, the number of SOE employees increased from 2.08 million to 2.51 million, while the number of employees in collectives decreased

Table 18.2 Employment Structure in Guangxi, 1980–2000

(Unit: %)

Year	1980	1985	1990	1995	2000
Rural	100	100	100.00	100.00	100.00
Primary sector	n.a.	n.a.	89.89	79.55	72.57
Secondary sector	n.a.	n.a.	3.99	6.41	6.93
Tertiary sector	n.a.	n.a.	6.12	14.04	20.51
Urban	100.00	100.00	100.00	100.00	100.00
SOE staff	83.20	74.70	75.98	67.64	59.66
Staff of collectives	16.00	18.21	14.96	11.23	7.84
Staff of other firms	0.00	0.00	0.59	3.11	8.56
Private businesses	0.80	7.08	8.48	14.91	21.32
Other employees	0	0	0	3.11	2.60
Guangxi	100.00	100.00	100.00	100.00	100.00
Primary sector	82.77	79.93	76.53	66.43	61.22
Secondary sector	8.09	8.76	9.82	11.83	10.83
Tertiary sector	9.14	11.31	13.66	21.74	27.94
Guangxi	100.00	100.00	100.00	100.00	100.00
Rural	83.87	83.80	83.83	82.44	83.61
Urban	16.13	16.20	16.17	17.56	16.39

Sources: Calculated from data in *Guangxi tongji nianjian 2001* (see note 5), pp. 51–52 and 195; Department of Comprehensive Statistics of NBS, *Comprehensive Statistical Data* (see note 19), p. 616.

from 0.40 million to 0.33 million. It is expected that the number of SOE employees will be cut further in the coming years due to the deepening of marketization and globalization. It is encouraging to see that the percentages of those engaged in urban employment in other firms and in private businesses have risen to 8.56% and 21.32% in 2000, respectively. Starting from a small employment base, these two categories of employment registered a significant expansion in the past two decades. Given that the SOE sector is expected to continue to shrink, other forms of economic ownership and private business have to be expanded greatly to create more jobs for the growing urban population.

It is also interesting to examine the changes in employment in the rural sector. The pressure on urbanization will be reduced if the non-agricultural sector and TVEs can provide many jobs in rural areas. According to Table 18.3, employment in the rural primary sector had declined by 2.03% in the period 1990–2000, while that in the secondary and tertiary sectors grew by 110.71% and 306.75%, respectively. It is interesting to note that in 2000, the rural tertiary sector employed 4.40 million people, even more than the total engaged in urban employment. Among rural non-agricultural employees in 2000, 3.53 million were employed by TVEs and 0.09 million by the private sector, while 0.72 million were self-employed. As there were

Table 18.3 Employment Growth by Sector in Guangxi

(Unit: %)

Year	1980–1990	1990–2000	1980–2000
Rural	35.98	21.36	65.03
Primary sector	n.a.	–2.03	n.a.
Secondary sector	n.a.	110.71	n.a.
Tertiary sector	n.a.	306.75	n.a.
Urban	36.36	23.39	68.26
SOE staff	24.52	–3.09	20.67
Staff of collectives	35.00	–35.29	–17.50
Staff of other firms	n.a.	1,700.00	n.a.
Private businesses	1,345.00	210.38	4,385.00
Other employees	n.a.	n.a.	n.a.
Guangxi	36.06	21.67	65.55
Primary sector	25.80	–2.66	22.45
Secondary sector	65.07	34.30	121.69
Tertiary sector	103.39	148.96	406.36

Sources: Same as Table 18.2.

only 0.51 million employees employed by TVEs in 1990, TVEs developed significantly only in the 1990s. This case again shows that economic transformation in Guangxi was delayed.[27]

For Guangxi as a whole, the percentage of those employed in the secondary sector increased slowly from 8.09% to 10.83% in the period 1980–2000, while the percentage employed in the tertiary sector increased dramatically from 9.14% to 27.94% (Table 18.2). This clearly indicates that industrialization was slow in Guangxi. Among the reasons for this are the lack of capital investment and the inability to compete in manufacturing. It is interesting to note that 1.29 out of the 2.78 million people in secondary sector employment and 4.40 out of the 7.17 million people in tertiary sector employment were found in the rural sector. Rural industries and trade services are small in scale with low efficiency and high environmental cost. How to integrate such rural economic development with urbanization is an important issue that needs to be handled properly.

Despite the significant increases in urbanization and urban growth, the level of urbanization is still low in Guangxi and its cities are also weak in terms of population size and economic strength. For example, in terms of the administrative status of a city, there were four municipalities directly under the administration of the central government and 15 cities with pro-provincial status in China in 1999.[28] A pro-provincial city 副省級市 enjoys certain administrative power of a province. The western region had one municipality and two cities with pro-provincial status. In terms of the size of the non-agricultural population, there were 13 super-large cities with a non-agricultural population of over 2 million, and 24 extra-large cities with a non-agricultural population of 1 to 2 million in China. The western region had 3 super-large cities and 5 extra-large cities. But none of the above cities were located in Guangxi. In this, Guangxi is similar to Qinghai, Ningxia 寧夏 and Tibet. However, these regions have much smaller populations, at 5.2, 5.6 and 2.6 million, respectively, than Guangxi. Although Guangxi has a population of 44.9 million, it lacks a leading city that can drive industrialization, technical upgrading and innovation.

There are 9 prefecture-level cities and 10 county-level cities in Guangxi.[29] Table 18.4 presents the ranks of 19 cities among all of the cities in the western region and in China in terms of non-agricultural population, GDP and GDP per capita in the urban districts in 1999. The capital and the largest city in Guangxi, Nanning, ranked only 39th in terms of non-agricultural population, 55th in terms of GDP and 114th in terms of GDP per capita among the 667 cities in China in 1999. Although Guangxi was

Table 18.4 Ranking of Guangxi's Cities in the Western Region and China in 1999

City	Non-agricultural population		GDP		GDP per capita	
	Western region	China	Western region	China	Western region	China
			Prefecture-level city			
Nanning	9	39	8	55	11	114
Liuzhou	11	51	12	91	10	110
Guilin	17	97	18	162	12	126
Wuzhou	37	219	47	367	19	145
Beihai	53	272	27	260	22	162
Fangchenggang	96	478	63	431	56	342
Qinzhou	68	347	33	283	86	476
Guigang	40	229	59	420	149	655
Yulin	60	313	51	386	100	530
			County-level city			
Cenxi	100	492	94	548	141	646
Guiping	74	389	70	471	153	660
Beiliu	80	412	60	422	133	625
Hezhou	102	498	54	389	105	539
Dongxing	158	664	133	630	27	203
Pingxiang	156	662	140	641	42	287
Bose	95	476	91	541	66	378
Hechi	104	510	88	532	53	334
Yizhou	118	555	64	435	80	459
Heshan	145	634	149	655	109	552

Source: Calculated from the data in *Zhongguo chengshi tongji nianjian 2000* (see note 28).

relatively more advanced than many other provincial regions in western China, its top city Nanning only ranked 9th in terms of non-agricultural population, 8th in terms of GDP and 11th in terms of GDP per capita among the 159 cities in western China in 1999. In total, only 3 cities, Nanning, Liuzhou and Guilin, in Guangxi ranked among the top 20 cities in terms of population and GDP in western China. Most interesting is that some county-level cities like Dongxing 東興 and Pingxiang also ranked high in terms of GDP per capita among the cities in the western region although their non-agricultural population was small. These two cities near the China-Vietnam border have clearly benefited tremendously in the 1990s from the border trade.

Table 18.5 Total Population and Non-agricultural Population in 2000 and Percentage Growth in the Non-agricultural Population in Cities of Guangxi, 1997–1999

City	Total population (Thousand)	Non-agricultural population[1] (Thousand)	Percentage of non-agricultural population[1] (%)	Percentage growth in the non-agricultural population 1997–1999 (%)
		Prefecture-level city		
Nanning	1,356	987	72.80	4.34
Liuzhou	907	793	87.40	2.11
Guilin	643	488	75.91	4.27
Wuzhou	335	257	76.74	0.75
Beihai	514	222	43.24	12.27
Fangchenggang	459	123	26.81	3.87
Qinzhou	1,171	182	15.52	5.36
Guigang	1,660	213	12.80	–16.09
Yulin	885	196	22.15	2.92
		County-level city		
Cenxi	777	115	15.26	3.50
Guiping	1,657	154	9.70	4.19
Beiliu	1,166	143	12.71	5.13
Hezhou	892	115	13.09	3.71
Dongxing	102	22	21.88	21.43
Pingxiang	102	29	28.50	4.40
Bose	325	121	37.64	4.94
Hechi	309	110	35.90	3.28
Yizhou	611	98	16.34	3.39
Heshan	140	61	42.96	–0.49

Note: [1] The data for county-level cities were for 1999.
Source: See Table 18.4; *Guangxi tongji nianjian 2001* (see note 5).

More detailed information on the population of various cities in Guangxi in 2000 is presented in Table 18.5. The non-agricultural population in Nanning approached 1 million in 2000. Liuzhou and Guilin, the most important industrial and tourist cities, respectively, also had sizable non-agricultural populations of 0.79 and 0.49 million, respectively. Most of the remaining cities had a non-agricultural population in the range of 0.10–0.25 million, as shown in Figure 18.2. The border cities, Dongxing and Pingxiang, only had a non-agricultural population of less than 30,000. The proportion of the non-agricultural population in the total population varied from city to city, depending on the scope of the urban districts under administration. The four largest prefectural-level cities had a non-agricultural population of over 75%, while seven cities had a non-agricultural population of under 20%. It is clear that there is substantial difference in socioeconomic conditions among the various cities in Guangxi. Table 18.5 also presents the percentage growth in the non-agricultural population of various cities. The most noticeable growth took place in Beihai and Dongxing whose non-agricultural populations grew by over 12% in the period 1997–1999. Most cities registered a modest growth of 2–5%, while the non-agricultural population in two cities, Guigang 貴港 and Heshan 合山, declined in the same period. The likely explanation is that increasing population mobility and urban competition in the post-reform period may cause the populations of some less developed cities to decline. The size of the temporary population was also small in Guangxi. In 1997, there was a registered temporary population of 0.72 million in Guangxi, of which 0.53 million came from within Guangxi and 0.19 million from other provinces. In 2000, Nanning and Liuzhou had the largest temporary populations of 0.18 and 0.10 million, respectively.[30] As a less developed region, Guangxi is not attractive to inter-provincial migrants and most of the temporary population is the result of increasing population mobility within Guangxi. This is significantly different from the case of Guangdong and Fujian 福建.[31]

Cities are centres of regional economies. It is useful to examine the economic strength of various cities. Table 18.6 presents the total GDP, GDP per capita and the GDP shares of primary, secondary and tertiary sectors in Guangxi. Nanning clearly dominated the urban system of Guangxi with a GDP of RMB21.52 billion in 2000. The industrial city, Liuzhou, came second, followed by Guilin. The top three cities accounted for 46.76% of the total GDP of all cities in Guangxi. Most other cities each only had a GDP of below RMB5 billion. In terms of economic structure, the tertiary sector had a greater share of GDP than the secondary sector in most cities except Liuzhou, Cenxi 岑溪, Beiliu 北流 and Heshan. The tertiary sector accounted for over 50% of GDP in five cities, including Nanning, Wuzhou, Dongxing, Pingxiang and Hechi 和池. The secondary sector was not strong in most cities. It accounted for over 40% of GDP only in four cities, including Liuzhou, Guilin, Yulin 玉林 and Heshan. On the other hand, the primary sector accounted for over 30% of GDP in eight cities, such as Beihai and Qinzhou 欽州. The cases of Beihai and Qinzhou were unexpected, as both were among the top three port cities in Guangxi. But they remained weak in manufacturing.

Table 18.6 GDP, GDP per capita and GDP Share of Primary, Secondary and Tertiary Sectors in Cities of Guangxi, 2000

City	GDP (RMB billion)	GDP per capita (RMB)	Primary GDP share (%)	Secondary GDP share (%)	Tertiary GDP share (%)
			Prefecture-level city		
Nanning	21.52	15,867	4.88	30.08	65.05
Liuzhou	14.30	15,771	2.46	55.03	42.52
Guilin	9.98	15,527	5.01	45.51	49.48
Wuzhou	5.01	14,951	2.14	36.50	61.37
Beihai	4.54	8,831	43.59	27.28	29.13
Fangchenggang	3.73	8,128	32.05	26.56	41.39
Qinzhou	6.35	5,421	51.60	14.97	33.43
Guigang	3.29	1,983	21.24	31.27	47.49
Yulin	4.34	4,904	25.65	41.05	33.30
			County-level city		
Cenxi	2.11	2,711	46.07	33.48	20.45
Guiping	3.06	1,845	51.07	18.10	30.83
Beiliu	3.96	3,396	39.09	33.91	27.00
Hezhou	4.38	4,909	39.91	26.74	33.35
Dongxing	1.21	11,832	26.53	16.19	57.28
Pingxiang	0.94	9,201	9.71	6.71	83.58
Bose	2.50	7,693	21.84	29.15	49.01
Hechi	2.52	8,166	13.81	32.20	53.99
Yizhou	3.69	6,047	30.61	25.55	43.84
Heshan	0.53	3,813	15.87	55.84	28.28

Source: Guangxi Zhuangzu, *Guangxi tongji nianjian 2001* (see note 5).

Five economic regions have been designated in Guangxi (Figure 18.2) and can be used to analyze the changing patterns of spatial development. It is noted that the border economic region is also part of the Guixi 桂西 and Guinan 桂南 economic regions and will not be analyzed here. The three largest cities, Nanning, Liuzhou and Guilin are located in the Guinan, Guizhong 桂中 and Guibei 桂北 economic regions, respectively. Among the five economic regions, the Guidong 桂東 and Guixi economic regions were the most populous, with over 13 million residing in each area in 2000. But, at less than RMB3,500, these two regions had the lowest GDP per capita in the same year. The most prosperous, the Guinan and Guibei economic regions, had a GDP per capita of RMB7,119 and RMB6,227, respectively, in 2000. Table 18.7 presents the percentage shares of GDP

Table 18.7 Percentage Share of GDP, Population and GDP per capita of Economic Regions in Guangxi, 1991–2000

(Unit: %)

Economic region	1991			1995			2000		
	GDP	Population	GDP per capita	GDP	Population	GDP per capita	GDP	Population	GDP per capita
Guidong	29.12	31.10	93.61	32.43	31.60	102.63	24.16	32.37	74.63
Guinan	22.44	17.15	130.81	22.88	17.37	131.74	27.29	17.68	154.39
Guixi	20.14	28.74	70.08	18.79	28.15	66.76	19.84	27.50	72.16
Guibei	11.79	10.64	110.84	11.42	10.47	109.14	13.70	10.15	135.04
Guizhong	16.51	12.36	133.56	14.47	12.41	116.58	15.00	12.31	121.89
Total	100.00	100.00	100.00	100.00	100.00	100.00	100.00	100.00	100.00

Sources: *Guangxi nianjian 1992*; *1996*; *2001* (see note 48).

Figure 18.5 Level of Development in Five Economic Regions in Guangxi, 1991–2000

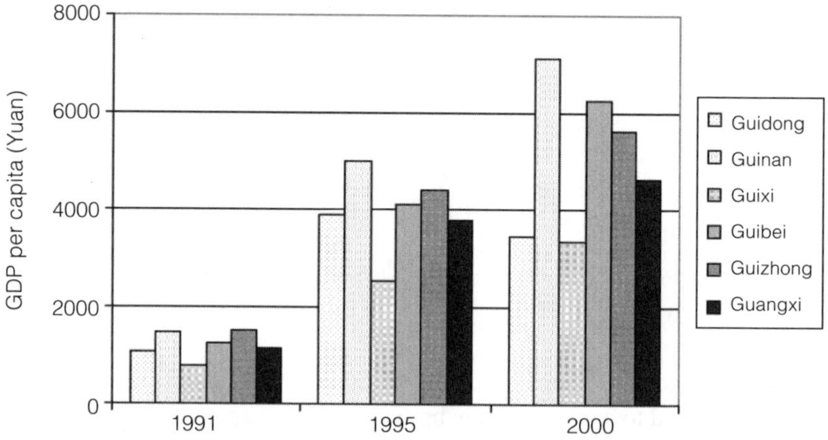

Sources: See Table 18.7.

and population, while Figure 18.5 presents the GDP per capita of various economic regions over the period 1991–2000. The percentage share of GDP per capita of an economic region relative to the average GDP per capita of the province is also presented. All of this information reveals the important spatial transformation that occurred in Guangxi in 1991–2000. Consistent data from the 1980s are not available. Thus, the analysis focuses on the 1990s, when economic reform in Guangxi was accelerating.

In the period 1991–1995, the share of Guangxi's GDP taken up by the Guinan and Guidong economic regions increased because of rapid development on the coast in the southeast region, while the GDP shares of the other economic regions decreased. In 1995–2000, the GDP shares of the Guinan and Guibei economic regions increased significantly. The boom in the Guibei economic region had much to do with the expansion in tourism, led by Guilin. Such an economic shift took place in a situation where population distribution was relatively stable. As a result, the spatial pattern in the level of development changed dramatically. In 1991, at RMB1,503, the GDP per capita in the Guizhong economic region was the highest, 33.56% higher than the average in Guangxi. By 1995, the Guizhong economic region had been overtaken in GDP per capita by the Guinan economic region. The GDP per capita in Guizhong was only 16.58% higher than the average in Guangxi, while the GDP per capita in Guinan was 31.74% higher than the average in Guangxi. Such a change has had the effect of slightly reducing spatial inequality in Guangxi, as the CV (coefficient of variation) of GDP per capita was reduced slightly from 24.66% to 22.92% in 1991–1995.

By 2000, the Guizhong economic region had also been overtaken by the Guibei economic region in GDP per capita. In that year, the GDP per capita in the Guinan and Guibei economic regions was 54.39% and 35.04% higher than the average in Guangxi, respectively, while the GDP per capita in Guizhong was 21.89% higher than the average in Guangxi. Rapid economic development in the Guinan economic region actually increased spatial inequality in Guangxi, as the CV of GDP per capita increased from 22.92% to 32.94% in 1995–2000. Clearly, economic development in Guangxi has had important spatial implications. the development in the Guinan and Guibei economic regions has been the most impressive. Indeed, the Guinan, Guizhong and Guibei economic regions form a development corridor with super infrastructure and good economic foundations. This development corridor, especially the Nanning-Qinzhou-Beihai-Fangchenggang area in the Guinan coastal region, should be the focus of further development. Effective government policies should be designed to attract capital investment and human resources to this area so that it can successfully compete in a globalizing economy.

Challenges and Opportunities in a Globalizing World

Previous sections have examined the resource and geo-political advantages of Guangxi and its current status in urbanization and regional development. This section will examine the challenges and opportunities facing Guangxi in the context of the western development strategy and China's entry into the World Trade Organization (WTO).

Impact of the Western China Development Strategy

As a less advanced area in China, Guangxi is included in the strategy to develop the western region of China, formally announced in 1999. This new development strategy involves the drive to mobilize national and local resources, and to attract an inflow of foreign capital to construct and develop the western region of China. The key objectives of this strategy are to reduce poverty, restore the region's ecological balance through environmental conservation and ecological construction, make use of natural resources and achieve economic development.[32] Since 2000, construction has begun in over 20 key projects, involving a total investment of RMB400 billion. The central government invested over RMB70 billion in each of the years 2000 and 2001.[33] Two major projects involving Guangxi are the construction of a sea passage for the greater southwest region of China and the transmission of electricity from the western region to the eastern region of China. Only the issue of the sea passage will be examined in detail in this section.

The central government decided to develop Guangxi, the only coastal provincial region in the southwest, as the sea passage for the greater southwest region in 1992 and as part of a major initiative to achieve development and regional integration in the southwest region of China.[34] Guangxi's ports are regarded as the best and closest outlets for goods from this region to be exported to foreign countries. For example, the distance from Chongqing to Qinzhou port is 1,029 km shorter than the distance from Chongqing to Shanghai 上海 port and 563 km shorter than the distance from Chongqing to Guangzhou 廣州. A consensus on development was reached between the central government and the Guangxi government. Thus, several railways, highways and seaports were under construction in the period 1992–1999, well before the announcement of the strategy to develop western China.[35]

The most significant is the construction of the Nan-Kun 南昆 (Nanning-Kunming 昆明) Railway in 1990–1997. The railway, 898 km long and involving an investment of RMB15 billion, passes through poor areas of Guangxi, Guizhou and Yunnan, and is considered a major project in poverty alleviation. The travel distance between some parts of the southwest and a seaport was reduced by 700 km. The Nan-Kun Railway has a capacity of 20 million tonnes a year. In 1998, it carried 1.08 million passengers and 5.5 billion km-tonnes of goods. With an annual operating revenue of RMB 0.52 billion, the new railway has been efficiently utilized, contributing to the economic development of the southwest region. Another, the Li-Qin 黎欽 (Litang 黎塘-Qinzhou) Railway, funded by Guangxi, is also significant, because it allows goods from Chongqing and Sichuan to be diverted to ports in Guangxi instead of to Zhanjiang 湛江 port in Guangdong. This locally invested railway was 156 km long and was constructed in 1996–1998 with a capital investment of RMB1 billion.

The construction of expressways in Guangxi began after 1992. The longest, the Guilin-Beihai Expressway, is 575 km and involved an investment of RMB10.5 billion. It was completed in 1999. The Guilin-Liuzhou Expressway, the first expressway in Guangxi, is one section of the Guilin-Beihai Expressway. It was constructed in 1993–1997, and is 140 km long and cost RMB1.86 billion to build. The second expressway, the Qinzhou-Fangchenggang 防城港 Expressway, was constructed in 1994–1997. It is 98 km long and involved an investment of RMB2.12 billion. By 2000, a network of expressways 812 km long had emerged, connecting major cities and seaports in Guangxi. The highways handled a total of 235.14 million tonnes of goods in 2000.

The construction of seaports is an important part of the plan to create a sea passage for the greater southwest. It has been estimated that 21 sites are suitable for the construction of seaports in Guangxi. The total capacity of these seaports can reach 0.2 billon tonnes if they are fully developed. There are currently three main seaports in Guangxi: Beihai, Qinzhou and Fangchenggang. The history of Beihai dates back to 1876. In 1984, it was designated by the Chinese government as one of the 14 open coastal cities. Its handling capacity has expanded since then, especially after 1992. From 1992 to 2000, its capacity increased from 1.90 to 3.04 million tonnes. The goods throughput in Beihai increased from 1.31 to 2.65 million tonnes in the same period. The construction of Fangchenggang only began in 1968. It is now the largest seaport in Guangxi.[36] The port has also expanded dramatically since 1992. Its handling capacity increased from 3.25 to 9.40 million tonnes in 1992–2000. The goods throughput also increased from 2.20 to 9.19 million tonnes in 1990–2000. Qinzhou was only a minor port in 1992, when it could only handle ships of 500 dwt. The port has been expanded dramatically and it can now handle ships of 30,000 dwt. Its total handling capacity was 2.60 million tonnes in 2000 and will reach 11.58 million tonnes when all construction is completed.

It is clear that, with the strong support of the central government, Guangxi has invested heavily in the construction of a sea passage for the greater southwest. The construction of railways, highways and seaports will benefit economic development in Guangxi. However, four major issues have to be considered. First, will all the provinces in the southwest use the seaports in Guangxi or Guangdong as their sea passage? According to a major study on the sea passage for the greater southwest region of China,[37] seaports in Guangxi are not used by some provincial regions in the southwest. In the case of Sichuan, most of its goods were exported via the ports of Tianjin 天津 (0.14 million tonnes) and Shanghai (0.09 million tonnes) in 1998. Similarly, Chongqing has chosen Shanghai as its main sea passage, making use of the Yangzi River 長江 for economic transportation. In 1998, Chongqing's 1.13 million tonnes of imports and exports were via river transportation, in contrast to 33,430 tonnes via rail transport.[38] Yunnan will rely on ports in Guangxi as sea passage is facilitated by the newly completed Nan-Kun Railway. A land passage towards Southeast Asia and South Asia, especially the proposed Pan-Asia Railway, may take quite a long time to realize, due to the problems of rail bottlenecks in nearby, mostly poor, countries and the difficulty of multi-country co-operation, although Yunnan is actively seeking such possibilities.[39] The main sea passage for Guizhou depends on ports in Guangxi and Guangdong, but Guizhou is adopting an open strategy towards four directions. Clearly, there is no consensus among the provincial regions in the southwest about using Guangxi as their main sea passage, except for Yunnan and Guizhou.

Second, ports in Guangxi are not the only choice for the export of goods via seaports in South China. Indeed, the port of Zhanjiang is located very close to the three main ports in Guangxi. For example, the distance from Chongqing to Qinzhou is only 51 km shorter than the distance from Chongqing to Zhanjiang. The savings in transport costs of using Qinzhou instead of Zhanjiang are negligible. Thus, the potential competition between Zhanjiang and the ports in Guangxi would be just another case of competition among local governments that is all too common in post-reform China. From the viewpoint of economies of scale, it is not wise to operate several seaports within short distances. In terms of competitiveness, Zhanjiang was the eleventh largest seaport in China, with a throughput of 20.38 million tonnes in 2000. It seems that the efforts of the Guangdong government have focused on the development in Pearl River Delta. It made no special attempts to strengthen the position of Zhanjiang when Guangxi was chosen by the central government as the sea passage for the greater southwest region. Nevertheless, Zhanjiang will continue to be a keen competitor of the seaports in Guangxi, and the result will be that none of them will become a giant seaport with a status similar to Shanghai, Guangzhou or Hong Kong. Currently, the Li-Zhan 黎湛 (Litang-Zhanjiang) Railway is considered the second sea passage for the greater southwest. Indeed, goods from Guizhou actually go through Beihai in Guangxi and Zhanjiang in Gaungdong, with similar shares between them. In 1998, Beihai and Zhanjiang handled 0.44 and 0.41 million tonnes of goods, respectively, from Guizhou.[40] The second track of the Li-Zhan Railway, 270 km long and involving a capital investment of RMB1.99 billion, was constructed in the period 1992–1999, increasing its transportation capacity from 12 to 31 million tonnes.[41] Its capacity will be further increased to 40 million tonnes by 2007 and it will be able to divert goods from Guizhou, Chongqing and Sichuan to Zhanjiang instead of to ports in Guangxi. The competition between Zhanjiang and the ports in Guangxi is demonstrated by the construction of the railway section connecting Litang to Qinzhou in a bid to divert goods away from Zhanjiang. The Li-Qin Railway, 156 km long with a capacity of 15 million tonnes, was totally financed by Guangxi itself, with an investment of RMB1 billion. It was constructed in 1996–1998. Unless a sufficient demand for transportation is generated locally, the combined capacity of the Li-Qin Railway and the Li-Zhan Railway will surpass that of Xiang-Gui 湘桂 (Hunan-Guangxi) Railway that feeds both of them from the north, resulting in a waste of capacity.

The third issue is the cost competitiveness of the seaports in Guangxi. They are not necessarily the most economical sea passage, even if their distance to the source of goods is the shortest. This is partly because of the high cost of land transport, high port service fees, poor service quality, low efficiency in port operations and less frequent shipping services in the ports of Guangxi.[42] Local railways (those financed, owned and operated by local governments), of which there are 728 km versus the 2,385 km of railway owned by the state, usually charge higher fees than do the state railways. Thus, although the nearest seaport for Chengdu 成都 is any seaport in Guangxi, the port of Shanghai is used because the total cost is lower. Similarly, transport down the Yangzi River to Shanghai is the main route for Chongqing, as it is over 50% cheaper than using rail transport to reach ports in Guangxi. The completion of the Three Georges Dam will increase the transportation capacity of the Yangzi River within Sichuan and

Chongqing from the current 10 million tonnes to 50 million tonnes by 2030, reducing the potential amount of goods destined for ports in South China.[43]

The fourth issue is the co-ordination of the development of the three main seaports in Guangxi. One study estimated that the total throughput in the seaports of Guangxi would reach 21, 42, 62 and 100 million tonnes in 2000, 2005, 2010 and 2020, respectively.[44] Given the above considerations, the projected dramatic growth in throughput is not likely to materialize. However, it seems that the three main seaports are positioning themselves for rapid expansion. Currently, the construction of Fangchenggang is mainly financed by the state, while the capital market is the main source of capital for the construction of the port of Beihai, through a company listed in the Shenzhen 深圳 Stock Exchange. As for the construction of Qinzhou port, it is being financed by some 20 pier owners with an investment over RMB 2.45 billion. This use of the market is a new approach to port construction, but the long-term planning of port development is difficult to achieve. Clearly, three different kinds of capital sources have been channelled into the three ports respectively, indicating a situation of market fragmentation, with different modes of port operation and degrees of local control. Without comprehensive planning and co-ordination, much-needed capital investment may be wasted on the over-construction of seaport capacity. Indeed, only 35% of the capacity was utilized in the port of Fangchenggang in 1998 while only 54% of the capacity was utilized in the port of Qinzhou.[45] According to the current planning,[46] the port of Fangchenggang will be the main port and sea passage for the southwest region, while the port of Qinzhou will be an industrial port serving a large coastal manufacturing base yet to be developed. The port of Beihai will expand modestly, and act as a port for commerce and trade. It is preferable to concentrate on one major port, such as Fangchenggang, to achieve economies of scale, with frequent shipping services, especially for containers. Some institutional changes in port financing are needed, so that market capital can also play a role in the major port, rather than being excluded and forced into the development of other secondary ports.

Economic Competitiveness and Border Trade

Guangxi has established a good economic foundation, especially since the early 1990s. Major industries include food manufacturing, machinery manufacturing, a non-ferrous metal industry and the manufacturing of building materials.[47] Sugarcane production is the most significant in the food manufacturing industry. Guangxi has been the biggest producer of sugarcane in China since 1993. The machinery manufacturing industry is focused on the auto-industry, especially on mini-cars. Indeed, the Liuzhou mini-car factory, the largest producer of mini-cars in China, has been designated by the state as the production base of mini-cars in South China. The non-ferrous metal industry focuses on the mining and processing of tin and aluminum.

Although economic reforms in Guangxi started at a much later stage, they have revitalized various enterprises, especially SOEs, which had been loss-making for many years. The reform of SOEs in Guangxi did not really begin until May 1998.[48] By 2000, the manufacturing sector as a whole generated a total profit of RMB3.59 billion and a total profit and tax of RMB11.70 billion. The SOEs generated a total profit of RMB1.27 billion and a total profit and tax of RMB4.77 billion, while the state-holding enterprises (SHEs) generated a total profit of RMB1.21 billion and a total profit and tax of RMB3.90 billion in the same year. Associated with economic development, the number of people living in poverty in Guangxi fell from 15 million to 1.69 million in the period 1985–1999.[49] Over 0.21 million people living in poverty have been resettled to areas with a better environment, although permanent housing has yet to be built for 42,769 migrants in 8,971 households. It is expected that a further 0.30 million impoverished people will be resettled via migration in the next 10 years. Over RMB11.71 billion is needed to subsidize these rural migrants, at a cost of RMB5,000–10,000 each, and to build roads for villages.

But Guangxi's economy and cities are relatively weak, especially in an age of regional economic integration and globalization. The state strategy of developing western China will certainly benefit Guangxi, especially through large-scale investment in infrastructure, such as railways, seaports and hydropower stations. But for sustained economic growth and prosperity, it is also necessary to enhance the competitiveness of the economic sectors in Guangxi.

Economic growth in Guangxi has relied heavily on state investment based on the development policy of the central government. Non-state or private sector investment remains weak. SOEs accounted for RMB32.88 billion, or 49.82% of the total investment in Guangxi in 2000. The inflow of foreign investment remains unstable. Actual utilized foreign investment increased from US$34.35 million in 1984 to a peak of US$1,282.54 million in 1998, then declined to US$752.81 million in 2000. Stagnation in capital investment is likely to slow down the rate of economic growth. Another feature of Guangxi is its heavy dependence on financial subsidies from the central government. Total fiscal revenue increased from RMB6.12 to RMB14.71 billion, while fiscal expenditures increased from RMB7.85 to RMB25.85 billion in the period 1992–2000. Thus, the fiscal deficit increased from RMB1.73 to RMB11.14 billion in the same period, despite an earlier decline in 1980–1983.[50]

The secondary sector remains weak, contributing only 36.4% to total GDP, lower than the tertiary sector in 2000. It accounted for only 10.8% of employment, in contrast to the 28.0% employed in the tertiary sector. The SOEs dominated the manufacturing sector, contributing 66.22% to total industrial output, while collective enterprises and enterprises with Hong Kong, Macao, Taiwan and foreign investment accounted for only 13.22% and 11.42% of total industrial output in 2000, respectively. The traditional manufacturing sector is not competitive, due to the less advanced technology, poor product quality, small-scale production, idle production facilities and low profit margins found in many enterprises. For example, in 1995, there were 105 sugar refinery factories with an average daily capacity of only 2,100 tonnes and 290 cement production factories with an average annual output of 70,000 tonnes.[51] Many local residents buy products from other provinces, reducing the demand for local production. Thus, as part of a large domestic market, Guangxi is already under the pressure of competition from other provinces.

China's entry to the WTO and the further opening up of the country to foreign trade and investment will further increase the pressure from competition. The standards for technology, environmental protection, hygiene and labour rights will be raised, making exporting more difficult. In the meantime, the domestic market for traditional products such as grain, sugar and automobiles will be squeezed by the importation of foreign products. Thus, Guangxi has no other choice but to upgrade its traditional industries using new technologies. In the meantime, efforts should be made to develop new industries, such as Chinese medicine and high-tech products. Market reforms should be consolidated to stimulate the efficiency of various economic sectors, especially the state-owned sector. It is also necessary to improve education and training and to attract skilled labour from other provinces.

Continuous efforts should be made to encourage regional co-operation, attract both domestic and foreign capital, and to expand international trade. In 2000, Guangxi received US$752.81 million in actual foreign investment, 57% of it from Asia. Among the total contracted foreign investment, Hong

Kong, Macao and Taiwan contributed 39%, North America 27% and Latin America 17%. Actual utilized foreign investment was concentrated in the manufacturing sector (28%), real estate development (22%) and the electricity and gas industries (14%). The top destinations for foreign investment were Guilin and Nanning, receiving actual utilized foreign investment of US$116 million and US$81 million, respectively.[52]

Two examples can illustrate how domestic capital has played an important role in the economic development of Guangxi. First is the Pingguo 平果 Aluminium Corporation, the largest producer of aluminium in Guangxi, based on huge recoverable reserves of 0.22 billion tonnes.[53] The company has planned to implement a second and third stage of development jointly with the China Aluminium Corporation, which will provide capital and technology. The annual production capacity of aluminium will be expanded from 0.50 million tonnes in 2000 to 1.5 million tonnes by 2005.[54] The second example is the development in the border city of Dongxing, a county-level city designated in 1996. The largest textile shopping mall in Southwest China named the Trade City of Zhejiang 浙江商業城, with a total floor space of 0.123 million m^2, was built with investment by two businessmen from Zhejiang. This example shows how domestic private capital can be used to develop high-quality trading facilities in Guangxi, contributing to the regional economic development.[55]

It will be useful to examine the role of border trade in Guangxi, which has been one of its geographical advantages. Trading with Vietnam, a developing country, needs special consideration. Vietnam had a population of 78.5 million in 2000. Its GDP grew from US$6.5 billion to US$31.3 billion in the period 1990–2000.[56] Its GDP per capita was US$390 in 2000. The value of the country's imports and exports was US$14.26 billion and US$14.45 billion, respectively. There was little border trade before 1978, because bilateral relations were overshadowed by over US$20 billion of Chinese aid to Vietnam. Following border conflicts in 1978–1979, hostile relationship between the two countries put an end to almost all border contacts in the period 1979–1987. The Sino-Vietnamese relations have improved since 1988, and normal relations were eventually restored in 1991. China and Vietnam have embarked on a similar path of economic reform and opening up to international trade and investment since 1978 and 1986, respectively.

Significant expansion in border trade occurred in the period 1989–1992, when the value of trade increased from RMB0.45 billion to RMB 2.60 billion. The initial expansion is said to have helped Guangxi export many products of not very high quality, such as beer and glass, which were facing great competitive pressures in the domestic market. Some border cities such as Pingxiang and Dongxing flourished in this period. However, as economic development in Vietnam grew and as the country's international trade expanded, the expansion in its border trade with Guangxi slowed down significantly. The total value of the border trade increased only slowly to RMB3.78 billion by 2000. There are several reasons for the slow growth.[57]

First, the border trade has become highly unbalanced, with a huge trade surplus in favour of Guangxi after 1995. In 2000, Guangxi's total exports were RMB2.60 billion, while import were only RMB1.18 billion. Second, the Vietnamese government has intervened in the border trade by introducing trade barriers to protect its domestic market and jobs, as well as national security. In 1992, Vietnam banned the import of 17 categories of Chinese consumer products such as electric fans, common light bulbs, fabrics and batteries, although such a ban was not very effective and the banned categories were reduced to only 3 in 1993.[58] Vietnam increased its border trade handling fees and import duties on chemical fertilizers and bicycles in 2000. Third, high-quality Chinese products from other provinces, such as beer from Guangdong, have replaced products from Guangxi. There was a lack of trust between Vietnam and Guangxi. Guangxi regarded Vietnam as a poor developing country, while to Vietnam Guangxi was a poor underdeveloped region in China. Both parties did not expect to gain much from trading with each other. Fourth, the border trade was originally limited to a small-scale cross-border trade and was liable to low tariffs in China. Thus, businessmen and trading companies from all over China intent on exporting their products moved into border cities like Dongxing, which reportedly hosts 180 representative offices. They abused the low tariff incentives for the border trade. Goods involved in the border trade came to include such items as tropical fruits and raw materials from Indonesia and North China. Thus, since 1993, the central government of China has attempted to limit the border trade to a cross-border barter exchange and coastal traffic to vessels of 2,000 dwt or less.[59] Fifth, the private businessmen engaged in the border trade are shortsighted. They pursue short-term profits, disregarding product quality and reputation. Thus, the share of the border trade in the total trade between Guangxi and Vietnam has declined. In 1999, the border trade amounted to US$0.68 billion, accounting for 60% of the total international trade between Guangxi and Vietnam.

Nevertheless, Vietnam was Guangxi's largest international trading partner in 1999, accounting for 31.3% of its total international trade, including border trade. Even excluding the border trade and considering only formal international trade, Vietnam was the third top destination for Guangxi's exports, after the U.S. and Hong Kong, according to trade statistics from the first 10 months of 2000.

Thus, the expansion of both the border trade and the formal trade with Vietnam is high on the agenda of Guangxi. One major measure is to seek approval from the central government to establish two border trading zones (BTZs) similar to free trade zones in other countries. One proposed BTZ is in Pingxiang, with an area of 3.50km^2, and another BTZ in Dongxing is to be upgraded from its previous status as border economic co-operation zone established in 1992, to have an area of 4.07km^2.[60] The Dongxing BTZ will be the counterpart of Vietnam's pro-provincial level Mong Cai 芒街 Special Economic Zone, just across a bridge from Dongxing, established in 1996. Guangxi as well as Yunnan has also been enthusiastic in improving railway and highway links with the border, in the hope of facilitating international trade. The building of an expressway linking Nanning with Youyiguan 友誼關, right at the Sino-Vietnam border, has been proposed.[61] However, such infrastructure will not be sufficiently utilized if no corresponding construction is made on the Vietnam side. For example, no train services between Nanning and Hanoi 河內, the capital of Vietnam, have been provided so far. It is clear that co-ordination is needed in the construction of infrastructure on both sides of the border. Railway, highway and river transportation on one side of the border should be matched with a demand for and timely construction of transportation infrastructure on the other side of the border.

Summary and Conclusion

Guangxi is one of the most favourable regions in China with all kinds of natural and geo-political advantages. A major state-led economic drive in 1992 to construct a sea passage for the southwest region of China has had a significant impact on the development of Guangxi. The recent state strategy of developing the western region of China will further enhance Guangxi's role as sea passage for the southwest and will offer the regions opportunities to realize its economic potential.

This chapter has examined Guangxi comprehensively, with a focus on several important issues. A brief assessment of the population, resources and environment indicated that Guangxi has a good resource base. But its population has increased rapidly in the past decades and the general level of education is low. As a region in the periphery of China, there had been little investment in Guangxi in the pre-reform period under the planned economy. In the post-reform period, an analysis of the development gap between Guangxi and China indicated that Guangxi's relative GDP per capita, using China's average as benchmark, declined significantly, especially in the early 1980s when GDP per capita based on fixed prices was used. If Guangdong was used as benchmark, the relative GDP per capita in Guangxi declined even more dramatically due to dramatic economic growth in Guangdong. This indicates the need to revitalize Guangxi's economy in the new century.

The process of urbanization has also lagged behind in Guangxi. The autonomous region lacks major economic centres. There is no super-large city or extra-large city in Guangxi. No city has a pro-provincial status. As the capital and the largest city in Guangxi, Nanning's rank was not high in terms of non-agricultural population, GDP and GDP per capita among the 667 cities in China in 1999. Thus, much has to be done to develop a strong metropolitan region, especially in the Nanning-Qinzhou-Beihai-Fangchenggang region, which is also closely related to the project of the sea passage for the southwest region.

Guangxi has been the focus of development since 1992, when it was chosen as the major gateway for the southwest region of China. There has been much investment in the construction of railways, highways and seaports. However, some issues have to be resolved to achieve the original objectives of development. They relate to the destination of transportation from the southwest, the cost advantage of using seaports in Guangxi, the competition and division of labour among seaports in Guangxi and between Guangxi and Guangdong. Service quality and efficiency also have to be improved to attract goods to Guangxi's seaports. In terms of seaport development, it is preferable to concentrate on one major port such as Fangchenggang to achieve economies of scale, with frequent shipping services, especially for containers.

With an estimated surplus rural population of 4 million in 2000 and an annual net growth in population of 0.4–0.5 million in the next 10 years,[62] Guangxi has to speed up industrialization and urbanization to provide more jobs, a situation similar to other parts of China. A weak agriculture and economy, lagging industrialization and urbanization, limited international trade and foreign investment, undeveloped science and technology, poverty and employment pressure, and problems of sustainable development are key problems facing Guangxi in the twenty-first century.[63] The key methods to solving these problems include further marketization, institutional reform, and technical upgrading and innovation to enhance the efficiency and competitiveness of Guangxi's government, firms, products and economy. Advancement in these aspects will also revitalize the border trade with Vietnam that is facing increasing pressure from competition after a period of boom in the mid-1990s.

Internally, Guangxi should further strengthen its traditional economies with resource advantages and foster the new economic sectors that are expanding worldwide such as tourism, electronics, transportation and communication. The major development should be focused on the coastal region, comprising the important cities of Nanning, Beihai, Qinzhou and Fangchenggang. The region will act as the node of the sea passage for the southwest, as well as the location of new industrial clusters that will reinforce each other. Comprehensive and dramatic reforms like those in Shenzhen and the Pearl River Delta in urban planning, land use, financing and administration are essential, so that capital and people will be able to agglomerate in this emerging metropolitan region. It would be ideal to concentrate on one development zone of high-tech industries, either in Nanning or Beihai, instead of the current four such zones or parks, as clustering and agglomeration have become critically important in technical innovation and modern industries. The tendency towards localism, in which each city wants to develop everything such as a high-tech park, software park and convention centre, should be overcome, so that limited financial resources can be most efficiently used. This may be achieved by the establishment of Guangxi-wide companies for the development of high-tech zones.

Externally, much effort should be made to attract more investment from domestic and foreign sources to make use of the advantageous coastal and border location and port facilities. Regional and international co-operation with provinces in the greater southwest, Guangdong and Hong Kong in South China, and Vietnam and countries in Southeast Asia should be enhanced to attract more investment and to expand regional and international trade.

Notes

1. Guangxi Tong 僮 Autonomous Region was established on 3 March 1958 to replace the previous Guangxi. In 1965, it is renamed the Guangxi Zhuang 壯 Autonomous Region. Its border with Guangdong was also finalized in 1965.

See Xiao Yongzi 肖永孜 (ed.), *Zhongguo xibu gailan: Guangxi* 中國西部概覽：廣西 (Introduction to the Western Region of China: Guangxi) (Beijing: Minzu chubanshe 民族出版社, 2000), pp. 8–9.

2. See Hans Hendrischke, "Guangxi: Towards Southwest China and Southeast Asia," in *China's Provinces in Reform: Class, Community and Political Culture*, edited by David S. G. Goodman (London: Routledge, 1997), pp. 21–47; Womack Brantly, "Sino-Vietnamese Border Trade: the Edge of Normalization," *Asian Survey*, Vol. 34, No. 6 (1994), pp. 513–28.
3. S. Ye, "Guangxi Cities: New Strategies for In-between Regions," in *Chinese Urban Reform: What Model Now?*, edited by R. Y. Kwok, W. Parish, A. G. Yeh and X. Xu (New York: M. E. Sharpe, 1990), pp. 213–29.
4. In addition to various data sources, some materials and observations were obtained for this study from an 11-day field trip to Guangxi during 15–25 May 2001, with the help of two professors in the Department of Environment and Urban Sciences of The Teachers' College of Guangxi, Nanning.
5. Population data in this section, unless specified, are drawn from Guangxi Zhuangzu zizhiqu tongjiju 廣西壯族自治區統計局 (ed.), *Guangxi tongji nianjian 2001* 廣西統計年鑑 2001 (Guangxi Statistical Yearbook 2001) (Beijing: Zhongguo tongji chubanshe 中國統計出版社, 2001).
6. For a detailed history of the minority population, see Xiao, *Zhongguo xibu gailan: Guangxi* (see note 1), pp. 194–213.
7. Guojia tongjiju renkou he shehui keji tongjisi 國家統計局人口和社會科技統計司 (ed.), *Zhongguo renkou tongji nianjian 2001* 中國人口統計年鑑2001 (China Population Statistics Yearbook 2001) (Beijing: Zhongguo tongji chubanshe, 2001), pp. 57–58.
8. Arable land and grain output per capita have been calculated by the author based on data from the National Bureau of Statistics (NBS) (ed.), *China Statistical Yearbook 2001* (Beijing: China Statistics Press, 2001).
9. Xiao, *Zhongguo xibu gailan: Guangxi* (see note 1), pp. 17–18.
10. Ibid., pp. 70–73.
11. Ibid., pp. 18–20.
12. Sites other than Guilin are also very attractive. Field observation, 15–25 May 2001.
13. Beihai was designated one of 14 open coastal cities in 1984. See J. Shen and Y. M. Yeung, "Free Trade Zones in China: Review and Prospect," *Occasional Paper* No. 122 (Hong Kong: Hong Kong Institute of Asia-Pacific Studies, The Chinese University of Hong Kong, 2002), pp. 1–36.
14. Hendrischke, "Guangxi" (see note 2).
15. For example, C. Cindy Fan, "Of Belts and Ladders: State Policy and Uneven Regional Development in Post-Mao China," *Annals of the Association of American Geographers*, Vol. 85, No. 3 (1995), pp. 421–49; J. Shen, "Urban and Regional Development in Post-Reform China: The Case of Zhujiang

Delta," *Progress in Planning*, Vol. 57, No. 2 (2002), pp. 91–140; S. X. Zhao, "Spatial Disparities and Economic Development in China, 1953–92: A Comparative Study," *Development and Change*, Vol. 27, No. 1 (1996), pp. 131–60; Y. D. Wei, "Fiscal Systems and Uneven Regional Development in China, 1978–1991," *Geoforum*, Vol. 27, No. 3 (1996), pp. 329–44.

16. *China Statistical Yearbook 2001* (see note 8), pp. 49 and 51; Statistical Bureau of Guangdong (ed.), *Guangdong Statistical Yearbook 2001* (Beijing: China Statistics Press, 2001), p. 119; *Guangxi tongji nianjian 2001* (see note 5), pp. 28 and 30.
17. See Y. M. Yeung and D. K. Y. Chu (eds.), *Guangdong: Survey of a Province Undergoing Rapid Change* (Hong Kong: The Chinese University Press, 1998); Shen, "Urban and Regional Development in Post-Reform China" (see note 15).
18. As the per capita GDP of Guangdong as a percentage of the per capita GDP of China is generally over 100%, its positive regression coefficient with time means there is an increasing gap in GDP per capita between Guangdong and China as the GDP per capita in Guangdong keeps growing.
19. The growth index of GDP per capita in Guangdong for the year 1978 was from the Department of Comprehensive Statistics of NBS, *Comprehensive Statistical Data and Materials on 50 Years of New China* (Beijing: China Statistics Press, 1999), p. 594.
20. See, for example, J. Shen, "Chinese Urbanization and Urban Policy," in *China Review 2000*, edited by C. M. Lau and J. Shen (Hong Kong: The Chinese University Press, 2000), pp. 455–80; J. Shen, K. Y. Wong and Z. Feng, "State Sponsored and Spontaneous Urbanization in the Pearl River Delta of South China, 1980–1998," *Urban Geography*, Vol. 23, No. 7 (2002), pp. 674–94.
21. *China Statistical Yearbook 2001* (see note 8), p. 101.
22. See J. Shen, "Rural Development and Rural to Urban Migration in China 1978–1990," *Geoforum*, Vol. 26 (1995), pp. 395–409; L. J. C. Ma and G. Cui, "Administrative Changes and Urban Population in China," *Annals, Association of American Geographers*, Vol. 77, No. 3 (1987), pp. 373–95; L. Zhang and S. X. Zhao, "Re-examining China's 'Urban' Concept and the Level of Urbanization," *China Quarterly*, No. 154 (1998), pp. 330–81.
23. See *Guangxi tongji nianjian 2001* (see note 5), pp. 39–40.
24. In the reform period, state benefits and welfare support have been reduced, especially in the areas of housing and employment. But the difference between the agricultural population and non-agricultural population remains significant. See Shen, Wong and Feng, "State Sponsored and Spontaneous Urbanization" (see note 20).
25. See Shen, "Rural Development" (see note 22).
26. Hendrischke argued that economic reform in Guangxi was slow in the 1980s and only took off in 1991. See Hendrischke, "Guangxi" (see note 2).

27. *China Statistical Yearbook 2001* (see note 8), pp. 110–11; Guojia tongjiju 國家統計局 (ed.), *Zhongguo tongji nianjian 1991* 中國統計年鑑1991 (China Statistical Yearbook 1991) (Beijing: Zhongguo tongji chubanshe, 2001), p. 380.
28. Most recent systematic data for all cities in China are for 1999, see Guojia tongjiju chengshi shehui jingji diaocha zongdui 國家統計局城市社會經濟調查總隊 (ed.), *Zhongguo chengshi tongji nianjian 2000* 中國城市統計年鑑 2000 (Urban Statistical Yearbook of China 2000) (Beijing: Zhongguo tongji chubanshe, 2001).
29. The difference between a prefectural-level city and a county-level city is their administrative status. The government of a prefectural-level city lies between the government of a province and the government of a county or county-level city.
30. *Guangxi tongji nianjian 2001* (see note 5), p. 173.
31. See J. Shen, "A Study of the Temporary Population in Chinese Cities," *Habitat International*, Vol. 26 (2002), pp. 363–77; J. Shen, X. Tang and Z. Lin, "Population Growth and Mobility," in *Fujian: A Coastal Province in Transition and Transformation*, edited by Y. M. Yeung and D. K. Y. Chu (Hong Kong: The Chinese University Press, 2000), pp. 455–85; C. C. Fan, "Migration and Labour Market Returns in Urban China: Results from a Recent Survey in Guangzhou," *Environment and Planning A*, Vol. 33 (2001), pp. 479–508.
32. See Chen Shupeng 陳述彭, Yeung Yue-man and Lin Hui (eds.), *Xinjingji yu Zhongguo xibu kaifa* 新經濟與中國西部開發 (The New Economy and China's Western Development) (Hong Kong: Hong Kong Institute of Asia-Pacific Studies, The Chinese University of Hong Kong); J. Shen, "Population Growth, Ecological Degradation and Construction in the Western Region of China," *Journal of Contemporary China*, Vol. 13, No. 39 (2004), in press.
33. The data were gleaned from the official website of the Office of the Leading Group for Western Region Development of the State Council at http://www.chinawest.gov.cn/.
34. This is formally announced in Document No. 4 of the Central Committee of the Communist Party of China in 1992. See Yang Jichang 楊基常 and Liu Xianyue 劉咸岳 (eds.), *Zhongguo daxi'nan zai jueqi* 中國大西南在崛起 (The Rise of Southwest China) (Nanning: Guangxi jiaoyu chubanshe 廣西教育出版社, 1994), p. 3; Hendrischke, "Guangxi" (see note 2), pp. 21–47; Liu Chaoming 劉朝明 and Zhang Xian 張銜 (eds.), *Daxi'nan zhengti kaifang zhanlüe yu chuhai tongdao jianshe* 大西南整体開放戰略與出海通道建設 (The Strategy of Comprehensive Opening and the Construction of a Sea Passage in the Great Southwest) (Chengdu: Xi'nan caijing daxue chubanshe 西南財經大學出版社, 2000), pp. 35–130 and 267.
35. Xiao, *Zhongguo xibu gailan: Guangxi* (see note 1), pp. 26–39; Li Fuchun 李甫春 et al., *Qiannian deng yihui: Guangxi shishi xibu dakaifa zhanlüe lilun*

gouxiang 千年等一回：廣西實施西部大開發戰略理論構想 (Once in One Thousand Years: Theoretical Consideration for the Implementation of the Strategy of Developing Western China in Guangxi) (Beijing: Minzu chubanshe, 2001), pp. 125–72.

36. Its port facility was very impressive, field observation, 15–25 May 2002.
37. Liu and Zhang, *Daxi'nan zhengti kaifang* (see note 34), pp. 35–130 and 267.
38. Ibid., pp. 70–73.
39. Ibid., pp. 97–105.
40. Ibid., pp. 126–30.
41. Ibid., p 224. See also Guangxi nianjian bianjibu 廣西年鑑編輯部 (ed.), *Guangxi nianjian 2000* 廣西年鑑2000 (Guangxi Yearbook 2000) (Nanning: Guangxi nianjianshe 廣西年鑑社, 2000), p. 211.
42. Liu and Zhang, *Daxi'nan zhengti kaifang* (see note 34), pp. 58 and 246.
43. Ibid., pp. 70–73.
44. Ibid., pp. 286–96.
45. Ibid., p. 26; *Guangxi tongji nianjian 2001* (see note 5), p. 252.
46. Xiao, *Zhongguo xibu gailan: Guangxi* (see note 1), p. 226.
47. Ibid., pp. 53–55.
48. As a peripheral area far away from the capital, reform came later to Guangxi. This loose relationships with the centre may also explain the serious case of corruption involving its former Governor and Deputy Chairman of the Standing Committee of the 9th National People's Congress, Cheng Kejie 成克杰. He was charged with accepting bribes of RMB41.09 million to intervene in the awarding of engineering contracts to specific companies, and to promote certain individuals to official positions. Cheng was executed on 14 September 2000 according to a verdict in a court in Beijing. He was the most senior official being sentenced to death in the reform period in China. See Guangxi nianjian bianjibu (ed.), *Guangxi niajian* 2001 (Nanning: Guangxi nianjianshe, 2001), p. 175.
49. *Guangxi tongji nianjian 2001* (see note 5), pp. 211–16; Liu Xianyue (ed.), *Guangxi jingji shehui xingshi fengxi yu yuce* 廣西經濟社會形勢分析與預測 (Analysis and Forecasting of the Economy and Society in Guangxi) (Nanning: Guangxi renmin chubanshe 廣西人民出版社, 2001), pp. 91–98.
50. *Guangxi tongji nianjian 2001* (see note 5), p. 99.
51. Liu and Zhang, *Daxi'nan zhengti kaifang* (see note 34), p. 279.
52. See Guangxi nianjian bianjibu (ed.), *Guangxi niajian* 2001 (see note 48), p. 282.
53. Field observation, 15–25 May 2001.
54. *Guangxi ribao* 廣西日報 (Guangxi Daily), 2 April 2001 and 21 January 2002.
55. Field observation, 15–25 May 2001. See also Chen Jianjun 陳建軍 (ed.), *Bianchui mingzhu Dongxingshi* 邊陲明珠東興市 (The Shining Border City of

Dongxing) (Dongxing: Zhonggong Dongxingshi weiyuanhui 中共東興市委員會 and Dongxingshi renmin zhengfu 東興市人民政府, no date).

56. Data from World Bank website at http://www.worldbank.org/data/countrydata/countrydata.html#DataProfiles.
57. Liu, *Guangxi jingji* (see note 49), pp. 63 and 224–32.
58. Brantly, "Sino-Vietnamese Border Trade" (see note 2), p. 506.
59. Hendrischke, "Guangxi" (see note 2), p. 42;
60. Liu, *Guangxi jingji* (see note 49), p. 71; Liu and Zhang, *Daxinan zhengti kaifang* (see note 34), pp. 201–16.
61. Liu, *Guangxi jingji* (see note 49), pp. 230–31.
62. Ibid., pp. 109–20.
63. Field observation, 15–25 May 2001.

19

Guizhou

Chen Zhilong and Zhang Min

Introduction

Guizhou 貴州 (Qian 黔 or Gui 貴 for short) is an inland province in the western region of China. It comprises 176,167 km^2, accounting for 1.8% of the total area in China.[1] The province extends 595 km from east to west and 509 km from south to north. As of 2000, Guizhou had a population of 35.25 million living in three prefectures (Anshun 安順, Bijie 畢節 and Tongren 銅仁), three autonomous prefectures (Southeast Guizhou 黔東南, South Guizhou 黔南 and Southwest Guizhou 黔西南) and three prefectural-level cities (Guiyang 貴陽, Liupanshui 六盤水 and Zunyi 遵義) (Figure 19.1).

Guizhou is located on the Yun-Gui (Yunnan-Guizhou) Plateau 雲貴高原, which has an average elevation of about 1,100 m above sea level. Topographically, mountains and hills account for 92.5% of the total area in Guizhou, with basins and flat land make up the remaining 7.5%. Guizhou has the largest area of karst landforms in China. It comprises 109,084 km^2 and accounts for 61.9% of the total area in Guizhou.

Guizhou is rich in energy and natural resources such as hydropower, coal, biological resources and scenic spots for tourism. It is one of the most important energy bases in South China. Hydropower reserves amount to 18.75 million kw, ranking the province sixth in China. Guizhou also has large reserves of all kinds of mineral resources. About 110 types are found in the province. Among the 76 kinds of mineral resources with proven reserves, 40 ranked in the top 10 nationally. Guizhou is also named the "garden province" because of its rich biological resources.

Because of its predominantly hilly terrain, Guizhou had only 1.84 million ha of arable land in 2000. The average amount of arable land per person was 0.05 ha, much lower than the average in China. Only a small proportion of the arable land was of high quality. The situation has become even worse with the rapid growth in population and the loss of arable land to industrial and urban development.

Guizhou plays an important role in the ecological security of China. The rivers in Guizhou mostly join the upper reaches of the Yangzi River 長江 and the Zhujiang 珠江. Soil erosion and pollution in Guizhou's river basins have had a significant impact on these two major rivers. The Miaoling 苗齡 Mountain is the watershed between the Yangzi River basin to the north and Zhujiang basin to the south. The areas of the two river basins are 115,747 km^2 and 60,420 km^2, respectively. Some 69 counties of Guizhou lie within the area of forest planned for the protection of the Yangzi River; they play an important role in the construction of the ecological environment

Figure 19.1 Guizhou in Its Geographical Setting

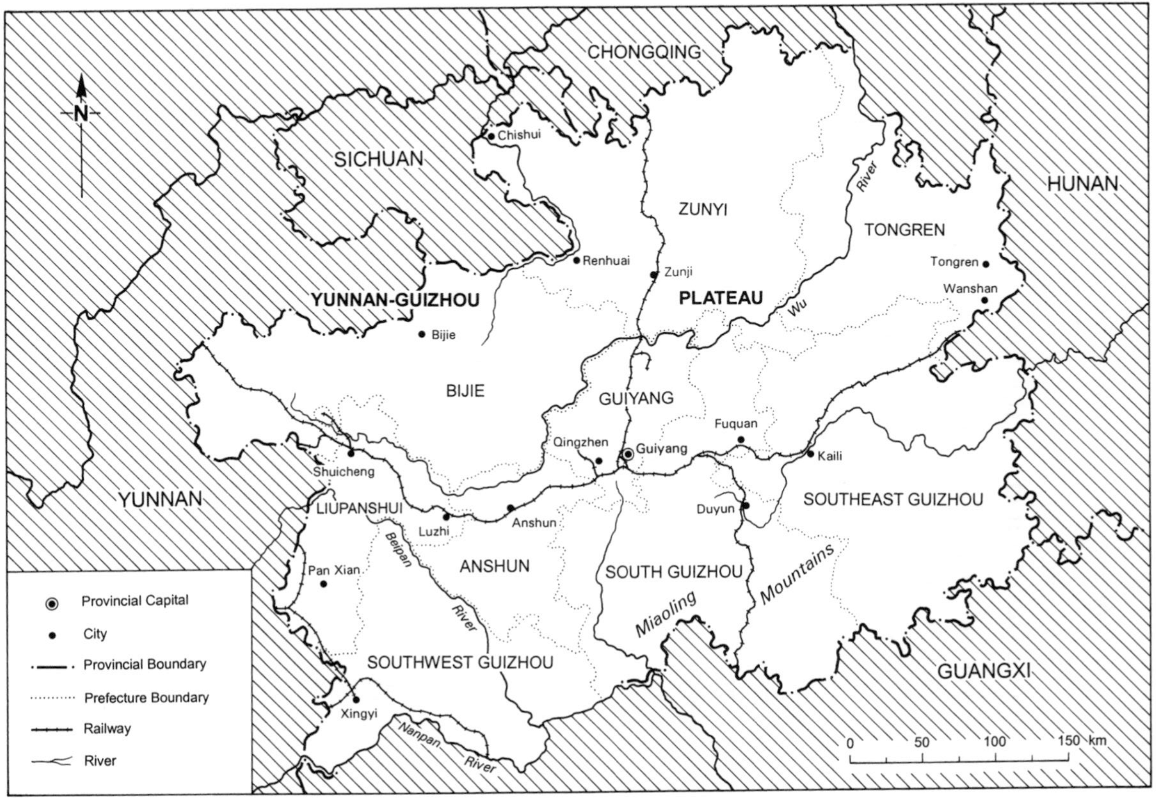

under the strategy of developing the western region.

This chapter examines Guizhou's economic development, industrial structure and persistent poverty in the reform period. Various constraints, problems and strategies for economic and industrial development in light of the strategy of developing the western region are discussed.

Economic Development in the Reform Period

There has been a significant amount of economic development in Guizhou since the implementation of economic reforms and the open policy in 1978. The main achievements can be summarized as follows.

First, Guizhou's economy has expanded a great deal in the reform period.[2] Table 19.1 presents the growth in GDP (gross domestic product) and GDP per capita in the period 1978–2000. In 1952–1978, the average annual GDP growth rate was 5.1%. In 1978–1993, it was 15.7%, and from 1993 to 2000, it was 12.2%. In 1978, Guizhou's GDP was RMB4.66 billion, 3.68 times what it had been in 1952. By 1993, it had reached RMB41.61 billion, 8.93 times the size in 1978. It further increased to RMB99.35 billion in 2000, 2.39 times greater than it had been in 1993. GDP per capita increased from RMB175 in 1978 to RMB1,255 in 1993 and to RMB2,662 in 2000.

Second, Guizhou achieved a preliminary level of industrialization and its industrial structure improved. In the 30 years following the founding of the People's Republic of China (PRC) in 1949, the emphasis in Guizhou was on heavy industry, and the development of agriculture and light industry was ignored in Guizhou. In 1978, the primary, secondary and tertiary

Table 19.1 GDP Growth in Guizhou, 1978–2000

Year	GDP[1] (RMB billion)	GDP per capita (RMB)
1978	4.66	175
1983	8.74	302
1988	21.18	683
1993	41.61	1,255
1998	84.19	2,318
1999	91.19	2,475
2000	99.35	2,662

Note: [1] Based on current year prices.
Sources: *Guizhou tongji nianjian 1995; 2001* (see note 2).

Table 19.2 Contribution of Primary, Secondary and Tertiary Industries to GDP, 1978–2000

Year	Primary industry (RMB billion)	Secondary industry (RMB billion)	Tertiary industry (RMB billion)	GDP share of primary industry (%)	GDP share of secondary industry (%)	GDP share of tertiary industry (%)
1978	1.94	1.87	0.85	41.7	40.2	18.1
1983	3.78	3.31	1.65	43.2	37.9	18.9
1988	8.52	7.86	4.80	40.2	37.2	22.6
1993	13.34	15.55	12.72	32.1	37.3	30.6
1998	26.49	32.60	25.10	31.5	38.7	29.8
1999	26.76	34.86	29.57	29.3	38.2	32.5
2000	27.10	38.79	33.47	27.3	39.0	33.7

Sources: *Guizhou tongji nianjian 1995; 2001* (see note 2).

industries accounted for 41.7%, 40.2% and 18.1% of GDP, respectively (Table 19.2). Farming accounted for 79.1% of the GDP in the primary industry. After 1992, the shares of the three industries in GDP changed drastically as the industrial structure improved significantly and the primary sector's share of GDP declined. By 2000, the primary, secondary and tertiary industries accounted for 27.3%, 39.0% and 33.7% of GDP, respectively. In that same year, the gross industrial output, of which state-owned industrial enterprises accounted for 79.3%, reached RMB63.16 billion.[3]

Third, the agricultural structure of Guizhou has been adjusted for the sake of efficiency and high quality. The amounts of land devoted to the growing of high-quality rice, high-quality corn, special cereals and organic potatoes were 192,700, 33,300, 33,300 and 66,600 ha, respectively, in 2000.[4] Farmers began to transform agriculture into a commercial sector. The rates of commercialization, the shares of products sold to the state or the market, in farming, forestry, fishing and animal husbandry were 36.5%, 45.1%, 53. 5% and 73.0%, respectively, in 2000. The government paid a great deal of attention to the construction of agricultural infrastructure. The gross output of rural enterprises amounted to RMB28.16 billion in 2000. The share of non-agricultural income in the total income of rural areas increased from 12.1% to 14.7% in the period 1995–2000.[5]

Fourth, living standards have improved while the number of people defined as poor has decreased. In the first eight years of efforts to alleviate poverty following 1986, the number of people below the poverty line declined to 10 million, although this still comprised 34.4% of Guizhou's total population.[6] A second poverty alleviation programme was implemented

Table 19.3 Key Indicators of Guizhou and Their Ranks in China, 2000

Indicator	Value	Rank in China	Indicator	Value	Rank in China
GDP (RMB billion)	99.33	26	Investment in fixed assets (RMB billion)	28.83	27
Population (million)	35.25	17	GDP of agriculture (RMB billion)	41.30	21
Urban disposable income per capita (RMB)	5,122	24	Gross industrial output (RMB billion)	63.16	27
Rural net income per peasant (RMB)	1,374	30	Imports and exports (US$ billion)	8.6	27
Expenditures for technical upgrading (RMB billion)	0.64	25	Foreign investment (US$ million)	25.01	27
Science and technology fund (RMB billion)	0.13	25	Vegetable oil output (thousand tonnes)	743	12
Educational expenditures (RMB billion)	3.18	22	Coal output (million tonnes)	36.77	9
Sales revenue of industrial products (RMB billion)	55.21	27	Wine output (thousand tonnes)	84	14
Total profits of industrial enterprises (RMB billion)	1.12	26	Tobacco output (thousand boxes)	1,874	6
Efficiency index of industrial enterprises	85.99	25	Chemical fertilizer (thousand tonnes)	841	13
Number of international tourists (thousand)	183.9	26			

Source: *Guizhou tongji nianjian 2001* (see note 2).

in 1994. The share of the impoverished population in the total population was further reduced to 9.74% in 2000. Seven million people have increased their income and crossed the poverty line since 1994. The living standards of poor people have improved significantly. Grain output per capita increased from 204 kg to 360 kg in the period 1993–2000, while income per capita increased from RMB335 to RMB1,260 in the same period.

It is clear that there has been a significant amount of development in Guizhou in the reform period, but that the province's level of development is still lower than that of other regions of China. Table 19.3 lists some important indicators in Guizhou and the province's ranking in such indicators in China. Except for a few items such as the production of tobacco, Guizhou ranks mostly near the bottom among the 31 provincial regions in Mainland

China. For example, the rural net income per person in Guizhou in 2000 was only RMB1,374, the second-lowest in China, just above Tibet. Thus, Guizhou is one of the poorest inland provinces in China. As a result, despite the many measures that have been taken, poverty is still a very serious problem in Guizhou. This is the focus of the next section.

The Problem of Poverty and Strategies for Poverty Alleviation

An Alarming Level of Poverty: The "Guizhou Phenomenon"

As mentioned before, Guizhou is one of the poorest provinces in China. The problem of poverty is a long-standing one. Historically, Guizhou was very backward and was known as a place where "people do not have even three cents" 人無三分銀. Today, poverty remains widespread in Guizhou. More than 15 million people, 57% of the rural population, lived below the poverty line in 1985. This number was reduced to 10 million in 1994, but this still accounted for 35% of the rural population. In 2000, Guizhou had 3.13 million rural residents with an annual net per capita income of below RMB625, accounting for 11.5% of the total impoverished population in rural China or 9.4% of the total rural population in Guizhou.

Poverty in Guizhou is also serious in degree. Engel's coefficient, the percentage share of income spent on food, is suggested by the Food and Agriculture Organization of the United Nations as a way to measure poverty. If Engel's coefficient is below 39%, people's living standards are very high. If it is in the range of 40–49%, people are comparatively well-off. If it is in the range of 50–59%, people are able to meet their basic needs. But if it is over 60%, then people have difficulty meeting their basic needs and are living in poverty. Table 19.4 shows that though the Engel's coefficient of rural residents has declined in recent years, it was still as high as 62.7% in 2000. This indicates that many rural residents in Guizhou still cannot meet their basic needs and that some do not have even enough to eat. The

Table 19.4 Engel's Coefficient, 1996–2000

(Unit: %)

Year	1996	1997	1998	1999	2000
Urban residents	53.4	51.1	48.2	42.2	43.0
Rural residents	72.5	69.5	69.2	67.5	62.7

Source: *Guizhou tongji nianjian 2001* (see note 2), p. 268.

characteristics of poverty described above are known as the "Guizhou phenomenon."

Causes of the "Guizhou Phenomenon"

The causes of the Guizhou phenomenon are extremely complicated. To begin with, Guizhou's history of poverty put the province in an unfavourable position in subsequent competition and development. Moreover, poverty in Guizhou is not just an economic problem but a comprehensive one, related to such things as social and cultural issues. Nor do the causes of poverty lie only in the province's weak economic foundation, but also in many other factors including the political situation, the regulatory regime and government policy. Three major causes are outlined below.

First, Guizhou's harsh natural environment places the province in a very unfavourable situation geographically. The typical karst terrain in Guizhou is a fragile ecological environment for agriculture. Natural disasters such as flooding and droughts are frequent, resulting in serious damage to agriculture. Without proper counter-measures, agricultural conditions will worsen over time. Furthermore, Guizhou's mountainous topography greatly hinders the transport of goods, the movement of people and the flow of information.

Second, the population, characterized by a low level of education and a high birth rate, has also contributed to poverty. Guizhou had a total population of 35.25 million in 2000. A high population growth rate exacerbated the problem. In the period 1996–2000, the birth rate was over 20‰ while the rate of natural increase was over 13‰ (Table 19.5). Rapid population growth has aggravated the pressure of population on the land, further worsening the fragile ecological environment. This has made it difficult to improve educational standards, as the limited educational resources are unable to meet the growing demand. There was little improvement in the educational level of the rural population in the period 1996–2000 (Table 19.6).

Third, poverty in Guizhou is also partly caused by government policies and by the socioeconomic system. In the pre-reform period, the central government was in charge of allocating resources in China. Mainly due to political considerations, the central government invested significantly in Guizhou, and built many large and medium-sized state-owned enterprises (SOEs) and several new industrial bases in the periods of the First, Second and Third Five-year Plans. As a result, the disparities between Guizhou

Table 19.5 Birth Rate and the Rate of Natural Increase of the Population, 1996–2000

Year	1996	1997	1998	1999	2000
Birth rate (‰)	22.05	22.15	22.02	21.92	20.59
Natural increase rate (‰)	14.36	14.48	14.26	14.24	13.06

Source: *Guizhou tongji nianjian 2001* (see note 2), p. 47.

Table 19.6 Share of Rural Labour Force by Level of Education

(Unit: %)

Level of education	1996	1997	1998	1999	2000
Illiterate or semi-illiterate	25.01	24.47	23.18	22.43	21.42
Primary school	37.86	38.08	38.45	37.50	39.77
Lower middle school	32.43	32.38	33.43	34.49	33.95
Higher middle school	3.75	4.14	4.15	4.57	3.27
Technical secondary school	0.84	0.80	0.73	0.97	1.37
Junior college and above	0.11	0.13	0.07	0.04	0.21
Average years of schooling of the labour force (year)	5.76	5.81	5.91	6.03	6.03

Source: *Guizhou tongji nianjian 2001* (see note 2), p. 268.

and the coastal provinces were controlled artificially. After the introduction of economic reforms and the open policy in 1978, the market has been playing an increasingly important role in resource allocation. This is disadvantageous for Guizhou because of its uncompetitive position in the market. Furthermore, China's open policy and economic reforms were first implemented in the coastal region. Thus, the coastal provinces enjoyed a more relaxed regulatory regime and various kinds of preferential policies not permitted in other provinces until much later. Guizhou faced an unequal starting point for competition in an emerging market economy and thus fell further behind during the reform period.

Strategies to Alleviate Poverty

The seriousness of poverty in Guizhou is due not to a single factor but to a range of factors. Thus, an integrated approach is needed to solve the problem, including the following measures.

First, the government should implement family planning regulations more strictly, to further limit population growth.

Second, the government should arrange for the migration of people who live in extreme poverty from areas with a harsh natural environment to places with more economic opportunities and higher living standards. Such a measure, if implemented properly, can lead to the alleviation of poverty in a short time. It can also help those who remain in poverty-stricken areas by reducing the stress of population on the land.

Third, it is more important to improve the economic capability and competitiveness of the poor. As the saying goes, giving a poor person a fish is not as good as teaching him how to fish. Based on the fact that many poverty-stricken areas have certain resource advantages, the government should take effective steps to help the poor to produce products that can compete in the market such as raw materials for traditional Chinese medicine, including banana taro 芭蕉芋, Chinese gall, the tung tree 油桐 and special fruits.

Fourth, local governments should make use of the development opportunities arising from the strategy initiated by the central government of developing the western region. They should make full use of various preferential policies and of the financial and material support offered to Guizhou by the central government.

Fifth, the government should pay attention to the ecological environment. The relationship between poverty alleviation in the short term and sustainable development in the long term should be considered. If poverty alleviation is achieved in short term at the expense of the ecological environment, it is unsustainable.

The Industrial Structure and Its Formation

The Industrial Structure and the Problems with the Structure

The persistence of poverty and the continued low level of economic development in Guizhou are due not only to historical, regional and political factors, but also to the province's inefficient and backward industrial structure. Guizhou's poor industrial structure is the cause of its poor competitiveness and low level of economic efficiency. The poor industrial structure has also hindered economic reform. This section examines Guizhou's industrial structure and its problems.

The most important aspect of the industrial structure in an economy is the composition of the primary, secondary and tertiary industries. In Guizhou, primary, secondary and tertiary industries contributed RMB

27.10 billion, RMB38.79 billion and RMB33.47 billion to the total GDP of RMB99.35 billion, respectively, in 2000.

The primary industry accounted for 27.3% of GDP and 69.9% of total employment in Guizhou in 2000. Although Guizhou is one of China's most important agricultural regions, its agricultural productivity and efficiency are relatively low. The secondary industry is the most important material base of an economy. Its development often determines the level and direction of economic development. The secondary industry accounted for 39.0% of GDP in Guizhou in 2000. This indicates that Guizhou still has a low level of industrialization. It is well known that the tertiary industry can generate more revenues with less investment than can the primary and secondary industries. Due to a large primary sector, the tertiary industry only made up 33.7% of the total GDP in Guizhou, much lower than the national average.

Generally speaking, a large proportion of the labour force in Guizhou is still engaged in agriculture. There is an urgent need to speed up the transfer of the labour force from the agricultural sector to the non-agricultural sectors. Indeed, the agricultural sector is dominated by farms with low productivity. The hilly topography and unstable climate actually give Guizhou no comparative advantage for farming. Forests and pasture are more suitable for Guizhou. But under the influence of the Maoist idea of "self-reliance," farming became a focus in Guizhou for a long time. The gross output from the primary sector was RMB41.30 billion in 2000. The output from farming, forestry, fishing and animal husbandry amounted to RMB27.96 million, RMB1.80 billion, RMB11.07 million and RMB0.46 billion in 2000, accounting for 67.7%, 4.4%, 26.8% and 1.1%, respectively, of the total primary output. It is clear that the land has not been used effectively according to its natural conditions. Under the pressure of dramatic population growth, over-planting has caused extensive damage to the ecological environment in Guizhou. Forestry and animal husbandry should become the focus of the primary sector in Guizhou.

In the secondary sector, a major problem is that light industry and heavy industry are not well co-ordinated. The output from heavy and light industries in 2000 was RMB42.53 billion and RMB20.63 billion, accounting for 32.7% and 67.3%, respectively, of the gross industrial output. According to the ranking of output value, important manufacturing industries in Guizhou included electricity generation, coal, gas and water supply, tobacco production, heavy metal manufacturing, chemicals, non-ferrous metal manufacturing, medicine production, non-metal mining, drinks and alcoholic beverages.

Among the total output of light industry, 89.0% was produced using agricultural products as raw materials, while 11.0% was produced using non-agricultural raw materials in 2000.[7] This means that light industry in Guizhou relies on agriculture as the source of raw materials. Among the total output of heavy industry in 2000, 8.5% was related to mining, 58.2% to rudimentary processing and 33.3% to manufacturing. It is clear that heavy industry does not supply much in the way of raw materials to light industry and that the industry production chain is short. In its trade with the eastern region of China, Guizhou often exchanges its energy products, raw materials or semi-manufactured products at low prices for consumer goods at high prices. A considerable amount of revenue is transferred from Guizhou to the eastern region through such trade.

As mentioned before, the tertiary sector is underdeveloped in Guizhou, although its share in total GDP increased from 22.6% to 33.7% in the period 1988–2000. The GDP of this service sector was RMB33.47 billion in 2000, ranking 27th in China. Its internal structure is problematic, with small contributions coming from important sectors in a modern economy such as the finance, insurance, information and consultation industries. The traditional sectors accounted for 42.5% of the GDP in the tertiary sector in 2000, including such industries as retail and wholesale, food and catering services, transportation, postal services and communications industries.

Guizhou has rich resources for the tourism industry. There are 8 national and over 40 provincial scenic spots in Guizhou. Despite active development since the 1980s, the tourism industry is still not highly developed. In 2000, 19.98 million domestic tourists and 0.18 million foreign tourists visited Guizhou. But other provinces in China attracted more tourists than Guizhou and Guizhou earned only 1.8% of the total revenue from foreign tourists in China. The limited revenue of the industry does not match its rich resources for tourism. Except for the preliminary development of tourist resources, the tourism industry has not been well planned and managed, resulting in the destructive development of tourist resources and historical heritage, and in poor tourism infrastructure in Guizhou. Such a situation undermines the potential of the tourism industry and must be dealt with as soon as possible.

Explaining the Formation of the Current Industrial Structure

The formation of the current industrial structure in Guizhou is a result of various factors. First, it has much to do with geographic conditions. As mentioned before, Guizhou has a harsh natural environment. Situated on the hilly land of the Yun-Gui Plateau, Guizhou is a region short of water resources and arable land. The arable land per capita is less than 50% of the national average. The uneven distribution of water resources has resulted in severe water shortages in the central and western parts of Guizhou. Guizhou's hilly terrain also means that it is difficult to improve the transportation infrastructure. Poor transportation, in turn, increases the cost of economic activities such as transporting production factors and developing Guizhou's rich energy resources. Guizhou's inland location, land-locked and far away from the sea, also constrains international trade and economic co-operation. All of this contributes to the low level of economic development in the province. The problem of Guizhou's industrial structure is simply a reflection of its undeveloped economy. The negative impact of unfavourable natural conditions on the economy cannot be eliminated by economic reforms, and is likely that such an impact will persist in the future.

Second, Guizhou had a very weak economic base in 1949 when the PRC was founded. Primary industry accounted for 80% of the total GDP of the province in that year. A poor economic base made it difficult for Guizhou to develop a strong economy in subsequent years. This is known as path-dependency, where the initial economic foundation has a significant impact on the path and speed of development of an economy.

Third, the bias in the pre-reform period towards the development of heavy industry directly contributed to the formation of a poor industrial structure. During the pre-reform period when highly centralized economic planning prevailed, Guizhou's economic development was virtually determined by the central government's macro-economic, industrialization and spatial strategies. Given its rich natural resources, Guizhou was chosen by the central government to be developed as a base for energy resources and raw materials. Under such a government policy, vertical specialization and the division of industries between Guizhou and other eastern provinces resulted. Guizhou assumed the role of a supplier of raw materials or preliminary products to the eastern region of China. The investment in secondary industry accounted for 66.8% of the total investment in fixed assets and the investment in heavy industry accounted for 95.6% of the total investment in the secondary sector in 1978. Such bias in investment towards heavy industry came at the expense of the development of agriculture and light industry. In 1978, the primary, secondary and tertiary industries accounted for 41.7%, 40.2% and 18.1%, respectively, of the province's GDP.

Fourth, the unbalanced regional development strategy in the reform period further affected Guizhou's industrial structure. From the late 1970s to the mid-1990s, the Chinese government adopted a strategy of "efficiency first while taking inequality into consideration" 效率優先、兼顧公平 to replace the previous strategy of balanced regional development. The coastal areas became the focus of economic development in China due to their excellent geographical location and good industrial foundation. These areas were also supported by the central government in various ways, such as through favourable policies on human resources, capital and technology.

In the reform period, state investment was concentrated on the eastern region. As Guizhou's economy, based as it was on heavy industry monopolized by SOEs, was more reliant on state investment than were the economies of the eastern region, the shift in the focus of state investment to the eastern region had a significant impact on economic development in Guizhou. More importantly, local governments in the eastern region were given a free hand to experiment with various approaches of economic regulation and management. Notable progress was made in the eastern region in the areas of institutional reforms and innovations. But Guizhou's economic reform and opening lagged behind not only the eastern region but also the country as a whole. Guizhou's weak private economy was a clear indication of such backwardness, which had worsened rather than improved Guizhou's industrial structure.

Industrial Strategies for Guizhou

An Evaluation of Two Industrial Strategies

From the above discussion, it is clear that Guizhou's industrial structure needs to be adjusted. Two strategies have been proposed.[8] The first is to develop the province's natural resources on a larger scale to transform the resource advantage into an economic advantage for economic competition. The second strategy is to expand the scale of basic industries, such as the production of basic materials and farming. Guizhou would then specialize in these industries. But in the light of slow growth in gross demand, surplus production capacity and intensifying competition, these two strategies are not viable.

Indeed, a resource-oriented strategy of industrialization has already failed in Guizhou. Guizhou has lost its traditional advantage in resource-based industries. Mineral resources and energy supply were once the bottlenecks in the Chinese economy. At the time, due to its rich reserves of energy and mineral resources, Guizhou had a comparative advantage in the production of energy and basic materials. But the situation has changed in recent years. Guizhou has gradually lost its traditional comparative advantage. Its market share of coal production, for example, has declined continuously for the following reasons.

First, the balance of demand and supply in the Chinese economy has changed fundamentally. There are surplus supplies of energy, basic materials and other mineral resources. Second, prices for energy and basic materials have declined in the international market, a situation that has had a negative impact on the development of natural resources in Guizhou. Third, the environmental cost of the large-scale development of natural resources has increased as environmental protection has become more and more important. Fourth, the competitiveness of the energy and mining industries in Guizhou has been reduced with the increase in foreign competition following China's entry to the World Trade Organization (WTO) in 2001.

In short, many factors such as natural resources, market competition and price advantage determine what Guizhou's advantages are in an open market. Guizhou cannot simply focus on its resource advantage. It is a good idea to turn its resource advantage into a competitive advantage for economic development. But it is very difficult to achieve such an objective. It should be noted that resource products always face unfavourable trading conditions in comparison to manufactured products.

Expanding the scale of basic industry and farming in Guizhou is consistent with the idea of forming an industrial gradient from the eastern region to the western region including Guizhou, but it is not a viable strategy for the following reasons. First, although Guizhou has achieved a rate of economic growth that is close to the national average by expanding the scale of animal husbandry and farming, such development is not sustainable as it comes at the expense of the environment. Second, the scale of basic industry in Guizhou is small and its technology is out-of-date. Third, conditions in Guizhou are not favourable for the large-scale development of basic industry and farming. These conditions include Guizhou's widespread karst topography, limited resources of arable land and water, and inconvenient transportation. Fourth, due to surpluses in supply in the national economy, basic industry and farming are facing insufficient levels of demand.

Consequently, it may be prudent for Guizhou not to adopt the two strategies considered above. What then can Guizhou do? This chapter argues that Guizhou should select some promising industries and then support their development with effective measures, as discussed in the next section.

The Third Strategy: Developing Promising Industries

The traditional manufacturing industries make up a large share of Guizhou's economy.[9] These traditional industries use less advanced technology and capital investment and have a low profit rate. Most of these industries only involve the early stages of the manufacturing process. This has led to a serious problem in product structure. Semi-finished products and basic products account for about 50% of the gross industrial output, while final products only account for 20% of the gross industrial output. Such an industrial structure is linked to Guizhou's natural resources. Sharing similar endowments of natural resources with adjacent provinces, Guizhou and these neighbouring provinces have similar industrial sectors, such as the manufacturing of tobacco, non-ferrous metals and automobiles.

Such similarity in the industrial structure is not easy to avoid. But generally, only industries with a strong level of competitiveness and which are not available in other areas can produce much profit. It is noteworthy that the traditional key industries of tobacco and wine production in Guizhou are now facing great challenges. Thus, Guizhou should not only make every effort to maintain its traditional advantage in these industries but also develop special industries of its own according to the principles of "no one comes close" 人無我有 or "second to nobody" 人有我精. The following promising industries are recommended.

First, there is the pharmaceutical industry, which should focus on the in-depth processing of Chinese medicine. The industry is characterized by an industrial sector that uses high technology and huge amounts of investment. It is highly profitable but also high-risk. It is one of the important industries listed in the "National Industrial Policy Outline" for the 1990s. Due to a surplus of pharmaceutical products, since the mid-1980s, the market in China has changed from one that is seller-driven to one that is buyer-driven. After China's entry to the WTO, competition in the pharmaceutical industry further intensified, although the Chinese pharmaceutical industry is also being provided with many opportunities in the international market.

Due to its rich varieties of climate and soil, Guizhou has the advantage in the production of all kinds of biological resources, especially in Chinese medicine. In recent years, the output of raw plant materials for Chinese medicine in Guizhou has accounted for 85% of the total in China.

Furthermore, the animal husbandry and coal industries also provide Guizhou with abundant raw materials for the pharmaceutical industry. The provincial government of Guizhou has provided much guidance and support to some big medical enterprises in recent years. These medical enterprises have successfully developed many new kinds of medicine. Thus, the Chinese medicine industry is a suitable one for Guizhou to specialize in and develop. It will become a new driving force for Guizhou's economy.

Second, green food is also a promising industry for Guizhou. Green food has become increasingly popular among consumers as living standards rise. Guizhou is extremely rich in agricultural resources. It has begun developing the manufacture of green food for the expanding market. Some big enterprises have emerged in the green food industry. Laoganma 老乾媽, for example, is a famous green food corporation in Guizhou. The Guizhou government should support the large-scale production of the following food and drink products: kiwi fruits, instant food, pepper, tea, plum juice and mineral water.

Third, the fine chemical industry is also valuable to Guizhou. So far, the province has focused on its coal and phosphorus industries. The main products of Guizhou's chemical industry are chemical fertilizer and its raw materials. The fine chemical industry, however, is a very promising one for Guizhou under the strategy of developing the western region. Three categories of products, involving a total of 18 series of products, are the focus in this industry. This is because these products have a promising market demand, while Guizhou also has rich raw materials. The three categories are fine phosphorus products for drink and food, fine coal chemical products and other fine chemical products. Guizhou should develop the following bases for the chemical industry: phosphorus fertilizer, manganese salt, bio-chemicals, rubber and carbon chemicals.

Fourth, information products and the software industry should also be a focus of development. Although it is still at an initial stage, there has been significant development in the electronics industry in Guizhou. A certain amount of progress has been achieved in the past 10 years in the following areas: computer systems such as new electronic components, telecommunications products and optical-machine-electronic products; information infrastructure such as telecommunications and broadcasting business; Internet products; and the application of information systems at various levels. Increased investment in the information industry and technical and human resource support from universities and research institutes are playing an important role in these developments. The information industry in Guizhou should focus on the manufacturing of telecommunications equipment and basic electronic components, and on the development of information technology.

Fifth, Guizhou can develop the electric power generation industry and export electricity mainly to Guangdong 廣東. Guizhou is rich in resources of hydropower energy, possessing a theoretical reserve of 18.75 million kw, of which 16.83 million kw can be effectively developed. Only 12% of the hydropower resources have been developed so far. Guizhou also has rich reserves of coal. In addition, Guizhou is not far away from other eastern areas that are in need of large supplies of power. For example, Guangdong does not have an adequate supply of electricity and demand is still growing. The increasing demand for electricity in the eastern region provides an indispensable market opportunity for Guizhou. Now, the project involving four hydropower stations and four coal-fired power stations is being implemented.

Sixth, with Guizhou's attractive karst landscape and minority cultures, there is great potential for the development of the tourism industry. Guizhou is famous for its beautiful mountains and natural scenery. The karst landforms consist of hills, rivers, forests and caves. The province has eight designated national scenic areas, two of which have been designated national forest parks, four natural conservation areas, nine national units for the conservation of ancient cultural heritage and other designated provincial scenic areas. Many minority people live in Guizhou, where they and their colourful cultures are to be seen all over the province. Rich tourism resources give Guizhou a great advantage in the tourism industry. Guizhou should make good use of these resources to develop the tourism industry taking the following approach. First, Guizhou should be developed as a famous trademark in tourism. Second, a series of international tourist products should be designed, including the Huangguoshu 黃果樹 Falls, minority festivals and natural ecological museums. Third, a serious of famous tourist products for the domestic market should be developed. Finally, all kinds of tourist goods and souvenirs should be manufactured and promoted.

Conclusion: Challenges and Strategies to Development

This chapter has examined the economic development, industrial structure and persistent poverty in Guizhou in the reform period. Various problems and measures for economic and industrial development have been discussed.

The implementation of the strategy of the development of the western region is certainly an opportunity for Guizhou. However, Guizhou will have to overcome a number of challenges and its development path will not be an easy one. This concluding section reviews the barriers to development in Guizhou and considers development strategies for the province in the coming years.

The Barriers to Development

Guizhou faces a number of barriers to development. Four of them are discussed here. First, the emerging market mechanism is not conducive to the flow of production factors such as capital and human resources into Guizhou. The current strategy of developing the western region is different from the development strategy of the 1950s and 1960s in the level of its impact on the movement of production factors. The previous strategy favoured the development of inland areas. Under the current strategy, production factors may not move into the western region as a result of simply following the instructions of the central government, as happened in the 1950s and 1960s. Instead, market principles determine the direction of the movement of production factors.

Due to its low level of development and poor transportation infrastructure, Guizhou has much difficulty attracting human resources and capital investment. On the one hand, Guizhou's senior personnel are ageing rapidly. But the province has a shortage of talented people. The situation has worsened with the migration of young and talented people to other parts of the country. There are also problems with the movement and redistribution of human resources within the province. Guizhou also faces a serious problem with capital investment. The state only makes limited investments in the province and there is little foreign investment in Guizhou due to its poor investment environment. Similarly, the domestic private sector in China has little interest in investing in Guizhou.

Second, the opening of China to the outside world has weakened the economic links between Guizhou and the eastern provinces in such areas as energy supply. In the years immediately preceding and following China's entry to the WTO, competition in energy and resources has intensified between foreign providers and Guizhou producers. Since the outbreak of the Asian financial crisis in 1997, energy prices have declined in the international market. Users in the eastern region prefer to import energy from foreign countries at a low price. This has seriously undermined

Guizhou's economy because the province has been relying on its revenues from the energy trade.

Third, the special "water problem" also constrains economic development in Guizhou.[10] Although Guizhou has a large supply of water resources, it still has a serious water problem. First of all, water resources are not evenly distributed. As cities in Guizhou tend to be located at the upper reaches of various rivers, they often experience water shortages. Secondly, reservoirs and other water facilities are poor in Guizhou. The karst landform makes it very difficult for the soil to retain water. Thirdly, water pollution has worsen the problem of water shortages.

Currently, about 4.52 million people in the province still have no access to clean drinking water. There are serious water shortages in 76 towns. It has been estimated that Guizhou will need 9.5 billion tonnes of water in 2005, when its GDP is likely to reach RMB153 billion, and its population an estimated 39.8 million. By the year 2010, the total demand for water will increase to 11.5–12.0 billion tonnes in Guizhou. Clearly, the problem of water shortages will become more acute at that time.

Fourth, poverty remains very serious in Guizhou.[11] As discussed previously, Guizhou has the most serious problem of poverty in China. People with incomes above the official poverty line also have very low living standards. It is very common for such people to be in and out of poverty. The poverty line was drawn at RMB300 in 1990 and was increased to RMB650 in 2000. It is estimated that 15% of the people who were above the poverty line have become poor again. Poverty-stricken areas have a weak infrastructure and it is difficult, if not impossible, to lift the inhabitants from their condition of poverty. Currently, the government is providing much support to meet the basic needs of the population defined as poor. But such dependence on government support is not sustainable in the long term.

Development Strategies

In order to solve the development difficulties mentioned above, the following strategies for economic development in Guizhou are proposed. First, Guizhou needs to speed up its economic reforms and offer an orderly but relaxed regulatory environment for economic development. Since it is in an unfavourable position to attract production factors under the market mechanism, it is crucial for Guizhou to accelerate its economic reforms and to set up a good regulatory framework to protect the interests of investors. This can promote inward investment. Introducing innovations to the system according to the situation in Guizhou is equally important for retaining capital and talent within the province, and for attracting capital investment and talents from other provinces.

Second, Guizhou needs to accelerate the construction of reservoirs to solve its problem of water shortages. As mentioned before, Guizhou is rich in water resources which are, however, not available at the time and place when needed. There has been an inadequate amount of investment in irrigation projects. Because irrigation projects are pubic or semi-public in nature, they will not be adequately funded under the market mechanism. Thus, to increase water supply, it is necessary for the government to increase its investment and build a series of irrigation projects as well as improve the maintenance of existing projects. Furthermore, the water management system should be reformed to optimize the distribution of water resources. It is important that water resources are used economically and efficiently.

Third, Guizhou needs to strengthen the construction of transportation infrastructure. Guizhou is neither a coastal province nor a frontier region. It is also not close to big rivers, and there are many mountains and hills in Guizhou. Such conditions make transportation in the province difficult and constrain economic development. It goes without saying that one needs to build roads first if one wants to get rich. According to the national plan, Guizhou is currently preparing for the construction of a highway network. By 2015, two national highways, one from Shanghai 上海 to Ruili 瑞麗 in Yunnan 雲南 and one from Chongqing 重慶 to Zhanjiang 湛江 in Guangdong, will pass through Guizhou. It will make Guizhou a highway pivot in the southwest region of China, which will facilitate economic development in Guizhou.

Fourth, further efforts should be made to change the old mindset of the people so that they become more open-minded and more aware of the market economy. Due to inconvenient transportation and little information exchange with the outside world, people in Guizhou are often conservative. Because the commodity economy has not been well developed in Guizhou's history, the local people also lack a tradition of business or trading. Furthermore, delayed market-oriented reforms in Guizhou have done little to improve the local people's market awareness. In order to develop the market economy of Guizhou, it is urgent that the current situation be changed. The mode of thinking, values and life styles that fit an emerging market economy should be advocated. The government should strengthen economic and cultural exchanges with the coastal provinces to broaden the minds of the local people.

Notes

1. *Guizhou nianjian 2001* 貴州年鑑2001 (Guizhou Yearbook 2001) (Guiyang: Guizhou nianjian chubanshe 貴州年鑑出版社, 2001), pp. 44–45.
2. Guizhou tongjiju 貴州統計局, *Guizhou tongji nianjian 2001* 貴州統計年鑑 2001 (Guizhou Statistical Yearbook 2001) (Beijing: Zhongguo tongji chubanshe 中國統計出版社, 2001).
3. Ibid.
4. *Guizhou nianjian 2001* (see note 1).
5. Ibid., p. 217.
6. Gong Xiaokuan 龔曉寬, *Guizhou zai xibu dakaifa zhong de zhanlüe dingwei he zhongda jucuo* 貴州在西部大開發中的戰略定位和重大舉措 (The Strategic Positions and Important Measures of Guizhou in the Development of Western Region), working paper, 2001.
7. *Guizhou tongji nianjian 2001* (see note 2).
8. Hu Angang 胡鞍鋼 (ed.), *Diqu yu fazhan: Xibu kaifa xinzhanlüe* 地區與發展：西部開發新戰略 (Regions and Development: New Strategies for the Development of the Western Region) (Beijing: Zhongguo jihua chubanshe 中國計劃出版社, 2001).
9. Gong Xiaokuan, *Guizhou* (see note 6).
10. Liu Zhouxiang 劉周祥 et al., *Guizhou gongcheng xing queshui wenti yanjiu* 貴州工程性缺水問題研究 (Study of Water Shortage Due to Engineering Reasons in Guizhou), working paper, 2001.
11. Gong Xiaokuan, *Xinshiji Guizhou fupin kaifa de zhongdian ji zhanlüe cuoshi* 新世紀貴州扶貧開發的重點及戰略措施 (The Focus and Strategic Measures of Poverty Alleviation Through Development in Guizhou in the New Century), working paper, 2001.

20

Yunnan

Gan Chunkai and Chen Zhilong

Introduction

Yunnan 雲南 is located in the southwest of China. It is also close to several countries in Southeast and South Asia. It shares a border with Myanmar, Laos and Vietnam. It is also close to Thailand, Cambodia, Bangladesh and India. Yunnan's geo-political significance cannot be under-estimated. In past centuries, Yunnan was China's gateway to India and Southeast Asia. About 2,000 years ago, the "Southwest Silk Road" 西南絲綢之路 began in Sichuan, then went through Yunnan, India and Central Asia, and finally ended in the Arabian region and in European countries. The famous "Mayuan Old Way" 馬援故道 in the early first century was a passage from southern Yunnan to Vietnam, ending in the South China Sea.

Yunnan is the eighth largest province in China. It has an area of 394,000 km^2, accounting for 4.1% of China's total area. It extends 847 km from south to north, and 990 km from east to west. In 2000, it had a population of 42.4 million. However, as a mountainous province situated on the Yun-Gui (Yunnan-Guizhou) Plateau 雲貴高原, 84% of the province's total area is comprised of hills. Plateaus make up about 10%, while river basins and wide valleys account for only 6% of the province's total area.[1] These natural conditions mean that there is a limited amount of arable land and Yunnan currently still needs to import grain from other regions.

Nevertheless, Yunnan is rich in many kinds of mineral resources. Some 154 kinds of mineral are found in the province, many of them in large quantities. For example, Yunnan has the largest reserves of plumbum, zincum, chromium, thallium, strontium and diatomite, and the second-largest reserves of titanium, stannum, nickel, germanium, cobalt, platinum, kalium and halite mines in the country.[2] The most important non-ferrous metal mines in Yunnan are plumbum and zincum, of which total proven reserves together amount to 23.12 million tonnes. Stannum is another important mine. Yunnan's estimated reserves of stannum are 5.37 million tonnes. Gejiu 個舊 is the most important base for stannum mining in China, producing 70% of the country's total output. With 18,000 species of plants and numerous species of wild animals, Yunnan is also remarkably rich in biological resources and is known in China as the "kingdom of plants" and the "kingdom of animals." So far, 1,704 kinds of amniotes and 100,000 kinds of insects have been identified.[3] However, until recently, the province's rich mineral and biological resources have not been effectively utilized for economic development.

During the period 1949–1978 when China was closed to the outside world, the above-mentioned geo-political features of Yunnan offered no advantages for economic development. Yunnan has been a relatively backward province for a long time. This is also partly due to its unfavourable natural environment and peripheral location. The difficulties of transportation between Yunnan and the rest of the country has impeded the province's economic integration with the nation.

As in other parts of the country, economic reforms and the open-door policy have been implemented in Yunnan for over 20 years, and Yunnan has achieved a significant amount of economic development during this period. Yunnan's geographical location also gives it a significant advantage in trade and co-operation with the countries of Southeast and South Asia. But many problems still exist, which will be reviewed later in this chapter.

In 1999, China began to implement the strategy of developing the western region. This will definitely stimulate the development of Yunnan's economy. To capture this development opportunity, Yunnan also needs to design relevant strategies, taking into account its own specific conditions. Yunnan will enter a new path of economic development in the twenty-first century. This chapter examines the economic development, changing economic structure, border trade and the role of government policies in Yunnan in the reform period. The chapter also outlines the current problems and future development strategies of the province.

Economic Development in the Reform Period

Since the implementation of economic reform and the open-door policy in 1978, economic development in Yunnan has been rapid. During the period 1978–2000, Yunnan's GDP increased from RMB6.91 billion to RMB 195.51 billion. On the basis of constant prices, GDP increased by nearly 7 times, with an average annual growth rate of 9.9% (see Table 20.1). Due to different situations and driving forces at different stages, Yunnan's economy did not grow at a constant rate. Specifically, there have been three different stages of development in the reform period.

The First Stage, 1978–1984

In this stage, the focus was on rural reform. Rapid rural development also stimulated the development of the tertiary industry. From 1978 to 1984, Yunnan's GDP increased from RMB6.91 billion to RMB13.96 billion (Table 20.1), for an increase of 72% at constant prices and an average annual GDP

Table 20.1 GDP Growth in Yunnan and China, 1978–2000

Year	Yunnan		China		Yunnan's share of the national GDP (%)
	GDP (RMB billion)	GDP growth rate (%)	GDP (RMB billion)	GDP growth rate (%)	
1978	6.91	21.7	362.41	11.7	1.91
1981	9.41	7.8	486.24	5.2	1.94
1984	13.96	14.5	717.10	15.2	1.95
1985	16.50	13.0	896.44	13.5	1.84
1986	18.23	4.3	1,020.22	8.8	1.79
1987	22.90	12.3	1,196.25	11.6	1.91
1988	30.11	16.0	1,492.83	11.3	2.02
1989	36.31	5.8	1,690.92	4.1	2.15
1990	45.17	8.7	1,854.79	3.8	2.44
1991	51.74	6.6	2,161.78	9.2	2.39
1992	61.87	10.9	2,663.81	14.2	2.32
1993	77.92	10.6	3,463.44	13.5	2.25
1994	97.40	11.6	4,675.94	12.6	2.08
1995	120.67	11.2	5,847.81	10.5	2.06
1996	149.16	10.4	6,788.46	9.6	2.20
1997	164.42	9.4	7,446.26	8.8	2.21
1998	179.39	8.0	7,834.52	7.8	2.29
1999	185.57	7.2	8,191.09	7.1	2.27
2000	195.51	7.1	8,940.35	8.0	2.19

Notes: 1. GDP data are based on current-year prices.
2. The growth rate of GDP is calculated on the basis of comparable prices.

Sources: Data for Yunnan comes from the *Yunnan Statistical Yearbook 2001* (see note 4); National data comes from the *China Statistical Yearbook 2001* (see note 4).

growth rate of 9.4%. The GDP contribution of primary industry grew from RMB2.95 billion to RMB5.73 billion, for an average annual growth rate of 8.7% at constant prices. The GDP of tertiary industry rose from RMB1.20 billion to RMB2.79 billion, while that of secondary industry grew from RMB2.76 billion to RMB5.44 billion. The average annual GDP growth rates of the tertiary and secondary industries, based on constant prices, were 12.0% and 8.9%, respectively.[4] During this stage, there was rapid and balanced development among the three industries. The release of economic potential previously constrained by institutional factors resulted in stable economic growth.

The Second Stage, 1985–1991

This stage of economic adjustment in Yunnan was characterized by drastic fluctuations in the rate of economic growth. During this period, Yunnan's GDP rose from RMB16.50 billion to RMB51.74 billion. Total GDP, based on constant prices, increased by 88%, with an average annual growth rate of 11.1%. There were drastic fluctuations in the annual rate of economic growth: high in 1985, 1987, 1988 and 1992, and low in 1986, 1989 and 1991. Such fluctuations were related to developments in both the macro and micro economy. From the perspective of the macro economy, there was a dramatic change in the structure of consumption due to rising income levels. But the production and supply of goods did not follow the changes in consumer demand. The mismatch between supply and demand resulted in both chaos and crisis in production. One important consequence, among others, was serious inflation. From the perspective of the micro economy, each micro economic entity (enterprises and households) knew little about market rules and was too sensitive to price fluctuations, although the market mechanism was playing an increasingly important role in the economy. Therefore, when prices changed, irrational panic buying occurred, undermining the stability of the economy. Another significant cause of economic fluctuations was the need to look for new driving forces for economic growth after most of the potential of constrained production had been released in the early stage. The uncertainty implicit in seeking such new opportunities also contributed to economic fluctuations.

The Third Stage, 1992–2000

In this stage, Yunnan's economy grew steadily at a high and rational rate. GDP rose from RMB61.87 billion to RMB195.51 billion, an increase of 100% based on constant prices, with an average annual growth rate of 9.1%. The growth rate was also very stable in this period. In 1992, the central government made the firm decision to establish a socialist market economy. Indeed, a high degree of marketization had been realized in all product and factor markets except for the financial sector. Enterprises and residents gradually adapted to market mechanisms, while the government attempted to influence the economy more skilfully through market approaches. All of these were important factors in the stable development of Yunnan's economy.

A detailed examination of Yunnan's economic growth in this period

Table 20.2 GDP, Investment and Consumption in Yunnan, 1992–2000

Indicator	1992 (RMB billion)	2000 (RMB billion)	Average annual nominal growth rate (%)
GDP	61.87	195.51	15.5
Total investment in fixed assets	14.07	69.79	22.2
Total retail value of consumer goods	23.46	58.32	12.1

Source: *Yunnan Statistical Yearbook 2001* (see note 4).

has revealed that investment was an important driving force. In 2000, the total investment in fixed assets in Yunnan was RMB69.79 billion, an increase of 396% (nominal increase) from RMB14.07 billion in 1992. The ratio of total investments in fixed assets to GDP increased from 22.7% in 1992 to 35.7% in 2000. According to Table 20.2, in 1992–2000, the average annual nominal growth rate of total investments in fixed assets in the province was 22.2%, 6.7% higher than that of GDP at 15.5% a year. In the same period, the average annual nominal growth rate in the total retail value of consumer goods was 12.1%, which was 3.4% lower than that of GDP. Thus, it can be concluded that investment in fixed assets contributed more to the expansion of GDP than consumption in Yunnan in the period 1992–2000. The rate of growth of consumption was smaller than the rate of growth of the economy as a whole. This indicates that the expansion in demand in Yunnan in that period was mainly driven by the expansion of investment-induced demand. The excessive expansion of investment-induced demand was the main reason for the high GDP growth rate.

It is also interesting to examine the role of foreign trade and foreign investment in Yunnan. As shown in Table 20.3, imports and exports increased dramatically, as indicated by high growth rates in the period 1992–1995. The dependence of GDP on foreign trade also increased. However, in 1996, Yunnan experienced a drop of US$0.19 billion in exports. After the 1997 Asian financial crisis, Yunnan's foreign trade further deteriorated. In 1999, exports declined by 18.9%. Overall, foreign trade played a very limited role in Yunnan's economy, in stark contrast to the situation in the coastal areas of the country.

Similarly, the role of foreign investment was also limited in Yunnan, although realized foreign investment increased from US$50.05 million in 1992 to US$221 million in 2000. The ratio of realized foreign investment to total investment in fixed assets increased slightly from 2.0% to 2.6% in

Table 20.3 Growth Rate of Foreign Trade and Economic Dependence on Foreign Trade in Yunnan, 1992–2000

Year	Growth rate of foreign trade (%)			Degree of economic dependence on foreign trade (%)		
	Total	Imports	Exports	Total	Imports	Exports
1992	21.8	16.4	36.4	6.0	4.1	1.8
1993	25.3	1.2	55.5	6.2	3.9	2.3
1994	60.0	74.1	36.8	11.8	8.1	3.8
1995	41.1	33.5	56.9	13.1	8.4	4.7
1996	−2.9	−14.2	16.1	11.5	6.4	5.1
1997	1.1	10.4	−2.8	10.2	6.1	4.1
1998	1.2	4.0	−3.1	9.4	5.8	3.6
1999	−17.5	−18.1	−18.9	7.4	4.6	2.8
2000	9.2	13.6	1.9	7.7	5.0	2.7

Source: Calculated according to data from the *Yunnan Statistical Yearbook 2001* (see note 4).

the same period. This was much smaller than the ratio of 15.1% for China as a whole in 2000.

Government Policies, Economic Structure and Pillar Industries

Economic development relies on the growth of various industries and structural transformations. For Yunnan, industrial policy is a key component of economic policy. This section reviews the economic structure and industrial policies in Yunnan.

The Evolution of the Economic Structure

From 1949 to the beginning of reform period, Yunnan was regarded as a backyard of China in case of the outbreak of war between China and other military powers. For several decades, the central government focused on political and military considerations rather than on economic development. As a result, capital investment in Yunnan by the central government was mainly concentrated in heavy industry, especially in areas related to national defence and military needs. Because capital investment by the central government was almost the only source of capital investment and economic construction in Yunnan under the centrally planned economic system, by 1978 when the policy of reform was introduced, an irrational and peculiar

Table 20.4 Changes in the Economic Structure of Yunnan, 1978–2000

Year	GDP (RMB billion)				Share of the three industries (%)		
	GDP	Primary industry	Secondary industry	Tertiary industry	Primary industry	Secondary industry	Tertiary industry
1978	6.91	2.95	2.76	1.20	42.7	39.9	17.4
1981	9.41	4.12	3.58	1.71	43.8	38.0	18.2
1984	13.96	5.73	5.44	2.79	41.1	39.0	19.9
1990	45.17	16.81	15.78	12.57	37.2	34.9	27.9
1991	51.74	16.95	17.96	16.84	32.8	34.7	32.5
1992	61.87	18.68	21.90	21.29	30.2	35.4	34.4
1993	77.92	19.17	32.71	26.04	24.6	42.0	33.4
1994	97.40	23.75	42.97	30.68	24.4	44.1	31.5
1995	120.67	30.53	53.66	36.48	25.3	44.5	30.2
1996	149.16	36.43	67.28	45.45	24.4	45.1	30.5
1997	164.42	39.15	75.00	50.27	23.8	45.6	30.6
1998	179.39	40.84	82.84	55.71	22.8	46.2	31.0
1999	185.57	41.22	82.51	61.85	22.2	44.5	33.3
2000	195.51	43.63	84.32	67.56	22.3	43.1	34.6

Note: GDP calculations are based on current-year prices.
Source: *Yunnan Statistical Yearbook 2001* (see note 4).

economic structure had formed in the province. In 1978, the primary, secondary and tertiary industries accounted for 42.7%, 39.9% and 17.4% of GDP in Yunnan, respectively (Table 20.4). Clearly, the primary sector dominated the economy in 1978. The main characteristics of the industries in these three sectors at the beginning of the reform period are examined below.

Although agriculture accounted for a large share of GDP, in the late 1970s, Yunnan's agricultural base was, in fact, very fragile. More than 50% of the arable land was not irrigated, while only 33.3% was effectively irrigated. Much arable land only had middle or low yields due to poor conditions for cultivation. Due to the inadequate production of grain in the province, in the period 1978–1980, Yunnan depended on allocations and transfers of grain from other provinces in the amount of over 400,000 tonnes a year on average.

The internal structure of the secondary industry was also problematic. The secondary sector was dominated by heavy industry, which accounted for nearly 60% of the total value of industrial output. However, this came at the expense of light industry, to the extent that, in the early 1980s, shortages in daily necessities resulted. The demand in the province for most daily consumer goods could not be met. The production chain in secondary industry was very short and the links among industries very weak. For example, few industries could provide auxiliary products and packaging material to other industries. The provincially competitive industries often relied on other provinces for supplies of raw materials. In the meantime, the raw materials produced by the province were not thoroughly processed. Most raw materials and preliminarily processed products were allocated and transferred to other provinces at low prices.

Moreover, the tertiary industry was underdeveloped. Except for officers working in the Chinese Communist Party (CCP), government and public institutions, employment in the tertiary industry was concentrated in the areas of commerce, wholesaling, retailing and warehousing. The finance and insurance industries had just begun to emerge. In the early 1980s, the underdeveloped transportation, postal service and telecommunications industries were bottlenecks in economic development.

After over 20 years of development since the beginning of reforms, Yunnan's economic structure has improved remarkably. In the early 1980s, the most important change was the rise in agricultural output due to successful institutional reforms in the rural areas. The contract-based household responsibility system was the core of rural reforms. The new system released the potential for production in agriculture that had previously been constrained. After the implementation of reforms in the rural economy, a series of policies aimed at developing various forms of ownership while maintaining public ownership as a main part in the economy were introduced. Such liberal policies brought about the rapid rise of private business and an emergence of a private economy mainly in the tertiary sector, in the areas of commerce, catering and services.

After basic problems in agriculture were solved, such as boosting supplies of grain and meat, economic development focused on industrialization. There were two goals for industrialization in Yunnan. The first was to achieve a balanced development of light and heavy industries. The second was to adjust the internal structure of heavy industry. As mentioned before, in the past several decades under the centrally planned system, Yunnan had focused on heavy industry, especially the production of raw materials. Consumer products were in short supply in the early 1980s. Thus, great efforts were made to develop light industry to change the economic structure dominated by heavy industry. These efforts have successfully resulted in the rising share of light industry in the economy and in increasing self-sufficiency in auxiliary products and packaging materials.

In the 1990s, there was stable and balanced development in the three industries. During the period 1991–2000, the average annual growth rates in the primary, secondary and tertiary industries were 5.0%, 12.2% and 10.3%, respectively. The development of the tertiary industry, especially the emerging industries of insurance, securities and telecommunications, was significant.

In summary, during the 20-year period between 1981 and 2000, Yunnan's GDP grew at an annual rate of 9.9% at constant prices, while the primary, secondary and tertiary industries grew by 6.7%, 10.3%, and 13.4%, respectively, per year at constant prices. The growth rate of the tertiary sector was especially rapid. By 2000, the shares of the primary, secondary and tertiary industries in Yunnan's GDP were 22.3%, 43.1% and 34.6%, respectively. In comparison with 1978, the share held by primary industry declined by 20.3%, while those of the secondary and tertiary industries increased by 3.2% and 17.2%, respectively (Table 20.4). The overall economic structure in terms of the three industries has been improving continuously. According to international experiences in industrialization, when an economy advances from the low-income level to the middle-income level, the share of primary industry will decline by 20% and those of the secondary and tertiary industries will increase by 10% and 15–20%, respectively.[5] This indicates that Yunnan's industrial structure is changing in the right direction.

It is also useful to review the current economic structure of Yunnan in more detail. In the agricultural sector, some agricultural production bases and pillar industries have been established, ensuring a sufficient aggregate production of agricultural products. Meanwhile, the restructuring of the agricultural structure has also induced the restructuring of the rural economy, especially in the area of rural industrialization. The secondary and tertiary industries in rural areas, especially rural enterprises, have experienced rapid development. In 1997, they accounted for 54.2% of the total value of rural output.[6] In that year, the output value of non-agricultural production exceeded that of agricultural production for the first time. This has changed the situation of the rural economy from one led by agriculture to one in which agricultural and non-agricultural production play equal roles.

In the secondary industry, the shares of light and heavy industries have been adjusted towards a rational structure. The processing industry using agricultural products as raw materials has developed rapidly. According to

Table 20.5 Light and Heavy Industries in Yunnan, 1978–2000

Year	Total industrial output value (RMB billion)	Light industry		Heavy industry	
		Total output value (RMB billion)	Share (%)	Total output value (RMB billion)	Share (%)
1978	5.54	2.38	43.0	3.16	57.0
1981	7.25	3.52	48.5	3.74	51.5
1985	13.63	6.59	48.4	7.03	51.6
1989	30.49	15.46	50.7	15.03	49.3
1990	34.53	18.11	52.5	16.41	49.5
1995	123.00	65.66	53.4	57.34	46.6
1998	150.32	77.47	51.5	72.85	48.5
1999	156.11	79.39	50.9	76.72	49.1
2000	158.94	80.27	50.5	78.67	49.5

Note: Total output value is based on current-year prices.
Source: *Yunnan Statistical Yearbook 2001* (see note 4).

Table 20.5, both light and heavy industries in Yunnan grew rapidly in 1978–2000. But light industry grew much more quickly than heavy industry. As a result, the share of light industry in the output value of secondary industry increased from 43.0% in 1978 to 50.5% in 2000. This indicates an improvement in Yunnan's industrial structure, as Yunnan has comparative advantages in the development of light industry, especially in the processing of agricultural products such as tobacco and food.

The internal structure of tertiary industry has also been improved. Traditional industries such as transportation, telecommunications, commerce, science and education achieved stable growth. Comprehensive transportation and telecommunications networks, with Kunming 昆明 as the centre, have been formed. In 2000, the value-added in the transportation, warehousing, postal service and telecommunications industries was RMB 8.25 billion, nearly 14 times greater than in 1978. Commercial circulation, both wholesale and retail, has expanded greatly. Preliminary product markets, factor markets and exchanges of various kinds have been formed. The total retail value of consumer products has increased steadily. The value-added in the wholesale, retail and catering industries in 2000 was RMB17.4 billion, which was nearly 10 times the value-added in 1978. Advancements in science and technology contributed 35%, 40% and 38% to GDP growth in agriculture, manufacturing and the whole economy, respectively. Along with the expansion of the traditional tertiary sector, new tertiary sectors such as the tourism, real estate, information and consulting industries have also experienced rapid growth in the reform period. For example, the number of foreign tourists increased from 1,299 in 1978 to over 1 million in 2000. The number of domestic tourists increased from 1.29 million to 36.73 million in the period 1978–1999.

Government Policies and Pillar Industries

Capital investment is an especially important spur to economic development in underdeveloped countries or regions. Compared with other provinces in eastern China, the private sector in Yunnan was underdeveloped, with a weak ability to accumulate capital. Thus, Yunnan relied mainly on government funds for capital investment. As a result, government policies had a significant impact on economic development in Yunnan.

The Third Plenary Session of the Eleventh Central Committee of the CCP in 1978 identified the need to solve structural problems in the Chinese economy. In April 1979, the working conference of the Central Committee of the CCP proposed guiding principles for the economic adjustment, reform, enhancement and improvement of the national economy. Serious structural problems were required to be generally solved in three years. Due to the focus on economic performance, this was regarded as an important change in China's industrial policy, although such a policy was still characteristic of the planned economy. Under the above guiding principles of the CCP, Yunnan attempted to promote industrial development. Officials in Yunnan changed their attitude and began to deal with real issues in Yunnan's economy. The first important task was to review the province's own conditions for development. Such viewpoint was emphasized in 1983 by He Zhiqiang 和志強, the governor of Yunnan at the time:

> Due to social and historic reasons, the economy in our province as well as science and culture is less developed. More and more comrades in our province have recognized this fact.... We acknowledge that Yunnan is backward, but we will not yield to such a backward situation.... Acknowledging this fact is the first step in changing such a backward situation. The next step is to find the right way to change this situation of backwardness.... Although Yunnan is backward, it is well known that Yunnan has rich natural resources and an advantageous geographical location.[7]

The above perception has been the basis of policy-making in the reform period. Faced with the situation of backwardness, the provincial government is keen to adopt a strategy of leap-frogging in industrial development. The industrial policies of Yunnan in the past two decades have focused on capital investment in infrastructure and on the development of pillar industries by concentrating on various resources, including policy measures and economic resources.

For a long time, economic development in Yunnan was constrained by the province's backward infrastructure and weak basic industries, such as energy and electricity generation, transportation and communications, education and R&D. For example, in the period 1981–1985, the elasticity coefficients for the production and consumption of energy and electricity were 0.59 and 0.56, respectively. At a time when there was no significant improvement in energy saving, the small coefficients indicated that there was a striking structural contradiction between energy supply and economic growth in Yunnan in the early 1980s. Supplies of energy and electricity could not meet the demands of economic development. Moreover, there was a shortage of skilled professionals in emerging industries such as insurance and R&D. To change such a situation, Yunnan adopted policies to support the development of infrastructure, mainly through capital investment. In the period 1982–1987, the total financial revenue was RMB 13.1 billion, while the total capital investment in electricity supply, transportation, agriculture, education, science and technology was RMB4 billion.[8] Such a heavy investment in infrastructure and in basic industries continued in the 1990s. As a result, the situation for transportation, communications and electricity supply improved dramatically by the late 1990s.

In terms of industrial policy in Yunnan, the first issue was to select pillar industries that would form the core of the economy. When selecting the pillar industries, Yunnan's own conditions and the changing economic situation had to be considered. Because of the changes of the past 20 years, the list of selected pillar industries had to be adjusted.

In the 1980s, Yunnan focused on the development of resource-based industries, including the manufacturing of tobacco, cane sugar and tea, and the mining of mineral resources. Considering the resource advantages and existing economic structure of Yunnan, it was appropriate to select these industries. However, all of the resource-based industries, except for the tobacco industry, involved simple processing, generating little value-added. These industries could not bring many benefits to Yunnan. Two kinds of measures were taken to change this situation. One was to technologically upgrade the existing pillar industries; the other was to develop new high value-added pillar industries.

By the early 1990s, the economic efficiency of traditional key industries such as the tobacco and mining industries had improved, while remarkable growth was also achieved in some new industries such as tourism and the processing of biological resources. Thus, in Yunnan's Sixth Congress of the CCP held in 1995, a strategy of developing four pillar industries was proposed, that is, the tobacco industry, the processing of biological resources, mining and tourism. The mining industry would focus on phosphorus chemicals and the processing of non-ferrous metals, while the tourism industry would feature scenic natural spots and diverse ethnic cultures. In December 1996, the provincial government confirmed its decision to speed up the construction of these four pillar industries in Yunnan. By the late 1990s, progress in the building up of the four pillar industries was palpable.

Border Trade and Changing Government Policies

Survey of the Border Trade in Yunnan

Yunnan is an inland province in China that shares a long land border with several countries. Such a geographic location is favourable for the development of border trading.[9] Border trading first took place in 1978 in Dehong 德宏. It then expanded to several prefectures or autonomous prefectures (*zhou* 州) such as Baoshan 保山, Nujiang 怒江, Lincang 臨滄, Xishuangbanna 西雙版納 and Simao 思茅 (Figure 20.1). Throughout the 1980s, most of the border trading in Yunnan took place in Dehong. When normal relations between China and Vietnam were restored in the early 1990s, border trading with Vietnam began to boom in Honghe 紅河 and Wenshan 文山.

The total value of imports and exports in the border trade was RMB 2,949 million for the whole province in 2000. This was an increase of 191.4% from 1989 and an increase of 55.2% from 1995. Table 20.6 presents the rates of growth in the border trade in Yunnan in the period 1989–2000. During this period, the average annual growth rate was 10.2%. Geographically, Yunnan's border trade was concentrated in 25 counties in 8 prefectures and autonomous prefectures. Indeed, for a long time, the border trade was concentrated in 4 prefectures and autonomous prefectures; that is, Dehong, Baoshan, Xishuangbanna and Honghe, in the order of their volume of border trade. In 1996, the total value of the border trade in these 4 prefectures and autonomous prefectures comprised about 92% of that for the province. Dehong actually accounted for nearly 50% of the total border

Figure 20.1 Yunnan in Its Geographical Setting

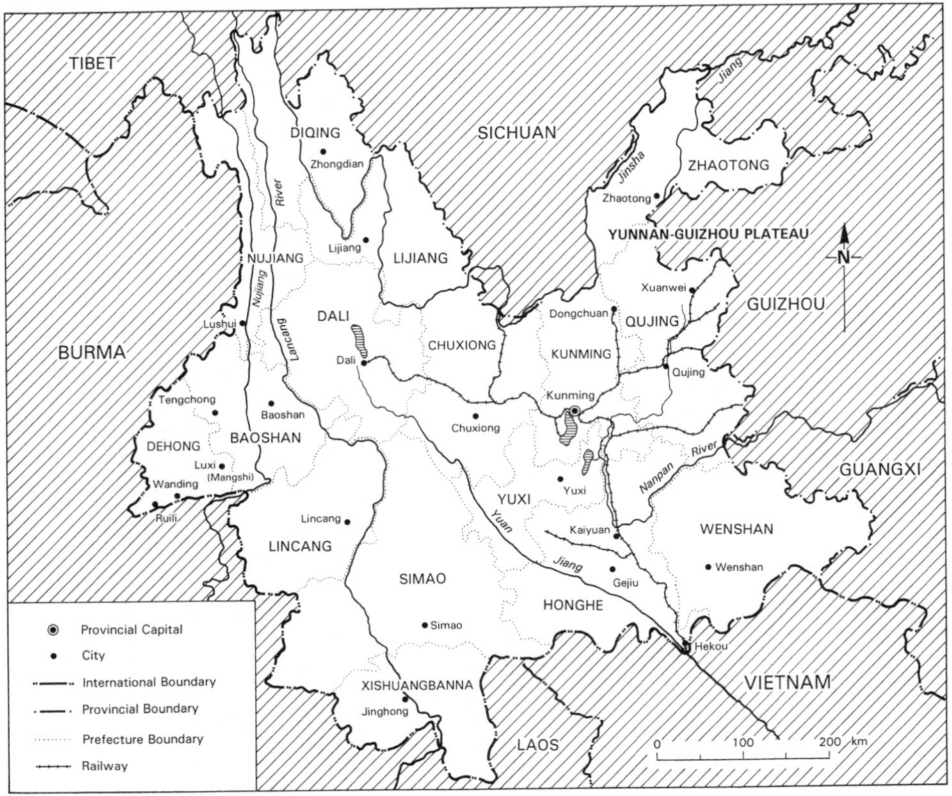

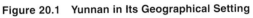

Table 20.6 Border Trade in Yunnan, 1989–2000

Year	Total of imports and exports (RMB million)	Imports (RMB million)	Exports (RMB million)	Growth rate of the total of imports and exports (%)
1989	1,012	676	336	—
1990	1,079	721	357	6.61
1991	1,278	844	435	18.52
1992	1,891	1,274	617	47.89
1993	2,345	1,713	631	24.01
1994	2,118	1,202	916	–9.67
1995	1,900	969	932	–10.27
1996	1,139	378	761	–40.05
1997	615	349	267	–45.98
1998	1,085	738	347	76.34
1999	2,382	1,919	463	119.52
2000	2,949	2,302	647	24.44

Source: *Yunnan Statistical Yearbook 2001* (see note 4).

trade. In 2000, the share of the four prefectures and autonomous prefectures in the total border trade of the province was still about 90%, although due to the rapid development of the border trade between China and Vietnam in recent years, the value of the trade in Honghe exceeded that of Baoshan.

Border trading has greatly stimulated the economic and social development of the border areas in Yunnan in the past 20 years. Taking Dehong autonomous prefecture as an example, the positive effect of border trade has been extensive. Many small border towns such as Ruili 瑞麗, Wanding 畹町 and Mangshi 芒市 have developed rapidly and become prosperous border cities. There has been a remarkable improvement in the transportation and communication infrastructure of the whole autonomous prefecture. Almost all highways in the autonomous prefecture had previously been constructed of gravel or dirt. Most of arterial highways in the prefecture have been upgraded to asphalt roads. Border trading is the main source of income in these areas. Most importantly, the development of border trading has changed people's traditional thinking, widened their scope of economic activity and nurtured many skilled people with business and management talent.

Impact of Government Policies on the Border Trade

Government policies have had a great impact on the development of the border trade in Yunnan. In 1980, the provincial government of Yunnan decided to resume petty trading, first along the Sino-Burma border. The State Council of China issued a document in 1984, making it clear that the small-volume border trade would be regulated and implemented by relevant provincial governments according to the "five points of the policy"; that is, "sourcing goods by oneself, selling by oneself, negotiating by oneself, balancing the payment by oneself and bearing the profit or loss by oneself." In accordance with this document, in 1985, the provincial government of Yunnan, taking into consideration the reality of the border area in Yunnan, issued a policy document entitled "Temporary Provisions on the Border Trade of Yunnan Province." The provincial policy further relaxed the state's policy on the border trade by permitting individuals or organizations to participate in the border trade rather than limiting participation in this trade to state-owned trading companies.

In June 1992, the State Council decided to extend the open policy to Kunming and other border cities. The policy for open coastal cities was extended to Kunming, while Hekou 河口, Ruili and Wanding were classified as open-border cities. Preferential policies for the border trade with Vietnam and Laos were also announced. All of this led to a large reduction in transaction costs for participants in the border trade. The result was a boom in trade.

However, when the State Council issued a document entitled "Notice on Relevant Issues on the Border Trade" in 1996, the policy environment changed dramatically. The document stipulated that quota licensing controls should be applied to imports and exports in the border trade. US dollars should be used as the currency of settlement instead of the RMB that was used in the Sino-Burma border trade. Certain restricted goods could only be traded by authorized companies. A total of 162 kinds of goods that had previously been exempted from import tariffs would be taxed at 50% of the normal tariff.

It was generally thought that the original intention of the 1996 policy was to replace the special border trade policy with the standard policy. This would enable the province to adapt to a more competitive environment in the future. However, the results were disastrous. Yunnan's border trade declined sharply from 1996 to 1997. The value of the trade decreased by 40.05% in 1996 and by 45.98% in 1997. Only 802 enterprises were authorized for border trade after registering with the Ministry of Foreign Trade and Economic Cooperation (MOFTEC), a decline of 60% from 2,010 enterprises in 1995. Most enterprises that failed to receive authorization went bankrupt or exited the border trade. Some enterprises that continued were mostly not profitable. This was in stark contrast to the previous situation, which saw most of these enterprises making good profits.

To a great extent, the 1996 policy did not reflect the realities of the trade. Yunnan's border trade had the following characteristics: It was dominated by small trade enterprises; the volume of each transaction in the trade was small; but the total number of transactions was large. This was due to the fact that the economies of Yunnan's partners in the border trade, especially Burma, tended to be small and fragmented and their level of solvency low. Strictly implementing a policy that was good for the coastal areas of the country to the border trade was like trying to help the growth of sprout by pulling it upward. In the end, the 1996 policy dampened the vitality of the border trade.

The 1996 policy greatly increased the transaction costs of enterprises engaged in the border trade. For example, the requirement that a transaction had to be settled in US dollars would necessitate extra intermediary foreign currency arrangements. Furthermore, there had previously been little circulation of US dollars in the border areas. According to economic principles, quota and licence management were likely to result in much rent seeking. This was aggravated by the fact that the regulatory system in the border areas was imperfect and supervision ineffective. In addition, the government departments in the border areas did not find it easy to adapt to the 1996 policy change. For example, the 162 kinds of goods that were exempted from imported tariff were taxed at 50% of the normal tariff. However, the local offices of state taxation insisted on collecting a value-added tax at the import stage on the half of the import tariff that had been exempted. The joint inspection teams of various departments were not well co-ordinated, and each department attempted to charge fees for its own reasons.

The 1996 policy was related to the important issue of the distribution of economic interest between local and central governments. Replacing special management procedures with ordinary trade management procedures for the border trade essentially meant that tax revenues would be transferred from local governments to the central government, which would significantly undermine local interests. For example, according to the provisions in the State Council's document, the state taxation bureau would collect at the import stage the value-added tax imposed on foreign businesses from 1 April 1996. This resulted in a reduction of over RMB40 million in the financial revenues of Dehong autonomous prefecture from 1995 to 1996.

Such a loss in revenue dampened the enthusiasm of local governments towards the border trade.

Fortunately, governments at various levels realized the importance of the problem. The governments of Yunnan and relevant prefectures or autonomous prefectures took measures to stop the decline in the border trade. In October 1998, the MOFTEC and General Administration of Customs also issued a series of documents, such as "Notice on Additional Regulations about the Further Development of Border Trade." According to these new documents, small border trading enterprises were also entitled to rebates in import tax. The new duties on the export of jade, timber, rattan and rawhide would be returned after they were levied.

The growth of the border trade in Yunnan resumed in 1998, although the total value of imports and exports that year was only RMB1,085 million, lower than that of any year in the period 1991–1996. Eventually, the total value of imports and exports in the border trade reached a peak in 1999, and again in 2000. It is clear that there is great potential for the further development of this trade. However, policy-makers have to resolve the following question: Is this the proper time to replace the border trade with ordinary international trade? From the perspective of the domestic economy, this may be a good opportunity to introduce policies designed to restructure various enterprises/organizations in Yunnan that are engaging in the border trade with different operational efficiencies. However, it is impossible to change the economic situation of neighbouring countries that are partners in the border trade. In these countries, most economic entities/organizations are small, and their operations are characterized by many transactions, each of a small volume. When trade is conducted between the combined large trading enterprise on the Chinese side and the numerous small organizations of trade partners, transaction costs for the Chinese side may not be reduced and may even increase. This reality has to be taken into consideration when planning the development of the border trade in Yunnan.

Conclusion: Problems and Strategies of Development

This chapter has examined economic development in Yunnan in the reform period. The changes in economic structure, border trade and government policy have been discussed. As indicated by its high rate of economic growth, Yunnan achieved significant economic development in the reform period. However, its level of economic development is still well behind that of the eastern coastal region. There are several problems with development in Yunnan.

First, the economic system has not been sufficiently reformed and the operation of the market mechanism falls short of expectations. The result is a low level of economic efficiency and difficulties in accumulating capital for economic growth. People in Yunnan have been used to depending on the central government for financial support. Such a dependence was formed in the pre-reform period when a centrally planned economic system prevailed. In Yunnan, government and public institutions such as the CCP, and other social organizations, are large in scale while the economic base is relatively weak. Thus, there are fewer enterprises to support various public institutions at various levels in Yunnan than in the eastern region, meaning that an enterprise in Yunnan has a heavier burden than one in the eastern region. This reduces the ability of an enterprise to accumulate capital. In the meantime, Yunnan does not have adequate tax revenues, thus constraining the effective operation of CCP, government administration and education in the province.

Second, the open-door policy has not been widely implemented and the investment environment is not satisfactory. Yunnan has not been able to attract much domestic capital and foreign investment. People still have the traditional idea that it is immoral to make profit by production and trading. Thus, external investment is not welcome. Furthermore, the planned economy still has a powerful impact on government behaviour in Yunnan. This results in unclear regulations, little flexibility, high costs and a great risk for enterprises.

Third, there are several problems in the areas of education and human resources in Yunnan. There is an insufficient amount of investment in human capital, funds for education are not used efficiently, and human resources are not well utilized. Educational levels in Yunnan are low and the province is short of human capital. There is no sign that these conditions will improve. Funding for education is not likely to increase significantly due to a tight government budget. The migration of many graduates to the eastern region will exacerbate the shortage of talent. Moreover, human resources are often not allocated efficiently. Driven by a "preference for official posts" (*guan benwei* 官本位) and practical interests, people with outstanding talent tend to find employment in many unproductive public institutions, while enterprises are deprived of skilled people.

Fourth, economic development is uneven in different areas of Yunnan and the alleviation of poverty is still a very arduous task. The central area of Yunnan, with Kunming as the centre, has the most developed economy. A considerable number of enterprises are located in this area and its people enjoy relatively high living standards. However, other areas in the province are generally less developed. By the end of 1999, there were still 3.5 million people in the province with an income below the poverty line. The average annual per capita income of farmers in the 73 counties designated as impoverished was only RMB855.[10]

As a key province in the "go-west" strategy, Yunnan needs to implement a development strategy to make use of such an opportunity. The following are some key areas to consider:

First, Yunnan needs to accelerate the reform of its economic system so that the market mechanism can operate effectively. At present, the core part of a market economy, that is, the price mechanism, has been well established. Most goods are traded according to market prices, although the prices of some goods are still distorted to a certain degree. Other important issues include the transformation of the role and function of the government and the establishment of a modern enterprise system.

An economy in which there is a great deal of administrative interference in the market is not a genuine market economy. In order to make the market mechanism work, the government must exit from the market. Government organizations should also be reformed. One key issue is to downsize the CCP, government and other public institutions.

The foundation of the modern enterprise system lies in free enterprise, meaning that enterprises can be set up freely, can enter and exit most industries freely, and can engage in production and management freely. For Yunnan, the strategic task is to focus efforts on building up an environment of "free enterprise," rather than to set up many large-scale enterprise groups. Such an environment will attract numerous investors to set up enterprises in Yunnan, while tax concessions offered by the preferential policy will also greatly improve an enterprise's return on capital investment.

Second, it is necessary to make full use of increased transfer payments from the central government to break the bottlenecks in development. Transfer payments from the central government can be used to support the expenditures of the CCP and government to some degree. This will reduce the tax burden on enterprises in Yunnan, so that factor input can have roughly the same rate of return in Yunnan as in the eastern region. This will also reduce the gap in income between people in non-productive units and those in production units, so that more people of outstanding talent will be attracted to work in the latter, improving the utilization and distribution of human resources. In addition, to make use of the preferential support for the construction of infrastructure in the western region, Yunnan should draw up rational plans for such areas as transportation and energy supply. Transfer payments from the central government can also be used for the construction of infrastructure. Moreover, transfer payments can also be used to develop greater access to basic education and to support a rational incentive mechanism to attract and maintain people of talent.

Third, further opening up Yunnan's economy can strengthen the province's economic vitality. It has been proven that outside investors can bring not only production factors, such as capital and technology, but also new ideas and methods in management. All of these are important factors in sustaining a prosperous economy.

Fourth, efficient institutional innovations require the support of the central government. These include innovations in such areas as finance, property rights, etc. For example, the land ownership system in Yunnan can be adjusted. Land-use rights for over 100 years may be granted, so that long-term returns can be guaranteed for investors. Under the macro-control of the state, land-use rights, as a kind of property right, could be traded on the secondary market after the land has been developed and evaluated. Land prices should also be reduced to make up for the low returns on capital investment in the western region. This should be accomplished through an open market mechanism so that the same policies apply to all investors.

Notes

1. For more detailed information on Yunnan's physical geography, see Shen Anbo 沈安波 et al., *Yunnan shengqing xinbian* 雲南省情新編 (The Situation in Yunnan Province, revised edition) on Yunnan xinwen wang 雲南新聞網 at www.yunnan.com.cn/ynsurvey/surveyyn.htm; Yunnan zhichuang wangzhan 雲南之窗網站 at http://www.yunnan-window.com.cn/.
2. For more detailed information about resources in Yunnan, see Zhang Huaiyu 張懷渝, *Yunnansheng jingji dili* 雲南省經濟地理 (Economic Geography of Yunnan) (Beijing: Xinhua chubanshe 新華出版社, 1988); Yu Zundian 余尊殿, "Zhongguo xibu dakaifa yu Yunnan de ziran ziyuan" 中國西部大開發與雲南的自然資源 (The Development of China's West and Natural Resources in Yunnan), *Yunnan dizhi* 雲南地質 (Yunnan Geology), Vol. 20, No. 3 (2001), pp. 221–28.
3. Che Zhimin 車志敏 et al., *Maixiang 2010 nian de Yunnan* 邁向2010年的雲南 (Yunnan Towards 2010) (Kunming: Yunnan renmin chubanshe 雲南人民出版社, 1998), p. 797.
4. Yunnansheng tongjiju 雲南省統計局, *Yunnan tongji nianjian 2001* 雲南省統計年鑑2001 (Yunnan Statistical Yearbook 2001) (Beijing: Zhongguo tongji

chubanshe 中國統計出版社, 2001). Unless specified, most of the data in this chapter has been drawn from this yearbook. Data on GDP have been adjusted by calculating growth rates according to the data in the general retail price index (*shangpin lingshou jiage zhishu* 商品零售價格指數) from National Bureau of Statistics, *China Statistical Yearbook 2001* (Beijing: China Statistics Press, 2001).

5. Hollis Chenery, Sherman Robinson and Moshe Syrquin, comp.; Wu Qi 吳奇 and Wang Songbao 王松寶 et al., trans., *Gongyehua he jingji zengzhang de bijiao yanjiu* 工業化和經濟增長的比較研究 (Industrialization and Growth: A Comparative Study) (Shanghai: Sanlian shudian 三聯書店, 1995), pp. 260–74.
6. Yunnan jihua fazhan weiyuanhui 雲南計劃發展委員會, *Yunnansheng nongye chanye jiegou tiaozheng yanjiu* 雲南省農業產業結構調整研究 (A Study of the Structural Adjustment of Yunnan's Agricultural System) (Neibu yanjiu baogao 內部研究報告, 1998).
7. He Zhiqiang, "Chengren luohou, gaibian luohou" 承認落後，改變落後 (Admit the Condition of Backwardness, and Change It), in *Yunnan de gaige kaifang yu fazhan* 雲南的改革開放與發展 (The Reform, Opening up and Development of Yunnan), edited by He Zhiqiang (Beijing: Zhonggong zhongyang dangxiao chubanshe 中共中央黨校出版社, 1995), pp. 2–7.
8. He Zhiqiang, "Zhengfu gongzuo baogao" 政府工作報告 (Government Working Report), in *Yunnan de gaige kaifang yu fazhan*, edited by He Zhiqiang (see note 7), pp. 17–48.
9. The data for this section come from Yang Changchun 楊長春, *Zhongxibu diqu de duiwai maoyi* 中西部地區的對外貿易 (Foreign Trade of the Central and Western Regions) (Beijing: Duiwai jingji maoyi daxue chubanshe 對外經濟貿易大學出版社, 2000); Zhu Zhenmin 朱振民, "Yunnan yu linguo de bianjing maoyi jiqi fazhan" 雲南與鄰國的邊境貿易及其發展 (Border Trade and Its Development between Yunnan and Neighbouring Countries), *Yunnan shehui kexue* 雲南社會科學 (Yunnan Social Sciences), No. 6 (2000), pp. 53–59.
10. Data from Zhu Wen 朱文 and Liu Ersi 劉爾思, "Ershiyi shiji Yunnan fupin mianlin de kunnan he wenti" 二十一世紀雲南扶貧面臨的困難和問題 (The Difficulties and Issues in Poverty Alleviation in Yunnan), *Yunnan caimao xueyuan xuebao: Jingji guanli ban* 雲南財貿學院學報：經濟管理版 (Journal of the Yunnan College of Finance and Trade: Economic Management Edition), Vol. 15, No. 2 (2001), pp. 74–77.

21

Tibet

Ng Wing-fai and Zhou Yixing

Introduction

Better known as "the Roof of the World," Tibet was at one time a dominating cultural force in Mongolia, Ladakh, Nepal, Sikkim, Bhutan and parts of northern Pakistan, northern India, western China and southern Russia.[1] Yet, save for a long list of reports by Jesuit missionaries, adventurers, soldiers and scholars who made their way to "the Forbidden City," Tibet's capital of Lhasa 拉薩, as early as the sixteenth century, Tibet was largely unknown to the outside world as recently as about 40 years ago.[2] This is partly because of the abrupt demise of the Lamaist kingdom,[3] and partly because of the systematic isolation of Tibet from world affairs since 1959. Among the first intimations in the West of Tibet's past was the caricature of the utopian Shangri-la 香格里拉 presented in the novel *Lost Horizon* and the depictions of a land of psychic mysteries detailed in more recent scholarly accounts.[4]

The description of Tibet as a highland civilization coincided with its modern search for nationhood in the early nineteenth century.[5] The quickening of the process of colonial expansion of the Western powers in Inner Asia, including not only Tibet, but also Manchuria 滿洲, Mongolia 蒙古 and Xinjiang 新疆, has caused Tibet to become more narrowly defined by religious sects and ethnic identity.[6] As the clashes of political and economic interests dominated, leading to the flight of Tibet's spiritual and temporal leader, the Dalai Lama 達賴喇嘛, in 1959, Tibet found itself in a more difficult position with regard to defining its regional economy.[7] Moreover, when China adopted a more lenient and open economic policy since 1979 towards its border regions, which are considered relatively backward and impoverished,[9] how can an interdependent relationship be evolved within the national boundary?

On the other hand, the growth of regional economies in China means that Southwest China cannot be effectively governed without the active role of Tibet, whether in terms of ecological protection or in generating economic growth in river source regions.[10] The immediate task is, therefore, to mend linkages through the mountain ranges, coupling national strength with the strategic repositioning of local and regional governments. To accomplish such a task, it is not sufficient to merely reach out via the modern world of cyberways, but also to create artificial linkages so that growth poles at different tiers can be adequately articulated.[11] For developmentalists, such linkages are necessarily administrative because of the goal of "balanced growth." Incrementalists, on the other hand, believe that "economies of scale" have to be achieved, such that nodal points of growth can be formed in the first place. Meanwhile, geographers regard the rectification of the core-periphery relationship as desirable, so that the siphoning-off of resources from the periphery to the core will become less likely to occur. Last, but not least, sustainable development has to be a moderating factor in selecting a development model.[12] All of these are core issues in our attempt to explore the question of the development of Tibet and the region.

Geography

Situated in southwestern China, the most prominent feature of Tibet, as exemplified in most textbooks, is its physical dimensions and characteristics. With an area approximating the size of Germany and France, Tibet measures about 2,000 km from east to west and 1,000 km from north to south; its area of 1,250,000 km^2 constitutes one-eighth of China's total. But, above all, Tibet is defined by altitude. Tibet has more than 100 mountains that are over 7,000 m above sea level, of which 10 are over 8,000 m above sea level, making Tibet virtually "an ensemble of peaks" averaging of 4,000 m in altitude.[13] In the northern part of Tibet are east-west mountain ranges — the Kunlun Mountains 崑崙山, Kekexili Mountains 可可西里山 and Tanggula Mountains 唐古拉山, separating it from Xinjiang 新疆 and Qinghai 青海. In the southern part of Tibet are the Himalaya Mountains 喜馬拉雅山, where the world's highest peak Mount Qomolangma 珠穆朗瑪峰 (Mount Everest) is situated (8,848.3 m above sea level) (Figure 21.1). In the central part of Tibet are Gangdise Mountains 岡底斯山 and Nyenchenthanglha Mountains 念青唐古拉山, dividing Tibet into the northern Tibet plateau and the southern Tibet valley. In the eastern part of Tibet is the north-south mountain range of the Hengduan Mountains 橫斷山, comprising the following mountains: the Ningjing Mountains 寧靜山, Taniantaweng Mountains 他念他翁山 and Boshula Mountains 伯舒拉山. The Jinsha River 金沙江, Lancang River 瀾滄江 and Nujiang 怒江 are south-flowing rivers, running parallel to each other and cutting through tremendous gorges. In the western part of Tibet is the 6,000 m high Karakorum Mountains 喀拉昆侖山, which is an extension of the Pamir Plateau from neighbouring Kashmir.[14]

By virtue of its particular physical features and geographical characteristics, Tibet can be clearly divided into four natural areas. The northern Tibet plateau accounts for about 40% of the area of Tibet and is a virtually uninhabited high-altitude alpine desert. The region is extremely arid and cold, with perennially frozen earth some 140–170 m thick. The alpine grassland region of Ngari 阿里 accounts for about 20% of the area of Tibet

Figure 21.1 Tibet in Its Geopolitical Setting

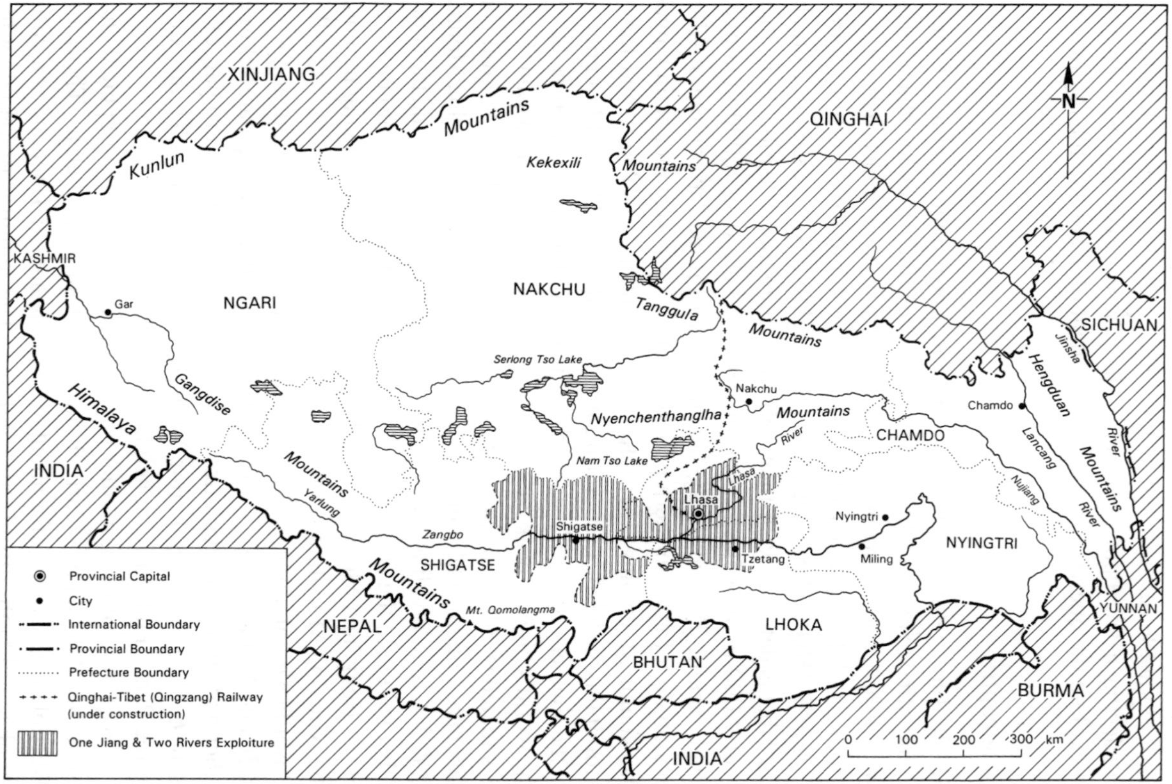

and is a pastoral area supporting nomads.[15] Although accounting for only 12% of the area of Tibet, the mountain shrub steppe and alpine steppe area of the southern Tibet valley is where the monsoons from the Bay of Bengal penetrate to the Yarlung Zangbo River 雅魯藏布江. The alpine meadow and alpine forest region of eastern Tibet accounts for about 20% of the area of Tibet and is described as "one of the richest areas of alpine flora in the world."[16]

All of the major rivers of Asia have their source in Tibet. The Indus, Ganges, Sutlej and Brahmaputra all arise in southwestern Tibet, while the Salween, Lancang and Yangzi all arise in central and eastern Tibet. Arising in the Gangdise Mountains, the Yarlung Zangbo is the largest river in Tibet, meandering through the central part of the southern valley. It runs for 2,057 km in the region, with a catchment area of about 240,000 km^2. Mid-stream, between Lhasa and Milin 米林, about half of the total population and arable land in Tibet is found. When it turns and runs through the world's largest gorge at 95°E,[17] it flows into India and is called the Brahmaputra. Although it is only the fifth-longest river in China, with its many tributaries and significant rapids, including the Tachok Zangbo River 多雄藏布河, Nyangchu River 年楚河, Lhasa River 拉薩河, Nyang Qu 尼洋曲 and Talung Zangbo River 帕隆藏布河, Tibet's hydropower reserves is the second-largest nationwide, accounting for about 47% of total reserves.

Approximately 100,000 km^2 of Tibet is an area of internal drainage, of which the largest inland river is the 409 km long Zagya Zangbo 扎加藏布, which drains into the Serlong Tso 色林錯 Lake. As the area is also weathered by glaciers, inland Tibet is dotted with several hundred lakes. The largest is Nam Tso 納木錯 Lake, which is 4,718 m above sea level and has a water surface of 1,940 km^2. As the rate of evaporation is low and the permafrost in many areas prevents water from penetrating to the surface, most lakes are deposited with salts and are natural sanctuaries for all kinds of wildlife.

As the northward advance of the heavily laden air mass of the Indian Ocean monsoon is blocked by the Himalayas, preventing the transfer of heat to the North Pole, Tibet has become the area with the greatest degree of climatic "continentality" on the planet. The climate of Tibet thus varies between sub-tropical to a frigid alpine zone, due to the existence of vast differentials in temperature and pressure. First, Tibet has abundant sunshine. For example, Lhasa has 3,005 hours of sunshine per annum, while Chongqing 重慶 on the same latitude has only 1,988 hours. Second, Tibet's weather is changeable, with the diurnal range of temperatures in the northern plateau reaching 22°C in January. Third, the incidence of rainfall at night is high. Rainfall between 8:00 a.m. and 8:00 p.m. in the northern and eastern plateau can account for 60–70% of the total annual rainfall, while it can be 80% for western Tibet. Fourth, it is windy in Tibet. In the Ngari region, northern Tibet and Shigatse 日喀則, in particular, the windy season can last for almost six months of the year.[18]

Ecology

The geography of the Tibetan plateau is very similar to that of the Rocky Mountain states of the United States, except that the altitude of the Tibetan plateau is about twice as high. As the plateau varies, with the altitude increasing from the southwest to the northwest, ecological zones vary from alpine meadow to alpine steppe and alpine desert. But, most significantly, about 60–80% of Tibet is ecologically fragile, including the following regions: the high region (above 3,500 m high), cold region (annual average temperature of below 0°C), dry region (annual rainfall of less than 250 mm), desert region (grassland coverage of less than 50%, or forest coverage of less than 5%), windy region (wind over grade 8 for 80 days annually), sandy region (sandy area of more than 80%), steep region (where the slope is more than 40°).[19]

In developing Tibet, a non-resource based approach has to be adopted in the face of the tough agenda imposed by the ecological zoning policy. The environmental protection of Tibet is basically carried out according to ecological zoning and regional zoning systems. The zones include: (1) a glacial ecological system: this includes all mountainous regions above the snow line and can further be classified into wet glaciers and dry glaciers; (2) a shrub ecological region: including shrubs and grasslands; (3) a water ecological system: thousands of lakes are formed when wet air penetrates the Qing-Zang (Qinghai-Tibet) Plateau 青藏高原 from the Indian Ocean; (4) a forest ecological system: in the deep valleys, there exist all kinds of climates found in the northern hemisphere, as well as a rare vertical distribution of the primeval forest containing a variety of species (about 5,760 botanical species and 3,045 animal species).[20] At present, there are 12 nature reserves, accounting for 27.1% of the area of Tibet and equalling the size of Finland. The objective is to protect the ecological system and rare species, and to stabilize ecologically fragile zones through establishing large-scale nature reserves. For example, (1) The Mount Qomolangma Nature Reserve and the Metok 墨脫 Nature Reserve are aimed at the protection of various types of ecological systems in the vertical zone; (2) The

Qangtang 羌塘 Nature Reserve, Riwoqe 類烏齊 Nature Reserve and Dongjug 東久 Nature Reserve are aimed at the protection of rare and precious animals; (3) The Nanxiang 南鄉 Nature Reserve and the Pagqi 巴結 Nature Reserve are for the protection of rare and precious plants. A four-river Nature Reserve co-funded by China and the U.S. has been proposed. The objective would be to protect the upstream areas of the four rivers (Jinsha River, Lancang River, Nujiang and Yarlung Zangbo). This ambitious project will affect highly populated regions along the Yangzi River, the Mekong Delta and the Ganges River Delta. It will involve China, Myanmar, Thailand, Laos, Kampuchea, Vietnam, Bangladesh and India, and cover aspects such as water conservation, disaster reduction, fisheries, water resources, and so forth.[21]

Characteristics of Regional Development

Apart from geographical and ecological issues, there are wider development issues of national significance to be addressed. The various strands need to be articulated in a coherent policy, from the perspective of Tibet as a regional economy. As such, it is necessary to deviate from the traditional theoretical framework, which tends to lessen the regional role of Tibet in the national economy, whether in terms of transport (the core-periphery theory), religion (historicism) or a dual economy (functionalism).[22] With regard to a positive-sum game, it is critical to explore what Tibet stands to lose and to gain in the Big Push. Therefore, in formulating a national policy, it is necessary to go beyond the issues of territorial integrity (geography) and the growth model (ecology), since there are more constraints to be resolved in putting all of these development issues into an integrated policy.

The most critical development issue is that although territorial isolation unites Tibet geographically, regional variations separate it. As at 1999, there were only 26,000 km of roads in Tibet, of which only 1,900 km were paved. Therefore, the attempt to homogenize the regional economy through the construction of infrastructure is an insurmountable task. It is essential to compartmentalize the regional economy and make the process of urbanization in Tibet rely more on regionalizing the economy (the small town strategy), rather than economizing the region (the large city strategy). In this sense, the construction of the 1,142 km long Qing-Zang 青藏 (Qinghai-Tibet) Railway is definitely an example of the former, in that it will disperse the dynamism of growth. Starting from Golmu 格爾木 in Qinghai, this feat of engineering passes through the highest point of the Tanggula Mountains Pass, which is 5,072 m above sea level, and enters

Tibet through Amdo 安多, Nakchu 那曲, Damshung 當雄 and Yangbajain 羊八井. It will open a new chapter in the history of railway transport in Tibet and is expected to vitalize its stalemated economy in the long term.[23]

The Spatial Structure of the Development of Tibet

How can an idealized model of regional development be derived to enable Tibet to shift to a "higher" platform of growth? The critical issue here is to explore the possibility of building growth poles outside the underdeveloped region of Tibet, such that cities as centres of economic growth, technological innovation and cultural production can actually be "relocated." Furthermore, as an artificial system of diffusion is to be established internally by the tripartite division of the regional economy of China, a model of regional development will be sustained, such that the local economy can be activated externally. In this vein, a more coherent pattern of regional growth based on the dual process of urbanization and regionalization will unfold to provide a more rational spatial context to resolve the problem of development, compensating for the regional variations that deeply divide Tibet.[24]

As such, the model of regional development practically works the opposite from the classical model, first by its emphasis on mending linkages, and second by its focus on effecting diffusion. Within the context of China's Western Development, a specialized model of the Big Push can be said to have been designed to rectify the shortcomings inherent in the development geography of Tibet. Economically, Tibet has been placed at the bottom of China's development ladder, being characterized as the so-called "zero-base taking-off point." Tibet is being gravely discriminated if the problem of hardware cannot be solved in the shortest possible time, leaving the problems of software to be placed in a hierarchy as problems of social development within a prescribed spatial order. Socially, the social structure of Tibet is very much an outcome of the Chinese mode of social mobilization. Only when an external institution can be established can the problems of social development be tackled. Politically, the economic and social development of Tibet can only be sustained by restricting Tibetan Buddhism to its own domain. The problem of regional development is necessarily an issue of national development whereby, during the interim period of economic and social transition, the problem of religion can be side-stepped.[25]

Therefore, if a transitory model focused mainly on changing track from a planned economy to a market economy and from a closed economy to an open economy in most parts of China, whereby "balanced growth" and "economies of scale" can be operated on the same platform, the paradigm of the development of Tibet dictates that a spatial structure for the development of Tibet must first be tackled. An alternative model of spatial development should differ from the existing pattern of regional growth, and growth can be sustained in realizing the national objective by making Tibet a discrete unit in regional development in the first place. Only in this way can Tibet realize its particular route of transition (from hardware to software, from politics to economics).[26]

In order to probe into issues of development and to the issue of the model for the regional development of Tibet, it is necessary to decompose the Big Push policy into the components of "balanced growth" and "economies of scale," and to provide both with a different spatial backdrop. While the former is an issue of national development, the latter can be more focused on the formation of a regional economy. The next section of this chapter places the Big Push policy in the context of dismantling the traditional core-periphery paradigm, such as to explore how a specialized model of the Big Push can be used to address the problem of regional development. Then, another section will demonstrate that an idealized spatial structure is possible by integrating both the consumption model and labour mobility model of Tibet more closely with those of eastern and central China. The last section questions the traditional model of regional development by relocating the growth pole outside the prescribed region, to address the opportunities and challenges brought about by the strategy of developing the western region.

The Big Push and Regional Development

The rivalry between "balanced growth" and "economies of scale" is deeply ingrained in Tibet's history of economic development in the last 50 years, as evidenced by the accelerating rate of transfer payments. As it stands, of all the regions, Tibet is currently the largest recipient of fiscal support from the central government. Aid to Tibet accounts for approximately 60% of the total input to China's underdeveloped regions. In terms of the absolute amount, the cumulative total from 1952 to 2002 was about RMB50 billion, and the total input in the last 10 years doubled that of the previous 40 years.[27] However, this does not help to create a regional economy in that Tibet ranks lowest in almost all counts of economic performance. For example, in 2000, its GDP was RMB10.56 billion, which was 0.14% of the national total and 1.18% and 0.54% of the regional averages of the western

Table 21.1 Economic Performance of Tibet, 2000

Items	Unit	Tibet	As % of China	As % of western China
Area	1,000 km^2	1,200	12.50	17.47
Population	Million	2.56	0.20	0.71
GDP	RMB billion	10.561	0.13	0.69
GDP per capita	RMB	4,262	65.20	95.07
GVIO[1]	RMB billion	2.40	0.06	0.38
GVIAO[2]	RMB billion	3.419	0.24	0.94
Fiscal revenue	RMB billion	0.935	0.08	0.44
Import and export	US$ billion	0.166	0.05	1.21

Notes: [1] GVIO: Gross value of industrial output.
[2] GVIAO: Gross value of industrial and agricultural output.

Source: Guojia tongjiju 國家統計局 (ed.), *Zhongguo tongji nianjian 2001* 中國統計年鑑 2001 (Statistical Yearbook of China 2001) (Beijing: Zhongguo tongji chubanshe 中國統計出版社, 2001).

and eastern regions, respectively. Table 21.1 presents a summary of Tibet's economic performance as at 2000.

Apart from its poor economic performance, issues of region and development issues regarding Tibet are in question, too. On the one hand, the rigidity inherent in a core-periphery relationship between the central government and Tibet has created a dual economy in the form of rural-urban income disparities. As at 1990, the region-wide rural-urban income ratio was 1:2.77. It rose, however, to 1:4.8 in 2000.[28] Moreover, much greater rural-urban income disparities are found in the "oasis of prosperity" represented by the central place of the *yijiang lianghe* 一江兩河 region. This elongated river plain measures about 500 km from east to west and 220 km from north to south, and comprises 18 counties that are inundated by the Yarlung Zangbo River, Lhasa River and Nyangchu River. On the other hand, Tibet's sectoral structure has been seriously dislocated, judging from the fact that the sectoral composition of primary, secondary and tertiary industries in Tibet has veered between 4:1:3 and 3:2:4 during 1990 to 2000.[29] The poor performance of the secondary industry implies that sectoral restructuring will not likely play a key role in salvaging the depressed regional economy, which has caused Tibet to be labelled an "atypical dual economy."[30] This not only deprives the central government of a tool to promote developmental growth, but also deprives the local government of a tool for regional expansion, both arguably important tools in invigorating the regional economy of the underdeveloped region. As a result, the issues of development have become less focused as the role of the region is declining. A typical example is the growth in the non-agricultural population in small townships. Until 1989, the agricultural population still exceeded the non-agricultural population in most small townships in Tibet, though the situation has been ameliorated since then.[31]

How the contradictory issue between developmental growth and regional expansion can be resolved depends on how the question is put in the national context. The prevailing view underwritten by China's nationalities policy is to put the question in a unitary system whereby Tibet, as well as Xinjiang, Inner Mongolia 內蒙古, Ningxia 寧夏 and Guangxi 廣西, are agglomerated under the banner of autonomous administration in the national theatre.[32] The fiscal policy is to work through sectoral restructuring, so as to boost the regional economy. This has been the main theme of the long-term plan to develop the ethnic minority regions, reflecting the contemporary process of nation-building in the multi-ethnic nation of China. This process is rooted in racial identification, religious harmony and territorial integrity. Both the development and regional issues have, therefore, been defined in broad and sweeping historical terms. Consequently, a holistic view of the historical legacy of Tibet is brought in, including the heritage of Tibetan Buddhism, the formation of the greater Tibetan region, and its former linkages with central Asia.

However, it has been suggested that the historical perspective is too large an aggregate by which to observe the practical problems of poverty alleviation, rural education, medical and healthcare, and so forth, particularly in an era of surging social demands. The central government has also realized that it is necessary to find a new platform for intervention, which is compatible with institutional changes induced by transforming the local economy into a more diversified mode of development. Therefore, since 1984, the central government has introduced a policy of paired assistance (*duikou zhiyuan* 對口支援) whereby a province in the more-developed coastal region provides support to its counterpart in the less-developed inland region. Such support ranges from setting up income-generating projects to catering for social services.[33] During this process, the involvement of the various levels of local government has been institutionalized to address the need for both developmental growth and regional expansion. This has led to an expansion of the role of the provincial government in the local affairs of underdeveloped regions, as the policy statement has been gradually expanded to encompass inter-provincial co-operation: "paired assistance, mutual benefit and joint development" (對口支援、互惠互利、共同發展).

This implies that both policies and institutions have become more diverse during the stage of economic transition, making room for the co-existence of fiscal policy and development policy, as well as sectoral policy and regional policy. In retrospect, such schemes are instrumental in shaping inter-provincial co-operation and in boosting economic and social development of the less-underdeveloped regions. Take, for example, the cases of Jiangsu 江蘇/Guangxi 廣西 and Fujian 福建/Ningxia 寧夏. It has been amply demonstrated that supply linkages in underdeveloped regions can be expanded considerably in response to market demand in the coastal region, causing a regional multiplier effect around the pair-assisted host counties.[34]

As compared with other pair-assisted underdeveloped regions, Tibet's scheme has gone much further, not only because all of its cities and counties have been designated in this way, but also because its policy statement has gone beyond the language of mere inter-provincial economic co-operation ("regional responsibility, paired assistance, staff rotation" 分片負責、對口支援、定期輪換). After the Third Tibetan Work Conference held in 1995, 15 provinces and cities in the coastal region were designated to provide assistance to 7 cities and prefectures in Tibet, including Beijing 北京/Jiangsu and Lhasa City, Shanghai 上海/Shandong 山東 and Shigatse City, Tianjin 天津/Sichuan 四川 and Chamdo 昌都 Prefecture, Hunan 湖南/Hubei 湖北 and Lhoka 山南 Prefecture, Zhejiang 浙江/Liaoning 遼寧 and Nakchu Prefecture, Hebei 河北/Shaanxi 陝西 and Ngari Prefecture, and Fujian/Guangdong 廣東 and Nyingtri 林芝 Prefecture. Starting from 1994, a staff of about 49 was dispatched to the pair-assisted cities or prefectures and it was intended that all of them would play a leading role in local affairs. In contrast to previous practice, all of the staff members dispatched to Tibet are responsible for financing and managing their assisted projects. The success and failure of the projects will have an impact on their political career. The paired assistance scheme will expire in 2004; however, in 2001, it was decided that the scheme should be extended for another 10 years after the Fourth Tibet Work Conference.[35] This implies that, within a period of 20 years (1994–2014), the socioeconomic life of the Tibetan people will be deeply affected by the flourishing economies of the coastal region.

An Externally Activated Model of Regional Development

The relationship between Tibet and the central government has occasionally been strained in the last 50 years, causing the central government to take a rather rigid approach to the Big Push. The central government tended not to prioritize "balanced growth" and "economies of scale" in whatever fiscal support it provided to Tibet. The events of the past few decades, including the peaceful emancipation of 1951, the closing down of private enterprises in 1956, as well as the establishment of the Autonomous Region in 1965, testify to the will of the central government to adopt more radical measures, such as transplanting the inland system of local administration and separating religion from politics. The result is an internally activated model of regional development, which seeks to expand the role of sectoral policy in the process of urbanization and to replicate an urban system characterized by a central city and rural-urban continuum. It aims to do this by diffusing a way of life and creating a spatial hierarchy and boundary in an underdeveloped region through a government fiscal scheme.

In the 1990s, it was noticed that the urban system existing in the *yijiang lianghe* region in central Tibet is remarkably similar to urban systems in the inland region. In this region, there exists an agricultural zone most suitable for modern farming.[36] An ambitious long-term development plan was launched in 1994, with the intention of transforming the region into the "bread basket" of Tibet. As self-sufficiency in food supply is the aim, the plan is to "produce one million tonnes of foodstuff, be self-sufficient in oil and meat supply, to eradicate rural poverty and to achieve a well-off living standard" by 2005. This region is also a centre of technological diffusion, extending not only to agricultural innovations, but also to high-end technologies such as telecommunications, solar energy, and so forth. In response to the demands for investment induced by sectoral restructuring, "43 Projects" and "62 Projects" financed by the central government were launched in 1984 and 1994, respectively, upon the conclusion of the Second and the Third Tibet Work Conference.[37] In reinforcing regional supremacy, the majority of these projects were located in the *yijiang lianghe* region, accounting for over 50% of the total investment (RMB480 million for the "43 Projects" and RMB3,700 million for the "62 Projects"). As infrastructure, transport and telecommunications have greatly improved, the *yijiang lianghe* region has become a focus of both agricultural and industrial production since 2000 (Table 21.2).

As economic activity accelerated, urban landscapes in the *yijiang lianghe* region have been dramatically transformed. From Tzetang 澤當 to Shigatse to Lhasa, the plan for urbanization stated in the Ninth Five-year Plan (1990–1995) has gradually taken shape: "The twin city of Shigatse and Lhasa should become the regional centre of economic activity, while

Table 21.2 Basic Economic Indicators for the *Yijiang Lianghe* Region, 2000

Items	Unit	*Yijiang lianghe*	As % of Tibet
Population	1,000	798.6	36.37%
Area	1,000 km^2	66.5	5.41%
Rural labour	1,000	298.5	50.40%
Arable land	1,000 ha	112	50.56%
Town	No	11	36.70%

Source: Li Tao, *Zouchu Xiangbala: Xizang yijiang lianghe liuyu xiangcun chengzhenhua yanjiu* (see note 31), pp. 46–50.

Chamdo should become a new growth pole and other prefectural seats should be developed more intensively."[38] During the period 2000–2010, the level of urbanization will reach 20%, while the number of towns will increase from 31 to 105.[39] Some cities like Baiyi 八一鎮 were virtually built from villages. Moreover, the urban functions have become more diversified, as witnessed by the key role played by county seats such as Tolun Dechen, Tzetang, and so forth.[40]

However, there are physical limits to the expansion of the *yijiang lianghe* urban system. With an area approximately 140% that of the expanded metropolitan region of the Pearl River Delta, in 2000, *yijiang lianghe* had only 3.8% of the latter's population and 3.1% of its industrial and agricultural capacity. With such vast differences, the dynamism arising from this urbanizing valley region and from similar valleys such as the Huangshui 湟水 Valley in Qinghai,[41] is quantitatively and qualitatively different from the well-tested models of town and village enterprises (the Sunan 蘇南 model), processing plus foreign trade (the Guangdong model) and exports plus foreign trade (the Zhejiang model) prevalent in the coastal region. Moreover, as the trajectories of outward-bound and inward-bound movements in Tibet's past urbanization are manifestly more selective, in order to sustain a model of regional development, it is perhaps necessary to differentiate two periods during which different methods to urbanize Tibet more intensively were attempted. Whereas the outward-bound movement dominated before 1994, the inward-bound movement has become more prevalent after 1994.

In order to break the physical barrier imposed by the natural environment, the aim of the outward-bound movement is to link Tibet with neighbouring regions. A typical approach is to treat Tibet as an integral part of the regional economy of the southwestern region, so as to make use of the trade route through coastal Guangxi. With such objective in view, Tibet has become an integral part of the Five Provinces and Seven Parties

Economic Co-operation Zone (5+7 Zone) 五省七方, launched in 1992, which includes Guangxi, Yunnan 雲南, Tibet, Sichuan, Guizhou 貴州, as well as Chengdu 成都 and Chongqing. As the prime objective of the 5+7 Zone is to increase the volume of trade within the bloc, bulk purchases of industrial and agricultural products are encouraged across the provinces. Such trade amounted RMB28.88 billion in 1992.[42] As factor endowments and comparative advantages are at work, regional centres have arisen from the increased levels of trade, such as Nanning 南寧 and Pingxiang 憑祥 in Guangxi, which provide maritime access to Southeast Asia and other parts of the world. The performance of individual provinces and cities has not been the same. While benefits arising from sub-regional co-operation have been reaped by Guangxi and Yunnan in the form of increased foreign trade, internal trade has also increased for power-rich Guizhou and labour-rich Sichuan. Although the impact has been unequal, the realignment with the new trading bloc has proven to be beneficial to inter-provincial as well as sub-regional trade, in both goods and services.

Against this background, however, the realignment of the *yijiang lianghe* region by linking Tibet with a larger economic region has been difficult for the following reasons. First, as the expansion of regional exchanges is not the aim, the design of the *yijiang lianghe* economy is more inward-looking, aiming mainly at self-sufficiency in food supply. Second, as the "43 Projects" and the "62 Projects" located in the *yijiang lianghe* region are primarily a form of transfer payment channelled through the central government, the level of participation of local governments is likely to be low, due to the one-off nature of the projects. Third, since 1985, the Qing-Zang (Qinghai-Tibet) Highway has out-performed the Chuan-Zang 川藏 (Sichuan-Tibet) Highway, Xin-Zang 新藏 (Xinjiang-Tibet) Highway and Dian-Zang 滇藏 (Yunnan-Tibet) Highway in terms of commodity transportation, accounting for some 85–90% of the total imports and exports of Tibet.[43] This has greatly undermined the attempt to revolutionize the regional integration of Tibet.

The inward-bound movement is less ambitious but has been more persistent after 1993. As a sliding scale has been prescribed for China's eastern, central and western economies, the aim is to invite enterprises in the east to invest in the development zone by providing preferential treatment, so as to energize polar growth in the host economy of Tibet. The cost effectiveness of this approach, however, depends not only on organizing demand on a large scale, but also on the existence of a leading sector to provide sufficient linkage to overcome the friction of distance. As it turns out, suburban farming such as the growing of greenhouse vegetables stands a better chance, since helping hands from Sichuan are more readily available. On the other hand, as enterprises are the most important vehicles for championing the cause of east-west co-operation, much will need to be provided to improve the business environment, such as financial and management services. In the absence of such improvements, instead of attracting enterprises at the high-end sector, such that technological innovation can be diffused, it is now cheap labour that is being utilized in Tibet. An example is the cement plant in Lhasa set up by the Nanjing Shuanglong 南京雙龍 Group, the labour for which mainly consists of prisoners sentenced to labour reform. As a result, there is little regional multiplier effect at the local level since the capital/labour ratio is low compared with similar efforts at industrial production in other inland provinces.[44]

A brief review of Tibet's history of urbanization has revealed that the linkages generated by a trading bloc are too haphazard, while the out-sourcing associated with most east-west schemes for co-operation is limited in scope. In order to make up for the shortcomings, both approaches have to be rectified, prioritized and synthesized, so that "minimum critical effort" can be obtained at the local level. With respect to the outward-bound movement, artificially created linkages have to be mounted to rectify Tibet's economic disadvantages. As evidenced in the regulations governing the paired assistance scheme, far fewer concessions are being offered by the host economy than given under most east-west co-operation schemes. In terms of considering the needs of "balanced growth" (as defined by the annual growth rate), underdeveloped regions are better protected because the terms of paired assistance are more favourable.[45] On the other hand, with regard to the inward-bound movement, a local process of regionalization needs to be generated, so that more sources of labour can be involved. In other words, instead of restricting labour mobility to the local labour market, it is now necessary to consider the possibility of importing labour from more diverse but direct sources, preferably linked to artificially created linkages. As such, the process of regionalization can be initiated not merely by utilizing local sources of cheap labour. As it is now cheaper to utilize imported labour, the needs of "economies of scale" (as defined by official design criteria) can be better catered for.[46] As stated in the regulations governing the paired assistance scheme, the staff that are dispatched to Tibet are better educated than the average and are thus helping Tibet participate in the regional labour market from the higher end. In the process of the partial globalization of China's economy, by virtue of the political influence exercised through the paired assistance scheme, Tibet can then compete on better terms and with better human resources.

In the context of this chapter, the process of regional development can only be initiated in the presence of artificially created linkages. The process is twofold in nature. While at the global level, the diffusing forces of coastal county economics are ushered in through the central government, the labour market has become more regionalized and homogenized at the local level. Since most of the regional multiplier effect happens outside the host economy of Tibet, the process of regionalization is termed "a model of regional development activated externally." A new question immediately arises: How can the reinforcing forces of paired assistance be differentiated from central fiscal support or from similar schemes applied to other underdeveloped regions? With respect to the issue of capital, the objective of extending fiscal support is to shorten the technological gap between Tibet and the coastal regions; therefore, the mode of entry is predominantly that of technical co-operation or technical assistance, so as to boost Tibet's technological competitiveness, resulting in a process of regionalization heavily subsidized by the central government.[47] With respect to the issue of labour, the objective of fiscal support is to alleviate poverty at the level of the community. Therefore, the mode of entry is the food-for-work programme or micro-financing, so as to maximize the utilization of cheap resources of local labour, resulting in a labour market that is heavily segmented along a rural-urban division.[48] In both situations, capital and labour cannot replace each other easily.

To sustain a strategy of long-term development and in order not to be diverted by issues of technology or cheap labour, it is necessary to make Tibet's regional policy more autonomous. More importantly, as regional policy is becoming more streamlined, it is now advisable for Tibet to integrate its economic growth with infrastructural facilities, which have so far been non-market-oriented. As most of these infrastructural facilities have not been incorporated in a regional framework activated from outside, the regional multiplier effect has been unduly misplaced, resulting in even more uncertain policy tools. Two coalescing forces must, therefore, be considered when following up on issues of regional development, namely, the "regionalization of the county economy" and "regionalization without labour mobility." Both are attuned to a particular form of spatial effect, linking regional policy at the local level and developmental policy at the global level.

Regionalization of the County Economy

It has been demonstrated that China's county economy has played the most active role in rural reform during the last decade, not only because it led in rural industrialization, but also because a spatial continuum can be constructed more autonomously by virtue of its marketing system or lineage society.[49] More importantly, as the traditional grassroots administration in Tibet has been gradually replaced by the tripartite system of county, township and village, the destruction of the monastery economy has created a vacuum that has been filled by township and village enterprises and functional bodies such as the Communist Youth Corps, women's unions, labour unions, peasants associations, etc. This has, on the one hand, speeded up the process of integration with the inland regions (in such areas as primary education) and, on the other hand, has given rise to the formation of administrative seats. As a result, it has become possible to create an "oasis of prosperity" by subjugating a particular county in Tibet under the administration of a coastal district or county, ensuring that both share the same development issues. In this connection, spatial contiguity as dictated by the principle of "economies of scale" can be bypassed to make way for the speeding up of regional development without resorting to substantial efforts at agglomeration such as the *yijiang lianghe* project or to designating areas as poverty-stricken areas.

However, paired assistance has contributed to popularizing a pattern of urban consumption by regionalizing the county economy. As opposed to the income approach prevailing in the inland provinces to resolve the peasant problem, the attempt is to improve patterns of consumption by expanding the provision of public goods. On the face of it, this is similar to the New Rural Movement advocated by Justin Lin 林毅夫 in 2001, in the sense that the provision of schools, water, sanitation, electricity, etc. has been encouraged. However, what should really be drawing our attention is the share of public goods at the township level in Tibet that is reaching the national average. As the per capita consumption of the donor and recipients counties draws closer due to the regionalization of the county economy through the mending of artificially created linkages, it can further be discovered that what has been initiated is not a process of rural industrialization, but rather a pattern of expenditure. According to reports derived from staff dispatched from Tibet, the pattern is even more evident when higher concentrations of population result.[50]

Regionalization without Labour Mobility

A non-migratory mode of labour mobility involving the localizing of social stratifications and expanding the portfolio of employment locally has been a significant factor in urbanizing the countryside in the eastern region. As such, the density of supply linkages has become an important indicator of project design within the region, since the regional multiplier effect at the receiving end is now a prime consideration. It is found that, the higher the level of localization, the higher the degree of local embeddedness. As surplus labour is immobilized, it has become much easier to urbanize the countryside, since the opportunity cost of using such surplus is almost zero, obviating the need to estimate a critical point from which to start the whole process of urbanization. As was evident in the 1980s, the rapid process of urbanization in the eastern region can be attributed to such a non-migratory mode of labour mobility.[51]

The process of urbanization is, however, based on the assumption that surplus labour exists in the first place. However, it is not clear whether such an assumption would be valid in the case of Tibet. First, in the absence of rapid social stratification, it remains to be seen how a township can emerge in a semi-agricultural and semi-pastoral economy such as Tibet's. Second, it is not cheaper to resettle social groupings accustomed to transhumance than to import labour from outside. The decision to build a township is, therefore, not a straightforward process. This is because, first, it is politically sensitive to import labour on a large scale from the outside and, second, the regional multiplier effect can be impeded in the absence of a strong industrial sector.

However, the problem of labour shortages arises from the institutional set-up rather than from the scientific approach of opportunity cost. A critical factor is the fragmentation of the labour market in Tibet along the lines of state-owned and private enterprises, domestic and non-domestic sources, and rural and urban sectors. As it is difficult to cross the line, an attempt has been made to revert to designated labour bases contracted by county enterprises, significantly pushing the process of recruitment to outside the region. Since the mode of entry is now the county enterprise, the labour market in the host economy can remain intact. Practically speaking, labourers can be relocated and the local labour value can be maintained without being further devalued, shifting the regional multiplier effect to a much wider spatial realm of concern.

Sichuan, Shaanxi and Hunan are the major sources of labourers recruited to work in Tibet, as well as in construction projects in the coast. Labourers are recruited from these places for most pair-assisted projects. The social cost of building towns can be greatly lessened since the labourers will return to their home provinces once the project has been completed. On the other hand, by sourcing labour from outside, Tibet can also tap into a larger labour market, including that of the central region. According to statistics for 2000, the relative percentages of contracted labour were: Hunan (2.70%), Chongqing (10.81%), Sichuan (67.57%), Shaanxi (2.70%) and Qinghai (16.22%), and they were distributed region-wide.[52] In the final analysis, it can be observed that the far-flung and sparsely populated region of Tibet can be involved in a process of regionalization merely by placing it at the starting point of the artificially created linkage brought about labour contracting activities.

Tibet's Unique Regional Development Model and Its Relationship with the Western Development Strategy

Viewed from the national level, it seems that Tibet has been excluded from the policy statement of the Western Development Strategy. First, in order to sustain economic growth, the fragile ecological conditions in Tibet imply that large-scale exploitation is not likely to happen if economic growth is to be sustained. Second, due to the existence of more complicated historical and geographical issues, the links between Tibet and other inland provinces cannot simply be described as economic or trading relationships. In particular, with the emergence of the paired assistance scheme endorsed by the central government, such a relationship has been re-aligned, witnessing the emergence of a more dialectic model of regional development.

Through the redeployment of the resources of other inland provinces, individual prefectures of Tibet have been placed at the receiving end of the paired assistance scheme, resulting in an outer circle characterized by a relationship of dependency. At the same time, as labour has been imported from the central region to other areas including Tibet, an inner circle characterized by labour bases in the central region has also resulted. With the spatial dimensions of Tibet substantially reconstituted by external forces, the inter-prefectural relationship has been weakened, while the influences of inland provinces have now become visible and more prominent.

Since a political process has been involved in sustaining a model of regional development, the development issues of Tibet have previously been described as being generated by a "diffusion-supply" relationship.[53] However, as the political process has increasingly come to be dominated by a local/local relationship, the traditional fiscal policy and sectoral policy have been replaced by a distinctive development policy and a distinctive regional policy, respectively. With regard to spatial formation, both the development issues and regional issues have been coherently described in terms of an inner circle and an outer circle. On the one hand, as a sub-national process of regionalization is contained in a national issue of developmental growth described by the outer circle, a political process can still be involved in sustaining a model of regional development at the local level. On the other hand, as regional issues are constantly being re-invented, within the confine of the outer circle, there are more new possibilities to deploy human resources and trade connections. Therefore, taking Tibet as a centre of centrifugal growth, a local pattern of regional growth becomes apparent, while Tibet's connection to neighbouring sovereign states remains a topic that is very much unexplored.

However, within the context of this chapter, it is apparent that the duality of the relationship that exists between Tibet and the inland provinces has set its experience of regional development apart from that of other provinces or autonomous regions designated by the Western Development Strategy. The most significant factor remains that the political process has been reinforced, implying that at least one event in the chain of activities is placed outside Tibet, regardless of whether an "inward-bound" or "outward-bound" policy is adopted in formalizing a process of regional development. This factor brings new opportunities to the emergence of possible models of regional development, while twists and turns are encountered in the process of developmental growth.

Opportunities: Regionalization Relying on the Division of the Eastern, Central and Western Regions

Ever since the establishment of the Tibet Autonomous Region in 1965, the regional problem has not been resolved. On the one hand, the links between Tibet and the surrounding Tibetan region have been considerably weakened, leaving ethnic cohesion a minor force in maintaining territorial integrity. On the other hand, a more precise regional division of labour has been impeded by an underdeveloped secondary industry. The issue of region involves the following dilemma. Should urbanization lead in advancing the cause of development with the expansion of the role of the existing central-place city? Or should territorial planning lead so that agricultural growth can be sustained, enabling Tibet to feed itself? In the former case, the *yijiang lianghe* basin has been designated for polar growth. While in the latter case, 10 food supply bases and 8 agricultural labour bases have been constructed. Self-sufficiency has, however, been undermined by the introduction of the paired assistance scheme, which has resulted in government concessions from the coastal provinces and a supply of labour from the central provinces. As the artificially created linkages are increasingly institutionalized, a process of urbanization can be initiated. The success of the Western Development Strategy depends on how well its development agenda can be integrated with such a process of urbanization. More specifically, by importing labour, how can the Western Development Strategy be tailored to local needs?

It is suggested here that, in the context of the development of Tibet, the Western Development Strategy has been modified by the splitting up of financial support, making it possible to diversify sources of funding, previously restricted to vehicles such as the Tibetan Development Fund (TDF). The financial scheme envisioned in the Western Development Strategy will concentrate on streamlining the sources of funding, with the aim of achieving a "3 × 80%" model, that is, the contribution of capital to GDP growth should reach 80%, 80% of the development fund should be sourced outside Tibet, and 80% of the development fund sourced outside Tibet should be from the central government.[54] The objective is, on the one hand, to avoid the duplication of development projects and, on the other hand, to produce a pattern of regional specialization that is beneficial to both town planning and territorial planning in the specialized region concerned.

In other words, within the broad framework outlined by the paired assistance scheme, the role of the Western Development Strategy as a financial tool is to sub-divide the given spatial milieu, so as to create the pre-requisites for town planning and regional planning. Under such conditions, the model of regional development arising from the given spatial division of labour is to: "focus on the central region, open up the western region, jointly develop the eastern region, leaving the northern region to seek wealth from husbandry and the mining industry."[55] As such, in realizing development issues, the opening-up policy (eastern region), resource management policy (northern region), regional trade policy (western region), as well as the polar growth policy (central region) have all assumed their unique spatial set-ups.

Challenges: Marginalization of Population Change

Since the process of urbanization in Tibet is underpinned by a duality of space instead of population change, it is obvious that the pattern of the regional division of labour is more prone to be influenced by shifts in the financial scheme instead of by changes in productivity. As such, the modernization of Tibet depends on how the central/local relationship is adjusted rather than being prescribed by a revolution in productivity. As a development policy is gradually shaped, Tibet's urban experience has become even more unique, since the goals of regional development, economic development and social development may not necessarily coincide.

As the programme of the modernization of Tibet has to be subjugated to the prevailing paired assistance scheme, regional policy has become not a statement to express development goals, but to constrain shifts in population. As the population is becoming increasingly compartmentalized, it can be further marginalized by altitudinal distribution.[56] Although the largest group of ethnic Tibetans are currently found in Tibet, it is also here that ethnic Tibetans are most sparsely distributed (13.67 persons per km^2 in other Tibetan regions as compared with 2.13 persons per km^2 in Tibet). As its altitudinal distribution is reinforced instead of being rectified, cities and townships in Tibet are more appropriately described as enclaves rather than as hubs of economic activities.

A formidable problem for the long-term development of Tibet is the need to keep the population under 3 million. This is a level sufficient to spare Tibet from the threat of marginalization, yet allow it to sustain a pattern of urban development that is not based on population change. There are few ways of solving this problem, since it has been demonstrated in the past decades that, even with a massive influx of people from the inland provinces, a desirable population structure cannot be sustained. It has further been proven that the age structure can become seriously distorted when economic activity accelerates. Such a trend can further be complicated when a "speciality economy" is encouraged under the Western Development Strategy, under which Tibet can be relinquished to the backwater of growth, since it can be excluded from the common market by virtue of the different trajectory of regional development it has pursued under the paired assistance scheme.

Conclusion

Tibet remained very much intact in the early 1980s, when most parts of China were opened up to a programme of modernization. Because of its breath-taking beauty and inaccessibility, it has customarily been described as a Shangri-la that will sooner or later be engulfed in an arbitrary process of "internal colonization."[57] As regional disparity deepens not only between Tibet and the more prosperous inland provinces, but also between Tibet and less-developed ethnic regions, it has become apparent that for the foreseeable future, Tibet will still have to rely on massive fiscal support from the central government. But is Tibet a unique case in the study of development geography? Or has the line of inquiry on regional economics reached its self-imposed limit? The lines of academic inquiry are only concerned with the emergence of the paired assistance scheme launched in 1995 to help underdeveloped regions, particularly those that are land-locked.

On the one hand, it has been discussed that, as Tibet is increasingly linked with the mainland, a conscious regional policy has become all the more necessary. By utilizing the separate components of the county economy and territorially bounded labour market, it has been discovered that both development and geography, as well as both region and economics, can be differentially combined through artificially created linkages, culminating in a pattern of regional development that is activated by outside forces. It can further be demonstrated that, with such an autonomous regional policy in place, the issue of the regional division of labour can actually be fully spatialized. On the other hand, as the general principles of development are rapidly being internalized, the reduction of its regional scale of application has invited new problems in the form of marginalizing population change.

As regional policy has become more localized and more compacted, the problems of development have to be streamlined and to be counteracted by appropriate development planning, preferably in the realm of institutional innovation. With the benefit of hindsight, it has become apparent that the agenda of the Western Development Strategy, including issues such as converting resource advantages to competitive advantages, realizing frog-leaped development, etc., has to be delivered by means that are practical for the region. The power of development thinking will definitely be weakened if it becomes too widespread and cannot be defined by a given spatial structure.

Notes

1. José Ignacio Cabezón and Roger R. Jackson (eds.), *Tibetan Literature: Studies in Genre* (Ithaca: Snow Lion, 1996), p. 11.

2. Among them are the accounts of the Jesuit father, Ippolito Desideri; the Hungarian linguist and explorer, Alexander Csoma de Koros; the English soldier, L. A. Waddell; the Russian historian, A. I. Vostrikov and the Italian scholar, Giuseppe Tucci. See a detailed account of the history of the West's discovery of Tibet in Wang Yao 王堯 (ed.), *Guowai zangxue yanjiu yiwenji* 國外藏學研究譯文集 (Translations of Overseas Tibetology Research) (Lhasa: Xizang renmin chubanshe 西藏人民出版社, 1992, 1994), Vol. 9, pp. 389–467 and Vol. 11, pp. 375–442.
3. Melvyn Goldstein provided an influential account of the list of historical events leading eventually to the "peaceful emancipation of Tibet" in 1951. See Melvyn Goldstein, *A History of Modern Tibet 1913–1951, The Demise of the Lamaist State* (Berkeley and Los Angeles: University of California Press, 1989).
4. See, for example, Rene de Nebesky-Wojkowita, *Oracles and Demons of Tibet: The Cult and Iconography of the Tibetan Protective Deities* (Graz: Akademische Druck-u. Veriagsanstalt, 1975).
5. Against the background of modern Tibet and Chinese political history, Warren Smith offered a comprehensive account of Tibetan nationalism and its close relationship with Tibet's ethnic, cultural and national origins, focusing particularly on the emergence of the Tibetan Buddhist state and its relation with China before 1950. See Warren Smith, *Tibetan Nation: A History of Tibetan Nationalism and Sino-Tibetan Relations* (Boulder: Westview Press, 1996).
6. For a detailed account of the interrelationships between tribal nations in Inner Asia, see Dennis Sinor (ed.), *The Cambridge History of Early Inner Asia* (Cambridge: Cambridge University Press, 1990). See also John K. Fairbank (ed.), *The Cambridge History of China, Volume 10, Late Ch'ing, 1800–1911, Part I* (Cambridge: Cambridge University Press, 1978), where Tibet is portrayed as an independent state occasionally in conflict with Chinese dynastic rule.
7. Wang Gui 王貴 et al. emphasized the legacy of Chinese rule. See Wang Gui et al., *Xizang lishi diweibian* 西藏歷史地位辯 (A Treatise on Tibet's Historical Position) (Beijing: Minzu chubanshe 民族出版社, 1995).
8. Some of the important works on the history of Tibet include Pedro Carrasco, *Land and Polity in Tibet* (Seattle: University of Washington Press, 1959), H. E. Richardson, *A Short History of Tibet* (New York: E. P. Dutton & Co., Inc., 1962) and Pradyumna P. Karan, *The Changing Face of Tibet* (Lexington: The University of Kentucky, 1976).
9. The most outstanding example is Xinjiang, which has recorded a conspicuous GDP 307% growth rate during 1990–1998, apparently by virtue of a 275% increase in internal trade in commodity crops, such as cotton. See Zhongguo Xinjiang weiwuer zizhiqu weiyuanhui xuanchuanbu 中國新疆維吾爾自治區委員會宣傳部, *Xibu dakaifa* 西部大開發 (Western Development) (Urumqi: Xinjiang renmin chubanshe 新疆人民出版社, 2000), pp. 150–51.

10. Preliminary ideas about river source economies have recently been raised to explore the possibility of developing Tibet into a nature reserve, so as to foster economic independence. The reserve would complement the green belt along the Euro-Asia Bridge in the northwest and the Chuan-Yu 川渝 (Sichuan-Chonging) urban corridor in the southwest. See Liu Fuxiang 劉福祥 and Lang Jiawen 郎家文, "Xibu dakaifa lilun tansuo: Heyuan jingjixue" 西部大開發理論探索：河源經濟學 (Theoretical Exploration of Western Development: River Source Economy), *Xibu fazhan pinglun* 西部發展評論 (Western Development Forum), No. 2 (2001), pp. 81–85.
11. Experts in China's transitory economy like Woo Wing Thye 胡永泰 believe that modern technologies such as telematics, mass agriculture, etc., can bring about growth. See *Hong Kong Economic Journal*, 28 December 2000.
12. "Balanced growth" and "economies of scale" are the two factors underlying the issues of equity and efficiency in the Big Push policy. See Christopher Bliss, "Trade and Development," in *Handbook of Development Economies, Volume II*, edited by H. Chenery and T. N. Srinivasan (Amsterdam: North-Holland, 1988), pp. 1190–94. Meanwhile, the core-periphery relationship and sustainable development provide a spatial and ecological backdrop to the "big push equals balanced growth plus economies of scale" formulation, p. 1193.
13. An Qiyi 安七一 (ed.), *Zhongguo xibu gailan: Xizang* 中國西部概覽：西藏 (An Overview of Western China: Tibet) (Beijing: Minzu chubanshe, 2000), p. 2.
14. The Tibetan plateau is considered the highest and the youngest plateau in the world. The Himalaya mountain range began to rise up about 13–15 million years ago, while the Tibetan plateau rose to its present average altitude of 4,000 m some 2–4 million years ago. See Ren Mei'e 任美鍔 (ed.), *Zhongguo ziran dili gangyao* 中國自然地理綱要 (An Outline of China's Physical Geography) (Beijing: Shangwu yinshuguan 商務印書館, 1985), p. 19.
15. An ethnographic study on pastoralism in Pali 帕里 was conducted in 1986–1988 in western Tibet. The study found that "Life in Pali today is closer to the traditional era than at any time since China assumed direct administrative control over Tibet in 1959." See Melvyn Goldstein and Cynthia Beall, *Nomads of Western Tibet: The Survival of a Way of Life* (Berkeley and Los Angeles: University of California Press, 1990), p. 183.
16. Zhao Songqiao, *Physical Geography of China* (Beijing: Science Press, 1986), p. 192.
17. The Yarlung Zangbo Gorge is 504.9 km long and is an average of 5,000 m deep (the deepest point is 6,009 m). Scientific research was undertaken by the China Geological Investigation Bureau and the China Academy of Sciences in 2000 in the Yarlung Zangbo Gorge, which is believed to have been caused by collision of the Euro-Asia plate and the Indian Ocean plate.
18. An Qiyi (ed.), *Zhongguo xibu gailan: Xizang* (see note 13), pp. 5–6.
19. Xu Fengxiang 徐鳳翔, *Xizang wushinian: Shengtai juan* 西藏50年：生態卷

(Fifty Years of Tibet: Ecology) (Beijing: Minzu chubanshe, 2001), pp. 182–83.

20. Ibid., pp. 34–37. The forest ranges from alpine grassland, alpine bush belt, conifer belt, mixed conifer and broadleaf tree belt to sub-tropical rain forest.
21. Li Zhiyong and Dogoin, *A Pure and Unspoilt Land: Tibetan Environment* (Beijing: China Intercontinental Press, 1994), pp. 29–34.
22. Theories on the development of Tibet mainly focus on the region's cultural, historical and economic aspects. See Ma Rong 馬戎, *Xizang de renkou yu shehui* 西藏的人口與社會 (Tibet's Population and Society) (Beijing: Tongxin chubanshe 同心出版社, 1996). For a cultural view, see Yu Zhen 余振 and Guo Zhenglin 郭正林 (eds.), *Zhongguo zangqu xiandaihua: Lilun, shijian, zhengce* 中國藏區現代化：理論、實踐、政策 (Modernization of China's Tibetan Region) (Beijing: Zhongyang minzu daxue chubanshe 中央民族大學出版社, 1999). For an economic view, see Sun Yong 孫勇 (ed.), *Xizang: Feidianxing eryuan jiegou xia de fazhan gaige* 西藏：非典型二元結構下的發展改革 (Tibet: Development and Reform under Atypical Dual Structure) (Beijing: Zhongguo zangxue chubanshe 中國藏學出版社, 2000).
23. The Qing-Zang Railway is the world's longest high-altitude railway line (960 km of the railway run on a plateau 4,000 m above sea level). The section from Xining 西寧 to Golmo in Qinghai (in total 814 km long) has been in operation since 1984. Work commenced on the section from Golmo to Lhasa commenced in June 2001. The line will be 1,142 km long, 550 km of which will run over perennially frozen earth. The project is scheduled to be completed in 2007, and the total investment is about RMB26 billion at the 2003 price level.
24. See Yue-man Yeung, "Globalization and Regional Transformation in Pacific Asia," in *New Regional Development Paradigms*, edited by Asfaw Rumssa and Terry McGee (Westport: Greenwood Press, 2001), Vol. 1, pp. 215–27, for a discussion of the dual processes of urbanization and regionalization triggered by globalizing forces. However, our discussion is more restricted as the emphasis is on the dialectic relationship between small townships and regional integration. See Zhang Xiaoshan 張曉山 and Hu Biliang 胡必亮 (eds.), *Xiao chengzhen yu quyu yitihua* 小城鎮與區域一體化 (Small Townships and Regional Integration) (Taiyuan: Shanxi renmin chubanshe 山西人民出版社, 2002).
25. See Ma Rong, *Xizang de renkou yu shehui* (see note 22), pp. 6–9, for a discussion on the issue of modernizing Tibet in the absence of religious reforms.
26. Seldom is the issue of developing Tibet discussed within the context of transitory economies. The exception is Pan Naigu 潘乃谷 and Ma Rong, *Zhongguo xibu bianqu fazhan moshi yanjiu* 中國西部邊區發展模式研究 (A Study on the Development Model for China's Borderlands) (Beijing: Minzu chubanshe, 2000).
27. See Xizang zizhiqu tongjiju 西藏自治區統計局 (ed.), *Xizang tongji nianjian*

2001 西藏統計年鑑2001 (Statistical Yearbook of Tibet 2001) (Beijing: Zhongguo tongji chubanshe 中國統計出版社, 2001), pp. 105–6.

28. Ibid., pp. 12–13.
29. The ratios indicate the relative importance of the three major sectors of industry. The higher the value indicated, the higher the importance of the sector, and vice versa. The different numerical values indicate the relative output values for each industry.
30. Sun Yong attributed this phenomenon to the highly centralized mode of governing Tibet. See Sun Yong (ed.), *Xizang: Feidianxing eryuan jiegou xia de fazhan gaige* (see note 22), pp. 299–309.
31. See Li Tao 李濤, *Zouchu Xiangbala: Xizang yijiang lianghe liuyu xiangcun chengzhenhua yanjiu* 走出香巴拉：西藏一江兩河流域鄉村城鎮化研究 (Beyond Shangri-la: A Study of the Urbanization of the Xijiang *Yijiang Lianghe* Region) (Lhasa: Xizang renmin chubanshe, 1999), pp. 176–77.
32. This has sometimes been described as a process of internalizing China's frontier provinces, which may otherwise be absorbed in Inner Asia. See Terry Cannon, "National Minorities and the Internal Frontier," in *China's Regional Development*, edited by S. G. Goodman (London: Routledge, 1989), pp. 164–79. Both Pan Naigu and Ma Rong have, however, viewed this as "borderland development" (see note 26).
33. Generally regarded as an ad hoc policy that was first conceived in 1984 to address the issue of regional disparity, the policy of paired assistance can be defined as: "To achieve the objectives of racial solidarity and joint prosperity by organizing economic activities among developed regions and nationalities and underdeveloped regions under the unified leadership of the state and all hierarchies of government." See Hou Jingxin 侯景新 et al. (eds.), *Dongbu xijin zhanlüe* 東部西進戰略 (Westward Strategy of the Eastern Region) (Nanning: Guangxi renmin chubanshe 廣西人民出版社, 2001), pp. 3–4.
34. There are quite a few in-depth studies on the paired assistance scheme, focusing mainly on different modes of pairing: (1) between provincial governments; (2) between provincial departments; and (3) between cities and rural areas. As found, rural enterprises are the most effective mode of entry into the host economy. See Hou Jingxin et al. (eds.), *Dongbu xijin zhanlüe* (see note 33), and Wang Yiming 汪一鳴 and Li Chongyang 李崇陽, *Minning hezuo: Dongli jizhi yu yunxing jizhi* 閩寧合作：動力機制與運行機制 (A Study of the Dynamic and Operational Mechanism of Co-operation between Fujian and Ningxia) (Yinchuan: Ningxia renmin chubanshe 寧厦人民出版社, 2001).
35. The Tibet Work Conferences were held in 1980, 1984, 1994 and 2001, respectively, and were generally chaired by the Party Secretary of the Chinese Communist Party. As the long-term plan for the development of Tibet was generally promulgated during these occasions, each working conference virtually marked a distinctive phase of development for Tibet. For example,

during 1995–2001, the provision of infrastructure for development was a major concern.

36. The 18 counties in the *yijiang lianghe* region are Lhasa, Lhundup 林周, Nyemo 尼木, Chushur 曲水, Tolun Dechen 堆龍德慶, Taktse 達孜, Medro Gongkar 墨竹工卡, Shigatse, Namling 南木林, Gyantse 江孜, Lhatse 拉孜, Thongmon 謝通門, Panam 白朗, Danang 扎囊, Gonggar 貢嘎, Sangri 桑日, Chong-gye 琼結 and Nedong 乃東.
37. In terms of distribution, 62.9% of the "62 Projects" are allocated for economic development, while for the "43 Projects" the figure is just 30.2%. In terms of regional distribution, 76.7% of the "43 Projects" are allocated in the *yijiang lianghe* region, while the figure is only 42.9% of the "62 Projects."
38. See Zhang Xiaoping 張小平 (ed.), *Zouxiang ershiyi shiji de Xizang* 走向二十一世紀的西藏 (Tibet in the Twenty-first Century) (Beijing: Zhongguo zangxue chubanshe, 1997), p. 24.
39. Ibid., pp. 32–33.
40. Li Tao has demonstrated the urban functions performed by Tolun Dechen and the foci of the rural-urban articulation of Lhasa and Tzetang. See Li Tao, *Zouchu Xiangbala: Xizang yijiang lianghe liuyu xiangcun chengzhenhua yanjiu* (see note 31), pp. 57–121.
41. Hou Jingxin et al. have identified 21 key regions in western China for more rapid economic growth and the development of Huangshui Valley as the most similar to the *yijing lianghe* region in terms of both size and economic capability. See Hou Jingxin et al. (eds.), *Dongbu xijin zhanlüe* (see note 33), pp. 384–403.
42. See Wushengqu qifang "Zhongguo daxi'nan zai jueqi" bianxiezu 五省區七方"中國大西南在崛起"編寫組, *Zhongguo daxi'nan zai jueqi* 中國大西南在崛起 (The Rising of Southwestern China) (Nanning: Guangxi jiaoyu chubanshe 廣西教育出版社, 1994), p. 10.
43. See Luo Li 羅莉 and La Can 拉燦, *Xizang wushinian: Jingji juan* 西藏50年：經濟卷 (Fifty Years of Tibet: Economy) (Beijing: Minzu chubanshe, 2001), pp. 124–27. According to Zhou Yixing 周一星 and Zhang Li 張莉, 83% of exports and 11% of imports go through Nepal instead of Guangxi. See Zhou Yixing and Zhang Li, "Zhongguo dalu duiwai jingji lianxi de kongjian" 中國大陸對外經濟聯繫的空間 (Spatial Structure of China's International Economic Linkages), *Jingji dili* 經濟地理 (Economic Geography), Vol. 20, No. 1 (2000), pp. 18–24.
44. The invitation to develop Tibet is exemplified by the "Regulations Regarding Inviting Merchants and Attracting Investment of the Tibet Autonomous Region" (西藏自治區關於招商引資的有關規定) promulgated in 1997, covering aspects such as mode of investment, leading sectors, concessionary policy, bonus schemes, preferential treatment, etc.
45. Particular ministerial regulations govern the practice of paired assistance,

covering aspects such as land acquisition and tax exemption. See, for example, "Management Rules for Ministry of Health Paired Assistance Scheme" (衛生部援藏管理辦法), promulgated on 9 October 1995.

46. In a field trip to Tibet in July 2001, the authors discovered that the county administration building and associated infrastructure such as roadwork in Chushur, which are pair-assisted projects by Yangzhou 揚州, a city in Jiangsu, tended to be over-designed since coastal building standards were being used.
47. An estimated 70% of the fiscal support takes the form of technical co-operation and technical assistance, especially for the "43 Projects" and the "62 Projects," in which 80% and 90% of the input, respectively, is technical. See Luo Li and La Can, *Xizang wushinian: Jingji juan* (see note 43), pp. 248–49.
48. See Zhang Xiaoping, *Zouxiang ershiyi shiji de Xizang* (see note 38), pp. 251–54.
49. An interesting study on county economy, which provides insights on aspects of the marketing system and lineage society, was undertaken by Bletcher and Shue in Shulu 束鹿 County in northern China. See Marc Bletcher and Vivienne Shue, *Tethered Deer: Government and Economy in a Chinese County* (Stanford: Stanford University Press, 1996).
50. Zhu Xiangdong 朱向東 has provided a clear indication of the importance of housing expenditure in the pattern of consumption in Tibet during 1985–1998. He found that the relative annual growth rates of expenditure on food, clothing, housing and services were 170%, 155%, 600% and 204%, respectively. See Zhu Xiangdong (ed.), *Zhongguo nongcun jumin xiaofei yu shichang* 中國農村居民消費與市場 (Consumption and Market of China's Rural Population) (Beijing: Zhongguo tongji chubanshe, 2000), pp. 430–34. Interviews conducted by the authors in 2001 revealed that the annual expenditure of residents in Shigatse, at RMB1,287, approached that of residents in suburban counties of Shanghai, at RMB1,431.
51. There is a huge body of studies on labour mobility. The more recent ones are those by Du Ying 杜鷹 and Bai Nansheng 白南生, *Zouchu xiangcun* 走出鄉村 (Escape from Villages) (Beijing: Jingji kexue chubanshe 經濟科技出版社, 1997) and Li Peilin 李培林 (ed.), *Nongmingong: Zhongguo jincheng nongmingong de jingji shehui fenxi* 農民工：中國進城農民工的經濟社會分析 (Peasant Workers: A Socioeconomic Analysis of Peasant Workers in Urban China) (Beijing: Shehui kexue wenxian chubanshe 社會科學文獻出版社, 2003).
52. See Xian Zude 鮮祖德 (ed.), *Xiao chengzhen jianshe yu nongcun laodongli zhuanyi* 小城鎮建設與農村勞動力轉移 (Small Township Construction and Rural Labour Mobility) (Beijing: Zhongguo tongji chubanshe, 2001), pp. 358–65.
53. See Ma Rong, *Xizang de renkou yu shehui* (see note 22), p. 223.
54. See Du Ping 杜平, Xiao Jincheng 肖金城 and Wang Qingyun 王青雲, *Xibu kaifalun* 西部開發論 (On the Western Development Plan) (Chongqing: Chongqing chubanshe 重慶出版社, 2000), pp. 320–21.

55. See Zhang Xiaoping, *Zouxiang ershiyi shiji de Xizang* (see note 38).
56. As estimated by Zhang Shanyu 張善余, about 71.33% of the total population of Tibet inhabited in mountainous region 3,500–4,000 m above sea level. See Zhang Shanyu (ed.), *Renkou chuizhi fenbu guilü he Zhongguo shanqu renkou heli zaifenbu yanjiu* 人口垂直分布規律和中國山區人口合理再分布研究 (A Study of the Vertical Distribution of Population and the Rational Redistribution of Population in Mountainous Areas) (Shanghai: Huadong shifan daxue chubanshe 華東師範大學出版社, 1996), pp. 174–83.
57. Donald S. Lopez, Jr. has captured such sentiments: "The Chinese takeover exposed Tibet's timeless culture to time, time that would cause the contents of the culture to wither and turn to dust like the bodies of those who dare leave Shangri-la." See Donald S. Lopez, Jr., *Prisoner of Shangri-la: Tibetan Buddhism and the West* (Chicago: The University of Chicago Press, 1998), pp. 7–8.

Glossary

5 North-South and 7 East-West 五縱七橫
5+7 Zone 五省七方
8 North-South and 8 East-West 八縱八橫
An-Shi Rebellion 安史之亂
banana taro 芭蕉芋
bianjing kaifang kouan 邊境開放口岸
chaganyide 查幹伊德
dates 大棗
dayuejin 大躍進
dianli zhuangji 電力裝機
donglin xitie, nanliang beimu, biandi shi mei 東林西鐵，南糧北牧，遍地是煤
Duhu Fu 都護府
duikou zhiyuan 對口支援
Dunhuang Grottoes 敦煌寶窟
(the) earthly paradise 人間仙境
Eastern Monsoon Zone 東部季風區
efficiency first while taking inequality into consideration 效率優先、兼顧公平
(the) Euro-Asian continental bridge 歐亞大陸橋
(the) fairyland 童話世界
(the) Far West 遠西部
(the) Foreign Industrial Movement 洋務運動
four supporting projects 四配套
ganshi didai 乾濕地帶
(the) greatest beauty under heaven 天下秀
guan benwei 官本位
Guanzhong economic region 關中經濟區
Guomindang 國民黨 (also Kuomintang)
gynostemma pentaphylla 絞股藍

Hanzu 漢族
hedi canliang 和糴殘糧
Hexi corridor economic region 河西走廊經濟區
Imperial ministers for Tibet 欽差駐藏辦事大臣
Lantian Ape Man 藍田猿人
Laoganma 老乾媽
(The) Legend Group 聯想集團
Lhasa's Potala Palace 拉薩布達拉宮
Mayuan Old Way 馬援故道
minorities 少數民族
(the) most impassable under heaven 天下險
(the) most secluded under heaven 天下幽
(the) Near West 近西部
no one comes close 人無我有
(the) northwest Sichuan high mountain plateau 川西北高山高原
Northwestern Arid Zone 西北乾旱區
one corridor, two cities, three bases and four pillar industries 一帶、兩城、三基地、四產業
paired assistance, mutual benefit and joint development 對口支援、互惠互利、共同發展
(the) Pearl River Transport Bureau 珠江航務管理局
people do not have even three cents 人無三分銀
ping liangang 平煉鋼
(the) project to beautify the mountains and rivers of northern Shaanxi 陝北山川秀美工程
(a) pro-provincial city 副省級市
Qinghai-Tibet (Tibetan) Plateau 青藏高寒區
qubie duidai 區別對待
regional responsibility, paired assistance, staff rotation 分片負責、對口支援、定期輪換
sanquan moshi 三圈模式
second to nobody 人有我精
shanpen moshi 山盆模式
shaoshu minzu 少數民族
Shengchan jianshe bingtuan 生產建設兵團
shengtai-shengchan moshi 生態生產模式
shidang fangkuan 適當放寬
Silk Road 絲綢之路
small but rich, small but strong 小而富、小而強

(the) southwest Sichuan mountain region 川西南山地
stringing points through lines, developing surfaces along lines 以線串點、以點帶面
Third Front 三線
tung tree 油桐
(the) west-east gas transmission project 西氣東輸工程
Wujin Sanjiao 烏金三角
wulanyide 烏蘭伊德
Xi You Ji 西遊記
Xi'an's terracotta warriors 西安兵馬俑
xiaomianji gao shengchan, damianji gao shengtai 小面積搞生產，大面積搞生態
yanbian kaifangdai 沿邊開放帶
Yiqi 一汽

Contributors

Y. M. YEUNG (楊汝萬) is Professor of Geography, Director of the Hong Kong Institute of Asia-Pacific Studies (HKIAPS) and Director of the Shanghai-Hong Kong Development Institute, The Chinese University of Hong Kong. His wide-ranging research interests have recently focused on China's coastal cities, South China, globalization and Asian cities. He has published extensively, including, as co-editor, editor or author, *Shanghai* (1996), *Globalization and the World of Large Cities* (1998), *Guangdong* (1998), *Fujian* (2000), *Globalization and Networked Societies* (2000) and *New Challenges for Development and Modernization* (2002).

SHEN JIANFA (沈建法) received his Ph.D. degree from the London School of Economics and is Associate Professor in the Department of Geography and Resource Management, The Chinese University of Hong Kong. His research interests focus on spatial population modelling, migration analysis, urban/regional governance and development. His recent publications include *China Review 2000* (co-editor, 2000), "Urban and Regional Development in Post-Reform China: The Case of Zhujiang Delta" (*Progress in Planning*, 2002) and *Resource Management, Urbanization and Governance in Hong Kong and the Zhujiang Delta* (co-editor, 2002).

CHAU KWAI-CHEONG (鄒桂昌) is Associate Professor specializing in Biogeography, Soil Geography and Resource Management in the Department of Geography and Resource Management, The Chinese University of Hong Kong. He obtained his Ph.D. in forestry at the Australian National University. His areas of interest are soil amelioration, agroforestry and biological resource management.

CHEN CAITI (陳材倜) graduated from Wucang College of Architecture Engineering and worked at various times in Chongqing Urban Construction Commission, Chongqing Architecture Design Institute and Chongqing

Urban Planning Bureau, dealing with planning design and planning management. As the Deputy Director of Chongqing Planning Bureau from 1983 to 2000, he participated in and organized the work of Chongqing Master Plan of 1983 and 1998, which were approved by the State Council. Currently, he serves as the Standing Director of Urban Planning Academy of China, Vice-Chairman of Urban Planning Association of China and Advisory Chief Planner of Chongqing Urban Planning Bureau.

DAVID Y. Q. CHEN (陳永勤) obtained his Ph.D. from The University of Georgia and is Assistant Professor of the Department of Geography and Resource Management, The Chinese University of Hong Kong. By training, he is a physical geographer with particular interests in hydrology and water resources.

CHEN YUE (陳悦) graduated from the Geography Department of Chongqing Teachers College and taught at the Technological School of Neijiang in Sichuan. Since 1987, she has been working on regional economics in the Institute of Economics, Chongqing Academy of Social Sciences. Currently the Deputy Director of the Institute, she has published several monographs and papers.

CHEN ZHILONG (陳志龍) received his master's degree in Economics in Wuhan University and is Professor in the School of Economics, Fudan University. His research interests focus on regional economics and regional development in China. His recent publications include *Infrastructure and Sustainable Development in Yangtze River Area* (1999) and "On the Role of Special Economic Area in Coastal Areas: Taking the Lead in Realizing Modernization" (*Special Economic Area Economy*, 2001).

FAN JIE (樊杰), a Ph.D. holder from the Chinese Academy of Sciences, is Professor in the Institute of Geographical Sciences and Natural Resource Research, Chinese Academy of Sciences (CAS). His research interests focus on regional development, regional planning and rural industrialization in China. His recent publications include *Regional Development Report of China* (co-author, 2003), *Countermeasures to Boost the Development of Minority and Poverty-stricken Areas in China* (co-author, 2001) and *Modernization Strategy in China's Coastal Areas* (co-author, 2001).

FANG CHUANGLIN (方創琳) currently is a researcher at the Institute of

Geographical Sciences and Natural Resources Research, CAS. Concurrently, he is the Deputy Director of the Research Centre for Regional and Urban Planning and Design. His principal research interests include sustainable regional development and regional planning. He has published extensively in the area of regional planning and development in academic journals and is also the author and editor of many books.

GAN CHUNKAI (甘春開) received his master's degree in Economics in Nankai University and is a Ph.D. student in Regional Economics in the School of Economics, Fudan University. His research interests focus on international economics and regional economics. His recent publications include *Economic Globalisation: Process, Trends and Countermeasures* (co-editor, 2000) and "An Analysis of Bank Credit Market Integration Process in EU" (co-author, *The Journal of World Economy,* 2002).

GU CHAOLIN (顧朝林) received his Ph.D. degree from Nanjing University and is Professor in the Department of Urban and Resource Sciences, Nanjing University. His research interests focus on urban and regional planning. He is a corresponding editor of the *International Journal of Urban and Regional Research*. He has published extensively, including recent articles on urban image space, regional polarization and "New Economic Geography."

HU XIA (胡霞), a doctorate graduate of Kyoto University in Japan, is Associate Professor in the Institute of Economic Studies, People's University of China. She has been trained in development economics and the rural economy. Her research interests lie in the regional economics and development issues in China's western region, with a special focus on poverty, population and environmental problems.

HUANG YEFANG (黃葉芳) received her B.Sc. from Shanghai Teachers University, M.Sc. from East China Normal University and Ph.D. from The Chinese University of Hong Kong. She is an instructor in the Department of Geography and Resource Management, The Chinese University of Hong Kong. Her research interests are in regional economic development in China, spatial modelling and spatial analysis. Her recent publication includes "Analysing Regional Industrialisation in Jiangsu Province Using Geographically Weighted Regression" (co-author, *Journal of Geographical Systems*, 2002).

JIN FENGJUN (金鳳君) is Professor in the Institute of Geographical Sciences and Natural Resources Research, CAS. His research focuses on transportation geography and regional planning.

LI TONGSHENG (李同升) is Professor of Urban and Resource Science in Northwest University, teaching regional development and urban/rural planning, and doing related research in rural development and rural urbanization, regional development, regional politics and economy. Since 1995, he has been in charge of 15 projects funded by national and local natural sciences foundations, published 2 books, and co-published 8 books and 36 papers.

LI XIAOJIAN (李小建) is Professor of Economic Geography and Vice-President of Henan University. He is the Vice-Chairman of the Economic Geography Committee of the Geographical Society of China. His current research interests include transnational corporations and regional development, spatial networks of small and medium enterprises, and sustainable development in the less-developed region. He has published extensively on regional issues in Chinese and international journals.

LIN HUI (林琿) graduated from Wuhan Technical University of Surveying and Mapping on the subject of aerophotogrammetric engineering and received his M.Sc. degree on remote sensing and cartography from the Graduate School of CAS and his Ph.D. in GIS from University of Buffalo. Currently, he is Professor in the Department of Geography and Resource Management, The Chinese University of Hong Kong. Professor Lin was elected academician of the International Eurasian Academy of Sciences in 1995 and President of Hong Kong Society for Photogrammetry and Remote Sensing. In 1997, he was appointed Director of the Joint Laboratory for GeoInformation Science of Chinese Academy of Sciences and The Chinese University of Hong Kong.

LIU QINGQUAN (劉清泉) served as Professor of Geography and Chairman of the Geography Department at Southwest China Normal University since graduation from The People's University of China in 1956. His major research focuses include economic geography and regional economic development. Since retirement in 1997, Professor Liu has continued to teach graduate courses at the University. Concurrently, he is Chairman of the Geographical Society of Chongqing.

LIU XIAOMING (劉笑明) is Assistant Lecturer in Northwest University and majors in regional economics and industrial organization.

LIU XUEMIN (劉學敏) is Professor in the Institute of Resources Science, Beijing Normal University. He holds a Ph.D. degree in economics. His main research fields are macroeconomics, regional economics and price management. Currently, he is conducting many projects, including the "Spark programme" project and the technical progress and sustainable development in western cities and counties. He has published 10 books, including *A Study on Price Management in China* and over 70 articles.

MAO HANYING (毛漢英) is Professor in the Institute of Geographical Sciences and Natural Resources Research, CAS. His research areas include sustainable regional development and regional planning. His publications have appeared in leading journals in geography and sociology in China.

NG WING-FAI (吳永輝) is by profession a chartered surveyor specializing in financial arrangements of large-scale infrastructure projects. He received his M.Sc. degree in Advanced Architectural Studies from the Bartlett School of Architecture, University of London and his Ph.D. in Geography from The Chinese University of Hong Kong. His major research interests are vernacular architecture, poverty alleviation and regional development in China's nationalities areas. He has also provided consultancy services on rehabilitation programmes for several non-governmental organizations in China.

NIU WENYUAN (牛文元) is Professor of the Institute of Science and Technology Policy and Management, CAS. He holds many prestigious positions in China and abroad, including Chairman of the CAS Study Group of Sustainable Development Strategies, member of the Chinese People's Political Consultative Conference, and academician of the Third World Academy of Sciences. Since 1999, he has been the principal author of the CAS annual reports on sustainable development strategies of China and played a leading role in the production of 4 volumes so far in the series. He has published 14 books and 209 articles, and won a national innovation award of China.

QIAO JIAJUN (喬家君) is Lecturer in Economic Geography at the College of Environment and Planning, Henan University. His research interests concern economic geography and sustainable development.

SHI PEIJUN (史培軍) is Vice-President of Beijing Normal University and Director of its Institute of Resources Science. Also a professor and supervisor of doctoral students, Professor Shi's main research fields are in environment changes, natural disasters and resources development. He is conducting several important research projects, including one on land use/cover change and its effect on agricultural ecosystem funded by the National Natural Science Foundation of China. He has published 20 books, including *The Methods and Practice in Land Use/Cover Change Study* and over 100 articles.

GARY M. C. SHIU (蕭滿章) was Research Officer at the Hong Kong Institute of Asia-Pacific Studies, The Chinese University of Hong Kong. Dr. Shiu received his Ph.D. in economics from George Mason University, U.S.A. His specialties include new institutional economics and public choice.

WANG GUIXIN (王桂新) received his Ph.D. degree from the East China Normal University and is Professor in the Institute of Population Research, Fudan University. His research interests focus on spatial population modelling, migration analysis, population, resources and environmental economics, urban and regional development. His recent publications include *Methods of Regional Population Projection and Its Applications* (2000) and *A Study on Population and Sustainable Development in Shanghai* (co-author, 2000).

WANG JING'AI (王靜愛) is Professor in the Department of Resources and Environment Sciences, Beijing Normal University. Her main research interests are on regional land use, land degradation and natural disasters. She has studied Inner Mongolia, especially the Farming-pastoral Zone in northern China, for many years. She has published more than 60 research papers.

YANG MINGCHUAN (楊明川) is Associate Professor of Institute of Resources Science, Beijing Normal University. His main research fields are land use/cover change, agro-industrialization planning, rural market planning and urbanization and environmental safety. He has published many books, including *Geography of Steel Industry* (1990), *Environmental Education of Sustainable Development* (English version, 1996) and *The Development Relationship between Yellow River and Yongding River* (1991).

YU TAOFANG (于濤方) is currently a Ph.D. student in the Department of Urban and Resource Sciences in Nanjing University. His research interest is on urban and regional planning and development.

ZENG GUANG (曾光) is a postgraduate student in the Institute of Geographical Sciences and Natural Resources Research, CAS. His research focuses on transportation geography.

ZHANG LI (張力) is Assistant Professor in the Department of Geography and Resource Management, The Chinese University of Hong Kong. His research areas, broadly defined, include migration, urbanization, and urban and regional development. His works have appeared in the journals such as *China Quarterly*, *Urban Studies*, *International Regional Science Review* and *Habitat International.*

ZHANG MIN (張珉) received her master's degree in Economics from Xiantan University in 2001. She currently is a teacher in Xiantan University and also a Ph.D. student in Regional Economics at Fudan University. Her research interests are in constitutional changes and regional economy.

ZHAO RONG (趙榮) received his Ph.D. degree from Peking University and is a professor and a doctoral supervisor in the Northwest University in Xi'an. His research interests focus on cultural geography, urban geography, tourism geography and regional economy. His recent publications include *Study on the Urban Development in Northwest China* (co-editor, 2001), *Human Geography* (co-editor, 2000) and *Study on the Cultural Landscape of Shaanxi* (co-editor, 1999).

ZHENG GUO (鄭國) received his master's degree from Northwest University in Xi'an and is a Ph.D. candidate in Peking University. His research interests focus on urban geography, tourism geography and regional economy. His recent publications include *Study on the Urban Development in Northwest China* (co-editor, 2001).

ZHOU YIXING (周一星) is Professor of Urban and Regional Planning, and Director of Geographic Science Research Centre at Peking University. His major research interests in urban geography are urban planning system, China's metropolitan interlocking region and suburbanization. He has published extensively, including *Studies on the Spatial Agglomeration and Dispersion in China's Coastal City-and-Town Concentrated Areas* and *Study on Suburbanization in Beijing*.

Index